Der Buddha-Christus als der Herr des wahren Selbst
Die Religionsphilosophie der Kyoto-Schule und das Christentum

The Buddha-Christ as the Lord of the True Self
The Religious Philosophy of the Kyoto School and Christianity

To my friend Harry Oliver
whose relationalism is
so much related to
pratitya-samutpada
    New year's day 1984
        Fritz

"To my friend Harry Oliver
whose relationalism is
so much related to
pratitya-samutpada
    New year's day 1984
        Fritz"

(Inscription in the translator's copy of the original text
and from which this translation was made.)

The Buddha-Christ
as the Lord of the True Self

The Religious Philosophy
of the Kyoto School and Christianity

by
Fritz Buri
(1907–1995)

translated and with an introduction by
Harold H. Oliver

MERCER UNIVERSITY PRESS
1997

ISBN 0-86554-536-7

MUP/H410

B
5242
.B8713
1997

The paper used in this publication meets the minimum requirements
of American National Standard for Information Sciences—
Permanence of Paper for Printed Library Materials, ANSI Z39.48-1984.

Library of Congress Cataloging-in-Publication Data

Buri, Fritz, 1907–1995
[Buddha-Christus als der Herr des wahren Selbst. English]
The Buddha-Christ as the Lord of the true self :
the religious philosophy of the Kyoto school and Christianity /
by Fritz Buri : translated and with an introduction by Harold H. Oliver.
xviii+416 pp. 6x9" (15x23 cm.)
ISBN 0-86554-536-7 (alk. paper)
1. Philosophy, Japanese—20th century.
2. Religion—Philosophy.
3. Buddhism—Relations—Christianity.
4. Christianity and other religions—Buddhism.   I. Title.
B5242.B8713   1997
294.3'372—dc21   97-15884
CIP

Contents

List of Illustrations

Abbreviations
of most frequently quoted journals

[Abbreviations in brackets = translator's additions]

JR	*Japanese Religions*
EB	*Eastern Buddhist*, new series
[EncB	*Encyclopedia Britannica*]
[ET	English translation]
MN	*Monumenta Nipponica*
PhEW	*Philosophy in East and West*
NAJTh	*Northeast Asia Journal of Theology*
ThZB	*Theologische Zeitschrift* (Basel)

[In the text, translator's remarks appear in brackets. Some such additions include the byline "—Trans."]

Translator's Introduction

The lengthy process of completing this translation culminated in the opportunity of spending two weeks in Basel in the company of Professor Fritz Buri at his home "Auf der Alp." In addition to the rewarding time we have spent together reviewing residual problems in the translation, there have been special personal moments when the three of us—Fritz, his wife Elsa, and I—have enjoyed reminiscing about our earlier times together in Basel (1963–1964) and in the States during their frequent visits during the 1960s, 1970s, and 1980s. This "personalized" conclusion to the project is not incidental to it, for it was undertaken not only to add to the English-speaking world further insights on the Kyoto School, but to share with a wider audience the profound wisdom on the East as well as the West of my former mentor, several of whose writings I translated early on.[1]

Buri's knowledge of Buddhism and Japanese philosophy was deepened by two year-long visits to Japan in 1968–1969 and 1978–1979, respectively. During the second visit he concentrated on the Kyoto Philosophy while living at the "House of Encounter" in Kyoto, during which time he engaged in zazen at the Tenryuji monastery and had extensive conversations with Takeuchi, Nishitani (d. 1990), Ueda, and Abe. For Buri, Buddhism in general and the "Nishida philosophy" in particular, represents a kind of *mysterium tremendum et fascinans*, in that while basically disagreeing with both, he appreciates their magnitude. As a religious thinker, Buri is so enamored of Buddhism as to suggest in his liberal way, that the Buddha and the Christ represent commensurate religions of redemption; as a Western thinker, he is critical of their attachment to "nonobjectifying thinking and speaking" about reality. Buri's stance is not surprising to those acquainted with his lifelong criticism of all "nonobjectifying thinking and speaking" directed principally against Heidegger and his theological followers (see *Journal for Theology and Church* 3 [1967]). While Heidegger & Cie. represent a philosophical legacy alien to his own, and the same is true finally of the Kyoto School, Buddhism—especially the Mahayana tradition—embodies a spiritual tradition which, though not his own, speaks to him profoundly. He acknowledges the impact of Buddhism on his own spirituality by admitting—in words adapted from Schleiermacher—that he is a "Christian or Buddhist of a higher order" (below, p. xvii).

Buri's study in his home on the "Bruderholz" is impressively appointed with symbols of Japanese and Korean culture, and he enjoys showing visitors his "Zen

---

[1] *Theology of Existence*, with Gerhard Onder, 1965; *Thinking Faith: Steps on the Way to a Philosophical Theology*, 1968; and the chapter on "The Reality of Faith," in his book, *How Can We Still Speak Responsibly of God?* 1968.

garden." This is the more remarkable to those of us who knew him thirty years ago as one whose "world" was wholly European. In point of fact, my own interest in the Kyoto School was generated by Buri who, upon reading an early draft of my book *A Relational Metaphysic*, pointed out to me in 1975 the striking parallel between my relational paradigm and Nishida's notion of "pure experience" which the latter first set forth in his book of 1911, *A Study of Good*. Buri has often indicated to me the similarity of my "Relationalismus" (as he calls it) to the Buddhist doctrine of pratitya-samutpada (dependent origination), as is evident, for example, in his inscription in the personal copy of *Der Buddha-Christus als der Herr des wahren Selbst* he presented to me in 1984. In view of these considerations, the reader will not be surprised by the fact that my own assessment of the Kyoto School is much more positive than Buri's. My students at Boston University, aware of this difference, have often asked me why I am investing this time in producing a translation of Buri's magnum opus on Buddhism and Christianity. I tell them that, in addition to the indelible bond that has characterized our relationship for almost thirty years, there is the consideration that this work on "The Religious Philosophy of the Kyoto School and Christianity" (to use its subtitle) is unique in representing the only major critical assessment of the Kyoto School to have been produced by a major Protestant systematic theologian. While Buri would be the first to admit that his is only "one voice" (below, pp. 339-40) on this subject, and that the Christian perspective he represents is not *the* Christianity, just as the Buddhism of the Kyoto philosophers is not *the* Buddhism (below, p. 1), this work of his is the culmination of an impressive career in the Academy and the Church.

The eight "inner" chapters devoted to the Kyoto philosophers seriatim are framed by an introductory and a concluding chapter which give the book a decidedly "Burian" character. In the first, he advances a novel theory of the similar "problematic of origins" of both Buddhism and Christianity. This theory reflects in part Buri's lifelong commitment to the neo-Schweitzerian School of Thoroughgoing Eschatology, with which some readers may not be able to identify. Yet there is no denying the strong eschatological element in Jesus' message and that of the early Church, so that even those who may hold to a "weaker version" of the thesis will find something of value in this chapter.

The final chapter culminates in a two-pronged estimate of Buddhism from Buri's perspective. Positively, it gives voice to a "spiritual affinity" which Buri acknowledges between Mahayana Buddhism and his own Christian experience which is illumined primarily by his insight that the symbolic—interpreted as the objectification of the Nonobjectifiable—is necessary to religion. Negatively, he faults the Kyoto philosophers for claiming that it is possible—even essential—to their Buddhistic philosophy, to avoid all "discriminating (that is, objectifying) thinking." Buri's rebuttal is that the "thought nothingness is not exactly nothing" (below, p. 128). Throughout, Buri taunts his Kyoto "Kollegen" with the question:

if there is no subject over against an object, who is the "subject" that makes this claim?

Buri raised the same question about my notion of "the relational self" in the reviews of my books, *A Relational Metaphysic* and *Relatedness: Essays in Metaphysics and Theology*, published in the Basel Theologische Zeitschrift (1982 and 1986), so I am not disposed to come to the defense of his "Kantian" commitments (my term), however mitigated they may be by existential components. I do believe, though, that Buri has framed the best case that a Western thinker can make based on this set of commitments. While the Kyoto philosophers are as "liberal" as Buri is in their own fashion, their "liberality" does not include the slightest concession on the issue about "discriminating thinking." Some of them would argue that Buri's thesis on the unavoidability of "objectifying thinking and speaking in theology" is not essential to the full articulation of Christianity, and that the time may have come to develop a theology that moves beyond the "Augustinian-Cartesian-Kantian" axis.

Saying this does not diminish my appreciation for the achievement Buri's book represents. It may well be the crowning achievement of a career rich in insights and endowed with courage. No one will fail to learn something from this book, and few will complete it without some appreciation for this "gift" Buri has given us.

As theology today is becoming increasingly aware of a new "world openness of Christianity" (to use the title of the Festschrift presented to Buri on his eightieth birthday in 1987), it may well be that what Buri has attempted in this volume vis-à-vis the legacy of Japanese culture, and especially of the Kyoto School, will need to be extended to other world religions—and could serve as a model for such undertakings. This must be done, not as a distracting aside within theology, but as an essential part of the theological task itself.

Those who study this volume will need to be aware that Buri's understanding of Buddhism and the Kyoto philosophers is based entirely on translations into modern European languages, and that in the decade that has followed the appearance of the German edition, there has been a wealth of further studies of the Kyoto philosophers based on very exact knowledge of the Japanese originals. This limitation of Buri's work is hopefully compensated by his vast experience in the arena of modern theological thought.

Declining the invitation to write an introductory word to this English version, Buri expressed to me his great interest in this project and his anticipation of the response it will find in the English-speaking world and among others elsewhere who have not been able to read the German original.

Translation Policy Statement

Buri's text quotes extensively from German and English sources, and in a few instances from texts that have appeared in both a German and an English version which often differ substantially from each other.

In those cases where there is only an English version of a text, it has been my policy to check the original English versions and to make Buri's citations of these conform to the original, thus avoiding the undesirable alternative of producing yet another English "version" of these quotations. This means, to give the most crucial instance, that the extensive citations from Nishitani's *Religion and Nothingness* in chapter 6 agree with the version found in the articles from *The Eastern Buddhist* rather than with the final English version in book form, with page numbers for the latter supplied for reference. In those cases where there exist independent German and English translations of the same Japanese work, I have chosen to translate the German version which Buri in fact cites, and to provide page numbers of the English version for reference purposes.

Acknowledgments

It is to Buri himself, and to his dear wife Elsa, that I owe the greatest debt of gratitude for the role I have had in producing this translation. Their hospitality and friendship over the years—and most especially during this visit to Basel—have been an inspiration to me in all aspects of my work.

The trip to Basel would not have been possible without the personal interest and financial support of John R. Silber, president of Boston University, and concomitantly of my dean, Robert C. Neville, both of whom have encouraged and enabled me to complete this translation under the best possible set of circumstances.

In Basel, my lifelong friend and former mentor at Emory University, Professor Martin Anton Schmidt, and his beloved wife Ruth, have graciously and generously provided for me during my stay here. It was they who ensured that I would not leave Basel this time without a few days in the Alps—mountains which symbolize for us the transcendent dimensions of nature itself.

To all of these I am truly grateful, as well as to many others who have encouraged and offered criticisms of my work. Crucial in this regard have been the services of my Boston University colleague, Professor Bodo Reichenbach, who, through President Silber's generosity, has reviewed the translation and spared me considerable embarrassment—as did Buri himself by reading the English translation in its entirety. In an undertaking as complex as this, where myriad minidecisions must be made, I cannot say that all the deficiencies have been eliminated. It remains to say, nevertheless, that final responsibility for the end product lies with me.

Many of my colleagues and graduate students at Boston University have given their support to me during this lengthy task. I would mention, in particular, Associate Dean John Berthrong, Professors David Eckel and Jennifer Rike, and my graduate assistants and students, Bockja Kim, Barbara Kauber, John John, B. J. Beu, and Hiroko Ueda. Of the various members of the staff of the library of the School of Theology who have been helpful in tracking down rare items, I should mention in particular Anne-Marie Salgat and Stephen Pentek.

It has not been easy for my wife Martha and daughter Daphne to endure the neglect that inevitably came with the hours of solitary work a task of this kind requires. They have encouraged and supported me in every phase of this task and for that I am deeply grateful to them.

Finally, I should like to thank Paul Haupt Verlag of Bern for giving me permission early on to publish this English version.

Basel, July 1992 *Harold H. Oliver*

Foreword

I should like to say something here about the origin of this book and its relation to my previous works. A few explanatory words, however, may also be in order about its title and the reactions to it that one may anticipate.

This book arose out of a preoccupation with the spiritual world of Buddhism which has extended over twelve years. While Buddhism was marginal to my interests earlier, a visit to Japan from the autumn of 1968 to the spring of 1969 gave me both the occasion and the opportunity to attend to it intensively. As guest professor at the International Christian University in Mitaka/Tokyo I had to give courses in "Introduction to Christianity" and "Ethics." In order to make this material intelligible to my hearers, most of whom were of Buddhist extraction, I was compelled to become more knowledgeable about Buddhism past and present. For this purpose the environment in which I lived, both near and far, with its temples, monasteries, and museums, provided abundant visual materials. When the lectures were cancelled in the third term due to student unrest, I was able to travel to Korea and to become acquainted with Buddhism there as well. Above all, I then had time to make personal contact with the Zen philosophers in Kyoto and to immerse myself in the literature of this school. (I have already published a report about this first "Meeting with Buddhist Thinking in Japan" in an account with this title (*Theol. Zeitschrift*, Basel [1969] and *Northeast Asia Journal of Theology* [1970]).

For many years since my return I have dealt with themes arising out of the issue of "Buddhism and Christianity" in lectures at Basel University. I reported on some of these at three congresses of the International Society for the History of Religion and also at other events at home and abroad. I was assisted in my study of Buddhism by students from the Far East, principally by a Korean couple who completed the doctorate with me on Buddhist themes, and also by the visits of Buddhist scholars from Japan.

On the basis of these scholarly works and connections, in 1978 I received an invitation from the Japan Foundation for a study visit in Japan which I spent in Kyoto from October 1978 to the end of February 1979, after a visit to Korea with my wife—our first visit there together. Here I not only immersed myself in the rich treasures of Buddhist culture and religious history, but also enjoyed the association with the professors of Kyoto and Otani Universities and participated in a seminar of Nishitani's and in Zen practice in the Tenryuji monastery. As I had visited the quarters of the Oriens Institute in Tokyo during my first visit, this time we were guests of the Ecumenical Institute in Nagoya, both of which—in contrast to the protestant Kyodan—also include Buddhism in the Oikoumene of religions, as do also the Jesuits at Sophia University.

After I had visited India on my way back home, having set out from Delhi to visit the original sites of Buddhism, the time had come to present in a more comprehensive way my experiences with Buddhism and the insights bound up with them concerning its essence, together with its relationship to Christianity. In order not to drown in the volume of material and also not to repeat the frequent mistakes of speaking of *the* Buddhism and of *the* Christianity while dealing with only one kind or with kinds of Buddhism and Christianity, I have selected as an example for demonstration the Buddhism I encountered in the so-called Kyoto School. I have confronted and rigorously evaluated it in terms of my own personal understanding of Christianity, without concerning myself in detail with other relevant positions. For the foundation of my Christianity and the debate with other professed Christianities I should refer to my numerous essays and writings—above all to the three volumes of my *Dogmatik als Selbstverständnis des christlichen Glaubens* (*Dogmatics as the Self-Understanding of the Christian Faith*)—in which I have sufficiently performed this service (see the bibliography in *Theol. Zeitschrift*, Basel, 1977) [Updated, *Theol. Zeitschrift*, Basel, 1987]. If in my theology I have represented a kind of Christianity different from that which the representatives of the Kyoto School customarily envision—and indeed one that is basically much nearer to them—so from my religio-philosophical position there arises nevertheless a criticism of their philosophy of religion that is no less sharp than that which they direct toward Christianity. I am concerned not so much with the Christianness of my theology, which can have quite different interpretations, just as the Kyoto School is itself not free from attack, but rather more with the truth of a self-understanding that is equally possible on the basis of the Buddhist and Christian tradition, if only the right use is made of it. If I understand this as an existential interpretation of traditional mythology and speculation, even in this respect I am in accord with the leading Kyoto philosophers insofar as they use this means of understanding their tradition. The title I have chosen for this book is the result of extending this view of both streams of tradition, in that herein I interpret their central figures in terms of the existential proximity in which they stand to each other, so that they become united in a symbol of authentic self-understanding: "The Buddha-Christ as the Lord of the True Self."

I am aware that this formulation of my concern will initially be met with some astonishment and shaking of heads; I should not even be surprised if some repudiate it outright. But I also fear that, if misunderstood, it could awaken false expectations. In anticipation of such diverse reactions, some remarks may be needed at this point in order to explain, justify, and preserve it from misunderstanding. Its inner historical justification, systematic necessity, and practical proof follow to be sure from the whole of the work and in special reference to the religious philosophy of the Kyoto School. Those who cannot be directly satisfied with the notion of the Buddha-Christ because it contradicts what they have presupposed by Buddha and Christ, are to be reminded that both figures have undergone many transformations in their long history. In consequence of these transformations they might not be able to recognize the picture of the Buddha or of the Christ in whom they trust. For in the course of this history both figures have entered into relationship with others, even those of other cultures. One has only to think of the joining of Jesus with the Christ and of the latter with the Logos, and that of Shakyamuni with the Buddha and of the latter, for example, with the Vahairocana, or of Christian Gnosis and of Shingon Buddhism. Why not then the symbol of the Buddha-Christ?

Both parts of the symbol no doubt stem from quite different worldviews and represent quite different conceptions of redemption. Simply stated, in one case one is dealing with a monism and self-redemption, and in the other with a dualism and a redemption beyond our human capacity. Nevertheless, a comparison of the two exhibits transfers and parallels, as for example in Amida Buddhism and in the synergistic forms of the relation of nature and grace in Christendom. Buddhists and Christians who here want to accentuate only the opposition and incompatibility of their standpoints are reminded not only of the problems in which they developed with their extreme forms of dogmatism, but also of the fact that the Buddha-Christ as we understand it could take on precisely the significance of an overcoming of the problematic on both sides.

I have already alluded to such a problematic in two of my early writings: *Prometheus und Christus: Grösse und Grenzen von Carl Spittelers religiöser Weltanschauung* (*Prometheus and Christ: The Grandeur and Limits of Carl Spitteler's Religious Worldview*, 1945) and *Kreuz und Ring: Die Kreuztheologie des jungen Luther und Nietzsches Lehre von der ewigen Wiederkunft* (*Cross and Circle: The Young Luther's Theology of the Cross and Nietzsche's Doctrine of the Eternal Return*, 1947). Further, in contrast to Paul Tillich who after his first visit to Japan explained that he had actually to reconceive his "systematic theology," as I composed the third volume of my *Dogmatik* while concurrently preoccupied with Buddhism, I felt threatened, not in my faith, but only in respect to the allotment of time for both spheres of my work. The present volume thus stands in no conflict with my *Pantokrator* (1969) and *Transzendenz der Verantwortung in der dreifachen Schöpfung des dreieinigen Gottes* (*Transcendence of Responsibility in the Three-Fold Creation of the Triune God*, 1978); rather it represents nothing but the application of my *Dogmatik als Selbstverständnis des christlichen Glaubens* to a special area of the History of Religions, and in this function belongs to the whole of my work as an organic unity.

The integral connection between this study of Buddhism and the *Dogmatik*—a connection clearly set forth in the introductory and final chapters—prompts me nevertheless to issue a warning against the false expectations of those who, because they are disappointed with Christianity and are therefore seeking redemption in the Far East, hope to find in my Buddha-Christ the Buddha of their dreams and longings, fantasies, and imaginings.

I am, however, much in agreement with their criticisms of Christianity. Most frequently it was such Far East enthusiasts who attended my lectures on the theme of Buddhism only sooner or later to disappear, because with me they were still subjected to too much theology. I cannot even speak of Buddhism without thereby stating what I mean by Christianity, both for its own sake and for the evaluation of Buddhism. For both—Buddhism as well as Christianity—are about the "Lord of the True Self."

For Buddhists, and especially for Zen Buddhists, "The Lord of the True Self" is a fundamental statement about Shakyamuni and their relationship to him, just as for Christians, especially from the perspective of Paul, the confession of Jesus as Lord is of central significance. With this Lord, if he really is the Lord, we are not dealing with a product of one's own heart, but with a "Beyond," with the Transcendence to which they experience themselves related. "The Lord of the True Self" is an expression for the transcendent relatedness of self-understanding. Every statement about this self-understanding which in its enactment is not objectifiable, but depends on objectifications for its enactment, is doubly threatened. It is in danger, first, of taking the transcendence into itself, that is, of regarding the transcendence as a mere dimension of the self, and second, of localizing the transcendence in a supraworld and thus making it into an object of a mythology or speculation.

Buddhism is more in danger of the former; Christianity, of the latter. But in both cases it means a loss of transcendence and simultaneously of the self. This fate, which threatens both Buddhism and Christianity in their inevitable dogmatizations, can only be eluded if the Buddha and the Christ prevail as statements of the self that is related to Transcendence. Because both the Buddha and the Christ can express that to which the self is related if it understands itself, and both obviate the dangers that threaten each in accord with its own essence by accenting their opposite features—Buddha through his more immanent, and the Christ through his more transcendent, character—I combine them in the Buddha-Christ as Lord of the True Self, as a symbol of the Transcendence to which we experience ourselves related.

More about this will not be said in this foreword. Whether the execution of the program herein announced actually corresponds to the intention—and it is a program with which I identify as a "Christian or Buddhist of a higher order," like Schleiermacher who in his time designated himself over against pietism as "a pietist of a higher order"—Christians and Buddhists, as well as those who number themselves with neither, will have to decide for themselves on the basis of what is subsequently set forth.

Once again: one must start from the self if one is to find its "Lord"; without him it cannot become the "true self." In comparison to this self-discovery, the name or names we give its Lord are of secondary significance. They are signs along the way at which one need not stop. The Buddhist says of the boat that carries one across the river, that one must not carry it farther on his shoulders. And as Albert Schweitzer testified at the conclusion of his history of Life-of-Jesus research, he comes to us, as to his disciples at the Sea of Genesaret, "as One unknown, without a name," and we can only experience "who he is" if we obey his command to follow him. The two directions supplement each other in respect to the heritage and future of our self-realization along the path for which the Buddha-Christ can be a sign, meant in the sense of the already mentioned references, to Buddhists and Christians and beyond these, to any seeker along the way. In my experience this is also possible because it indicates a path on which we can leave behind the means of travel once they have rendered their service, in order to follow on our own feet the call of the Lord of our true self, to realize in freedom that to which we experience ourselves destined through him. To go this way will not be simple, for it is not *the* way. But it *is* one way, and we can encounter along this way quite unexpected fellow travelers, as, for example, a Confucius who in discussing the "Book of Changes" in his "Addresses to Pupils" is said to have declared against every absolutizing of a standpoint:

> It is the way (Tao) of Heaven that when something is completed, it changes. That something can long survive at the summit of fullness is unprecedented. That means: whoever regards himself as wise, his ears do not perceive the good words in the world . . . whoever knows to bring about the correct measure in fullness and emptiness, he is not full of himself, he is able to create what lasts (ch. 14,8, according to the translation of Richard Wilhelm).

These words we wish to note as travel advice for our progression through the religious philosophy of the Kyoto School under the sign of the Buddha-Christ as the symbol of the transcendence of self-understanding, in the hope that in this way there might be fulfilled something of that which the other great translator of Far Eastern wisdom had in mind when he wrote vis-à-vis his "Rendering of the Bi-Yän-Lu into German":

> One never knows whether there shall in the future not arise a completely new myth which narrates that the Buddha and the Christ had become united in one and the same person, so as to live in the heart of every man who opens himself to this highest potency (Wilhelm Gundert, 125).

Basel, Auf der Alp 3, Beginning of October 1981   *Fritz Buri*

Chapter 1

Introduction
A Critical Comparison of
Buddhism and Christianity

1. The Historical and Systematic Structure of the Comparison

In the long, diverse history of their encounters, Buddhism and Christianity have constantly confronted each other in formulations quite special to each. It was not *the* Christianity the Nestorians brought to China in the seventh century, but one which was rejected and persecuted as a heresy. Similarly, it was not *the* Buddhism that caused Francis Xavier, when he landed in Japan in 1549 and entered into conversation with the Buddhists, to exclaim: "The cursed Lutheran heresy is already here!" He was apparently dealing with representatives of Amida Buddhism, of which Karl Barth explained in a well-known remark that it was indeed right, but in its understanding of faith it should speak of Christ rather than Amida. Even within Buddhism Amida faith has itself not gone unchallenged past and present, and the disciples of Nichiren, for example, with their exclusive reliance upon the Lotus Sutra, are not outstripped by biblicism. The dialogue between the two religions and within each is today still burdened by exchange of the proper conception of the true form of the religion with one of the different forms that has appeared in the course of history. The more or less openly highlighted claim to exclusivity for their Christianity, or their Buddhism, makes their representatives unworthy of faith and incapable of dialogue.

The best cure for such rigidities is the knowledge of the history of Christianity and Buddhism since the time of their origins—a history in which so many diverse forms have emerged and continue to do so. In this way not only can a wholesome relativizing of their respective positions emerge, but also the insight into certain inner necessities of this development and its sequels. The answers that have been given to the final questions in the religions have a history, arose in definite situations, and have contributed to their alteration, but have also generated new questions. Their history is a problematic history, and, as it can only be understood as such, so their representatives can only understand one another by their acknowledgement of this. From the circumstances of opposed solutions to problems a common history of problems has developed.

Thus in the religious philosophy of the so-called Kyoto School which forms the object of our investigation we are not dealing with *the* Buddhism, nor again with *a* definite form of Buddhism, but at the very least with two essentially different kinds of Buddhism: principally with Zen Buddhism, but partially also with Pure Land Buddhism, or a combination of both. Comparably, the Christianity the representatives of this school have in view is not *the* Christianity. Rather, definite conceptions of Christianity are dealt with which are in no way shared by all its representatives today—to say nothing of the fact that they correspond to those of earlier times in all sections.

For these reasons we preface our investigation of the religious philosophy of the Kyoto School and the role Christianity played in it with a critical comparison of two magnitudes in question—a comparison that is just as indispensable as it is instructive for the understanding of this Buddhist philosophy of religion and its evaluation of Christianity. On such a basis we not only arrive at an appropriate understanding of the Buddhism of this philosophical movement, but can in all probability contrast its Buddha with a Christ who has more in common with him than the devotees of both who fail to take this problematic history into account are inclined to think—much less avow.

In order to provide an overview of this problematic history we begin with the determination that—despite all their differences and oppositions—Buddhism and Christianity share three factors in their origin and history.

> First, Buddhism and Christianity are both concerned with redemption, that is, with a knowledge of the problematic of the meaning of existence in the world and with its resolution in its fulfillment of meaning.

> Second, precisely in respect to the possibility of the fulfillment of the meaning of existence which they represent and the ways that lead to it, both have in the course of their history become quite different from what they were in their origin, and this in very different formulations on both sides.

> Third, this historical fate is connected with a problematic contained in the forms of their origin which works itself out in their history.

All three points are matters of scholarly, historical investigation, and our insights about them may raise the claim of universal provability. A difficulty, to be sure, consists in the fact that we possess no authentic testimonies concerning these origins, because neither Buddha nor Jesus recorded their teachings, and we are also dependent upon later sources concerning their persons. A scholarly, historical justification of our view of the problematic of origin and their unfolding in history issues precisely from the fact that the reason the two so-called founders did not record their teachings, lies in the presuppositions of the salvation announced by them: in the assumption of the imminent end of history on the part of Jesus, and in the nonattachment to things as the fundamental command of the Buddha.

Just as for Jesus and his disciples a recording of their preaching was rendered unnecessary by their expectation of the end of the world, so for Buddha and his disciples a literary deposit of their teachings would have been understood as a sign of attachment to the existing world and its things—an attachment they rejected, having recognized it as the cause of misfortune. Both presuppositions subsequently proved to be untenable: the early Christian expectation of the end, by the delay of the end; and the Buddhist nonattachment to things, by the necessity of attachment to the doctrine of nonattachment to things so as to hold on to this doctrine. Just as Christianity from the very beginning found itself with its expectation of the end to be in contradiction to the actual state of the world, and this became the presupposition of its continuation in history, so Buddhism, through the nature of its doctrine as teaching, felt compelled to develop it in a way that contradicted its central command of nonattachment to any kind of thing whatsoever. While Jesus' and Buddha's neglect of the literary recording of their preaching represents an immediate consequence of their fundamental presupposition—whether of the imminent end of the world or of nonattachment to things—the formation of a canon of holy scriptures stood in express opposition to those external and internal points of departure and is as such the consequence and simultaneously the proof of their problematic.[1] To be sure, still other factors

---

[1]In theories about the origin of early Christian literature and its later canonization it has been customary, since the time of Franz Overbeck, to take into account the eschatological character of the original situation or, rather, the suspension of that factor. Surprisingly, however, in Buddhism research no account is taken of the motif of the nonattachment to things, which we consider being parallel, as an essential cause explaining the lack of any written records from the hand of Buddha and of the relatively late recording of his doctrine; instead, this lack is here attributed to the custom of reciting sacred traditions and to other circumstances of history, culture, and religion. And yet one might precisely in this context make the point that in either case this transformation, whether effected earlier or later, was caused both by the intention to prevent the forming of sects as well as by a certain secularization; in Christianity in the Great Church, in Buddhism in Mahayana. Just as, for its survival, the Great Church needed a canon to which it could appeal against the multitude of spiritual testimonies, so in Mahayana one no longer felt that metaphysical speculations as advocated in the Abhidharma were a contradiction to the third "Noble Truth" of nonattachment to things; rather it was thought that one could therein see direction to pursue such speculations because they served to prove the nonexistence of the world of things. The course of doctrinal development in Christianity and Buddhism thus offers indirect proof that one must understand the fact that neither Jesus nor the Buddha fixed their teachings in writing in connection with the eschatological expectation in which the former lived, or with the instruction about nonattachment to things which the latter represented. The actions of both reflect a specific negative attitude toward the world which later ages were unable to sustain because they found themselves surviving with a doctrine that one needed to record so that one could hold fast to it. It is for that reason that this point of view is recommended here to the attention of Buddhism research and, to the extent it is not there considered, also to the origin of Christianity.

would have to be mentioned in order to explain this phenomenon of the original lack of records and the later rise of such. Even among those aspects we have considered it represents only one element of the much more comprehensive *problematic of the origin of Buddhism and Christianity* which deals not merely with the formal quest for the tradition and its emergence but of its content, that is, with the question of the redemption it proclaims and its presuppositions. The problematic inherent in Buddhism and Christianity from their inception is grounded in their essential nature as messages of salvation and in their presuppositions about the world. This problematic that stamps their entire history we have next to consider.

But their histories show both to be not only under the sign of this problematic of their origins; even more significant are their attempts to solve it—attempts which are characteristic of their respective histories. On both sides there is a continuous series of attempts to master this problematic and thus to understand the original message in ever new modifications as a way of realizing the meaning of existence in the world. This happens in such a way that new problems arise out of each attempt to solve it. Therefore our second task consists in working out the problematic of Buddhist and Christian attempts to solve the problematic of their origins.

On the basis of this presentation of their attempts throughout history to solve the problematic of their origins we are in a position—thirdly—to develop a *typology of the problematic of redemption in Buddhism and Christianity*, from an epistemological and metaphysical as well as an ethical and historical-philosophical perspective.

In this typology we are dealing not only with the problematic of Buddhist and Christian doctrines of redemption as they present themselves to us from their history under their respective points of view, but also with something like a treasury of symbols of truth which have been operative in them, which are surely something quite different from their conceptual objectifications, which can be maintained only by forfeiting the truth intended in those symbols. In our presentation of the philosophy of religion of the Kyoto School and its relationship to Christianity we are seeking finally to arrive at these symbols of truth in the Buddhist and Christian doctrines of redemption. Because we appeal thereby to a history of the problem of Christianity understood in the sense of Albert Schweitzer's consistent eschatology, in the conclusion of this introductory chapter attention will be given to a comparative survey of the Kyoto School and the School of Thoroughgoing Eschatology, which also serves as a transition to the main section of this study.

Together with the concluding systematic chapter the following historical survey forms the frame of our preoccupation with the philosophy of religion of the Kyoto School within which its nature and significance can be determined. For this purpose we shall have an opportunity in this introduction—as indicated—for some systematization which then will serve as the foundation for our concluding position in the last chapter of this work.

2. The Problematic of the Origins of Buddhism and Christianity

Despite all their material difference, in their origins Buddhism and Christianity exhibit a structurally mutual twofold problematic, which is grounded in the nature of redemption as the overcoming of the problematic of the meaning of human existence in the world.

The Buddha and Jesus both view the question of meaning which moves them—and which they answer—in the context of a specific traditional view of Being which already contains a certain solution to the question of meaning which they nevertheless found insufficient and which therefore was decisively transformed by them.

For the Buddha this cosmic presupposition consists in the idea of reincarnation in samsara, the beginningless and endless becoming and passing away in accord with karma, that is, in accord with earlier behavior, and in the expectation of being freed from this fate in Nirvana sometime in the future. In this context the Buddha sees life as suffering amidst transiency, evident in the evils of aging, sickness, and death until it is extinguished in Nirvana after countless reincarnations.

On the contrary, Jesus views human existence in relation to God's history with creation, which has a beginning and will come to an end, whereby the history which occurs between beginning and end is determined by the conflict of God with the powers which, although fallen from him, struggle against him—powers under whose dominion humanity not only gets entangled in all kinds of evil, but also in guilt before God. Here a conclusive and final redemption is also envisaged, whereby through his Messiah God prepares an end for the evil world and will establish his kingdom on earth or in his new world. In place of a karma-judgment which perpetuates itself in samsara—a judgment which determines the stages of reincarnation, there is here a judgment at the end of time, in which God or his Messiah will decide on those who do and those who do not belong to the Kingdom of Glory.

These views of human existence in the world, of its absurdity and fulfillment of meaning, taken over by Buddha and Jesus are nevertheless transformed by both in fundamental ways, especially in terms of a possible fulfillment of meaning. For both, this transformation derives from a special insight which they shared: Buddha in his Enlightenment under the Bodhi tree,[2] and Jesus, at his bap-

---

[2]Karl Eugen Neumann, *Übertragungen aus dem Pali-Kanon* (Zurich: Artemis Verlag/Vienna: Paul Zsolnay Verlag, 1956) 1:188ff., 276ff., 641ff.

tism in the Jordan, in the revelation of the Spirit that he was destined by God to be the future Messiah.[3]

Buddha's Enlightenment contained two elements. First, the insight that the cause of suffering is desire, which leads us astray due to ignorance about the true nature of the world, and the attachment to things arising from it. Attachment to things is senseless because there are no things to hold onto; everything—even the "I" attached to things—is only a momentary uniting of nonsubstantial elements which constantly disintegrate. Second, to free humanity from this insane attachment to nonexistent things he recognizes as a task from the compassion which is likewise grounded in the relation in which all beings stand by virtue of "dependent origination" (pratitya-samutpada). Out of compassion he will teach suffering humanity this insight and the resultant nonattachment to things. Therefore, to the first three of the "Noble Truths," which contain his fundamental insight, he adds as a fourth the "Eightfold Path" which leads from the acceptance of the teaching about moral behavior to the attainment of Enlightenment.[4]

---

[3]Mark 1:9-11 and parallels.

[4]For the basic insights of the Buddha brought into connection with his Enlightenment by the tradition one should consult its presentation and commentary in Hermann Oldenberg's *Buddha* (Goldmanns Gelbe Taschenbücher, 103-26, 211-66 [ET: *Buddha: His Life, His Doctrine, His Order* (London: Williams and Norgate, 1922) 72-94; 138-56], and Helmuth von Glasenapp's relevant notations in the same volume, 411-77); Etienne Lamotte, *Histoire du Bouddhisme Indien*, 2nd ed. (Louvain, 1976) 25ff.; Edward Conze, *Der Buddhismus*, 6th ed. (Urban Taschenbücher, 1977) 39ff. [ET: *Buddhism: Its Essence and Development*, Harper Torchbook (New York: Harper & Brothers, 1951) 27ff.]; Hajime Nakamura, "Die Grundlehren des Buddhismus. Ihre Wurzeln in Geschichte und Tradition," in *Buddhismus der Gegenwart*, ed. Heinrich Dumoulin (Herder, 1970) 9-34 [ET: "The Basic Teachings of Buddhism," in *Buddhism in the Modern World* (Macmillan, 1974) 3-31]; excerpted from *Saeculum* 20 (1969): 173-98. The "Four Noble Truths" and the schema of "dependent origination" are here cited from the work last mentioned (following the German edition).

The Four Noble Truths:

1. "This, O Monks, is the noble truth of suffering: Birth is suffering; old age is suffering; sickness is suffering; death is suffering; to be yoked with what is not loved is suffering; to be separated from one's loved one is suffering; not to attain what one desires is suffering. Briefly, the five aggregates which arise from attachment are suffering."

2. "This, O Monks, is the noble truth about the origin of suffering. It is desire which causes reincarnation, accompanied by sensual joys which here and there finds its satisfaction, the longing for lust, the longing for becoming, the longing for non-existence."

3. "This, O monks, is the noble truth about the annihilation of suffering. It is the annihilation of the longing, so that no wish still remains. It is the

Also in the preaching of Jesus such an appeal to a definite attitude is proposed on the basis of a change of thinking: "Change your thinking for the kingdom of God has drawn near," is the way the Synoptics express the summary of his preaching.[5] Just as nonattachment to the world does for the Buddha, so for Jesus the imminent end of the world forms the ontological foundation for the attitude which brings fullness of meaning. If this ontological foundation is already actualized in the miracles Jesus performed, the same could be said for his forgiveness of sins and condemnation of the impenitent as anticipation of his messianic function in the Last Judgment. In contrast to the Buddha, however. Jesus is not only a teacher but one who acts in the event of being; and his decisive intervention consists in his sacrificial death through which he took it upon himself to facilitate the turn of the aeons, just as he then also understands his messianic task in the sense of the "Suffering Servant of God" to be the enactment of a vicarious atonement.

As for the Buddha, so for Jesus these corrections of the traditional concept of redemption are connected with a problem of conformity with being.

---

surrender, letting-go, becoming free from and discarding this craving."

4. "This, O monks, is the noble truth about the way to the annihilation of suffering. It is this Noble Eightfold Path which includes: right faith, right decision, right word, right deed, right life, right striving, right thinking, right meditation" (21).

The Formula of the Causal Nexus (*Pratitya-samutpada*) is here rendered in the following form:

1. Because of ignorance the forms(sankhara) arise. Literally *sankhara* means what is formed or what is shaped, formed and set alongside. Frequently the translation "element of Being" or "karmic forms" is appropriate;

2. Because of the forms knowledge arises;

3. Because of knowledge name and corporeality (namely, psychophysical existence) arise;

4. Because of name and corporeality the six sense organs (the sixth is thinking) and their objects arise;

5. Because of the sense organs and their objects touching arises;

6. Because of touching perception (sensation or feeling) arises;

7. Because of perception desire (or longing) arises;

8. Because of desire seizing arises;

9. Because of seizing becoming (or worldly existence) arises;

10. Because of becoming birth arises;

11. Because of birth, old age and death, pain and lamentation, suffering, grief and despair arise. —All these comprise suffering in general" (23) [ET, 15].

Oldenberg describes the Buddha's attainment of these insights in biographical connection from the legends of his youth up to the Benares sermon (Oldenberg, *Buddha*, 98-132).

[5]Mark 1:15 and parallels.

The Buddha dissolves the fate of samsara by the disclosure of the error in respect to "dependent origination" and through a corresponding nonattachment to things. Is samsara therefore only a delusion or at best a fanciful notion that arises out of the futile attachment to things, a mythological image for a human attitude and its consequences—but in no case a transhuman ontological reality? But the Buddha seems to conceive the whole chain of events from samsara through reincarnation and karma to Nirvana as such a reality existing independently of humans and encompassing them. Can reincarnation occur even if there is no individual that can be reincarnated? Has Karma not therefore lost its object?[6] The Nirvana at the end, however, becomes superfluous if it can already

---

[6]It is interesting to pursue how a modern scholar of Mahayana Buddhism of the rank of a Hajime Nakamura deals with the problem of the self. He first establishes by means of a passage from the Benares sermon that for the Buddha there is "no self" or "ego" in the sense of a "metaphysical substance." By appealing to the doctrine of the five skandhas, i.e., "perceptions, feelings, physical corporeality, formations, knowing" as "impersonal powers, movements, functions, and processes," he explains: "Buddhism swept away the traditional concept of a substance called 'soul' or 'ego' which had up to that time dominated the minds of the superstitious and the intellectuals alike," and posited in its place "the principal of *anatta* (nonself) which has held throughout Buddhism." Anatta means: "The relationship between its components is constantly changing, it is never the same for two consecutive moments. It follows that no sooner had individuality begun than its dissolution, disintegration, also begins." To the Theravadins who understood this principle as a "denial of the ego" Nakamura nevertheless makes the objection: "The Buddha clearly told us what the self is not, but he did not give any clear account of what it is." It is therefore completely "wrong to assume that Buddhism holds that there is no self at all." The Buddha did not deny the self; rather he remained silent about it. Rather than affirming or denying the existence of the atman, the Buddha advocated a philosophy that recognizes the limits of philosophy." Accordingly, Nakamura believes that the "No Self theory in the Buddha's original meaning does not mean the complete denial of the self." By referring to the ethical instructions of the Buddha he emphasizes that the Buddha "acknowledges the existence of the self as the subject of human activity in its practical and ethical respects." "The self is for him no graspable, concrete thing, but can be realized only when we act according to universal norms of human existence. When we act morally the true self manifests itself. Thus, the self of Buddhism was not a metaphysical entity, but a practical postulate" (*Buddhismus der Gegenwart*, 17-20 [ET, 8-11]; cited here from the German version).
On this struggle with the problem of the self in its metaphysical or nonmetaphysical, empirical and ethical aspects one should consider the relevant statements which Glasenapp in his discussion of the doctrine of the skhandas offered as an extension of Oldenberg's presentation of the theory of the Dharma by which the state of affairs with respect to this one basic question of Buddhism is

be attained in the Enlightenment in which the Eightfold Path culminates. And yet in his teaching the Buddha presupposed this entire conceptual world as a subsisting in Being (Seinsbestand), although he explains it in his teaching and through its observance as nonexistent. So what are we to believe? That the traditional teaching nevertheless consists in an affirmation of (the world's) Being, or that for the sake of the fulfillment of meaning by appealing to Enlightenment and through a corresponding attitude it is unmasked as a mere delusion?

A corresponding ambiguity is present also in the radicalizing of the expectation of the Kingdom of God into an imminent expectation or an inbreaking of the end of the world in Jesus' preaching and conduct. Through its radicalization into an event fulfilling itself in the present the traditional expectation of the end, which presupposes a fulfillment that is not yet being enacted, is rendered problematic. And yet Jesus still presupposes it as a reality—as the Buddha presupposed the traditional notion of Being. The difference from that of the Buddha consists only in the fact that Jesus did not make the tradition out to be an illusion, but radicalized it accordingly into an imminent expectation and believed himself and his disciples to be in a situation that is irreconcilable with the traditional conception, because the nearness of the Kingdom or indeed its presentness in the one who knows himself destined to be the coming Messiah is not anticipated in it. The old framework remains, but the picture which it contains is replaced by another. The picture no longer fits the frame and the frame no longer fits the picture.

To this inner problematic of their teaching about salvation which pertains equally to the Buddha and Jesus there is now added a second, equally pertinent to both, which derives from their environment, and which is connected to the problematic of the former. For the Buddha this consists in the fact that he—on the one hand—establishes his admonitions with pronouncements about Being in the sense of pratitya-samutpada, in consequence of which there are neither individual things nor an individual ego, but on the other, rejects a discussion of metaphysical questions—whether the world has a beginning or is eternal, and whether there is a life of the soul after death—as useless and detrimental. Instead of such discussions which in his eyes only lead to controversy and amount to an attachment to things, he admonishes his disciples to follow after him in traversing the "Middle Path" which takes the middle course between denial of and involvement in the world[7] and is comparable to a "having as though having not"—only with a different grounding than with Paul.[87]

---

certainly not made simpler (Oldenberg, *Buddha*, 415ff.). It is not even surprising that in his treatment of the problem of the self in Buddhism Conze makes reference to Hume, William James, Herbert Spencer, and Schopenhauer (Edward Conze, *Der Buddhismus*, 17 [ET, 19-20]).

[7]In this connection compare the illustrations of the Buddha's "Stance against

There were problems, however, inherent both in those negative and these positive instructions. How far should one go in the practice of asceticism? Is it

---

other Philosophers and Religions," his "Silence about Metaphysical Problems" and his conception of the "partial truth of the Ideas" with which Nakamura opens his contribution to *Buddhism der Gegenwart*. There he enumerates the questions to which the Buddha customarily gave no answer:
Whether or not the world is eternal?
Whether or not the world is infinite?
Whether the soul is or is not to be distinguished from it?
Whether or not a person exists after death in any way whatsoever?
Further, he illustrates the silence of the Buddha with his "Parable of the Man Injured by a Poisoned Arrow": "The one struck by the poison arrow was rushed to the doctor who wished to extract the arrow. The wounded man however did not permit it, but cried: 'The arrow will not be extracted until I know the man whom I chanced to meet, the family to which he belongs, whether he is tall, short, or of medium build, whether his skin color is black, brown, or yellow. . . . ' Just as the one struck by the poison arrow would die before he could experience the answer to his question, so would the disciple curious about salvation succumb to the sufferings of the world before solving all metaphysical questions" (*Buddhismus der Gegenwart*, 10; text here does not appear in English version). As proof of the merely partial truth of metaphysical teachings Nakamura supplies the "Parable of the Blind Person and the Elephant": As the blind persons who have touched the parts of the elephant say, "An elephant is this way and not another, he is not like that but another," until they eventually quarrel and beat one another, so it happens with the ascetics and Brahmins who have respectively seen only a part of the truth and assert: "The truth is this way and not that, truth is not like that, but like this . . . " (ibid., 11).
As a positive addition to the silence in respect to the questions that lead nowhere, but only cause strife, the Buddha understands his "purely ethical" "philosophy as the path," as a "vehicle" for crossing the river of life, in order to travel successfully "from the shore of the mundane experience of non-Enlightenment, of ignorance (avidya), craving (kama) and of suffering to the other shore of transcendental wisdom (*vidya*), liberation (moksa) from bondage and suffering." "There one builds a raft and can thus reach the other shore. 'What would you think of this person?" asks the Buddha. "Would he be a clever man if, upon reaching the other shore, he—out of gratitude for the raft which carried him over the stream to certainty—should get attached to the raft, put it on his back and wander around with its weight.' The monk replied: "No." And the Buddha concluded: "In the same way the vehicle must be discarded and abandoned, when once the other shore of Enlightenment is reached" (ibid., 14-15 [ET, 4]). For the ethic of the middle rank see especially Oldenberg, *Buddha*, 267-352, and Nakamura, "Die Grundlehren des Buddhismus. Ihre Wurzeln in Geschichte und Tradition," 30-34 [ET, 25-30]).
[8]1 Cor 7:29ff.

not possible that in the striving to attain Enlightenment an effluence of the thirst for life and egoistic attachment to illusory things is just as operative as in attachment to the world? And how is denial of the world even possible in a specific measure and in such moderation as the Middle Path requires if there is no individual who can determine the measure and will it? Is a person in a position to fulfill such demands and thus to effect his or her own salvation, or is he or she therein not dependent upon aids—not only proximate ones but those from a higher world, as religions have long since taught them—even those with which the Buddhist community loved to surround themselves? If one however seeks to attain Nirvana through his own power and undertakes his own salvation, one thereby contradicts "dependent origination" which connects every mundane event and human act and from which issues the Buddha's compassion for suffering humanity and all creatures. If holiness suffices and is realizable at all, is it possible for one to separate himself from the world in such a way? Is it possible to succeed without metaphysics and psychology, or can one stop halfway in dealing with these questions and cut off discussion by silence, thus leaving them unanswered, as the Buddha did?

These are the questions put to the Buddha by his disciples and with which they concerned themselves after the death of the master. Were they not required to enquire further, especially in view of the fact that the master said to them in his last address: "Be your own lights!"?[9]

Even more radically than the Buddha and his disciples, Jesus and his community saw themselves rendered problematic by the actual course of the world—Jesus, at the latest, on the cross and the disciples after his departure—through the manner in which an attempt was made to solve the problem of meaning in the expectation of the immediately imminent end of the world. Through his proclamation of the nearness of the Kingdom of God and in his atoning death for the purpose of effecting the turn of the aeons Jesus had not only done away with an illusion—as the Buddha intended in his teaching—but proclaimed a world situation and demanded a corresponding conduct in order to participate in God's Kingdom; and with his own conduct he had attempted to reach a goal which, like his preaching, proved to be an illusion. Contrary to the actual course of history, an inbreaking of the new form of the world could be seen in the resurrection of the crucified one, in his appearances, in the receiving of the Spirit and its effects, and the fulfillment of the End Time which, already begun in a preliminary way, could be expected in the distant future.[10] But on the one hand these happenings dealt with only a portion of the promised and

---

[9]Cited by Nakamura, "Die Grundlehren des Buddhismus. Ihre Wurzeln in Geschichte und Tradition," 20 [ET, 11].

[10]Cf. Acts 1:4-11; 2:22-40; 3:18-21.

anticipated end event, and on the other, the necessary postponement of the end contradicts its earlier imminent expectation.[11] This required becoming reconciled with the world and becoming "at home" in it, and this in a way which contradicted the demands on which Jesus had made the attainment of the fulfillment of meaning in the Kingdom of God dependent.[12]

We have accordingly outlined the twofold problematic with which Buddhism and Christianity saw themselves confronted in their origin in structurally analogous ways. With their first appearance in history they spoke of the realization of meaning in a conceptual form which was actually diverted from the intended realization of meaning, and simultaneously the realization of meaning so envisaged in the situation in which each found itself with it was perceived as insufficient and was rendered problematic by reality. The history of Buddhism and Christianity is the history of attempts to solve the problematic of their origins and proves itself to be no less problematic than these.

3. The Problematic of the Attempts of Buddhism and Christianity to Solve the Problem of their Origins

Corresponding to the specific problem of their form of origin, there are for Buddhism and Christianity two ways, respectively, in which the attempt can be made to overcome the problematic of origin. For the Buddha's community the point of departure consists in striding the "Middle Path" by which Nirvana, into which the Buddha has already entered, is attained, while his followers are still located in the world "on the way." In a corresponding way Jesus' community still remained in the world in the expectation of the Parousia of their exalted Lord for the purpose of inaugurating the Kingdom of God, in which they prepared themselves to participate. Over against the fulfillment of their strivings and hopes stands the world in the form of samsara or under control of demonic powers. Both face the situation that the world, as both the Buddha and Jesus envisaged it, must be overcome.

Among the successors of the Buddha this redemptive overcoming of the world has been attempted in two ways, both of which represent a radicalization or an outgrowth of his admonition about nonattachment to things. The one believed that the uncertainty which pertains to distancing oneself from the world and resigning oneself to the world in the instruction of the "middle path" could only be resolved by choosing to distance itself from the world, not only because,

---

[11]Cf., e.g., Matt 16:28 and Rom 13:11 with 2 Thess 2:1ff. and 2 Pet 3:4, 8, 9, 14-16.

[12]Cf., e.g., the sayings about marriage, possessions, and domesticity in Matt 19:12-21, 2, and 1 Cor 7:29ff. with 1 Tim 2:15; 4:1-5, and the relation to authority in Matt 19:25ff. with 1 Tim 2:1-4 and Titus 3:1.

being the more difficult, it promises more success for a higher rebirth, but because it is more beneficial for the immersion that leads to Enlightenment than all preoccupation with the world. Thus in intending thereby to be especially faithful and zealous followers of the Buddha they became ascetics who by extreme denial strived to actualize the ideal of holiness. Against our stated objection that in different ways they run counter to the instructions and ideal of the Buddha, they sought to obviate this by collecting the doctrines and stories transmitted from him in the so-called Pali Canon. In the 300 years following the Buddha's departure the tradition had become so copious that this arhat ideal could emerge from it. Because compliance with it was only possible for a small circle of adherents, this monastic community—in whose salvation the masses could win a portion only by patronizing them—was called Hinayana, the "Small Vehicle."

The Hinayanists obtained their name from the representatives of the "Great Vehicle," the Mahayana, while for themselves and their devotees they claimed they represented "the teachings of the elders" (Theravada). By contrast the Mahayanists emphasized that in accord with the "middle path" it is possible to connect even surrender to the world with world denial. For this they could appeal not only to the doctrine of "dependent origination" from which there issued for the Buddha his goodwill toward every being, but also to his instruction about nonattachment to things in that it extended this explanation of the origin of suffering to the sphere of knowledge and saw in the discriminating knowledge directed at objects, and in its conceptuality, the sources of the illusory world of images. In contrast to the phenomenalism represented by Kant 2,000 years later according to which in our understanding we have to do not with mere illusion (Schein-maya) but with appearance, they assume, whether rightly or wrongly, behind illusion—not like Kant who posited behind appearance a "thing in itself"—the nothing. Nothingness underlies the illusion as its cause, and the unenlightened one only deals with a fanciful world of illusion, while to the enlightened Nothingness emerges as the true being of everything which putatively exists.[13]

---

[13]These different formulations of Buddhism are described extensively in Etienne Lamotte, *Histoire du Bouddhisme Indien* (see note 4), and more concisely in Edward Conze, *Der Buddhismus* (see note 4), and with special reference to the teaching in Erich Frauwallner, *Die Philosophie des Buddhismus*, 2 vols. (Berlin, 1936, 1958); Ninian Smart, *Doctrines and Argument in Indian Philosophy*, 2nd ed. (George Allen & Unwin, 1969, [1]1964); Hans Wolfgang Schumann, *Buddhismus. Philosophie der Erlösung* (Dalp Taschenbücher: Bern, Francke, 1963), *Buddhismus, Stifter, Schulen, and Systeme*, 2nd ed. (Olten and Freiburg: Walter-Verlag, 1978) (both only for Indian Buddhism); Helmut Glasenapp, *Die Philosophie der Inder*, 3rd ed. (Kroener, 1974). Further bibliography in Heinrich

As the comparative reference to Kant indicates, this doctrine of Nothingness (*sunyata*) represents an equally awesome and complicated formulation of epistemological reflections and metaphysical speculations in which—in connection with and on the assumption of the corresponding methods of sublimation—the world which stands in the way of Nirvana turns out to be Nothingness. By equating this philosophical concept of Nothingness with the mythological image of Nirvana, samsara as the essence of the world becomes identical with Nirvana, in whose emptiness things appear in their fullness, as they truly are from this vantage. This sunyata philosophy extends itself through the whole of Mahayana Buddhism, from Nagarjuna (ca. AD 200) to the most representative current Japanese philosopher, Keiji Nishitani.[14]

In view of these mental accomplishments, and the sutras and doctrinal writings growing out of them, the question arises as to the effect of the Buddha's silence about metaphysical questions. In addition to this sunyata philosophy there are in Hinayana, and especially in Mahayana, numerous other metaphysical speculations in which the Buddha is equated with the universe and is accordingly to be found in all things.[15] In addition to such ontology there is nevertheless also

---

Dumoulin, *Begegnung mit dem Buddhismus* (Herderbücherei, 1978) 163ff. A comprehensive presentation of his own research and of the history of research in this sphere is offered by Hajime Nakamura in his latest work, *Indian Buddhism: A Survey with Bibliographical Notes* (Kufs Publication, Japan, 1980), reviewed by Fritz Buri in *Theologische Zeitschrift* 38 (1982): 61.

[14]An interesting comparison of the philosophy of Nothingness, especially that of Nagarjuna, with Kant's philosophy can be found in T. R. V. Murti, *The Central Philosophy of Buddhism: A Study of the Madhyamika System*, 2nd ed. (London: Allen & Unwin, 1974) 123ff. Murti sees in the philosophy of both a "Copernican revolution against dogmatism and speculative metaphysics."

On Nagarjuna, cf. Frederick Streng, *Emptiness: A Study in Religious Meaning* (Nashville: Abingdon Press, 1967) with rich text interpretations; K. Venhata Ramaan, *Nagarjuna's Philosophy* (Delhi: Motilal Banarsidass, 1975), the standard work of Theodore Stcherbatsky, *The Conception of Buddhist Nirvana*, 5th ed. (Delhi: Motilal Banarsidass, 1978, [1]1968); and the essay by Karl Jaspers, *Die grossen Philosophen* (Munich: Piper Verlag, 1957) 934-56 [ET: *The Great Philosophers*, ed. Hannah Arendt, trans. Ralph Manheim, vol. 2 (New York: Harcourt, Brace and World, 1957, 1964) 416-33]; on Keiji Nishitani's sunyata philosophy, cf. the two chapters especially concerned with sunyata in his principal religiophilosophical work *Was ist Religion?* [ET: *Religion and Nothingness*] (cf. our chapter on Nishitani, pp.).

[15]Cf. Ed. Conze, *Der Buddhismus*, "The Old Wisdom School," and "The Mahayana and the New Wisdom School," 84-135 [ET: 89-143].

an idealistic philosophy of consciousness for which everything is "only consciousness,"[16] as well as maxims of Zen masters which ridicule all logical thinking.[17]

Besides this philosophy or unphilosophy of Zen the other great achievement of Mahayana consists in the formulation of a rich sphere of divinities by adopting the deities from the areas into which Buddhism extended itself, and the world of the Bodhisattvas, that is, those holy and enlightened ones who out of compassion for those who are ignorant refuse entry into Nirvana in order to accompany them on the way to salvation. Through the cultic veneration of the vast numbers of Buddhas and Bodhisattvas Mahayana Buddhism became a world religion, which it certainly was not in the beginning.

In this connection one figure among the countless hosts of Buddhas and Bodhisattvas is especially emphasized: the one that arises from the myth of Dharmakara—the monk who became king—who on his way to Bodhisattva-hood

---

[16]Of fundamental significance for this "*Nur Bewusstsein* (One-Mind)" philosophy is the treatise of unknown provenance stemming from the first or second century AD, *The Awakening of Faith: Text with Commentary* (Columbia University Press, 1967), supplied with more than 170 commentaries, among them one by the Korean Buddhist Wonhyo (617-86), whose philosophy Ock Hee Pyun compared with that of Karl Jaspers in her Basel dissertation of 1976 entitled "The Understanding of Faith in Wonhyo and Karl Jaspers and its Significance for the Christian Faith in Korea" (partially reprinted under the title "Man in Wonhyo and Karl Jaspers," in *Journal of Korean Cultural Research Institute*, 29 (Ewha Women's University, Seoul, 1977): 289-312.

[17]These Zen maxims and their related stories and commentaries have been made available to us in two German translations: the *Bi-Yän-Lu, Niederschrift von der Smaragdenen Felswand*, 3 vols., by Wilhelm Gundert (Munich: Karl Hanser Verlag, 1964/1965/1973), and *Mumonkan: Die Schranke ohne Tor*, by Heinrich Dumoulin (Mainz: Gruenewald, 1975). While Gundert translated and elucidated only 68 fragments, the English edition, translated by Thomas and J. C. Cleary, contains all 100 instances: *The Blue Cliff Record*, 3 vols (Boulder and London: Shambala, 1977). Shortly after Heinrich Dumoulin's translation of the Mumonkan, there appeared two others: *Zu den Quellen des Zen* (Munich: O. W. Barth, 1976), and Walter Liebenthal, *Zutritt durch die Wand* (Heidelberg: 1977). The great promoter and interpreter of Zen sayings and stories is D. T. Suzuki in whose numerous works are to be found a host of such anecdotes and koans, as well as rich critical studies of the Zen thinking corresponding to them. Heinrich Dumoulin, in *Zen, Geschichte und Gestalt* (Berlin: Francke, 1959) [ET: *A History of Zen Buddhism* (New York: Pantheon Books, Random House, 1963)], provides a survey of the history of Zen and its different forms.

vowed not to enter into Nirvana until he has led all living beings to this way and therewith into the "Pure Land." By exclusive trust in this vow the devotees of Amida hope to find salvation.[18]

Higher than all other Buddhas, however, stands the divine Buddha which the historical Buddha became in Nirvana. After he represented an incarnation of Amida Buddha on earth, he was elevated into the series of Buddhas who each rule an age of the world and is as such the Lord of the present age. The relationship in which his modes of being stand to each other is governed by the Trikaya doctrine, the three bodies of the Buddha, in which a distinction is made between Nirmanakaya, his earthly body of transformation; the Shambhogakaya, his radiant body of glory; and the Dharmakaya, the body of the doctrine, in the form of which he represents the corporealizing of the one truth that enlightens the whole world and causes it to appear—again, only to the Enlightened—as the Nothingness in which samsara and Nirvana are one.

The changes the figure of the Buddha experienced in the course of time can be traced quite impressively in the history of its pictorial representation.[19] In the springtime of Buddhism there were no pictures of the Buddha, but use was made instead of the symbol of the wheel of the doctrine, which the Buddha set in

---

[18]No less than for Zen, D. T. Suzuki is also the great authority for Amida Buddhism as translator of and commentator on Shinran's major work, Kyogyoshinsho, newly edited in 1973 on the occasion of the 800th birthday of Otani University. Besides Suzuki's essays on Shin Buddhism, a second volume of this monumental work contains also the biography of Shinran (Godensho) and the catechism of Shin Buddhism (the Tannisho) composed by one of his pupils. For the conclusion of the Kyogyoshinsho, which is lacking in Suzuki's translation, one should consult the edition published in 1966 by Ryukoku University. In addition, the Shin Buddhism Translation Series edited by the Honganji International Center in Kyoto makes available *Letters of Shinran* (1978) and his *Notes on One-calling and Many-calling* (1980), both with extensive notes. On the life and teaching of Shinran together with many quotations, cf. *The Contemporary World*, edited by the Nishi Honganji Commission on the Promotion of Religious Education (Kyoto, 1974). A German translation of Tannisho by Ryogi Okochi and Klaus Otte, together with a conversation of the two on "Encounter between Buddhism and Christianity," appeared in 1979 from Origo Verlag, Bern. Two years earlier the Hompa Honganji in Kyoto had already published a German translation, together with interpretations, by Michio Sato.

[19]On the history of the images of the Buddha the Luxury Volume, *The Image of Buddha*, with an excellent accompanying text, was edited by UNESCO in 1978, as well as *Pure Land Buddhist Painting* (Zurich: Kodansha International & Boxerbooks, Inc., 1977).

motion, or representations of his feet or footprints, especially as decoration for stupas in which his relics and those of other holy ones were preserved. Statues of the Buddha appeared only under Hellenistic influence in the Ghandara period—statues which later, in accord with the art styles of the countries where Buddhism spread, experienced specific configurations and thus represent at the same time a history of the changes of Buddhist doctrine.

Beside these ascertainable influences of the West in art, such may also be assumed in the doctrine, and indeed in two directions: from the side of the Nestorians in China in the likely approximation of the redeemer figures—Christ and Amida, Mary and Kannon, as well as from the East to the West where the Buddha became unconsciously taken up among the saints of the Church through the legend of Barlaam and Josaphat, and a mutual influence may have occurred also in the formulation of the legend. Because of all these similarities in the legends about the Buddha and Christ, as well as in the narrative materials, it is not possible to establish the priority of origin.[20]

What can be established nevertheless is the parallelism between the problematic historical emergence of Buddhism and Christianity. For all their material differences and the temporal shifts that appeared earlier and later on, the historical problematic of the two bears a remarkable resemblance in its basic structure. Because the sources bearing on its origin date further back for Christianity than is the case for Buddhism, and the former have been more extensively researched than the latter and their content has proven more amenable to a conceptual grasp than the formation of the Buddhist doctrine which presents a logical confusion for our concepts, a clear image can be formed of the history of Christianity—even if everything in it is not always logical. In any case, however, the structural parallelism is apparent.[21]

---

[20]On this much treated theme, cf. the bibliography in *RGG* III, s.v. "Buddhism und Christentum," and in *NAJTh* 20/21 (1978) as well as Shanta Ratnayak, "A Buddhist-Christian monastic Dialogue," in *The Maha Bodhi* (June-Sept 1979): 158-72, esp. on Barlaam and Josaphat.

[21]Very instructive for this parallelism is a comparison of the presentations of the problematic of historical origins in *Buddhismus* by Junjiro Takakusu, in *The Essentials of Buddhist Philosophy*, ed. Wing Tsit Chan and Charles A. Moore, 3rd ed. (Honolulu: University of Hawaii, 1956); Hajime Nakamura, *Ways of Thinking of Eastern Peoples: India-China-Tibet-Japan* (1964); as well as the three volumes on *The Indian Mind*, *The Chinese Mind*, and *The Japanese Mind*, all published by the East-West Center Press, Honolulu, in 1967; and for *Christianity* the works by Albert Schweitzer, *Die Mystik des Apostels Paulus*, 1930 [ET: *The Mysticism of Paul the Apostle* (1931)]; *Reich Gottes und Christentum* (1967) [ET: *Kingdom of God and Christianity* (1968], both by J. C. B.

As in Buddhism—after initial convergence—the "Small" and "Great" Vehicles virtually immediately became opposed with their world-denying arhat ideal and world-affirming Bodhisattva, respectively, so the Great Church developed on the foundation of Christianity out of holy congregations which awaited the return of the Lord and from all kinds of syncretistic formations—with the exception that, in contrast to Hinayana, it collected the canon and established rules for its exposition in order to combat its heretical use and individual prophetic spiritualists, and, as well, instituted a corresponding hierarchical organization. From the community of the saints arises the sacral corporate body supposedly instituted by Christ which is in possession of the saint and is used by him in respective institutions for the salvation of the believers. Rudiments of this development are already evident in the canonized tradition and are reflected in new spiritual horizons corresponding to the course of history and with the aid of its interpretive possibilities. The end of the world from whose imminent inbreaking early Christianity expected salvation was transferred to the far future due to its nonarrival, and in its place appeared the Church in whose own revelation and aids to salvation Christ is present and effects redemption based on faith and the use of the sacraments. As in Buddhism, Nirvana can be attained in the future Beyond as well as in the present, so also the Church holds out the prospect of a future salvation in the Beyond, which can however begin here and now as the starting point of a path to salvation which leads to Paradise. In both Buddhism and Christianity the concepts are quite diverse and vary from an immediate spiritual event to its inclusion in a strongly regulated cult and ritualism. It is understandable that Catholic theologians today find in Buddhism phenomena which are related to their mysticism, their cultus, and their meditation practices.[22] In the history of both, monasteries also play an important role, both as places of Nirvana, or the Kingdom of God, as well as innerworldly agents of culture. Both also experienced doctrinal controversies for whose settlement councils were summoned and in which mundane powers became involved.[23]

Mohr/Paul Siebeck, Tübingen; Martin Werner, *Die Entstehung des christlichen Dogmas* (1941) [ET (abridged): *The Formation of Christian Dogma* (New York: Harper & Brothers, 1957), *Der protestantische Weg des Glaubens*, vol. 1 (Bern: Paul Haupt, 1955) and Fritz Buri, *Dogmatik als Selbstverständnis des christlichen Glaubens*, 3 vols. (Bern and Stuttgart: Paul Haupt, 1956, 1962, 1978).

[22]Examples of this are Heinrich Dumoulin's *Östliche Meditationen und christliche Mystik* (Munich: Karl Alber Verlag, 1966) and Hugo M. Enomija-Lassalle's *Zen Meditation für Christen* (Weinheim: Otto Wilhelm Barth Verlag, 1969).

[23]In the expansion of Christianity and of Buddhism and in the establishing of councils, the Emperor Constantine and King Asoka (273-232 BC) play a

Just as the formative process which occurred in Mahayana by contrast with early Buddhism produced rich metaphysical speculation, so Christian theology also developed from the transformation of eschatological Christianity into the great Catholic Church. Just as there, so here the new understanding of salvation arising in a changed environment necessitated a new formulation of the nature of the Redeemer who effects this salvation. Just as from the Mahayanistic turning toward the world there emerged from the historical Buddha an analogous cosmic Buddha and the figures of the Bodhisattvas, so the historical Jesus who was defined as the coming Messiah of the turn of the aeons no longer corresponds to the new conception of redemption in terms of sacramentally mediated immortality, necessitated by the delay of the Parousia—quite apart from the unclarity about these matters—and must be replaced by a new redeemer figure in view of the newly conceived notion of salvation. Deification of the flesh could only be brought about by a redeemer who was himself God in person—not merely an incarnation of the divine Logos.[24] While for Buddhism a place in the series of heavenly Buddhas doubtless remains for the Buddha who appears as God on earth as one of their incarnations, and only the earthly and supraearthly modes of appearance of the Buddha must be brought into one relation, the problem is significantly more difficult in Christianity because of its monotheism and its concepts of substance and person. Therefore the doctrine of the trinity and the two-nature Christology represent a much more complicated and a much more essential configuration for orthodoxy than does the Trikaya doctrine in Buddhology. But both speculations are quite far removed from the notions in which the historical Buddha and Jesus understood their mission, but are the consequences of the problematic which was connected with the original understanding of being in both.

Analogously this connection in the problematic of history is evident also in the remaining ingredients of the whole of Buddhist and Christian doctrine in its

---

similar role, except that the latter through his personal religiosity took a greater interest in such than the former.

[24]The parallelism in this process of forming the figures of the Buddha and of the Christ is beautifully presented in the section "Buddha und Christus als Heilandgottheiten" (185-217) by Gustav Mensching, *Buddha und Christus—ein Vergleich* (Stuttgart: Deutsche Verlags-Anstalt, 1978). For the significance of the new conception of the notion of the Redeemer caused by the delay of the Parousia for the transformation of Christology one should refer to the extensive presentation in Martin Werner, *Die Entstehung des christlichen Dogmas*, 468-635 [ET, 193-211]. A presentation of the Buddhist doctrine of the Redeemer and of redemption corresponding to the investigation of the Christian history of dogma is unfortunately still not available in the rich relevant literature.

different formulations, although it is not possible to deal with it in this presentation. Instead of this, as an example for the parallelism in the development of doctrine reference will be made to the Reformations which occurred from similar
principles and with corresponding consequences in thirteenth-century Japan and
300 years later in the West. Japanese Amida, Zen, and Nichiren Buddhism were
founded by monks inspired by forms of Chinese Buddhism. The first named with
its emphasis upon the grace of Amida is something like the Protestantism of
Buddhism;[25] Zen corresponds to the late medieval mystics;[26] and Nichiren
Buddhism, with its appeal to the Lotus Sutra as the sole source of revelation
reminds us of the value assigned to the biblical writings by the Reformers and
their descendants. Just as in the West, Pietism and the Enlightenment followed
from the Orthodoxy that arose out of the Reformation and from these the so-
called new Protestantism developed, so in the Meiji period Japan also experienced its Enlightenment under Western influence. In the Myokonin of Amida
Buddhism[27] it had its Pietism and in the so-called "New Religions,"[28] a parallel
to Neo-Protestantism. Both of these represent a mixture of tradition widely
secularized by different forms. Since the introduction of Western science and
technology, Japan has stood under the sign of secularization. As in the West
dialectical theology and the philosophy of existence, and in its wake demythologizing and existential interpretation, arose as a protest against it and as its further

---

[25]On this cf. my lecture at the International Congress for the History of
Religion in Lancaster in August 1975: "Der Begriff der Gnade bei Paulus,
Shinran und Luther," *ThZB* 31 (1975): 274-88, and "The Concept of Grace in
Paul, Shinran and Luther," *EB* 9/2 (1976): 21-42.

[26]Cf. Shizuteru Ueda, *Die Gottesgeburt in der Seele und der Durchbruch zur
Gottheit. Die mystische Anthropologie Meister Eckharts und ihre Konfrontation
mit der Mystik des Zen-Buddhismus* (Gütersloh: Gütersloher-Verlagshaus Gerd
Mohn, 1965).

[27]D. T. Suzuki offered a glimpse of Shin Buddhism and the lay piety of the
"wondrously, happy men" of the Myokonin which grew out of it in his two
essays, "The Myokonin" and "A Tariki Mystic," in *The Collected Writings on
Shin Buddhism* (Kyoto: Shishu Otaniha, 1973) 78-110.

[28]On the "New Religions" cf. Werner Kohler, *Die Lotus-Lehre und die
modernen Religionen in Japan* (Zurich: Atlantis Verlag, 1962); H. Neill
McFarland, *The Rushhour of the Gods* (New York: Macmillan, 1967), *Rissho
Kosei-Kai* (Tokyo, 1966), *The Arnold Toynbee and Daisaku Ikeda Dialogue*
(Tokyo, 1976); Ofudesaki, *The Holy Scriptures of Ocmoto* (Kameoka, 1974);
Frederick Franck, *An Encounter with Ocmoto "The Great Origin": A Faith
rooted in the Ancient Mysticism and the traditional Arts of Japan* (New York:
West Nyak, 1975).

development, so in modern Japan the representatives of the Kyoto School are still influenced by Barthianism, but—in the wake of Heidegger—also attempt to demythologize Zen and Amida Buddhism, and to interpret them existentially.

These latest phenomena in Christianity and Buddhism show precisely that these attempts to overcome the problematic contained in their origins have all but failed, and that this problematic of origins is pervasive. This determination nevertheless signifies a negative judgment neither in view of the present situation nor of the whole preceding history. In our view, the truth of Buddhism and of Christianity is rather contained in this problematic common to both despite their different forms. In order to validate this truth it is necessary to recognize the problematic of their vessels and to draw the necessary consequences from them.

With this intention we shall next summarize in a typology of antitheses the problematic of Buddhism and Christian evident in their history from several essential perspectives.

4. Typology of the Problematic of Redemption in Buddhism and Christianity

From the preceding outline of the historical problematic the following four points of view offer themselves for a comprehensive characterization of the typically Buddhist and typically Christian conception of redemption.

First: What is the nature of the knowledge on the basis of which Buddhists and Christians think they are able to speak of redemption?
Second: What do they understand ultimate reality to be, and what significance do they assign to it for redemption?
Third: How and through what means does redemption take place?
Fourth: What is the historical situation of persons who expect redemption?

The first question is epistemological in nature. The second deals with the possibility and nature of Transcendence. The third is of a soteriological-anthropological nature, while the fourth deals with the philosophy of history.

a. The Epistemological Question

In this respect, three factors are characteristic for Buddhism. First, it regards objectifying knowledge as a reprehensible attachment to things. Like all other attachment to things, cognitive [attachment] thinks there are things which can be grasped or conceived in concepts. According to the understanding of being in the doctrine of *pratitya-samutpada* this claim is nevertheless false. According to this doctrine there are no self-contained substances; rather all fleeting elements of being change into one another in a ceaseless becoming and perishing. This is true of the course of events in the inner world no less than of those of the outer world. But according to this teaching even the distinction between the inner and the outer world is false: there is neither a knowing subject nor a knowable object.

Second, to become free of the error of this juxtaposition of subject and object is the goal of meditation, of becoming immersed. Along the steps leading to immersion the maya-world of objectivity dissolves in ever increasing measure, the ego loses its egoity and the world its worldhood; subject and object become a Nothing.[29]

Third, this Nothing is however not nothing, not a nonobject, but as emptiness it is "the place" in which the "true I" appears, and things show

---

[29]The following advice for the immersion bound up with the "Great Doubt"—cited by Nishitani—serves as an example of this.

> You are to doubt regarding the subject in you that hears all sounds. All sounds are heard at a given moment because there is certainly a subject in you that hears. Although you may hear the sounds with your ears, the holes in your ears are not the subject that hears. If they were, a dead man would also hear sounds. . . . You must always doubt deeply, asking yourself what the subject of the hearing could be. Pay no attention to the various illusory thoughts and ideas that may occur to you. Only doubt more and more deeply, gathering together in yourself all the strength of your entire self, without aiming at anything or expecting anything in advance, without intending to be enlightened and without intending not to be enlightened; become like a child within your own breast. . . . But if you go on doubting, you will find it impossible to locate the subject that doubts. You must explore still further just there, where there is nothing to be found. Doubt deeply in a state of singlemindedness, looking neither ahead nor behind, neither right nor left, becoming completely like a dead man, unaware even that you exist. When this method is practiced more and more deeply, you will arrive at a state of being completely self-oblivious and empty. But even then you must bring up the "Great Doubt," "What is the subject that hears?" and doubt still further, all the time being like a dead man. And after that, when you are no longer aware of your being completely like a dead man, and are no more conscious of the procedure of the Great Doubt but become yourself, through and through, a great mass of doubt, there will come a moment, all of a sudden, at which you emerge into a transcendence called the Great Enlightenment, as if you had awakened from a great dream, or as if, having been completely dead, you had again become alive.

Keiji Nishitani, "Was ist Religion?" *Philosophical Studies of Japan* 2 (1969) 39ff.; cf. also *Was ist Religion?* Vom Verfasser autorisierte deutsche Übertragung (Frankfurt; Insel Verlag [ET: *Religion and Nothingness* (Berkeley: University of California Press, 1982) 20-21; cited here following the German edition].

themselves as they really are. For the Buddhist this is the nature of Enlightenment, in which true knowledge (*prajna*) is thought to occur.[30]

This way of knowledge leading to Enlightenment in the emptiness of Nothingness doubtless has something in its favor. Now knowing presupposes a subject that knows and an object that is known. That is true even of the image of the mutual reflection of two mirrors which the Buddhist uses for the subject- and objectless Prajna-wisdom. For, first, this image presupposes a subject that makes use of it as its object; and second, there must be something between the mirrors that can be reflected as something between, and quite different from them. Should this mirror itself be this something as subject and object, this could serve as its self-understanding, but it would remain inconceivable how the things appear in it as they really are. Wherever these things come from, and whether or not they emerge like a wave out of the water in order only to disappear again in it—there the enlightened one finds a criterion for the claim that in his condition and in his knowledge of Enlightenment, he is dealing with his true self and with things as they really are, and not merely with reflections of his illusions.[31]

---

[30]The use of the term "place" (*topos*) in this sense in Buddhist philosophy stems from Kitaro Nishida. On this cf. Robert Schinzinger, "Introduction to the Intelligible World" in his translation of Three Philosophical Essays under the title *Kitaro Nishida, Intelligibility, and the Philosophy of Nothingness* (Honolulu: East West Center Press, 1966) 29-39.

[31]Especially instructive for this use of the mirror in Buddhist, and especially Zen Buddhist, epistemology and the dilemma it encounters with this image are Hisamatsu's comments on it in reference to Kant's *Bewusstsein überhaupt*:

"Everything that is proceeded from the one and only heart." That is not merely a wish-projection nor pure faith, but the true confirmation of the one and only heart. The reality we experience every day is, as Kant says, not completely independent of our heart, nor existing outside of it, as we usually imagine it, but is rather that which has arisen from our heart. Thus, if we replace what we call the external world by the phrase, "everything that is," we arrive at the statement that everything that is proceeded from our heart. Yet the "all-originating heart" of Buddhism is Kant's so-called *Bewusstsein überhaupt*, and that is nothing other than the heart which is comprised of what it apprehended from Kant's idea of the *Ding an sich* by virtue of his category of *Bewusstsein überhaupt*. Such a heart is like a mirror that reflects all things unchanged which fall upon it from outside. What is reflected in the mirror cannot be separated from it, as long as it changes itself only via reflection. If there is merely a mirror, but nothing falling on it from outside, no reflected image can arise; from within the mirror there can emerge no

No less problematic than in Buddhism, though different, is the problem of knowledge in Christianity—at least in average traditional Christianity, just as the Buddhist precisely imagines it from the way it encounters him. In Christianity the emergence and the existence of mankind and of the world of things present no problem. God has created the world and mankind and sustains them even after the Fall, and wishes to obviate the consequences of the latter nevertheless through the salvific work of His Son even in time and to complete it in eternity. One can know something about creation, providence, and also of his sinfulness and its effects on the basis of reason and conscience. In this consists the general natural knowledge of God. To be sure, this is not sufficient for knowledge of salvation. The knowledge of salvation rather constitutes the object of the special supernatural revelation of God, which God has communicated through the Holy Spirit to the prophets and apostles, and finally in His Son. This revelation of

---

image. In Buddhism, however, the image showing in the mirror does not originate outside, but from within. It rises from the mirror itself, reflects itself within it and thus attains appearance; it disappears within the mirror and leaves no trace as it recedes. In Buddhism, the heart referred to by the phrase "Everything that is proceeded from the one and only heart" is like this mirror. The thing reflected never comes from the outside and thus this "heart" is likewise altogether different from Kant's *Bewusstsein überhaupt*. Yet a mirror producing a reflection from within can never be reality; for the heart of the Buddha, therefore, the analogy of the mirror is but an improvised expedient. Thus, in the likeness of the mirror, one often uses in Buddhism the comparison with a wave, which is better suited as a symbol for the creative power of the heart. A wave does not fall into the water from outside, but originates within the water without separating itself from it; it disappears and returns to the water as to its origin and in so doing does not leave the faintest trace. From the perspective of the wave, it arises from the water and returns again to whence it came. From the perspective of the water, the wave is motion of the water. The water forms a union with the wave, and yet the water neither originates nor disappears as waves originate and disappear, nor is it by their action diminished or increased. To be sure, water arises and disappears, in forming a wave, yet it neither arises nor disappears as water. Thus water forms waves thousand- and ten-thousand-fold and yet remains consistent and unchanged within itself. The one and only heart from which all things proceed is like the water.

Shin'ichi Hisamatsu, *Die Fülle des Nichts* (Pfullingen: Verlag Günther Neske, n.d.) 53-55 [ET: "The Characteristics of Oriental Nothingness," *Philosophical Studies of Japan* (1960) 2:95ff. Text here follows the German version cited by Buri. -Trans.].

salvation which is contained in Holy Writ and can however continue to occur—in connection with it—through the witness of Holy Spirit, is not a thing of reason, but of faith effected through the Holy Spirit. This faith in revelation can also involve the powers of reason, just as the latter even in their own sphere are dependent upon the former because of their sinful condition.

Quite apart from the fact that this dogmatic system appears in the context of contemporary knowledge of nature and history as a formulation of temporally conditioned mythology and speculation, it also inherently contains unsolved problems, primarily in connection with the epistemological problem. How far does the damage of the Fall extend, and in what way can it be rectified through revelatory faith? The answers that can be given to these critical questions in Christian theology [Glaubenslehre] are quite diverse and refute themselves in their oppositeness. They reach from one extreme, in consequence of which in the believer God himself is a believer in a way which corresponds to the mutual reflection of two mirrors without anything coming between them, to the other in which for reason faith dissolves into an inconceivable Nothing. In between lie a host of variations of a connection of revelation and reason, which are nevertheless more truly restatements of the problem than solutions to it, as this is expressed in the postulate of a faith-knowledge. Faith-knowledge is an oxymoron.[32]

This problematic of the Buddhist and Christian conception of knowledge is also operative in the attempts to answer the question of the nature of reality which arises from it. Thus is posed

b. The Question of Metaphysics

Buddhism gives a threefold answer to this question. First, the nature and ground of reality is Nothingness, emptiness. Second, reality is the true self of the enlightened one. Third, Buddha is the sole true reality, who is at once Nothingness and the Enlightened One in one.

Here two questions pose themselves. Is there a reality outside enlightenment? If so—is this unenlightened reality also Nothingness like the enlightened? That would signify that they are not to be distinguished from one another. Or is there only the enlightened reality? In this case why is enlightenment still necessary, and how then is the enlightened one to be distinguished from the unenlightened? Is the Nothing an ontological expression that refers solely to reality and is it valid quite apart from the way in which persons understand themselves? Or in this matter is it dealing with an *existential*, that is, with a specific expression of human self-understanding relative to the meaning of existence in the world?

Buddhism leaves undecided both the question of the relation between enlightenment and nonenlightenment, and the distinction between ontological and

---

[32]Cf. Fritz Buri, *Dogmatik als Selbstverständnis des christlichen Glaubens*, Bd. 1, 47ff.

existential statements. It regards this discriminating thinking as an erroneous attachment to being and therefore this either-or is a question posed quite erroneously. It opposes the law of identity, *a* is *a*, with the logical principle, *a* is not *a*, therefore *a* is *b*. Therefore it counters the law of the excluded middle with "nonduality," that is, one is neither one nor two, which when applied to Nothingness means that Nothingness is beyond the opposition of being and nonbeing, or with the claim with respect to Enlightenment, that whoever says he is enlightened is not enlightened. Curiously, he is able to transcend all differentiation only by means of the discriminating thinking he casts aside. But even this claim does not touch him, because it consists of discriminating thinking. Therefore he will not refute it, because he would thereby make himself guilty of discriminating thinking, of attachment to things, of not being enlightened.

Again, Christianity is quite different. Here God as Creator is strictly distinguished from humanity and the world as God's creation. The world is neither without beginning nor endless. God created it from Nothing and preserves it in his omnipotence. This preservation is necessary because the world would otherwise lapse into the Nothing and humanity would completely fall into the hands of the Evil One. Apparently the Nothing, or as the Bible puts it, Chaos, was not completely overcome in creation and invades God's first creation in the form of the Evil One, with the result that God must replace it with a second, new creation.[33]

Two critical questions emerge. First, despite what is intended, is not God essentially restricted by being defined at least in his existence by means of reason and in his nature on the basis of his special revelation for faith, as the concept of definition implies? It is understandable that attempts have constantly been made to construct a *theologia negativa*; but when it is not exhausted in the legitimate critique of what is *menschlich-allzumenschlich* in theology but is absorbed into the Nothingness of mysticism, it thereby annuls the possibility of statements about God. On the other hand, the question arises over against positive theology as to the Whence of Chaos and the Evil One. Either God has also created these powers and preserves them, or he is not omnipotent—hence the problem of teleology and of theodicy.

The riddle of Being cannot be solved by the Nothing of Buddhism which annuls all distinctions nor by Christian trust in God's governance of the world. But neither Buddhism nor Christianity could be content with the insolubility of this burning question of human existence. As religions of redemption they intend to answer the question of the possibility of the meaningful actualization of existence in the world. This shared intention leads us to the third point of

---

[33]Cf. Buri, *Dogmatik als Selbstverständnis des christlichen Glaubens*, vol. 3, "Die Schöpfung aus dem Nichts," 41ff.

comparison of the common problematic: to the question, how they consider redemption to be possible.

c. The Question of Human Redemption

The problem of "self-redemption or other-redemption" has been discussed in Buddhism ever since the rise of the Mahayana. In contrast to the historical Buddha and to the Hinayana, it teaches that humans cannot free themselves from the fate of samsara by their own power, but that they need outside help for this, or that such is available to them. There are enlightened saints who refuse entrance into Nirvana in order to attend to the unenlightened in the world of samsara and they are petitioned by them for their help and, because of their help, honored by them. According to legend the Buddha overcame the temptation to reserve enlightenment for himself and preached his way of salvation to the world. But neither he nor Mahayana Buddhism dealt with other-redemption in the strict sense, for the help here took the form of an appeal to the act of making oneself free from attachment to things, and second, the assisting will of the Buddha and of the Bodhisattvas derives from the knowledge of enlightenment about the universal relation of "dependent origination" and is grounded in it insofar as in those who are dependent upon this enlightenment there is—by virtue of this *pratitya-samutpada*—also a receptivity to enlightenment and a corresponding attitude.

The parallels to Christ and the saints are obvious, as they are to the capacity—not just the need—for salvation on the part of those entangled in the world. Just as Buddha and the Mahayanists appeal to the *pratitya-samutpada* which permeates everything in the world, so the Church appeals to the love of God which encompasses everything, which fills the saints and for whose revelation sinners wait. As the Buddhists speak of a Buddha nature in a man which is to be awakened, so the doctrines of the Church assume in man an image of God (*imago Dei*), which was not completely lost through the Fall, as a point of contact for the divine revelation and the assistance of grace and as a presupposition of cooperation with it. Even here it is appropriate to speak, not of an exclusive other-redemption, but of a cooperation, a synergism of nature and grace.

Over against this relative other-redemption there arose in Japan as in the West a new view of redemption connected in each case with a reformation, accompanied in both cases with an appeal to origins.[34] In both it was a catastrophic world situation and pessimistic mood which led two monks—Shinran Shonin and Martin Luther—to doubt their own efforts at holiness and to find salvation in the unconditional acceptance of Amida's undeserved grace, or of

---

[34]On the course of the Japanese "reformation," see Joseph M. Kitagawa, *Religion in Japanese History* (New York & London: Columbia University Press, 1966) 86ff., and Gerhard Rosenkranz, *Der Weg des Buddha* (Stuttgart: Evangelischer Missionsverlag, 1960) 243ff.

Christ's, and their message of grace, of redemption without good works, *sola gratia*, awakened a powerful echo in the hearts of thousands. Both abandoned the cloister, renounced the priesthood and married, and undertook to show in a substantial literary activity that they alone understood their tradition correctly, planted their piety in the hearts of their adherents by writing songs and so became the founders of new forms of Buddhism and Christianity.[35]

For both their denial of the necessity of good works for attaining salvation also caused difficulties in their estimate of natural human capacities and their ethical validation. Thus their followers again attempted to connect other-redemption with dimensions of self-redemption. In Old Protestant Orthodoxy and in its confrontations with Catholicism this became apparent in the controversies over justification and vindication in faith whose hopelessness in the neo-Protestantism of the Enlightenment led to new talk of the goodness of man and of creation. In contemporary Buddhism in which, along with the so-called "New Religions," Zen and Shin Buddhism count the most numbers of adherents, their spiritual leaders attempt to combine self-redemption and other-redemption in such a way that Zen philosophy sees in Nembutsu—the formula for sole trust in the grace of Amida—a koan that annuls discriminating thinking, while the Shin Buddhists regard their devotion to Amida as simultaneously an absorption into Nothingness. The unavailability of conceptual thinking for conceiving of grace allowed various kinds of mysticism to arise in the West as in the Far East—the mysticism of God and Nothingness, and Christ- and Amida-mysticism.[36]

In both, discussions were not limited to the redemption of the individual, but extended on both sides of the tradition to the question of the universal-historical aspects of redemption.

d. Historical, Cultural, and Philosophical Aspects of the Question of Redemption

To be sure Buddhism was acquainted with a universal-cosmic perspective on history. It consists of the succession of temporal epochs of individual kalpas, each beginning in a perfect form and then—in descending steps—ending in equally complete ruin.[37] Each of these kalpas has its own Buddha who descends from the Tushita heaven to bring redemption and then returns. As a whole, however, this endless series of kalpas belongs to the category of samsara which

---

[35]Cf, Fritz Buri, "Der Begriff der Gnade bei Paulus, Shinran und Luther," *ThZB* 31 (1975): 281.

[36]For two different points of view on this see Heinrich Dumoulin, *Östliche Meditation und christliche Mystik* (Verlag Karl Alber, 1966) and Maruus Heinrichs, *Katholische Theologie und Asiatisches Denken* (Mainz: Mathias Gruenewald, 1963).

[37]Cf. Conze, *Der Buddhismus*, 45ff. [ET, 48ff.].

comprises them and completes itself in reincarnation which occurs in accord with karma. In the individual kalpas there is redemption only for individuals; the world as a whole remains unredeemed. Therefore the Buddha turns way from it, abandons it to its fate and concerns himself only with those living beings with whose totality he knows himself to be connected. Redemption is through Enlightenment alone, and it consists in fleeing the world and entering Nirvana, which can however occur in such a preliminary or more complete way that one who is in the world is already in Nirvana, for Nirvana is simultaneously samsara and samsara, Nirvana. This is the source of the paradoxical simultaneous withdrawal from and readiness for the world on the part of the Buddhist who knows himself to be free from the world while in it.

Being free from the world in the world is the impressive thing about Buddhism, but is also its problematic. This attitude toward the world and even the conception its representatives have of themselves and their attitude toward one another lack an ultimate seriousness, an ultimate engagement and a final accountability. The Buddhist withdraws from all this into a final detachment in which he can just as easily appeal to the interconnection of all things in nonthingness, as he can refute it. The vow of the Bodhisattva to save all living beings is quite touching.[38] But what does he "touch" in this conception if the other is for him only his "shadow" as Buddhists, when queried about this, state in countering a critical partner in dialogue? This thoroughly corresponds however to the notion that the objectified "I" is not the "true I." As the ethical commandments of the Buddhist path to salvation serve only for the attainment of enlightenment in meditative immersion, Buddhism also assigns no value to the powerful accomplishments it has brought to completion in the spiritual, cultural, aesthetic, and religious history of mankind; they are rather only shadowy forms destined for extinction in Nothingness in Enlightenment. The ascending ramps of decaying Borobudur which lead past countless representations of the Buddha and Bodhisattvas end in the Nothingness which the Buddha is, and the Buddha sinks into the silence of Nothingness.[39]

---

[38]The vow of the Bodhisattva which is recited at the end of every Zen festival goes like this:
> However innumerable beings are, I vow to save them;
> However inexhaustible the passions are, I vow to extinguish them;
> However immeasurable the Dharmas are, I vow to master them;
> However incomparable the Buddha-truth is, I vow to attain it.

D. T. Suzuki, *Manual of Zen-Buddhism*, 5th ed. (New York: Grove Press, 1960) 14. Cf. also his description of the compassionate forms which the All-Compassionate-Bodhisattva [Kwannon] assumes to save all beings (33-38).

[39]*Borobudur, Kunst und Religion im alten Java 8. bis 14. Jahrhundert*

No less problematic than the Buddhist, is the Christian conception of history and the course of spiritual and cultural history—especially in view of its "having as though not having"—which it has completed on its own soil. Although the Buddhist view is similar, the Christian is grounded differently. Here we are not dealing with an eternal cycle of kalpas dissolving into one another, but with a history that begins with creation and runs toward its goal under divine guidance. As there is only *one* history, there is only *one* Messiah whose Parousia brings about its fulfillment. But because, contrary to its original expectation, the Parousia has been delayed, the *provisorium* of the end of history has become its lasting condition which as it were still stands under the sign of the fulfillment of history expected in the future, but at the same time necessitates a sufficiently positive attitude toward what exists provisionally. In this way the notion of creation, as well as of a continuing creative activity of God, is of considerable significance for the conception of history. Out of a history of decline a history of progress emerges which, in view of the new problems which result from this progress, proves to be so problematic that at times confidence in the providence of God active in the world no longer suffices, in consequence of which the individual souls again escape to hopes in the Beyond or even to more or less realistic notions of an end of the world through the return of Christ to establish his sovereignty upon a new earth. Whether conceived naturally or supernaturally, as a fulfillment here or in the Beyond, this Christian concept of history is presided over by the Cross of Christ as its sign of victory with the result that to Buddhists it appears in all its various interpretations as a sign of the will to sovereignty which represents to them the opposite of the Buddha's immersion in silence.

The contrast between the Buddhist and Christian conception of redemption could scarcely be expressed more abruptly than in the representations of the Buddha lying prone, near to the earth and surrounded by animals, dying in majestic peace, and of the Christ hanging in pain on the cross and shedding his blood. Buddhists have frequently used this contrast in this sense, and Daisetz Suzuki, who has succeeded above all others in providing Westerners access to the nature of Buddhism, thought he could see in the exalted Christ's position on a cross elevated above the ground a sign of the Christian will to sovereignty and did not refrain from repeatedly expressing his abhorrence of the notion of a redemption through blood—which is spoken from the heart quite conceivably by

---

(Zurich: Kunsthaus, 1978), and Karl Jaspers, *Der philosophische Glaube angesichts der Offenbarung* (Munich: Piper Verlag, 1962) 399ff. [ET: *Philosophical Faith and Revelation*, Religious Perspectives 18, trans. E. B. Ashton (New York: Harper & Row, Publishers, 1962) 265ff.]

a Buddhist and also by not a few Christians.[40] But a no less negative attitude

---

[40]D. T. Suzuki, *Der westliche und der östliche Weg* (Ullstein, 1974), "Kreuzigung und Erleuchtung," 121ff.:

> Always, when I see a picture of the crucified Christ, I have to think of the deep cleft that lies between Christianity and Buddhism. The cleft is symbolic for the psychological difference between East and West (121). . . .
>
> The symbolism of Christianity has a great deal to do with human suffering. The symbolism of the crucifixion is the culmination of suffering. Buddhism often speaks of suffering, but for it the Buddha sits smiling under the Bodhi tree at the river of Niranjana. Christ bore his suffering up to the end of his earthly life, while the Buddha ended it while living and continued to preach the gospel of Enlightenment until he departed gently under the twin sal trees. The trees stand upright, while the Buddha in Nirvana lies horizontal like eternity itself. Christ hangs helpless, full of sadness, on the vertically towering cross. For Eastern sensibility the sight is completely intolerable. Buddhists are accustomed to the sight of Jizo-Bosatsu (Kshitigarbha-Bodhisattva) on the streets. The figure brings to mind tenderness. It stands upright, but what a contrast to the Christian symbol of suffering.
>
> Permit me to introduce a geometrical comparison, as it were, between a statue which sits with crossed legs in meditation and a crucifix. The verticality (of the crucifix) first awakens the impression of action, movement, and upward dynamic. The horizontal—as in the case of the reclining Buddha—makes us think of peace and completion. A sitting figure mediates to us the idea of trustworthiness, firm conviction and aplomb. The body sits with hips and crossed legs firmly on the floor. The center of gravity lies in the hips. That is the most secure position that a two-legged creature can assume in life. At the same time it brings to mind images of peace, quietness, and self-reliance. The upright posture generally awakens the impression of militant spirit, in defense or attack. It gives to one moreover the feeling of its own significance which is born out of individuality and power (124-25). . . .
>
> The crucified Christ is a horrible sight, and in my thinking I cannot but connect it with the sadistic impulse of an exaggerated phantasy. . . . Christianity has a tendency especially to emphasize the corporeality of existence. Hence the crucifixion and the symbolism of the eucharist, the eating of flesh and the drinking of blood. To non-Christians the thought of drinking blood is repulsive (127).

Suzuki also expresses the same thoughts—somewhat more moderately—in an essay on "The Doctrine of Shin Buddhism" in his *Collected Writings on Shin-Buddhism,* 59ff.

toward the Buddhist doctrine of redemption arises also from the Christian side. It is true that the Catholic Church today recognizes that there may be truths in Buddhism, but always with the proviso that the full truth is to be found only in its faith.[41] Protestants, furthermore, who are astonished at Shinran's Buddhism of grace, have only raised the objection—following a famous example—that he did not use the correct name for his redeemer. He should call him Christ rather than Amida, before there could be discourse with him and his devotees.[42] While

---

[41]In the "Declaration of the Relationship of the Church to Non-Christian Religions" of the Second Vatican Council it states [in specific reference to Buddhism]:

> The Catholic Church rejects nothing which is true and holy in these religions. She looks with sincere respect upon those ways of conduct and of life, those rules and teachings which, though differing in many particulars from what she holds and sets forth, nevertheless often reflect a ray of that Truth which enlightens all men. Indeed, she proclaims and must ever proclaim Christ, 'the way, the truth, and the life' (John 14:6), in whom men find the fullness of religious life, and in whom God has reconciled all things to Himself (cf. 2 Cor 5:18-19).

Konzilsdekrete 2 (Reklinghausen: Paulus Verlag, 1966) 30 [ET: *The Documents of Vatican II*, ed. Walter M. Abbott, S.J. (New York: Guild Press, 1966) 662.

[42]Karl Barth, *Die kirchliche Dogmatik*, 1/2:372ff. [ET: *Church Dogmatik*, 343]:

> Only one thing is truly decisive for the distinction of truth from error. And we call the existence of Yodoism a providential disposition because with what is relatively the greatest possible force it makes it so clear that only one thing is decisive. That one thing is the name of Jesus Christ. Methodologically, it is to be recommended that in face of Yodoism, and, at bottom, of all other religions, our first task is to concentrate wholly upon this distinction, provisionally setting aside whatever other deference we think we recognize. It is not merely a matter of prudentially weighing the various possibilities of heathen development, which might eventually catch up with the differences we teach, but of a clear insight that the truth of the Christian religion is in fact enclosed in the one name of Jesus Christ, and nothing else. It is actually enclosed in all the formal simplicity of this name as the very heart of the divine reality of revelation, which alone constitutes the truth of our religion. It is not enclosed, therefore, in its more or less explicit structure as the religion of grace, nor in the Reformation doctrines of original sin, representative satisfaction, justification by faith alone, the gift of the Holy Spirit and thankfulness. All this, as Figura shows, the heathen, too, can in their own way teach and even live and represent as a church. Yet that does

Suzuki, for example, is quick to concede that Amida with his vow is "not a historical person, but a testimony of religious consciousness,"[43] a myth, some Christians think that the strength of the Christian doctrine of redemption over against that of Buddhism consists in the fact that an historical person stands at its center, without noting that an essential reason for its problematic lies precisely in this fact, with which Buddhism on its own admission is not concerned.[44]

5. The Kyoto School
and the School of "Thoroughgoing Eschatology"

With this fourfold typology of the question of redemption, which resulted from a historical comparison of the problematic of their origins and of attempts at their solution in Buddhism and Christianity, we have gained the perspectives from which we can present the philosophy of religion of the special kind of Buddhism in the Kyoto School and its attitude toward Christianity. These four perspectives of epistemology, metaphysics, soteriology, and cultural history are those which we encounter time and again in the works of the representatives of this school in special forms and in different emphases and interconnection, depending on its major ideas. These are also the essential elements of the cultural history of Christianity, so that in this view we have to deal with a real encounter between the two and will repair to a systematic evaluation of them.

To be sure we do not have to deal with Buddhism as it meets us in the whole of its two and a half thousand year history, but with what is by compari-

---

not mean that they are any the less heathen, poor, and utterly lost.

On this cf. the position of the Shin Buddhist Bando Shojun, in *Gott in Japan*, ed. Yagi Seiichi and Ulrich Lutz (Munich: Ch. Kaiser Verlag, 1973) 72-93, and Gempo Hoshino, "Das Verhältnis des buddhistischen Denkens zu Karl Barth," in *Antwort: Festschrift zu Karl Barths 70. Geburtstag* (Zurich: Evangelischer Verlag, 1956) 423ff.

[43]In the explanations of his translation of the Kyogyoshinsho, *Der westliche und der östliche Weg*, 204.

[44]Masatoshi Doi's text, *Search for Meaning through Interfaith Dialogue* (Tokyo: Kyobunkwan, 1976), based on Tillich, represents an example of the problematic of Christian theology's appeal—in contrast to Buddhism—to the decisive saving significance of an historical event for faith. In dialogues with Buddhists in Japan and Asia Tillich himself seems to have found no appreciation of his understanding of history, which is not surprising in view of its problematic nature. (Cf. the discussion of Hisamatsu's "Dialogue with Tillich," below, pp. [ch. 5, sec. 4]). The sections on "Christianity and Buddhism in Encounter," and "The Buddhist Interpretation of History" by Doi, 158-76, are especially illuminating.

son only a section of it. The same holds for the Christianity that will be discussed here. There are specific forms of Christianity to which the philosophers of the Kyoto School make reference, and what we set over against them as Christianity is a special view of its nature which is offered to us by this history. But this restriction to a special kind of Buddhism and to a confrontation with a conception of Christianity that is by no means universally recognized protects us from a undifferentiated and correspondingly dogmatic speaking of Buddhism and Christianity as is regularly the case in the previous as well as the newly emerging dialogue between the two—to the detriment of both.

That we have selected from the rich Buddhist voices the philosophy of religion of the Kyoto School as a dialogue partner derives not only from the fact that the writings of its representatives are available to us to a considerable degree in translations, and that they concern themselves in large measure with Western Christian cultural history, but is based on the fact that this philosophy of religion doubtless belongs to those phenomena of contemporary Buddhist culture which have to be dealt with from the Christian side and with which a confrontation would also be fruitful for both sides. To be sure, in the thought processes and images of this religious philosophy something is dealt with which is quite different from what Western tourists get to see in Buddhist temples and ceremonies, and quite different from what is currently today propagated and practiced in the West as Zen. But neither those spectacles nor these articles of export, from which individual principals of our school of philosophers expressly distance themselves on occasion, can furnish the appropriate basis; for an essential and suitable dialogue between Buddhism and Christianity one must come to terms with the material content of a philosophy of religion as it is represented today in a remarkable way in the Kyoto School on a par with the Western tradition of thought.

It is to be similarly noted that the perspectives we have used in the historical comparison just previously carried through, do not deal with those of a Christianity as it is represented in missions or in theologies to which the representatives of the Kyoto School appeal, although it must be said that at least some individuals among them are not unacquainted with "the conception of the school of thoroughgoing eschatology of early Christianity and of its history." They cannot be faulted for failing to draw the necessary consequences from it, because it would not be reasonable to demand of them what has not even occurred in the theology which confronts them with the claim to be *the* Christian one—and this even less so since Buddhism does not begin to ascribe the significance to history that Christianity assigns to it.

In view of this state of affairs which is frankly to be conceded, it must be said that two "schools" are juxtaposed in our confrontation: the Kyoto School with its Buddhist philosophy of religion and the School of Thoroughgoing Eschatology with its conception of the nature and history of Christianity which issues from it. In contradistinction to other attitudes toward Buddhism currently undertaken from the Christian side—even of those which concern themselves especially with Zen Buddhism—the advantage of the view of thoroughgoing eschatology and the systematic perspectives bound up with it, which we espoused in the previous discussion in respect to the history of Christianity and in the following have now to apply to the individual representatives of the Kyoto School, consists in the fact that we neither have to abandon what is especially Christian in favor of what is Buddhist nor talk at cross purposes with Buddhism from a supposedly *proprium Christianum*, but are in the position of discussing with one another the religious philosophy of the Kyoto School and our conception of what is normatively Christian in such a way that the intentions of both are validated and an encounter can occur that takes them into account and is promising for the future of both.

As the "School of Thoroughgoing Eschatology" appeals to Albert Schweitzer, so the Kyoto School also possesses its principal in its founder Kitaro Nishida, whose influence can be established not only upon his contemporaries but also in the two subsequent generations of the Kyoto School, just as the representatives of thoroughgoing eschatology extend to three generations running temporally parallel to those of the Kyoto School. Named as the representatives of the first generation of the Kyoto School, besides Kitaro Nishida, are Daisetz Suzuki and his successor at Kyoto University, Hajime Tanabe, as well as the somewhat still younger Shin'ichi Hisamatsu who in any event had meanwhile died, like the two previously named. The middle generation is represented today by Keiji Nishitani and Yoshinori Takeuchi, sometime colleagues at Kyoto University who have already been emeriti for a long time, but whose productivity continues in a rich activity of lectures and literary work. As their pupils, Shizuteru Ueda who holds the chair of Nishitani and Masao Abe who taught formerly at Nara and later at Claremont represent the third generation of Kyoto philosophy.

Nishida's philosophy and Albert Schweitzer's conception of Christianity exhibit a certain parallelism not only in terms of the fact that both formed schools which lasted for three generations, but also in their inner structure and in the fact that in the course of the change of generations remarkable differences developed. Although Schweitzer, like Nishida with respect to Buddhism, originally formulated his understanding of Christianity in discussion with the Western philosophy of the late nineteenth and early twentieth centuries and each remained fastened to this origin despite all the criticism, in their later years both nevertheless occupied themselves—again each in his own way—with the philosophy of existence and the dialectical theology which grew out of a collapse of this tradition. A positive influence from the former and a confrontation with the latter occurred in both schools, nevertheless, only in the second and third generations, in which different relations with their respective principals became manifest.

In the development that we must subsequently present, such a divergence is already evident in Tanabe's criticism of Nishida and the different significance both assigned to Zen and Amida Buddhism, respectively. Although essential elements of both kinds of Buddhism—not to speak of other differing components of Buddhist tradition, to which they admittedly assigned different weight—are evident in all the representatives of the Kyoto School, it is nevertheless proper, in view of the the decisive influence imparted to the Buddhism of grace by Tanabe in the course of his religious development, to speak of a religious philosophy within this school directed more or less to Zen or Amida, respectively. This difference is most sharply evident between the Zen philosophy of Hisamatsu and Nishitani and the devotion to Amida of Tanabe's disciple Takeuchi, whereas Daisetz Suzuki was indebted to both directions.

In a similar fashion, in the theology which developed from the work of Schweitzer different directions were taken, according to the ways each estimated its philosophical presuppositions and the different forms of existential philosophy entered into each, the result being that, for example, the evaluation we give to Buddhism differs from that represented by Schweitzer in his day, especially since he took no notice at all of the Kyoto School that we have subsequently to present in terms of its individual representatives. Just as the differences peculiar to the Buddhist tradition did little to hinder those interpreters from participating in the discussion from reworking the different forms of these in their systems of thought, our departure from Schweitzer's position does little to prevent us from appealing to the perspective of thoroughgoing eschatology and the systematic perspectives it offers in our presentation of the religious philosophy of the Kyoto School and in our confrontation with it and with its conception of Christianity.

Chapter 2

Nishida Kitaro (1870–1945)
Japan's Great Philosopher
and Founder of the Kyoto School

1. From Pure Experience to the Logic
of the "Place" (Topos) of Nothingness

To experience means to know events precisely as they are. It means to cast away completely one's own inner workings, and to know in accordance with the events. Since people usually include some thought when speaking of experience, the word "pure" is here used to signify a condition of true experience itself without the addition of the least thought or reflection. For example. it refers to that moment of seeing a color or hearing a sound which occurs not only before one has added the judgment that this seeing or hearing relates to something external or that one is feeling this sensation, but even before one has judged what color or sound it is. Thus, pure experience is synonymous with direct experience. When one experiences directly one's conscious state there is as yet neither subject nor object, and knowledge and its object are completely united. This is the purest form of experience.

Nishida's first work, *A Study of Good*, which appeared in 1910, begins with these programmatic sentences.[1] They could serve as a motto for his entire philosophic work, for they contain the fundamental perspective which he sought to carry through with increasing vitality in the course of the changes of his thought; further, they permit us to recognize the twofold background which was the basis for his philosophizing: the experience of Zen and modern Western thought, both of which have to do basically with the relationship of subject and object in knowing. That the postulated ways of knowing which Nishida deals with in the passage cited are those of Zen is already evident from its description as "pure experience." For in the exclusion of the objectifying intellect which has as a consequence the fact that one no longer stands over against the contents of consciousness, but remains with them, so that one becomes aware of reality as

---

[1]Nishida Kitaro, *A Study of Good*, trans. V. H. Viglielmo (Tokyo: Japanese National Commission for Unesco, Ministry of Education, 1960). [Cf. the new translation: Kitaro Nishida, *An Enquiry into the Good*, trans. Masao Abe and Christopher Ives, introduction by Masao Abe (New Haven CT: Yale University Press, 1990).]

昭和18年2月
Nishida Kitaro (1870–1945)

it is originally—in this exclusion we find the methods and goal of Zen practice. This is true whether it consists now in the form of Soto Zen as "pure sitting" or in that of Rinzai Zen as the concentration on an enigmatic expression or saying (Koan) which cannot be solved by our usual thinking, or, for example, even in the practice of archery in which bow, target, and shooting have become a unity.[2] It is known from Nishida's diary that he participated in Zen practice both before and after the composition of his book *A Study of Good* and that it is attested that he attained enlightenment (*satori*).[3] Moreover, throughout his life he was a close friend of his classmate Daisetz Suzuki and died in a cloister in Kamakura where their graves lie side by side. Thus it is not surprising that in his writings one encounters pronouncements of Zen masters and citations from the Zen tradition, often not distinguished as such, but always in a meaningful connection.

Even the definition of "pure experience" cited initially could be read and used as an instruction for Zen meditation, although this is not Nishida's intention—at least not directly. What he intends with his references to Zen sayings and with the use of his insights gained from Zen is rather to show that these can also be expressed in the forms of Western thinking, and that they are suited to correct or overcome what seems to him to be unsatisfactory or faulty in Western thinking.[4]

---

[2]Eugen Herrigel, *Zen in the Art of Archery* (New York: Random House, 1989); D. T. Suzuki, *Zen and Japanese Culture* (London: Routledge & Kegan Paul, 1959); Philip Kapleau, *The Three Pillars of Zen* (New York: Doubleday. 1980).

[3]Lothar Knauth, "Life Is Tragic. The Dairy of Nishida Kitaro," MN 20/3-4 (1965): 335-58. Shibata Masumi, "The Dairy of a Zen Layman," MN 14/2 (1981): 121-31.

[4]David Dilworth, "The Initial Formations of 'pure experience,' in Nishida Kitaro and William James," MN 24/1-2 (1969): 93-111. On this, cf. what Nishida wrote to Nishitani Keiji in a letter of 19 Feb 1943: "It is said that Zen forms the background of my thinking. That is absolutely incorrect. . . . Zen deals with the authentic grasp of actual reality. As impossible as it may seem, I should like somehow to bring this into connection with philosophy. That has been my dream since I was thirty" (Nishida, *Collected Works*, 19:24-25; cited in *Bulletin* 5:38, of the Nanzan Institute for Religion and Culture, Nagoya, in a report on its third symposium on "Absolute Nothingness and God. The Nishida-Tanabe Tradition and Christianity."

This passage is also mentioned in the article by Shibata Masumi, accompanied with an energetic protest against conceiving his philosophy in "Zen categories." Against those who attempt this, Nishida says that they understood "neither Zen nor his philosophy" (MN 2 [1981]: 131).

With this we arrive at the other background already evident in the initial citation, which distinguishes Nishida's thinking no less than its origin in Zen: his relation to and entry into Western thinking, above all its modern and to him contemporary expressions. But while the connection with Zen persisted throughout his life, and in the second half of his life the Buddhist character of his thinking became manifestly sharper and more decisive than at the beginning, his relation to Western thinking underwent great transformations. This is due not only to the increasing attainment of the completed form of his philosophy as one that is typically Far Eastern in contrast with that of the West, but also to the fact that Western thinking—as far as it can be conceived as a unity in contrast to that of the Far East—does not represent the kind of unity found in the Far East, but appears in quite diverse forms even today.

Ever since Japan opened its doors to the West at the beginning of the Meiji period (which prevailed from 1868 to 1912) after two hundred years of seclusion, it has been under the influence of Western science and technology, as well as of Western philosophy. Thus, modern Japanese philosophy which arose in this era displays the entire spectrum of modern and contemporary philosophy, from German idealism and its countercurrents to empirical psychologism, Neo-Kantianism, phenomenology and existentialism, including the heritage of the West and of Christianity.[5]

These different forms of Western thinking, or an encounter with them, are ascertainable from Nishida's philosophy, even to the point that its development can be divided into three or four segments precisely by means of its treatment, or neglect, of such forms of Western philosophy. The succession of these different periods of his philosophical thinking runs strikingly parallel to the external changes in his teaching career and finally to the fate of his people in the context of world history.[6] In contrast to many of his contemporaries Nishida nevertheless

---

[5]Gino K. Piovesana, S.J., *Recent Japanese Thought 1862–1962: A Survey*, rev. ed. (Tokyo: Sophia University, 1968).

[6]On Nishida's biography and literary production in which the changes in his philosophy are mirrored, cf. Piovesana, ibid., 85-112; Robert Schinzinger, *Kitaro Nishida, Intelligibility and the Philosophy of Nothingness* (Honolulu: East-West Center Press, 1966 [repr. of 1st English ed., 1958]) 21ff. A German edition had already appeared in 1943 from Walter de Gruyter, Berlin. Cf. also Shimomura Torataro, "Nishida Kitaro and some Aspects of his Philosophical Thought," appendix to *A Study of Good*; also the following works of Yoshinori Takeuchi: "Hegel and Buddhism (Nishida's Philosophy and His Dialectic of Absolute Nothingness)"; *Il Pensiero* 7/1,2 (1962): 7-20; "The Philosophy of Nishida," JR 3,4 (1963): 1-32; "Japanese Philosophy (Nishida's Philosophy as Representative of Japanese Philosophy)," *Encyclopedia Britannica* [EncB] (1966): 959ff.; "Nishida Kitaro," EncB (1967): 532; "Nishida Kitaro," EncB (1974): 118ff. Note also the works of David A. Dilworth: "Nishida's Early Pantheistic Voluntarism,"

did not succumb to Westernization, but only utilized Western forms of thinking to express in them the nature of his specific Buddhist and Japanese thinking and feeling and finally to abandon them in his own philosophy, which entered into the history of the philosophy of his country as "Nishida philosophy" and by which he became the founder of the Kyoto School, and to replace them with a different kind of Far Eastern logic. But even though therein he praised "the authentic spirit of Japan," he did not, like so many others, succumb to the danger of nationalism in the fateful and difficult hours of his country, but remained true to its greater spiritual heritage.[7]

In his *A Study of Good*, which he composed as a still unknown school teacher, Nishida made use of the categories of an empirical psychology and the *Lebensphilosophie* of Bergson in articulating his Zen experience and appealed to its relationship to Christian mysticism. The writing was well received, not only because it mediated hitherto unknown Western forms of thought, but also because it showed how Buddhist experience and thinking could be expressed in them as valid modern forms. It also earned the author a call to the then Imperial University of Kyoto, at which he soon became its most influential teacher.

In the time when he taught at Kyoto University, which lasted from 1912 to 1927 and represents the second period of his spiritual creativity, Nishida was preoccupied above all with the epistemological problems of what was then his philosophy of consciousness. To deal with this, empirical psychology and its mystical speculations nevertheless no longer sufficed, and he expanded or replaced them with logical deliberations and investigations. He was dependent for this on the great German thinkers from Kant to Hegel, as well as Neo-Kantianism and the phenomenology which was then emerging with which he however critically argued. A whole series of writings stemming from this time bear witness to Nishida's success with epistemological and logical, as well as ethical, problems. In the last text of this series, whose publication coincided with his departure from the University in 1927, there emerged the concept of "Place," of Topos (Japanese = *basho*), which he probably took from Plato's later philosophy but to which at the same time he gave a quite different meaning, namely, the sphere of Nothingness around which Buddhist thought has ever revolved.[8]

PhEW 20/1 (1970): 35-49; "The Range of Nishida's Early Religious Thought," PhEW 14/4 (1969): 409-21; "Nishida's Final Essay: The Logic of Place and a Religious Worldview," PhEW 4 (1970): 355-67; translator's preface to Nishida Kitaro, *Fundamental Problems of Philosophy* (Tokyo: Sophia University Press, 1970).

[7]Nishida Kitaro, "The Spirit of Japanese Culture," in *Sources of Japanese Tradition*, 2nd ed., ed. William Theodore de Bary (New York: Columbia University Press, 1958) 350ff.

[8]The title of this untranslated text was "On Dealing with Seeing" (1927). In

The second half of Nishida's creative activity, which was spent in Kamakura from the time he retired from teaching till his death in 1945, was devoted to working out this logic of Nothingness. Within this, two periods can be distinguished insofar as he first set out in a number of essays to unfold the "fundamental problems" of his own philosophy, by then well established, which no longer appeared in the garb of Western thought, but as a product of the Zen logic of the identity of absolute contraries, only then in his last decade to draw consequences for the understanding of history, culture, and religion.

Nishida's total literary work, which established him as the dominant philosopher of modern Japan, is available today in nineteen volumes, issued in a second edition in 1965, of which only a few have been translated into English to date, and fewer into German. Fortunately in these translations we possess at least one, and in part even several, examples from each of the four periods of creativity of Nishida's philosophy. For the original form, psychologically oriented, we have available *A Study of Good*, which has already been mentioned, and for the period of transition from psychology to the transcendental logic, *Art and Morality*. The third period is represented by three essays edited by Robert Schinzinger first in German, and then in English under the title *Intelligibility and the Philosophy of Nothingness*, and by the volume *Fundamental Problems of Philosophy*. From the last period of his life several essays on comparative history of culture and Nishida's religious worldview are available in translation, in part completely and in part only in extracts and portions. Nishida is generally deemed—even by Japanese—difficult to understand.[9] This judgment is especially confirmed in a preoccupation with his philosophic work which is dependent on only parts of it—and these in translations. Nevertheless it seems to me to be possible to make

---

the notes to his journal Nishida had nevertheless remarked that he had already written about *basho* in the years 1918 and 1919 (Knauth, *Life Is Tragic. The Diary of Nishida Kitaro*, 355).

[9]E.g., D. T. Suzuki in his instruction, "How to Read Nishida," which prefaces *A Study of Good*, writes: "Nishida's philosophy of absolute nothingness or his logic of the self-identity of absolute contradictions is difficult to understand, unless one is passably acquainted with Zen experience (iii), and Shimomura Toratora noted in his appendix to this work that because of its "spiraling" course, Nishida's philosophy "after *A Study of Good*" "not only was extremely difficult but had to be difficult" (206-207). Thus Nishida's "firstborn" work belongs to the most extensive philosophic writings in Japan, but preoccupation with Nishida's thought is mostly limited to this one. An example of this is Shizuteru Ueda's contribution to the *Festschrift* for Carl Ratschow, *Denkende Glaube*: "Das denkende Nicht-Denken: 'Zen und Philosophie' bei Nishida unter besonderer Berücksichtigung seiner Frühphilosophie der reinen Erfahrung" (Berlin/New York: Walter de Gruyter, 1976) 331-41.

a picture of his thinking on the basis of what is available to us, at least as far as its main lines and principal intentions are concerned, all the more if we see that we are in agreement with those who know the entire corpus, whose references are useful to us, even when we do not agree entirely with their view of the whole.

While among his disciples in the modern Kyoto School (1) Nishida's concept of Nothingness is basically emphasized and viewed in connection with the original Buddhist concept of emptiness (sunyata), (2) the identity of absolute contraries with which Nishida fills this "emptiness" is nevertheless suppressed or bypassed, or through the "ontological difference" of existential philosophy expanded or replaced, and (3) they usually regard him in his preoccupation with Western philosophy as a Buddhist thinker, it seems to us that his agreement with Western philosophy goes much deeper; and we are of the opinion that his logic of contradiction is just as much the result of the attempt to overcome the opposites of Western thinking as it is an expression of Buddhist sunyata. Because with his Zen heart he travelled Western paths of thinking on the stilts of Western concepts the course of his thinking is equally difficult to follow for Buddhists and Westerners, but it also becomes understandable that he finally abandoned these erroneous paths, discarded the stilts and found his Buddha as the "Place of Nothingness."

2. The "Newborn" Text on the Good

In order to establish our view of Nishida's philosophy as just explained we will attempt in the following to trace the course of his thinking by means of the documents available to us. In this way attention to two characteristics which already dawn on us in his "newborn" text, *A Study of Good*, may be shown to be necessary and helpful for understanding his philosophy.

First, in view of the fact that Nishida initiated this text with his definition of "pure experience," which we have identified in reference to the relevant notes of his journal as a consequence of his Zen experience, it is determined that he did not derive this "pure experience" from psychological investigations, but brought it with him in order to make it into an object of psychology and in this way to allow its general validity to be confirmed. This priority of Zen experience holds for the later stages of Nishida's course of thinking in which he attempted to conceive that experience philosophically.

Second, as its title might lead us to suppose, this text does not represent an expressly ethical essay. "The Good," as the theme of ethics appears rather only in the third part of this text, while the first part is devoted to the epistemological aspect of "pure experience." In the fourth part, when he takes account of Christianity and Buddhism, he finally concerns himself with the question of "religion," whereby—as already in the third part—the behavior of the individual is also seen in cultural, historical connections. This disposition not only shows the context in which Nishida would like to answer the question of ethics according to the meaning of existence and the possibility of its actualization, which is central for him, but it also corresponds to the four perspectives under which we have brought Buddhism and Christianity into connection with each other in the first chapter. By means of these formulations the difference of our position in answering the material questions about the meaning of existence will become even sharper—first in relation to the first form of Nishida's philosophy present in this text, and then in view of its transformations in its further unfolding.

Just as in connection with the designation of what is for him the normative nature of "pure experience" in *A Study of Good*, Nishida characterized the epistemological theory represented by him therein by explaining that this experience "can exist only in present consciousness" and is therefore to be examined as a "psychic phenomenon" in view of its components.[10] How he conducts this analysis of consciousness specifically by appealing principally to William James and other contemporary representatives of an empirical psychology we can here omit. What is essential about it is that he ascribed to the different components specified by him, among them principally the will,[11] a "unifying function"[12] and believed that, by disavowal of an individual "carrier" of the same[13] and in its replacement, he was able to derive this from a "universal unifying power."[14]

The warrant for the grounding of the existence of this "universal unifying power" and the assumption of its subjectless activity as a perceiving, thinking, feeling, willing and intuitive contemplation—rather than an "I perceive, think, will, etc."—I leave undecided. What we must observe with astonishment is the apparent fact that this discriminating analyzing of "pure experience" is something different from it and that it does not happen without a subject; rather Nishida is its subject, and "pure experience" is its object. This is true not only of the knowing practiced here by Nishida, but of all conceptual thinking in so far as this transpires in the subject-object scheme of consciousness and is not satisfied with an unconsciously occurring unification. Nishida was apparently aware of this basic problematic of his epistemological theory, for he believed that he was able to explain or sublate it. For the negative explanation he appealed in a later connection to the myth of the Fall.[15] The loss of paradise occurs where we exit the unity of consciousness, proper to the "newborn child," by "separating subject

[10]*A Study of Good*, 1-2.
[11]Ibid., 20ff.
[12]Ibid., 31.
[13]Ibid., 45.
[14]Ibid., 57ff.
[15]Ibid., 181.

and object,"[16] and—instead of letting the powers of consciousness work—conceive of ourselves as its subject.[17] In so far as this individualization belongs to the development of consciousness one could think of the doctrine of consciousness espoused by the Yogacarins—something Nishida certainly does not do.[18] To the contrary, Nishida sees the positive dissolution of this fate in artistic creativity and in the enjoyment of a work of art,[19] or even in handworking activity which through practice becomes artistic skill.[20] The creation of the gifted artist becomes for Nishida the archetype of true knowing, in that in this work the inspiration working unconsciously assumes a form and continues to work creatively as a "something created"—"from the created to the creating," as the expression Nishida frequently used put it—in artistic creativity as in the one who shares in its experience by its creations. In this knowing that corresponds to this process, in which the separation of subject and object is constantly *aufgehoben* anew we are dealing—according to Nishida—with the true nature of reality.[21]

As the presentation indicates, this epistemology already possesses metaphysical character. The universal unifying power which Nishida assumes to be efficacious in the individual forms of consciousness is a metaphysical speculation; and the question of the nature of reality which he wishes to answer is a question of metaphysics. In order to answer it he needs only to extend the lines of his analysis of human consciousness, which in their starting points are already of a metaphysical kind, into the universal in order to arrive at its metaphysics. His universal metaphysics is a metaphysics of consciousness expanded into the cosmic. In human consciousness the same unifying power is operative as in the Universe.[22] Through it person and world are ultimately a unity. As for the "Consciousness-only Philosophy" of the Yogacara, so for Nishida "consciousness [is] the sole reality."[23] The knowability of the world rests on the identity of the unifying power of our consciousness with that which works in the world.[24] Spirit and matter are only different aspects of the unifying power which facilitates

---

[16]Ibid., 4.

[17]Ibid., 160.

[18]Edward Conze, *Der Buddhismus*, 6th ed. (Urban Taschenbücher, 1977) 163ff. [ET: *Buddhism: Its Essence and Development*, Harper Torchbooks (New York: Harper & Brothers, 1959) 161ff.

[19]*A Study of Good*, 19, 32, 52, and 95.

[20]Ibid., 80.

[21]Ibid.

[22]Ibid., 58.

[23]Ibid., 42ff., 62.

[24]Ibid., 66.

knowledge—objectifying in the mental, objectified in the material appearances.[25] In contrast to the forms of nonhuman nature, priority is assigned to the human Geist in that its mere preliminary unitedness attains completion through it. But in order for this to happen, man has to become one with nature. "When one sees a flower, it means that the self becomes a flower," is a well known Zen proverb quoted by Nishida is this connection.[26] Thus his metaphysics once again flows into epistemology, which is not surprising in view of the connection in which for Nishida they stand with each other.

Before Nishida draws the relevant consequences of these epistemological and metaphysical speculations for his concept of religion,[27] he sets forth in a further chapter their implications for answering the ethical question as to what is to be done as "the good."[28] What is to be done and how it is possible to do it both result for Nishida from the universal power operative both in consciousness and in the world. As such this power does not operate in us so as to exclude "free will,"[29] for this belongs to the inventory of our consciousness of being a responsible person,[30] but it does not permit us to follow our own egotistical wishes; rather, if we allow it to work in us, it turns us into social being, which finds its fulfillment in love. For—as Nishida understands his ethical pronouncements—"our true self is the basic substance of the universe, and if one knows the true self, one is not only linked with the good of mankind in general, but melts with the basic substance of the universe and is divinely united with the will of God."[31] Only by acting in this way do we attain to the "realm of the unity of subject and object" wherein lies "the final meaning of religion and art." In Christianity this is called "rebirth"; in Buddhism, "enlightenment."[32]

Thus Nishida here once again attests that, for him, knowledge, the realm of metaphysics and ethical action form a totality, which as such simultaneously comprises the essence of religion, to whose presentation he devotes the final chapter. Just as in the treatment of the themes of the previous chapter the relation of subject and object repeatedly shows itself to be the central problem—as when he there asks, Can "pure experience" be the object of psychological analysis? Can reality properly be conceived as consciousness? Is it possible to unite personal being with operational power?—so this problem is posed in its final

---

[25]Ibid., 69.
[26]Ibid., 86.
[27]Ibid., 85ff.
[28]Ibid., 91ff.
[29]Ibid., 100ff.
[30]Ibid., 103ff., 140ff.
[31]Ibid., 156.
[32]Ibid., 157.

depth when Nishida says that in religion we call this power "God,"[33] and when he identifies it with the world[34] and the "true self,"[35] as the "unifier of the world [universe]."

But as he had already at the end of the earlier chapter pointed to religion as the solution of its problems, so here also he now not merely notes its problems—evil and the Evil One[36] and our weakness before them[37]—but also sees in religion their overcoming. For him, the opposites belong to the harmony of the whole,[38] and these are actualized in our becoming one with God, which is at the same time a becoming of God in our consciousness.[39] For this he appeals to Christian mystics, like Meister Eckhart and Jacob Boehme,[40] to the christological God-Man dogma,[41] [[42]citation in text missing] to Jesus' injunction to his disciples to take up their cross,[43] and to the word of the Apostle Paul about the Christ who "lives in me,"[44] but also to Shinran's Buddhism of Grace (*tariki*) and the possibility of its connection with self-salvation (*jiriki*) in Zen Buddhism.[45]

Thus he concludes the chapter on "Knowledge and Love" in A Study of Good with the confession that the teachings of the Vedas, Neo-Platonism and Zen Buddhism are "identical in essence" with Christianity and Shin-Buddhism despite all their differences, insofar as in them the knowledge of the Unknowable is fulfilled in the "intuition of love."[46]

These are all the aspects which we also encounter differently in the later works of Nishida, which he also has again principally taken up in his final essays, although there he more hints at, than explains, them. After the publication of his "newborn" text he principally deals with the epistemological, metaphysical and ethical problems of his philosophy of religion contained in it. That problems of an epistemological sort—beyond those already noted—are especially present in it becomes somewhat apparent from the fact that, on the one hand, in the ethi-

---

[33]Ibid., 167.
[34]Ibid., 171, 180.
[35]Ibid., 182.
[36]Ibid., 183.
[37]Ibid., 184.
[38]Ibid., 154, 184.
[39]Ibid., 189.
[40]Ibid., 174-75.
[41]Ibid., 165.
[42]Ibid., 181ff.
[43]Ibid., 181ff.
[44]Ibid., 158, 163.
[45]Ibid., 188.
[46]Ibid., 189.

cal chapter he admits the necessity of conceptual knowledge,[47] and on the other, stresses to the contrary that neither the self nor God can be grasped in concepts.[48]

3. The Search for New Ways: A Transitional Phase

During the years he taught at Kyoto University Nishida was occupied primarily with epistemological problems. In discussing them he examined above all the presuppositions not only of the empirical-psychological-speculative knowledge hitherto represented by him, but of knowledge as such. He was prompted in doing so not only by the methodic and material problems of his previous philosophizing, but also by a deeper penetration into Kant's transcendental philosophy, German Idealism and Neo-Kantianism, as well as becoming acquainted with phenomenology and its conception of the relation of the act and object of thought in their intentionality. Here it is a matter no longer merely of experience, but of the laws of thinking always operative in knowledge, that is, of the a priori of all experience and all knowledge. In the course of the attempt to conceive his Zen experience with the aid of Western psychology along the lines of Western logic, Nishida—at the end of the second portion of his philosophic journey—attained to an expressly Eastern logic different from this Western type, which unlike the latter had the capability of corresponding to that from which he began his thinking.

The text on *Art and Morality* published by Nishida in 1923[49] is a typical example of the transitional phase in which he attempts to ground now more transcendentally and with the help of intentionalism the metaphysical unity of subject and object, which he believed he had demonstrated in his "newborn" text in an analysis of consciousness. If he here unfolds this new approach by the examples of art and ethics, this corresponds throughout to the significance which he had always attributed to the creative nature of art and to ethical willing and acting—with the exception that what he had earlier explained about them psychologically he now wished to validate transcendentally and intentionally.

For this purpose Kant's Transcendentalism did not satisfy him, because its "Ding an sich" remained inconceivable,[50] and the categorical imperative, with whose help Kant wishes to overcome this cleft, appeared to Nishida as too abstract, since it lacked content.[51] On the contrary Fichte's conception of the "fact" (*Tathandlung*) in consequence of which the I posits the world in order to

---

[47]Ibid., 138.

[48]Ibid., 168, 172, 175, 178.

[49]Nishida Kitaro, *Art and Morality*, trans. David A. Dilworth and Valdo H. Viglielmo (Honolulu: University of Hawaii Press, 1973).

[50]Ibid., 7.

[51]Ibid., 87ff.

overcome it, better corresponded to Nishida's intention of the creative will.[52] In this Fichtean conception of the *Tathandlung* he now sees the transcendental-aprioristic grounding of the "universal unifying power" postulated by him in *A Study of Good* from a psychology of experience.

Just how close Nishida comes to subjective Idealism in this phase of his struggle with Fichte's subject-object problem, while simultaneously rejecting its absolutization of the self, is shown by the position he takes on "Francis of Assisi's 'Hymn to the Sun'."[53] After emphasizing "in sun, moon, stars, wind, and clouds there is nothing that was not a symbol of God" he wishes "to deepen this viewpoint even further by employing a Zen saying to this effect: "Heaven and earth are of the same root as the self, and the myriad things are of the same substance as the self." If it is questionable whether with his concept of symbol Nishida conformed to the saint's belief in the Creator, he did apply to his intentional deepening of the "Hymn to the Sun" through the image of the "same root" a concept which Francis, despite all his relatedness to nature, did not here utilize.

Probably in allusion to the childlikeness of piety he cited, following Matthew 18:3, "unless one become an innocent child, one cannot enter into the Kingdom of Heaven," yet he observed on this that the "spiritual state of the child is not directly the state of the religious spirit." Whoever wishes to attain the Kingdom of Heaven must "first penetrate to the root of the self." But that means for him attaining to the "non-distinction" of "enlightenment" and "samsara" which is possible neither in the horizon of pure non-reflection nor of innocence.[54]

Thus Nishida engaged in reflection in the sense of Fichte's transcendental philosophy in which the self-reflecting self is one with itself and in this inner "activity" appear the "innumerable things," that is, the external world, as "the modes of expression of the self." But while in the aesthetic intuition of the poet and artist this unity of self and world is immediately actualized, for the inner activity of judging and for the ethical activity directing itself to the external condition of the world it represents an unending process in which man becomes conscious of his finitude through religion. This religious feeling is the opposite of Fichte's creative I in knowledge and will, for it consists in an "absolutely humble attitude" in which the self "as intellectual, and even as emotional and volitional" "is completely effaced" and "one's entire person" abandoned.[55]

Nishida introduces a twofold dialectic into Fichte's aprioristic "Tathandlung," in that he sees in the intuition the presupposition of conceptual knowledge, yet at the same time holds it to be dependent upon the inner and outer volitional

---

[52]Ibid., 11, 125.
[53]Ibid., 78ff.
[54]Ibid., 78.
[55]Ibid., 100ff.

activity and regards this as not merely positing being but as the reality over against him which is never finished. Nevertheless, he then brings this conception of the aesthetic and ethical self into dialectic relation with the religious, by permitting it—although it consisted of self-extinction—to encompass art and ethics and to bring them into a unity in this way.[56] Thus for Nishida religion, which is itself dialectical, in that it consists for him in the sense of Zen both in an extinction of the self and also in an attaining of "the true self" which sees things "as they are," represents the "point of unity of the true, the good and beautiful," which contain severally a dialectic in themselves, as well as standing in dialectic relation to each other and to religion.

On the basis and in the unfolding of this much convoluted dialectic Nishida developed the nature of the two realities named in the title of this writing. His exposition was dialectic in that he simultaneously presupposed what was to be unfolded and accounts for it in its unfolding. Despite the differentiated execution it provides no fundamentally new insights on the essential nature of art and ethics in comparison with those in *A Study of Good*. What is of concern to him in both domains even now is already found in the "newborn" text. What is altered meanwhile is only the mode of argumentation, in that the psychological-speculative has been replaced with the no less speculative transcendental-logical.

For the dialectic character which the transcendental-logical speculation has assumed for Nishida, however, the apriori of the Fichtean "Tathandlung" now also proves inadequate for the philosophical definition of the unity of subject and object in the Zen experience. Fichte's "Tathandlung"-thinking is also dialectical in that the self posits the non-self in order to sublate it. But in view of the "extinction of the self" in Zen it is still too onesidedly idealistic and self-assertive and too little allows the things to show themselves as they are in themselves. On this basis Nishida could not be content with Fichte's absolute self in which he believed he found the transcendental-logical analogue to "universal unifying power," but had to look for a logic which stood opposed to the onesidedness of Fichte's Subjectivism and Personalism and validated the apersonalism of thinking and the objectivity of its content, which had been of interest to Nishida from his empirical-psychologistic beginnings.

Nishida found one way of thinking which takes his intention into account in the transcendental philosophy of the phenomenological intentionalism of Brentano, which was quite different from idealism.[57] In place of Fichte's positing and sublating of the non-self by the self there appears here the intentional directedness of thinking toward an object, the intention of the noetic, in which the essence of what is thought, the intention of the noema, is validated, when the

---

[56]Ibid., 104.
[57]Ibid., 6, 101, 123.

latter corresponds to the former.[58] In the agreement of the intentionality of thinking with what is thought it arrives at the "unity of subject and object."

In opposition to epistemological subjectivism, Nishida had already referred at the beginning of *Art and Morality* to Zen's characteristic possibility of "seeing things through things";[59] and in the further course of his thought he attained—in the "internal unity of object and act"—the apriori[60] from which he sought to interpret Fichte's *Tathandlung* as a "being-embraced" by "the narrower and wider horizons."[61] But while he here allowed this polar transcendental logic still to be enacted in consciousness, in the later writings in which he arrived at his own characteristic philosophy he then localized this in the "field of Nothingness," in which—he is convinced—the nonobjectifiability of the self and of Being can only really be thought.[62] At the conclusion of *Art and Morality* he confesses that we "must pass through the gate of truth" in order to enter the realm of the beautiful and good. On "this side of the gate" in which he on his own admission is located in this text, "the self that we see in general consciousness" is merely a shadow of a darker instinct. From this concluding sentence and the other of the foreword: "I must first censure the inadequacy of my own thought,"[63] it follows that Nishida knows that in this text he is at a decisive turning point of his philosophizing.

From our perspective we have only to ask about the nature of this "gate" which Nishida holds we must penetrate, whether the "shadow" turns into the "gleaming darkness" of which he speaks with the mystics, or into the night in which—as Hegel says—all cows are grey, and how it is with the "darker instinct." Nishida is occupied with Hegel and Schelling no less than with Kant, but also with the origins of this thinking and its transformations in Western history. By following further this course of thought which he has taken Nishida arrives at his own philosophy.

4. Characteristic Nishida Philosophy

Two of Nishida's writings are available to us from this third period of his philosophy in which it reached its final form: *The Intelligible World* from the year 1930 and his *Fundamental Problems of Philosophy* which appeared three years later. In both writings Nishida's course of thinking leads into the "Place of Nothingness"—in the first under the aspect of mutually encompassing horizons and

---

[58]Ibid., 6ff.
[59]Ibid., 9.
[60]Ibid., 8.
[61]Ibid., 49.
[62]Ibid., viiff. (foreword by David A. Dilworth).
[63]Ibid., 4.

in the second under that of the polar unity of opposites which are absolutely exclusive; thus each explicates one of both possibilities, already envisaged in *Art
and Morality*, of an overcoming of the subjective onesidedness of the idealistic
philosophy of consciousness. Transcendental logic which formerly was perennially captured in consciousness is now transformed into a "logic of Nothingness."

In an essay on "Nishida's Philosophy of 'Place' "[64] Masao Abe has shown
how, by means of a critical analysis of the nature of judgment, Nishida overcame
the danger of subjective idealism which he exposes by equating reality with consciousness in his "newborn" text and also again in his appeal to Fichte's
"Tathandlung." Abe points out that, like Hegel who distinguished between an
"abstract" and a "concrete" universal, Nishida distinguished between two kinds
of judgment, a "conceptual universal" and a "universal of judgment." While the
abstract or conceptual universal robs the individual of its particularity, the concrete universal or universal of judgment which contains the principles of
particularization in itself facilitates their unfolding. But because Hegel conceives
the concrete universal as an idea in dialectic self-unfolding, it still represents an
objectification of self-reflecting consciousness, and accordingly is something
which cannot be the last, and neither determines itself nor leaves self-determination to the individual. This deficiency can only be corrected, according to
Nishida, if in lieu of the objectifying "grammatical subject" the "place" of the
judging is considered, and this "place" is the "absolute Nothingness." This
"absolute Nothingness" as "Place" enables the concrete individual to determine
itself and, *pari passu*, the individuals to determine themselves in mutuality.

Abe illustrates this not only with the example of a dog, Ralph, which can
only then be this definite dog if it "stands in the unfathomably deep Nothingness" and "neither an idea nor a creative activity of God" maintains or grounds
its existence," but with the famous Mu-koan as well: "A monk once asked his
master: 'Does a dog have a Buddha nature?' Joshu says: 'Mu!' " Abe interprets
this koan to mean that with his answer, "Nothing!" the master wished the monk
to understand that with his question he was still imprisoned in the "duality of
being and nonbeing" as if the Buddha nature were a something one could "have
or not have," whereas it is precisely [the] "completely nonobjectifiable Absolute
Nothingness." But because this Absolute Nothing is "not an empty Nothing,"
Joshu could answer on another occasion: "U!" that is, "having being." Only in
the Place of the Absolute Nothingness can the things show themselves as they
really are. In view of the space-creating effect of this koan Abe calls it a "sword
that cuts both ways." In accord with this example of an interpretation of Nishida

[64]Masao Abe, "Nishida's Philosophy of 'Place' "; Japanese in *Riso* 541 (June
1978). Manuscript of the English translation still unpublished.

by a Japanese Zen philosopher we wish to see how we can find our way around in this "space" on the basis of linguistic and conceptual avenues at our disposal.

In the extensive essay "The Intelligible World"[65] Nishida begins with the conceptual thinking which includes everything in its judgment, but which is itself included in self-consciousness whose self can as little be made into its object as can the whole of Being. Thus the self—conceptually conceived—and its content reach beyond themselves into the sphere of insight, of intelligibility, in which the thinking subject in its noetic function perennially stands over against what is thought, the noema. The split of self-consciousness which points beyond itself is thus posited in the intelligible sphere and gets expressed in religion in which human beings who know about values to which they do not correspond, stand over against God as sinner. But even this objectification must still be experienced—which is only possible in the "self-consciousness of the Nothingness which can be Nothingness as well as Being," because it is "indefinable"—but in such a way that everything which is, is allowed to appear as that which it is.

Nishida illustrates this vertiginous course of thinking in which everything seems to dissolve into a self-reflection of mirror images—but which puts the one who dares it in touch with true reality—by means of an old Chinese poem of unknown origin[66] which tells how a rice farmer ploughs his field on a cliff overhanging an abyss. The ploughshare strikes a rock so as to cause sparks. For a moment the man is in danger of losing his grip. If he loses control over the instrument he will plunge into the depths. The fear that overtakes him allows him to experience the sparks as a cosmic conflagration in which he is consumed. But

---

[65] *The Intelligible World* in Nishida Kitaro: *Intelligibility and the Philosophy of Nothingness. Three Philosophical Essays*, trans. Robert Schinzinger (Honolulu: East-West Center Press, 1958 and 1966) 69-141.

[66]Ibid., 137ff. Cf. Hans Waldenfels, *Absolutes Nichts* (Freiburg: Herder, 1976) 60 [ET: *Absolute Nothingness. Foundations for a Buddhist-Christian Dialogue*. Trans. J. W. Heisig (New York: Paulist Press, 1980) 43-44]. Waldenfels translation of the poem reads as follows:
The poet says:
From the cliff,
Eight times ten thousand feet high,
Withdrawing your hand,—
Flames spring from the plough,
World burns,
Body becomes ashes and dirt,
And resurrects,
The rice rows
Are as ever,
And the rice ears
Stand high.

he proceeds further, firmly holding the plough in his hand, and has a mental image of the harvest for whose sake he engages in his dangerous work. In this he experienced enlightenment in which the world has come into being anew.

The poem is equally suited to the inner course of a Zen meditation as well as to the philosophical transcending step by step, from the encompassing to the one who encompasses and then to the all-encompassing which is not actualizable, but realizes itself by passing through its different forms, which Schinzinger in his introduction to this essay correctly sees as parallel to Jaspers' metaphysics.[67] Letting what is conceived wander belongs to the progressing, but it is preserved in this as a preliminary step in order finally to arise anew in its true form in Nothingness.

Nishida developed this course of thinking in a somewhat different and more extended way in the volume of essays devoted to the *Fundamental Problems of Philosophy* and so titled.[68] While in the preceding single essay he approached Nothingness vertically into the heights or in a spiral movement running into the depths, his thinking here moves specifically between two poles which stand on one plane with each other in such a relation that they mutually cancel each other, with the result that this plane proves to be "the Place of Nothingness."

Framed by a "Foreword to Metaphysics" placed at the beginning as a summary of the whole and a concluding chapter which with his comparison of "classical Eastern and Western forms of culture" draws the relevant consequences from the metaphysics and indicates the problematic sphere with which Nishida especially occupied himself in his final years, the central section of this work consists of two parts. The first of these has as its theme the dialectic relation of "self and world," while in the second the "dialectic structure of the world" is unfolded. In the transcendentalistic transition phase of his philosophy Nishida had already conceived the relation of these themes in a dialectical way and had there already entertained the possibility of the "Nothingness" as "boundary."[69] But now this transcendental-intentional view of the relation of the thinking subject and thought object seems to him to be still too much "seen from outside"[70] and as too "rationalistic."[71] That does not mean that he now thinks that it is no longer possible to think this mutual relatedness at all. It may only not be thought in such a way that the two poles—either from the side of the subject in Fichte's

---

[67]Ibid., 30-31.

[68]Nishida Kitaro, *Fundamental Problems of Philosophy*, trans. with an introduction by David A. Dilworth (Tokyo: Sophia University, 1970).

[69]*Art and Morality*, 123, 158, 201ff.

[70]*Fundamental Problems of Philosophy*, 1, 95, 113.

[71]Ibid., 3.

sense or Hegel's[72] or phenomenologically by taking into account the intentionality appropriate to the object[73]—can be brought into a noncontradictory system.

To assume such a standpoint outside of the polar contradictions of the world
and thereby theoretically and practically to bring the contradictions into a system
which overcomes them, is, according to Nishida, denied us because we already
always find ourselves as thinking and acting beings—spatially and temporally—to be contradictory beings in a contradictory world.[74] We may not and cannot
abstract from this state of affairs in which we find ourselves; rather to do justice
to it requires a "concrete logic.".[75] True dialectic consists not in the elimination
of the contradictions, but in recognizing them as reality. That does not mean that,
because it seems to us contradictory, it does not exist, but rather the opposite:
because it is contradictory it is therefore true. Put into logical formula this
means: A is not A, therefore it is A. The contradiction is truth. The true is in
itself contradictory.

Thus Nishida opposes the undialectic logic of identity with the dialectical
"logic of the identity of absolute contradictories" with which alone he believes
it is possible to do justice to the world and existence in it. The meaning of this
logic is not to sublate the contradictories; rather, the meaning of Nishida's logic
of contradictories is to sublate the logic which only speaks of contradictories to
be sublated. The sphere in which this happens he calls the "Place of Nothingness," which can neither be thought in the logic he rejects nor made into an
object by the logic he represents, because it is the "Place of Absolute Nothingness." As such it corresponds to the "final encompassing" to which he attains in
the essay on intelligibility by transcending the boundaries of what is no longer
perceivable.

In *The Fundamental Problems of Philosophy*, however, he constantly thinks
in this "topos," in that he allows the objects to become unities of contradiction
through their mutual conditioning of each other.[76] Thus his metaphysics here consists of discussions of pairs of concepts, like individual and universal, subject and
predicate, time and eternity, being and the ought, I and Thou, community and
society, God and humanity. By being defined and actualized, the first concept
becomes the second and its content; but by losing its nature therein, it becomes
active in this self-abandonment and so alters the sphere inimical to it—so that the
concept "lives as it dies and dies as it lives."[77] This metaphor of "living by

---

[72]Ibid., 21ff.
[73]Ibid., 125ff.
[74]Ibid., 232.
[75]Ibid., 13.
[76]Ibid., 6-7.
[77]Ibid., 7, 41, 45, etc.

dying" repeatedly used throughout the entire work shows that for Nishida it is
not intended to deal merely with a dialectic of concepts, but with a dialectic of
existence and understanding—based on Zen experience and remembered in
Christian belief in the resurrection—from which he then derives as its meaning
"love" in the sense of agape[78] and of which he emphasizes that it is not merely
a human thing but is based on belief in the "Word of God" which is to be heard
in the contradictory nature of the world. Christianity believes in this "through the
Christ event." Mahayana Buddhism reaches this in "self-enlightenment in
absolute negation" by which one attains to "absolute affirmation" if and when he
"realizes the anxiety of deep self-contradiction in the very depths of the self."[79]

In several publications of the following years Nishida expanded the consequences of his metaphysics delineated at the conclusion of these two parts in
ethical, cultural-historical and religious perspective.

5. A Religious-Ethical Hypothesis of Culture
as the Goal of Nishida's Philosophy

In a chapter added to *The Fundamental Problems of Philosophy*[80] Nishida had
already drawn a parallel between the nature of Israelite-Christian, Greek, Indian,
Chinese, Modern Western, Russian, and Japanese culture. While he critically
evaluated all others—with the exception of the last-named—from the perspective
of his metaphysics by estimating their essential characteristics, the treatment ends
with a hymnic doxology on the culture of Japan, a fact which awakens in us
objections to establishing culture the way Nishida does. What in his eyes confers
upon Japanese culture its special worth is its being anchored in feeling which
bursts forth in the splendid blossoms of the cherry tree and "crystalizes into
swords forged a hundred times" whose blades even "cleave iron pans."[81] To see
"the source of national polity"[82] in a "culture of feeling" as "form of the form-

---

[78]Ibid., 105-106.

[79]Ibid., 235.

[80]Ibid., 237ff.: "The Forms of Culture of the Classical Periods of East and
West Seen from a Metaphysical Perspective."

[81]Ibid., 254. Nishida is here citing the battle hymn stamped by the Neo-
Confucianism of the Sung period, which reads in full:
Heaven and earth are the great vitality. How purely it cherishes the land of
the gods [Japan], whose essence is manifested in its unique mountain [Fuji],
lofty and majestic through one thousand autumns. Its flowing rivers become
the great ocean. How wide and deep it encircles the eight islands. It bursts
forth into a myriad of cherry blossoms, beyond the compare of other
flowers. It crystalizes into swords forged a hundred times, whose blades can
cleave through iron pans.

[82]Ibid., 249.

less" can produce no other fruit than what Nishida saw wonderfully emerging from "Goethe's metaphysical background."[83]

Nishida seems to have become aware of this dangerous possibility as the "problem of Japanese culture" in a series of lectures held at Kyoto University in 1938,[84] in which he warned of the then raging nationalism and emphasized that feeling must be combined with the Western intellect in order to prevent self-destructive purposes. But even here he did not transcend the "contradictory self-identity" as he saw it intimated in a connection of "No-mindedness [in Zen Buddhism] or effortless acceptance of the grace of Amida [in the True Pure Land teaching]."[85]

In his two final works, "Towards A Philosophy of Religions with the Concept of Preestablished Harmony as Guide" (1944) and "The Logic of Place and the Religious Worldview" (1945), Nishida extends this project of a synthesis of culture, both under a religious aspect as well as by accenting its fulfillment in a combination of Zen and Shin Buddhism as the authentic goal of his philosophy. In the former essay,[86] which represents a preamble to his religiophilosophical testament, he criticizes Leibniz for the fact that, in his cosmic view of the mutual mirroring of the One and the Many and of the Many arranged beneath each other as a creation of the One, namely, God, he falls into an untenable contradiction in this system between a pantheistic monism and a dualism of God and world. This reproach of Leibniz consisting of his own presuppositions rests on his Aristotelian logic in which independent assertions can be made in the predicate about the subject as a substance of space and time. According to Nishida, the correct intention of Leibniz' Monadology could only be achieved if his abstract logic is replaced by "the concrete logic of the historical individual" which in the "depths of his self" understands himself passively and actively as "self-identity of contradiction" of the self-expression of the world. This has to do no longer with substance but with structures which realize themselves in him as Past and which simultaneously in view of the future he realizes as the "creative

---

[83]Schinzinger, "Goethe's Metaphysical Background," 145-59, in *Kitaro Nishida, Intelligibility and the Philosophy of Nothingness*. Cf. German version in Goethe, *Viermonatsschrift der Goethe-Gesellschaft des dritten Bandes*, Zweites Heft (Weimar: Verlag der Goethe-Gesellschaft, 1938) 136-41.

[84]An excerpt in English translation, with an introduction by Masao Abe, appeared in *Sources of Japanese Tradition* (New York: Columbia University Press, 1958) 857ff.

[85]Ibid., 869.

[86]Nishida Kitaro, "Towards a Philosophy of Religions with the Concept of Preestablished Harmony as Guide," EB 3/1 (1970): 21-46.

point"—as the "eternal present" and the unity of necessity and freedom in the "Place of Nothingness."[87]

In this view of the unity of world history and the awareness of the "true self" the nature of religion consists for Nishida in the way in which he sees it embodied in the Christian notion of revelation, the Fall, reconciliation and divine Providence, but better in the Buddhist notion of Karma in connection with trust in the Buddha's compassion and the "seeing of nonseeing" in Zen.[88] If in this connection Nishida speaks of an "eschatological perspective," he intends this not in the sense of an end to history, but as an awareness of "the absolute Present" in the mutually mirroring self-determination of the world and the self-determination of the individual.[89] The true self is "the call of God," and there is "nothing which is not religious."[90] "Every moment is the beginning and the end of the world."[91] "Religion is the problem of the self,"[92] and "the world is religious."[93]

Nishida characterizes the ethic which results for him from this religious view of the world by means of two sayings of the founder of Rinzai Zen according to which the man who understands himself and the world in the prescribed sense is surely "master of himself wherever he may go" and "no matter how he stands, everything is right with him." In agreement with Spinoza's thought of the indistinguishable identity and in allusion to Paul's word that "there is neither male nor female" (Gal 3:28)—omitting to be sure the "in Christ" in the latter—he is convinced that "out of the depths of such 'nonego' infinite compassion wells forth."[94] But he also stresses that it would be wrong to think that religion has to do only with individual "peace of mind" in consequence of which one would not see in it a "question of nation."[95] Although he must concede that modern Buddhism has forgotten "the true meaning of Mahayana" which Nishida requires for his philosophy, he holds nevertheless that for it "Eastern culture," if it rises to the meaning prescribed for it, is destined "to contribute a new light to world culture." "As the self-determination of the absolute Present" he believes it is possible from this perspective to see "in the national polity of Japan a norm of historical action."[96]

---

[87]Ibid., 31.
[88]Ibid., 43-44.
[89]Ibid., 36, 45.
[90]Ibid., 37.
[91]Ibid.
[92]Ibid., 37.
[93]Ibid., 46.
[94]Ibid., 44-45.
[95]Ibid., 45.
[96]Ibid., 36.

What he says of the politics of his country, that in it "the true spirit of Mahayana is in the East preserved only in Japan,"[97] holds for nations absolutely. "Nations are the forms of the self-formation of the world." In view of the fact that "every individual self fundamentally mirrors the world of the absolute Present," the nations can be conceived "as the sources of morality."[98] For Nishida, in this way "morality and culture are grounded on the religious."[99]

As much as Nishida's harmonious view of the—truly "preestablished"—meaning of human existence and the history of nations agrees with Leibniz' preestablished harmony, we must not overlook the great difference between them. This difference consists not only in the fact that in Leibniz' thinking, the contradictions of the world's existence are united in a universal unity of meaning while Nishida makes contradiction a principle of his logic, but rather fundamentally in the fact that for the latter this becomes in a sense a matter of existence. Whereas Leibniz sees no problem in the fact that he thinks the world and understands his thinking as world transforming—but that indeed he solves the problems, Nishida sees therein a "deep contradiction, anxiety and anguish, in the existence of the self itself" which "cannot be eliminated by the power of the self," certainly not "through moral efforts" because "it is our very existence . . . the very essence of our life." "Moral action is a process grounded on such a self-identity of contradiction," and in it is to be sought "the root of man's religious exigency."[100]

To illustrate this fact Nishida cites both the Zen thinker Daito Kokushi: "Buddha and I, separate through a billion kalpas, yet not separate for a instant; encountering each other the whole day through, yet not encountering each other for an instant,"[101] as well as Augustine: "Our hearts will never rest, Oh Lord, until they rest in Thee."[102]

This self-understanding is to be understood "not in a psychological way as expressed in Descartes"[103] but in the sense of Dogen's instruction for Zen meditation: "To learn the way of the Buddha is to learn the self," it consists in forgetting the self and becoming enlightened by the Dharmas.[104] With respect to Augustine Nishida speaks, not of enlightenment, but faith which, according to Luther, consists in a complete conversion of life, effected in us by God, as the

---

[97]Ibid., 36.
[98]Ibid., 45.
[99]Ibid., 46.
[100]Ibid., 41.
[101]Ibid., 35.
[102]Ibid., 102.
[103]Ibid., 40.
[104]Ibid., 42.

"Self-determination of the self-identity of contradiction."[105] Closely connected with the "nonobjectifiable knowing" which leads into "absolute Nothingness" is the *docta ignorantia* of the negative theology of Nicholas Cusanus insofar as he does not still think in Aristotelian logic and speak "under Christian influence" of a "mystical way" of a becoming one with God. For Nishida, to the contrary, God—insofar as he uses this expression—is nothing but "Absolute Nothingness" in which "there is nothing which can be negated."[106]

In his last essay, "The Logic of the Place of Nothingness and the Religious Worldview,"[107] Nishida basically adds nothing new to this Buddhist interpretation of the preestablished harmony—at least in the middle section available [to me]—but is satisfied with explanations and an expansion of what had already been developed by him. But the section represents a highly compact collection of high points of Nishida-philosophy. Informative for the existential character of the nonobjectifiability of the self and of Being, or Nothingness, represented in it, is here the reflection on death and in connection with it, on the "Kenosis of God." Nishida argues here in such a way as to distinguish between a merely represented or thought death and "eternal death." The first is not "one's real death," because we stand in contrast to it as something imagined or thought and thus are not really concerned with it.[108] Only when we become aware of the nonobjectifiability of our death do we have to do with the "eternal death" before which we can say with Isaiah in the sight of God: "Woe to me, for I am undone. . . . "[109] In this "contradictory correspondence" we find our "complete self" in encounter with the Absolute.[110]

---

[105]Ibid., 42.

[106]Ibid., 40ff.

[107]Nishida Kitaro, "The Logic of Place and the Religious Worldview," 1946: the central section appeared in German translation with Notes by Yagi Seiichi, published under the title "Was liegt dem Selbstsein zugrunde?" in *Gott in Japan*, ed. Yagi Seiichi and Ulrich Luz (Munich: Chr. Kaiser Verlag, 1973) 94-112. Prior to this German translation there appeared the same section with the title "Religious Consciousness and the Logic of the Prajnaparamita Sutra from the Logic of Place and a Religious Worldview," MN 25/1-2 (1970): 203-16, trans. David A. Dilworth. Cf., by the same author, "Nishida's Final Essay: The Logic of Place and a Religious Worldview," PhEW 20/4 (1970): 355ff. [Version used by translator is from Nishida Kitaro, *Last Writings: Nothingness and the Religious Worldview*, trans. David A. Dilworth (Honolulu: University of Hawaii Press, 1987) 47-123.]

[108]Ibid., 96 [ET, 67].

[109]Ibid., 97 [ET, 68].

[110]Ibid., 96 [ET, 67].

What is true of the self, is true also of the Absolute. Also it "must itself be identical with itself in contradiction"; for to be absolute, it must distinguish itself from something else; but if there is something outside of it, it is not absolute. Once again Nishida illustrates this with the concept of God: "A God who does not create is an impotent God, is not God"[111] He says the same also about the world as the unity of the "One and the Many,"[112] in which "the individuals frame the creative world as the creative moments of the creative world," so that Nishida believes he can even see in this "Place" the Trinity of Father, Son and Holy Spirit.[113]

Insofar as the world can be understood "atheistically," "without God," and death as well as the "freedom of the self"[114] belong to it—both of which can be misunderstood—Nishida speaks of it as the "world of absolute evil," the "Satanic world."[115] But even though he says, "Even one who speculates errs,"[116] he incorporates—in a speculation proceeding from the contradictory unity of personal being and with reference to the Sacrifice of Isaac, understood in a Kierkegaardian way—the presence of the Satanic world into the will of God as an expression of the "self-negation" belonging to God's nature. "God as the true absolute must be Satan, too." "A God who merely opposes, and struggles with, evil" remains "a relative God." "The absolute God must include absolute negation within himself," that is, he "descends to the ultimate evil." For "Absolute Agape must reach even to the absolutely evil man."[117]

Nishida speaks of the "Place" of this event in the image of a sphere of infinite diameter, whose center is everywhere, because it has no circumference, and which—since it has no transcendent ground outside itself—reflects itself within itself.[118] In this "Place" Nishida thinks creation as well as redemption can find expression; a creation without a "transcendent *dominus*,"[119] but as a "self-negation of the Absolute One,"[120] and redemption as the awareness of the contradictory unity of the self, for which "the sacrifice of the Son of God, who is sent into the world of man," and "the power of the Other," namely, of Amida

---

[111]Ibid., 97 [ET, 68].
[112]Ibid., 100 [ET, 71].
[113]Ibid., 102 [ET, 73-74].
[114]Ibid., 100 [ET, 71].
[115]Ibid., 103 [ET, 74].
[116]Ibid., 105 [ET, 76].
[117]Ibid., 103 [ET, 74-75].
[118]Ibid., 105 [ET, 76].
[119]Ibid., 100 [ET, 71].
[120]Ibid., 120 [ET, 95].

Buddha, can become expressions[121] if they do not become misunderstood in objectifying thinking, and in cultic activity become the "magic" of "magical forms,"[122] but are understood "on the basis of our selfhood" as "the call of God or Buddha, the act of God or of the Buddha."[123] This is the way Nishida wishes Zen Buddhism to be understood rather than in the usual—and to him wrong—way as the "difficult way of redemption by one's own power" which is just the opposite of Shinran's Buddhism of grace. To appeal to the "alien power of grace" could be even more difficult than the practice of self-power because it is equally mistaken. In contrast to both positions and therefore to that of Christianity he recommends the behavior of the one who extinguishes a "fire on his head" as quickly as possible. "Anyone who has awakened to true religious consciousness must act as strenuously as a man attempting to be cured of a fever."[124]

In this image, with which Nishida concludes the central section of his final essay we observe once again the intention which moved him in his entire course of thinking and the insights which dawned on him. The "fire on his head" represents the religious and philosophical worldviews and conceptions of life which are intellectually conceived, and represented and practiced in this form, and which Nishida encountered on this path. For him the fire which he experienced in Zen enlightenment and which he had fueled in participating in Zen practices and in the deeper penetration into the Zen tradition, is not a "fire on his head," but in his "religious heart."[125] But it also became for him a "fire on his head" when he attempted at the beginning to conceive it in the categories of a mystical psychology and later in those of an intentional transcendental philosophy. Nishida was constantly occupied in his later philosophy with the extinction of this "fire

---

[121]Ibid., 108 [ET, 79].

[122]Ibid., 106, 108 [ET, 77, 79].

[123]Ibid., 107 [ET, 78].

[124]Ibid., 109 [ET, 80]. [Buri's reference to the "fire on his head" is based on Sei'ichi Yagi's translation of Dogen's saying into German ("Was liegt dem Selbstsein zugrunde?" in *Gott in Japan*, 109). Nishida's original Japanese for the "fire on his head" is *zunen* (   ), which means "urgent problem." Yusa Michiko's rendering of the Japanese by the words "as if one's hair were caught on fire" (Nishida Kitaro, "The Logic of Topos and the Religious Worldview," trans. Yusa Michiko. EB 19/2 [1989]: 29) is more accurate—at least more literal—than Dilworth's expression "as a man cured of a fever." Dogen uses *zunen* (   ) in *Gakudo Yojin-Shu* which is not part of the *Shobogenzo* but an independent work. Dogen says "Exercize the way as if your hair were caught on fire" (   ). (This note to the English version was supplied by Hiroko Ueda. —Trans.)]

[125]Ibid., 95 [ET, 65].

on his head" in order to let the fire of his heart newly arise out of the ashes. With the long and mighty breath of his thinking he fans the sparks of the contradictory unities and provides conceptual fuel for them in whose consumption they illuminate the world and our existence in it, with the result that against the background of an impenetrable darkness and from this can appear things as they really are and the "true self."

In view of the way Nishida concerned himself also with Christianity and the figure of its Redeemer on this path of Buddhist enlightenment which dissolved all objectifications and thus first validated them in their true significance, it may not seem inappropriate to see him not only on the path of the Buddha but also with Jesus and two of his disciples on the road to Emmaus and there holding communion with them.[126] In the way in which the Evangelist lets a cult meal of the resurrected one shine through in a profane meal in the inn and lets the participants recognize him as this one in the breaking of the bread and also to disappear from their sight, we have a parallel to the quick extinguishing of the objective "fever" demanded by Nishida in favor of the nonobjectifiable fire of the heart. Concerning the extinguishing of the vision of the Resurrected One the disciples asked themselves: "Did not our heart burn within us as he spoke to us on the way, as he disclosed to us the scriptures?"[127]

But only the one for whom "religion becomes an existential question" knows of this burning heart. That it was for the disciples of Emmaus an existential question is evident. It is another question whether and to what degree it is such a question for the Evangelist and those who transmitted his traditions, or whether and to what degree it became in the tradition a "fire on the head," which according to Nishida must be quickly extinguished. It is possible to go with Nishida to Emmaus, but one cannot accompany him "back to Jerusalem" into the community which believes that it possesses strong proofs of the resurrection of its Lord and proclaims them as the salvation of the world.

---

[126]Luke 24:13ff.
[127]Luke 24:32.

Hajime Tanabe (1885–1962)

Chapter 3

Hajime Tanabe (1885–1962)
Philosophy of Repentance
and Dialectic of Death

1. The Other Pole of the Kyoto School

Hajime Tanabe was a younger contemporary of Nishida's who was born only fifteen years later, but survived him by seventeen years. For the most part their literary and academic activity occurred at the same time and even at the same university.[1] Tanabe's first work[2] appeared in the same year as Nishida's "newborn text," and from 1918 on they taught together at Kyoto University. But they had already taken notice of each other earlier, which is not surprising considering the stir Nishida's *A Study of Good* awakened, and in view of the fact that Tanabe in the work mentioned referred to thoughts already well known from Nishida.[3] At that time as well as in the following years both were interested in the same German philosophers, especially in Rickert and Cohen and their discussion of the relation of the natural and the social sciences. Tanabe composed *inter alia* an essay on "The Limits of Rationalism in Epistemology," with which Nishida is said to have expressed agreement. But whereas Nishida only knew Neo-Kantianism and phenomenology from books, from 1922 to 1924 Tanabe studied in Berlin and Leipzig, as well as in Freiburg with Husserl and Martin Heidegger,

---

[1] For the biography of Tanabe and a list of writings, reference is made to the following: Gino K. Piovesana, S.J., *Recent Japanese Philosophical Thought 1862-1962. A Survey*, rev. ed. (Tokyo: Sophia University, 1968) 145-58; Yoshinori Takeuchi, "Tanabe's Philosophy of Metanoetics," art. "Modern Japanese Philosophy," in EncB (1966): 961; introduction to the Philosophy as Metanoetics," JR 5/2 (1967): 29-47; Seiichi Yagi, "Einleitung zu Hajime Tanabes Memento mori," in *Gott in Japan* (1973) 113; Johannes Laube, "Westliches und östliches Erbe in der Philosophie Hajime Tanabes," *Neues Zeitschrift für syst. Theol.* 20 (1978): 1ff.

[2] "On the Ontological Judgment," 1910, in which—according to Takeuchi—Tanabe attempted to conceive the original form in which the subject-object split originated and in which the Pure Land experience was changed into a judgment.

[3] Tanabe's name appears for the first time in Nishida's journal as early as 1913.

who was then a lecturer there.[4] In the time they shared in Kyoto (1919–1928) the philosophy of both not only matured, but, owing to significant changes, assumed for each of them a quite different form. Whereas Nishida took leave of the Western philosophy he had used up to that time and attained for his Zen logic the "logic of the Place of Nothingness," Tanabe increasingly turned in the same years to Kant and Hegel,[5] in order to reach—beyond Hegel's dialectic—to a "logic of species," helpful in the area of mathematics as well as of politics.[6]

As for Nishida the identity of opposites occurred in the Topos of Absolute Nothingness, so for Tanabe, in the species as the sphere of mediation between the general and the individual.[7] It is obvious that the different solutions which the two thinkers represented in regard to the same problematic must have led to controversies between them which were fought out on a high spiritual plane. The polarity of their respective positions was evident in the degree to which Nishida, after his retirement from Kyoto University which ensued in 1928, constructed his philosophy of the "self-identity of absolute contraries in the Place of Absolute Nothingness" in ever new leaps, while Tanabe as his successor up to the time of his retreat from academic office which followed in 1944, was occupied with the unfolding of his logic of species.[8]

Like Nishida's death in 1945, this retreat also stood in the shadow of the defeat of Japan in the Second World War which was always clearly in the background and finally was fulfilled, and the bitter experiences which were connected with it for Japan. The experience of this difficult time had as a consequence for both thinkers a deepening of their philosophy with respect to religion. But while Nishida's last essay on "The Significance of the Topos Logic for a Religious Worldview" represented his philosophical testament, for Tanabe the distress of that year became the occasion for a religious conversion and for the hour of birth of a new thinking as a "philosophy of repentance,"[9] which gave a religious foundation to his species logic, and to the development of which he devoted the remaining years of his life. For not only was Shinran and his Buddhism of the "Pure Land" (Jodoshinshu) of decisive significance for him, but also Christianity with whose philosophy and theology, above all in the figure of Kierkegaard, he concerned himself in several works.[10]

---

[4]Cf. Tanabe, "Todesdialektik," in *Martin Heidegger zum 70. Geburtstag: Festschrift*, ed. Günther Neske (Pfullingen: Neske, 1959) 94.

[5]*Kant's Teleology*, 1924.

[6]Collected essays on the "Logic of Species," for the years 1932–1941.

[7]"The Logic of Species against the Logic of Place," 1934.

[8]"The Dialectic of the Logic of Species," 1945.

[9]*Philosophy as Metanoetics*, 1946.

[10]"Existence, Love and Praxis," 1947; "Dialectic of Christianity," 1948.

The difference between the two thinkers persisted, although a certain approximation occurred between the two in the way in which, on the one hand, Nishida in his last essay introduces Christian ideas of faith and connects his Zen Buddhism with Shinran's Buddhism of grace, and on the other, Tanabe in his metanoetics connects redemption through "other power" with redemption through "one's own power" and thus from his understanding of grace came to appreciate Zen Buddhism. This difference is due to the fact that Nishida proceeds from Zen experience and finds the philosophical form for it in his "Logic of Place," whereas for Tanabe the completion of his species logic took shape as metanoetics in the sense of Shinran, which resulted not only in the differences in attitude of the two philosophers toward the state, but also in their different approaches to Christianity.[11] As Nishida became the founder of the Kyoto School not only through the intuitive-transcendental-logical form of his earlier works, but also through his "Logic of Place," so Tanabe is counted among the most representative members of this school not so much because of the scientific-theoretical investigations which he composed before his conversion, but rather because of his "philosophy as metanoetics," and the ensuing writings based on it.

The local and spiritual proximity of the two thinkers pertains to their essential characteristics, in that some of the successors were more under the influence of Nishida, and others more under that of Tanabe, and can lead both to the denial of one to the advantage of the other as well as to the connection of both into a synthesis, so that the Kyoto School as a whole represents a "self-identity of absolutely contraries"—except that "place" is not nothingness, but even Kyoto itself. Outwardly this symbiosis between Zen Buddhism and Shin Buddhist philosophy appears in the fact that Keiji Nishitani, who having been outspoken for Zen Buddhism, after becoming emeritus from the State University conducted his seminar at the Shin Buddhist Otani University, and in the fact that *The Eastern Buddhist* which is obligated in both directions is edited in the seminar room of this university. This coexistence corresponds to the narrow relation in which the two kinds of Buddhism—despite their separate temples and different cults and religious practices—stand to one another in Japanese culture.

This state of affairs which forms the background of the personal and philosophical relations between Nishida and Tanabe and continues today among their successors, is promoted by the circumstance that there are within Zen Buddhism and Pure Land Buddhism many different types which—especially since they derive from the same source and in view of their common history—despite their lines of demarcation suggest and justify borrowings from one or the other side in essential points. Thus today, for example, the founder of Soto-Zen, Dogen, is

---

[11]"The Pressing Need according to a Political Philosophy," 1946; "An Introduction to Philosophy," 1945–1952.

respected and cited by Shin Buddhist philosophers as an authority, just as Zen Buddhists delve into Shinran's Kyogyoshinsho, both of which were typical for Nishida and Tanabe. Numerous publications have been devoted to both from the Zen as well as the Shin Buddhist side during their lifetime and especially since their death.

More regrettable than the circumstance that this secondary literature is not available to us—with the exception of the presentations of Takeuchi and Piovesana mentioned in note 1—is the fact that of the literary work of Tanabe's, which initially did not lag behind Nishida's,[12] much less has appeared in translation than of the latter. Only two sections from the *Philosophy as Metanoetics*,[13] one section from *The Logic of Species as Dialectics*,[14] and the short essay "Memento mori"—the last also into German—have appeared in English translation.[15] There also belongs to the list the German translation of his contribution to the Heidegger *Festschrift*, which carries the title "Todesdialektik" ("Dialectic of Death").[16] Besides these few, there is also available to us—thanks to the kindness of Professor Takeuchi—the manuscript awaiting publication of his recently completed English translation of Tanabe's *Philosophy of Repentance*. As much as we regret being necessarily oriented only secondhand to the prehistory of the works of Tanabe belonging to this work, we appreciate the fact that through these translations in manuscript form we are able by means of these to construct an original picture of the decisive turning point in Tanabe's philosophy, which has here found its sediment and is visible in its consequences. The circumstance that Takeuchi belongs to the most trusted of Tanabe's pupils, convinces us that in his translation he has done justice to the intention of his revered master, which

---

[12]*The Collected Works of Tanabe* appeared in 15 vols. in 1963/1964, and in a reprint in 1972/1973.

[13]"Introduction to 'Philosophy as Metanoetics'," JR 5/2 (1967): 29-47, trans. Yoshinori Takeuchi [PM, xlix-lxii; text follows JR]; and "A Comparison of Metanoetics with the Philosophy of Freedom (Part I from Chapter 4 of the *Philosophy as Metanoetics*)," JR 8/2 (1971): 50-75, trans. Gerald Cook and Yoshinori Takeuchi.

[14]"The Logic of Species as Dialectics," MN 24/3 (1969): 273-88, trans. David Dilworth and Taira Sato.

[15]"Memento mori," in *Philosophical Studies of Japan*, compiled by the Japanese Commission for UNESCO, published by the Japan Society for the Promotion of Science (Tokyo: Ministry of Education, 1959) 1-12, trans. V. H. Viglielmo, and into German by Seiichi Yagi, in *Gott in Japan* (1973) 114-26, with introduction and notes.

[16]"Todesdialektik," in *Martin Heidegger zum 70. Geburtstag* (Neske, 1959) 93-133, trans. Koichi Tsujimura and Harmut Buchner.

is not always easy to grasp, and has been able to communicate its meaning to us. For these reasons, in our presentation of Tanabe's philosophy we can limit ourselves, not only of necessity, but with substantial justification, to the principal elements of his metanoetics and can use the excerpt from the species logic and the essays mentioned only as expansions of what is already presented in that central work. They become helpful for us especially as expanded contributions to the religious character of Tanabe's philosophy and its relation to Christianity. For this side of Tanabe's thinking that is especially interesting to us there are available to us notes on the contents of "Existence, Love, Praxis" (1947) and "Christianity and Dialectic" (1948)—for which we thank a pupil of Takeuchi's, Hisao Matsumaru, who is presently studying in Basel—which are important in this connection but are not translated and are either not dealt with, or not sufficiently so, in the secondary literature available to us.

The work to which we primarily devote our attention in view of its significance, and whose content we wish to present in its main lines in the following, because it is for the most part unavailable to those unfamiliar with Japanese, consists of an "Introduction to Philosophy as Metanoetics," and of eight chapters in which Tanabe developed step by step the program sketched in this introduction—from the origin of this philosophy in his personal experience and its philosophical interpretation, to its confrontation with Western thinking and the way it is brought into connection with Shinran's Buddhism of grace, up to the significance which is ascribed to it for the grounding of a salvatory religious theory of society.

2. On the Origin of the Philosophy of Repentance

In the introduction we mentioned, which was published in English translation,[17] of special importance is the description Tanabe gives therein of the hopelessness of the situation in which he found himself with his people in the summer of 1944, and of the consequences that resulted for him in and from this experience. Due to increasing American air attacks, Japan had come to a cul-de-sac: the government, because it was at its wit's end, and dared not admit the true state of affairs to the people, but forbade any kind of criticism of its policies; the populace, because they were not able to bring about a change of course due to the rule of the military.[18] For Tanabe, however, the situation was more difficult, because, on the one hand, as a philosopher he knew it was his duty to serve his

---

[17]Cf. n. 13.

[18]"Introduction to 'Philosophy as Metanoetics'," JR 5/2 (1967): 29 [PM, xlix]. For the "avowed remorse" Tanabe uses the Japanese word *zange*, or the Greek terms *metanoesis* and *metanoia* in the sense of an existential reversal of thought.

nation with his thinking and fearlessly to express his understanding to the
government, but on the other, he feared that through his advice he might—insofar
as it lay in his power—create a division among the people and thus do more
harm than good in the situation of war. What should he done, therefore: keep
silent or speak, but say what? His indecisiveness and inability to determine an
appropriate solution led him completely to doubt his profession of teaching philosophy. "But," so he continues in the description of his doubting condition, both
from within and without,

> at that precise moment a wondrous thing happened. In my profound stress,
> I surrendered myself, humbly admitting my own incapacity, and then I was
> suddenly led to a new insight! My remorseful confession, metanoesis
> (*zange*), unexpectedly turned me back from things external upon my own
> inwardness. It was now out of the question for me to teach and correct
> others under the circumstances, I who could not deliver myself and do the
> correct thing. The only thing for me to do in this situation was to resign
> myself frankly to my weakness, to examine my own inner self with humility,
> and to explore the depths of my powerlessness and lack of freedom.[19]

He devoted himself to this task before which he saw himself placed at that
moment rather than to his previous philosophy, and it did "not matter to [him]
whether this was called philosophy or not," since he had "realized [his]
incompetence as a philosopher." Like the decision to undertake a "philosophy
which is not a philosophy" which was "attained through the way of *zange* or
metanoia," so is therefore its implementation not a matter of his "own power,"
which he had "abandoned in despair," but of "Other-Power" (*tariki*) which
"turned" him in a "new direction" and from the "realization of [his] utter
helplessness" to "start afresh."[20]

But just as little as the designation of his philosophy of metanoia as
"unphilosophy" hindered him from claiming that its "purpose is to fulfill the
functions of ultimate thinking and radical self-realization which are the very
goals of philosophy," so just as little did the stress on "Other-Power" as the
power in repentance and in its development into a "philosophy of metanoetics"
hinder him from taking account of "consciousness" and its I. True, he can confess: "It is no longer I myself who pursue philosophy, but rather *zange* itself
which does its own thinking." But at the same time he says of this philosophizing: it is "a philosophy as self-realization of my *metanoetic consciousness*." He

---

[19]Ibid., 30-31 [PM, 1].
[20]Ibid., 31 [PM, 1].

brings both factors together in the sentence: "As I practice my metanoesis, metanoesis itself demands its own self-realization."[21]

In order to understand this relation of being determined by one's own enactment of consciousness and of the other power at work in it—a relation that represents a paradox for conceptual-logical knowing—it is necessary to consider that in this connection Tanabe uses not merely epistemological, but also ethical-religious categories. "Metanoesis (*zange*)," so he defines it,

> signifies a repentance for the wrongs which I have done, with the concomitant torment of knowing that there is no way to expiate my own sins. It also signifies shame for my lack of power and ability which have driven me to despair and self-abandonment. But [as he continues], insofar as this is an act of negating my own self, paradoxically it cannot be my own act even though at the same time it is mine. Rather, it is prompted by a Power outside of myself. This Other-Power brings about my conversion so that I am turned in a new direction to tread a path hitherto unknown to me.[22]

This is the way his relation to this Power attains religious significance. "I entrust my entire being to Other-Power (*tariki*) and, by practicing my *zange* and by maintaining faith in this Power, I have the truth of my own conversion-and-resurrection experience confirmed." Thus "the practice, faith, evidence (*gyo-shin-sho*)" of [his] *zange* becomes the philosophy of [his] "regenerated being." and this he understands by "metanoetics" as an "Other-Power-philosophy." "I have died to philosophy but have been resurrected by *zange*."[23]

For Tanabe, metaphysical significance is also to be ascribed to this religious existentially understood "awakening," because he connects it with the concepts of transcendence, of the Absolute and of Nothingness. Since it is connected with the denial of the former way, it cannot consist of any kind of "repetition" of the same, but only of a transcending, a "Self-transcendence." "I no longer live by myself but live because life is granted to me from the transcendent realm of the Absolute which is neither life nor death. The Absolute may be defined as Absolute Nothingness because in this way it is the negation and transformation, that is, conversion, of all the relative." That in this interpretation of the "experience of conversion and awakening" we are dealing with specific Buddhist metaphysics is evident from the fact that for Tanabe Absolute Nothingness is identical with love. "Absolute Nothingness which grants me a new life of resurrection, is

---

[21]Ibid. [PM, 1].
[22]Ibid., 31-32 [PM, li].
[23]Ibid., 32 [PM, li].

experienced by me as Nothingness qua Love." In this experience it is attested
that "the Great Nay is in itself the Great Compassion."[24]

Despite the emphasis upon the experiential foundation of his "dependence
upon *tariki* (Other-Power)," Tanabe also concedes that this "may sometimes be
accompanied by resurrection," and that for him the resurrection experience could
even become the occasion for "self-complacency," to imagining himself to be "a
wise man." "Only through continuous *zange* (repentance)," explains Tanabe, "can
we obtain the faith and witness (*shin-sho*) of continuous resurrection." "Death"
as the loss of repentance and the renewed despair growing out of it can only be
the occasion for repentance, from which resurrection takes place anew. In this
"circular movement" repentance proves to be not only "in accordance with the
development of actuality," but there is revealed also "its own infinity and
eternity," and in this way "the dialectical unity between the Absolute and the
relative is affirmed." This is, however, also "the basic principle of history."[25]

Before Tanabe further develops this reference to the possibility of an application of his thinking about repentance to the understanding of history into a
"radical historicism," he inserts into his introduction several remarks on the
relation of his decisive experience and the metaphysics grounded in it to Shinran
and his conception of the Pure Land.[26] For him everything depends primarily
upon making two things clear. First, that he attained to his conversion and the
insight contained in it independently of Shinran; second, that only from the
perspective of this personal experience did the correct understanding of Shinran's
doctrine [come] to him—a doctrine which, in comparison with Zen, all too
easily, because of its emphasis upon the grace of Amida, devolves into a misunderstanding of "The Easy Way to Salvation." His natural inclination was more
toward Zen, although he had never practiced it and therefore had not entered
"into the profundity of its holy truth." He had certainly studied its literature and
after he became involved anew in Shinran's work after his conversion, in his
belief in Other-Power he "felt closer than ever to the spirit of Zen which
[advocated] Self-Power."[27] By adopting the general Mahayana notion of the
Bodhisattva's "return to this world from the Pure Land," Tanabe already
expressed in this connection the "collective responsibility," which is essentially
bound up with redemption as he understands it.[28]

---

[24]Ibid. [PM, li].
[25]Ibid., 33 [PM, li-lii].
[26]Ibid., 33-34 [PM, lii].
[27]Ibid., 35 [PM, lii].
[28]Ibid., 36-37 [PM, liv].

Although Tanabe claimed that he attained to his conversion, which corresponded to Shinran's doctrine, "in the philosophical realm,"[29] and describes how he had devoted himself from August 1944 on to the task of developing his "metanoetics into a form of philosophy,"[30] he emphasizes nevertheless that it is not a "philosophy of metanoesis" in the sense that it treats an object termed "metanoesis." Metanoesis is "a philosophy which should be erected at the place where all prior philosophical standpoints and methods have been entirely negated." This "destruction" "is even more radical than Cartesian methodological skepticism." Metanoetics "is based on the action-evidence of religious existence in death and resurrection." Unless one practices metanoesis himself, there can be no talk of Metanoetics. In the course of his investigations he attained to a "logic," which "is effective throughout metanoetical thinking" and represents an "absolute criticism."[31]

In his last lectures held at Kyoto University in the winter of 1944/1945, amidst great external and health-related difficulties, he applied this method of an "absolute criticism" to European philosophy from Kant to Heidegger, with special attention to Meister Eckhart, Pascal, and Kierkegaard.[32] In these lectures he not only showed how these—with the exception of the dialogue partners mentioned last—lacked critical self-questioning, but also developed its positive complement which consists in the "reciprocal mediatory transformation between the Absolute and the Self" on the basis of an "action-evidence through Other-Power,"[33] as this arises for him from a "metanoetic interpretation of the Kyogyoshinsho."[34]

In the summer of 1945 Tanabe withdrew to the mountains in order—in their quietness and solitude—to work on this lecture for the purpose of publishing it,[35]

---

[29]Ibid., 33. [PM, lii].
[30]Ibid., 37-38 [PM, lv].
[31]Ibid., 38. [PM, lv].
[32]Ibid., 41 [PM, lviii].
[33]Ibid., 38ff. [PM, lvff.].
[34]Ibid., 34 [PM, lii].
[35]Ibid., 43 [PM, lix]. As he had already done when discussing the last lectures held in Kyoto, and the political dangers connected with giving them, Takeuchi in the foreword to his translation gives us a moving description also of this sojourn, which was marked by illness and privation. The remarks about the literature which he was at that time to convey to Tanabe at the latter's request confirm on the one hand Tanabe's emphasis on not having experienced his conversion under the direct influence of Shinran's writings, but on the other hand also the fact that he let himself be guided by Shinran's spirit in the particular manner in which he developed the significance of these writings in his own

because he was convinced that its content was of significance not only for his country, but for the whole of mankind after the defeat which would follow in August of that year. In this difficult time he had himself experienced "the power of metanoetics," in that he did not "fall into despair," but "was lifted to a spirit of detachment by being transformed by the Absolute," or—as he expressed it religiously: "I felt the grace of being resurrected by the compassion of Other-Power, after a thoroughgoing self-assessment in humility of my powerlessness."[36] He commended such a sincere attitude of repentance derived from his own practice to the people of his own country, especially in view of "the shamelessness of the leaders, who, most responsible for this defeat, are now recommending the repentance of the entire nation only to conceal their own responsibility." "Collective responsibility," for which he stood, demands that "all of us should practice metanoesis collectively."[37] Over against the pain of despair about the outer defeat he placed the inner pain necessarily associated with the attitude of repentance—a pain which is transformed by the other-power working in it into joyfulness and thankfulness and lets one hope in resurrection and renewal. This necessary renewal is attainable not only by political and economic changes, as much as it is connected with them, but alone "by transforming the self-affirmation of the ego into nonself through the mediatory activity of Absolute Nothingness."[38] Only in this way will mankind "enter into a realm of absolute peace, where, in reconciliation and cooperation, they will help each other for the sake of their mutual emancipation and salvation." Precisely in view of the difficulties which resist the realization of this goal of mankind, "all nations have their own need to perform metanoesis," and "metanoetics must become [the] philosophy not only of Japan, but of all mankind."[39]

It is significant for the way in which Tanabe at the end of his introduction raised this claim for the universal validity of his philosophy of repentance, that in this connection he recalled both the prophet Jeremiah,[40] and the fact that Shinran explained that he had "no disciple at all."[41] Also Tanabe assured us that he had no "intention of directing the world by this idea, for such an intention would be contrary to the spirit of metanoetics."[42] He can speak of it only like Shinran when he said: "Now it depends on your decision, whether you accept

---

Philosophy as Metanoetics.
    [36]Ibid., 42-43 [PM, lix].
    [37]Ibid., 43 [PM, lx].
    [38]Ibid., 46 [PM, lxii].
    [39]Ibid. [PM, lxii].
    [40]Ibid., 46 [PM, lxi].
    [41]Ibid., 47 [PM, lxii].
    [42]Ibid., 46 [PM, lxii].

nembutsu[43] or reject it."[44] As Jeremiah appeals to the word issued to him for his preaching of repentance and interprets the destiny of his people from the content of this experience in which he participated, so Tanabe derives his "philosophy of metanoetics" from his *zange*-experience understood as the working of the "Great Compassion" in order to speak from it his word for the hour in a "turning point of world history."[45]

As is evident from the foregoing, the description which, in this introduction, Tanabe gives us of the historical "origin" of his metanoetic philosophy[46] is already richly bound up with philosophical and religious interpretations of his personal experiences (*Erlebnisse und Erfahrungen*). Yet they also already contain various references concerning its execution, which he had conceived in eight chapters from the time of his conversion to the composition of that introduction in October 1945.[47]

3. The Contents of the Metanoetics

In the first five chapters of the "Philosophy of Repentance," Tanabe develops from different sides the nature of his metanoetics in interaction with Western philosophy and—without naming him—that of his former colleague at Kyoto University, Kitaro Nishida. Then he devotes two chapters to the teaching of Shinran and his own metanoetic interpretation of the same. In the last chapter, finally, Tanabe draws the consequences which arise for him from his philosophy for a religious theory of society.

The individual chapters carry the following titles:
1. The Philosophical Meaning of Metanoetics
2. Absolute Critique: The Logic of Metanoetics
3. Absolute Critique and Historicity
4. Metanoetics and the Philosophy of Freedom
5. Absolute Mediation in Metanoetics
6. From Pascal to Shinran: Metanoetics as Absolute Genso
7. Metanoetics and the Theory of the Three Minds
8. Metanoetics as a Religious View of Society.[48]

---

[43]An abbreviation of the cult formula of Pure Land Buddhism, Namu Amida Butsu (I place my full trust in Amida Buddha).

[44]Ibid., 47 [PM, lxii].

[45]Ibid., 46 [PM, lxii].

[46]Ibid., 41 [PM, lviii].

[47]Ibid., 47 [PM, lxii].

[48]Tanabe Hajime, *Philosophy as Metanoetics*, trans. Takeuchi Yoshinori with Valdo Viglielmo and James Heisig (Berkeley: University of California Press, 1986). [Buri cites from the manuscript of the ET by Takeuchi. —Trans.]

To begin his explanation of "the philosophical meaning of metanoetics," Tanabe employs a criticism which could be raised against this concept, or the way in which he intends to react to it. The criticism he undertakes claims that he coined this novel term only out of the desire to be original and made use of it to conceal the obsolescence of his thought. If the way in which Tanabe advances this objection makes us think rather of a self-criticism than of a suspicion voiced in his circle, so it does not surprise us how he reacts to it. Not only is he prepared to accept this objection and to admit a correspondingly questionable attitude also in other connections; he even believes that in such self-examination he can still see a symptom of his intention to deceive himself and others.

This result of his moral dissection of himself is for Tanabe nevertheless anything other than merely negative, but rather is positive in the highest degree, in that it gives him reason for the remorseful recognition of his guilt, or proceeds from such an attitude of repentance and allows him therefore to experience not only its agony but its liberating power as well. If he would not like to appear to himself and to others as unassailable with respect to his sincerity, and if for him the acknowledgement of the justification of this moral questioning is also painful, he happens upon "a wondrous power," for which he says he "has a deep gratitude," "because it abolishes the torment of my shameful deeds." *Zange* is like a "balm for the pain of repentance." It is also like "the source of absolute light that paradoxically makes the darkness shine without expelling it." "The experience of accepting this transforming power of *zange* as a grace from *tariki* (Other-Power) is the very core of metanoetics."[49]

In this way Tanabe, from the perspective of the experience of repentance which he makes into his own philosophy of repentance, attains to insights about the state of affairs which, according to him, are valid not only for this philosophy, but for philosophy as such. Not only is metanoetics philosophy, but philosophy is really possible only as metanoetics, as philosophy of repentance. Tanabe develops this claim especially in two directions: one, epistemologically, and the other, in religioethical respects, and this in such a way that the first named perspective leads him to separate himself from any other kind of Buddhist philosophy, namely, Nishida's philosophy, while the second offers him the opportunity to clarify his relation to Buddhist mythology, especially that of Amida.

From an epistemological perspective, Tanabe is convinced that in the self-consciousness of repentance we are dealing with an "objective reality" elevated beyond all doubt, and, because the one repenting raises the objection that his repentance is not genuine, he therefore restlessly acknowledges and practices repentance for the sake of his sincerity. The truth in which he finds himself in the continued practice of repentance is neither generally provable nor a matter

---

[49]Ibid., 2.

of mystic contemplation in which the I transcends into the Beyond. Metanoetics is precisely not metaphysics, but a "breaking-through" of the self out of reflection into a mode of being which can be understood and expressed only paradoxically as a "continuous practice of death and resurrection" in a "new dimension of absolute Nothingness beyond denial and affirmation"—a breakthrough that occurs only in one's own enactment of repentance.

It is the apparent proximity in which Tanabe finds himself with his philosophy of repentance to Nishida's philosophy of the "identity of contradictories in the place of nothingness" that causes him here—without mentioning the name of his colleague—to point to the difference which in his view obtains between the two proposals. According to Tanabe, Nishida's logic of nothingness, in which the contradictories dissolve into identities, is still a system of metaphysical speculation which is not only constructed without remorse about human incapacity, but its "Logic of the place of nothingness" permits no emotional disturbance through repentance. Because Tanabe did not observe the turn to Shin Buddhism which Nishida executed at the same time in which the former composed his "philosophy as metanoetics," he could see in Nishida's Topos-logic only self-redemption to which he opposed his metanoetics which rests on redemption through Other-Power.

The peculiarity of this second characteristic of Tanabe's philosophy consists in the dialectical conception of the relation of self- and other-power in the redeeming repentance and in the use of "Amida's Great Compassion" as a symbolic expression of this—independent of that dialectic of tariki and jiriki attained philosophically. Tanabe expressed over and again that for an "ordinary," "unlearned man" as he understands himself according to the example of Shinran, as well as of Socrates, self-redemption does not emerge as a possibility—even in the form of metaphysical speculation. But this dependency on grace otherwise attested by him and which does not stand at our disposal, likewise expressly points to the fact that this can only become efficacious in cooperation with one's own power. Remorse, repentance, and conversion are in any case always our own acts, but in such a way that through them and in them Other-Power realizes itself in the world. Both spheres interpenetrate each other and are reciprocal to each other. Metanoia is our own act and simultaneously not merely our own act. In its relativity it mediates the Absolute. Only as one's own power (*jiriki*) does Other-Power (*tariki*) become absolute.

From the vantage of this dialectic, paradoxical, reciprocal definition of the relation of self- and other-redemption Tanabe takes his stand with the central Shin Buddhist doctrine of the Great Compassion of Amida Buddha, and this in two respects: he warns of a conception of the vow of Amida which excludes human cooperation in redemption and the remaining sinfulness of man. On the other, in view of such possible misunderstandings of traditional doctrine he holds firm to the independence of his philosophy as metanoetics. His philosophy can make use of the tradtional doctrines as symbols; but as little as it is dependent on them, so little does it lie in its power to annul them. Mythology and meta-noetics are two different ways which—if rightly used—can lead to the same goal. Metanoetics reaches it through a logic of absolute critique.

For this "absolute critique as a logic of metanoetics,"[50] Tanabe appeals to Kierkegaard and Augustine, while he reproaches Kant and the speculative idealists for not being sufficiently radical in their critique of reason. Kant's critique of reason is uncritical because it is executed in discursive logic and does not finally put itself in question, but eludes the radical crisis in the distinction of a phenomenal and noumenal sphere. Even with Hegel the subject remains iden-tical with itself and returns into Being instead of into absolute nothingness, which is "neither life nor death," as Goethe anticipated it in his "Die, and become!" and is understood by Augustine and Kierkegaard in their experience of crisis as resurrection.

Under the aspect of the "relation between absolute critique and historicity"[51] Tanabe develops this cultural confrontation further with special reference to Martin Heidegger, whose philosophy he faulted for the same deficiency as ideal-ism and Nietzsche, namely, that he—like these—did not attain to the historicity of thinking because of the lack of absolute critique, but always held on somewhat unhistorically to the Absolute. The freedom of "project" which is not present apart from its realization must precede the being-like "thrownness" and its acceptance.

This confrontation with Heidegger gives Tanabe the occasion for a compari-son of "metanoetics and the philosophy of freedom."[52] Freedom, which is neces-sary for becoming aware of the thrownness of Dasein and its acceptance, cannot be objectively proven, but only subjectively realized. This happens in the "dying" of the self in the inscrutable contradictories in which it finds itself, which, how-ever, because it enacts this dying itself in repentance, or lets it happen to it, at the same time is a "becoming resurrected." "The acting subject and objective reality correspond to each other and presuppose each other, so that the death of the self is brought about by the antinomies that arise out its confrontation with reality, and, on the other, the antinomies of the real world are brought into being with the free action of the self serving as the determining factor."[53] Besides "death and resurrection," Tanabe uses the pair of terms "nothingness" and "Great Compassion" to designate this state of affairs. Just as "nothingness" corresponds

---

[50]Ibid., chap. 2.

[51]Ibid., chap. 3.

[52]Ibid., chap. 4. The beginning of this chapter is reprinted in JR 7/2 (1971): 5-72.

[53]Ibid., 121 [JR 7/2 (1971): 57].

to the mutual annulment of all statements, so the "Great Compassion," to the self-attainment of the self in renouncing all will to self-assertion. The "self-less Self" which "acts without acting," possesses and mediates "naturalness," that is, "unhindered freedom."[54]

Although Tanabe establishes a relationship of "nothingness" with the "Ungrund" in Schelling's philosophy of freedom (*Philosophische Untersuchungen über das Wesen der menschlichen Freiheit und die damit zusammenhängenden Gegenstände*, 1809), and of the "Great Compassion" with the factor of "love" in Schelling's theogony, he sees his metanoetics as an existential ontology in the authentic sense in contrast to the understanding of existence in Heidegger's unsatisfactory existential ontology. He faults Schelling for ascribing ontic significance to ontological concepts in an uncritical way. In Heidegger who does not make this mistake, he missed the insight into the ethical problematic of existence and its overcoming through genuine religious faith which is grounded in "Other-Power." This, however, is "neither transcendent nor immanent," but rather consists in the "absolute mediation between transcendence and immanence."[55]

Under this aspect of "absolute mediation in metanoetics,"[56] Tanabe discusses the dangers of the misunderstandings of the self which threaten all religions—Zen and Shin Buddhism, as well as Christianity—if they regard as absolute the redemption they confuse with one of the forms that mediates it, that is, a form of mediation—satori, nembutsu, or a specific conception of the cross of Christ—instead of experiencing their suitability for mediating the Absolute in their relativity. Just as false as making no distinctions is absolutizing the distinctions. Over against the "both-and" of the former and the "either-or" of the latter Tanabe represents a "neither-nor" that leads beyond the analytical thinking of the subject which is identical with itself to "faith" as the mediation of the Absolute in the relative. Tanabe recognizes koan exercise as the means to overcoming discursive thinking, but his view of the Buddha nature to be found on this way of self-redemption fails to correspond to the true nature of man who does not experience himself as one with the Absolute, but rather, in his relativity and imperfection, as dependent on the Other-Power of the Great Compassion of Amida Buddha which becomes efficacious only in the sphere of the finite, and in such a way that it makes use of it as its means.

On the one hand, Tanabe in this connection recalls the paradoxes of the warning of the Apostle regading complete effort despite complete dependence on God (Phil 2:12, 13). On the other, he emphasizes also that this paradox of "absolute mediation" is allowed to be expressed, not ontologically, but only in

---

[54]Ibid., 120 [JR 7/2 (1971): 55].
[55]Ibid., 150.
[56]Ibid., chap. 5.

an "analogy of nothingness." "Without breaking the bonds of suffering and worldliness," says Shinran, "it is possible to participate in the nature of Nirvana."

This is what Tanabe found in Shinran from his own experience and from which he believes he can understand his teaching, and thus, after developing the basic structures of his philosophy of repentance in five chapters, he then devotes two chapters to Shinran: "From Pascal to Shinran: Metanoetics as Absolute Genso"[57] and "Metanoetics and the Theory of Three Minds" in Shinran's principal work, Kyogyoshinsho.[58]

By the example of Pascal's *Pensées*, Tanabe especially points to the danger that metanoetics and nembutsu, like Pascal's *esprit de finesse*, are still forms of self- instead of other-redemption—contrary to their intention. It seems to Tanabe that this danger of self-misunderstanding of the faith of grace can only be overcome by trusting in the power of grace—instead of removing it by any kind of dialectic of thinking—by making use of the means (*upaya, hoben*) that correspond to its intention. For this use of what is inappropriate for faith as well as of what is appropriate for it Tanabe appeals, with Shinran, to the nineteenth, twentieth, and eighteenth vows of Amida in the *Sutra of Eternal Life* and to the final chapter of the *Kyogyoshinsho* which deals with the *upayas*. By means of different forms of "upright," "deep," and the mind that "transfers merit," which are simultaneously conceived as "one" mind, he believes he can show how redemption can be realized and grasped in its essence, not through the thinking of the self, but through the working of other-power in the self-less self. Therefore for him the Pure Land school represents the "apex of the development of Buddhism," insofar as it leads to metanoetics and can only properly be understood as metanoetics. As it has led him out of the cul-de-sac into which he had come in Western philosophy, so to it is ascribed human significance. This human significance of his Shin Buddhist metanoetics Tanabe develops—at the end of his deliberations and as its practical goal—in the form of a "religious theory of society."[59] After first analyzing in their nature and above all in their insufficiency different types of the notions of redemption as they emerged in the course of history in the West and the Far East, he postulates "love" as the overcoming of their deficiency and the fulfillment of their ideals. This "love" as "Absolute Nothingness" forms "the foundation of an independent Dasein of a relative nature"; or said in a Buddhist way: self-power is used as the means to other-power. With this is meant concretely neither "friendship" in an Aristotelian, nor "love" in the Christian sense, but "brotherly seniority," that is, cooperation in the priority and reciprocity of the master-pupil relationship. For realizing this personal under-

---

[57]Ibid., chap. 6.
[58]Ibid., chap. 7.
[59]Ibid., chap. 8.

standing "conversion and transformation" are certainly necessary, which is quite different from Nishida's "intuition of place," which is not sufficient.

This is the one place where Tanabe mentions his counterpart by name, and this shows how important to him are the political consequences of his metanoetics, which as such, as well as in its political consequences, is very different from Nishida's "Logic of Place" and the politics that issues from it. In this connection Tanabe characteristically comes to speak of the concept of species as the midpoint between the typical and the individual, whose application to the state preserves this both from false nationalism as well as from a perverted democracy, and, as "brotherhood," can widen into a "new social ideal" of a "synthesis of the freedom of the capitalistic society and the equality of the socialistic state. As for the peculiarities which are especially important for social ethics, he gives prominence to the Mahayana Buddhist notion of the Bodhisattva and its associated idea of the return from the Pure Land, in which absolute "Other-Power" makes use of the self-power of relative beings for redemption. Like the father, Tathagata leaves it to his brothers to complete their redemption in mutuality. What is true of the individual within the family and of the families within the nation, is true also of the nations and their cultures within human community and mankind as a whole.

For the basic principle of his metanoetic theory of society, in consequence of which the Absolute is mediated in the mutual mediation of relative being, Tanabe appeals both to the word of Jesus, "Whoever keeps his own life will lose it. But whoever will lose it for my sake, will find it," as well as to the Buddhist "nonattachment to things," that is, to "an existence grounded on nothingness," which "lives in and through its dying." On this basis Tanabe decisively rejects the objection that metanoetics deals only with redemption from guilt in the ethical sense and not also with redemption from fate of the rebirth determined by karma, by emphasizing that through the redeemed-redeeming relation of man in history, nothingness, that is, Nirvana, is reached—for which he can also use the expression "the Kingdom of God."

In both mythologies—the Buddhist as well as the Christian—Tanabe sees both the question of Being and the question of meaning: the question of the origin of Being and the question of the meaning of history. But he also believes he can find therein an answer if he interprets them as symbols of his metanoetic understanding of the self. Strange to say, Tanabe offers in this place no information about how he interprets the Christian redeemer myth, but only notes in respect to Plato's dualistic worldview, that we are not well served by such a theory of two worlds, which he apparently also assumes for Christianity. As a unique, profound redeemer symbol, to the contrary, he praises the myth of the Bodhisattva existence of Amida before his becoming a Buddha as an expression of "absolute mediation" in the mutual interpenetration of the two worlds. The image of the "lotus in the fire" or, still better, of a revolving peony reflected in a mirror, seems to him eloquently to express this redemption in an incomparable way, and can serve not only for Japan but for all nations as instruction for repentance and can assist them "to build a new society based on brotherhood," as is also "the meaning of the philosophy of metanoetics."

4. The Logic of Species

Before, during, and after the composition of the *Philosophy as Metanoetics*, Tanabe was exhaustively occupied with the concept of *species* used in its final chapter, both formally-logically as well as in material political and culture-philosophical respects. In the first respect it is a designation for a "middle group between genus and individual"; in the second, for the cultural uniqueness of races which determines their individual characteristics as well as how these differ from the universally human. In this sense species corresponds to Hegel's concept of objective spirit as a "specialization and limitation of the absolute spirit" and as a power which binds and controls the subjective spirit.[60] Whereas the absolute or divine spirit, which permeates all things and takes them into itself, returns to itself, species represents "the expedient means" (*hoben*) in which the individuals "edify and save each other." In the absolute spirit the opposition between national society and the individual is "transformed into a mutual mediation."[61] Thus "the nation" becomes "the expedient means of the divine redeeming love for the individual." "The governments . . . become the mediation for the religious foundation of the Kingdom of God."[62] For Tanabe this mediation is "religious" because he sees it in connection with the "Pure Land" and with the "death and resurrection" in "conversion."

The relation of species and individual is paradox, in that species confines the individual, but simultaneously provides its substance.[63] The species which mediates the individual is at the same time "the limit of self-identity."[64] This putting into question of self-identity Tanabe sees as acknowledged in the word of the Apostle Paul in Gal 2:20: "It is no longer I, but Christ who lives in me," while he faults every intuitive-aesthetic, speculative-mystical speculation as the arrogance of finite-relative man over against God.[65] Although he illustrates this deficiency in religion, that is, its trust in other-power and the abandoning of the

---

[60] "The Logic of Species as Dialectics," MN 24/3 (1969): 274.
[61] Ibid., 275.
[62] Ibid., 276.
[63] Ibid., 280.
[64] Ibid., 281.
[65] Ibid., 282-83.

self, by the example of Plotinus, it is nevertheless clear that he basically has in mind Nishida and that his critique is intended for him.[66]

Tanabe believes that with the dialectic of species logic, both in its religious as well as political respects, he can transcend Nishida's "logic of the self-identity of opposites." If this exchange between Nishida and Tanabe creates mutual misunderstandings within the context of the Buddhist conception of self-power and other-power, or immanence and transcendence, so the positions of both become problematic in the respect to the Bible and Christianity, for example, to the passage Gal 2:20, cited here by Tanabe and elsewhere by Nishida.

Here Paul is dealing neither with a "persistent self-identity in death and life," as Tanabe suspects in the mystical conception of the passage, nor—as he claims for his understanding of it—with a "leap into a new life" effected by "absolute Nothingness" and enacted in "faith in Other-Power."[67] It may well be that Paul recognizes a change of the subject which excludes an identity of the earlier self, to which he has died, with the new which has arisen in him.[68] On the other hand, this new being does not consist for him merely in self-understanding reached by a "leap" of faith enacted by himself; rather, he understands himself as being "in Christ" on the basis of the new world which has broken in with his resurrection, in which he participates "with Christ" through his dying and rising. In comparison to this final event to which Paul appeals for his self-understanding, Tanabe's "leap of faith"—no less than the intuitive-speculative nonmysticism of Nishida's—appears to be a matter of the self finally identical with itself.

As Jesus died in order to hasten the end of the existing world, so the turn of the ages assumed to have been put in place through the death of Jesus forms the presupposition for the fact that Paul can understand himself as a new creature. While Jesus distinguishes between his own person and his future appearance as heavenly "Son of Man,"[69] and Paul, both in respect to Jesus and to himself, distinguished between the pneumatic and the fleshly form which is to be forgotten,[70] Shinran and Tanabe always deal with one and the same person, who is understood either—in an insufficient way, according to them—as on the way to the Pure Land, or in accord with the Bodhisattva ideal, as returning on the way from the Pure Land into the world. Although Nishida in the final formulation of his philosophy reckoned with this second possibility, Tanabe has in mind Nishida's topos-logic in which the contradictories prove to be identical in nothingness, which is possible without appealing to the vow of Amida.

---

[66]Ibid., 279n.7.
[67]Ibid., 282.
[68]Rom 6:3-4; 1 Cor 15:50ff.; 2 Cor 5:17.
[69]Cf., e.g., Matt 16:28; 24:30ff.
[70]2 Cor 5:16.

But—whether in a Zen or Shin Buddhist way—salvation occurs here in any case in a self-understanding which makes use of a myth for its enactment, or in the context of a definite logic, while in the New Testament, and especially in Paul, the proclamation of, or faith in a cosmic situation which precedes them and is therefore independent of them refers to the situation of the eschatological turn of the aeons already in course as its being-ful foundation.

As will be discussed in a later section, prejudices and unfavorable judgments are connected with both sides. In a preliminary way we can point to the fundamental difference that obtains between an understanding of death and resurrection and the significance of nothingness in the context of Shin Buddhist mythology and Zen Buddhist logic, on the one hand, and the role these play in the eschatological events presupposed in early Christianity on the other. Neither Nishida nor Tanabe take sufficient account of this difference, which is grounded in early Christian eschatology, between the significance which is ascribed to death and resurrection in Paul and themselves, in that they understand the respective statements either dialectically—so Nishida—or interpret them existentially—as occurs with Tanabe. If with respect to the Buddhist tradition this represents a modernization—which to be sure goes as far back as Nagarjuna—so in respect to the early Christian tradition, with which this process as well as its entrance into history is set in motion, it can be grasped as such in its nature and in accord with its cause only in the course of its centuries-long historical development. Without a doubt the discrepancy between eschatological expectation and the actual course of history depends on the fact that in Western thinking which encountered this problematic, history and its meaning became a central motif, and ever new attempts were made to answer these questions in the context of a supernatural-divine *Heilsgeschichte* or even in its secularizations. Far Eastern thinking, to the contrary, knows neither of an origin of the problematic of the meaning of the world and of human existence nor of its overcoming in history; rather, as existence in the world as such lacks salvation, so salvation consists in becoming liberated from it in Nirvana, which like its opposite can occur only in the timeless moment of the absolute present.

For this reason Buddhism is neither interested in its history nor possesses an understanding of the intention which binds Christianity to its history. As it does not view its history and the development of it in a line from the past to the present and beyond this into the future, but as moving in concentric circles around the present, so it uses categories of Western historical thinking in terms of its quite different understanding of being, in that it interprets them in this sense. A typical example of this is the way in which Tanabe, in his species logic—in contradistinction to Nishida's logic of nothingness as the self-identity of absolute contradictories—speaks of the "self-identity of death and life" and uses the term species for it.[71]

Whereas for Nishida the individual and the universal, which exclude each other as logical opposites, can paradoxically appear in the sphere of nothingness as identical or can be stated dialectically from its opposite, Tanabe does not permit the individual and the universal to collapse into an indefinable one, or into nothingness, but as different forms of a species, to assist one another mutually to realization. To the degree that this happens, dying or living is completed rather than diminished and what is imperfect is rectified. This is something quite different from the beyond of good and evil and the possibility bound up with an absolutizing of something finite, such as we meet in Nishida's ethic, and especially in his doctrine of the state.

But Tanabe's positive estimate of species as the "expedient means," despite its questionableness, is to be distinguished from the evaluation of the human situation in the time before the immediately imminent end, or during the turn of the aeons already in course. The eschatological situation presupposed by Jesus and Paul in different degrees of progress does not permit us to assume a lasting condition justified by it—neither of one which is godless nor of one that consists of the law and judgment of God, as this is assumed in the continued "living dying" and "dying living" as a lasting condition. What counts for Tanabe as redemption, is represented in Paul only as something preliminary, a passage from the old to the new aeon in the context of the eschatological event. Just as little as the "dying one" remains for Paul "one who is dying," but death is overcome as the "last enemy,"[72] just as little does "the godless" remain "a godless one," but becomes "in Christ" a "new creature,"[73] which is executed in this time amidst the still existing "form of flesh" as preparation for the future completion.[74]

When they speak of Christianity—whether they agree with its individual notions or concepts, or distance themselves from them or reject them—neither Nishida nor Tanabe can be faulted for considering, not its original eschatological forms, but forms which arose in the course of its history, as, for example, Nishida does with late medieval mysticism, or he and Tanabe do with Hegel's speculation, or the latter does with so-called existential philosophy. Like many other phenomena of Western cultural history, they are products of the demythologizing which ensued due to the delay of the end of history which early Christianity expected imminently. Nishida and Tanabe correctly refer in this connection to modern science and technology which are characteristic for the West. While its

---

[71]"The Logic of Species as Dialectics," 282-83.
[72]1 Cor 15:26.
[73]2 Cor 15:26.
[74]Rom 6:5ff.

achievements could be viewed for some time as a substitute for the delayed super-natural completion of the end, they have become in the atomic age a danger which threatens the future of mankind, which represents a "Memento mori" not to be ignored. That, however, is the situation in which Tanabe believes the diffi-culty, in which the West finds itself with its Christian or even its unchristian "philosophy of life," can be overcome through the "dialectic of death" of Far Eastern thinking in which life is death and death, life. How this seems possible to him he attempts to develop in two essays composed in his final years of life—1958 and 1959—which carry the titles, "Memento mori," and "Dialectic of Death."

5. The Philosophy of Death

In both essays Tanabe deals, on the one hand, with the questionableness of natural science and technology and its "philosophy of life," and on the other, with a philosophy which knows of an overcoming of death by taking seriously its inevitability, its relatedness to life, and therewith of resurrection. Both factors are connected in the fact that he thinks, with Heidegger, that the development of science and technology can no longer be brought under the control of those who use them.[75] But going beyond Heidegger, he would like to do this without losing faith in a final meaning of this development, but in the restless preparation for taking over our destiny, even if this means our downfall. *Amor Fati* or "love of absolute Nothingness" is resurrection in death.[76] Not a life after death, as the eschatological myths describe it, but the attaining of life in the freely affirmed permitting of life, is "the Eschaton."[77]

Tanabe speaks of love not only in respect to the attitude toward destiny; rather for him love belongs also to the mediation of this insight and its realiza-tion from man to man. In the essay, "Memento mori," he illustrates this state of affairs with a Zen story in which it occurred to a monk only after the death of the master that he owed his enlightenment to him.[78] As in the consideration of this koan, so Tanabe, in his "Dialectic of Death," uses the figure of the Bodhisattva for this mediation out of compassionate love as its personification.

Although Tanabe is prepared to see such an attitude also in "Christian love," he thinks, nevertheless, that it occurs in the "Mahayana Buddhist Bodhisattva" "in more concrete ways," "because the deed of the Buddhist Bodhisattva consists in concern for the awakening and redeeming of other men before his own

[75]"Todesdialektik," 108.

[76]Ibid., 109; *"Memento mori,"* 118 [ET: "Memento mori," *Philosophical Studies of Japan* 1 (1959): 5].

[77]"Todesdialektik," 112.

[78]"Memento mori," 117ff. [ET, 4].

awakening, whereas in Christian love the redeeming and carrying through of one's own faith and the proclamation for others are realized simultaneously with one each other."[79][80] In order to clarify in what the nature of love of neighbor consists in terms of Bodhisattva-being, and with it "also the meaning of Christian love of enemies,"[81] he again seizes upon the concept of species,[82] in which according to him individuality and community are connected in human existence.[83]

It apparently derives from the circumstance that, for "the dialectic unity in which a subject contains another in itself, and at the same time preserves its self-identity," Tanabe appeals to the Leibnizian concept of the monad,[84] that he now further speculates with Leibniz and states the same of God as of the "monad of monads,"[85] namely, that the "love of God (subjective genitive) can be realized through "the love of man for God (objective genitive)," which however can only occur through love of neighbor and of enemy. "As for the love of man to God, it has as the love of finite man nothing in itself which could contribute to God's being. Only through the love for a neighbor who is at the same time a dreadful enemy may man indirectly participate in the love of God and cooperate with it."[86]

In view of the abstractness of the thoughts in which Tanabe further develops this relation of "divine transcendence" and "finite existence,"[87] it could be asked how he arrives at regarding the Bodhisattva attitude as "more concrete" than the "practical action of man" in the sense of "Christian love,"[88] for these speculations—even when they are developed by Tanabe in connection with Leibnizian metaphysics—are anything but "Christian" in the sense of the New Testament or of dogma, but are certainly to be regarded as typically Buddhist, due to the role which is assigned to the concept of nothingness. It is even more questionable why in both essays Tanabe appeals for the "Buddhism" he represents—as he did in his philosophy of repentance—not to Amida Buddhism, but to Zen, since in his essay, "Memento mori," he explains "nothingness as love" with a Zen story used as a koan, and in the "Dialectic of Death" praises and uses Zen as "the

---

[79]Ibid., 119ff., 123 [ET, 6-7]; "Todesdialektik," 113ff.
[80]"Todesdialektik," 113ff.
[81]Ibid., 122.
[82]Ibid., 118.
[83]Ibid., 122.
[84]Ibid., 120.
[85]Ibid., 121.
[86]Ibid., 123.
[87]Ibid., 124ff.
[88]Ibid., 113.

exemplary religion of the Far East."[89] Where Tanabe appears to be closest to Christianity, he is actually farthest away. But that is due not only to his misunderstanding of Christianity, but has its cause also in the Christianity's misunderstandings of itself.

6. Laube's Presentation of Tanabe and a Necessary Expansion

In connection with our presentation of Tanabe we should like to refer to two articles by Johannes Laube published in 1978 in the *Neue Zeitschrift für systematische Theologie*: "Westliches und östliches Erbe in der Philosophie Hajime Tanabes" ("Western and Eastern Heritage in the Philosophy of Hajime Tanabe") and "Die 'Absolute Dialektik' von Hajime Tanabe ('The Absolute Dialectics' of Hajime Tanabe"); the reason for this is that their author can appeal to material which is instructive for the understanding of this thinker which is not available to us for linguistic reasons. Both of them are marked by valuable citations and exact references to sources and attest to Laube's familiarity with the work of Tanabe and his place in his spiritual world.

In the first of the two essays[90] Laube projects an overview of Tanabe's thinking by means of the different spiritual sphere from which he emerged, only then to pursue its development in seven stages, thereby emphasizing that Tanabe raises a "total claim" for each of these as "the uniquely possible philosophy for today."[91]

In the "heritage" of which Tanabe takes possession and which he engages, Laube distinguishes three parts: First, Western thinking from its beginnings in Greece and in Christianity up to Martin Heidegger and dialectic theology, of which Tanabe says, he was "raised" in it and feels delegated "to lead himself in it to death and resurrection"; second: "the heritage of Eastern philosophy," whose different rationalizations in Dogen and Shinran were for him the occasion for his "dialectical mediation of jiriki and tariki," of "absolute and relative." And third: "the heritage of Nishida's philosophy, of which Tanabe is reported to have said in his "neo-Kantian" period: "Apart from Nishida I have no teacher."[92]

In introducing Tanabe, Laube established three things common to each and three differences between the great teacher and his pupil who goes his own way. What is common is that for both the Absolute can be thought "only as absolute nothingness, and not as absolute Being"; that the "nature of philosophy" consists in the "self-consciousness of the religious act which, at the same time, is act, activity"; and that "the eternal Now" and "Absolute Nothingness" are as ideas

---

[89]Ibid., 117.
[90]*Neue Zeitschrift für syst. Theol.* 20 (1978): 1-15.
[91]Ibid., 2.
[92]Ibid., 3.

"something which both separates and connects." On the contrary, the two philosophers are different in the fact that Nishida connects activity with "intuition," while Tanabe connects it with "faith"; that for Nishida dialectic has an "integral" character, that is, existence in every historical situation can be "creative," whereas for Tanabe it possesses an "infinitesimal" character," representing at every point a cul-de-sac which must be broken through with resolve toward death ("acting and believing"), in such a way that the relative becomes the "symbol of Absolute Nothingness"; and Tanabe from a "social-ethical" perspective attempts a connection of Zen Buddhism and Amida Buddhism and of both with Christianity, by subordinating Nishida's "pure experience" to the "absolute (self)criticism of reason in Kant's sense, and therefore—as one "too subtly formulates" it—comes not from religion to philosophy, but from philosophy to religion."[93]

Laube—by appealing to a Japanese presentation of Tanabe's philosophy—works out "seven stations" in Tanabe's "way of thinking," which becomes visible in the changing attitudes toward different streams of tradition, and thereby chronologically classifies the writings of his philosopher which belong to it.[94]

The *first* section (1908 to 1922) he characterizes as "Early Critique," which is determined by the fact that Tanabe in its "thoughts of Kant and Neo-Kantianism, as well as taking up Nishida" concerned himself in the form of an "idealistic realism" with questions of the natural sciences (*The New Natural Science*, 1915; *Sketch of Natural Science*, 1918; *Studies in the Philosophy of Mathematics*, 1925).

Under the title "Later Critique," he specifies a *second* section (1922 to 1927), the beginning years of which Tanabe spent in Germany and there became personally acquainted with the representatives of Neo-Kantianism as well as with Husserl and Heidegger, whereby besides nature, history came into his view. From the repeated engagement with Kant there arose in 1924 the writing on "The Teleology of Kant."

A *third* section (1927 to 1934) was marked by "theory-related speculation" and the "Marburg School," from which Tanabe criticized the idealistic, or materialistic dialectic of Hegel and Marx, and juxtaposed to both an "absolute dialectic" as "negation of negation" in the "emptiness" of "Absolute Nothingness," in such a way that it is for him at the same time a "dialectic of action." For this Laube cites Tanabe's explanation: "The equation 'nothingness = being' is not an ontological sentence. It is nothing other than the symbol of the self-consciousness of the deed. Positively and materially said, it designates the active love that constantly denies itself. Therefore for a man who does not himself stand

---

[93]Ibid., 5.
[94]Ibid., 6ff.

on the standpoint of nothingness, that is, who does not practice this love himself, there is no "equal" of the equation or nothingness." Appealing to Koichi Tsujimura's translation he remarks in a notation on the concept of "self-consciousness," that it does not deal with a "psychological phenomenon," but with "something similar to Fichte's 'Tathandlung' (Self-consciousness of the transcendental I)," a "becoming aware of myself" that becomes as such a "becoming aware of Absolute Nothingness (the true Self)."[95]

So understood, Tanabe's conception of the true self would correspond to our thesis that the self—and being, as well—in its inconceivability for conceptually objective thinking proves to be a "nothingness" in the enactment of its self-understanding with which it makes use of the concepts as symbols of what is non-objectifiable and experiences itself as related to transcendence, which to be sure—other than as Laube says of "God" as "Absolute (Nothingness)" in Tanabe[96]—does not remain merely absolute nothingness, but is revealed in the enactment of the self-understanding in a special way as a transcendence whose nature can be expressed only in "personal symbols." Just as little as the "God" of the true self is the "absolute Being," is he "Absolute Nothingness"; rather—in contradistinction to both speculative concepts—he is a special revelation of a reality—still falsely objectified in them—of an experience of the self of being determined by its transcendent ground to unconditional responsible being in community as an attitude for which Tanabe uses the expression "love." This is a view Laube does not consider, and that does not become clear in Tanabe.

It corresponds thoroughly to the questionableness of the speculative character of Tanabe's concept of the transcendence of Absolute Nothingness and to the vain attempt to derive from it the demand of love, that Laube designates the *fourth* section in Tanabe's philosophy of the years 1934 to 1944 as "Praxis-related Speculation (Social Philosophy)." What is new is the concept of "species" which Tanabe inserted as an essential definition of the nation between the concepts of genus and the individual used by Nishida for mankind and for the individual historical subject, respectively, in order to mediate between them. As we know from our review of the last chapter of Tanabe's metanoetics, he has succeeded neither there nor in the essays worked out at the same time first individually and then as a whole after the metanoetics and published in 1947 under the title "The Dialectic of the Logic of Species," in saying univocally what he actually means by his "human state." Laube also reports that, before the Second World War, Tanabe was reproached by the fascists who said "he neglected the

---

[95]Ibid., 8-9.
[96]Ibid., 11n.42.

3. Hajime Tanabe (1885–1962)

Japanese nation state"; and after the war, the accusation by the liberals and
Marxists was that "he had absolutized the state as such."[97]

In the foreword to his later reworking of one of these essays on the "Logic
of Species" Tanabe confesses—apropos of his theory of remorse that had meanwhile arisen—that in the earlier formulation, the concept of "remorse," which had
become so important in the time of crisis during the Second World War, was
missing, with the result that Laube titles the *fifth* section of Tanabe's course of
thinking in which he sees "philosophy as the way to remorse or philosophy as
metanoetics" represented, "Speculation Related to Religion (Philosophy of
Religion)." The conclusion of a longer citation is given here because from it, it
follows that "the Absolute as Absolute Nothingness," for which he thanks his
"rebirth," is for Tanabe apparently not "pure Nothingness," and as such trans- or
unpersonal, when he says: "Because that nothingness allows me to be reborn, it
is experienced by me as nothingness = love."[98]

From the *sixth* section, 1949 to 1956, entitled "Art and Science-Related
Speculation (Aesthetic Theory, Scientific Theory)," Laube gives prominence
especially to Tanabe's "Introduction to Philosophy," (1949–1952); he also mentions, however, without going more into them, the works "Natural Science, Philosophy, and Religion" (1950), "The Philosophical Aesthetic of Valéry" (1951)
and the incomplete essay "Philosophy, Poetry, and Religion" (with the subtitle
"Heidegger, Rilke, Hölderlin") composed from 1953, from which we can observe
some of the areas to the treatment of which Tanabe has applied the fundamental
philosophical-religious conception of his metanoetics.

The *seventh* section, 1956 to 1962, entitled "Speculation Related to the End
(Death)," Laube devotes to Tanabe's articles, "Todesdialektik" and "Memento

---

[97]Ibid., 10. In addition to the concise characterization of the "Logic of
Species," the first part of a detailed presentation of the same by Johannes Laube
is available under the title "Kritik der 'Logik der Spezies' von Hajime Tanabe
(1. Folge)," in *Neue Zeitschrift für systematische Theologie* 23/3 (1981): 297-318,
in which the history of its development is described and the contents of the first
eight different formulations of "The Logic of Social Being," which appeared in
1934–1935, are analyzed. This deals primarily with the relation of mankind as
genus, state (here especially "Totem Society") as species and individual, as we
know it from the metanoetics.

Laube announces in a note that his *Habilitationsschrift* on "Dialektik des
Absoluten Vermittlung—die Philosophie von Hajime Tanabe in religionsphiloso-
phischer und religionsgeschichtlicher Sicht" is ready for publication.

[98]Ibid., 12.

mori," which we already presented earlier, and in this connection explains the koan which we have dealt with, "Neither death nor life."[99]

In his second article, entitled "Die 'absolute Dialektik' von Hajime Tanabe,"[100] Laube describes by means of Tanabe's "Introduction to Philosophy" from the year 1932, how Tanabe sought on the way of a critique of Hegel's idealistic and Marx's materialistic dialectic, to attain to his "absolute dialectic" as a "dialectic synthesis of both."[101] In a "critical stand on Tanabe's absolute dialectic,"[102] Laube shows that only through a misunderstanding of the intentions of Hegel and Marx does Tanabe believe he can surpass their positions, and that he himself still represented an idealism of the "moral freedom of the person," which—on the basis of Japanese history between 1931 and 1945—he abandoned in the work "Philosophy as Metanoetics," conceived in 1944.[103]

Thus we have confirmed for us the ununified, vague character that constitutes for us the person and literary work of Tanabe. The strengths and weaknesses of his philosophy consist in the fact that it constantly surpasses itself in each of its forms, and in this respect has something in common with that of Nishida. But it is apparent that this peculiarity is the reason both thinkers have been so interesting to their pupils.

A critical expansion of Laube's presentation of Tanabe's philosophy is nevertheless necessary because in neither of his essays does he go into Tanabe's relation to Christianity, with which the latter was extensively occupied in his later years. Therefore reference is made here to at least two of essays which give evidence of it—essays which were not mentioned by Laube in his accounting of Tanabe's works, concerning whose content my pupil Hisao Matsumaru informed me and who has partially translated several essential parts for me. These two essays which stand temporally and materially near to each other are "Existence, Love, and Praxis" (1947)[104] and "The Dialectic of Christianity" with an appendix, "Christianity, Marxism, and Japanese Buddhism" (1948).[105]

In the second of these two treatises Tanabe explains: "The God of Judaism, who is defined as absolute Being, and the God of Hellenism, who is known as beyond Being, were first transformed in Christianity into the God of love." Of this "love of God" he says that it "realizes itself in human love" which is due to

---

[99]Ibid., 14.

[100]*Neue Zeitschrift für syst. Theol.* 20/1,3 (1978): 278-93.

[101]Ibid., 281ff.

[102]Ibid., 288ff.

[103]Ibid., 293.

[104]*Collected Works*, vol. 9.

[105]*Collected Works*, vol. 10; for both cf. Gino K. Piovesana, *Recent Japanese Philosophical Thought*, 152-54.

the fact that man has occasion to thank and praise God for the "self-negation" necessary for love of neighbor and enemy—a self-negation he cannot bring about by himself, but which can only be received by participating in the "rule of love" as "grace." Thus Tanabe distinguishes three elements in love, which mutually "mediate" one another: "love of God," that is, God as love; "love to God," as thankful affection; and "love of neighbor." In this "trinity of love" "God reveals himself in the brotherhood of men," and man experiences "death and resurrection."[106]

In the tractate "Existence, Love, and Praxis," Tanabe connects the Johannine definition "God is love" with the "Great Commandment" (Matt 22:36-40) in such a way that the first commandment of love to God, who is love, forms the basis for the second commandment of love for one's neighbor which is equated with the first, so that love of neighbor as thankfulness for the love of God is represented as its "unfolding" and "breakthrough." By referring to the concepts of *oso* (Amida's grace) and *genso* (return to the world for the redemption of others, he distinguishes "the ascending phase of religion" as "grace" from the "descending" in the "act" of love for neighbor, so that the latter is the "confirmation" of the former. He faults Kierkegaard and existentialism for not "bringing about the unfolding of the descending phase," and Marxism for being concerned only with the "reforms of societal organization." According to Tanabe, "rebirth of the soul" and "social revolution" do not stand opposed to one another as opposite standpoints, and in this sense he would like to connect Kierkegaard and Marx, since, despite their oppositeness, they stand "in unison" in the fact that they attempted, over against "Hegelian conservatism," to renew the human world."[107]

On our theme Laube only remarks: "In Tanabe the ethical and ethical-social approach predominates. From this ethical-social approach he seeks to connect the truths of Zen Buddhism with those of Amida Buddhism (especially the Jodoshinshu). He seeks to establish an analogous mediation between the truths of Buddhism and those of Christianity. The mediation is realized not as a new syncretistic religion, but as Tanabe's philosophy."[108]

If this characterization, which intends to present Tanabe's "difference" from Nishida, is questionable in its generality, the same is probably true of Laube's view that "The word 'God' must be conceived by Tanabe as *the* Absolute (Nothingness). In no case may it be misunderstood as a personal, theistic God or as Absolute Being."[109] The way Tanabe accedes to the Christian notion of God in both of the treatises we have engaged and argues from it against Marxism, or

---

[106]"Dialectic of Christianity," *Collected Works*, 10:240ff.
[107]"Existence, Love and Praxis," *Collected Works*, 9:326-30.
[108]*Neue Zeitschrift für syst. Theol.*, 20 (1978): 5.
[109]Ibid., 11n.42.

seeks to connect Marx with Kierkegaard, contradicts this interdiction of Laube—quite apart from the fact that the Amida of Jodoshinshu, to whose vow Tanabe appeals in his metanoetics, bears personal traits. What Tanabe turns against is only the mythical objectification of this figure. As such, however, the myths serve him as symbols of a religious self-understanding. In this sense Takeuchi even understands his revered teacher as a religious existentialist, whereas Laube incorrectly disregards this basic feature of Tanabe's philosophy.

Chapter 4

Daisetz Teitaro Suzuki (1870–1966)
Zen and Shin Buddhism
for the West

1. Suzuki the Genius

It can be asked whether Daisetz Suzuki, who belongs to the same generation as Nishida and Tanabe, is also to be numbered among the founders of the Kyoto School, and to what extent he would consider it appropriate to be included in this context. There are grounds for this thesis, and others that can be advanced against it.

The fact that Suzuki, like Nishida and Tanabe, set about to understand anew and justify the truth of Buddhism by taking into account Western thinking which had exerted great influence at that time in Japan, speaks generally and fundamentally for such an inclusion in this circle. This mutual leadership received a special personally determined stamp from the fact that all three dealt with the Buddhism they represented—if with different accents—namely, both with Zen and Shin Buddhism. A further reason for viewing Suzuki among the co-founders of the Kyoto School results from the fact that he taught with Nishida and Tanabe in Kyoto in its years of origin, from 1921 to 1941—to be sure, not at the then Royal University, but at the Shin Buddhist Otani University, with which he remained connected his whole life. In this regard reference should be made to the friendship which had bound Suzuki to Nishida since their school days. This bond worked itself out, for example, in the fact that Suzuki wrote a deeply perceptive introduction to the English edition of *A Study of Good*, just as Nishida had earlier composed an introduction to Suzuki's Japanese publication, *Culture and Religion*, in which he testified how much he was indebted to the personality and stimulation of his friend for his own philosophical thinking.[1]

There are, however, arguments—both negative and positive—that speak against summarily including Suzuki in the Kyoto School. Suzuki left behind a literary life work which, with its one hundred Japanese and more than thirty English publications,[2] exceeded in volume the collected works of Nishida and those of Tanabe as well. But while the writings of these two dealt with the systematic unfolding of their own philosophy, those of Suzuki deal principally

---

[1]EB 2/1 (1967): 35.
[2]Ibid., 121, and "Chronology and Bibliography" in ibid., 208-29.

with editions and translations, anthologies and commentaries of the Buddhist tradition. His translations of the *Lankavatara sutra* and the *Kyogyoshinsho*, together with related explanations and studies, as well as the three volume *Essays in Zen Buddhism* and his *Zen and Japanese Culture*, belong to the standard literature in these fields.[3] Moreover, Suzuki was a tireless narrator of Zen stories and his favorites were the Myokonin, the "special saints" of Shin Buddhism.[4]

If Suzuki represented his Buddhist philosophy in such a casual rather than developed way, and for this reason more personally and directly, this reminds us of the way he once, as a justification of this method of philosophizing, appealed in his Eranos Lecture to Kierkegaard's parable of the philosopher who lived, not in the palace of his system, but in a modest hut he constructed for himself. He could, so continued Suzuki, only live in that building if there were no difference between the building and the builder, with the builder understanding himself as his building.[5] Like Kierkegaard, with this image Suzuki wished to clarify the difference between an objective and a no-longer objectifying thinking which he identifies with himself, the first of which he regarded as typical for philosophy and theology, while the second he reserved for the "spiritual man, the "religious spirit," which he sees realized in Zen, when he explains:

> Zen is concerned with a person, a living person, who acts and does not spend his life in mere thinking. With him thinking and acting are one. He builds a house and the house is he. With him the house is not an object erected beside him. He is the builder and the building while being engaged

---

[3]*Studies in the Lankavatara Sutra* ([4]1972; [1]1930) and *The Lankavatara Sutra* (1932), both from Routledge and Kegan Paul (London); *The Kyogyoshinsho and Collected Writings on Shin Buddhism*, both from Shinshu Otaniha (Kyoto, 1973); *Essays in Zen Buddhism*, 3 vols. (London: Rider, 1949–1953; 5th eds., 1974 and 1975; 4th ed., 1977, in different formats); *Zen and Japanese Culture* (London: Routledge and Kegan Paul, 1959; also in many editions and translations). It is to the credit of Edward Conze that he drew to the attention of the Western, especially the Anglo-Saxon world, in which Suzuki became known as the propagator of Zen, the extensive research Suzuki devoted to this field, by publishing a Taschenbuch edition of individual essays of Suzuki on the forms of Indian Mahayana Buddhism, in *D. T. Suzuki on Indian Mahayana Buddhism*, ed. with an introduction by Edward Conze, Harper Torchbooks (New York: Harper & Bros., 1968). In addition to those selected, the titles of Suzuki's other English works in this field are also noted.

[4]"Japanese Spirituality," Japanese National Commission for UNESCO (Japan Society for the Promotion of Science, 1972) 167-215; *Collected Writings on Shin Buddhism*, 78-110.

[5]"The Awakening of a New Consciousness in Zen," *Eranos-Jahrbuch 1954* 23 (Zurich: Rhein-Verlag, 1955): 288-89.

in building. The builder is never away from the building, he is building himself. Zen wants us to take hold of this builder in the building—the building not as an object but as the subject himself, as the one who is engaged in the act of building.[6]

Suzuki does not wish thereby to render superfluous the philosophy he conceives to be intellectualist, but only if it does not exchange the pointing finger for the moon. According to Suzuki, "conceptualization" becomes an "unnecessary luxury" for what he understands by "experience." Before one can attain to it, "intellectualizing" is not only "inevitable," but can even be useful—like the pointing finger.[7] Suzuki is thoroughly aware of the epistemological problems he touches on thereby, and he disposes of them not always—even though quite frequently, as in connection with the passage cited—by narrating one or several drastic Zen episodes, in which blows are exchanged and noses twisted or in which one yells "Kwatz" and runs away. As is yet to be shown, he is also thoroughly equipped to deal with these questions also in a way that corresponds to Western modes of thought.

But in contradistinction to Nishida and Tanabe, in these discussions Suzuki does not engage in a confrontation with the positions of Kant and of German idealists or of Neo-Kantianism or of existentialism. From the spiritual tradition in which he moves, in the figures of his Zen masters and Amida devotees he encounters these problems much more directly and deals with them in an elementary way, tolerating no objection and brushing aside our head shaking with a smile. Here there is nothing of the abstractness of a transcendental philosophy like Kant's or Fichte's and of Hegel's or Kierkegaard's dialectic. Only what stands behind their use in Nishida and Tanabe remains and is aggressively expressed in a Zen saying or a Nembutsu formula.

For this reason Suzuki is often reproached for being neither scientific nor philosophical, which is correct when he neither exposes the limits of science in a generally demonstrable way but rejects this possibility in advance as merely "scientific," nor allows the "emptiness" attained in this way to be really empty but turns it into a showplace of scientifically and philosophically problematic "experiences" and their testimonies in words and deeds. To be sure, the Zen stories used by Suzuki in this way—through the shocking effects which are described therein and are felt by those who enact them—make scientific procedure and philosophical consciousness seem to be mere intellectualism and in their place bizarre assertion and displays of scurrilous behavior are made to appear as evidence of a special spirituality and religiosity. But apart from the liberation from falsely absolutized science and audacious philosophical

---

[6]Ibid, 289.
[7]Ibid., 288n.8.

Daisetz Teitaro Suzuki (1870–1966)

speculations which they bring about, nothing is attained in this way of the spirituality that does justice to the problems of human existence in the world and of a religiosity that does not appear superstitious in another way.

Suzuki is not satisfied simply to describe and expand these strange stories and figures of Buddhist tradition, but demonstrates their significance for individuals and society in the past as well as the possibility of renewing their effects in the present—in their psychological and metaphysical as well as their cultural religioscientific aspects. Examples of the first two of these are to be found in all of Suzuki's works, especially in *Essays in Zen Buddhism* as well as in works and lectures published outside this collection which attempt to introduce Westerners to what the Easterner understands by "Enlightenment" and the "true self." These psychological and metaphysical notions get treated also in Suzuki's cultural and religioscientific investigations, just as investigations of this latter sort are also to be found in the essays on Zen Buddhism. Typical of the cultural-historical manner of his understanding of Buddhism are his long term investigations of the significance of Zen for Japanese culture and the lectures he gave on "Japanese Spirituality" during the Second World War.

Nishida and Tanabe spoke and wrote on all these problems—partly at the same time. But if the way in which they do it is compared to that of Suzuki, it will become apparent that—except for a few assertions in specific situations—they are scarcely heard and understood beyond a narrow philosophical circle, while Suzuki became an apostle of Buddhism not only in Japan but worldwide and enjoyed great popularity.[8] In this way what became known through him in the West as Buddhism was above all Zen Buddhism, while for him—even more expressly than was the case with Nishida and Tanabe—Shin Buddhism represented something equivalent to it. Nishida was already at home in Zen Buddhism early on and positively espoused faith in Amida in his last writing, even though he became acquainted with it from his mother.[9] As for Tanabe, he acknowledged that he never fully subscribed to Zen,[10] and Amida became significant to him in connection with a crisis he experienced at the end of the Second

---

[8]As partial proof of the recognition accorded him one can point to the special issue of *The Eastern Buddhist*, dedicated in his honor a year after his death, with thirty-eight contributions by scholars from around the world (EB 2 [1967]: 1).

[9]"Die Logik des Ortes und die religiöse Weltanschauung" in *Gott in Japan*, ed. Yagi and Luz, 108-109. [ET: see David A. Dilworth, "Nishida's Final Essay: The Logic of Place and a Religious Worldview," PhEW 20/4 (1970): 355ff. (repr.: Nishida Kitaro, *Last Writings: Nothingness and the Religious Worldview*, trans. David A. Dilworth [Honolulu: University of Hawaii Press, 1977] 47-123).

[10]Tanabe Hajime, "Introduction to Philosophy as Metanoetics," JR 5/2 (1967): 35 [cf. *Philosophy as Metanoetics*. trans. Takeuchi Yoshinori with Valdo Viglielmo and James Heisig (Berkeley: University of California Press) liii].

World War—and then quite decisively. By contrast Suzuki concerned himself with both forms of Buddhism quite early, in that during his studies at Tokyo University he spent his free time as a novice in the Zen monastery at Engakuji in Kamakura and during his first visit to America immediately thereafter he translated a work on Amida from English into Japanese and one on the life of Shinran from Japanese into English.[11] From then on for decades he was occupied with research on and translation of texts from both branches of Buddhism—especially in the journal *The Eastern Buddhist* which he founded in 1921—just as when he was in Japan he was the Zen specialist at the Shin Buddhist Otani University where the editing of *The Eastern Buddhist* is still located.

But not only in his being equally at home in Zen and Shin Buddhism and in his preoccupation with their traditions did he surpass both of his colleagues—as far as this can be established—but it is also biographically evident—in view of his long life—with respect to the sphere of his engagement with the Western world and his recognition and effectiveness with it. Nishida was still a teacher in the provinces and Tanabe still a student when Suzuki accompanied his Zen master as translator on a lecture tour to America where he resided from 1897 as an assistant in a publishing house.[12] On his return trip to Japan he visited Europe for the first time and continued these visits to the West with lectures at most of the great universities on both continents until quite advanced in age. At ninety-four he spent two weeks in New York, and then finally—as previously—attended the (fourth) East-West Philosophers Conference in Honolulu where he spoke once again of Shinran. Through these opportunities he became personally acquainted with numerous famous contemporaries from the world of philosophy and religion. This familiarity with the West was due also to his marriage to an American and the ability, not only to teach without an interpreter, but to publish without depending upon a translator. The echo of this did not stop, but continued in innumerable invitations and honors. The professorial existence of Nishida and Tanabe which was scarcely known beyond the boundaries of their own country does not compare with the world notoriety he enjoyed for more than seventy years. Nishida never travelled abroad and Tanabe only left for a two-year stay as student in Germany. Whereas of their works only a few were translated and most of these after their deaths, already in Suzuki's lifetime a large number of his lesser as well as extensive publications appeared in English, most of which he himself wrote in the English language in which he had taught from age nineteen.[13] For this reason his different positive and negative

---

[11]Shojun Bando, "D. T. Suzuki's Life in LaSalle," EB 2/1 (1967): 137ff.; cf. "Chronology," 208-209, and "Bibliography," 216ff., in the same issue.
[12]Ibid.
[13]Ibid.

positions with respect to Christianity became better known than those of Nishida and Tanabe, while the thorough evaluation of Christianity in the later writings of the latter is still unavailable to us in translation. While Suzuki's engagement with Christianity, like Tanabe's, resulted from faith in Amida, Tanabe's handling of this theme is incomparably more comprehensive and systematic than Suzuki's more cursory and apodictic treatment, which makes the lack of a translation all the more regrettable. It remains to be said that Tanabe's positive attitude toward Christianity represents an exception, while Suzuki's negative posture agrees with that of Nishida if not with Buddhist philosophy generally, especially with the Zen direction within the Kyoto School.

If—as we think—the critical juxtaposition of the Buddhist tradition, especially that of Zen and Shin Buddhism, with the West belongs to the essential characteristics of the Kyoto School, then Suzuki has a legitimate place within it; also, in view of the source material which he made available to the remaining representatives of this school he can be counted among its founders. If the philosophy which he developed principally through commenting on this traditional material appears as only an excavation site or contractor's hut in comparison to the palatial systems of Nishida's and Tanabe's, in scope and content it does not rank below theirs. But no less than the builders of those constructions of thoughts identified with them—in any case, Tanabe—Suzuki did this with the texts he translated and explained, and the edifices that he often erected upon them.

How this worked itself out in his extensive writings is to be illustrated in the following examples. For this we neglect the more historical works in favor of the expressly systematic expositions in which he not only materially supported the Kyoto School, but also augmented it in his own manner.

2. Two Lectures before the Tenno on the Nature of Buddhism

As the first example we latch onto the two lectures on "The Essence of Buddhism" delivered by Suzuki before the Emperor on the 23rd and 24th of April 1947 at his invitation to the Imperial Palace in Tokyo—lectures which in the same year appeared in English translation double in size.[14] In the first lecture Suzuki makes the metaphysically and ethically important distinction between the sphere of immediate perception of meaning and its conceptual reconstruction on the one hand, and that of spirit and religion on the other.[15] The latter discloses

---

[14]"The Essence of Buddhism," Imperial Lectures, enl. and rev. ed. (Hozokan Kyoto, Matsuzaka Bunko, 1947; [2]1967). [The first of the two lectures was reprinted in *The Essentials of Zen Buddhism: Selected from the Writings of Daisetz Suzuki*, ed. Bernard Phillips (New York: E. P. Dutton, 1962) 383-414. —Trans.]

[15]Ibid., 1 [Phillips, 383].

itself to human consciousness only on the basis of the experience of the problematic of meaning in the former,[16] but it would be an error to assume that we are therein dealing with two different worlds. That Being does not represent a unity for us is due to the conceptuality of the intellect which we cannot escape, but which nevertheless is an illusion.[17] The bifurcation also contradicts our experience which certainly cannot be conceived with customary logic, but only with the "Buddhist logic of self-identity,"[18] in consequence of which "the two worlds are at once one and not one."[19] The origin of the error as of all evil is the self that belongs to the intellect[20] and this must first be disposed of in order to make a place in the "Great Death" for "nondiscriminating wisdom (*prajna*)."[21] This is not distinguished from conceptual thinking, but consists in becoming aware of the boundaries of discriminating thinking.[22] In order to attain to it, "Enlightenment" is necessary.[23]

Suzuki believes this can be located also in the "terms of Christian experience" as "living in Christ by dying to Adam or as Christ's rising from the dead."[24] In Christianity the "divine revelation" corresponds to the "unthinkable" in Buddhism.[25] But "words are needed to transcend words, and intellection is needed to rise above the intellect."[26] This holds especially for the concept of karma, since being bound to karma means overcoming karma,[27] insofar as "self-appraisement" forms the "key to self-deliverance."[28] As Suzuki emphasizes, that is not intended in the moral sense of a supposedly free personality, nor as merely being delivered over to a law of nature. Rather the privilege of the person consists in his knowing that he is bound to karma from which comes suffering, not only in the natural, bodily sense but also in a personal and spiritual manner. This contradictory state of affairs which is not conceptually capable of being unified refers beyond this sphere of meaning and intellect to that of the "self-identity of contraries" in the Buddhist logic of prajna intuition. The Enlightened person does

---

[16]Ibid., 2-3 [Phillips, 384-85].
[17]Ibid., 4-5 [Phillips, 385].
[18]Ibid., 7 [Phillips, 387].
[19]Ibid., 8 [Phillips, 388].
[20]Ibid., 9 [Phillips, 388-89].
[21]Ibid., 10ff. [Phillips, 389ff.].
[22]Ibid., 12 [Phillips, 390].
[23]Ibid., 17 [Phillips, 394].
[24]Ibid., 20 [Phillips, 396].
[25]Ibid., 22 [Phillips, 397].
[26]Ibid., 27ff. [Phillips, 402ff.].
[27]Ibid., 28ff. [Phillips, 402ff.].
[28]Ibid., 31ff. [Phillips, 403].

not distinguish his nondistinction from distinction. "Thus it belongs to a world of distinctions, but at the same time it is above it."[29] Embedded in the wheel of rebirth he is simultaneously released from it. Whoever is united to this wheel cannot escape from it,[30] but experiences it in such a way that "the spirit is master of itself,"[31] and attains thereby "immortality, as Christians would say."[32]

True to form, Suzuki concludes the exposition of this prajna enlightenment—which from a Buddhist perspective is liberating—with a Zen story. To the question, how one can escape the change from summer to winter, a Zen master answers: "Why not go to the place where there is neither winter nor summer?" and to the further question, where can one find such a place?: "When winter comes you shiver; when summer comes you perspire."[33] To this Suzuki adds the exclamation that should be made according to the legend of the newborn Buddha: "Above heaven and below heaven I alone am the Honored One," in order to connect it with the promise that every one has this magnitude in himself and, like the Buddha, realizes it in the "supreme affirmation: when hot, we perspire, when cold, we shiver."[34]

In the second lecture Suzuki expands the concept of the "Great Wisdom, *Mahaprajna*," expounded in the former, by that of the "*Mahakaruna*, the Great Compassion," which in their own way are one and—personified as such in the *Dharmakaya*—become the "principle of vitality in the world of sense-intellect."[35] He developed this matter here on the basis of Kegon philosophy, that is, of the Avatamsaka sutra by means of its key terms *Ji* (distinction, form) and *Ri* (nondistinction, sunyata, emptiness). With certain reservations—Suzuki thinks—*Ri* can be compared with the concept of God or the universal, and *Ji* with human individuals and with the individual. But differently from these opposite terms in Western thinking they belong together in Buddhist thinking in such a way that "form is emptiness, and emptiness form,"[36] with the result that their connection represents "a perfect, mutual, unimpeded solution." This becomes expressed grammatically with the famous "soku" which does not mean identity, because therein a duality is still presupposed, but rather "how it is" or "thus-ness." This is a characteristic that is not expressed in concepts, but can only be experienced

---

[29]Ibid., 40 [Phillips, 410].
[30]Ibid., 42 [Phillips, 412].
[31]Ibid., 40 [Phillips, 410].
[32]Ibid., 43 [Phillips, 412].
[33]Ibid., 43 [Phillips, 412].
[34]Ibid., 45-46.
[35]Ibid., 46.
[36]Ibid., 48.

intuitively.[37] It can only be intimated metaphorically, for example, in the self-reflection of a lamp in ten mirrors arranged around each other or by the relationship of the material and form of a golden lion, as is used in Kegon philosophy in many modifications as a model for *Ri* and *Ji*.[38]

That with which Kegon philosophy and with it Suzuki deals in the world perspective, in which all things mutually encompass and interpenetrate each other and thus represent a unity in diversity and a diversity in unity is the "Great Compassion" made possible in this way, or the "Great Compassionate Heart" as the world-principle that permeates all things and which is only conceivable in the intuitive enlightenment wisdom that cannot be objectified.[39] Of it Suzuki explains: "Buddhists personify it in different ways: *Amida* (*Amitabha*, "infinite light") is one of these personifications, the most popular one in Japan. His followers belong to the Pure Land School of Buddhism."[40] The conclusion of the lectures is devoted to the exposition of this faith in Amida, in which, as Suzuki conceives history, the historical and systematic are not to be separated. This furnishes him the opportunity for interesting comparisons with Zen Buddhism and Christianity.

That Amida with his vow is not historical but legendary does not detract from his saving significance for the believers, in that, for them, he is "just as real and lively and historical as they are themselves." As enlightened ones they have been bound up with him since his enlightenment in the spiritual world, "where he and we and all the rest of beings are one and not distinguished one from another, and therefore his Enlightenment means our enlightenment and ours, his."[41] Only "as long as we remain in the world of dualistic logic, this world . . . controlled by the Great Compassion will be unintelligible."[42] But if we hear his "gentle voice"[43] and obey it, we ourselves become "not an arhat, but a Bodhisattva," in whose heart Amida is present and revered as in a temple."[44] He is reinforced therein by the other personification of the great compassionate heart, *Kwannon* (*Avalokitesvara*), because trust in its help makes us fearless and capable of compassionate devotion.[45]

---

[37]Ibid., 50-51.
[38]Ibid., 54ff.
[39]Ibid., 53, 54.
[40]Ibid., 64.
[41]Ibid., 65.
[42]Ibid., 66.
[43]Ibid., 69.
[44]Ibid., 73.
[45]Ibid., 75ff.

In this connection Suzuki distinguishes Zen and Pure Land Buddhism by saying of the former that it represents the *prajna* phase of Mahayana," "inclines toward the arhat ideal," and is "studied by the scholars," while the latter "appeals to karma," "tends toward the Bodhisattva ideal," understands that "too much learning is calculated to prevent the growth of the spiritual life," and therefore is more "for the masses."[46] In his eyes both forms of Buddhism are to be distinguished from Christianity with its dualistic thinking with respect to God and the world[47] and its societal- and world-constituting ethic,[48] to which he juxtaposes the example of a Zen master who is ready to go to hell for a poor sinful woman[49]—without taking into account that such a self-sacrificial love is to be found also in the New Testament and that the Christ who embodies it descended into Hades for the salvation of the condemned.[50]

It is indicative of Suzuki's attitude toward Christianity that he points out correspondences between Buddhism and Christianity and employs them to make Buddhist peculiarities understandable. When he tries to point out something special in Buddhism, he neglects to provide comparisons in a positive sense, but rather is content to interpret Christian motifs in not very understandable ways to their disadvantage. Because of his close relationship to the West, Suzuki frequently speaks of Christianity in his works and numerous examples of this attitude are to be found even in those publications we draw upon in the following in order more closely to characterize his Zen Buddhism and Shin Buddhism.

In order to illustrate Suzuki's concern with both kinds of Buddhism—a concern which issues not merely from historical interests, but in personal participation—we select from the materials available to us three examples which are informative for his systematic conception of Zen and Amida Buddhism.

3. Concerning Zen and Zen Psychology

Two years after the programmatic presentation before the emperor, in which he took account of Zen and Shin Buddhism, Suzuki spoke at the Second East-West Philosophers Conference at the University of Hawaii in 1949 on the theme of "The Buddhist Conception of Reality,"[51] in which he appeals exclusively to Zen philosophy and develops his conception of reality on this basis. He did this in such a way that his expositions would appeal to non-Buddhists, especially

---

[46]Ibid., 77.

[47]Ibid., 76 and 86.

[48]Ibid., 81.

[49]Ibid., 82.

[50]Matt 26:28; Rom 4:25; 1 Cor 15:3; Gal 1:4; 1 Pet 3:18; Heb 9:26; also 1 Pet 3:19.

[51]"The Buddhist Conception of Reality," EB 7/2 (1974): 1-21.

Christians, by making use of Christian concepts, like God, creation, Christ, and faith—but in any case not as they are used in traditional dogmatics.

Here also Suzuki makes a distinction between two kinds of knowledge: the "objective method" of the logical intellect,[52] which approaches things "from the outside,"[53] and the method of *"prajna* intuition,"[54] which he also calls "faith,"[55] and which deals with the "innerliness of things."[56] Despite their differences of approach and result they do not mutually exclude, but mutually reinforce each other, since the former ends in questions which only the latter is able to answer. These questions are of two kinds. The one asks, "Why are we here?" and the other, "What is the significance of life here?"[57] But just as in relation to the ways that can be followed in answering them, so for him these questions stand in relation to each other. "This questioning about the meaning of life" is for him "tantamount to seeking after ultimate reality."[58]

He takes up the latter in order to ascertain the impossibility of framing an answer by means of the intellect. The intellect "raised the question," but "this does mean that it is qualified to answer it."[59] To be sure, it is useful in commerce with "the affairs of daily life," but it exceeds its limits if it deals with "the question of reality" which "lies behind all things of nature and spirit." "Creation out of nothing," with which Christianity answers this question, is "the most baffling question for the intellect."[60] According to Suzuki, one would have to become atman, or if one is a Christian, God himself—which naturally appears to the intellect to be an impossibility—or [the intellect] would have "to kill itself and to let something else take its place."[61]

This other that has to replace the spectator attitude of the intellect if the question of reality is to be answered, is in Suzuki's eyes a "faith," in which we undertake the "grand experiment," "become conscious of the fact that man is God" and is created in the image of God, or without question and doubt participates in the Buddha nature. That is what Buddhist philosophy teaches and Christ means when he rebukes his disciples for their little faith.[62] It therefore does not

---

[52]Ibid, 2-3.
[53]Ibid., 4.
[54]Ibid., 15.
[55]Ibid., 6.
[56]Ibid., 20.
[57]Ibid., 1.
[58]Ibid., 1.
[59]Ibid., 2.
[60]Ibid., 3.
[61]Ibid., 4.
[62]Ibid., 5-6.

deal with becoming something we are not, but with relocating to where we were before we adopted the spectator approach of the intellect in the distinction between subject and object.[63]

To understand itself and another in this way is for Suzuki "creation out of nothing," not as an event in grey antiquity, but as something which "is taking place every moment of our life."[64] To distinguish this act epistemologically he makes use of Nishida's notion of "pure experience."[65] In this way is expressed the "intellectual co-meaning of true enlightenment," which derives from the fact that the intellect conceals a faith that corresponds to a system of cosmic unity.[66] "The intellect seeing itself is no other than reality becoming conscious of itself," and this "not in its psychological sense, but in its metaphysical bearing" insofar as here neither the subject nor object are at hand, but "an experience experiencing itself," which, by contrast with that of everyday, represents "in its most eminent sense" what can only be approximated in words.[67]

The ultimate reality of Buddhist philosophy "goes beyond definability," is *sunyata*, emptiness. This emptiness is nevertheless not something without content, but the "fullness of things," "a grand integration which is before subject and object are intellectually differentiated," "the cosmic or divine Unconscious becoming conscious."[68] As an example of this Suzuki uses the "first cry of a newborn," which—just as little as the famous exclamation of the newborn Buddha—wishes to be "interpreted" or to be imitated by an adult as proof of "wisdom." Although Suzuki remarks meaningfully that for Buddhist masters, as for Christians, little children belong to privileged beings, he does not neglect to warn against a striving after their undeveloped spiritual condition. "What is important is to remain ourselves in every way possible with all our faults, moral as well as intellectual, and yet be 'wise' as babies."[69] For Suzuki this is the meaning of life which issues from his experience with being.

Suzuki also comes to terms with the question of the meaning of existence in the lecture he delivered five years later at the Eranos meeting at Ascona, entitled "The Awakening of a New Consciousness in Zen,"[70] except that here—more expressly than in the preceding one—he sees "reality" under the aspect of the question of meaning. The "world" is considered insofar as its condi-

---

[63]Ibid., 6-7.
[64]Ibid., 7.
[65]Ibid., 8.
[66]Ibid., 9.
[67]Ibid., 11-12.
[68]Ibid., 14-15.
[69]Ibid., 18.
[70]*Eranos-Jahrbuch 1954* 13 (1955): 275-313.

tion gives us reason to seek beyond it for a better one. To actualize the fulfillment of this longing, which Suzuki sees as the essence of religion,[71] he conceives
of two ways: an "outward," "intellectual and objective" one and an "inward,"
which—in contrast to the other—cannot be called "subjective or affective or
conative," because to characterize it differently from that one would no longer
be the "inward way," since its essence consists in that fact that "no contrast
exists between the inward and the outward."

Although Suzuki concedes that this may be a "logical contradiction," he continues to provide distinguishing traits for both ways. The "outward" way consists
of an "never ending procession" in the constant "opposition of two terms, subject
and object," and because it lacks "finality," is bound up with a "sense of
insecurity." On the inward way the mind turns "inwardly to see what is there
behind all this endless procession of things."[72] In contrast to the intellect of the
outward way the movement inward does not stop for the sake of self-assertion,
but consists in "taking the things as they are," in their "is-ness" or "suchness."
To speak of being as it happens in these terms is not quite appropriate to the
inward way. "It is much better to lift a finger and say nothing about it." In its
"orthodoxy" it generally avoids appealing to language, though it never shuns it.
Suzuki further describes it by saying that—in its use of the terms "one" and "all"
as mutually interchangeable—it is perfected in "absolute nothingness," and that
this happens especially in Zen.[73]

At this point Suzuki recalls that the Japanese Buddhists use the term *kokoro*
for this "abyss of absolute nothingness," which means psychologically "heart or
mind," metaphysically "substance," and ethically "verity, faithfulness."[74] In
Western terminology the term can be regarded as parallel to "God or Godhead,"
from whom, or from whose "spontaneity," the world sprang.[75] To it there corresponds in man "the eternal longing" "to transcend this world of particulars"—a
longing "for something which has vanished from the domain of the outward way
of intellectualisation,"[76] but which still represents a "shadow of the original
kokoro" which "is cast in the track of the inward way," and therefore is only
erroneously held by us to be permanently lost, as this is meant in Christianity by
the "Father's mansion" as our "original abode" which cannot be lost, and in Shin
Buddhism by Amida who holds us "firmly in his arms" even if we wish to run

---

[71]Ibid., 276.
[72]Ibid. 277.
[73]Ibid., 278.
[74]Ibid., 279.
[75]Ibid., 281.
[76]Ibid., 282.

away.[77] The "new consciousness" awakened in Zen is "the restoration or re-cognition" of our original face which we possessed before our birth, the "face of innocence" which we had "before our eating of the tree of knowledge" which is "the outward way of intellection."[78] The inward way, to the contrary, corresponds to faith as Asvaghosha understands it as a matter of enlightenment, that is, as becoming aware of " 'Original Enlightenment' in which we were and are."

To this explanation of the nature of faith as Zen understands it Suzuki attaches the observation that God cannot be proven objectively, and that those who attempt to do so do not have to do with God either subjectively or objectively. To the foolishness of the question of the "objective existence of God" he counters, "As soon as [they] have faith, they have God. Faith is God and God is faith. . . . It is not God who gives us faith, but faith that gives us God. Faith is God coming to his own knowledge."[79]

After this expansion of faith into metaphysics, Suzuki in accord with the title of his lecture, turns in its second part once again to the psychological sphere of consciousness in order to apply the distinction between outward and inward now also to the consciousness which we can and should have of ourselves.[80] Con-sciousness, so he explains here, is ordinarily "always conscious of something other than itself." In such a dichotomy "the self cannot be conscious of itself." It can only be known "when it remains itself and yet goes out of itself." "Understood on the level of the outward way" this is a contradiction. Therefore, in order to "realize" the significance of self-consciousness "to its full depths" one must rise above this level to the "inward way" on which "consciousness turns inwardly into itself." This is a "homecoming," "the seeing of one's own 'primal face', which one has even before one's birth."

For Suzuki this is the same as "God's pronouncing his name to Moses," "the birth of Christ in each one of our souls," and his "rising from death."[81] But while at this point he provides no commentary for the application of these Christian symbols, in the third section of his lectures he subsequently interprets the "Ten Ox-Herding Pictures"[82] to mean that the ox represents the self in such a way that as one who has run away and is sought by the shepherd it corresponds to the person who imagines himself to be the possessor of his self and in his dualistic delusion seeks his self until it disappears, although he has never really lost it. Only he who thinks that he can objectify his self on the "outward way" of

---

[77]Ibid., 283.
[78]Ibid., 284.
[79]Ibid., 285.
[80]Ibid., 294ff.
[81]Ibid., 295.
[82]Ibid., 297ff.

knowledge, thinks he has lost his self and vainly seeks it on this way. On this basis the ox which symbolizes this falsely contrived and sought self first appears black in an older series of pictures, but becomes white to the degree that the error is understood, until he completely disappears with the ox in enlightenment and only "the fullness of the nothing" remains.[83] The oxherd attains the primary "inward way" by following the tracks of the ox and subdues it with reins and a whip until he brings it back into its shed. As the texts accompanying the pictures explain, the tracks symbolize the instructions contained in the tradition, and the subduing of the ox signifies the Zen training which the observer of the series of pictures has adopted up to the time he participates in enlightenment, and from the Nirvana disclosed therein he can return as a Bodhisattva saved and saving to the "marketplace of the world," as is represented in the last picture of the more recent series.

Suzuki sees in this series of pictures both a rendering of the stations which the one who practises Zen must go through, as well as a representation of the kokoro personified in Amida, from which the Shin devotees cannot escape. Also they make him think of the "lost and regained paradise" in Asvaghosha's notion of the prenatal home in the maternal body of Tathagata and in modern depth psychology.[84] These viewpoints which he characteristically advances as the interpretative possibilities of this classic "Story of the Ox and its Oxherd" and its pictorial representations often repeated up to the present time document not only its extraordinary symbolic power, but also the richness of Suzuki's spiritual word.

Suzuki returns once again to the perspective of depth psychology just mentioned in the extensive contribution which he makes under the title "Lectures on Zen Buddhism" to the work *Zen Buddhism and Psychoanalysis* jointly published in 1960 by the psychiatrists Erich Fromm and Richard de Martino.[85]

In the first lecture he clearly reveals the difference between the Eastern and Western kinds of spirit through a comparison of a haiku of Basho with a poem of Tennyson's on the same theme which consists in reactions to the sight of a flower. Whereas Basho, a Japanese poet from the second half of the seventeenth century, in the seventeen syllables of his haiku would sooner conceal than indicate what transpires between him and the unpretentious flower that he has discovered in a hedge, Tennyson describes how he plucks the flower together with its roots and in gazing at it, has thoughts of God, the world, and himself.

---

[83]Suzuki brings the older Chinese versions together with the more recent Japanese version in his *Manual of Zen Buddhism* (New York: Grove Press, First Evergreen Printing, 1960 [15th ptg.]) 127-44; cf. also the reissue of this series of pictures in *Essays in Zen Buddhism*, first series (London, 1949; ³1975).

[84]*Eranos-Jahrbuch 1954*, 298.

[85]D. T. Suzuki, Erich Fromm, and Richard de Martino, *Zen Buddhism and Psychoanalysis*, A Harper Colophon Book (New York: Harper & Row, 1960).

After a thorough analysis of the two different types of behavior which he characterizes as "the scientific method" whose representatives approach its object from outside and the Zen approach that consists in a self-identification with the "object," in the second lecture he speaks of "the unconscious" in Zen Buddhism.[86] The Zen way is the "pre- and post-, and even indeed antiscientific way." While the scientific kills the object in order thereafter to reassemble the dead pieces, "Zen plunges itself into the source of creativity and drinks from it all the life there is in it. This source is Zen's Unconscious." Suzuki says of this unconscious, following Basho's meaning, that he "awakens the flower from the unconscious" when he looks at it without knowing whether it [the unconscious] is in him or in the flower[87]—but in any case he is like the creative artist "in him" as the "Cosmic Unconscious."[88]

The unconscious is "scientifically not accessible," but is a matter of the feeling which refers to the emergence of the unconscious out of the ocean of the unconscious, so "we can realize that our fragmentary existence gains its full significance,"[89] which—as Suzuki assures his dialogue partners and hearers—is the best help against neuroses and psychoses which arise from doubt about the meaning of life. Zen awakens persons to be "artist[s] of life,"[90] "free from the constrictive motivations of consciousness," but "in direct communion with the great unconscious" his life is to be formed in "creative" ways into a work of art, as "master of himself wherever he may be found."[91] As much as this is a matter of naturalness and immediacy, it does not deal with a mere instinctualness, but with a "trained unconscious in which all the conscious experiences [he has gone through since infancy] are incorporated as constituting his whole being"—in the individual as well as in the "cosmical history of life."[92] Because the unconscious works in the conscious, it must be constantly purified of its contamination by the egoism of the intellect. One must become free from anxiety and uncertainty as the consequences of that which is meant in the biblical myth by "the loss of 'innocence' or the acquirement of 'knowledge' " and in Buddhism by "the interference of the conscious mind predominated by intellection," if "the 'trained' unconscious operat[es] in the field of consciousness."[93]

---

[86]Ibid., 10ff.
[87]Ibid., 12.
[88]Ibid., 13.
[89]Ibid., 14.
[90]Ibid., 15.
[91]Ibid., 16.
[92]Ibid., 19.
[93]Ibid., 20.

In the following chapter which is devoted to the "concept of the self in Zen Buddhism,"[94] Suzuki attempts to show above all by appealing to "The Sayings of Rinzai"[95] that "the true self" deals with "a kind of metaphysical self" which stands "in opposition to the psychological or ethical self" "which belongs in a finite world of relativity."[96] For this "real self" of which Suzuki says on the one hand that it is something quite different from the merely negative non-I of the Buddha's *annata* doctrine with which Zen Buddhism is not satisfied,[97] which however, on the other, according to him can be grasped in no conceptual objectivity[98] and can be striven for in no way[99]—for this self he uses Rinzai's image of the "true man with no rank in the mass of naked flesh,"[100] whose name is "secret"[101] and who is the "master of himself wherever he goes and for whom "all is right" wherever he stands.[102]

Since the Chinese Zen master Rinzai is the founder of the Rinzai Zen named after him, which distinguishes itself from Dogen's Soto Zen through the use of koans as aids to meditation, it seems appropriate that Suzuki, as on other occasions, [103]devotes a chapter in this series of lectures to the theme of the koan.[104] The purpose of koan mediation consists in breaking through the objectifying conceptuality of the intellect which stands in the way of the meeting with reality. But when in contrast to his dialogue partners Suzuki also stresses that the sphere of the unconscious reached in this way does not belong "to the domain of psychology," but rather transcends it, he does not wish thereby to be "take[n] as an anti-intellectualist." Rather, he defines his position by saying that the "intellect is needed to determine—however vaguely—where the reality is. And the reality is grasped only when the intellect quits its claim on it."[105] This way of knowledge is not only symbolized but practically realized in the practice of sitting (*zazen*) in which thinking takes place not with the head but with the

---

[94]Ibid., 24ff.
[95]Ibid., 33ff.
[96]Ibid., 32.
[97]Ibid., 31-32.
[98]Ibid., 35ff.
[99]Ibid., 41.
[100]Ibid., 32.
[101]Ibid., 35.
[102]Ibid., 38.
[103]E.g., in *Die grosse Befreiung. Einführung in den Zen-Buddhism* (Zurich: Rasher, 1958) 137-63.
[104]*Zen Buddhism and Psychoanalysis*, 43ff.
[105]Ibid., 49.

stomach.[106] For this reason in China corpulence counts as a sign of the wisdom of the Bodhisattvas,[107] with whose fourfold vow to redeem all Suzuki concludes his "Lectures on Zen" after answering many questions.

We should not overlook two meaningful references to parallels to Christian ideas of redemption which Suzuki makes in this koan chapter. For the satori experience in which "ordinary consciousness" becomes the "borderland between the conscious level and the unconscious" and "becomes infused with the tidings of the unconscious," he refers to "the moment when the soul hears directly and inwardly the voice of the living God," like, for example, Moses on Sinai,[108] and for prajna intuition, to "perfect knowledge" ("face to face" in 1 Cor 13:12).[109]

But the experience of Moses on Sinai in which God reveals to him his name, and the image of the mirror which the Apostle Paul uses for his knowledge of God and the self are at best appropriate in a formal way for enlightenment with which Suzuki deals insofar as in both instances a "breakthrough" occurs. For neither with Moses nor with Paul does this breakthrough consist of an over-flowing of ordinary self-consciousness from the sphere of the unconscious, however much it deals with extraordinary happening. But as little as "the voice of the living God" belongs in Zen enlightenment, does Suzuki wish to assert that in prajna intuition he "see[s] God as he is in himself." Such objectifications are not compatible with the nature of satori and prajna. Thus in a discussion of the content of the phenomena which he regards as somewhat related, Suzuki refrains from examples drawn from the biblical sphere. Basically they are meant only to serve to bring the Far Eastern Buddhist thought world, which appears to the Western Christian hearer or reader strange and difficult to follow, closer to him and to make it more understandable.

No less valid than these parallels of the relation to transcendence of the Buddhist and Christian types of spirituality is the opposition which Suzuki constructs at the end of the entire series of lectures between the conceptions of love which mutually issue from them, as he explains:

> Love as it is understood by the Buddhists lacks the demonstrative feature of eroticism which we observe strongly manifested by some of the Christian saints. Their love is directed in a very special way toward Christ, whereas Buddhists (Suzuki thinks, in this connection) have almost nothing to do with Buddha but with their fellow beings, nonsentient as well as sentient. Their

---

[106]Ibid., 33ff.
[107]Ibid., 54.
[108]Ibid., 47.
[109]Ibid., 57.

love manifests itself in the form of ungrudged and self-sacrificing labor for others.[110]

Actually in their love the Christians—and not only "several of their saints"—are "directed," like the Buddhists, in a "totalistic intuition" "to the infinite, which envelops everything finite," but "in very special ways to Christ," because "the infinite" is revealed in a very special way and becomes effective—and this precisely in the way Suzuki claims exclusively for Buddhist love.

As for the rest there is in addition to Zen Buddhism also Amida Buddhism which knows—even if not unequivocally—of the "infinite" in its personification in different manifestations of the Buddha in Amida who is more similar to Christ and who among his devotees approaches mystical eroticism no less than do "several Christian saints,"as is especially the case with the Myokonin, the "wonderfully happy men" of Amidism. Since Suzuki is just as concerned with this form of Buddhism as with Zen and takes a stand with respect to Christianity based on it, this gives us a reason in the following to attend to his conception and representation of Shin Buddhism.

4. Shin Buddhism and Christianity

As a more substantial document than that of the chapter on "Crucifixion and Enlightenment" in his book *The Western and Eastern Way* which we dealt with earlier,[111] we select from his *Collected Works on Shin Buddhism* the comparison he made *between Christianity and Buddhism* in a longer "Miscellany on the Shin Teaching of Buddhism" in order to present *Suzuki's Shin Buddhism* and his attitude toward Christianity.[112] Of the ten different points he develops here in twelve pages in a very compact, systematic way he says that it is equally appropriate to "understand the characteristic teaching of Shin as a development of the Pure Land doctrine and also as a school of Mahayana Buddhism."[113]

First, Suzuki emphasizes that, in contrast to the Christian conception of God, Amida is "neither creator nor author of evil"; rather, "all [evils] in the world are our own doings." He even says that what we do as karma-conditioned individuals is "necessarily evil," and explains this by saying that we "are always conscious of what we do" and that it is "this very awareness that destroys the merit of goodness." For "good men cease to be good as soon as they become conscious of their goodness and attempt to make something out of it."

---

[110]Ibid., 75.

[111]Cf. 46-47n.40 in chap. 1.

[112]*Collected Writings on Shin Buddhism*, 57-69. The foreword to this collection in which this "5th Miscellany" is to be found is dated "May and August 1949 Kamakura and Honolulu."

[113]Ibid., 57.

But Amida knows of this being determined by *karma* which in Suzuki's view appears in place of the authorship of evil in the thoughts about the Creator and makes "the idea of selfhood" a "hindrance to entering into the Pure Land." As "the pure embodiment of love" Amida makes "no distinction between evildoers and good men." He "has no idea to discipline beings" and "keeps away from the responsibilities and relativities of this dualistic world," but is rather "a kind of melting-pot of good and evil in which faith alone retains its absolute value." "Whoever believes in him as saviour is sure of being taken up by him into his Pure Land."

Second, Suzuki establishes that in Christianity "God requires a mediator," who "is sacrificed as an innocent victim in order to save souls," while "in Shin Amida performs to some extent the office of God and also that of Christ" through his vow, so that here "the vow is the mediator." In the Christian doctrine of redemption God's action does not seem "fair" to him in view of the fact that the souls to be redeemed "are not necessarily responsible for their unrighteousness because they are born so." He always concedes that "the Christian experience has at least demonstrated a pragmatic value for it." He also concedes that in Christianity "concrete images" are used, whereas in Shin "words and phrases, more or less abstract in a sense," are available for the work of the mediator, as is apparent from the Namu Amida Butsu.

Third, if however the Christians for their religion like to appeal to "historical facts" as its solid and objective foundation, and Shin Buddhism on the contrary is a "metaphysical reconstruction" of general religious ideas, Suzuki actually views this as the "basic difference" between Christianity and Shin; but he remarks at the same time that "truth is neither subjective nor objective," and that there is "no more reality in what is known as a so-called historical fact than in what is considered psychological or metaphysical." In many cases "historicity is a mere fiction." As a spatiotemporal magnitude history depends upon "intellectual reconstruction." Yet religious faith wants to "grasp what is not conditioned by time and space," and arises out of "what lies behind historical facts," namely, a "Reality that transcends the polarization of subject and object." History is *karmic,* but Shin strives for the *"akarmic* or that which is not historical." Yet this is Amida's way. He stands akarmically "above *karma,*" that is, "all historical facts, all *karmic* events have their origin in [him] and return to him."

The *fourth* pair of opposites Suzuki holds before us is that of the "crucified Christ" and the Buddha, who "at his Nirvana lies quietly on his bed surrounded by all beings including the birds of the air and the beasts of the field" or is also "represented as sitting in meditation, symbol of eternal tranquility." The following position should serve as a certain explanation of the way Suzuki here gives renewed expression to his abhorrence of the image of the Crucified attested in other places:

The agony of crucifixion, death, and resurrection making up the contents of the Christian faith, have significance only when the background impregnating old tradition is taken into consideration, and this background is wholly wanting in Buddhists who have been reared in an atmosphere different not only historically but intellectually and emotionally.

Whereas there seems to be accordingly no access for Suzuki to an understanding of the significance of the crucifixion, he would like to assume—*fifth*—a certain "correspondence" between the Christian concept of vicarious atonement and the Buddhist concept of merit-transference, but only in relation to the "transference" insofar as "it is the merit accumulated by the Bodhisattva that is desired to be transferred to other beings" in order thereby to bring the whole creation to enlightenment—but not in the sense of an atonement which consists in "somebody being sacrificed for the fault of others" for "there is no idea of atonement in Buddhism, especially in Shin." According to the teaching of Shin, Amida "has no intention to interfere with the working of *karma*, for it has to run its whole course in this world." Everyone has to pay for his guilt "by himself—not by another." "But the mysterious power of Amida's Name and Vow—which is the mystery of life to be simply accepted as such, all the logical contradictions notwithstanding—lifts his offender from the curse of karma and carries him to the Land of Purity and Happiness, where he attains his supreme enlightenment." In a way similar to "how Christians feel assured of vicarious atonement when their faith is confirmed in Christ," "the akarmic power works quite unknowingly to the karma-bearer himself." "But he begins"—as Suzuki describes the "transfer of merit" which ensues—to realize this "fact" of the effective power of the Buddha, that is, the secret power of Amida's name and vow, "as soon as faith in Amida is awakened in him." "Faith works this miracle in his consciousness. Although he knows he is subject to the law of karma and may have to go on committing deeds of karma in spite of himself, his inmost consciousness, once his faith is established, tells him that he is bound for Amida's Land at the end of his karmic life on this earth. It is by this inmost consciousness in the Shin devotee that the truth of merit-transference is demonstrated." "Whatever theological and ethical interpretation may be given to this, the truth or fact, psychologically speaking, remains the same with Christians and Buddhists; it is the experience of a leap from the relative plane of consciousness to the Unconscious."

After breaking off any discussion which simultaneously opens the possibility of a new dialogue it is not surprising when Suzuki suddenly assigns a possible positive use not only to Christian notions like resurrection and ascension, but also to the notions of crucifixion and resurrection which he previously so decisively rejected, explaining the first in the sense of "rebirth in the Pure Land and enlightenment," while bringing crucifixion and death into connection with the "abandoning of self-power" (*jiriki*) which occurs for the Shin followers "at [the] moment they utter from the depths of their being the *Namu-amida-butsu*."

Supposing that "Christians may not agree with this form of interpretation" because they "love to ascribe all such experiences to Christ himself while their individual human salvation is regarded to come from believing in supernatural events"—which in his opinion thoroughly corresponds to the "genius of the Jewish tradition"—Suzuki questions whether when they say "to die in Adam and live in Christ," they mean "going through all the spiritual experiences individually and personally of Christ himself" "or a "believing in Christ as divine mediator."

Sixth, after the critical conclusion of this substantial and conciliatory section we are not surprised when Suzuki strikes a different note in the next. By means of the Bodhisattva ideal and a certain Christian future blessedness he believes that he can demonstrate here "that the Buddhists work for salvation of their fellow beings whereas the Christians are busy with their self-salvation and that the former are socialistically motivated and the latter individualistically." The return of the Bodhisattvas from the Pure Land is grounded in the compassion with which they are filled in contrast to the still unenlightened and which allows them to use the Pure Land only as a kind of "railroad station" between departures and return, but also in that fact that they "would be bored to death" in the land which should provide life. He caricatures the Christians because "when once in Heaven [the Christians] show no desire to come back to their former home, although they may not know what to do up there in company with Christ and the angels." This is the reason "some Christians of modern days bring the kingdom of God down on earth, the realization of which is their aim while here."

This point is hardly more substantially expanded in section *seven* under the rubric of the "difference between redemption and enlightenment." "Shin followers desire enlightenment and not salvation." "Christians aim at salvation and not at enlightenment." Suzuki arrives at these assertions which do not exactly arise from enlightenment because he thinks "Christian piety" consists of "saving one's soul from damnation," whereas Buddhists know that there is no redemption from the karma corresponding to sins, but only rebirth in the Pure Land which is the same as enlightenment.

After this identification of enlightenment with the Pure Land it remains for Suzuki—*eighth*—to answer the question as to where it is neither in terms of "orthodox Shin interpretation" nor purely rationally. "Do not ask questions, for their solution is in you and does not come from the mouth of the teachers." As an example of this he mentions a Shin follower who, when asked whether Amida is capable of helping us out of karma, answered: "You are not helped by him!" Such "genuine religious faith" he recommends even to Christians.

Ninth, he explains "the mysterious power of Amida's name and vow, which "has nothing corresponding to it" in Christianity, religiously as magic; epistemologically by reference to the "creativity of the naming"; psychologically, pedagogically, as it occurs in the recitation of *Na-mu-a-mi-da-bu-tsu* in the Jodo Shu; and metaphysically, that is, authentically, as the answer of the "inner Amida" who is "awakened in us in faith" and in reference to the call of Amida who is "the Buddha of Infinite Light and Eternal Life," in accord with the understanding of the Jodoshinshu. The ideal solution consists in the fact that repeated "pronouncing of the name (*shomyo*)" in meditation becomes identical with "the thinking of the Buddha (*Nembutsu*)," which Suzuki sees as the ultimate possible common feature of the two manifestations of Honen's Pure Land Buddhism and Shinran's followers.

But Suzuki does not widen the gap farther, for he not only combines the two schools of the Pure Land with respect to their ultimate intention, but—at least in one sentence—refers to the historical connection between Pure Land Buddhism and Zen, of which he writes: "Historically the shomyo practice is related to the koan exercise in Zen Buddhism." He refers to this in his deliberations in the second volume of his *Essays in Zen Buddhism*,[114] where he extensively wrote on the "Koan Exercise and the Nembutsu," and clarified why and how Zen and Amida Buddhism are related to each other, for which Suzuki Shosan is presented as an impressive example.[115]

After this extension of Nembutsu praxis to its possible relation to the koan praxis in Zen and even to the use of the daranis, the magical formulas of mantric Buddhism, it suits Suzuki once again to emphasize the uniqueness of Shin, and he does this by stating at the conclusion of his *tenth* point that "the Original Vow is the expression of Amida's Will or Karuna (Love or Compassion) which he cherishes over all beings." The Original Vow is "Amida's heart which is with him from the beginningless past." "[It] awakens in us what corresponds to it but lies in us quite latently." When Suzuki says of Amida's Will and our faith that they are consubstantial, that is, "there is a perfect correspondence between the two concepts of reality," this prompts us to think of the *consubstantialitas*, which obtains between God and his Son according to the trinitarian-Christological dogma, whereby prajna assumes the function of the Holy Spirit, and the emergence of Amida from his meditation in order "to communicate with [us] karma-bound beings," of the redemptive event of the *Opera Trinitatis ad extra*, wherein Amida, who is "also the embodiment of Karuna," corresponds to the incarnation of God in Christ.

Suzuki finally characterizes the parallelism and difference between the two doctrines of salvation as follows:

> The mysterious power abiding in the Original Vow is the mystery of Amida himself, who, in the terminology of Shin, is Infinite Light and Eternal Life.

---

[114]*Essays in Zen Buddhism*, 2nd ser. 5th ed. (London: Rider, 1974) 146-99.
[115]Cf. Winston King, "Suzuki Shosan, Wayfarer," EB 12/1 (1979): 83-103.

In Christianity God's will or love of humanity, I may say, is expressed in the crucifixion of his only son, that is, as a concrete event in the history of karma-bound beings; whereas in Shin Buddhism Amida's will takes the form of intense determination and its solemn declaration. The latter may seem insipid, inane, and evaporating compared to the Christian realism. But in point of fact the Shin together with its parental Jodo has been the most irresistably inspiring power in the history of Far Eastern Buddhism, and this power has been exercised without ever shedding blood, without committing cruelties, without persecuting heresies.

As an expansion of what Suzuki has developed in these ten points about Amida and his vow, an essay on "Amitabha, the Buddha of Infinite Light" can be drawn upon which appeared at approximately the same time as the prior one referred to from the lectures apparently delivered in California.[116] In a somewhat

---

[116]"Infinite Light," EB 4/2 (1971): 1-29. The essay is included in the *Collected Writings on Shin Buddhism*, 129-52.

Besides this and the other essays contained in this collection on Shin Buddhism, two other publications may be mentioned which stem from a series of lectures on this subject which Suzuki delivered in 1958 in New York, and in 1963 at Otani University, which are instructive for his understanding of this brand of Buddhism and show that he—precisely in confrontation with Christianity—understood himself equally as a Shin or Zen Buddhist: *Amida—der Buddha der Liebe* (Bern: Wilhelm Barth and Scherz Verlag, 1970 (German translation from the English original, *Shin Buddhism*) and "Thoughts on Shin Buddhism," EB 13/2 (1980): 1-15; 14/1 (1981): 13-25; 14/2 (1981): 1-10.

In both lecture series Suzuki once again takes up the theme of God's revealing his name to Moses which was mentioned without commentary in the Eranos Lecture of 1954 (n. 8), seeing in the "I am that I am" (Exod 3:14) a self-assertion of the Enlightened One. In the New York lectures he justified this interpretation with the "spiritual" vagueness of the Chinese and Japanese language which facilitates it, especially in relation to the use of pronouns ("Amida, der Buddha der Liebe," 83). In the second lecture at Otani University he appealed to the "softness or flexibility of heart" of believers in Amida that "pervades . . . and accept[s] everything that is," and makes him confess: "Whether we say, 'I am that I am,' or 'I am the God who is,' either way it means the same thing (i.e. what Shakyamuni was supposed to have said after his Enlightenment) as 'Above the heavens, below the heavens, I alone am revered' " ("Thoughts on Shin Buddhism," EB 14/1 [1981]: 17ff., 22, 23-24).

In the third lecture—by appealing to the notion that the name, in contrast to a mere sign, is simultaneously the named reality (EB 14/2 [1981]: 2-3)—he describes the identity-in-difference of the awakened believer with the Namu Amida Butsu as the effect of the "power of Amida's Vow" (ibid., 6-7), which, like the "music of the Harp of Asura," flows spontaneously without a player (ibid., 9), yet at the same time letting him attain a "second childhood" in

Scholastic way, from the concept of Infinite Light and the statements about it contained in sutras and hymns, Suzuki even derives the power penetrating hell[117] which bestows "the other power" upon the vow of Buddha[118] which as "other power" overcomes its "self-power" in our "empirical self" and in "faith [as] enlightenment experience"[119] secures acknowledgement for the vow.[120] This "our inmost experience" rests for him likewise on "scriptural authority" in that he says that the latter is "supported" by the former,[121] as this is attested in the tradition, above all in the "Wasan," Shinran's "Songs in Praise of Amitabha,"[122] and the Myokonin.[123] But he includes himself and his hearers in this tradition by explaining: "From the point of view of the religious consciousness Ananda and the whole congregation including the Buddha himself are no other than ourselves who are gathered here tonight."[124] Therefore he deems it necessary after he discusses the three most important of the forty-eight vows of Amida[125] and had related vows seventeen and forty-seven to these,[126] to "translate" the former three "into more humanly understandable language."

---

existence as play.

[117]EB 4/2 (1971): 5ff. [CW, 133ff.].

[118]Ibid., 19ff. [CW, 146ff.].

[119]Ibid., 21 [CW, 147].

[120]Ibid., 23ff. [CW, 150ff.].

[121]Ibid., 11 [CW, 139].

[122]Ibid., 2, 7, 14 [CW, 129, 135, 142].

[123]Ibid., 8, 12, 17 [CW, 135, 140, 144]. On Suzuki's high estimate of the Myokonin, cf. the instructive article by Bando Shojun, "D. T. Suzuki and Pure Land," EB 14/2 (1981): 132-36.

[124]Ibid., 15 [CW, 142].

[125]Ibid., 19ff. [CW, 196-97].

[126]In his translation of and commentary on all forty-eight vows contained in the "Sutra of Eternal Life" (*Collected Writings on Shin Buddhism*, 42ff.) Suzuki indicates that Shinran did not understand the twentieth vow which corresponds to his doctrine of grace in its original historical sense, in that he read the Chinese characters in such a way that—instead of a turning of the merits of those who have died toward Amida—there results a turning of the merit of Amida toward the believers who are dependent upon his "grace alone" (ibid., 50 and 72ff.). Cf. his discussion of *eko* ("turning over," that is, "merit-transference") in the glossary to his translation of the Kyogyoshinsho [*The Kyogyoshinsho: The Collection of Passages Expounding the True Teaching, Living, Faith, and of Realizing the Pure Land*, trans. Daisetz Teitaro Suzuki, ed. the Eastern Buddhist Society (Kyoto: Shinshu Otaniha, 1973) 213ff. —Trans.] and in *Essays in Zen Buddhism* 3:334n.1.

In order to compare this "translation," which represents an existential interpretation of the mythology of the Pure Land in the best sense, the three vows which are to be demythologized and explained existentially are reproduced here:

18. If, upon my obtaining Buddhahood, all beings in the ten quarters should not desire in sincerity and trustfulness to be born in my country, and if they should not be born there by only thinking of me for say, up to ten times, except those who have committed the five grave offences and those who are abusive of the true Dharma, may I not attain the Highest Enlightenment.
19. If, upon my obtaining Buddhahood, all beings in the ten quarters awakening their thoughts to enlightenment and practicing all deeds of merit should cherish the desire in sincerity to be born in my country and if I should not, surrounded by a large company, appear before them at the time of their death, may I not attain the Highest Enlightenment.
20. If, upon my obtaining Buddhahood, all beings in the ten quarters hearing my Name should cherish the thought of my country and planting all the roots of merit turn them in sincerity over to being born in my country, and if they should fail in obtaining the result of it, may I not attain the Highest Enlightenment.

And now Suzuki's "translation":

After a good night's sleep, I get up. The sun is shining into the room, a refreshing breeze comes through the windows, I breathe deeply. Probably I had a dream, but I do not remember now what it was. I am ready for the day's work. I meet people, greet them, and they greet me back. They look pleased, so am I. As I am a writer, I sit by the desk, take up my pen, or have the typewriter ready. I collect my thoughts, or look up books needed for reference. After some hours' work I feel tired. I go down into the garden, take a walk among flowers, for I like them, and the garden is filled with them. About this time of the year in Japan, the morning glories begin to shoot out their young tender leaves. It is interesting to watch them grow. They have to be carefully taken care of if we wish to see them bloom fine in summer. When the summer comes the first thing I do in the morning is to go around in the garden and admire the flowers refreshingly full of life. They can well be compared with those lotus flowers blooming in the water of merits in the Pure Land. Nature is generally thought to be dumb, but the trouble is not on her side, but on ours: she speaks eloquently in her own way and it is we who fail to understand her. In the Pure Land every tree, every leaf, every flower is described as singing in praise of the triple treasure. So do things on this side of the world. Swedenborg's doctrine of correspondence holds good in Buddhism too. Amida's light illuminates this *sahaloka* [land of suffering] as much as the Pure Land. Amida attained his enlightenment and his Pure Land came into existence. We attain ours and this *sahaloka* too must transform itself into a Pure Land. When we have our absolute faith established firmly in Amida, we do not go to Amida's Pure Land, but the Pure Land comes to us along with Amida. Amida is born in our minds with his Land. This *sahaloka* becomes a Pure Land, and we Amida. For are we not devoted followers of tariki, the other-power? After this musing I come back to my study and resume my work. The inner world is another "nature." Beautiful flowers are here along with rampant weeds; the sweet-singing birds are here along with poisonous snakes; the star sprinkled skies reflect themselves on mud-filled ponds perhaps harboring noxious plants. All kinds of bonno [illusions] are in company with high-flying ideals and a tenderly yielding heart.[127]

After such a swift "mental journey" in his Pure Land at Suzuki's side, one could only wish that he had tested the existential interpretation, whose mythological form appeared strange to him, by the Christian tradition which appeared strange to him—as it does in many respects to us—or had at least taken notice of the fact that today not a few of his Christian contemporaries do precisely this. They do so, to be sure, not merely—to speak further in his language of flowers—as enthusiastic strollers but as gardeners who know themselves to be entrusted by the master of the garden with its care and therefore do not permit everything to grow and live, but uproot and discard some—as this happens in the real Japanese garden, as is well known, whereby the artificiality and deformation of nature seem to be less adequate—even in the thoughts of both Buddhists and Christian theologians! That must await future encounters.

---

[127]EB 4/2 (1971): 26 [CW, 152].

Chapter 5

Shin'ichi Hisamatsu (1889–1980)
Atheistic Buddhism

1. A Learned Zen Master

Hoseki Shin'ichi Hisamatsu does not belong to the founding generation of the Kyoto School, for he was nineteen years younger than Nishida and Suzuki, and although he survived Tanabe and for decades was the much respected Nestor of the Kyoto School, he has not attained the commanding significance which was ascribed to those three in the history of the school. But he belonged to it as far as his education and scholarship were concerned, but also with respect to the form of his philosophy in which specific characteristics of this school found expression.

As far as his university training is concerned, Hisamatsu studied under Nishida at the then Imperial University of Kyoto from 1912 to 1915, and after concluding his studies, upon Nishida's recommendation he entered a Rinzai Zen monastery. After he served as Privatdozent at several universities, he worked from 1932 to 1949 at Kyoto University where from 1943 on he held a professorship of Philosophy of Religion and Buddhism. After his resignation from this position he delivered further lectures at universities in the environs of Kyoto, as well as also in America, such as, for example, in 1957/1958 simultaneously with Suzuki at Harvard University, where he met with Paul Tillich. Following this visit to America he undertook a lecture tour through Europe, the Near East, Iran, and India, where he spoke of Zen culture. Returning home, he transformed the "Seminar for Learners of the Way"—founded through his initiative at the University of Kyoto at the end of the world war and directed by him—into the F.A.S. Zen Institute. F.A.S. is the abbreviation for "Formless Self—All Mankind—Superhistorical History," by which its meaning and purpose are known, and for whose realization this institute was intended.[1]

But it is not only the lengthy relationship to Kyoto University that connects Hisamatsu to its great philosophical tradition; rather, he stands in close

---

[1] Cf. the statements about the author in Hisamatsu's *Die Fülle des Nichts* (Neske, 1975) 66-67, and in *Die Fünf Stände* (Neske, 1980) 87ff., above all EB 14/1 (1981) with seven contributions on the person and work of Hisamatsu as well as an index of his writings, photographs, and one of his calligraphic works. On the significance of F.A.S. see "Redemption" in EB 8/2 (1975): 57ff., and F.A.S. newsletters edited by the FAS Society Office in Kyoto.

Shin'ichi Hisamatsu (1889–1980)

relationship to this by his philosophical work, and through the fact that therein two special possible forms appear: on the one hand, its possible atheistic character and, on the other, its applicability in the understanding of art and culture. With respect to the first-named characteristic Hisamatsu differentiated himself from his teacher Nishida and especially from Tanabe, in that for him a positive connection of Zen and Shin Buddhism is possible only on an "atheistic basis." Nevertheless, he shared the interest in art and culture with Nishida and above all, with Suzuki. As the long-term elder and, in his way, special representative of the Kyoto philosophy, he emphatically represented the line that leads from Nishida, continues in Nishitani, but stands in opposition to that of Tanabe and his student Takeuchi.

If the literary work of Hisamatsu is not as extensive as that of his predecessors—his *Collected Works* which have appeared since 1970 comprise nine volumes—because of its two special directions we mentioned it nevertheless forms an important bridge connecting the earlier and contemporary generations of the Kyoto School.[2] Precisely because of his rejection of any theism in favor of an "autonomous heteronomy," Hisamatsu became—as he was called—the "Reformer of Zen Buddhism in Japan,"[3] but also an interesting conversation partner for Christian theology, as is evident from the Christian philosopher Katsumi Takizawa, who translated Hisamatsu's essay on "Atheism" for a colloquium held at the Missionsakademie of the University of Hamburg in 1978.[4] Also his conversation with Dr. and Mrs. Tillich and Richard de Martino represents a piece of evidence for the significance of the personality of Hisamatsu for East-West dialogue.[5] Hisamatsu's text on "Oriental Nothingness" already published in 1939, proved very helpful for the dialogue between East and West—a text that has since appeared both in English as well as German translation.[6] A contribution by

---

[2]In his contribution to the volume of tribute to Suzuki, entitled "Daisetz Suzuki and Shin'ichi Hisamatsu," Jikai Fujiyoshi reported that Hisamatsu called Suzuki his "Uncle in the Dharma," whereas Nishida was for him his "Father in the Dharma." EB 2/1 (1967): 193.

[3]*Die Fülle des Nichts*, 67.

[4]"Atheismus, mit Vorbemerkungen von Hans Waldenfels," *Zeitschrift für Missionswissenschaft und Religionswissenschaft* 4 (1978): 268-96.

[5]"Dialogues, East and West. Conversations between Dr. Paul Tillich and Dr. Hisamatsu Shin'ichi," EB 4/2 (1971): 89-107; 5/2 (1972): 107-28; 6/2 (1973): 87-114.

[6]"The Characteristics of Oriental Nothingness." *Philosophical Studies of Japan*, vol. 2 (Japanese National Commission for UNESCO, 1960) 65-97; Hisamatsu, *Die Fülle des Nichts: Vom Wesen des Zen* (Neske, 1975). [Text here follows German version cited by Buri.]

Hisamatsu on "satori" was rightly included by Yagi and Luz in their collection *Gott in Japan*.[7] Moreover we have available to us a series of essays by Hisamatsu that appeared in English translation in *The Eastern Buddhist*, the most important of which are "Ultimate Crisis and Resurrection," "Ordinary Mind," "Zen: Its Meaning for Modern Civilization," and "Zen as the Negation of Holiness."[8] To his revered friend Suzuki he dedicated a very personal "Mondo" in the memorial volume for the former.[9] His work on *Zen and the Fine Arts*, which is most characteristic of his special interest, represents the most extensive publication of Hisamatsu's available to us, a work in which he, in terms of rich material, presented his philosophy as the key for the understanding of Japanese Zen art.[10]

With these we have indicated the most important of Hisamatsu's publications available to us, on the basis of which we can form a picture of his philosophy which, despite its impressive comprehensiveness, exhibits many inner tensions and evident problems. If the publications we previously mentioned furnish sufficient occasion for critical reflections, we shall at the conclusion of this chapter make reference to two publications that appeared after Hisamatsu's death on 27 February 1980: his deliberations on "Die fünf Stände von Zen-Meister Tosan Ryokai" ("The Five Stations of the Zen Master Tosan Ryokai"), and his exposition of the "Rinzai Text." Also for this purpose we shall take into consideration a qualified evaluation of his "Philosophy of Awakening" (cf. the bibliographical items in nn. 205 and 236).

His "The Characteristics of Oriental Nothingness" which was the first to be translated into English and has since been translated into German, is best suited to serve as an introduction to Hisamatsu's thinking, principally because we are familiar with its epistemological foundations. Therefore we shall begin with it in order to represent the connection in which this thinking of Nothingness stands to Hisamatsu's understanding of Zen art. A pursuit of his conversation with Paul Tillich and relevant references from his individual essays already mentioned will serve us in making the transition to the resulting anthropology, metaphysics, and ethics. For those central themes of his philosophy we shall appeal to the important essays on "Ultimate Crisis and Resurrection" and "Atheismus," both of

---

[7] "Satori (Selbsterwachen). Zum postmodernen Menschenbild," in *Gott in Japan*. ed. Yagi Seiichi and Ulrich Luz (Chr. Kaiser, 1973) 127-38.

[8] "Crisis and Resurrection. Part I. Sin and Death," EB 8/1 (1975): 12-30; "Part II. Redemption," EB 8/2 (1975): 37-66; "Ordinary Mind," EB 12/1 (1979): 1-29 (Japanese, 1941); "Zen: Its Meaning for Modern Civilization," EB (1965): 22-47; "Zen as Negation of Holiness," EB 10/1 (1977): 1-12 (orig. 1937).

[9] "Mondo: At the Death of a 'Great Death-Man'," EB 2/1 (1967): 29-34.

[10] *Zen and the Fine Arts* (Kodansha International, 1971; [2]1974; European ed., Boxerbooks [Zurich]).

which belong to his final publications and represent a survey of his view of Buddhism and his discussion with Western thinking and Christianity.

2. The Tractate on Nothingness

The treatise on "The Characteristics of Oriental Nothingness," or *Die Fülle des Nichts,* which stems from the year 1939,[11] with its differentiated conceptuality seems like a medieval scholastic tractate, which is all the more remarkable because its object is no object and for this reason cannot be conceived in concepts. But "in order to help the seeker for truth" Hisamatsu is prepared to take upon himself "the insurmountable fate that awaits any conceptual explanation of this nothingness."[12] In a "negative delineation of Zen Buddhist nothingness"[13] he presents by means of five "ordinary" terms for nothingness what nothingness is not, in order then in the second half to attempt to present its nature positively.[14]

The distinctive artful systematization does not quite succeed, in that in the first part the usual concepts of nothingness which are measured by the essential characteristics of Zen Buddhist nothingness and are judged as unsatisfactory for these. Although Hisamatsu explains that "those are univocally distinguished from these,"[15] he acknowledges at the conclusion of this contrast that "strong similarities" obtain between them, to which he then appeals in the second positive part, in which he undertakes "to express in words what is directly observed in deep experience."[16]

In the first part the Zen contents of experience (*Erlebnis* and *Erfahrung*) are contrasted with the otherwise usual concepts of nothingness, are not completely mutually exclusive, but blend with each other, because in their nature they form a whole, and are confronted as such with differentiating conceptual thinking and therefore cannot adequately be comprehended by it. The result is that this fundamental structural difference of the two realms gets worked out only in the second part in that the contrasts only partly observed previously are displaced, because the positive characteristics of Zen Buddhist nothingness are now so abundant that, like the two, they are partly related to one of the terms which are

---

[11]If not otherwise noted, we cite in the following from the German translation of *Die Fülle des Nichts* prepared by Takashi Hirata and Johanna Fischer and edited by Eberhard Cold (Neske Verlag), whose cover is illustrated with the characters from the Japanese word "Mu" (Nothingness) painted by Hisamatsu in "meditative concentration."

[12]*Die Fülle des Nichts.* 9-10.

[13]Ibid., 11ff.

[14]Ibid., 25ff.

[15]Ibid., 13.

[16]Ibid., 22.

judged to be unsatisfactory. Accordingly the scale vanishes and their "fullness" extends beyond the original five and requires a sixth aspect.

The principal difficulty with the cognitive conception of Zen Buddhist nothingness which is here attempted consists in the fullness of meaning of the expression "kokoro" or "shin" which corresponds to it as the place of experience in human—terms which are rendered in English translation by "mind" or "mindfulness" and in German by "Herz" (heart) or "Herz-Natur" (heart-nature)—and of which one never knows whether in its enactment it is subject or object, because it transcends the subject-object schema of conceptual thinking. The thought nothingness is not exactly nothing, just as the thinking self is quite different from the thought self. But let us see how Hisamatsu carries out his conceptual systematization of nothingness which resists both concept and system—a nothingness which for him is at the same time the "true self"—and whether he succeeds in making it familiar to us as "something alive"!

The five types of nothingness Hisamatsu considers as "failing to correspond to the nothingness of Zen" are:

First: "Nothingness as the negation of being," whether of an individual being or of all being.

Second: "Nothingness as a predicative negation," whether concerning an individual subject or whether as a total negation in the sense of "all other than" or permitting no subject at all.

Third: "Nothingness as an abstract concept," that is, nothingness in contrast with being.

Fourth: "Nothingness as a conjecture" of a definite thing or person, for example, in statements like": I am not," or "The whole of Being is not."

Fifth: "Nothingness as absence of consciousness," in so far as for a person in deep sleep or in unconsciousness or in death or in a wakeful state of un-consciousness there are no definite things or no things at all.[17]

By means of Zen sayings[18] partially very forcibly interpreted by him on the basis of which he also engages in criticism of traditional Buddhist concepts,[19] he contrasts these five types of nothingness with the nature of "Zen Buddhist nothingness."

---

[17]Ibid., 11-12.
[18]E.g., ibid., 13.
[19]E.g., ibid., 16 and 18, 20-21 and 43-44.

First, in respect to the first example, not in "negation of being," but "only in nothingness as Zen itself, or otherwise stated, in self-awakening"[20] there is "nothing which as being could be so addressed."[21]

Similarly he remarks on the second example, that—in contrast to its nothingness as a negative predication about something—Zen Buddhist nothingness excludes every statement and conceptual determination about itself." For this reason it deals with something quite different than when in Christianity God, or in Buddhism, the Buddha nature or Nirvana is occasionally defined as nothingness.[22]

Over against the idea of nothingness in the third example he holds that its nothingness "necessarily stands in contrast to Being" and therefore is different from the Buddhist "emptiness" of "absolute nothingness," which is located beyond being and nonbeing."[23]

Because the nothingness of Zen Buddhism is quite different from the "conjecture" of the fourth example, he refers [us] to the "immersion in the Buddha image" which is only genuine when "heart and object" are forgotten and "the looking itself is the Buddha nature."[24]

The same holds true with respect to the "unconsciousness" of the fifth example, because the "Great Death," which is at the same time "the Great Awakening," is not a matter of "unconsciousness," but of a "state of extreme clarity" comparable to a "polished mirror."[25]

After this fivefold contrast Hisamatsu notes nevertheless: "False interpretations are bound to arise because the similarities are so strong."[26] But, he continues, "unless one draws upon these aspects of everyday nothingness, the nothingness of Zen can scarcely be expressed."[27] The concept of similarity which Hisamatsu repeatedly uses as a designation of the relation of the concept of nothingness to what is meant by them in Zen obviously represents a parallel to the Catholic doctrine of analogy,[28] except that for Hisamatsu it is not a matter of an analogy of being, an *analogia entis*, but of an analogy of nothingness, an *analogia nullius rei*. If he says of nothingness, of which he can only necessarily

---

[20]In the English translation it reads: "in and for Oriental Nothingness-in-itself or in-Its-Self-Inner-Realization" (68).

[21]*Die Fülle des Nichts*, 13-14.

[22]Ibid. 16ff.

[23]Ibid., 16-17.

[24]Ibid., 18-19.

[25]Ibid., 20-21.

[26]Ibid., 22.

[27]Ibid., 23.

[28]*Inter creatorem et creaturam non potest similtudo notari, quin inter eos maior sit dissimilitudo notanda* (Denz., 806).

speak in inadequate concepts, that it must be "immediately experienced in itself," and that "for the nothingness of Zen personal experience is an unconditional necessity";[29] and if he cites a Zen saying in this connection in which it says, "Yet since man is ignorant and caught in delusion, many Buddhas again appear on earth and give it (the truth) a provisional name,"[30] it follows that he is not dealing merely with an *analogia nullius rei*, but—*sit venia verbo*—with an *analogia nullius rei in experientia naturae Buddhae*, which would be parallel to the *analogia entis in Christo*.[31]

We need to return to the perspective that is important for understanding and evaluating Hisamatsu's philosophy. As is always the case with him, so in the second part in a series of aspects which corresponds somewhat to the division of the first, he develops with the aid of conceptual distinctions what constitutes the "true nature" of Zen Buddhist nothingness on the basis of his "own experience" in "direct perception" and "direct knowledge," in relation to which, because it is said to be "direct being," that is, nothingness' "one's own knowledge of the true essence," "a conceptual formulation is completely excluded."[32]

It turns out that these "positive explanations of Zen Buddhist nothingness,"[33] whose subject is Hisamatsu himself who makes these statements, while according to his statements it is a matter of his "own knowledge" of nothingness, in which this "demonstrates itself,"[34] can only result in logical contradictions which above all have the effect that one does not know who is actually speaking here, and what is meant in the speaking. This logical inconsistency and conceptual vagueness already appears in the first section of "positive delineations,"[35] which is entitled "The 'Not a Single Thing' or the Complete Indeterminability," and is related to the first two examples of "negative delineations." Of the state to be attained in "immersion," in which the self becomes nothingness, he here writes: "But as long as there is consciousness in me which contains the nothingness as object, I am not really in a state of nothingness."[36] In the following section on "emptiness"[37] we read nevertheless: "But Zen Buddhist nothingness is in no way

---

[29]*Die Fülle des Nichts*, 22-23.

[30]Ibid., 23.

[31]On this Christological-existential doctrine of *analogia entis* and *analogia fidei*, cf. my *Dogmatik als Selbsverständnis des christlichen Glaubens*, vol. 3, the chap. on analogy, 632ff.

[32]Ibid., 24.

[33]Ibid., 25ff.

[34]Ibid., 24.

[35]Ibid., 25ff.

[36]Ibid., 27.

[37]Ibid., 30ff.

something unconscious and unexperienced," like "emptiness" is, but is the subject which "clearly and distinctly knows itself."[38] Who really knows of this subject in "self-forgetfulness"[39] or "emptiness" which is said to be "very similar," but may "not be identified" with it, because—in distinction to nothingness and its "heart nature"—it "possesses no heart"?[40]

The two sections on "Emptiness" and "The Heart"[41] together correspond to the "idea" as the third example of the first part. But while he there juxtaposes "emptiness" and "the absolute nothingness, which is to be found beyond being and nonbeing,[42] with "nothingness as idea" only as its negation which is of course logically correct, here where he attempts a "positive delineation," he falls into logical contradictions and paradoxes, because he says of the "heart" at the same time that it "is conscious of itself"[43] and that it maintains "the function of consciousness" "in the state of nonthinking," which is "the heart of the nonheart and nonthinking."[44]

What could be meant by this "heart" becomes clearer in the section on "The Self" which forms the "positive" correspondence to what is elucidated in the "negative" part on "conjecture."[45] Here he explains of this "true heart,"[46] that it is "not a heart" "which stands over against me as an object," but a heart which has become in me the subject, whose "activity" "means not being directed toward an object," but a subjective being."[47] In a way which is highly instructive for his view of the relation of Buddhism and Christianity he here exemplifies what he means by the "self," by appealing—in contrast to the way in which God in the Christian religion and, "very frequently also in Mahayana Buddhism," the Buddha are regarded "as the Other who stands over against"—to the Pauline "I live, yet not I, but Christ lives in me" (Gal 2:20) and to the corresponding commandment of the Jodo Shin sect, "to leave oneself in the hands of Buddha-Amitabha," with the result that "Christ and Amitabha can be designated as Other and at the same time as the subject."[48]

---

[38]Ibid., 34.
[39]Ibid., 29.
[40]Ibid., 39.
[41]Ibid., 39ff.
[42]Ibid., 17.
[43]Ibid., 40.
[44]Ibid., 41.
[45]Ibid., 42ff.
[46]Ibid., 41.
[47]Ibid., 42.
[48]Ibid., 43.

As meaningful as this paralleling, or identification, of Christ and Amitabha is, and he correctly contrasts it with the "subject as the naive self of modern Humanism,"[49] yet one cannot overlook the fact that with the Apostle Paul there is no passage in which he conceives his "Christ lives in me" as being identical with the Christ, or in which he thinks that Christ is "nothing other than one's own heart," as Hisamatsu represents them both in relation to the Buddha on the basis of numerous Buddhist texts. The "being in Christ" of the Apostle is quite different from the being-Buddha of the "true self" of the Buddhists, just as the Pauline dying and becoming buried with Christ is different from the "Great Death" of the Zen Buddhist which consists only in dying from one's self and in the knowledge of "one's own heart." Paul is rather to be found on the side of the Jodo-Shin-shu which Hisamatsu reproaches for presenting a "superficial exposition" of Dogen's demand to present body and soul to the Buddha and to conform to what occurs from it, and contrasts it with "the absolute subject" of the "Buddha heart."[50]

After Hisamatsu had already described differently the ethical consequences of the "self-hood character of Zen Buddhist nothingness"[51] in the preceding section,[52] he comes to speak expressly of the foundation of ethics in the "nothingness of Zen Buddhism" in the section entitled "Freedom and Unfetteredness."[53] To be sure, he emphasizes that Zen sayings such as "If you wish to go, then go; if you wish to sit, then sit" or "When you hunger, then eat; when you are exhausted sleep," do not mean "arbitrary freedom," but "unfetteredness" from all the bonds "of the absolute subject," which are acquired when "reason in the form of the discriminating understanding [is acknowledged] as the origin of all errors," as not only Buddhism teaches this, but also the biblical story of the Fall indicates.[54] "The task of religion" is to transcend the distinctions of right and wrong, good and evil, which indeed occurs in the Christian religion and in Jodo Shin Buddhism, but only in incomplete ways through the distinction between God and man, Buddha and the world, and the conception of God and the Buddha as "transcendent objects," whereas it is attained only in the "samadhi of the miraculous mirror" in the nothingness of Zen."[55]

---

[49]Ibid., 44.
[50]Ibid., 44-45.
[51]Ibid., 46.
[52]Ibid., 29, 32, 36, 38, and 44.
[53]Ibid., 47ff.
[54]Ibid., 48.
[55]Ibid., 50.

We need further to consider the "creative power" issuing from it, to the discussion of which Hisamatsu devotes a sixth section,[56] because we have already cited a lengthy excerpt from it in an earlier connection and have pointed to the problematic contained in it.[57] The expression "creative power" and the circumstance that Hisamatsu here contrasts the "God of Christianity" as the "perfect ideal of the Creator"[58] with "the 'heart which brings forth all things' of Buddhism,"[59] provide for us an occasion to represent the way in which Hisamatsu—following the example of his teacher Nishida—pursues this dimension of the creative in the realm of art and like Nishida, from an ethical perspective.[60]

3. Zen Art and Zen Ethics

While Nishida develops his connection of art and ethics in a very general and very abstract theory of artistic creativity—but in any case inspired by Zen—Hisamatsu in his richly illustrated volume *Zen and the Fine Arts* is concerned especially with Zen art, in order to portray on the basis of a fine-tuned analysis of a host of art works—as Suzuki does in *Zen and Japanese Culture*—how the nothingness of Zen has attained expression and received form in them. As in the writing on *Die Fülle des Nichts* whose inconceivability he attempts to conceive in the abstractness of differentiating conceptuality, so here he undertakes the same by means of distinctions of the peculiar characteristics of the forms of aesthetic expression. In this way this volume on art represents a visual presentation for the exercise of thinking in the tractate on nothingness.

For the systematic elucidations which he provides as descriptions of the pictorial materials comprising some 278 in all,[61] Hisamatsu uses a method similar to that of *Die Fülle des Nichts*, with the result that the two treatises are also comparable to one another in their structure. To the five examples of the "ordinary," "everyday aspects of nothingness" there correspond here "the seven essential characteristics," which can be established for Zen art—quite the same whether they deal with painting, calligraphy, ceramics, and so forth—and which make them recognizable as something special. They are (1) Asymmetry, (2) Simplicity, (3) Austere Sublimity or Lofty Dryness, (4) Naturalness, (5) Subtle Profundity or Deep Reserve, (6) Freedom from Attachment, and (7) Tranquillity.[62] If by means of the explanations and examples Hisamatsu supplies,

---

[56]Ibid., 52ff.
[57]Cf. chap. 1, p. 38n.31.
[58]Ibid., 53.
[59]Ibid., 54.
[60]*Art and Morality*, e.g., 23ff., 58ff.
[61]*Zen and the Fine Arts*, 11-60.
[62]Ibid., 28-38.

one simply concurs with his characterization of Zen art, one nevertheless experiences it as a somewhat too generalized idealization if he thinks these characteristics are—or at least have been in the past—typical for East Asian culture as such and, in contrast with Western [depictions], are traceable to "the people's daily life."[63] On the contrary, however, his emphasis upon and description of the interconnectedness and inseparability of these characteristics seem to us to be more correct.[64]

As in the writing on nothingness the positive delineations consist in setting forth the characteristic traits of Zen by juxtaposing them with the ordinary aspects of nothingness, so in this consideration of art Hisamatsu also inserts a description of the nature of Zen in order to show on this "Zen basis" the characteristics of Zen art previously described as forms of expression of the "formless self," of which the one who practices Zen can become aware if satori, "self-awakening," takes place in him. This section on the "significance of Zen" which deals with "nonobjectifiability" (Formlessness), the "authentic subject" (Fundamental Subject) and the "activity" of "self-awareness,"[65] belongs to the best that can be found in the literature with respect to the philosophical formulation concerning this inmost essence of Zen. In strong conceptuality Hisamatsu distinguishes from objectifiability of sense experience and that of self-consciousness which is distinguished by it, the "Self-awareness" of the "true self" that in its enactment is no longer objectifiable—a self-awareness that, in contrast with self-consciousness, can no longer be distinguished from its surroundings and as such is not communicable, but becomes effective as the center of the formation of life and can find in artistic creativity the special expression most adequate to it.

In this sense Hisamatsu distinguishes "two aspects" of "awakening": "the process or direction of attaining freedom from what has (objective) form and of Awakening to the Self without Form (the nonobjectifiable self); and the process in which, through its activity (its enactment), the Self without Form comes to assume form." "When this is attained," continues Hisamatsu, "a new kind of form arises: not ordinary form, but that which is 'wonder-full'. For Zen, therefore, it is this world of 'wonder-full being' that constitutes the world of differentiation."[66]

Hisamatsu exemplifies this constituting of the world through the "formless self," of which he remarks that it ensues only "after awakening—something like seeing a tree"—in the following manner: "When . . . a tree is seen, the seeing is the activity of the Formless Self, and the tree that is seen is the tree that has

---

[63]Ibid., 37-38.
[64]Ibid., 36-37.
[65]Ibid., 45-52.
[66]Ibid., 51-52.

its being there. Since in the *perceived* tree the Formless Self expresses itself, it is no ordinary tree; it is rather a 'wonder-full' tree seen as the self-expression of the Formless Self, and is not separate from the perceiver. As the self-expression of the Formless Self, the tree comes to have a meaning that it did not have previously, just as the perception of the tree through the eye is now realized to be an activity of the Formless Self. It is in this sense," Hisamatsu continues, "that the world in which the Self Without Form expresses itself becomes the world of the Buddha; for by the Buddha is meant nothing other than such a self." In reference to an "ancient verse" according to which "The mountain colors are the Pure Body; the voice of the mountain stream is the broad, long tongue," he further stresses that it would be an "animistic misunderstanding" if one took it to mean "that an object such as a mountain or a tree is inhabited by a soul . . . [or] that the Buddha is such a soul." "Buddha is not an image or the like; but rather whatever is seen or heard or arises in the mind is the Buddha."[67] Therefore he decisively denies a "God [such as that] of Christianity, who is other and objective, in whom one has faith, and upon whom one relies," for the sake of "the bottomless depth of the human being which is the Fundamental Self, that is, Actively Nothing." At the same time he claims for its "metaphysical basis" the fact that it is "the One" in the "plurality of the phenomenal world," in which "men unavoidably suffer due to inequality," and that it "makes all men equal" and "free." He is concerned not so much with these redeeming, ethical consequences, however, but—corresponding to the goal which he pursues in these elucidations—with "a philosophy unique to the Orient," whose "artistic expression" is "the creation of a uniquely Oriental art."[68]

On this basis Hisamatsu indicates in the third part[69]—parallel to the "positive delineations of Zen Buddhist Nothingness" in the tractate of "The Characteristics of Oriental Nothingness"—how "each of the seven characteristics is rooted" in "an aspect of the Formless Self," whereby even here the different aspects of the rootedness form a whole in their artistic ways of appearance. Corresponding to Zen's character of wholeness they deal not only with aesthetic qualities, but all the more essentially with attitudes of life and ways of behavior, even if these are primarily of an aesthetic sort. They show that Zen is a matter of aesthetics and finds its fulfillment in art—understood in the widest sense. In the same sequence as the "seven characteristics" of Zen art, Hisamatsu describes the "aspects of the Formless self" corresponding to them as (1) No Rule, (2) No Complexity, (3) No (claim to) Rank, (4) No Mind, (5) No Bottom, (6) No Hindrance, and (7) No Stirring. The short elucidations to both series are expanded by "Appreciations of

---

[67]Ibid., 52.
[68]Ibid., 53.
[69]Ibid., 54–60.

Selected Plates" of painting, calligraphy, architecture, ikebana, gardens, crafts, and theatre from the realm of Zen[70] which are in principle very helpful for considering these artistic creations of Zen, and together with these, for understanding the nature of Zen.

What occurs to us in considering this rich documentation of Zen art and concerning the attempt to execute the self-understanding announced in it, is finally the insight into the difficulty, if not the impossibility, of understanding what it deals with, and this not only in a formal, but also material regard, because we see ourselves here over against conception of the world and of life which is strange to our senses, whose ethical consequences appear objectionable to us. Probably we can value the fact that Hisamatsu undertakes to introduce "absolute nothingness" in categories of Western thinking to a Westerner who has still not attained "awakening," and that he wants to awaken us in this manner to the mood of human being[71] which we have forgotten. But still more than the fact that he assists us in this respect is the fact that he awakens in us critical questions with respect to his delineations. These are the critical questions of an epistemological, metaphysical, and ethical kind which for Hisamatsu are closely related to each other.

As for the three following areas of questioning to be taken up next, they are for Hisamatsu bound into a whole by his interest in man, the quest for the "true man" and "its realization"—a whole that appears as such in the outer and inner conduct of man. Thus Hisamatsu's analysis of Zen art undertaken primarily under aesthetic perspectives results in characterizations which—like these art works themselves—are valid for the nature and conduct of man which is expressed in them, so that it could be said that, as for all aesthetics, art is for him an ethical matter.

But as much as art is valued by Hisamatsu as an abode of the ethos, it is for him in no way limited to this sphere, but as it works itself out in the other areas of life, he derives it then not merely from that of art, as happens in the context of this work on Zen art; rather, the ethical arises for him on other occasions directly out of the nature of man, without consideration of the sphere of art, that is, out of the awareness of the true self in its final metaphysical depths which are not conceivable in objectifying knowing. In other ways than is the case in this analysis of Zen art, the nature of the Zen ethic becomes evident in these expositions which take no account of Zen art and in the ways in which their problematic is worked out.

---

[70]Ibid., 61-102.
[71]Ibid., 60 (cf. the opening of *Die Fülle des Nichts*).

"Zen,"—as he elucidates it, for example, in the essay with this title—is "the negation of holiness."[72] Hisamatsu places the verses from the story of "the ox and the oxherd" at the beginning as a motto:

Worldly passions fallen away,
Empty of all holy intent,
I linger not where Buddha dwells
And hasten by where no Buddha is.

In contrast to the differing conceptions of "holiness" in Windelband, Nathan Söderblom, Rudolf Otto, and the dialectical theologians, in which the Holy is regarded in every kind of way as something Transcendent which is set over against the world and man,[73] he explains here that Zen is not acquainted with this distinction, because for it "the true Buddha" is not thing-like but is "no-thing"; [rather] the Buddha and the human world mutually interpenetrate each other, so forming a unity. In this way he brings "the sacred from the reaches of transcendent views or objective forms [back into] the folds of human subjectivity," thus "affirming "what is sacred in man.""[74]

In the essay on "Zen: Its Meaning for Modern Civilization,"[75] Hisamatsu infers the following from the unity of man and the Buddha as the actualization of the "Buddha nature" of the "true man": "The fundamental aim of Buddhism is to attain freedom from every bondage arising from the dualities of life-and-death, right-and-wrong, good-and-evil."[76] He does not here unfold the consequences of this conception for man, but concerns himself with the significance of this independence of Zen from the historical tradition[77] and also in respect to the nature of art.

With all desirable clarity the ethical consequences of that "beauty which is the free functioning itself"[78] come to light in the essay which carries the title, "Ordinary Mind."[79] This mind (spirit) characterized by Hisamatsu as "ordinary," that is, "everyday,"[80] "just as [it is],"[81] is not only something different from

---

[72]"Zen as the Negation of Holiness," EB 10/1 (1977): 1-12.
[73]Ibid., 1ff.
[74]Ibid., 11f.
[75]"Zen: Its Meaning for Modern Civilization," EB 1/1 (1965): 22-47.
[76]Ibid., 29.
[77]Ibid., 22ff.
[78]Ibid., 45ff.
[79]"Ordinary Mind," EB 12/1 (1979): 1-29.
[80]Ibid., 23-24.
[81]Ibid., 28.

Hegel's idea of speculative mind,[82] but is also different from scientific knowing,[83] as well as from Bergson's "intuition"[84] or Dilthey's "*Lebensphiloso-phie*,"[85] because all of these—albeit in different ways—still deal with attempts of an objective, fixed seizing of the "living flow" of things,[86] whose methods and results can be taught and learned[87] and are valid as "norms" for conduct.[88]

Over against such attempts to attain knowledge of ethical norms which he holds to be just as typical for academic "Western-style" ethics as they are decep-tively convincing,[89] Hisamatsu places a "fundamentally subjective" ethics as a "lived ethic" in comparison to which "even the best scholar of ethics in the Western sense may be a poor scholar of Eastern ethics," for which he points to the Analects of Confucius as an example.[90] According to Hisamatsu this lived ethics must be grounded and constituted in a "total life act" in which man becomes an "ultimate unity" from which issues an "elucidation [of] the total Being in a total manner."[91] But whereas Hisamatsu says of the person who enacts this elucidation, that he is an "ultimate unity," he restricts it—in relation to what obtains between that which is elucidated and that which elucidates itself through him—to "neither one nor different," because he only permits "the task of what is elucidated" to elucidate itself through what is elucidated. Yet at the same time he explains that "the total being, which is itself the task, illuminates itself in a total manner."[92]

This being-in-and-with-one-another of what is different-from-one-another as a "philosophical" act of life Hisamatsu sees embodied in the war art of the samurai[93] or otherwise in the "masters of [traditional] arts,"[94] and even in the one who answers the question as to what he should do in view of life's total dedica-

[82]Ibid., 13.
[83]Ibid., 7.
[84]Ibid., 2, 15.
[85]Ibid., 14.
[86]Ibid., 2.
[87]Ibid., 7 and 14.
[88]Ibid., 19.
[89]Ibid., 8 and 10-11.
[90]Ibid., 9-10. Cf. on this *The Chinese Mind*, ed. Charles Moor; *Kungfutse, Gespräche. Lun Yü*, verdeutscht und erläutert von Richard Wilhelm (Diedrichs, 1955).
[91]Ibid., 11-12.
[92]Ibid., 12.
[93]Ibid., 6.
[94]Ibid., 17.

tion to death: "Coming to tea, I take tea; coming to a meal, I take a meal."[95] Such men are for him "the saints and sages" on the "Great Way of humanity,"[96] whom he poetically illustrates with the Zen verse: "In spring, flowers; in summer, the cool breeze; in autumn, the moon; in winter, snow,"[97] or with the somewhat trivial formulation which nevertheless stems from Zen: "When hungry, I eat; when tired, I sleep."[98] The "ethical principle" so far as one can speak of such, consists for Hisamatsu not in any kind of "transcendent norm," but in "immediate response to circumstances,"[99] which does not lack the "greatness and depth," necessary for "the freedom to make decisions and to act,"[100] if it issues in awareness of "the abyss of history,"[101] whose "overcoming" represents at the same time "dying the Great Death."[102] In this sense he can say: "Everyday actuality itself, in and of itself, is the ideal, the end," and "each and every being is perfect as it is."[103]

If, in this essay on "the abyss of history" first published four years before Hiroshima—an "abyss," which he thought he could counter with his ethic of the "Way without an exit"— Hisamatsu writes that it is "as if one were to hold a thousand-ton bomb and stare down into a ten-thousand-foot pit,"[104] then "the religious dialectic" of the Great Death may be—for the one who dropped the bomb and for those who are the victims and contemporaries of this dropping of the bomb—"the ultimate 'overcoming,' the ultimate unification." But there is the further question whether an ethic of this kind is suited to preserve mankind from the fact that "the total *sapiens-faber*-man" continues in the construction of such means of destruction and so makes such use of it that the "Great Death" it effects permits no "Great Awakening." But "the contradictions of history" are no more able to be solved by "temporizing and drinking tea" than are those of "everyday life"!

The causes that lie behind the insufficiency of his Zen art ethic, which are made evident in the ethical consequences of Hisamatsu's "ordinary mind," are the epistemology and metaphysics in which they are grounded. In a dialogue with Hisamatsu, Paul Tillich referred to these epistemological and metaphysical prob-

---

[95]Ibid., 29.
[96]Ibid., 15 and 17.
[97]Ibid., 28.
[98]Ibid., 19.
[99]Ibid., 5 and 25.
[100]Ibid., 5-6.
[101]Ibid., 26.
[102]Ibid., 27.
[103]Ibid., 23.
[104]Ibid., 26.

lems of his Zen philosophy.[105] Not only because we share the objections Tillich raised against Hisamatsu's position, but also because the conversation in large measure turns on art and Hisamatsu refers therein both to this text on nothingness and also to his work on Zen art which had appeared by that time,[106] following the course of this substantial conversation offers us the opportunity to continue our encounter with Hisamatsu precisely in respect to the two points that have been mentioned.

4. The Conversation with Paul Tillich

The dialogue between Tillich and Hisamatsu occurred in the fall of 1957 when both taught at the Harvard Divinity School, and took place with the help of two translators, an American and a Japanese, who later produced the written version by means of a tape recording. The conversation which Tillich opened with the practical question of the possibility of calmness in the midst of a busy lecture activity,[107] is immediately deepened by Hisamatsu who explains that calmness is a matter of "the Self that transcends calmness and busyness," of the "formless Self" which cannot "be conceived psychologically,"[108] but is actualized only in "object- and subject-less" Zen meditation.[109] When Tillich asks in this connection, how one can know of this "true self" without "the help of words,"[110] and in relation to Meister Eckhart's "detachment"[111] speaks of the Logos[112] as the

---

[105]"Dialogues, East and West: Conversation between Dr. Paul Tillich and Dr. Hisamatsu Shin'ichi," EB 4/2 (1971): 89-107, 107-28; 5/2 (1972): 107-28; 6/2 (1973): 87-114. Jong-won Kim develops an instructive parallel to the conversation between Tillich and Hisamatsu in a confrontation between Tillich and Suzuki, in his article, "Paul J. Tillich and Daisetz T. Suzuki: A Comparative Study of their Thoughts on Ethics in Relation to Being," JR 10/1 (1977): 38-56; 10/2 (1978): 42-67. The problematic of an ontological grounding of ethics in Buddhism and Christianity—as correctly seen by the author of this article—a problematic which is evident even in this conversation between Tillich and Hisamatsu and which we meet again and again in our engagement with the other representatives of the Kyoto School—we shall take up in accord with the preceding individual discussions, in a concluding stand in our final chapter, and indicate as its overcoming a connection between Being-in-Christ and Buddha-Being, as it is contained in the symbol of the Buddha-Christ as the Lord of the True Self.

[106]EB 4/2 (1971): 100ff.; 6/2 (1973): 87.
[107]EB 4/2 (1971): 90.
[108]Ibid., 93.
[109]Ibid., 97.
[110]Ibid., 93.
[111]Ibid., 95.

"power of Being,"[113] the two points of divergence are already evident in the plan which is carried out through the whole conversation, as it is explained, but not resolved, in the first round by means of examples of Western art.[114]

At the beginning of the second round of conversations[115] De Martino summarizes very well the opposition between the two philosophers of religion in this way: that Tillich deals with the "depth of Being," "which possibly leads to God as the ultimate source of Being," while for Hisamatsu this is "not God, but the Self, that is, the true or formless Self of man."[116] In the ensuing discussion about what constitutes "true and justifiable religion,"[117] the conception of the self and its nature proves to be—more clearly than in its discussion by means of art—the decisive point of divergence. Already in the latter, in which Tillich could agree after all with Hisamatsu on the point that the work of art represents an expression of the self of the artist, in whose regard the self of the one making the judgment can enter into a specific relation to that of the artist, Tillich—in contrast to Hisamatsu—emphasizes the difference between the two selves and proposes as an alternative to the "depth dimension of art" "the dimension of the Ultimate"[118]—which Hisamatsu rejects by saying that in Western art "one is not completely awakened," so that one has to do merely with "surface expressions."[119]

This anthropological and metaphysical dualism which Hisamatsu rejects[120] becomes even more apparent for Tillich in the way in which, in answering the question about the nature of religion, he attempts to validate "the Ultimate" in a threefold manner as "the creative ground" of the finite, as "the judge of the finite," and as the "reunion with the finite."[121] If the way he does this on the basis of his "theological thinking," as well as the way he treats the time-eternity problem[122] and distinguishes between the potentiality and actuality of evil in God,[123] is itself extremely questionable, in this he correctly points to the ethical and metaphysical problematic of Hisamatsu's Zen philosophy. If, in contrast to

---

[112]Ibid., 97.
[113]Ibid., 99.
[114]Ibid., 100ff.
[115]EB 5/2 (1972): 107-28.
[116]Ibid., 110.
[117]Ibid., 110ff.
[118]EB 4/2 (1971): 100ff.
[119]Ibid., 103.
[120]Ibid., 98-99.
[121]EB 5/2 (1972): 110-11.
[122]Ibid., 114-15, 121.
[123]Ibid., 119-20.

Tillich's emphasis upon the difference between the eternal Ground and temporal
being which is entailed in the distinction between good and evil[124] and the role
assigned to the individual,[125] Hisamatsu appeals to "breaking through" this
dualism in the "awakening" brought about by the "Great Death,"[126] Tillich is
correct in holding to the contrary that this "breakthrough" has to occur at a
definite time in a definite person—for example, at a definite point in the life of
Hisamatsu and "not in Hitler."[127]

As is evident in the further discussion of the core problem[128] in the third
conversation with reference to concepts of the Kegon and Tendai philosophy[129]
and Pseudo-Dionysian and Neoplatonic speculation,[130] both Hisamatsu and
Tillich—in their efforts to speak somewhat conceptually of nothingness, or
Being, and of the true self—lapse into paradoxes, which as such appear only as
merely meaningless and arbitrary, if they are understood in connection with conceptual thinking which necessarily founders in each case—which occurs differently for each conversation partner: for Tillich, as he still argues in his
concluding sentence from "experience," while Hisamatsu—according to the
insightful explanation of De Martino—argued from his Zen existence as a
"nonduality embodied" in him—which gets expressed—better than in logical contradiction—in a Zen master's fashion as a "push in the stomach."[131]

What Hisamatsu in dialogue with Tillich merely suggested as the basis
which stands behind his questions and forms their presupposition—his anthropology and metaphysics—which for him represent, together with their ethical consequences, a unified whole as soteriology, this he has extensively and in systematic
form developed in the two essays which carry the titles "Atheism" and "Ultimate
Crisis and Resurrection," which are so indicative of the position of their author.
In both, as a way of explaining historically the contemporary situation and of
grounding his position—as the singularly defensible "postmodern religiosity"—he
makes use of a definite schema of the religio-cultural development of mankind,
to which he devoted a thematic treatment in the shorter essay on "Satori."

---

[124]Ibid., 114.
[125]Ibid., 124.
[126]Ibid, 122ff.
[127]Ibid., 124-27.
[128]EB 6/2 (1973): 93.
[129]Ibid., 102ff.
[130]Ibid.
[131]Ibid., 114.

5. Postmodern Religiosity and Its Problematic

In the article on "Satori,"[132] Hisamatsu explains "the nature of man in four typical ways of being": as "1. The Humanistic Picture of Man"; "2. The Nihilistic Picture of Man"; "3. The Ethical Picture of Man"; and "4. The Self-Awakening Picture of Man." This series results for Hisamatsu not so much, although also, as something religiohistorical—for therein the theistic view of man has to be abandoned—but under a systematic-normative aspect. That he has both in view is evident from the fact that he writes: "If the first picture of man is that of modern humanism, the second is that of nihilism which presses against the boundaries of humanism. In the third picture of man the second, nihilistic way of being is completely converted through God as the other; it is the picture of man in medieval theism in which the independence and autonomy of man are lost."[133] The deficiencies of these three "pictures of man," or "ways of being," Hisamatsu regards as overcome (*aufgehoben*) in that of "Self-awakening," in which the "hopelessness of nihilism" is radicalized into "the dying of the Great Death,"[134] wherein simultaneously the "frivolous wishful thinking" of religions, as well as of idealism and materialism, are abandoned.[135] To be sure, Hisamatsu concedes that "the resurrection in Christianity and the crossing over into the Pure Land of Blessedness in the 'true school of the Pure Land'—if we understand them critically"—could correspond to what is meant in Zen by "the Great Death and the subsequent resurrection." By "critically understood" he means "freed from premodern mythology."[136] This means with respect to Buddhism that: "Outside this mode of being of self-awakening there is nothing that can be designated as the Buddha. As something else the Buddha would only be a projection of this human mode of being, a self-objectification, nothing but an embodied Buddha nature and therefore not a true Buddha." Only in one form will Hisamatsu acknowledge a "personified Buddha as another," and this consists for him in "the fact of compassion itself, in which the mode of being of awakening as the true Buddha guides the unenlightened person to self-awakening."[137]

Irrespective of this ethical consequence of the "mode of being of this awakening—that is the Buddha"—Hisamatsu arrives in this discussion principally at two factors: first, to free "the mode of being of self-awakening" for the sake

---

[132]*Gott in Japan*, ed. Yagi Seiichi and Ulrich Luz (Munich: Kaiser Verlag, 1973) 127-38.
[133]Ibid., 132-33.
[134]Ibid., 132.
[135]Ibid., 129-30.
[136]Ibid., 137.
[137]Ibid., 136.

of its "absolute autonomy" from every "theistically dependent mode of being of premodern heteronomy,"[138] and second, despite its "atheistic" character[139] to settle on it as the unique possibility of a "postmodern religion."[140] He develops this program in the two larger essays already mentioned which follow.

In the essay on "Atheism"[141] Hisamatsu confesses that he has "been atheistic for a long time,"[142] and maintains "that we should become more radical atheists,"[143] and both for the sake of the "true religion,"[144] which for him can only be a "religion without God."[145] In such directness these formulations nevertheless do not satisfy him, for he asks: "Am I then only simply atheistic?" in order to admit of the "present state of his heart": "I certainly incline toward atheism, yet I cannot say that I am simply an absolute, unconditional humanist. I cannot cease being atheistic. Yet I cannot also believe, like a modern man, that man can create his good fortune alone through his human power. In this contradictory situation my existence consists in the present. Insofar as I cannot return to theism, I am thoroughly atheistic. Yet I can exist neither purely anthropocentrically nor purely theocentrically."[146]

As a "modern man" himself Hisamatsu sees the situation of religion past and present as similarly complex. Thus he can say of the "Atheismus" with which Fichte was charged: "Over against the usual faith in God his faith brings disbelief to expression,"[147] and can see the problematic of medieval faith in God in this way, that it was "no mere heteronomy, but rather theonomy." Because "the Christian God was the subject of the law, it is a matter "within human nature" of "a heteronomy, which was carried over into autonomy," of whose "immediacy" Hisamatsu says that "it must simply be known and recognized as such." But he emphasizes just as much that this "medieval theonomy" must be rejected—because it "becomes a theonomy that transcends autonomy" rather than "containing in itself the autonomy"—and as such could only be repudiated by

---

[138]Ibid., 137.
[139]Ibid., 136.
[140]Ibid., 133, 137.
[141]"Atheismus," *Zeitschrift für Missionswissenschaft und Religionswissenschaft* (1978): 268-96. Cf. also Helmuth von Glasenapp, *Der Buddhismus—eine atheistische Religion* (Munich: Sczczesny Verlag, 1966).
[142]Ibid., 272.
[143]Ibid., 278.
[144]Ibid., 277.
[145]Ibid., 281.
[146]Ibid., 275.
[147]Ibid., 274.

"modern autonomy," by which the latter must simultaneously necessarily become "atheistic."[148]

But as much as Hisamatsu sees in atheism the inevitable consequence of this religious and social development, and according to him all the vestiges of a "medieval theonomy" should be "eliminated" in Buddhism,[149] all the less would he like the "autonomous self-consciousness of modern man"—from which atheism issues—to suffice;[150] rather he would like to develop therein the historical dialectic of heteronomy and autonomy into an "autonomous heteronomy."[151] In this, in place of God as the "wholly other" and of its exclusive revelation in God or the Buddha, Shakyamuni or Jesus, a theonomy or heteronomy of the "true self" as the "total self" would have to appear.[152] "The future religion," so he proclaims, "must so to speak be a heteronomy which includes the autonomy in itself." In this autonomous theonomy or heteronomy the person awakened to his autonomy will develop in accord with the "religious law" which arises in him and is known by him.[153]

This "religious law" consists in nothing but the "self-awakening" of the man to his "true self," for which Hisamatsu uses the expression "resurrection" and then goes on to define it exactly in such a way that it deals with a "resurrection" or "springing forth" which issues "from the self's own ground" or from "its own original core"—in any case, with a completely autonomous process, in which nothing other than the self is itself engaged.[154]

Hisamatsu reiterates that "apart from this awakening to one's self" there is in Buddhism "no Buddha,"[155] and in this sense even the "going out (*oso*)" to the Pure Land and the "return (*genso*)" from thence, as they are taught in Jodoshinshu, are corrected in such a way that therein—"in accord with the authentic teaching of Buddhism—they do not deal with "the transforming power of Amida," but with the "autonomous, transforming going out and returning" of the I-self, which is "the Buddha in the most original sense." Nevertheless, he is prepared to assign to "the theistic Buddha which appears in Buddhism" the role of a "mediator" (hobenbutsu), for which he appeals also to the trikaya doctrine.[156] The problem of "theocentrism and anthropocentrism" before which he places

---

[148]Ibid., 275.
[149]Ibid., 277-78.
[150]Ibid., 281.
[151]Ibid., 278.
[152]Ibid., 279ff.
[153]Ibid., 280.
[154]Ibid., 281ff.
[155]Ibid., 283.
[156]Ibid., 285, 286ff.

himself in this way,[157] and with which he sees Christian theism principally concerned—even in Eckhart's mysticism—[158] he resolves in such a way that he refers to "the doctrine" and "the nirvana" of "prajna knowledge," in which "the formless self,"[159] which is attained through the "great Death," is "the true self."[160] As an image for this state of affairs in which the true self does not arise through an operation which comes from outside the self, but represents a self-awakening, and in which what is awakened is identical with the unawakened self, Hisamatsu employs the emergence of a butterfly from a cocoon, whose cause is not the incubation, but lies in the nature of the cocoon, which becomes apparent in the butterfly as such.[161] Every kind of theism is excluded by Hisamatsu because for him becoming Buddha deals with a self-awakening to authentic being. The same can be said for what he rejects as "anthropocentrism," in that the self-awakening must pass "through the absolute crisis which lies at the base of humanity,"[162] which he even calls the "decisive zero point, that is, its own negation."[163]

Without a doubt Hisamatsu succeeds in making clear with this image what he means by the self-awakening which transcends anthropocentrism and theocentrism. But two questions remain unanswered for us. First, the question Why is there something rather than nothing?—applied to the image used by him: Why are there cocoons and a world in which butterflies can emerge? without the image: Why is there a world and everything that belongs to it?—a world whose existence man cannot only raise as a question, but which even forms the presupposition for the fact that it can be thought of or repudiated. These are the questions to which the theism that Hisamatsu rejected attempts to give an answer—in however questionable ways.

With the reference to the problematic of theism which Hisamatsu offers, its intention is in any case not settled even if it is recognized that, by passing over the question of being in favor of the question of meaning, Hisamatsu takes up the other intention, assuming that theism in its different forms is still more important than the question of the ground of being, namely, the question of the ground of meaning of human existence. In the interest of the question of the meaning of existence and the behavior which corresponds to it, theism asks the question of the ground of all being and gives it a form which not only seems to

---

[157]Ibid., 283.
[158]Ibid., 288.
[159]Ibid., 284.
[160]Ibid., 287-88.
[161]Ibid., 288-89.
[162]Ibid., 287.
[163]Ibid., 288.

give information about the meaning of being, but through it even the realization of this meaning seems to be guaranteed.

But this grounding of the meaning of existence in the ground of being is beset with many difficulties. Not only must its representatives reckon with the fact that, with such a universal construction of meaning, they exclude themselves with the not unjustified suspicion that it deals with a illusory wish projection, but that the more univocally they conceive the ground of being as a guarantee of the meaning of the existence of themselves and the world, the more must they ask from whence stems the apparent split in the meaning of Being as a whole, namely, the evil in the world and in human existence. Epistemologically considered, it is believed that this problematic can be solved by postulating a higher way of knowing different from knowledge of the understanding, and metaphysically, by differentiating layers of the ground of being, of an *Abgrund* or *Ungrund*, with which even what is nonsensical can be brought into connection, and an activity directed to the fulfillment of meaning which is embodied in special redeemer figures, like Christ or Amida.

Although one must assume that Hisamatsu would roundly have rejected that representation of the problematic as not applicable to his position, he is nonetheless familiar with it from Christianity and Amida Buddhism, and he sees in Zen Buddhism an overcoming of the problematic of both of these forms of religion, with the result that it is quite appropriate to evaluate his position in the framework of the problematic situation just described and to ask whether he is able to show a way out of it or whether he is affected by it, despite his denial. Epistemologically considered, over against the "usual religion in which it is established that God can be neither known nor proven but only believed," and according to which the believing subject is related to an "object of faith" attested to him on the basis of a "canonical text" as the "Word of God" or "Word of Buddha"—over against this religion he places the "true religion" of "awakening" in which the "formless self" in a "formless faith" attains to "certainty of itself," which is just as "absolute" as it is "autonomous."[164]

In this way the position which Hisamatsu assumes for metaphysics has already been characterized. For him there is no metaphysics in the sense of a differentiation between appearance and being as such; rather "all appearances are the true reality."[165] "In authentic Buddhism the Buddha is neither transcendent nor immanent," but "rather present."[166] The Buddha is present in the "true self." "Outside of this awakening to one's self there is in Buddhism no Buddha."[167] Of

---

[164]Ibid., 284, 293.
[165]Ibid., 284.
[166]Ibid., 290.
[167]Ibid., 283.

this awakening to the true self in which alone the Buddha is present, Hisamatsu also says that therein "one reaches to his most authentic state." "That the ordinary person becomes a Buddha means nothing other than that a person living in an inauthentic way becomes a person existing in an authentic way." The "basis" for this possibility of becoming Buddha, Hisamatsu, appealing to the Buddhist tradition, calls "Buddhahood," which "every thing living has," and for its realization uses the image of the hatching of the chick from the egg which occurs "simultaneously by being pricked from within and pecked at from without."[168]

In Hisamatsu's development of this state of affairs which is central for him both epistemologically and metaphysically, there becomes evident the problematic of his position in which he does not get beyond those conceptions which he rejects, but contributes a new variant. If he distinguishes between inauthentic and authentic existence and connects the former with unenlightened, and the latter with enlightened-being, namely, with discriminating knowledge and prajna wisdom, respectively, he thus apparently makes the distinction which theism does between two kinds of knowing. As radical faith in revelation explains that it can only be understood in itself and not from outside, so Hisamatsu thinks that only when the conception of becoming a Buddha, outside of which there is no Buddha, is considered "from the perspective of one who does not exist in authentic being," can it be "designated as something quite different." But while revelatory faith holds to the distinction between statements of faith and those of unbelief, for Hisamatsu the distinctions in the sayings, which for him are the result of two modes of being, collapse, so that he continues: "But this other cannot be the Absolute-Other. To that extent one must nevertheless designate what is most authentic in man as Not-Absolute-Other." In this regard it first appears that he believes that in the quid pro quo of the "most authentic mode of being of man"—according to the Buddhist tradition—he can see "Tathata, that is, the truth of being as it actually is,"[169] by which the noetic conception of truth is ontologized.

Out of this ontologizing of the Buddha nature of man there issue, for Hisamatsu, important soteriological and ethical consequences. In contrast to the theism of Christianity and of Amida Buddhism neither God nor Amida is needed to bring aid to man by which he as the "ordinary being" becomes "the true subject which freely wanders to and fro and works in the midst of this world";[170] rather this happens wholly from out of itself and occurs as such in accord with its "original, authentic mode of being," "just as the butterfly, breaking out of the envelope by itself, freely flies around." As evidence for this he cites the sentence

---

[168]Ibid., 294.
[169]Ibid., 94.
[170]Ibid., 290.

from the Buddhist tradition: "Playing in the midst of the forest of sins, to practice the divine power which penetrates all things without hindrance; entering into
the garden of birth and death, to help every corresponding need of man."[171]

Hisamatsu fails to give us an answer to two questions which here so
unhesitatingly present themselves. To be sure, he can positively ground "the true
self's" "loss of self," "which has its own ground in itself and nothing else which
can constitute its ground of being," by means of the model of the Bodhisattva
who renounces the Pure Land by pointing out that only such a relationship corresponds to the nature of the true self, and negatively with the argument that the
assumption of a ground of being that lies outside the self would bring this into
a "relation of dependency," which would not be commensurate with the being
of the true self.[172] But from whence comes it, that there is "Being" and "self" at
all rather than nothing? With the argumentation that this is a completely
inappropriate way of posing the question, because therein the character of being
and the self as nothingness is misunderstood, this question is not obviated, for
even this "dis-allowance" of its appropriateness presupposes an existent in the
world, both of which as such are not nothing. The other question also remains
unanswered for Hisamatsu, namely, from whence does it come about that not
only such questions which he regards as inappropriate can be posed, but that a
butterfly does not emerge from every cocoon nor a chick from every egg; or put
without the image: not every man "attains to his most authentic state"; that "the
truth"—according to the citation he brings forth—"dwells in the midst of the
sinful world."[173] Significantly he repeatedly speaks in this connection of
"becoming," "must" and "obedience" and confirms it by stating that there is not
only the possibility of Buddha-being, but also its opposite, namely, that one
"can," "must," and "will miss" the fulfillment of the meaning of existence.[174]

To be sure, theism—in the forms such as Hisamatsu envisages it in
Christianity and Amida Buddhism—does not answer the question of the ground
of being and ground of meaning of human existence in a satisfactory manner.
But neither does his "atheism" do justice to them, but can only produce a metaphysics which in rejecting a mythological creator God acknowledges a mystery
of Being, which for our conceptual thinking represents a nothing, and distinguishes from it a special revelation of this mystery whose mythological "mediator
figures" are to be understood as symbols of the special possibilities of meaning
of human existence.

---

[171]Ibid., 291.
[172]Ibid., 293.
[173]Ibid., 294.
[174]Ibid., 289ff.

In our view, from the perspective of this metaphysics there flows also an understanding of "love or compassion" different from that of Hisamatsu's: not merely as an innocent cosmic play in an "absolute autonomy," in which man is "dissolved" "in the midst of the difference from all differences,"[175] but through a special activity of the mystery of Being, experiences himself as distinguished from the riddle of meaning of all beings and thereby from his own through the determination of the realization of meaning in compassionate love over against every being which clamors for the fulfillment of meaning. In this case, it is certainly not sufficient that we have become "self-less" in the Buddhist sense. For how then could the "active" becoming of self-lessness expressly demanded by Hisamatsu be brought about? To be sure, attachment to a self, egoism, represents a hindrance to love, and only a man who has become free from attachment to his self is capable of a loving relationship with the other. As much as this ethical attitude must be our attitude, it does not arise out of our own natural being in which we experience ourselves as embedded in the superethical mystery of being and of its riddle of meaning. We must be rescued from the cruel play by an "Other-Power" which makes possible for us a mode of being other than the "usual" one, as this is provided by the mediator-figures of the Christ and of Amida. Because Hisamatsu does not make this distinction in metaphysics, and with "theism" understands these mediator-figures only in mythological objectivity, instead of existentially, he can only reject them as incommensurate with true self-being.[176] The consequence of this misunderstanding, of which Christianity and Amida Buddhism are certainly not innocent, in that they rather occasion it, consists in the fact that its appeal "fundamentally to invert and affirm reality,"[177] metaphysically considered, only leads into "emptiness."

Whereas in his article on "Atheism," Hisamatsu—through the way in which he uses the image of the butterfly and its chrysalis and even more so of the hen and chick emerging from the egg and through the fact that he believes in this connection that he can assign a "expedient" function to the "mediator-figures" like Amida or Christ—after all provokes the question whether a specific character of transcendence can be ascribed to these figures because of their function as redeemers, such a possibility seems initially excluded in the treatise on "Ultimate Crisis and Resurrection,"[178] in that here he extends the elimination of metaphysics with respect to the question of Being to the question of meaning. In both, the elimination consists in a failure to hear the question, why is there something rather than nothing? But while in the article on "Atheism" he comes to grips

---

[175]Ibid., 291.
[176]Ibid., 295.
[177]Ibid., 296.
[178]EB 8/1 (1975): 12-29; EB 8/2 (1975): 37-65.

with the "theism" which answers this question—albeit always in unsatisfactory ways—at least in respect to its treatment of the question of meaning or of redemption, and rejects the theistic doctrine of redemption as incommensurate with absolute self-being, he in no wise agrees with its metaphysics, but, in a positive way, develops "resurrection" and "redemption" purely from the side of the nature of the "true self."

With this rejection or neglect of any kind of relatedness to transcendence both ontologically and soteriologically, Hisamatsu is emphatically concerned to show the "raison d'être of religion."[179] On his own he confesses that he is "one who seeks religion," not for the sake of religion to be sure, but of man—a religion without which man could not be man, also a religion grounded in human nature. Other than in this anthropological aspect he sees himself obligated to no religion,[180] and from the standpoint of the understanding of religion he then criticizes "ordinary Buddhism"[181] and even certain strictures of Zen.[182] But when, over against a "narrow intellectualism" and an uncritical humanism, he also emphasizes that religion "transcends man,"[183] this "transcending" occurs for Hisamatsu according to all three directions from and to man, namely, in the "depth" of the true self, in its "width" as "brotherly love for all humanity," and in its "length" as history, by which the formation of history is said to be meant in terms of the first two dimensions named.[184]

The main section of the elucidation of this program is devoted to the aspect of the depth of the self, as it makes its appearance on the one hand as sin and death[185] and on the other, as "value and antivalue" and "existence and nonexistence" in space and time.[186] In respect to the Christian concept of original sin Hisamatsu sees in sin and death as a unity an expression for the insurmountable limitedness of humanity,[187] in that not only in death, but in the interrelation of sin and death that is apparent even in the antinomies in the moral and aesthetic realm,[188] there lies the "antinomian structure" of human being, the "extremity-situation of reason," the *"abyss of man."*[189] In the existential awareness of this

---

[179]EB 8/1 (1975): 15ff.
[180]Ibid., 16.
[181]EB 8/2 (1975): 47; EB 8/1 (1975): 14.
[182]EB 8/2 (1975): 63ff.
[183]EB 8/1 (1975): 17-18.
[184]Ibid., 12-13.
[185]Ibid., 18ff.
[186]EB 8/2 (1975): 41ff.
[187]EB 8/1 (1975): 18ff.
[188]Ibid., 20, 25.
[189]Ibid, 21-22.

situation, in which man becomes a "great doubting mass," it is the "Great Death"[190] in which "the breaking through" to the "awakening" of the "true self" occurs in a leap.[191] As in the "Great Doubt"—in contrast with Descartes' doubt—the one who doubts and that which is doubted" are one,[192] so—in contrast to the Christian notion of redemption—the "awakening" occurs not through an "other-power,"[193] but as the "breakthrough" of the "Buddha-nature" or "Buddha-being,"[194] which is characteristic of all beings, by virtue of which the unredeemed is already redeemed and needs no redeemer;[195] rather the true self can be called "Creator."[196]

After Hisamatsu has "solved" the problem of meaning in this way by the liberating adoption of the ultimate crisis in the "depth of the self," he must then ask himself how this solution works itself out in the "width dimension" of the self, that is, in its environment in space and time.[197] Here there are not only "values" and conflicts of value, but in view of these the question poses itself, how in this context the redemptive "breakthrough" enacts itself and develops as the true self. In order to answer this "very difficult" question[198]—as he calls it—he distinguishes between "relative" and "ultimate" difficulties.[199] The former arise from the fact that man thinks he can solve the problems which arise for mankind from his embeddedness in nature and the attempts to become its master by technical mastery, by means of reason. The "ultimate, absolute difficulties" however have their ground in the "antinomian structure" of reason and of existence as such and in the attempts to eliminate them in illusory religious notions, scientific-technical investigations and philosophical theories.[200] Hisamatsu illustrates this state of affairs with the "discovery and uses of atomic power" arising from the amazing progress of moderns—a power that today threatens mankind and fills it with anxiety.[201]

In order to counter this and other dangers of the contemporary development of humanity, in 1958 Hisamatsu founded his F.A.S-Zen Institute whose three

---

[190]Ibid., 23ff.
[191]Ibid., 27ff.
[192]Ibid., 26.
[193]Ibid., 28; EB 8/2 (1975): 38-39.
[194]EB 8/1 (1975): 29.
[195]EB 8/2 (1975): 38.
[196]EB 8/1 (1975): 29.
[197]EB 8/1 (1975): 41ff.
[198]Ibid., 48.
[199]Ibid., 41-42.
[200]Ibid., 42ff.
[201]Ibid., 54.

initials symbolize the "Formless self" which is to be awakened in "All humanity" and is to arise from the one "Superhistorical history." From the program which he sketches at the conclusion it is not evident how a "world-forming and historically creative activity" can result from the awakening to the true self which has been "freed from every fetter,"[202] and in what this "wondrous" activity should consist. Hisamatsu probably not unjustly accuses the "ordinary political movements" that in them what he understands by the "Formless Self" has regularly been "forgotten completely," and it is not without warrant that he warns the representatives of "religion" in Buddhism and especially in Zen Buddhism that in "accenting the formless self" they limit themselves to the "silent illumination" which only has to do with this self and thus "fall into the 'devil's cave.'"[203] For him the essence of religion consists in the actualization of the F.A.S. and in it alone he believes he can get a glimpse of the "ultimate Mahayana."[204]

The way in which Hisamatsu, in his "Search for the True Religion," of which he gives testimony for us in this essay, concerns himself almost exclusively with the "depth" of the self, while the activity of its width and length is explained, so to say, dependently as postulates, could give rise to the apprehension that, with his religion of self-redemption, he becomes captive to the fate of which he warns his religious contemporaries. A conception of religion which thinks it can abolish transcendence in every form seems unable to escape from this fate. If the self has to redeem itself, this is such an "amazing activity" that it neither can nor will escape from it, but rather finds full sufficiency in the "fullness of nothingness" with which it has to do therein.

In order to arrive at a conclusive position on this religious philosophy of Hisamatsu there are available to us from recent times three more extensive publications which we wish to consider in the following section.

6. Hisamatsu's Interpretation of the "Five Stations" and the "Rinzai Text" as Well as an Evaluation of his "Philosophy of Awakening" by Masao Abe

A lecture series, which Hisamatsu delivered in the framework of the fall and winter semesters of the year 1960 at his F.A.S. Zen Institute in the Myoshin Temple in Kyoto on "The Five Stations of the Zen Master Tosan Ryokai," and which has recently appeared in German translation, can serve as an example for the previously indicated problematic of the "amazing activity" of "formless self" in the "fullness of nothingness" in its world-forming ethical aspect.[205] In his

---

[202]Ibid., 61.
[203]Ibid., 63.
[204]Ibid., 65.
[205]The eight lectures were published in 1974, in the fourth volume of Hisa-

"structural analysis of awakening" carried through by use of the schema of the "five stations," Hisamatsu deals on the one hand with the understanding of the self and of Nirvana as emptiness and, on the other, with the deduction of the redeeming activity of the Bodhisattva as the "Great Compassion" from the "One Position of Positionlessness" of this emptiness.

The intention of the attainment of absolute emptiness Hisamatsu carries through in a dialectic of the two attitudes he designates as "upright" and "aslant" and for which he frequently employs the distinctions of Yin and Yang, dark and bright, host and guest, master and servant, which are used in the tradition. According to Hisamatsu, the nature of the first two stations consists in the fact that in them the two sides interpenetrate, so that "in the upright, the aslant," and "in the aslant, the upright"; or, philosophically spoken: No identity without difference, no One without plurality; rather both are One in difference. In a negative way he illustrates this result as the fruit—which appears suddenly in its indisposability—of a long way of practice[206] in Soto Zen, which in its "Only sitting" can lapse into "mere indifference, stillness, egoity and law," and in Rinzai Zen, which is threatened by the same "errors of awakening," if it thinks

---

matsu's *Collected Works* and appeared in a somewhat abbreviated form under the title *Die fünf Stände von Zen-Meister Tosan Ryokai* in a translation by Koichi Tsujimura published with Neske Verlag in Pfullingen in 1980, together with the author's calligraphy of typical Zen sayings and an afterword by the translator. In reference to these "final great calligraphies of the ninety-year-old master," which he produced for the German edition shortly before his death, the translator regards this text together with those of *Die Fülle des Nichts* as the memorial of the author in Germany (19). In comparison with the "Oxherd Pictures" he characterizes their significance in this way, that the latter, unlike the former, were intended not for beginners, but for the "advanced," because they wish to protect them from the "insistence of the ones who have once won awakening" (89). He emphasizes however that Hisamatsu, in his "structural analysis of awakening" does not understand the five stations "statically and in a contemplative way," as is the case in the Tradition, but interprets it "anew as active-dynamic" (90).

A presentation of the traditional conception of the "Five Stations" which still stands under Confucian influence (I-Ching) is offered by Heinrich Dumoulin in the context of his description of the "five houses" of Zen in the Tang period and the following periods of the five dynasties, by which he represents Tosan Ryokai under the name of Ts'ao-shan along with other founders of the Soto Zen Tungshan, and explains both dialectics—as Hisamatsu also does—by means of the image of a circle that changes between black and white colors (Dumoulin, *Zen, Geschichte und Gestalt* [1959] 116ff. [ET: *A History of Zen Buddhism*, 1963, 106ff.]).

[206]Ibid., 8.

that in its koan practice it has to do merely with "difference, movement, plurality, and things."[207]

Over against both possibilities of failure Hisamatsu places the famous "Parable of the wave and the sea" as an image of the position of positionlessness, in which both stations, without being robbed of their particularity, are one.[208] In this sense he holds that "Without the heart, no Buddha,"[209] and that Nirvana is that "essence-less essence" of the self in awakening. But while he speaks in this connection of the nonobjectifiability of the self and of Nirvana, he nevertheless repeatedly emphasizes that it is here not a matter of logical, intellectual deduction in the manner of "European" or even "Chinese" thinking,[210] but initially and in all its stations of the "position of positionlessness" of the awakening in "practical exercise," which can be spoken of in "silence," as Shakyamuni is said to have expressed it in his forty-nine years of preaching.[211]

If one should like to gain some understanding from the perspective of our Western thinking—despite its negative evaluation by Hisamatsu[212]—for the course of thought in which he develops his first intention, insofar as we know of a "looking through" the objectivities to something nonobjectifiable that is common to them, of which he is aware from the perspective of the self, and can agree with him to some extent in our self-understanding from afar, it is difficult for us to go along with him vis-à-vis the second intention which he attempts to validate by means of the three other structural forms which he characterizes as "issuing from the upright," "coming together," "returning home together."[213]

As these indicators make us aware, he wishes here—in extending the criticism already expressed with respect to certain forms of Zen[214]—to go beyond a merely static conception of awakening as a persistent and satisfying condition of redemption, and to arrive at certification of its necessary, but rightly understood redemptive activity in the "Great Compassion" of the Bodhisattva. According to the notation on the indication of the fourth station[215] and according to the condition that the upright and aslant cannot be satisfactorily expressed in the five stations,[216] the tradition to which he appeals in what appears to be a scholastic

---

[207]Ibid., 41-42.
[208]Ibid., 42ff.
[209]Ibid., 20.
[210]Ibid., 20, 28, 44ff., 53, 67, and 80.
[211]Ibid., 58.
[212]Ibid., 79.
[213]Ibid., 51ff.
[214]Ibid., 12, 32, 41, 42, and 46.
[215]Ibid., 10.
[216]Ibid., 45.

way presents some difficulties for him. The way in which he attempts to resolve this is contradictory both to his rejection of Chinese thinking in that—without noting it—he makes use of its basic perspective, and to a consequence which he draws from it, which is possible only on the basis of the objectivity of the conception of reality in Western thinking which he also rejects, without [which] this latter goes into the void in the "emptiness" of Zen Buddhism and makes all world-altering acts illusory.

In opposition to his demand of "becoming free" from "Chinese philosophy and cosmology,"[217] Hisamatsu—in order to go beyond a mere "contemplating Zen"[218] in his use of the "precious mirror" "which allows not only external things to be reflected in it," but can form and change them"—appeals to the designation of the "upright position" of a central notion of Taoism, as this occurs already in the sixth Chinese patriarch, Hui-neng. When Hisamatsu says of this "precious mirror," "It does not simply show things, but changes them, in a way that exactly corresponds to them, and creates what was not. Accordingly it creates nothing because it creates something; it makes nothing, changes nothing, because it makes and changes something,"[219] this is exactly what Lao-tzu said of the Tao in the Tao te Ching. Only by inserting the Wu-wei of the Tao does Hisamatsu succeed in bringing movement into the persistent stillness of awakening and thus in finding in this nonactivity the occasion and space for the activity of the Bodhisattva for whom the object of his "Great Compassion" is still missing.

But Hisamatsu is not troubled by this lack of an object of compassion in emptiness. As if he had not previously judged the entire world of objects to be an illusory product of the thinking of consciousness which he rejects while wishing to regard awakening as the sole reality, as being at the same time Buddha- and Nirvana-Being,[220] now as though he were a Western Christian, he speaks of "the other self," to which the self must "arrive from the upright," in order to realize the "gathering together" of the "upright" and the "aslant," and to complete itself in the "coming home together." But in contrast to Christian love, which does not seek its own (1 Cor. 13:5) he emphasizes that the "going out" to the "aid-of-the-other" takes place for the sake of the "aid of the self." "Whoever looks back to the way through which he has reached his self, sees that he was not in the true self; he wishes that the others also attain to the true

---

[217]Ibid., 44.

[218]Ibid., 48.

[219]Ibid., 45. On Hisamatsu's relation to "Chinese philosophy and cosmology," or "becoming free" of it, cf. Toshihiko Izutsu, "The Absolute and Perfect Man in Taoism," *Eranos-Jahrbuch 1967* (Zurich: Rhein-Verlag, 1968) 379-441.

[220]Ibid., 28, 51.

self."[221] From this argumentation it will not only not be apparent why the movement toward the "going out" as the "aid for the other" arises from the insight into nontrue self-being which was the case earlier but now is apparently overcome, but Hisamatsu radically excludes the ready-to-hand appeal to a sympathy with the other—whether from its own selfishness, insofar as one cannot be happy without the other, or from a sensitivity to his suffering—in that he explains: "The suffering being, which is said to be rescued, is nowhere to be found, and this is the basis of the compassionate deed for the suffering being."[222] He himself expresses the judgment on this grounding of the compassionate deed when he speaks of compassion as something "groundless" and regards every other grounding of the same as an illusory idealism. Only in this way does the self experience itself as "absolutely free,"[223] having need of "neither God nor the Buddha;"[224] it recognizes no "rules and laws" for its acts,[225] and is beyond good and evil without being imprisoned therein.[226]

Hisamatsu expresses the existential seriousness of the conception of life through the image of "dying and resurrection" and emphasizes that both must occur "during life."[227] But when he sees this way of life of the "true self" symbolized in the orbit of the moon and its change from "new moon to full moon,"[228] and compares the five stations with the unfolding, fanning and refolding of a fan, the question arises whether he has succeeded in making dynamic what is static in the traditional structure of awakening, and whether it has been illumined by him not merely in its naturalistic and aesthetizing aspects, but also ethically. If the Zen sayings which he presents in his calligraphy and which he prefixes as mottoes to his elucidations on the "five stations of awakening" stimulate us to deep thought: of a 'memorial of the author,' as Tsujimura thinks of it, we cannot speak in view of the "structural analysis of awakening," which Hisamatsu undertook by means of that memorial of Zen Buddhist tradition, but we see in it rather its crumbling and dissolution under the disintegrating influence of an atmosphere of Far Eastern, as much as of Western nihilistic thinking. In the Far East as in the West nihilism proceeds from the assumption that man—for the sake of the freedom of his Self—thinks he can make his self as substance or as emptiness into his own Lord and therefore attain to an existence which

---

[221]Ibid., 80.
[222]Ibid., 66.
[223]Ibid., 77.
[224]Ibid., 78.
[225]Ibid., 71.
[226]Ibid., 81.
[227]Ibid., 78.
[228]Ibid., 74.

Hisamatsu designates as "free of all ties";[229] "having forgotten all attributes";[230] "coming home" in "our authentic, ordinary mode of being";[231] "without changing the true world" and "without wiping the dust;[232] "sitting in silence"[233] only temporarily using the fan for "fanning" and sinking in "One Silence."[234]

Hisamatsu correctly declined the arrangements of a funeral, the gathering of his remains and the erection of a tombstone—as Tsujimura reports—and instead, leaves behind as his "legacy" several poems, one of which reads as follows.[235]

> Awakened to the formless self,
> I die death immortally
> Born to the unborn life,
> I play in three worlds.

Playing in paradoxes, every form dissolves into the formlessness of an emptiness as "redemption of redemption" in Nirvana, and what is left is a poem as the reflection of enlightenment—to be enacted in practice.

It is evident that from this perspective every kind of Christian conception of redemption can only be rejected as a sign of unredemption, as Hisamatsu repeatedly suggests in this treatise. He can and need not do more than suggest this opposition, because he would otherwise have to abandon the "position of positionlessness" and the "form of the formless." But it is precisely in this that the incommensurability of his conception of Zen with every form of Christian faith becomes evident. For a real encounter of the two worlds it would be necessary to transcend the Christ of Christianity, as Hisamatsu postulates for the Buddha of Buddhism. In this he is a genuine Zen Buddhist and shows in this way, as few others have done, what Buddhism ultimately means for Christianity and what decisions it faces in the encounter in its most radical forms.

To characterize this situation and further to elaborate the position we have represented over against it, we can make use of two contributions which appeared in two of the most recent numbers of *The Eastern Buddhist*, one of which stems from Hisamatsu's own writings and the other from the pen of one of his best disciples, and in both of which the nature and problematic of Hisamatsu's thinking once again confronts us.[236]

---

[229] Ibid., 77.
[230] Ibid., 73.
[231] Ibid., 55.
[232] Ibid., 57.
[233] Ibid., 73.
[234] Ibid., 82.
[235] Ibid., 91.
[236] "On the *Record of Rinzai*," EB 14/1 (1981): 1-12, and 14/2 (1981): 11-21;

The first article taken from the collected works of Hisamatsu consists of lectures "On the *Record of Rinzai*," which Hisamatsu delivered in 1962 in the course of a Zen Sesshin. He begins his deliberations with a citation from the beginning of Rinzai's work—[237]

> If I were to demonstrate the Great Matter in strict keeping with the doctrine of the Patriarchal School, I simply couldn't open my mouth—

in order to see therein the norm both for his elucidations on this work as well as for the attitude to be exhibited toward it by the hearers, and to draw from it for both not only a negative, but a positive consequence. For him as well as for the hearers who follow his expositions nothing depends upon how much or how little he expresses from Rinzai's text. His "entire *Record*" can be grasped "in the fullest sense by means of just one of its words and phrases," as in the one just cited, which fill "every page" "with vitality and life."[238] It is also valid not to read them according to the "manner of historians, that is, as a document of the early period of Chinese Zen." For then it would be "a mere record of the past," and we would not have in it "the words and actions of our living Self here and now."[239]

With this latter definition Hisamatsu goes far beyond that which we could initially imagine as the "immediately present truth"[240] he mentioned earlier, which "manifests itself in all of its majesty," being the result of a so-called existential understanding. Then the text would still have to serve as a "means" to the understanding of something meant therein. This is just what Hisamatsu means by appealing to Rinzai's conception of his preaching of the Dharma, in consequence of which "the Hearer and Rinzai are never two,"[241] and he would deliver us a blow in accord with the well-known method of Zen masters if he remains as "an *object* of our respect and devotion" "outside of us."[242] As "religious seekers," according to Hisamatsu, we must "seek" Rinzai's record "within ourselves." For "Rinzai is in us." "Because the words and effects of the living Rinzai emerge out of ourselves," we must "emerge out of ourselves," must "free ourselves from his record." Therein consists "the critical spirit" of "authentic Zen." "Studying and practicing Rinzai's way" consists in "making one's self free of him."

Masao Abe, "Hisamatsu's Philosophy of Awakening," EB 14/1 (1981): 26–52.
[237]EB 14/1 (1981): 1.
[238]Ibid., 2.
[239]Ibid., 3.
[240]Ibid., 1.
[241]Ibid., 2.
[242]Ibid., 4.

Although Hisamatsu's repeated reference to the Dharma in his use of Rinzai's "I could not open my mouth"[243] makes us think momentarily of the function which in a certain theology of revelation is assigned to the Word of God on the one hand, and on the other, to the Incarnation, the replacement represented there of existential with a "theological exegesis" is categorically excluded for Rinzai and Hisamatsu by the appeal to the famous Zen saying: "Encountering a Buddha, killing the Buddha; encountering a patriarch, killing the patriarch." When he says of such figures that attachment to them is "apt to restrict us and to involve us in complications,"[244] one can only agree with him in view of the things which are connected with the theology of the Word of God. In Zen, on the contrary, the difficulties of the Dharma-"transmission from mind to mind" in the "awakening" to the "original Face" are dissolved in Rinzai's "True Person without Rank" as the "true self,"[245] as Rinzai demonstrates when he delivers a blow to his teacher Obaku and thereby becomes in "genuine child-like piety" "the heir of his Dharma." In this sense, explains Hisamatsu, "we must all actualize Rinzai in our selves, and his record as our own words and acts."[246]

In one of the following lectures Hisamatsu elucidates this hermeneutical program in more detail.[247] In the face of the rejection of the "methods of the historians" which he previously demanded and of the warning which he issues about a "mere copying of Rinzai's behavior,"[248] he here undertakes the beginning of "the circumstances surrounding his decision to begin Zen practice and the events involved in his great Awakening."[249] Although the picture he arrives at of the difficulties Rinzai apparently had with "scholastic Buddhism"[250] and of the way in which he "left the lecture halls,"[251] and the parallels he supplies from other Zen stories[252] confirm the fact that they all ultimately and solely deal with the realization of the "true self," he is nevertheless dealing with "historical" facts which he proposes to his hearers as prototypes for their behavior. Hisamatsu's descriptions differ from historical methods only in the fact that he no longer makes a distinction between the subject and object of research, because in "awakening" both get obliterated, or "killed" and Rinzai, the Buddha and the true

---

[243]Ibid., 2.
[244]Ibid., 3.
[245]Ibid., 2.
[246]Ibid., 4.
[247]Ibid., 5ff.
[248]Ibid., 3.
[249]Ibid., 5.
[250]Ibid., 7.
[251]Ibid., 8.
[252]Ibid., 6ff.

self of the awakened one, "lecturer or hearer," become "one" "right now beyond past, present, and future,"[253] so that we can no longer speak of a mere imitation, because the awakening is "nothing special"; rather the "formless self" assumes form "freely and without hindrance."[254]

Thus the nature of the treatment Hisamatsu assigns to the Rinzai text in his explanations of it consists in letting it work in such a way that it makes its hearers free from it—as indeed of every entanglement in conceptualities—therefore in an exegesis that leads to absurdities, as this corresponds to the basic Zen principle of the "transmission outside the teaching."[255] But from this, according to Hisamatsu, no method can be created in the sense of an "essence of Buddhism" or of "Buddhist precepts,"[256] for if he regards it as constitutive for the "sudden awakening" he represents in contrast to the "gradual," that is, for the "Great Doubt, Great Resolution or Great Death,"[257] yet at the same time he emphasizes that this only starts to work in immersion if one does not think of it.[258] When, at the beginning of his essay, Hisamatsu recalls that Rinzai's text has "a well-established reputation for being quite impenetrable," it must be said after these lectures that he likewise completely corresponds to it in this regard, which is due to the fact that he does not wish for it to be taken as an object and to be regarded as such. Still less than this hermeneutic can both the tangible illustration which Hisamatsu provides for it in a thorough description and commentary of the exchange between Rinzai, Obaku, and other Zen masters and the way they insult each other and slap each other in the face in the second part of this contribution, be recommended for imitation. One is accordingly anxious to see whether a master disciple like Masao Abe can succeed in making "Hisamatsu's Philosophy of Awakening" more accessible and capable of execution.

Abe begins his essay which carries this title with a general characterization of Hisamatsu's philosophy in connection with several typical characteristics of the nature and origin of his experience and thinking which exhibits a great similarity with what Hisamatsu highlighted as characteristic for Rinzai and which distinguishes both from Western philosophers.

Abe first emphasizes that Hisamatsu's philosophy is nothing other than the "free and unrestricted self-expression" of the "awakening" he experienced as the "fundamental self-realization" of his human being. As such it is expressed by him not merely as philosophy, but equally so in "calligraphy, painting, and

---

[253]Ibid., 7.
[254]Ibid.
[255]Ibid.
[256]Ibid., 11.
[257]Ibid., 9.
[258]Ibid., 10.

poetry," in the "tea ceremony" of which he was "especially fond," in fact in "everything about his life, his everyday conversations, his way of receiving callers, his laughter and silence," and in a floral arrangement he created as in an "ordinary word of greeting." Because it is grounded in figure and form in awakening, this philosophy is to be distinguished from "ordinary philosophy," both from that of Hegel, because it does not consist in a "speculative conceptual structure," but also from that of Kierkegaard, because Hisamatsu was not like him, namely, a "Christian-in-the-making" (*Werdender Christ*), but "one who has become a Buddha." Although it possesses "greater affinity" with the philosophy of Socrates—on account of its "unity of knowledge and action" and his admonition, "Know thyself'—and that of Spinoza—because of its "intoxication with God"—these do not, in Abe's eyes, attain the stature of the philosophy of awakening, because they do not "break beyond the frame of reason," as is the case in the "self-negation" of the latter, and thus it is not merely philosophy, but at the same time "religion," or rather: "philosophy and religion are one" in a "total person."[259]

After this fundamental characterization of the essence of this existentially religious philosophy of awakening, Abe illustrates its individual features in the following four sections of his essay by means of Hisamatsu's "Memories of My Student Life," which is still untranslated.[260] From the citations from these memoirs and their elucidations by Abe there emerges the following picture of the origin of Hisamatsu's "philosophy of awakening" and of its nature in particular. Hisamatsu, who was raised in a devout Shin Buddhist family, was according to his own words "a steadfast young believer" and wished to become a "man of religion." But already during his high school period doubts began to arise in him, and his departure from school was for him, as he writes, characterized by "a conversion from the religious life of naive religious belief which avoids rational doubt, to the critical life of modern man based on autonomous judgment and empirical proof." He remarks, however, that "at the same time, his rational awareness of sin deepened," from which he wished to be freed, even though he did not think "he was destined for hell, nor did he long to be "reborn in paradise." He rather hoped that he could resolve this "dilemma" in "rational inquiry," and for this reason began "the study of philosophy under Nishida Kitaro at Kyoto University." This great teacher "revived his fundamental religious concern, and opened up for him a new philosophical perspective on religion," not only through

[259]Abe, "Hisamatsu's Philosophy of Awakening," 26-28.
[260]Ibid., 28-37.

his lectures but in a different way, by "advising him to do sanzen (Zen practice)."[261]

What happened to him in the eight years of his study at Kyoto is summarized by Hisamatsu, who in his sketches constantly refers to himself in the third person, as follows: "He cast off the religion of medieval belief, turned to philosophy grounded in modern reason, broke through the extreme limit of rational philosophy based on objective knowledge, and awakened to the free and unhindered True Self."[262] This is the result of the reciprocity and cooperation of the central perspective of the "self-contradictoriness of autonomous reason" of Nishida's philosophy[263] with the "Great Death as Great Awakening," in which the one who in Zen practice becomes the "Great Mass of Doubt," participates in *kensho*, that is, "seeing one's nature, insight into the self."[264]

Abe makes several explanatory observations about this "experience" which according to Hisamatsu occurs on the philosophical way he pioneers after abandoning the religion of his parents. Thus he recalls that after Hisamatsu's "faith was destroyed by rational skepticism," his "rational awareness of sin became increasingly acute and he earnestly longed to free himself from it." He sees the cause of this in the fact that "as a result of the religious atmosphere in which he had been brought up, this faith was deeply ingrained in him in the early years before he turned to philosophy," so that for him "philosophical inquiry was a problem neither of the theoretical cognition of the world nor of the objective validity of values," as was the case with Nishida's "philosophy of pure subjectivity." Insofar as Hisamatsu's "philosophical understanding remained objective cognition, he was completely unable to solve the total, existential problem at hand."[265] It was "autonomous reason" which "spurred on the hidden, yet unchanged desire to live the truth and brought it to light," but at the same time it "permitted him to remain discontented," and thus led him "beyond philosophy to Zen." In Zen it has always been known that "at the bottom of the Great Doubt lies the Great Awakening," but—according to Abe—"until Hisamatsu, the kind of self-contradiction found in autonomous reason had never before constituted the dynamics behind the establishment of the Great Doubt."[266] Abe draws the conclusion from Hisamatsu's report on his Zen experience that Hisamatsu's Great Doubt and the following Great Awakening "were sharpened

---

[261]Ibid., 28ff.
[262]Ibid., 32.
[263]Ibid., 30-31.
[264]Ibid., 32n.4; cf. 29.
[265]Ibid., 31.
[266]Ibid., 33.

and clarified by his realization of the self-contradictoriness intrinsic in autonomous reason."[267]

If Abe wishes to see in this connection of satori and the self-contradictoriness of objective knowledge—which for him was typical of the origin and nature of Hisamatsu's "philosophy of awakening"—not only the norm of Zen thinking, but also the proof of its superiority over every other kind of thinking, and that means especially of the Western kind, it must be objected that all objectifying thinking presses self-understanding to its limits, except that the one who becomes aware of these limits becomes a "Great Doubting Mass," and "suddenly" in "total darkness" attains a break-through into a realm in which the "Great Doubt" becomes simultaneously the "Great Awakening." The second crisis which Hisamatsu falls into on his course of thought has its ground apparently in the fact that he thinks the first, in which he with his "medieval faith" had been offended by becoming acquainted with modern science, could only be solved by its logic and then with a absence of contradiction supported by Zen practices.

What Abe systematically developed concerning this in the further sections of his essay as Hisamatsu's "religion" as "self-redemption of the absolute self,"[268] represents—first—a worldview in which there is "neither God nor man, transcendence nor immanence" nor any kind of differentiation, but only "the world of pure Nothingness," in which there is no single thing, not even what one could call "awakening," but only "the emptiness of all things."[269] Reaching this state is a matter of the "self-redemption of the awakened self" in "absolute autonomy"—and—second—it is bound up with a "cosmological character,"[270] because in it things appear as they are with one blow, freed from the "subject-object duality."[271] Although Hisamatsu sees in it a peculiarity of the "spiritual heritage of the East," he nevertheless maintains that it belongs to the nature of man in the East as well as the West,[272] and on this—third—he grounds also his demand for a "new humanism" as the "creation of history" of universal human proportions.[273]

Unfortunately Abe fails to develop in detail these three traits of Hisamatsu's "philosophy of awakening," but rather remains content to clarify its fundamental presuppositions in Hisamatsu's philosophical development and reserves its elucidation for a subsequent article.[274] But from what he has developed it already

---

[267]Ibid., 34.
[268]Ibid., 37ff.
[269]Ibid., 37.
[270]Ibid., 38.
[271]Ibid., 40.
[272]Ibid., 38.
[273]Ibid., 41.
[274]Ibid., 42.

appears that a confrontation with this "philosophy" is excluded because a stand-point would have to be assumed over against it, which is rejected by it a limine as the fate of the subject-object split of consciousness. This cannot be discussed with an "enlightened one" because whatever are allowed to be submitted as critical objections against its enlightenment derive according to it from non-enlightened being and therefore lose any positive significance for it. In view of all the hopelessness of finding a hearing among the representatives of the "philosophy of awakening," we would nevertheless like to pose this question: how can a self, which according to its essence is nothing, save itself or to what extent can this be a self-redemption if it is the 'deed' of nothingness? Further, what is the case with this "expansion of the self" into a "spatial and temporal boundlessness?"[275] Further, how is it possible to arrive at the "creation of history" as a "true humanism?"[276] We can only agree with the conception of the self as nothingness—as Hisamatsu has experienced it—by not allowing it to be grasped in the framework of the subject-object schema of conscious thinking, for it represents for this a nothingness. But this becoming aware of its character as nothing-ness for the objectifying consciousness is not a matter of nothingness, but of this self that, having become aware of the limits of its grasp, exhibits itself in this nonobjectifiability as the "true self." As such, however, it is identical with neither being nor nothingness, but represents a special phenomenon within this sphere, which can be identified with neither. With its self-absolutization as "creation" it would betray its finiteness of which it is to be aware precisely at its limits. In be-coming aware of its finiteness it experiences a special power of the mystery of being, or of nothingness, and therefore grounds the nature of history in distinc-tion from natural occurrence. The formation of history, however, presupposes con-ceptual differentiation, and therefore the opposite of an "expansion into spatial and temporal boundlessness." History occurs where man does not suppose that he generates the world, but experiences himself as destined for its meaningful formation, which can actually become for him "a cause for the discovery of great surprise and joy,"[277] but not without the simultaneous experience of its proble-matic. This problematic of meaning constitutes the nature of history, whose over-coming and fulfillment is also the goal of Hisamatsu's F.A.S. program.[278] But this is realizable only on the basis of a "true self" which is conscious of its specific significance in the framework of the universe—a self which is conscious in terms of discriminating thinking, of its being destined for a world-redeeming function. For this purpose the mythology of the Christ could serve as a symbol

---

[275]Ibid., 40.
[276]Ibid., 41.
[277]Ibid., 40.
[278]Ibid., 41.

in an existential interpretation, as Hisamatsu, for example, undertakes it with the
true self of the 'man without rank" as a explanation of the task of humanity in
the cosmos and its problematic. With this cosmic expansion of the self and its
dissolution into nothingness Hisamatsu may not be able to do justice to this state
of affairs. Here two different self-understandings stand in irreconcilable opposition: a conceptual thinking of consciousness which is conscious of its finitude
and problematic nature and becomes intellectually effective on this basis, and an
ontological speculation of a unity for which the thinking in the subject-object
schema of consciousness represents only a secondary deprivation of the 'original
awakening." Between these self-understandings we have to choose without the
benefit of retroactive ontological-speculative authentication, but alone in terms
of their cultural effects. "Oriental Nothingness" or "Being in Christ"—that is the
basic decision before which we find ourselves inevitably placed. Without the
"Great Doubt" and the "Great Death" it cannot take place, but it appears to us
to be possible only in the second way to come to the "Great Awakening" which
really deserves the name and can benefit the "whole of humanity."

Chapter 6

Keiji Nishitani (1900–[1990])
Zen as Philosophy of Religion

1. The Development and Intention
of Nishitani's Philosophy

After the death of Shin'ichi Hisamatsu at the beginning of 1980, Keiji Nishitani became the oldest surviving representative of the Kyoto School. He was born in 1900, studied under Nishida at Kyoto University, became associate professor in 1935, and then full professor of philosophy and successor to Tanabe in 1943. Since becoming emeritus in 1964 he has taught at Otani University in Kyoto, whose campus is the site of the editing of *The Eastern Buddhist*, in which Nishitani was engaged. He is also president of the Eastern Buddhist Society and of the International Institute for Japan Studies and is regarded as one the most important philosophical thinkers of modern Japan. In numerous publications and through participation in international programs as well as lectures in Europe and America he has been engaged in the interchange between Western and Far Eastern culture and the encounter of Buddhism with Christianity.[1]

About his personal development Nishitani reports that even before he heard Nishida's lectures, he felt strongly moved by Nietzsche, Dostoevski, Emerson, and Carlyle, but also by the Bible and Francis of Assisi, and that among Japanese authors he loved above all Natsume Soseki (1867–1916) and the two Zen masters Takuan and Hakuin. In these he was most intrigued by the "doubt about the true self," and therefore with "something like the Buddhist 'Great Doubt'," and this is what turned him to Zen. This led him further to a preoccupa-

---

[1] For Nishitani's biography, cf. Jan van Bragt, "Nishitani on Japanese Religiosity" in Joseph J. Spae, *Japanese Religiosity* (Tokyo: Oriens Institute for Religious Research, Tokyo, 1971) 271-84 (with numerous excerpts, partly from untranslated writings of Nishitani); Hans Waldenfels, *Absolutes Nichts* (Herder-Verlag, 1976) 67ff. [ET: *Absolute Nothingness: Foundations for a Buddhist-Christian Dialogue* (New York: Paulist Press, 1980) 35ff.]; Gino K. Piovesana, S.J.; *Recent Japanese Thought, 1892–1962*, 2nd ed. (Tokyo: Sophia University, 1968) 192-93, 200ff., 253. All three authorities give information about Nishitani's publications. For further literature on Nishitani, cf. Hans Waldenfels, "Absolute Nothingness. Preliminary Considerations on a Central Notion in the Philosophy of Nishida Kitaro and the Kyoto School," MN 21/3-4 (1966): 354-91; Jan van Bragt, "Notulae on Emptiness and Dialogue," JR 4 (1966): 50-78; Joseph Spae, *Buddhist-Christian Empathy* (Chicago, 1980) 35ff.

tion with German Idealism, above all with Schelling, whose text on freedom he translated, and with the medieval mystics, especially with Meister Eckhart [cf. King in Nishitani, *Religion and Nothingness*, xxxiv-xxxv].

Shortly before the Second World War Nishitani studied for some time with Heidegger in Freiburg. His influence seems to have made itself most noticeable in the way in which Nishitani concerned himself with the problem of the nation during the war. The two writings "Philosophy of Fundamental Subjectivity" (1940) and "World Conception and Conception of the State" (1941) stem from this period. Nishitani also coauthored a newspaper article with two colleagues which deals with Japan's position in world history and with themes such as "The Philosophy of Total War."

In an understandable apology, Piovesana notes that "it was practically impossible during the war to speak about such themes, without making a place more or less for nationalistic tendencies," and that the authors were "left with no other choice."[2] Following his refusal to cite passages taken out of context, we also refrain from citing objectionable passages to be found in these two texts; rather we shall point out that in them Nishitani also emphasizes that only a "religion which does not become a tool of politics" can serve politics with its "true power," and that already here he espoused thoughts about the crisis of culture and secularization as well as the possibility of their being overcome religiously in terms of Zen, and the significance which is ascribed therein to Zen, which he then unfolded in a series of books and essays after the war.

Only after the war did Nishitani's philosophy of religion attain the form with which we have to be concerned here. To characterize the initial phases of this unfolding of his own philosophical work, to which Nishitani is indebted for the standing which he attained in the contemporary cultural life of Japan and beyond its borders, we shall mention primarily the titles of two untranslated writings: "Nihilism" (1946) and "God and Absolute Nothingness" (1949). The series of his publications which were translated into English or German began with his contribution to the International Congress for the History of Religion, held in Tokyo in 1958, which he entitled "Die religiöse Existenz im Buddhismus."[3] An essay published in Japanese in 1958 on "The Problem of Time in Shinran," first appeared in English translation in 1978.[4] Nishitani also participated in the debate

---

[2]Piovesana, *Recent Japanese Thought, 1892-1962*, 193. I am indebted to my former doctoral student Keiji Kasai for knowledge of the contents of these writings.

[3]In the *Proceedings of the IX. International Congress for the History of Religion* (Tokyo, 1958) 577-83, and in *Sein und Sinn. Ein philosophisches Symposium*, ed. Richard Wisser (Tübingen: Max Niemeyer, 1960) 381-97. Here the title reads: "Die religiös-philosophische Existenz im Buddhismus."

[4]EB 9/1 (1978): 13-26 (with additions and emendations).

over demythologizing inspired by Bultmann with a comprehensive and significant essay published in German in 1960, with the title "Buddhismus und Christentum."[5] Already by 1960 there had appeared an English translation of the first chapter of his principal work *Religion and Nothingness*, which had hitherto been published only in Japanese.[6] Whereas this chapter was separately published one year before the Japanese edition of the whole volume by UNESCO in *Japanese Studies of Philosophy*, the other five chapters only made their appearance during the years 1970–1980 in *The Eastern Buddhist*. As the notations to the individual chapters indicate, Nishitani had extensively reworked them for the English translation, and above all had significantly expanded the last two.[7]

In the time between the appearance of the first and second chapters of *Religion and Nothingness*, *The Eastern Buddhist* brought out the three additional essays from Nishitani's pen under the title, "Science and Zen,"[8] "The Awakening of Self in Buddhism,"[9] and "On the I-Thou Relation in Zen-Buddhism."[10] Moreover, he wrote an Introduction to two of Heidegger's speeches reprinted in this

---

[5]*Nachrichten der Gesellschaft für Natur- und Völkerkunde-Ostasiens/Hamburg* (Wiesbaden: Kommisionsverlag Otto Harrassowitz, December 1960) 5-32. It appeared with the title "Eine buddhistische Stimme zum Thema Entmythologisierung," in *Zeitschrift für Religions- und Geistesgeschichte* 13 (1961): 244-26 and 345-635.

[6]*Japanese Studies of Philosophy*, comp. by the Japanese Historical Commission for UNESCO, vol. 2 (Tokyo, 1960) 21-64.

[7]Chap. 2: "The Personal and Impersonal in Religion," EB 3/1 (1970): 1-18; 3/2 (1970): 71-88. Chap. 3: "Nihilism and Sunyata," EB 4/2 (1971): 30-49; 6/1 (1972): 55-69; 5/2 (1972): 96-106. Chap. 4: "The Standpoint of Sunyata," EB 6/1 (1973): 92-110; 6/2 (1973): 58-86. Chap. 5: "Emptiness and Time," EB 9/1 (1976): 42-71; 10/2 (1977): 1-30. Chap. 6: "Emptiness and History," EB 12/1 (1979): 49-82; 12/2 (1979): 55-71; 13/1 (1980): 9-30.

According to all reports, Nishitani is thought to have incorporated significant modifications in the still unpublished German translation of this work. A comparison of this with the English translation which is the basis for our work should prove instructive for the understanding of his thinking and its development. But it should be noted that the English translation, in contrast to the original Japanese text, already exhibits "numerous revisions and additions" (EB 3/1 (1970): 1n.1. Presently an edition of the work which appeared piecemeal in *The Eastern Buddhist* is being prepared in book form in English. [See *Religion and Nothingness*, trans. with an intro. by Jan van Bragt, foreword by Winston L. King (Berkeley: University of California Press, 1982). —Trans.]

[8]EB 1/1 (1965): 79-108.

[9]EB 1/2 (1966): 71-87.

[10]EB 2/1 (1969): 71-87.

Keiji Nishitani (1900–1990)

journal,[11] and in 1968 provided a contribution to *The Japanese Christian Year-book* under the title, "A Buddhist Philosopher looks at the Future of Christiani-ty."[12] It remains for us to mention only a still unpublished translation in which Nishitani supplied information on "The Standpoint of Zen." Reference should be made to the article by Jan van Bragt on "Nishitani on Japanese Religiosity" for Nishitani's autobiographical statements which are available only in Japanese, especially with respect to his attitude toward Christianity.[13]

From this survey of Nishitani's literary corpus which is available to us in translation, it follows that in these essays we are dealing with individual essential aspects of his philosophy and the areas to which he applied his philosophy of religion, in that in the latter he gathered together those individual attitudes toward specific problems into a whole under the question of the nature of religion. In accord with this state of affairs we shall proceed in our presentation of Nishitani's philosophy of religion in such a way that we try to understand these essays *seriatim* in order then to turn to the conceptualization of their intention in the work in which he was engaged for decades and which represents his authen-tic lifework. It will correspond to his basic intention if we indicate the main features of what Nishitani understood by religion and how he took up a position on Buddhism and Christianity from his conception of religion.

In each of these essays we are dealing with the whole of Nishitani's thought in condensed form, both with respect to the areas he addressed and the problems he discovered in them, as well as to the solutions he believed himself capable of offering to counter solutions that appeared to him untenable. Above all he dealt with the world and mankind and its quest for the meaning of existence, with science and religion which attempts to answer these questions, with the nihilism which threatened modernity and the possibility of overcoming it which in his view is available only in the concept of religion in Zen philosophy. The indi-vidual essays are to be distinguished from one another only insofar as Nishitani proceeds from the world-picture of science in the one and from the conception of the self in the other, or concerns himself with special worldviews and notions of redemption as they encounter him in his own tradition and in Christianity or outside of both of them. But in each we are always dealing with the basic thoughts of the program of salvation in a more or less developed form.

Typical of the programmatic nature of these essays is the lecture on "Die religiöse Existenz im Buddhism" which Nishitani composed in German and

---

[11]"Preliminary Remark" to Heidegger's "Ansprachen zum Heimatabend" and to "Über Abraham a Santa Clara," in EB 1/2 (1966): 48-59.
[12](Tokyo, 1968) 108-11.
[13]Cf. n. 1.

delivered in 1958 at the congress of historians of religion in Tokyo.[14] He sets out from the problem of "religion and science" which in his opinion "pervades" "the history of all higher religions," and that consists in the fact that the attempts "to draw a line between them" or—as may be needed—"to find a common ground in which they are mutually rooted" turn out to be "unsatisfying," and that "one of the main elements" of this difficulty lies in the "concept of God" which has hitherto been regarded as such a ground. As at the beginning, he expresses his conviction "that Buddhism has long since prepared the basis for overcoming this difficulty," and for evidence of this, points to the concept of anatman as a denial of the reality of an essence, like e.g. the atman, that is, of that which "prevails in every individual being as the permanent and unified carrier of its identity."[15] In this way is denied both the concept of "substance" and the "Cartesian ego" as well as every idealistic or materialistic "fundamental principle." including the Christian concept of God and of his *creatio ex nihilo*, because these concepts have to appear in opposition and "hinder mankind from breaking through to itself in a fundamental way."[16] The "Universe" never suffices as a parable of anatman or the "subject-less;" rather, anatman itself constitutes the place for extended space as well as for everything physical, psychic and spiritual." It is what is "absolutely open" which stands "beyond all opposition: the "place" in which "everything is grounded" and finds its "ultimate truth," and "in which each can break through to himself, come to himself and can know himself."

In order to clarify what this is about, Nishitani recalls the story of a monk who upon asking what "the primal truth of Buddhism is," sustained a kick from his teacher, so that he fell to the ground and thereby attained to the "break-through," for which reason he explained with "loud laughter": "O Miracle! O Miracle! I have all at once at the point of a needle discovered the origin of the countless wonderful truths, the primal ground of all things."[17] Nishitani inter-preted this Zen story to mean that it does not deal with a mystical union, but makes the point that the "trinity," namely, the existence of the man in the men-tioned event, the origin of all things, and the one who knows, is the "same," which means that the monk "at the moment of falling" became in his "not being the subject" (*Da des Nicht-Subjektums*) the "primal ground of all things" which "revealed" itself to him in this event as the "origin of all truth."[18] The equiva-lence of "absolute difference" and "absolute identity," as in that "trinity" in the monk's "knowing," persists—according to Nishitani—also between the monk and

---

[14]Cf. n. 3.
[15]Ibid., 577.
[16]Ibid., 578-79.
[17]Ibid., 580.
[18]Ibid., 581-82.

his teacher, in that their relationship deals with "the most immediate communication" which is "nevertheless not genuine communication," because with each everything flows out of its own origin, and "because here there is no communication, and no communicants."

When he concluded his lecture with the admission that "the customary kinds of communication" "always remain somewhat half or unfulfilled" and—in order to make good this lack—"always o'ervault themselves and must return to that manner of communication" "which is actually no longer communication,"[19] this reminds us not only of the close of the dialogue between Hisamatsu and Tillich;[20] rather, this mark of Buddhist philosophizing corresponds as well to the situation in which Nishitani may have found himself with his hearers, and in which we also find ourselves if we attempt to imitate his thoughts. It taxes us even more to see how he developed on a later occasion what he only "attempted to explain" here in his own words as a "reference to the religious existence on the basis of anatman."

2. The Existentializing of Science and Religion

The essay on "Science and Zen"[21] which appeared seven years after the contribution to the congress of historians of religion, in which Nishitani referred not merely to the concept of anatman, but also made use of the remaining Buddhist terminology belonging to the theme, serves as an example of such a penetrating presentation of "religious existence" and now makes more apparent the relation of "science and religion" which he merely mentioned in the previously cited lecture. In place of the story about the swift kick there appears here in connection with another Zen story the image of the kalpa fire which, in the demythologized existential interpretation in which he articulates it, acquires the same function of calling forth the "breakthrough" as the swift kick.

When Nishitani here writes, "In the religiosity of Zen Buddhism, demythologization of the mythical and existentialization of the scientific are contained in one and the same process,"[22] this surprisingly calls to mind Rudolf Bultmann's thesis about the necessity of the "demythologizing and existential interpretation of the New Testament kerygma." As will be shown later by means of another essay, Nishitani was thoroughly concerned in the interim with the demythologizing debate instigated by Bultmann. One should be careful here, however, to take note of the significant differences between the two programmatic formulations.

---

[19]Ibid., 583.

[20]Cf. above [162ff.].

[21]EB 1/1 (1965): 79-108. Repr.: *The Buddha Eye: An Anthology of the Kyoto School*, ed. Frederick Franck (New York: Crossroad, 1982) 111-37.

[22]Ibid., 92.

Whereas with Bultmann demythologizing and existential interpretation refer in equal measure to the New Testament kerygma, Nishitani distinguishes between "demythologizing the mythological" and "existentializing the scientific"—despite the fact that they belong together. The former he shares with Bultmann who did not speak of an "existentializing of the scientific," but only made use of science to demythologize the tradition in order to understand this subsequently in existential terms as the "kerygma" of a saving act of God that is not graspable scientifically. For Nishitani, to the contrary, there is neither such a once-for-all historical fact of salvation nor a transcendent God from whom it could originate; rather for him there occurs in the "existentializing of the scientific," that is, in the existential amazement at the breakdown of the scientific world-picture, that for which Bultmann carries out his "demythologizing." The kalpa fire becomes "demythologized" for him in such a way that he no longer views it as a merely mythological event in some kind of future, but that it becomes for him an image for what man today experiences as the catastrophic consequence of his science and technology—but which can at the same time become in Zen the "field" or "place" of "salvation,"[23] of which a Zen master says: "in the midst of the all-consuming kalpa fire there is an unspeakably awesome cold."[24]

Now how does Nishitani describe in detail this "numinous"[25] experience of salvation in the encounter of "science and Zen"? He does this in three steps, in that he first uncovers the human problematic of meaning brought about by modern science, then explains this "bottomlessness" "existentially" by recourse to the "Great Death" in Zen Buddhism, in order therein to attain to a new conferral of the meaning of Dasein in an existence understood by him as "religious."

The nature and effect of this "modern" science, here considered in the sense of the natural sciences, consists for Nishitani in the fact that through its mechanistic-materialistic explanation of the world the world is dedivinized and mankind is rendered homeless. He does not positively consider the fact that science can become aware of its limits; rather, in terms of Nietzsche's nihilism he judges such undertakings as "naive" attempts to elude a "fate" understood in Heidegger's sense. In a way that reminds one of Jaspers' speech on the collapse of the protective *"weltanschaulich* housings" he employs the picture of a dismantled "greenhouse,"[26] and further expands it eschatologically: "Science has

---

[23]Ibid., 93.

[24]Ibid., 90.

[25]I use the term "numinous" because the Zen saying corresponds to what Rudolf Otto meant by this term, and because in 1951 Nishitani was preoccupied with Rudolf Otto in his essay "God and Absolute Nothing," published only in Japanese.

[26]Ibid., 80, 88.

descended upon the world of teleology like an angel bearing a sword, or rather like a new demon."[27]

Nishitani not only deals in the present with a "world of death" described by him, but is acquainted with it, as he explains in the course of its presentation, from the Zen Buddhist tradition.[28] So it is not surprising that he ranks alongside the picture of the "angel with the sword" which stems from biblical apocalyptic, another derived from the eschatology of Buddhism, that of the kalpa fire. From the sentence with which he introduces this section it is evident what he intends with the use of this mythology. It states:

> That the usual state of the universe is explained by science in terms of life-less materiality means for a thinker who faces science existentially, that is, who accepts it as a problem concerning his own existence as such, that the universe is a field of existential death for himself and for all mankind, a field in which one is necessitated, to use again a Zen term, "to abandon him-self and to throw away one's own life," a field of absolute negation.[29]

At the end of the preceding section he had already explained, following Nietz-sche, that it is valid to "take science upon oneself, as a fire with which to purge and temper the traditional religions and philosophies, that is, as a new starting point for the inquiry into the essence of man." Here it is for him no longer a matter of a scientific investigation in which "the borderless universe" is still re-garded "from the viewpoint of science" as "nothing more than a material process, and the death of the living beings merely one aspect of the same process." Here "this constant feature of the universe and the death of living beings" is rather to be entertained as an "existential problem" in a "totally different way."[30]

As an example of this—as he says—"change of attitude" demanded by our philosophical and religious consciousness,[31] Nishitani seizes upon the "Zen koan about Tai-sui and the kalpa fire" whose importance to him resides in the fact that in it the notion of the world conflagration is "existentially interpreted"—as has happened in Buddhism from time immemorial—and thus at the same time "demythologized." It occurs in this instance in such a way that Tai-sui who, when asked by the monk whether in the "kalpa fire now raging" in which all worlds are consumed, even "this One"—by which this monk apparently means his "original self"—also perishes, answers: "It perishes." To the second question, whether "'it' goes off with the other" he answers: "It goes off following the

---

[27]Ibid., 85.
[28]Ibid., 85.
[29]Ibid., 88.
[30]Ibid., 87.
[31]Ibid., 87.

other." It must be destroyed—as Nishitani explains the matter—because as the monk understands it and aspires to it, it is still some kind of "other," that is, world.[32]

In this connection Nishitani does not hesitate to recall Hiroshima and scientific theories of the end of the world and so acknowledges that in these is manifested "an element of hidden scientific actuality as an actuality within the human realm." But he explains in reference to the verse added to the koan, "A question was asked within the glare of the kalpa fire; the monk tarries before a twofold barrier," that through Tai-sui's answer the "dagger of death," which "modern science has become for teleology," has become a "dagger of death in a religious sense" that is "at the same time a dagger of life."[33]

This "at the same time" of death and life he expounds in such a way that he primarily shows how through the "decision to accept the universe with its feature of bottomless death as the place for the abandoning of oneself and the throwing away of one's own life," "the life-inhibiting world of modern science is thereby exposed as a field in which death in the religious sense, or the Great Death as it is called in Zen Buddhism, is to be realized existentially." In this way the "myth of eschatology [is] realized and turned into the religiosity of the Great Death."[34] But in the fact that one makes "the universe . . . an expression of himself or, rather, a revelation of his own selfhood," "the sword that kills is here at the same time a sword that gives life." The monk who understands himself in the sense of Tai-sui's answer is "likened to 'a piece of ice glistening in the midst of a fire' . . . in the midst of a kalpa fire which burns up all things."[35] In such a way, Nishitani continues, "the monk . . . is brought to the dimension where he can find his salvation, the dimension in which he exists truly as himself, in which he is in his *Alētheia*," just as "the universe as itself and the kalpa fire . . . [are] each of them in its own *Alētheia*." In this way the monk realizes "the unborn for himself" which is as such "imperishable" because it is something beyond "the duality of life and death." Through the "Great Death" he becomes "free from all things as well as from himself" and by giving up "his egoistically small self," realizes "in the Unborn his own great Selfhood." This "existential path of self-deliverance" is what is also called in Zen Buddhism "the Great Compassion."[36]

After Nishitani has demythologized and existentially interpreted a portion of Buddhist eschatology in the manner we have described, he then expressly poses

---

[32]Ibid., 88-89.
[33]Ibid., 90.
[34]Ibid., 91-92.
[35]Ibid., 92.
[36]Ibid., 93.

the truth question, especially in the sense that he is in quest of the truth of religious existence in its relationship to the "truth" of scientifically establishable actuality.[37] On the one hand he characterizes the demythologized kalpa fire as an "expression of a scientific actuality"[38] as having the same "character of fact and truth" which he did not challenge for the results of science in other areas.[39] To be sure, over against them he holds firm to the "bottomlessness" connected with the Great Death, in that he points both to the difference of "quantitative and qualitative terms"[40] and to the "impossibility" of deriving from them "an original whole,"[41] as well as to the fact that man in his creative activity is always more dependent upon nature than the "original creator" insofar as everything has "its origin in the bosom of nature."[42]

On the other hand, however, he then stresses also that "in the eschatological idea" which deals with that "bottomlessness," "is contained something more" than a "scientific actuality"[43] and that this "dimension of bottomlessness" represents "the field" of the "place" "where concrete facts of nature emerge presenting themselves as they actually are and of more 'truth' than when they are ordinarily experienced as true facts."[44] In this connection he recalls Leibniz's distinction between *vérités des faites and vérités éternelles*—except that in contradistinction to Leibniz he speaks not of the universal Being of the central God-Monad—but just as idealistically and monistically—of the "Sole Self-exposed One"[45] of "the authentic self" on the "field of emptiness (*sunyata*) or absolute nothingness" of religious existence which as "the None in contrast to, and beyond, the One . . . enables the manifold phenomena to attain their true Being and realize their real Truth."[46]

On this "field of the Great Death" occurs the opposition between the pictures of the world and of man grounded religiously and mythologically or speculatively and philosophically, and the scientific one which challenges them, as well as the difference between these and "religious existence" as Nishitani understands it; for here "appears" "the ultimate truth and ultimate reality" of the "ultimate self" in the fact that all things (or phenomena) are hidden in the "unreal and untrue

---

[37]Ibid., 93ff.
[38]Ibid., 94.
[39]Ibid., 95.
[40]Ibid., 94-95.
[41]Ibid., 95.
[42]Ibid., 97.
[43]Ibid., 94.
[44]Ibid., 95.
[45]Ibid., 96.
[46]Ibid., 98.

realized in the "Great Death" so that in the unveiling of their illusoriness these are at once a real fact and an unreal appearance, "at once a 'truth' and untruth and are of more 'truth' and of more 'fact' even than they are in themselves."[47] As a picture of this "true Suchness" (*Tathata*), Nishitani uses the Buddhist saying about the wooden man who sings and a stone woman who dances[48], and—without mentioning the concept—allows "the mechanistic view of the world" and its "[existential acceptance] as the field of the Great Death of Man" to "interpenetrate each other" in the "vision of the mental eye" in accord with the sense of *pratitya-samutpada*.[49] In this he believes that he has found the "basic standpoint of man's religion," which in its "universality is similar to that of science." Since he explains by way of conclusion that this "standpoint of a religion with the above demanded universal character has already been realized, at least basically, in Buddhism, especially in Zen Buddhism, even though there are in Zen, in its traditions and actualities, various points to be amended, complemented, or perhaps radically reformed," he thereby simultaneously offers the program of his philosophy of religion.[50]

---

[47]Ibid., 101.

[48]Ibid., 103.

[49]Ibid., 107.

[50]Ibid., 136. In addition to this presentation of Nishitani's conception of the relation of "Zen and Science" reference should be made here to the quite different position Fritjof Capra represents respecting this problem in the work *The Tao of Physics. An Exploration of the Parallels between Modern Physics and Eastern Mysticism* (Boulder CO: Shambala Publications, 1975), which has in the meantime appeared in French and German translation (*Le Tao de la Physique* [Paris: Editions Tchou, 1979]; *Der kosmische Reigen* [O. W. Barth Verlag]. While Nishitani only envisions the mechanistic natural science derived from Newton and Descartes with its catastrophic consequences for a teleological picture of the world and of history and praises Zen for overcoming it, Capra appeals to contemporary atomic and astrophysics based on relativity and quantum theory to uncover, not oppositions, but quite fundamental commonalities between them and Far Eastern thought, especially Zen—and this is the case both with respect to methods and results. According to Capra the koans and even the myths assume the same function as the formulas and models of quantum theory, namely, as witnesses to the view of reality that is not imaginable in logical conceptuality but finally forms a harmonic whole. Like Capra, Nishitani held that the mystics, in contrast to what is the case with the physicists, did not annul the logic through the recognition of the logically inconceivable nature of reality but only indicated within its boundaries what is not possible without logical thinking. The reference to the boundaries of discriminating thinking is only possible through discursive thinking. The "nameless Tao" of the Tao Te Ching, like the "Nothing" of Zen, is an expression of the ineffable and presupposes as such the validity of the rules

3. Buddhistic Existential Philosophy

As examples of portions of an elaboration of this program of an existentialistic interpretation of Buddhist, and in particular of Zen Buddhist tradition, two further essays of Nishitani's may be mentioned, one in a still unpublished English translation which carries the title "The Standpoint of Zen"[51] and one which appeared in 1969 entitled "On the I-Thou Relation in Zen Buddhism."

---

of logical thinking. This is the point at which the physicist is to be distinguished from the mystic, in that he does not sink into silence but makes his calculations and tests their results for accuracy; however, this does not hinder him, but in fact requires him to take account of the true significance of those "mystical" symbols.

The erroneous notion that logic must be abandoned because it is refuted by experience rests on the assumption that its rules are laws of being rather than laws of thinking. But it is precisely this thinking in the service of the laws of logic that determines these contradictions in the reality of experience, and apart from the laws of logic these contradictions cannot be established. What is refuted by experience is not logic, but the misconception or expectation that reality is logical, univocal, in itself without contradiction and causally accountable, or the intention to interpret it in this sense. Such conceptions, expectations and intentions are belied by reality. To abandon the logic of thinking without acknowledging this fact would make thinking into a nonthinking, and allow us no longer to distinguish the talk of "harmony" from a wish-determined illusion and to speak of the "Nothing" in such a way that no one knows what is actually meant by it. If this is what is meant by the "parallels between modern physics and Eastern mysticism," then the lofty expectations in respect to mankind's future, which Capra connects with them, would be built on sand; and Nishitani's existentializing of the mechanistic worldview would be preferable, because in it—at least to some extent—our current situation in science and technology is recognized more clearly; even though one might draw other consequences than does Nishitani, whose existentializing likewise amounts to an ontologization of noetic statements.

Presentations, as for example those of Tokuyo Yamauchi on "Problems of Logic in Philosophy East and West" (JR [1964]: 1-7) and Yoshifumi Ueda on "Thinking in Buddhist Philosophy" (*Philosophical Studies of Japan* [Tokyo: Japanese National Commission for Unesco, 1964]), which stem from the same time as Nishitani's "Science and Zen" and are typical for Buddhist thinking, can only reinforce us in our insistence on not by any means abandoning the logic of thinking in conceptually objective terms—despite full recognition of its limits—and also strengthen our conviction that one can speak appropriately of what is nonobjectifiable only on the basis of and within this objectivity—even if this runs counter to the intention of these authors. The same holds true of the further expositions of Nishitani.

[51]English translation by John C. Maraldo.

In the former treatise Nishitani makes the bold attempt to explain the central concept of *Alaya-* (that is, Store-) Consciousness of the "philosophy of consciousness only," stemming from the third or fourth century, in terms of the existentialism of his Zen understanding which opposes every kind of philosophy of consciousness. He begins by developing in psychological and literary-historical ways the nonobjectifiability of the self in its "simple existence" which precedes all objectifications but still operates in them. By means of the Socratic "Know Yourself," of Cartesian doubt and its flight to the *veracitas Dei*, and of the Augustinian "God and Soul" he uncovers the pronounced "egoistic" character of Western thinking which in his view derives from Christianity, to be sure as a consequence of objectifying the self and its transcendence. In the third section he counters the "homocentricity" of Western thinking with the "cosmocentricity" of Buddhism and, for this, appeals to the doctrine of consciousness—developed in Mahayana—as a universal trait and especially to its eighth step, the root- or store-consciousness which in inseparable ways is both the "hidden root of discriminatory thinking" and the "becoming aware of this 'falsehood'." It deals with a kind of corporealizing of the problem of the nonobjectifiability of the self, whose solution is contained in becoming aware of it. In Buddhist terminology this means: In Alaya-consciousness is rooted both the karma-consciousness of attachment to the "world of things" as well as the possibility of "severing" its roots, which according to Zen happens in the "Great Death." In the fourth section Nishitani describes the relationship in which Zen stands to the speculation of the philosophy of consciousness as parallel to Kierkegaard's critique of Hegel's speculation. Zen is the existentialized version of the "completely fulfilled true nature" of Only-Consciousness-theory. How this true nature is to be found and in what it consists he finds expressed in a poem contained in the 34th section of the Zen collection of the Bi-Yän-Lu, which [in Wilhelm Gundert's translation] reads as follows:

> Highest reason forgets feeling and speech.
>> Where is a parable for it to be found?
> At the end the moon sinks into night and ice-cold
>> Abandoned to the abyss
> The fruit, ripened, hangs still heavier with monkeys.
>> The length of the mountains deceives me on the path.
> I look up: there remains a rest from brightness!
>> . . . As constantly in the West, when I head for home.

Nishitani remarked about this that the everyday existence in its transitoriness described here is not, as it was for Goethe, "only a parable," but "eternity itself." This Zen poet seeks no parable for eternity—he lives it in his everydayness.

In the essay "The I-Thou Relation in Zen Buddhism,"[52] Nishitani presents deep reflections on the theme of the title by means of another everyday incident: the meeting of two men who ask each other their names, and how in the previous essay it happened that he could speak of the significance of this incident only in the form of "poetry" because it dealt with a "spiritual divertissement."[53] The scene stems from the *Bi-Yän-Lu*: Kyosan meets Sansho and asks him his name. The latter calls himself by the name of the one who asks, leading him to reply: But that's who I am! Then Sansho gives his real name, whereupon Kyosan breaks out into loud laughter.

Nishitani sees in this curious Zen mondo an expression for the problem of human encounter because through the naming which comes to distinguish individuals, the individuality is threatened by being generalized, and simultaneously a real encounter is rendered problematic because two individuals, in asserting themselves and thereby misunderstanding themselves and the other in their true nature, stand over against one another in the sense of Hobbes's *homo homini lupus*. According to Nishitani this fate of the "man-wolf," of which the medieval mystic Heinrich Seuse speaks, can be overcome neither by Kant's "dignity of the person" nor Martin Buber's "personal I-Thou relation," nor the "*communio sanctorum* of the Christian Church," nor through the proclamation of "human rights" and "civil laws,"[54] because these attempts always eventuate in "totalitarianism" or "anarchy" or always "[wobbled] between these two [problems]."[55]

As a Buddhist, Nishitani sees the "source of the conflicts that cut mankind in two" in "self-attachment which puts one's 'self' at the center and so discriminates between 'self' and 'other'." This "self-attachment," again, is rooted in the "*Ignorance (avidya)*, to be found in the eighth, or 'store' consciousness (*alayavijnana*), the foundation on which all human consciousness is based." The "blindness" and "illusion" "at the very root of the human intellect" cannot be overcome by "civil, moral, and divine law; rather through such "ideologies" "one falls into pride in one's country, into moral pride, pride in one's gods or buddhas," that is, to a "self-attachment on a higher plane." Even so the "nonduality of the self and the other" as it is illumined in the "light of the Great Wisdom"—even if it is made into a "concept of nondiscrimination"—"is only another form of "attachment to law" and must therefore be "broken through."[56] Only where this breakthrough ensues, on which everything depends in Zen Buddhism, is "true reality attained for the first time," and of which Nishitani says in

---

[52]EB 2/2 (1969): 71-87. Repr. in Franck, *The Buddha Eye*, 47-60.
[53]Ibid., 85ff.
[54]Ibid., 72ff.
[55]Ibid., 76ff.
[56]Ibid., 84-85.

a surprising turn, that "a contest of 'fragrant freshness' goes on between the self as the self, the other as the other, and law as the law." Then "the everyday encounters between all men are something of infinite freshness, pervaded with an infinite fragrance."[57]

Nishitani derives these expressions from a poem about spring which a Rinzai Zen priest of the fourteenth century, who established the Daitoku-ji Temple in Kyoto that still carries his name, composed in reference to the Zen koan mentioned at the beginning of this article.[58] With Daito, Nishitani sees in this "poetry" a "superreality" which has occurred in the encounter between Kyosan and Sansho. In the playful controversy about their true names, in which they find themselves amidst "roaring laughter" in their self-identity of nonduality, they participate in reality as it is real. This real nature of reality can only be conceived "poetically," or better said: it becomes speech in the poetizing, which is the same as "when the struggles in the ultimate ground of hostility become sport or play."[59] Nishitani explains that this deals with a "pious" event and cites for it a passage from a description of a cult of spring by the poet Hakuin.[60]

When he stresses that "this is not a poetry of Romanticism but of radical realism" it is still proper to probe how this spring-like "awakening of the self in Buddhism" works itself out in the political reality with which he brings it into connection in an essay with this title.

He begins this essay with the admission that Buddhism today—in contrast to earlier times—exercises only "little influence upon people's lives." This decline in the public influence of Buddhism he believes can be traced back to the fact that "most people today separate 'transforming men' and 'transforming society' from one another, and think that "the former takes precedence over the latter," whereas Buddhism, although it possesses no "social theory of its own," may have possessed in the past "as great a force for moving society as Christianity," the reason being that it "transforms man's innermost mind radically."[61]

In Nishitani's opinion "the very idea that social revolution should take precedence over man's inner transformation," as is assumed by many of the "progressives" of his country, represents "a not insignificant part of the crisis itself."[62] Differently from such illusionary and destructive ideologies, Buddhism with its "altogether revolutionary view of the essential nature of man" opens up "a more fundamental and permanent principle of social transformation than could

---

[57]Ibid., 85.
[58]Ibid., 71.
[59]Ibid., 85.
[60]Ibid., 86.
[61]EB 1/2 (1966): 1.
[62]Ibid., 2.

ever be offered by a mere ideology." As the most important elements of the Buddhist path to salvation he lists "[emancipation] from the innumerable attachments that arise spontaneously from within ourselves and tie us to things of this world," that is, Nirvana, or "the extinguishing of the fire"; "an awakening in which we become aware of our original and authentic nature (our *Dharma*-nature)" and a living "in accord with it"; the "[attainment] of enlightenment," which "depends upon ourselves alone," because the ability to attain it "lies deeply hidden . . . in the Dharma-nature of each one of us"; and "[becoming] 'homeless' in the world" by "[cutting] the threads of attachment."

As the great example for the world-historical significance of this doctrine of salvation represented by Buddhism from its beginnings, Nishitani cites "the community of Buddhists, the *samgha*" as a "brotherhood . . . of revolutionary character," in which "all 'worldly' differentiations, social as well as psychological . . . between the rich and poor, the learned and the unlearned, and so forth, and in particular the distinction between castes" are negated.[63] As evidence of the denunciation of the brahmanic caste system he not only mentions the fact that the first disciples of the Buddha came from different castes, but cites extensive passages from the Diamond Needle Tract attributed to Asvaghosha, in consequence of which "the nobility of the fundamental character of man [was] based on morality"[64] and "a Brahman can be called a Sudra and a Sudra can be called a true Brahman."[65]

If one had expected Nishitani to show how, based on this basic position and the historical illustrations of the principle issuing from it, this concretely operates in contemporary social problems, one would be disappointed, for instead he occupies himself in the second half of this essay with a certainly very impressive confrontation of the "realization of the human grounded precisely on the Buddhist standpoint of nonego" which emerged "for the first time" in the reversal of the caste system,"[66] with the problematic of the "realization of man" in the West. According to Nishitani the problematic of the Western idea of man derives from the fact that in its origin in Christianity it is based on a "dogmatically God-centered"[67] "personal relationship of man to God" which stands in tension with "[m]an's autonomous existence" realizable only through the "process of social and cultural 'secularization'." The nature of the secularization that results "inexorably" from this historical origin Nishitani sees not only in the atheistic character of its "realization of the self as *ego*" which is his right, but—connected

---

[63]Ibid., 3.
[64]Ibid., 5.
[65]Ibid., 6.
[66]Ibid., 6.
[67]Ibid., 8.

with this self-assertion of the ego—in the replacement of love which is grounded religiously with the abstract rational ideal of "liberty, equality, and brotherhood" of the French Revolution.[68]

If now, however—in contrast to the West—Nishitani calls to mind the "mendicant way of life" of the Buddhist monk and the "begging bowl as the Buddha's badge of sovereignty [which he] received . . . as the reward of rejecting the position of world ruler,"[69] and explains that in comparison to the "kingly characteristics" of the true man," the proletarians—including "aristocrats and bourgeois"—remain proletarians "with the highest standard of living,"[70] reference is thereby made to the different course of social history in the West and in the realm of Buddhism. Not only is "love" in the Christian sense understood as something quite different from mere surrender and compassion; rather what has issued from the Buddhist conception cannot be compared with what bourgeois society and the proletariat have accomplished in social formation.

The obvious prejudice Nishitani displays in respect to this should not however prevent us from acknowledging the justification of his view of the problematic of the history of Christianity and its origin. What he only hints at here, he has presented more thoroughly in his larger treatise, "Buddhism and Christianity"—even if no less unsatisfactorily as far its the result is concerned.

4. Demythologizing in Buddhism and Christianity

Before we concern ourselves with the treatise just mentioned, it is appropriate to mention his "Preliminary Remark on Two Addresses of Martin Heidegger"[71]—not only because Heidegger's philosophy of existence, with which Nishitani knows himself to be connected, lies behind Bultmann's "demythologizing and the existential interpretation of the Kerygma" with which Nishitani deals in that treatise, but also because in it he makes several statements essential to the theme of "Buddhism and Christianity" in the context of the "meeting of East and West." Here he sees the positive significance of the secularization effected through science and technology in the fact that men in the East as well as the West are freed from "dogmatic prisons" so that they are able to meet each other "as a 'son of man' who has nowhere to lay his head,"[72] and in the succession of the Buddha who elected "homelessness" in order to "awaken to the true self."[73] As Heidegger in his "Address to the Homecoming (*Heimatabend*) in Meszkirch"

---

[68]Ibid., 7.
[69]Ibid., 9.
[70]Ibid., 10.
[71]EB 1/2 (1966): 48-59.
[72]Ibid., 51.
[73]Ibid., 53.

finds a home (*Heimat*) in the "undomestic (*Unheimischen*)," so Buddhism and Christianity have the task "of indicating the way home to a wandering humanity" and can by doing so—together with other religions—come nearer to and understand one another.[74] Thus Nishitani finds the same spirit of Zen in the utterance of Abraham a Sancta Clara cited by Heidegger in the second address: "Man—this five-foot-long Nothingness,"[75] or in the other, that "a man who dies before he dies, does not die when he dies,"[76] and in the image of the "silverwhite swans" "who carry the snow over the waters" on their wings.[77] To take notice of this would seem useful in order to understand Nishitani's position on Bultmann's "existential method of interpretation" and the demythologizing debate which he established in some detail in the treatise on "Buddhism and Christianity" already mentioned.

By way of introduction Nishitani appropriately points to the connection and difference that obtains between Bultmann's hermeneutics and Heidegger's fundamental ontology,[78] to determine directly and correctly that "the question of demythologizing did not first begin with Bultmann,"[79] but "that in Christianity, from its very beginnings, that deeply rooted problem was always hidden just below the surface." In view of this problematic history illustrated by several of its phenomena Nishitani surprisingly notes "that the vitality that Christianity still exhibits today has its guiding principle in the hidden presence of this threatening problem," in order to explain of Buddhism which "was free of this problem already in the beginning years": "There where this lively and far-reaching debate enters into our circles a tepid and stupid Buddhism in its present condition appears as a kind of geological fossil from primeval times."[80]

In the following Nishitani shows himself to be strikingly familiar with the debate which at that time had developed around Bultmann, in that he essentially accepted the objections raised against Bultmann, as, for example, "that on the one hand in the way in which he regarded myth from the perspective of the modern worldview as passé he did not do justice to its significance,"[81] and then on the other side in contradiction to this thesis, held to a mythological "remain-

---

[74]Ibid., 54.

[75]Ibid., 55.

[76]Ibid., 56.

[77]Ibid., 57.

[78]In the *Nachrichten der Gesellschaft für Natur- und Völkerkunde Ostasiens/Hamburg: Zeitschrift für Kultur und Geschichte Ostasiens* (1960): 5.

[79]Ibid., 6.

[80]Ibid., 8.

[81]Ibid., 8ff.

der" when he spoke of an "act of God" like an "event in space."[82] Nishitani
maintains, not incorrectly, that the demythologizing debate "in the context of
Christian theology" has reached a "dead point." The exact cause of "the complexity of this dead point" which in his view "lies at the root of Christianity and
is dragged along through its entire history,"[83] he seems not to recognize, for
otherwise he would not think he could clarify it with the example of the dogma
of the "Immaculate Conception" nor see in the use of that dogma as the model
of the Buddhist doctrine of "nonduality" the solution to the myth problem that
vexes Christianity.

Nishitani is doubtless correct when he discovers in his discussion of this
dogma how the theology that represents it undeniably falls into the "dilemma"
of the "double truth" because it makes statements about "one and the same
course"[84] which are grounded naturally and supernaturally in several points that
mutually contradict each other.[85] He sees, as it were, in this "double truth" of the
simultaneous "defilement and undefilement" of the conception of the Virgin an
embodiment of the Buddhist doctrine of "nonduality" and by appealing to
Nishida's formula of "absolute paradoxical identity"[86] regards it as valid not only
for Mary but for "every beloved woman," because in it is expressed "the natural
nature of human existence."[87] In this way nothing is said about the historically
provable origin of the dogma, but a specifically Buddhist interpretation is presented which however stands in express contradiction to its original intention
which can be demonstrated on the basis of the history of dogma—whether or not
it is assumed that its founders and representatives were unconscious "anony-
mous" Buddhists.

In his understanding, or misunderstanding, of Christianity Nishitani actually
proceeds from this presupposition, in that he cites with approval the saying of the
Zen Master Hakuin: "All sentient beings are originally Buddha existences,"[88] and
summarizes his solution to the myth problem[89] by saying "that a fundamental and
basic demythologizing of all myths and an 'existential' interpretation of mytho-

---

[82]Ibid. 11-12. On this and what follows, cf. my exchange with Rudolf Bult-
mann in "Entmythologisierung oder Entkerygmatisierung der Theologie,"
Kerygma und Mythos 2, ed. H. W. Bartsch (Hamburg, 1952) and "Theologie und
Philosophie," ThZB 8 (1952): 116-32.

[83]Ibid., 13.

[84]Ibid., 14-15.

[85]Ibid., 19.

[86]Ibid., 16.

[87]Ibid., 17.

[88]Ibid., 20, so also 22.

[89]Ibid., 14-15.

logical notions are possible only by breaking through to the horizon of absolute 'emptiness' or of the absolute 'Nothing'."[90] As a foundation for this he then elucidates in a longer "notation" the concept of "nonduality" as "the primal category in Mahayana Buddhist thinking."[91]

Nishitani touches on the point of view which in our opinion is decisive for the understanding as well as for a solution to the myth problem in Christianity when he confronts Bultmann together with Jaspers, whose position he presents with obvious sympathy,[92] with the position of Heidegger, and reproaches Bultmann and Jaspers for an inadmissible use of the "Heideggerian 'existential' analysis" "for understanding the 'Christian existential' human being"[93] as well as for "the claim" for the "revelatory once-for-all-ness and absoluteness of Christianity" which is incompatible with the "openness to reason."[94] With his *Skandalon*[95] Bultmann stands in the company of those theologians who in their *Heilsgeschichte* assert the "incarnation of God" as "historical fact" and thus arrive at an "ambiguous" speaking of facts—"facts of faith" which science "regards as pure superstition."[96] It is in this connection that Nishitani comes to speak of the problem of transcendence,[97] and this in such a way that he brings the assumption of a "vertical transcendence"[98] into connection with the assertion, which he meets in Christianity, of a supernatural, divine fact of salvation, which cannot be exhibited in the secular sphere of science, but—if one wishes to takes it into account nevertheless—can only assert itself as the "factual breaking in of the supernatural into our world."[99]

Without noticing it, Nishitani has struck upon the historically establishable problematic of the historical origin of Christianity, which consists in the fact that the "breaking in of the supernatural into our world," which was actually expected in early Christianity in the form of an eschatological event and assumed to be already in progress, has not taken place, so that Christianity, if it does not wish to abandon its expectation of salvation, sees itself required to ground it differently than the way it happened originally, as e.g. with the dogma of the Virgin Birth, which Nishitani believed he could "radically demythologize" with the help of

---

[90]Ibid., 26-27.
[91]Ibid., 21-22.
[92]Ibid. 28ff.
[93]Ibid., 29.
[94]Ibid., 31.
[95]Ibid., 11.
[96]Ibid., 14-15, 23.
[97]Ibid., 23ff.
[98]Ibid., 25.
[99]Ibid., 23.

"Buddhist *prajna* wisdom"[100] and in relation to Jaspers' "cipher thinking."[101] Interesting parallels to this can be cited from Western Gnosis in which the attempt was made in a "Great Wisdom" opening up into "emptiness" to deal with the problem of the eternal in time as a once-for-all universal salvation event in history.

But still another reference is in place here, dealing not with more or less Christian parallels to Nishitani's treatment of the problem of demythologizing, but with the fact that this problem is present not only in Christianity but also in Buddhism—certainly not in its 'early years," as Nishitani rightly saw, but probably shortly thereafter in different forms, above all, in Amida Buddhism in which the vow of Amida plays the role of a salvation event, similar to that of the Christ event, and with which Nishitani was occupied in some detail even before he concerned himself with its parallels in Christianity. Although only eight years separate the first appearance of his essay on "The Problem of Time in Shinran"[102] and his contribution to the Bultmann debate, it is reasonable to think that in this latter work he had forgotten what he had undertaken in the former. For while he speaks in the latter of the necessity of demythologizing, as if this were no problem in Buddhism, and Christianity needs to learn from Buddhism to solve its problems, Nishitani was concerned already in the earlier essay with demythologizing the famous original vow of Amida, in consequence of which the latter as a Bodhisattva praised as Dharmakara vowed that he would not enter the Pure Land before all sentient beings attained to true insight and are thereby redeemed—with the exception that he spoke here not of "demythologizing" but thought he had found in Shinran's conception of "faith" as "true trust" the answer to the question how that vow could prove to be a salvation event for all times. In the form and content of its tradition this vow is different from the Christian message of salvation. But as Bultmann wrongly ascribed his demythologizing already to the Apostle Paul, so Nishitani with his existential conception of time in the sense of Kierkegaard's "simultaneity"[103] of the historical past and present decision is not able to convince us that in Shinran's understanding of the vow of Amida we are not dealing with a "myth in the usual sense." For on the one hand, an existential interpretation of the time with which we have to do in myth presupposes myth, and on the other, it is not clear why this demythologizing should not deal with a "general human possibility," as Nishitani has con-

---

[100]Ibid., 31.
[101]Ibid., 28-29.
[102]EB 11/1 (1978): 13-26.
[103]Ibid., 18.

tended, and still less, why—contrary to Nishitani's denial—even the doctrine of predestination could not be understood in this existential sense.[104]

As Christian theology affirms that the traditional and proclaimed salvation event which occurred in the past actualizes itself in a faith that decides that it is valid for it personally and sees in this realization the effect of that event, so Nishitani here describes the "fulfillment of the vow of Amida" as an event which occurs in the "now of the moment" for all times, in which Shinran decided that he was personally meant and that he owed this "self-realization" to the "power of the vow." Actually here only the names of the redeemers and the scenery in which the salvation event plays itself out are different, but in both the event is existentially intensified.

Although in this essay Nishitani declines to take a position and aimed only to work out the understanding of time as it follows from Shinran's "faith," it could be thought that with the concept of a "religious" or "existential" time thus attained—while he is thereby influenced by Western philosophy and theology—he is concerned to show Buddhists and Christians a way to a better understanding of their tradition, by which they can better understand each other. In any case it is understandable under this aspect that he could designate himself occasionally both as a "becoming Buddhist" as well as a "becoming Christian"—with the difference to be sure that he understands himself "as one who has become a Buddhist," but as such not "one who has become a Christian." Because he could "not bring himself . . . to regard Buddhism as a false doctrine," he "could not have acceded to the faith of Christianity." He is conscious both of the "deficiency of Buddhism" as well as the "strengths of Christianity." But he is all the more convinced that, "as a Buddhist, with the help of Buddhist dialectic and always from the perspective of Buddhism," he could work at the solution of the existing problems.[105]

From this vantage it is not surprising that, in his contribution to *The Japanese Yearbook* of 1968, "How a Buddhist Philosophy sees the Future of Christianity?"[106] Nishitani challenged Christianity to a "new interpretation" of its traditional concepts of faith and revelation, Christ and God. Instead of permitting faith on one hand and science and philosophy on the other to oppose each other, a mutual dialogue must come about between them. For the sake of its future, faith must rely on free thinking. In respect to the concept of God the relationship of a personal God to ultimate being must be envisaged, and the prison walls be

---

[104]Ibid., 15, 19-20.

[105]Cited by Jan van Bragt in his contribution "Nishitani on Japanese Religiosity" in *Japanese Religiosity*, ed. Joseph Spae (1971) 280-81.

[106]"A Buddhist Philosopher looks at the Future of Christianity," in *The Japanese Christian Yearbook* (1968): 108-11.

broken through, in which a divine I-Thou relation which is valid for all persons dominates, as was attempted by Tillich, Bonhoeffer, John Robinson and the Death of God Theology. Only in this way could Christianity overcome its intolerance and exclusivity and fulfill its task even in Japan.

After this survey of the available sections in the translated essays and treatises from Nishitani's philosophy of religion we now have to see how these individual pieces of the mosaic get joined together into a systematically ordered whole in his principal work, *Religion and Nothingness*, which he has to thank for his representative position in contemporary Japanese philosophy of religion.

5. The Principal Work: *Religion and Nothingness* (chapters 1 and 2)

What Nishitani deals with in the essays on various themes in the preceding material and why they exhibit changing points of view is the problem of "Science and Religion"—the question of its origin, its significance and its possible solution. The cause of the origin of this problem he sees in secularization which renders it problematic with just as much necessity as is the case with Christianity. But in the degree to which modern science and technology, in which this fate of the West has taken shape, have become effective in the Far East, Buddhism sees itself threatened by secularization. In both, secularization means not only the rendering problematic of the meaning which religion gives to existence, but the opening up to nihilism in the disclosing of the illusoriness of their own ersatz-constructions of what they have abandoned. But while for Nishitani Christianity is essentially responsible for this unwholesome course of history, he believes that in Buddhism there is a way out of this fate and thus, a solution to the problem of "science and religion."

This view of the fateful development of Western, originally Christian, cultural history and the Buddhist conviction about the significance of humanity arising from it forms the basic scheme of Nishitani's principal work *Religion and Nothingness*, except that it is here more comprehensively grounded and expresses its individual aspects more extensively and in constant interchange with Western thinking in its consequences for a "religious" attitude toward life. Basically his answer to the question "What Is Religion?" is already presented in the first chapter, which carries this title. But the fact that he develops his conception of the nature of religion as an overcoming of Western nihilism with reference to the problematic of the personality of the Christian concept of God provides the occasion for him to focus in the second chapter on "The Personal and Impersonal in Religion." The third chapter is devoted to a comparison of "Nihility and Sunyata" in which it is shown how nihilism which issues from the problematic of personhood can be overcome only by the complete emptying of the self and, pari passu, of its view of the world. Thereby Nishitani attains "The Standpoint of Sunyata" which he develops in the fourth chapter. From this standpoint of emptiness he unfolds in the following two chapters the nature of time and the nature of history arising from it, in exchange with Western conceptions of time and history and in relation to the Buddhist doctrines of samsara and Nirvana. Thus the fifth chapter is superscribed, "Sunyata and Time," while the sixth chapter carries the title "Sunyata and History."

Accordingly, in this work we are dealing with a systematic presentation of Nishitani's philosophy of religion, in which the individual aspects of his essays are gathered up into a whole and in this overview become further expanded and grounded in greater detail—all for the purpose of showing the superiority of "religious existence" in Buddhism, especially of Zen Buddhism, over the science, philosophy and religion of the Western world. In this way Nishitani gives us the occasion and opportunity with this sixth chapter—of its course of thought and the problems which get expressed in its development—to test how it applies to this Zen Buddhist philosophy of religion and its critique of Christianity.

Right at the beginning of the first chapter Nishitani, by means of two examples, clarifies the nature of his concept of religion in more formal and material regard in order to concretize these two essential elements by appealing to Buddhist forms of thought as well as in confrontation with Western thinking consciousness, existentialistic atheism and Christian theology, the result being that we already have in this first chapter the basic structure of his philosophy of religion. It consists in an elucidation of the question which forms the title of the whole work, and at the same time of this first chapter, holding that it is not intended as a question—posed from a standpoint outside of religion—about its purpose, but as a question which "breaks in" upon us if in definite experiences under such a perspective a "void" is opened up and all meaning of life disappears into a Nothing.[107]

The positive side of the experience that appears primarily as merely negative, that therein reality is brought to experience as it is in truth,[108] is illustrated by Nishitani by means of a passage from *The House of the Dead*, in which Dostoyevsky describes as an experience from his Siberian imprisonment how for him the things which surrounded him dissolved over the Western horizon, so that he was moved to tears, believed he saw "God's world" and could forget his "wretched self."[109] Over against Dostoyevsky's description of his experience

---

[107]Keiji Nishitani, "Was ist Religion?" *Philosophical Studies of Japan* 2 (1960) 23-24. [ET: *Religion and Nothingness* trans. with an intro. by Jan van Bragt, foreword by Winston L. King, Nanzan Studies in Religion and Culture (Berkeley: University of California Press, 1982) 2-3. Page numbers of this final English version given for reference only. —Trans.]

[108]Ibid, 25ff. [R&N, 5ff.].

[109]Ibid., 27ff. [R&N, 8].

which he expanded in other passages through the assumption of "a great harmony among all things in the universe that brings them into being" Nishitani places our "thinking consciousness" in which we do not just forget ourselves, but, what is more, make ourselves the center; but this has to do neither with our world nor ourselves but only with our notions about this outer and inner world.[110]

Nishitani cites Descartes as the most important instigator and representative of this thinking consciousness centered on the I and separated from reality.[111] Although he acknowledges as an "incontrovertible fact" that "the self of contemporary man is an ego of the Cartesian type,"[112] he is of the opinion that the "self-consciousness of the *cogito, ergo sum* . . . needs to be thought about [by leaving its subjectivity as is] and proceeding from a field more basic than self-consciousness"[113]—in order to escape not only from the "dead world" of scientific technology,[114] but also from epistemological principles, because the self is not able to fathom itself in the framework of thinking consciousness; rather it involves itself in an endless chain of notions of itself, but never with their origin.[115] Only in a "deep awareness of its subjectivity" in a "breaking through the field of consciousness and self-consciousness" may the self "reach" "the ground of everything that exists," which—because it can in no way be objectified"—reveals itself as the "Nothing" into which it "transforms" itself and, because it can "no longer distinguish between 'inner' and 'outer', at the same time proves to be the otherwise "concealed" ground of "everything in the world."[116]

In distinction from Cartesian consciousness in whose doubt the "I" still asserts itself and then can also become an object of psychology and depth psychology,[117] Nishitani brings this "breaking through" in which "the self and all things in their *esse* have become a single question mark and a single problem," into connection with so-called "existential thinking," and says of it that it is "the specific contribution of religion, and indeed of religion alone."[118] As the outstanding example of a "corporeal" realization of Nothingness in the "extinction of consciousness," in which "the doubter can no longer be distinguished from the doubted," but rather we ourselves become "changed" in "transcending" this difference "together with the things into a great mass of doubt," Nishitani cites

[110]Ibid., 29ff. [R&N, 10].
[111]Ibid., 30 [R&N, 11].
[112]Ibid., 33 [R&N, 13].
[113]Ibid., 34 [R&N, 15].
[114]Ibid., 31 [R&N, 11].
[115]Ibid., 34ff. [R&N, 15].
[116]Ibid., 35 [R&N, 15].
[117]Ibid., 37 [R&N, 16].
[118]Ibid., 37 [R&N, 16].

a Zen sermon[119] about the "Great Death" with which the "immersion" (*samadhi*) of Zen practice is concerned, and which leads to "Enlightenment" in which is disclosed "the true reality of the self and all things."[120]

Already in the dimensions of this existential way of knowing of the "great Wisdom"[121]—Nothing, true self, new view of the world—and in the concepts which Nishitani uses to describe its implementation and its results—in limit situations[122] characterized by "Angst" and radical Doubt[123]—immersion, dying, enlightenment—its religious character becomes apparent. There first rightly follows its connection with the realm of religion which goes beyond science and philosophy when he brings it into connection in the following section with "redemption" from "original sin" and "karma" in "faith" in Christ or Amida.[124] Proceeding from Kant's "radical evil"[125] and its existential interpretation in Kierkegaard,[126] he sees in the Christian idea of original sin and the Buddhist notion of karma equally "corporeal" and "existential" forms of expression of our "responsibility" and "personal existence" as they are to be found "only in the realm of religion" and ethics.[127] In reference to the controversy between Karl Barth and Emil Brunner over the "point of contact" in which the latter maintained a residue of the image of God undamaged by the Fall, Nishitani explains that "the awareness of our total corruption and incapacity for redemption" as the "open field of the Nothing," is the "place"—understood in Plato's sense—in which in Christianity the "Love of God," and in Buddhism "the saving power of the vow of Amida," is received, and that it deals "in both cases" with "faith" as a "bodily experience"—there in the effecting of a "real connection between man and God" through the Holy Spirit; here through the fact that Buddha's compassionate vow to redeem all sentient beings reveals the substantial identity of the Buddha and "profane" beings.[128]

In paralleling the Christian and Buddhist understandings of redemption Nishitani takes no offence at the distinction of names and the salvation connected with them, but rather sees what is common to both in the uniqueness which is ascribed respectively to the Buddha or the Christ, and in the way salvation can

---

[119]Ibid., 39 [R&N, 20-21]. We have already cited it verbatim on 37n.29.
[120]Ibid., 37ff. [R&N, 21].
[121]Ibid., 41 [R&N, 23].
[122]Ibid., 40 [R&N, 22].
[123]Ibid., 37 [R&N, 21].
[124]Ibid., 41ff. [R&N, 23-24].
[125]Ibid., 41 [R&N, 23].
[126]Ibid. [R&N, 23].
[127]Ibid., p. 43 [R&N, 24].
[128]Ibid., 46 [R&N, 26-27].

be understood on both sides as an event in "faith" in which the self in its sinfulness or karma existence—and that means, in its "ego-centeredness"[129]—is absolutely denied and simultaneously absolutely affirmed,[130] and in this "turn or conversion" breaks through to its "true reality."[131] In this "rebirth" there occurs in
the faithful what Paul said of Christ: " He gave himself for my salvation" and
what Shinran said of Amida, that he made his vow which issued from contemplation lasting five aeons solely for Shinran's salvation.[132] When, in doubt and
enlightenment, as well as in sin and faith, "we ourselves are thrown into the
reality of evil or faith in such a way as to become ourselves the realization of
their realness, a conversion takes place within reality itself."[133] In this
sense—without expressly mentioning Barth's "No" to Brunner's point of contact
with respect to faith—he cites the word of his "Eastern ancients": "The channel
forms as the water flows."[134]

    Because he referred in the previous material to "God and Tathagata
(Buddha)," while today "atheism has been elevated to the position of serving as
a substitute for theistic religions," for which he sees in Sartre a typical example,
he deems it necessary to concern himself with his *L'Existentialisme est un
humanisme.*[135] Precisely because he sees in Sartre's atheistic nihilism a consequence of Cartesian thinking consciousness, he reproaches him for holding onto
the "I" of self-consciousness and not reaching the "Great Doubt" which would
mean the "bankruptcy of the Cartesian 'ego'," and for remaining therefore stuck
in what in Zen is called "living in the Demon's Cavern" "instead of attaining the
"Buddhist Sunyata." While Buddhism represents "Absolute Sunyata" "in which
even a denial of Sunyata is denied," the "negative attitude of nihilism" "turns
everything into un-reality" instead of attaining "Absolute Emptiness" in which
"all things . . . become present as bottomless realities" and in their bottomlessness are shown as they truly are.[136] "For as long as we do not step beyond the
field of a fundamental separation of subject and object" Nishitani thinks it is not
possible at all, and he maintains in contrast to Sartre's talk of absolute, free, self-
creative acts which "sounds like words of Zen disciples" that "an act is only
absolutely free" if it realizes itself "from the far side (or even more from this
side) of consciousness or self-consciousness, that is, of the field of the 'I'" and

---

[129]Ibid., 47 [R&N, 27].
[130]Ibid., 48 [R&N, 29].
[131]Ibid., 49 [R&N, 29-30].
[132]Ibid., 47 [R&N, 27].
[133]Ibid., 49 [R&N, 30].
[134]Ibid., 20 [R&N, 28].
[135]Ibid., 49-50 [R&N, 30].
[136]Ibid., 53 [R&N, 34].

thus "ceases being 'my' or 'your' action, although at the same time we are the ones who act."[137]

After this excursus Nishitani turns once again, and this time thematically, to Christianity, because on the one hand he sees in religion the sphere in which Sartre's position can be "broken through" and thereby the insufficiency for which he reproaches it can be overcome, and, on the other hand, sees Christianity—albeit on another level—bound up with the same problematic as Sartre's atheistic existentialism. For this problem which connects them he points out that "the alienation of modern man from religion" was caused by the fact that in "traditional Christianity" the religious content of original sin and life in God was expressed in such a way that it could not be reconciled with the subjectivity of modern man growing out of them and thus fell victim to secularization. While he only briefly makes reference to this cultural connection at this place,[138] he does concern himself exhaustively with the immanent problematic of the "Christian concept of God, especially of transcendence and the personal character of God" which represents the cause of this development.[139] Although he notes as the goal of his criticism also the possibility of a "higher synthesis" between the radicalization of existentialistic nihilism in terms of Buddhism and "the religious freedom which surfaced in the Christian tradition," he ignores it in this chapter, explaining that by doing so he can uncover the problematic of the Christian concept of God indicated by him in terms of the omnipresence and omnipotence of God.[140]

Regarding the problem of the omnipresence of God he refers to the difficulty bound up with the Christian concept of Creator insofar as it contains therein both the concept of an "absolute transcendence" before which we stand as before a "iron wall," as well as an "immanence of God" in all things created by him.[141] The same "paradox" is present in eschatology insofar as the "appearance of Christ," which in the "proclamation of the nearness of the Kingdom of God" compels "man to decide in reference to death and resurrection," represents a "turn" which is "contained in God himself."[142] Because in both instances this simultaneity of transcendence and immanence is understood not merely "ontologically" but "existentially,"[143] it appears as "impersonal," thus "negating" man while admitting that he is "personal," in consequence of which under this aspect

---

[137]Ibid., 54 [R&N, 35].
[138]Ibid., 55 [R&N, 36].
[139]Ibid., 56 [R&N, 37].
[140]Ibid., 56ff. [R&N, 38ff.].
[141]Ibid., 58 [R&N, 39-40].
[142]Ibid., 59 [R&N, 40].
[143]Ibid. [R&N, 40].

of God's omnipresence "the relationship between God and man" is "so to speak an impersonal-personal or personal-impersonal one"—a characterization that is equally vaild "of God himself and the world permeated by his Spirit."[144]

Nishitani proceeds in similar fashion with the "concept of omnipotence," in that primarily by virtue of the question asked in jest "whether God could sneeze" he leads it into an absurdity,[145] and from this proceeds to discuss the "theodicy problem"[146] in order to show in ironically trivial and deeply dialectical ways that this concept and its corresponding biblical statements can only appropriately be understood existentially, whereby "the concept of the personality of God and man" could be expressed on a plane upon which "the contraries of 'personal' and 'impersonal' are transcended" and at the same time "the horizon" be opened in which "the problem of religion and science" could really be dealt with as such.[147]

In this way is formulated the theme to whose treatment Nishitani devotes the second chapter which he entitled "The Personal and the Impersonal in Religion" and which begins with a discussion of the problems just mentioned.[148]

Corresponding to his method of presentation of briefly recapitulating long elaborations before he proceeds further in his argumentation, Nishitani—at the beginning of the third section of this chapter—summarizes the two preceding sections on the historical development of the relationship of "science and religion" and its fundamental significance for the way the modern problem is developed as is it known to us from different essays of his,[149] in the following two points.

First, the "idea of personality" which has up to now been applied to "God and man" is in need of "modification" because the laws of nature in the modern concept of nature are so "completely indifferent" to man and his intention that a world ruled by them appears as something that "runs contrary to the personal relation between God and man of which religion consisted in earlier times."

Second, the "death of God" represents the culmination of subjective consciousness which arose in modernity in connection with the change in the concept of nature and is realized by modern man as an "abyss" which yawns at the basis of his existence, and in which he may attain "ecstatic transcendence" and thus become aware in a true sense of his subjectivity as something truly free and independent.[150]

---

[144]Ibid., 59ff. [R&N, 41].
[145]Ibid., 60 [R&N, 42].
[146]Ibid., 61 [R&N, 42ff.].
[147]Ibid., 61-62 [R&N, 45].
[148]Cf. n. 7.
[149]Above all, from the essay on "Science and Zen."
[150]EB 3/1 (1970): 12-13 [R&N, 57].

Because this development is closely connected with Christianity, Nishitani wishes to treat the theme of this chapter in this connection, and for this purpose begins with a comparison between the command to love one's enemies, which has reached its "completion" in the fact that, like God, it makes no "distinctions of good and evil, just and unjust," and what in Buddhism is called "nondifferentiating love beyond enmity and friendship." The nature of this nondifferentiating love, for which he uses the New Testament term "agape,"[151] he sees in both Christianity and Buddhism in a "self-emptying" which provides the occasion for him to present the conceptuality used in Christianity and Buddhism in connection with the doctrine of kenosis or Sunyata.

Without expressly citing the locus classicus for the Christian doctrine of kenosis, Phil. 2:4ff., he explains the expression here used of Christ, that he emptied himself of his divine form (*heauton ekenōsen*), to the effect that "within God himself is included the meaning of "having made himself empty." He bases this conception on the claim that the self-emptying of the Son happened "in accordance with the will of God" so that its "origin [is] in God," that is, in God's forgiving love in which his "original perfection" consists, so that in the Son's work of *ekkensosis* the nature of the Father is fulfilled as *kenosis*.

That this derivation of the "emptiness of God" from the self-emptying of the Son represents a typically Buddhist interpretation Nishitani confirms by the fact that he expressly explains that "ekkenosis in the case of the Son" and "kenosis in the case of the Father" signify in Buddhist terminology anatman or muga, that is, nonego or selflessness, and takes this occasion in a longer note to present the "similar concept" of "emptiness," *sunyata*, in its significance in Buddhology. According to the Buddhist doctrine of the three bodies of the Buddha the perfection of the eternal Buddha consists in the sunyata of the "Dharma of Buddha." As such it is "simultaneously the ground of *Sambhoga-kaya* (or Body of Reward), that is, the "way of Buddha-being in his self-manifestation as compassionate Tathagata." This so-called "Great Compassion" has its basis in "emptiness" and, "moreover, this emptiness identical with the Great Compassion is the ground of *Nirmana-kaya* (the "Transformation Body") of the Buddha, that is, of the way of Buddha-being in its manifestation in the form of man as the *Tathagata* Shakyamuni." This taking of twofold form, notes Nishitani, means "essentially an *ekkenosis* (making oneself empty), although it seems at first to be the contrary," for the "transition from being form-less to being in form means selflessness and compassion, as in the case of a school master playing with his children." The use of the image, which in any case is not occasioned by the Apostle Paul, nevertheless does not detain Nishitani, but gives him all the more reason to conclude this elucidation with the remark that "especially in the

---

[151]Ibid., 14 [R&N, 58].

Mahayana the concepts of emptiness, compassion and selflessness are seen to be inseparably connected" and "the Buddhist way of living, as well as the way of thinking, are permeated by *kenosis* and *ekkensosis.*"[152]

On the basis of this understanding, Buddhistically stamped, of the God of the Christian doctrine of kenosis as a being that consists in the fulfillment of his self-less love which makes no differentiation, Nishitani believes he can say that it "has something in common with the great compassionate heart of Buddhism." But simultaneously he holds that besides this "impersonal" aspect in Christianity there is also the contrary conception of a "personal absoluteness" of God who "elects the people Israel" and who "loves the justified and punishes sinners." Nishitani does not reproach Christianity for considering—with few exceptions—"in the past in general only the personal aspect of God," instead of connecting with the "transpersonal." Thus he sees in it the reason why Christianity could hitherto offer no solution to the problem of religion and science.[153]

One of the promising "exceptions" in Christianity Nishitani sees in "negative theology" and especially in its most thoroughgoing form in Meister Eckhart. On this basis he devotes an extensive discussion to his "birth of God in the soul" in which the soul in complete "abandonedness" is not a matter of being "united with God (*Deo unitum esse*) but [of being] One with God (*unum esse cum Deo*), that is, with the "Ground of God" which Eckhart calls the "desert of God."[154] The agreement of Eckhart's conception of the "desert of God" as the "place of the soul's absolute death" which is for him at the same time "the spring of eternal life,"[155] with the Buddhist basic formula of "nonduality"[156] in the relation of "life and death," "being and Nothingness" as "absolute self-identity" toward which this presentation moves, is signalled by Nishitani already at the beginning in a notation in which he points out that this deals with a unity that cannot be thought in the conceptuality of the subject-object schema, but understood in its nonobjectifiability, but is "only possible existentially, through immediate experience."[157]

---

[152]Ibid., 15n.3 [R&N, 288n.4].

[153]Ibid., 18 [R&N, 61]. On the Buddhistic interpretation of the doctrine of kenosis, cf. the section on "Die Sinnmitte des Buddhismus: Kenostase" in Peter Antes, *Die Botschaft fremder Religionen*, Topos Taschenbücher 107 (Mainz: Matthias Grünewald-Verlag, 1981).

[154]EB 3/2 (1970): 71-72 [R&N, 62ff.].

[155]Ibid., 87 [R&N, 75].

[156]Ibid., 88 [R&N, 76].

[157]Ibid., 73n.2 [R&N, 283n.8].

This "new consideration" of Eckhart's thinking which he judges to be timely[158] is developed by Nishitani by juxtaposing the existentialism that still "asserts
itself" in its nihilism with the theological personalism standing "before God" as
the "breaking through of the Nothing" to the "true self."[159] While traits related
to Eckhart he finds mostly in the later Heidegger,[160] and in Nietzsche's "Midnight
Song,"[161] there is for Nishitani complete correspondence in the inscription which
a Japanese Zen master—a contemporary of Eckhart after all—supplied with his
self-portrait:

> The conscious mind of this shadowy man
> At all occasions is to me most familiar—
> From long ago mysteriously wondrous,
> It is neither I nor other.[162]

and in the "Death Poem" of the same Zen Master:

> It is ninety-one years
> Since my skin and bones were put together;
> This midnight, as always,
> I lay myself down in the Yellow Springs
> (the underworld).[163]

In these verses what is at stake in Nishitani in his thematizing of the relation of
the "personal and impersonal in religion" again becomes clear. What matters to
him is that the "selfhood" "within the innermost depth of the personal self"
becomes "aware of itself as the absolute, nonobjectifiable nothingness beyond all
time."[164] Therefore he can say of it that it not only represents the "highest
idea,"[165] but also, "as being in oneness, with absolute nothingness," that is, in its
nonobjectifiability, it represents for him "the highest Being."[166] But when he
wishes to assert the same validity of the "idea of God as personal Being"[167] then
here—if one thinks of the Christian Creator and redeemer God which Nishitani

---

[158]Ibid., 77 [R&N, 66].
[159]Ibid., 75ff. [R&N, 63ff.].
[160]Ibid., 80 [R&N, 68].
[161]Ibid., 87 [R&N, 75].
[162]Ibid., 84 [R&N, 72].
[163]Ibid., 75 [R&N, 75].
[164]Ibid., 85 [R&N, 73].
[165]Ibid., 80 [R&N, 69].
[166]Ibid., 83 [R&N, 71].
[167]Ibid., 80 [R&N, 69].

has in mind—the relation of personal and impersonal is something quite different. What is conceived of in the Christian conception of *Heilsgeschichte* as creation out of nothing and new creation through the redeemer is in Nishitani replaced by the awareness of the nothing, in respect to which he explains: "The so-called 'outer world' emerges here as a self-realization of nonobjectifiable nothingness, or rather, it comes to appear, as it is, in oneness with the nothingness."[168] In place of the "outer creation" by God, a "turn" in the "innerness" of man has entered. When Nishitani also emphasizes that its significance can only be understood in its enactment experienced existentially, he is thus convinced that "only on this level" is a fruitful discussion of the problem of science and religion possible.

6. Sunyata as the Overcoming of the Nihilism of Science (chapters 3 and 4)

In the third chapter, which carries the title "Nihility and Sunyata," Nishitani also takes up this problem in such a way that he raises the question of the "horizon" of the "objectivity of the laws of natural science" and its "cosmological" presuppositions.[169] He very perceptively develops the different aspects under which one and the same event can appear as something quite different, according to whether it is regarded physically, biologically, psychologically, or under the viewpoints of Spirit or personality, whereby the relevant means of explanation or understanding not only stand in relation to each other, but in their sphere of application prove to be limited and therefore relative.[170] As an especially complex, but consequential phenomenon he analyses in detail the connection in which the investigation of the laws of nature are useful to technology. On the one hand, in the technical application of the laws of nature, in which one submits himself to these through their recognition, he attains freedom from nature. On the other, however, he stands in the danger that out of this freedom an even greater servitude can develop through the control of nature if he understands the world and himself merely in terms of the laws of nature, for then that would appear to him meaningless and he would himself become a "desire-driven" being of "naked vitality,"[171] with the result that this "mechanical world-picture of modern science" leads to nihilism and to the "crisis of culture" as we experience it today.[172]

Nishitani makes no secret of the fact that he can see in this development only a "perversion" of the "authentic relation which naturally ought to be

---

[168]Ibid., 85 [R&N, 73].
[169]EB 4/2 (1971): 30ff. [R&N, 77-118].
[170]Ibid., 32ff. [R&N, 79ff.].
[171]Ibid., 34ff. [R&N, 86].
[172]Ibid., 38ff. [R&N, 84ff.].

between man and the world,"[173] because—as he expressly says—"man's personality or spirituality is indispensable for the correct human mode of being.[174] On
this basis he would like to recognize both in the "traditional religions" as well
as in the philosophical development "since Descartes" the traceable intention of
a resistance against science and an overcoming of its ultimately nihilistic consequences—only to show that its implementation is insufficient and to set over
against it Buddhist Sunyata as the sole "field" on which "person and spirit" can
appear in the "true form" of their reality and "nihilism can truly be overcome."[175]

    In the execution of this program which constitutes the entire remaining con-
tent of this chapter, the Christian faith in revelation, creation, providence, and redemption serves him as an example of "traditional religions,"[176] while from the
"history of philosophy" he considers especially Kant,[177] Nietzsche[178] and Heidegger,[179] but reaches back among all others to Aristotle.[180] As is to be expected on
the basis of the preceding chapter, from the circle of these Western thinkers only
Eckhart's "absolute Nothing as 'ground' of the personal God" and his "detachment"[181] stand up under the judgment of the "Great Death" of "emptiness" and
seem comparable to the ensuing "resurrection of one's true self,"[182] while in
Nishitani's judgment all other representatives of "Western Geistesgeschichte"[183]
lapse into an erroneous "objectivizing of what is nonobjectifiable" of the "being
of things and of the self" in the "subject-object duality" of logical thinking,[184]
and appear to unite with science as the pioneer of nihilism. Not only Kant's Ding
an sich and Nietzsche's "Overman" but also Heidegger's "abandonedness into
the Nothing"—not to speak of Aristotle's concept of substance and the statements of Christian Heilsgeschichte—Nishitani sees as within the boundaries of
a thinking consciousness that falsely ontologizes its content.[185]

    Judged from the standpoint of these different traits of Western thinking,
which deal with "person and spirit" and in whose attainment and preservation its

---

[173]Ibid., 41 [R&N, 87].
[174]Ibid., 43 [R&N, 89].
[175]Ibid., 44-45 [R&N, 91].
[176]Ibid., 44-46 [R&N, 91ff.]; EB 5/1:65 [R & N, 104].
[177]EB 5/2:98 [R&N, 111].
[178]Ibid. [R&N, 111].
[179]EB 5/1:56 [R&N, 96].
[180]EB 5/2:101 [R&N, 114].
[181]EB 5/1:59, 67 [R&N, 99, 106].
[182]EB 4/2:45 [R&N, 90-91]; EB 5/2:98ff. [R&N, 110ff.].
[183]EB 5/1:65 [R&N, 105].
[184]EB 5/2:99 [R&N, 112].
[185]EB 5/2:95ff. [R&N, 108ff.].

representatives along with Nishitani see "the core of genuine humanity,"[186] one could think that in these deliberations he has lost sight of his goal of overcoming the nihilism that arises through the idea of the hegemony of the sciences or that with his argumentation its attainment gets stuck halfway. For not only does he fail to consider thinking's striving for meaning but, in a manner reminiscent of Nietzsche, appears rather to greet the heritage of nihilism, because he expects from its completion in the "great Death" the "resurrection of the true self." Is it not the case that he claims a world-creative function when he explains with the author of "Questions and Answers in a Dream," that "Hills and rivers, the earth, plants and trees, tiles and stones, all of these are the self's own original part" and are brought forth "from the realm of this original part,"[187] as the idealists do in reference to their "subjectivity" and the pantheists and theists do of their "God"? Is it not the case that the objectivity striven for in science is different from the "true being" of things, evident from the fact that "one enters into them,"[188] and that this is due not merely to the fact that one has at one's disposal demonstrable proofs for it, while the latter by comparison must be highly subjective? But to whom does reality "announce itself" or where should it realize itself, if the self must "extinguish itself" for this to happen? Is the "field of Nothingness" something different from the sphere of nonobjectifiability against whose relative boundaries critical science pushes and at whose absolute boundary philosophy arises?

That these determinations and the questions resulting from them, to which his presentations have given rise, are not unknown to Nishitani; rather, the fact that he has rather taken them into account and taken a position on them is evident in the fourth chapter in which he thematically develops "The Standpoint of Sunyata."[189] With the exception of two factors to be mentioned, this chapter offers nothing essentially new, but expands and deepens the previous perspectives and positions. Without taking up again the question of meaning he posed for discussion at the beginning of the third chapter in view of the nihilism that issues from the mechanistic world-view, here he enters further into a discussion of the question of being, in respect both to concepts of substance[190] and of the subject,[191] especially in confrontation with Kant,[192] but also in reference to the pre- and post-Kantian philosophy, in order to juxtapose rationalistic and idealistic

---

[186]EB 4/2:44 [R&N, 89].
[187]EB 5/1:69 [R&N, 108].
[188]EB 6/1 (1973): 77-78 [R&N, 128].
[189]EB 6/1:68-91 and 6/2:58-86 [R&N, chap. 4, 119-67].
[190]EB 6/1:74ff. [R&N, 125ff.].
[191]Ibid., 1ff. [R&N, 127ff.].
[192]Ibid., 82ff. [R&N, 132ff.].

thinking consciousness with *"Samadhi"*-being[193] in whose "emptiness" the things—through their own "power" or *virtus*[194]—"settle [their] position"[195] and can thus be what they are, "freed from all hidden connections with a subject."[196]

Whereas Nishitani, as previously, demands as a condition of true knowledge the "extinction" of the subject, and here illustrates this "paradox" with a "death poem"[197] that reads

> Having now become deaf,
>   I distinctly hear
>   the sound of dew,

he explains in connection with this subject that it always consists of a "unity of two orientations": "on the one hand, the direction of its pure subjectivity, of its being definitely not an object," and, "on the other hand, the direction of its relating, in that capacity, to objects, of its knowing objects. At the point of inter-section the subject comes into being with the structure of self-consciousness, that is, it contains a consciousness of itself as something persistently unobjective and, nevertheless, always opposed to an object"; said differently: "its 'being' origi-nates in its self-reflection, in the reflective knowledge of itself as the unity of the two above directions." From this perspective Nishitani draws the conclusion that "subjectivity is nothing else than the self-in-itself projected onto the field of con-sciousness" and that "reflective knowledge," in which the self knows itself and objects (as such) becomes "possible by the fact that the self-in-itself is 'Not-knowing'."[198]

What is special in this passage cited consists not in the stress on the nonob-jectifiablity of the authentic self and its originality in the sense of being the "essential ground" of all objectivity, but rather in that fact that here Nishitani—in contrast to the *docta ignorantia* otherwise represented by him in this view—speaks expressly of "two orientations" of knowledge, one of which deals with the nonobjectifiable and the other, with the objectifiable, so that the non-objectifiable self "sees itself as standing over against an object" in which—if it is also a "projection of the self onto the field of consciousness"—"reflective knowledge" in which it knows itself *and objects* (issuing from us), becomes possible. Nishitani therefore not only distinguishes here between a "nonknowing" of the "self-in-itself" in a transcending of the subject-object split of consciousness

---

[193]Ibid., 78, 89 [R&N, 128, 139].
[194]Ibid., 73 [R&N, 123].
[195]EB 6/1:78 [R&N, 128].
[196]Ibid., 89 [R&N, 154].
[197]EB 6/2:71 [R&N, 154].
[198]Ibid., 73 [R&N, 155ff.].

and in a "reflective knowing" occurring in this field, in which the self knows itself and objects," but regards the latter as indispensable for the realization of the former." Although he speaks of the significance of reflective knowledge only in an aside and counterbalances it by stressing the "non-knowing" of the "self-in-itself" as the original element, in distinguishing between the two kinds of knowledge and the ordering of the former in the latter he nevertheless makes use of conceptual discriminating thinking and thereby confirms that it is formally indispensable for knowledge—even for the knowledge of "Not-knowing."

If Nishitani wishes to take account of the dependence of the thinking of what is non-objectifiable about the self and being upon the objectifying thinking of consciousness at whose boundaries it experiences its limits, the projection of the nonobjectifiable into the objectivity of consciousness—a point he rightly makes—would not have to be transformed into the "illusoriness"[199] of a phantom world, as it produces the "magician" mentioned by him[200] and as this happens for him in his highly idealized equation of the being and knowledge,[201] rather "the things" could reveal themselves in their "true being," not in a poetic, phantasmagoric imagination, but in a rationality conscious of its relative and absolute boundaries.

The state of affairs worked out with respect to the certainly instructive position of this chapter in immanent critique as a considerable inconsistency in Nishitani's thinking does not present anything new with respect to his preceding statements but is true of them from the beginning and in their entire course. One could speak of something new that appears here only insofar as in the manner in which Nishitani here unfolds the "standpoint of sunyata," its problematic appears in epistemological perspective, as we have already indicated previously in an especially pregnant passage.

Of a second specific element that meets us in this chapter—at least as far as its conceptual formulation is concerned—something should be said about a term newly introduced by Nishitani, which in Japanese is "egoteki" and rendered by the translator of this chapter, the Catholic theologian Jan van Bragt, by the term "circumincessional" associated with the doctrine of the Trinity. In the doctrine of the Trinity the relation of the three divine persons is described by *circumcessio* or *circumincessio*, Greek *perichoresis*, a mutual enveloping of one another and mutual interpenetration in which both their unity and personal distinctiveness are said to be preserved, according to the basic innertrinitarian formula: *una divina essentia (substantia) in tribus personis.* If one disregards the concepts of substance and person presupposed in this trinitarian doctrine of *perichoresis*,

---

[199]Ibid., 76 [R&N, 158].
[200]Ibid., 79 [R&N, 160].
[201]Ibid., 64ff. [R&N, 147].

which are naturally alien to Buddhist sunyata, and considers them solely as their representatives intended as a mutual enveloping and mutual interpenetration with the distinction of their subjects preserved, then the term *circumincessional* could to some extent correspond to what Nishitani intends when he says "that it is one moment of what makes each of the others 'be,' that it puts each of the others in the position of self-autonomy," which means that they are both in the position of servant and master. If this "Buddhist" *circumincessio* does not deal with a determinate relation in the sphere of divine transcendence, as the Christian term does, but is assumed for things in the world, then a certain correspondence does obtain between these conceptions, insofar as these relational determinants hold true for realms—Transcendence or "emptiness"—which are closed to the discursive thinking of understanding and demand a spiritual faith or an extinction of the I attached to things. If one nevertheless recalls the role which is assigned to the *ratio* in the formulation of the Christian doctrine of the trinity and considers the significance of consciousness as the sphere of the projection of the nonobjectified self, as Nishitani assumes, then the parallelism of both positions as well as also of their epistemological problematic becomes apparent.

What is completely new is this determinate relation for which Nishitani coins the term *egoteki*—translated by Jan van Bragt by the word *circumincessional*. But it is not new to the extent that it is nothing other than the epistemological formation of the state of affairs already intended in the early Buddhist *pratitya-samutpada* which is described with the image of "water and wave" in their simultaneous difference and inseparability. Nishitani develops this beloved image only insofar as he constructs an ontology by presupposing the field of emptiness, in consequence of which every "thing" has its "self-being" in that of the other, so that the boundless circle of its center expands to a boundless circle whose center is everywhere. Here there is neither a unitary being in which everything loses its own existence nor a disparateness, without unity, but rather a unity that is simultaneously diversity, and a diversity that is simultaneously a unity.[202] It is not surprising that Nishitani compares this "web" of circumincessional mutual interpenetration of all things to Leibniz' system of monads as "living mirrors of the universe, reflecting one other"[203]—but with the difference that with him, in place of Leibniz' divine central monad, there appears the nonobjectifiable "home ground" of man, from which the world and all things originate."[204] To be sure, he says however that as this "selfless subject" that has its "home ground" likewise "in all things," just as "all things are also in the home ground of our

---

[202]Ibid., 60ff. [R&N, 143ff.].
[203]Ibid., 67 [R&N, 150].
[204]Ibid., 69 [R&N, 152].

self,"²⁰⁵ we become a "son of god or a son of the Buddha,"²⁰⁶ and he brings this into connection with the "Great Light" of the all-penetrating "wisdom of the Buddha."²⁰⁷

The fact that at the end of the doctrine of sunyata epistemologically and ontologically developed in this chapter Nishitani mentions these mythological notions of the Buddhist tradition and—in reference to samadhi ²⁰⁸—speaks of "absolute freedom"²⁰⁹ and of a specific understanding of time realized therein which includes "simultaneity" with "Shakyamuni and Jesus, Basho and Beethoven"²¹⁰ and "the fullness of time" in a being within and outside of time,²¹¹ signifies that in this "ontology" of emptiness he is dealing with a universal ontology in which the question of meaning should find a solution.

7. The Understanding of Time and History in the Philosophy of Sunyata (chapters 5 and 6)

After the previous hints about the role which, in view of the goal of his presentation, is assigned to the understanding of time it is evident that Nishitani would have to occupy himself more thoroughly with the problem of time, and this he does in the fifth chapter, which is entitled "Sunyata and Time."²¹² In this he proceeds in such a way that in its first half he shows how the notions of samsara and nirvana that are fundamental for the Buddhist understanding of time are not only to be demythologized and existentially interpreted, but are to be realized in such understanding, in order in the second half to juxtapose it with the Christian notion of *Heilsgeschichte* and the Western thinking about history derived from that notion.

Nishitani was certainly concerned with the latter already in the first half of this chapter and indeed in a threefold manner. First, in that he refers to the insufficiency of the Hegelian concept of thinking for the understanding of the significance of the doctrine of rebirth (Samsara) adopted by Buddhism; second, in that he sets the existential interpretation which this doctrine has found in Buddhism in parallel to existential philosophy which arose in the West according to the trajectory from Kierkegaard through Heidegger and which supersedes that

²⁰⁵Ibid., 77 [R&N, 159].
²⁰⁶Ibid., 76 [R&N, 158].
²⁰⁷Ibid., 78ff. [R&N, 160].
²⁰⁸Ibid., 84 [R&N, 165].
²⁰⁹Ibid., 78 [R&N, 160].
²¹⁰Ibid., 80 [R&N, 161].
²¹¹Ibid., 78 [R&N, 159-60].
²¹²EB 9/1:42-77 and 10/2:1-30 [R&N, 168-217].

philosophy of consciousness; and third, in that he lets this existential thinking be dissolved and completed in a specifically Buddhist form.

The critical reference to Hegel is here quite concise, and actually presupposes the following two points of Nishitani's argumentation. Citing Hegel gives him opportunity for the evaluation of the concept of an "infinite finite" as a "bad infinity."[213] Nishitani sees such an "infinite finite" brought to expression in the mythological image of the "endlessly rotating wheel"[214] of being reborn and dying, in which all being is entangled. To the contrary, in the logic of his conceptual thinking Hegel is able to see in this only a "logical contradiction"; his speculative overcoming of it in absolute reason"—in contrast to the "Nothing" as the "transcendence as ecstasy" of existentialism—remains stuck in the "immanence" of an anthropologically understood world and its Logos.[215]

However, to the idealistic understanding of time he juxtaposes—in reference to Heidegger—not only that of existentialism as the becoming aware of the finiteness of man, but also—and this partly to the latter—the Buddhist understanding of time as based on an existential conception of the doctrine of rebirth strangely demythologized in Buddhism since the time of its origin. For the "existential understanding" of this tradition "in Heidegger's sense"[216] and its "demythologization" in parallel to that of Bultmann's,[217] he appeals to the early Buddhist conception of existence as suffering[218] and the "fateful causality" of karma "as a result of our own acts."[219] But over against Western existentialism he emphasizes that demythologizing did not first arise—as in the West—as a consequence of the sciences but was operational from the time of the origin of Buddhism throughout its entire history and conferred on it a "unique character" that "distinguishes it from other religions."[220] Similarly he thinks that only in the universality that is assigned in Buddhism to suffering through the inclusion of all sentient being and of all spaces and times,[221] is the "anthropocentricity"[222] that is peculiar to Bultmann's self-understanding and to a certain degree also to Heidegger's understanding of *Dasein* overcome, which is according to Nishitani

[213]EB 9/1:44 [R&N, 170].
[214]Ibid., 43 [R&N, 169].
[215]Ibid., 46 [R&N, 171].
[216]Ibid., 43 [R&N, 169].
[217]Ibid., 48 [R&N, 174].
[218]Ibid., 45 [R&N, 170].
[219]Ibid., 44 [R&N, 169].
[220]Ibid., 48 [R&N, 174].
[221]Ibid., 47, 49, 50-51 [R&N, 172, 175, 175-76].
[222]Ibid., 50 [R&N, 175].

only possible on "the standpoint of emptiness," and is attainable only through the dying of the "great Death" in which the "true self" is awakened.[223]

Insofar as this deals with an "understanding" both of the self and the world, as well as of relevant tradition, and in this understanding deals with a "realization" of the reality of the self, and of what is meant in the tradition by "in reality," Nishitani—without mentioning it—has something in common with Heidegger and Bultmann, namely, in reference to the conception of "understanding as realization." Only to Heidegger's "being-in-the-world," which is quite different from "human-being-in-the-world" and to his statement "the world 'worlds' (*weltet*)" does he accord a certain recognition, but in them he sees that "emptiness" is not yet attained.[224] On the contrary he does not espouse Bultmann's "eschatological" understanding of reality at all.

For his "understanding of understanding" as "realization of reality" he appeals to Dogen's "well-known words" out of his *Shobogenzo*: "Just understand that birth-and-death itself is nirvana, only then can you be free of birth-and-death"; or, "This present birth-and-death itself is the Life of the Buddha." Nishitani comments on these words by saying that according to Dogen the paradoxical equation of samsara and Nirvana represented in Mahayana Buddhism is realized when we understand ourselves in our existence in this sense, and that reality realizes itself in this understanding—in new ways for us—as that which it is. With this it runs into the same threefold ambiguity that is known to us from Heidegger's and Bultmann's existentialism: first, on one hand, understanding deals with a matter of the attitude of man toward a reality existing independently of him, in which he is located, which however through the way in which he attunes to it, takes on a different significance for him. On the other hand it is to be emphasized that the appearance of reality, how it appears to him, does not deal merely with the significance appropriate to it, but with "Being in itself." Second: On the threatening dissolution of reality into meaning, which is indistinguishable from delusion, something should be said of a "self-revelation of reality," of its self-realization. Apart from the fact that, prior to its realization, reality cannot be decided, the question now arises, how this understanding that precedes what is realized is related to this self-realization of "reality in itself." Just as little as Heidegger was able to justify the above equation of thinking and being by understanding the "thinking of being" at the same time as a subjective genitive and an objective genitive, so little does Nishitani give us a satisfactory answer to the subject of realization in understanding. The third element that connects him to Heidegger and Bultmann, is that he, like they, knows about this question and attempts to answer it in a similar way. Just as Heidegger speaks of

---

[223]Ibid., 51, 59 [R&N, 176, 183].
[224]Ibid., 50-51 [R&N, 175].

an "advent of Being," and Bultmann of an eschatological presence of Christ—as Christianity in general appeals to the working of the Holy Spirit—so in this connection does Nishitani introduce the "spirit of Tathagata (the one thus come)" and says of him: "The Buddha-spirit is reflected—and thus exhaustively in it—in the nature of the existence of man or his "spirit," in that it effects in him a radical turn and self-transcendence and simultaneously his spirit is reflected in itself." For this unifying of Tathagata or the Buddha-spirit and the human spirit he uses the image of two mirrors mutually reflecting each other without any intervening image," and explains this to this effect, that in understanding, the *kokoro*, that is, the significance of a matter, is presented "like the solution of a riddle." A fourth problem common to Nishitani and his Western kindred spirits is the fact that they emphasize that this, as in all individually understood understanding, does not deal with a process in the sphere of the intellect and its conceptually objectifying thinking, and not even with a understanding of symbol, but with an existential self-understanding or event of being, although both can speak of it only in an objective, even partially mythological, conceptuality and despite their use can speak of them only in such a way.[225]

Although using "Buddhist terminology," Nishitani in a twofold way surpasses the existentialism so widely shared by him, believing that he is able to elude its apparent problematic of understanding in a more radical way: first, by letting this "understanding as reality" complete itself in "emptiness," which he simultaneously understands as an *existential* for Nirvana,[226] and then by explaining in a longer elaboration Dogen's instruction on shikantaza, that is, only sitting, in which "body and spirit are allowed to merge," as the method of Zen practice, in which that "emptiness" can be attained.[227] In the "King Samadhi"[228] as a "consummate form of religious existence in Buddhism"[229] "all things are just as they are, and at the same time, as they ought to be."[230] and the "King Samadhi" who becomes aware of his emptiness is master of every situation[231] and "lord of universal being,"[232] in the "open field, where leap year comes one year in four, and every morning the cocks crow at dawn,"[233] that is, in the middle of time time is

---

[225]Ibid., 53ff. [R&N, 178ff.].
[226]Ibid., 55, 58 [R&N, 179, 182].
[227]Ibid., 60-71 [R&N, 184-193].
[228]Ibid., 65 [R&N, 187].
[229]Ibid., 60 [R&N, 184].
[230]Ibid., 69 [R&N, 192].
[231]Ibid., 70 [R&N, 192].
[232]Ibid., 71 [R&N, 193].
[233]Ibid., 64-65, 71 [R&N, 188, 193].

annulled, 'time' is time, because it is not time,"[234] and therefore precisely is "authentic time."[235] "With empty hands"[236] he possesses the power of a "king,"[237] and when he "forgets no sentient being" but vows to save them all,[238] he thus lives his "everyday life" "beyond all care and afflictions," in that he "takes things as they come," "not in fatalism or resignation," but in the "indestructible" nature of the "Dharma body," whose "manifestations" are the "transitory things" but which is not to be conceived of in "conceptual logic," but only in the "logic of existence (*sive/non*),"[239] which—as the "falling away of body and spirit" emphasized by Dogen proves—is ecstatic nature, the "ecstasy" of which Nishitani speaks in numerous other passages in respect to nihilism and all the more in respect to sunyata.

While Nishitani gets to speak on other occasions of the Christology and soteriology of the Apostle Paul, he limits his reference here to only a word which, considering the apparent similarity of Paul's being-in-Christ with Dogen's "King *Samadhi*," seems truly remarkable. To be sure, between these two notions of redemption—with respect to their spatial as well as their temporal conceptions of redemption—there is a fundamental difference. While for Paul redemption possesses no universal dimension, but is primarily limited to the sphere of the Christ event whose completion is still outstanding and in which there are those who will not participate in it, for Dogen as well as Nishitani, the Buddha nature has always been all-encompassing, and a completely different conception presents a delusion about the true state of affairs that already obtains. But what the Apostle says in reference to the redemptive effect of the Christ event corresponds in many respects to what Dogen describes by "sitting," in whose "emptiness" spaces and times are engulfed, that is, become manifest in their state. A certain parallelism appears between the distinction of God and Christ also in Nishitani's emphasis on Tathagata as the "thus come Buddha." But this specific function of Tathagata which reminds us of the Christ whose advent is still outstanding, is likewise again compensated for by its being incorporated in the universal and timeless being of the Buddha.

As Nishida's consideration of the instruction on not caring in the Sermon on the Mount and its mention of the Kingdom of God yields merely examples of "nondiscriminating thinking,"[240] he pays no attention to their eschatological

---

[234]Ibid., 66 [R&N, 189].
[235]Ibid., 67 [R&N, 190].
[236]Ibid., 64 [R&N, 188].
[237]Ibid., 68 [R&N, 190].
[238]Ibid., 64 [R&N, 189].
[239]Ibid., 67 [R&N, 190].
[240]Ibid., 57-58 [R&N, 182]

grounding which they have in common with the Pauline Christ-mysticism. In the fact that the eschatological expectation of the imminent or incipient turn of the aeons has not been fulfilled in the further course of history, but rather in place of the expected kingdom the Church appeared, lies the true cause of the problematic of Christianity and its conception of time and history. Instead of concerning himself with the problematic of the origin of Christianity and with its existential truth—which arises in connection with sunyata philosophy, in the second half of the chapter[241] Nishitani confronts its understanding of time with the Christian belief in *Heilsgeschichte*,[242] the alteration of its secularization into the modern belief in progress,[243] and its change into nihilism which Nietzsche supposedly tried to overcome with the "will to power" of his "eternal return" and the replacement of the salvation event asserted in Christianity as an "historical happening" by a Dionysus mythology.[244]

To be sure, Nishitani in this way also gets around to speaking of the problem of eschatology and history, but in a way that does not do justice to this special situation in early Christianity, because it distinguishes itself in one essential point from that which has been dogmatized in the Christian Church as *Heilsgeschichte* and which Nishitani has in view in his discussion of that problem. His casual mention of the Japanese national myth of the "descent of the heavenly grandson of the sungoddess" as a "once for all, nonrepeatable event"[245] causes him to compare this with the messianic self-consciousness and behavior of Jesus as well as with the Christian conception of *Heilsgeschichte* which arose as a compensation for the catastrophe of this actualization of the eschatological mythology and thereby to establish the relationship and difference of these three conceptions.

To a certain degree Nishitani carries through the comparison suggested here, but without succeeding to a real clarification of the situation which is here under discussion. Apparently he is concerned here to refute Arnold Toynbee's conception of the relation of "nature and history in Buddhist philosophy" as a "cycle of events ruled by an 'impersonal' law." In order to prove that only if the universe is regarded "from the perspective of nature" does this "so-called circularity" result, Nishtani points to the fact that there was already operative in an old Japanese rice harvest offering a historical factor which does not appear with as much "clarity" as is the case in the myth of the "grandson of the sun goddess."[246] It is

---

[241]EB 10/2:1-30 [R&N, 193-217].
[242]Ibid., 17ff. [R&N, 206ff.].
[243]Ibid., 20ff. [R&N, 209].
[244]Ibid., 23ff. [R&N, 211ff.].
[245]Ibid., 11-12 [R&N, 201ff.].
[246]Ibid., 16 [R&N, 205ff.].

also not appropriate—he holds—on this basis to ascribe a greater significance to the "historical consciousness of the Jewish people" which was developed in Christianity into a "consciousness of original sin, freedom and the once-for-allness of time" in respect to the overcoming of mythological cyclical thinking.[247] When he explains that "this kind of religion stands on a plane much higher than the mythological one,"[248] he seems to identify myth with the "cyclical" conception of history" in the sense of an event of nature—as is the case with Bultmann[249]—in contradistinction to the examples of mythologies of history from the Japanese and Western spheres which he also mentions.

Instead of indicating on the one hand the commonality of the mythological conception of history in these diverse types—to which even the relationship in the self-understanding of the Japanese and the Jewish-Christian people of God would belong—and on the other, the differences in the historical realization of these selected peoples and in relation to their mediator figures, Nishitani proceeds to reproach Christianity *en globo* for its inner untruthfulness uncovered by Feuerbach and Nietzsche,[250] its claim to absoluteness and the temporary intolerance that follows from it,[251] the untenability of its expectation of the end in view of the "actual" course of history,[252] and the fact that its story of the Fall is unbelievable.[253] Without noting that in all these points in Christianity—both between the New Testament and the dogma of the Church as well as also within both of these dimensions—there exist powerful differences which have their cause in the expectation of the Parousia, or its delay, Nishitani believes that he can see the "roots" of all these questionable features of Christianity, which have arisen in the course of its history, in the "personalism" of its concept of God and of man and in the "self-centeredness" common to both.[254]

From the criticism which Nishitani directs at the noncyclical understanding of time in the Christian conception of *Heilsgeschichte* and at the egocentricity of its depiction of God and man, one could conclude that what strikes him as ideal is an understanding of history which would be as free from the historical problematic of Christianity as from the egocentricity of its personalism in which he sees its cause. That and how such a cyclical and at the same time not merely

---

[247]Ibid., 16-17 [R&N, 206ff.].
[248]Ibid., 17 [R&N, 207].
[249]Ibid., 15 [R&N, 205].
[250]Ibid., 14 [R&N, 204].
[251]Ibid., 18, 21 [R&N, 207, 209].
[252]Ibid., 19-20 [R&N, 208ff.].
[253]Ibid., 25 [R&N, 213].
[254]Ibid., 13, 12, 26ff. [R&N, 203, 202, 214].

cyclical feature can be possible on the basis of a selfless personality is then the goal of the concluding chapter of Nishitani's philosophy of religion.

With respect to the preceding material this sixth chapter devoted to the theme of "Sunyata and History"[255] offers nothing fundamentally new, but in a renewed confrontation with what he understands by "Christianity" and by "nihilism"—as the overcoming of both—he brings to bear on the nature of history what he has already repeatedly developed about the "selflessness of the true self" and the "infinite finitude of existence" with "nihilism." He relates it frequently to what he had already presented earlier, the result being that this chapter forms the crowning conclusion of the entire work, in which all its threads run together and become interwoven into an artful whole which seems like a mandala image before which the viewer sinks into Nothingness and for whom the world and his existence may become "new." Because the individual parts of this system are of a dialectic kind, so their juxtaposition represents a configuration of a higher dialectic, whose completion through the kinds of arguments—at times monotonous and then again erratic—in which Nishitani develops them is not easy. But if one cannot follow each step in his thinking, one nevertheless knows—by this time already in advance—what he aims at with his pro and contra. In the middle of the scheme of his figures of thought which emerge and then again dissolve sits the figure of the Buddha—identical with Nirvana, penetrating and illumining everything. Everything proceeds from this "essential ground" so as in it to return from "ignorance" (*avidya*) to "Enlightenment," as Nishitani has set it forth in his existential interpretation of the samsara mythology, and in which it serves him as the basis of his understanding of history.

As a refutation of Toynbee's misunderstanding of the notion of samsara as a "purely cyclical" conception of time and of the world process, with which Nishitani already concerned himself in the preceding chapter, he points here to the notion—which belongs to Buddhist eschatology—of beginningless and endless succession of kalpas—just like samsara. Through a combination of both notions he arrives at a cosmic model of time, by means of which it can be assumed of each individual "now" that it moves "simultaneously in a circle and a straight line, and that there is revealed to that individual in its necessary return with such necessity simultaneously what has never been, but only is newly to be actualized—over an "abyss of openness" without beginning or end.[256]

The validity of this model is exhibited not in its logical-speculative constructability, but in the fact that it represents a notional expression of the existential experience of being-in-the-world, or an existential interpretation of samsara and kalpa mythology to which the karma notion also essentially belongs. The

---

[255]EB 12/1:49-82; 12/2:55-71; 13/1:9-30 [R&N, 218-85].
[256]EB 12/1:49-50 [R&N, 119].

entire first half of this concluding chapter is devoted to the unfolding of the existential interpretation of the mythological understanding of time and its confrontation with the Christian conception of *Heilsgeschichte*, of the nihilism which arises from its secularization and its remythologizing in Nietzsche's teaching of the eternal return,[257] by which the notion of kalpa specified at the beginning conspicuously recedes behind that of karma. The "simultaneity of what is opposite" which is initially demonstrated in relation to the series of kalpas is connected principally with the karma idea in the further course of the presentation, because the latter is more suited to existential interpretation than the former.[258]

In an impressive way Nishitani presents the "essential ambiguity of our existence" from all sides. On the one hand, time requires us to do something in its incessant change in order to maintain ourselves in it, and on the other, at the same time it gives the "possibility of creative freedom." But not only because this possibility is placed upon us; rather, because we can never exhaust it, it represents at the same time "an infinite burden." The act by which we exhaust our debt is the seed of a new one,"[259] as this is expressed in the doctrine of rebirth and its karma notion. But precisely in their interconnection these doctrines point to the fact that we are embedded in this being of time not only externally but also through our own nature, which consists in "desire." On this view the ambiguity of our existence goes still deeper into time, in that it consists in a simultaneity of our "attachment of things" and of their causal connections, of its own inner behavior and external necessity,[260] whereby its own behavior is ambiguous in itself, in that desire is spontaneously and simultaneously a compulsion.[261] The question about the why and wherefore of this situation Nishitani answers by pointing to the fact that the phenomenon of time is without beginning and end, that is, he resigns himself to the recognition that it has no answer.[262] But while he knows neither of a ground of being nor of the meaning of our existence, he sees the "origin of the infinite impulse, which is revealed in our self-consciousness on the basis of our own 'being' and 'acts' as the ground of our factual existence," in the "self-satisfaction " which is derived on its own side from the "fundamental avidya" and is the cause of endless karmic activity.[263]

---

[257]Ibid., 49-82 [R&N, 219-50].
[258]Cf. ibid., 50, with 68ff. [R&N, 219 with 236].
[259]Ibid., 51 [R&N, 220].
[260]Ibid., 52 [R&N, 221].
[261]Ibid., 78 [R&N, 246].
[262]Ibid., 54-55 [R&N, 223].
[263]Ibid., 74 [R&N, 242ff.].

With this designation of "self-centredness" as the "ultimate ground of karma"[264] Nishitani arrives at the point from which there results for him the possibility of an overcoming of the "meaninglessness"[265] of that "simultaneity of ambiguity," several features of which he locates in Christianity, secularism, nihilism and Nietzsche, but always in sketchy forms, from which the "turn" that leads to salvation cannot ensue, but according to him is only possible in the emptiness that transforms self-centeredness into selflessness.[266] In the second half of this last chapter Nishitani concerns himself with the positive presentation of this genuine Buddhist doctrine of redemption in its orientation to Nirvana and the ethic of compassion issuing from it.[267]

As guidance for the realization of "emptiness" he reverts to what he had already set forth in reference to Dogen's "dropping off body and spirit" in the "royal *samadhi*"[268] and for the theoretical grounding of its ethical consequences in universal compassion, to the previously developed metaphysics of the all-encompassing "mutual interpenetration" of all things.[269] In the emptiness realized in immersion the will also falls away, which in its operative form entangles man in the law of karma, and with the liberation from self-centeredness man becomes free from the notion of circularity growing out of it,[270] because now there is no longer a "self" that can become entangled in this circle. Nevertheless, Nishitani—in a way similar to Nietzsche's Zarathustra in his liberating "Yea-saying to the eternal return"—speaks of an "acceptance" and "bearing" of the "burden of guilt" out of the "free will" which is at the same time liberation from this burden, and—likewise like Nietzsche—stresses the "play"-character of this "spontaneous work."[271]

Whereas Nishitani holds that in Christianity the self-centeredness is "not completely overcome," but remains especially active, for example, in the consciousness of election,[272] in connection with the ethical consequences of the doctrine of the "interpenetration of all things" he not only recalls once again the motto of Luther's "freedom of the Christian man" already cited,[273] but also St.

---

[264]Ibid., 78 [R&N, 245].
[265]Ibid., 60 [R&N, 229].
[266]EB 12/2:55ff. [R&N, 250ff.].
[267]EB 12/2:55-71 and 13/1:9-30 [R&N, 250-85].
[268]EB 12/2:55, 57, 70; 13/1:21 [R&N, 250, 252, 264, 276-77].
[269]EB 12/2:63, 65, 69; 13/1:20, 26, 30 [R&N, 258, 259, 263; 275, 280-81, 285].
[270]EB 12/1:74ff. [R&N, 242ff.].
[271]EB 12/2:58, 64 [R&N, 252ff., 258].
[272]Ibid., 56 [R&N, 251].
[273]EB 13/1:20 [R&N, 275].

Francis' Hymn to the Sun[274] and the latter's behavior during his eye operation[275] as manifestations of that doctrine in the sign of God's love and of the cross as a sign of "emptiness." The most perfect expression of the "boundless connection to the world" is represented for Nishitani by "the four vows of the Bodhisattva": "However numberless sentient beings, I vow to save them; However inexhaustible the deluding passions, I vow to extinguish them; However limitless the Dharma Gates, I vow to practice them; However supreme the Buddha way, I vow to achieve it."[276] Despite his high estimate of Kant's categorical imperative in consequence of which the person is always an end in itself and may never be used merely as a means to an end, he regards this formulation as unsatisfactory and lagging behind the vows of the Bodhisattva because of the self-determination of the person it demands.[277] However, he can acknowledge a certain correspondence to the vows in Christian "conversion," if it is understood not merely as a realization of the individual components of Christian *Heilsgeschichte*, while "from the standpoint of the way of the Bodhisattva each individual moment of infinite time carries the solemn weight of those designated components in Christianity" (i.e. of its historical facts of salvation), and as "monads of eternity," unite the weight of all time in themselves.[278]

This comparison of Christian *Heilsgeschichte* with Bodhisattva being is typical both for Nishitani's attitude toward Christianity and to all other forms of religion, as well as for his understanding of the nature of history per se, with which this chapter finally deals. Not in the biblical-Christian *Heilsgeschichte* in its traditional form as a divine saving event comprised of a past, present and future, but alone in its existential interpretation in the "conversion" of the individual does he see a possible positive relationship to his concept of redemption, despite the difference of metaphysics presupposed in them. Thus he can say that, as far as "practicing the Buddha Way," he does not "suggest that the true face of existence in religious praxis obtains only in Buddhism." It is rather contained "in all true religious life."[279] In his existential interpretation of *samsara*, karma and Nirvana, which he defines in this connection once more by the formula "Existence is real as understanding," only to confront it in the further course of his thought once more with "Kant's epistemological 'Copernican revolution'"[280] and in this connection, with the Western concept of the subject as

---

[274]Ibid., 26 [R&N, 281].
[275]Ibid., 28-29 [R&N, 283].
[276]Ibid., 15 [R&N, 270].
[277]Ibid., 17ff. [R&N, 272ff.].
[278]Ibid., 16-17 [R&N, 271].
[279]EB 12/2:67 [R&N, 261].
[280]EB 13/1:19 [R&N, 275].

such,[281] he is not dealing "with any kind of especially religious or philosophical view"—even over against different conceptions of karma in the "doctrine of the power of the other in the Buddhist schools of the Pure Land." His "goal" is rather "the original nature of reality and of 'man,' who is a part of this reality, inclusive of both antireligious and antiphilosophical standpoints, such as, for example, Nietzsche's nihilism and the scientism of 'secularization'." If he "repeatedly" represents the "standpoint of Buddhism and especially of Zen Buddhism," this happens "principally" because it seems to him that therein the "original form of reality appears most clearly and error-free," which does not preclude that "the same view is to be found among the representatives of Nembutsu" and with Shinran. "In his discussion of emptiness and karma" he does "restrict this to only one of the Buddhist forms."[282]

What Nishitani—even with this openness—cannot accommodate is the notion of the biblical-Christian *Heilsgeschichte*. Certainly he can establish the connection of several of its parts to the corresponding forms of the Buddhist doctrine of redemption—above all, death and resurrection—but always with the proviso of a completely different kind of understanding. As a whole however he can only finally reject it, because it is "history," and "history" for him is immersed in, or has to sink into, emptiness, because emptiness is its fulfillment. This fulfillment it finds in the enlightenment of the individual in which "the world becomes new" to this one. To the one who already belongs to the Christ as the bringer of the new aeon and the one-in-Christ as one who in this passing world already belongs to the new world there corresponds the Buddha-Tathagata (the thus-coming one or one already come), for example, in the form of Amida, and the Bodhisattva who refuses entrance into Nirvana for the sake of those to be redeemed from their unknowing. Whereas in Christianity the Parousia—whether imminent or in some kind of future—is still awaited and therefore history—if also in different, partly very problematic forms—is assigned an essential meaning, in Buddhism the enlightened one already experiences himself in the present and as displaced in this world to the "far shore" of the stream of time, except that this terrain—at least for the disciples of Zen—is not decorated with the trees of paradise and no river flows out of it; rather in it he sees "mountains and trees" "as they really are." Since he himself takes over the function of the redeemer, he need no longer await his appearance. In place of the messianic expectation there appears here a messianic action, such as Luther required in the text on freedom cited by Nishitani, when he there writes that we should "become Christ each to the other."

---

[281]Ibid., 17ff. [R&N, 272ff.].
[282]EB 12/2:67-68 [R&N, 262-63].

Under this ethical aspect issuing equally from an existentially understood Buddhology and Christology history neither becomes dissolved into an "emptiness" nor defaults to a divine governance of the world, but manifests itself as the task each of us must master. If this is what the word "field" means in the sentence with which Nishitani concludes his work, namely, "Unless man's thinking and doing take place on that field, the various problems that beset humanity can never really be solved";[283] then we can agree with him in thinking that on "this field" a fruitful conversation between Buddhism and Christianity becomes possible. But as Nishitani here lets "emptiness" be his final word and ends abruptly with it, so Christian theology has hitherto believed that it must oppose Nirvana with its Kingdom of God. After what has been set forth we are of the opinion, to the contrary, that only if the problematic of both views is looked into and taken into account can Nishitani's concluding sentence become valid in the positive sense as testimony to an obligation with respect to human history.

Having presented Nishitani's philosophy of religion in such a way and taken a position with respect to it, it is advisable for purposes of comparison to throw light on the most extensive presentation and evaluation that has been allotted to this philosopher from the Christian side.

8. Waldenfel's Book on Nishitani[284]

This book, entitled *Absolutes Nichts*, which appeared from Herder-Verlag in 1976 (ET: *Absolute Nothingness: Foundations for a Buddhist-Christian Dialogue* [New York: Paulist Press, 1980]), is the fruit of a thirteen-year-long preoccupation with the religious philosophy of Keiji Nishitani and its Buddhist heritage as well as with the Kyoto School and its spiritual surroundings. As is evident from the bibliography, a series of smaller publications on this subject preceded it. The fact that it was accepted by the theological faculty of the University of Wurzburg as a *Habilitationsschrift* in the field of the history of missions indicates the change which has occurred in the Catholic Church since Vatican II in respect to the concept of mission. In his accompanying word Nishitani attests of this work that it represents "the first attempt on the part of the West to enter deeply into the heart of problems that have become the focal point of the contemporary discussion between Christianity and Buddhism."

The book consists of three parts which carry the titles "Background," "Keiji Nishitani and the Philosophy of Emptiness," and "Stepping Stones for Dialogue."

---

[283]EB 13/1:30 [R&N, 285].

[284]Cf. my review of this book in EB 12/1:153-56, as well as my lecture on "The Fate of the Idea of God in Keiji Nishitani's Philosophy of Religion" given at the XII. International Congress of Historians of Religion in Stockholm, in 1970, from which parts of this section are taken.

In sketching the historical background Waldenfels refers to the "homelessness" of the Buddha and his silence respecting questions of metaphysics, as well as to the concept of anatman and the doctrine of dependent origination (*pratitya-samutpada*); further, to Nagarjuna and the Madhyamika philosophy. There follows a short sketch of the history and nature of Zen Buddhism, which ends in a concise characterization of Kitaro Nishida's course of thought from "pure experience" to the "absolute self-identity of contradictories."

Already in this presentation of the religious and philosophical heritage of Nishitani Waldenfels takes into account not only statements of other representatives of the Kyoto School, but for comparison quotes passages also of Western philosophers, above all, Nietzsche and Martin Heidegger. This is especially true for the discussion of the sunyata philosophy of Nishitani. He also divides this main part of his book into three sections. A first is devoted to "Stimuli" which Nishitani has experienced for his thinking; a second, to his journey "from nihilistic doubt to the emptiness of the open hands"; and a third indicates which "estimate of world, history, and man" issues from the perspective of "emptiness." Besides other writings and individual essays, Nishitani's principal work of 1961, "Religion and Nothingness," forms the principal object of his thorough analysis. For several central terms, as, for example, that of Nothingness and of "nondifferentiated difference," he appeals to explanations of Masao Abe and Shizuteru Ueda or notations of Daisetz Suzuki and Hisamatsu, or Christian thinkers like Tillich, Takizawa, and Yagi. Thus we possess here a picture not only of Nishitani's philosophy, but also of the concerns of the Kyoto School as a whole and its role in contemporary East-West dialogue.

The worldwide actuality of Nishitani's sunyata philosophy issues for Waldenfels from its starting point in the dilemma in which modern man in the East as well as the West sees himself located due to modern science and technology, in that he falls victim either to nihilism or to a no less destructive superstitious science. While according to his view, Christianity and Western thought per se cannot prevail against them, Nishitani believes he is able to find the solution in the way of Zen that leads through the "Great Doubt" to the "true self" of "enlightenment" and beyond these, to the "wonderful self."

If already in a formal way the enactment of the Zen thinking of Nishitani which transcends the conceptuality of thinking consciousness and its subject-object split is in Waldenfel's presentation no simple matter, so the statements about the ineffable grow into what is unintelligible in his attempt to indicate the material consequences of this thinking for the understanding of nature and history and for the role to be assigned in it to God and man. But this obvious denial by Waldenfels relative to the intelligibility of representing Nishitani's philosophy is not so much the special burden of the former, but is grounded in the nature of what he attempts here to accomplish. Only stammering and silence would correspond to the ineffable, but would be bound up with a loss of the self and its transcendence, about whose attainment the Buddhist Nishitani and the Christian Waldenfels each go their own ways.

In this equally endangered and mutual intention, Waldenfels seeks to take into account what he believes he can set forth in the concluding chapter of his book as "stepping stones to conversation." They consist, on one hand, of hermeneutical comments on the necessity of combining "kataphatic-positive" and "apophatic-negative" discourse about God and man and of an understanding of mystical texts as "mystagogy"—that is, as leading to existential praxis in the loss of any kind of self-assertion—whether intellectual or dogmatic. On the other hand, it consists of taking seriously the "Christian claim of revelation" in faith in the "God-man Jesus" and the strongly related doctrines of the Catholic Church on the trinity, the *analogia entis*, and the Christological-theological background of the doctrine of kenosis, whose neglect by Nishitani is faulted by Waldenfels in his presentation of Nishitani's philosophy.

It is obvious that very different kinds of stepping stones are dealt with from which no foundation for an edifying conversation can result. With the first kind, that of general hermeneutics, the Buddhist could immediately agree. But with the second, in which Waldenfels announces the special revelatory claim of the Christian faith, he finds himself in contradiction to the principles of the first kind that he recognizes. This self-contradiction of the Christian, to which "the enlightened Buddha" can only answer with a "smile," constitutes the cause of the "tortured countenance of the crucified Jesus"—although in a different way from that which Waldenfels intends.

This not only "unpretentious" but disappointing result of Waldenfel's confrontation of Christian faith and Buddhist philosophy can furnish the occasion for representatives of both positions to remember that the "enlightenment which radiates love and the love that radiates enlightenment" can occur wherever a distinction is made between being and oughtness and responsibility is assumed, for which defect Waldenfels reproaches Buddhism; but he himself fails to draw out the consequences, placing the burden on his Christ. The Buddhist can no longer, as Nishitani loves to do, use the Pauline word, "Christ in me," merely as a bewildering koan, but can see in it the correspondence to his becoming a Buddha, an invitation that one should become to the other a Buddha or a Christ. Then we should have to do therein no longer merely with the "Nothing" or the "abyss in God," but against the background of bottomless depth, with the equally groundless depths of the special revelation of transcendence in its incarnation as our incarnation which represents a universal possibility transcending all dogmatization, technologization and institutionalization. In order to solve its mutual problematic Christian theology must draw the consequences out of its historical problematic, and Buddhist philosophy must acknowledge that its speculation about Nothingness stands in contradiction to the silence of the Buddha.

As a way of summarizing the critique utilized at different points in the context of our presentation of Nishitani's philosophy of religion, we shall formulate five critical questions which are quite different from those advanced by Waldenfels, but which relate to his position insofar as it agrees with that of Nishitani, in order by way of conclusion to suggest the corresponding positive considerations from which, in our opinion, a fruitful conversation with Nishitani could become possible.

First, how is a statement understandable for one's own consciousness and the consciousness of another still possible beyond the subject-object structure of thinking consciousness? A statement presupposes a subject which makes it, or attempts to understand it, and intends an object by which it expresses something. Even a mere gesture or inarticulate sound, if it is said to have a meaning, becomes an object for the agent or the receiver who plays the role of subject over against them both—or else one sinks into silence and has nothing more to say, or into unconsciousness and can then neither communicate something to oneself or another. A nonobjectifying thinking and speaking, on the contrary—equally in Buddhism or Christianity or any kind of space—appears as empty chatter or a self-deception.

Second, where is the place of the "Great Doubt" or the "Great Death" and the "conversion" to a new life or of an "awakening of the true self"—these salvation events about which Nishitani has so much to say, in which he—mutatis mutandis—correctly sees parallels even in the Christian doctrine of redemption and in contemporary Western philosophy? With his "great mass of doubt" to which the Zennist supposedly comes in the "Great Death" Nishitani finds himself in a difficulty which is not less than that with which the Christian belief in resurrection is burdened with respect to the relation of the old and new being.

Third, in these contradictions can authentic existence be ascribed to the actually non-objectifiable nature of human personhood? With what right does this personal event—and it cannot deal with something other than such if it is about something rather than nothing—become expanded into a cosmic event, to a world creation (Buddhist or idealist) or in Western—Christian and non-Christian—speculation into a universal teleology? Does not this special event of the opening up of the radical question of meaning in man and the possibility of attaining through being led by this question to a special realization of human existence in midst of the experienced loss of the meaning of life and of the world, therefore lose its special character, its genuine character of a new being, which is "not of this world"?

Fourth, it is significant that Buddhism as well as Christianity in this situation take flight to mythologies and speculations of a Nothing or of a redeemer who differs from the creator God and yet is bound up with him—to Buddha or to Christ. But in their dogmatic Buddhological or Christological formulation are these figures—quite apart from their historical contingency and relatively human significance—quite different from symbols of human self-understanding, especially for the special situations in which and through which man experiences himself as redeemed from the riddles of existence and in which he prepares himself to behave properly toward them in the world?

The fact that a "theology after the death of God" has arisen on Christian turf and an "atheistic Christianity" is demanded, represents a parallel to the fate of the thought of God in Nishitani's philosophy of religion, only with the difference that in the latter God does not need to die, because he was never really alive.

Over against both phenomena we see ourselves, in view of their metaphysical character, brought to the question whether they do not deal with inadequate metaphysical constructions of meaning because they are not able to give an answer to the question of the ultimate ground of the presence of a world to be redeemed and of its redeemer.

Fifth, do trust in the vow of the Buddha as a guarantee for attaining the rebirth in the Pure Land, the ideal of the mendicant monk and the thought of "innocent play," which Nishitani recalls with respect to the social problems which confront us today, represent a way to solve these problems, or do they—like certain Christian conceptions of the Kingdom of God and of grace—actually only deal with an "opium for the people," whose use prevents us from changing the world—instead of merely interpreting it further—and that on the basis of what we are able to know and realize within insurmountable boundaries?

From such critical considerations, which we miss in Waldenfels' book, the prospect for a possible understanding with Nishitani could eventuate, insofar as in his philosophy of religion starting points are evident from which a thought of God could be attained, which represents a symbol of true incarnation and thus also corresponds to what Waldenfels strived for, but did not reach.

We agree with Nishitani that being, inclusive of man, can be ultimately objectified neither in its essence nor in its origin, but for our unavoidably objectifying thinking is dissolved into an ungraspable nothing. In this sense God and the "I," like Being as a whole, constitute for our knowledge an unfathomable abyss. Without the recognition of this "emptiness" to our grasp there is no legitimate application of the thought of God.

With Nishitani we intend further not to end in nihilism but to succeed to the awareness of our true self—to be sure, not in an abandoning of consciousness and a collapse of thinking, as is the case for Nishitani, but in the realization of personal being which in its conceptually fulfilled self-understanding—which in this enactment is no longer objectifiable—understands itself to be responsible for its acts. Although Nishitani rejects this way and its goal, in his philosophy of religion—despite its different logic and his experiential background—he locates himself with us on this journey; for he poses as its author and seeks to convince us therein of his view.

For such personhood, which he also lays claim to and to which we appeal in conversation with people like Nishitani, consists no longer merely in a "complete emptiness"; rather in it we experience ourselves destined to its specific realization which cannot be expressed with the image of the "innocent play" of the being of "water and waves," but is rather related to it like fire to water, and includes a struggle toward realization and the obligation to change the world in the sense of facilitating personal being in community.

Christian theology speaks here of Christ as the special revelation of God and of being-in-Christ that corresponds to it. But doesn't the Buddhist also know of the Buddha's delayed entry into Nirvana for the sake of his work as Bodhisattva and for determining man to Bodhisattva-hood to save the world?

It is true that in Christianity and Buddhism redemption is conceived differently: here is the point at which not only in Nishitani's philosophy of religion, but in philosophy of religion per se—of the East as well as the West—a turning point could enter the "fate of the thought of God." In this sense we agree with the conception repeatedly expressed by John Cobb, that the encounter between Buddhism and Christianity cannot remain at the stage of "dialogue," in which its partners become acquainted with the differences and antagonisms of their standpoints, yet persevere in their unchanged attachments and claims to validity; rather the representatives of both must, through insight into the insufficiency of their positions, reach a new conception of the same, in which faith or philosophy yield to each other as their necessary completion.[285] This is not the case with Waldenfels, because as a good Catholic he is not in a position to question the claim to absoluteness of his Church.

---

[285]John Cobb, Jr., "Buddhism and Christianity as Complementary," NAJTh (March/Sept 1978): 19ff.

Yoshinori Takeuchi (b. 1913)

Chapter 7

Yoshinori Takeuchi (b. 1913)
Buddhist Religious Existentialism

1. Amida Priest and Disciple of Tanabe

Yoshinori Takeuchi was thirteen years younger than his better known and—
philosophically regarded—more important colleague Nishitani, with whom he
taught philosophy of religion at Kyoto University. He also published less. If even
Nishitani's work was less voluminous than that of his predecessors, this is still
more the case with Takeuchi's. He limited himself in Japanese to four publications, all of which were concerned with Shinran, his Kyogyoshinsho, his significance for the present and especially his view of history.[1] This exhaustive treatment of Shinran is connected with the fact that Takeuchi belonged to the
Jodoshinshu in which he attained a high rank and owns a temple of this school
at which he still works as a priest. Since becoming emeritus at Kyoto University
in 1976 he has lectured at the Aichi gakuin University. Besides his academic
career and priestly obligations he has concerned himself with the founder of the
type of Buddhism he represents as well as with his teachings, but has paid attention to Buddhism in general, especially to its origins and its formulations in the
fathers of the Kyoto School, Nishida and Tanabe.

His research on the origins of Buddhism and his personal understanding of
these matters are attested in four essays which appeared in German in 1972
under the general title "Probleme der Versenkung im Ur-Buddhismus" ("The
Problems of Contemplation in Early Buddhism"), among which there is a longer
one devoted to "Stufen der Versenkung im Ur-Buddhismus" ("Stages of Contemplation in Early Buddhism") which has supplied the name of the collection. The
three others are lectures which Takeuchi delivered from 1960 to 1968 in Europe.[2]

The results of his preoccupation with Nishida and Tanabe he reported on in
two longer articles which appeared in English in two journals[3] and in three con-

---

[1]"The Philosophy of the Kyogyoshinsho," which appeared in the journal published by the philosophical faculty of Kyoto University, *Philosophical Studies*
vols. 24 (1939), 25 (1940), 26 (1941), 28 (1943), and 29 (1944/1945); "Shinran's
View of History" and "Shinran and the Present" in the journal *Riso* #485 (1974).

[2]"Probleme der Versenkung im Ur-Buddhismus," *Beihefte der Zeitschrift für
Religions- und Geistesgeschichte* 16 (Leiden: E. J. Brill, 1972).

[3]"Hegel and Buddhism," *Il Pensiero* 7 (1962, Urbino): 1-2; "The Philosophy
of Nishida," JR 3 (1943): 4.

tributions to the *Encyclopedia Britannica*.[4] Moreover, lectures he delivered at
Columbia University in 1961–1962 form the basis for a journal article.[5] Despite
the succinctness of these articles they are among the best that have been written
in English about Nishida and Tanabe and are extraordinarily helpful for understanding what is not easy to grasp. If Takeuchi has done justice to both thinkers
and has developed an interesting comparison of their differences as well as of the
convergence of the ideas of both, it is clear nevertheless that in his own thought
he stands more on the side of Tanabe than of Nishida. In contrast to Hisamatsu
and Nishitani who emphatically continued the line of Nishida, Takeuchi is an
outspoken devotee of Tanabe to whom he was joined in a close teacher-pupil
relationship.

A gripping testimony to the intensity of the personal relationship of Takeuchi
to his revered teacher is presented in the proposed introduction to his translation
of Tanabe's *Philosophy as Metanoetics* which—with the exception of two hitherto published segments[6]—is only available in manuscript form [at the time Buri
wrote —Trans.]. In view of the complexity of Tanabe's way of expressing himself philosophically and the difficulty of translating him, the effort which
Takeuchi exerted on it over many years might even be designated his lifework.
The sympathetic attention of the thoughts of another belong authentically to the
personality of Takeuchi which—corresponding to his religiosity—is deeply one
which serves in openness and self-giving. One becomes aware of this not only
in personal association with him, but also in the way in which he reacts to Western thinking and the peculiarities of the Christian faith. With all the limitation
which he readily concedes, there is nothing here of a hidden and finally
intransigent air of superiority which one so often painfully experiences in his
predecessors and colleagues. Also, much Western "Christianity" would be
shamed by the humility of his Amida piety.

Takeuchi is a pious existentialist without Nietzsche's *ressentiment*. Those
who do not know Japanese already encounter this characteristic of his nature and
thought in his first English publication in his contribution to the *Festschrift* for
Paul Tillich, entitled "Buddhism and Existentialism: The Dialogue between
Oriental and Occidental Thought,"[7] and the impression is deepened in the essays

---

[4]"Modern Japanese Philosophy," EncB 12 (1966) 958-62.

[5]"The Philosophy of Nishida," JR 3/4 (1963): 1-32; also in *The Buddha Eye:
An Anthology of the Kyoto School*, ed. Frederick Franck (New York: Crossroad,
1982) 179-202.

[6]"Introduction to 'Philosophy as Metanoetics'," JR 5/2 (1967): 29-47 [cf. also
Hajime Tanabe, *Philosophy as Metanoetics*, xxxi-xlvii]; "A Comparison of
Metanoetics with the Philosophy of Freedom," JR 7/2 (1971): 50-75.

[7]"Buddhism and Existentialism. The Dialogue between Oriental and Occidental Thinking," in *Religion and Culture. Essays in Honor of Paul Tillich* (New

collected under the title "Probleme der Versenkung im Ur-Buddhismus," in that here Takeuchi—despite maintaining the difference between Eastern and Western thinking in respect to Being and Nothingness—expressly acknowledges a religious existentialism of Buddhist persuasion. For this reason we designate Takeuchi's thinking as a "Buddhist religious existentialism" and begin its presentation with a review of his essay on "Buddhism and Existentialism" in order to expand and deepen this characterization of his position by means of additional essays and his deliberations on Nishida's and Tanabe's philosophy. It is generally to be noted in respect to Takeuchi's style of thinking that—in contrast to the other Buddhist philosophers we know who are often erratic and difficult to follow—he is pleasantly distinguished by clear organization and orderly thinking. Thus he divides the "Dialogue between Eastern and Western Thinking," which he advances in this essay by means of a comparison of "Buddhism and Existentialism," into three main sections and this again into several subsections which issue from one another and together form a systematic whole.

2. Buddhism and Existentialism

In the first, brief section of the essay which carries this title[8] Takeuchi expresses his satisfaction that the problem of "Being and non-Being" which has occupied Buddhism from the beginning has been brought up for discussion by the philosophy and theology of existence. For him this portends not only a better mutual understanding between East and West, but also means that it will be possible on this common basis effectively to counter the dehumanization by modern technology which threatens them both. In this sense the theology of Paul Tillich appears to him to be especially helpful. To be sure he does not refrain from pointing to a twofold fundamental difference which consists in the fact that in the East the emphasis is upon nothingness, while in the West the focus is on being, and that in the latter nothingness is understood differently than in the East. Whereas Western thought is interested in the relation between beings and being, Eastern thought deals with the question how nonbeing is related to absolute negativity. From this parallel way of posing the problem there issues for both the question of how "being-itself, or absolute negativity, [is] related in God or in the Absolute." On both sides, nevertheless, the deepest experienced consciousness of finitude and the transience of human existence represents "a first step to religious awakening." It is in this sense that the three basic words of the Buddha on the impermanence of all things, on their nature as suffering, and on nonbeing are to be understood.

York: Harper & Brothers, 1959) 291-318.
[8]Ibid., 291-93.

For Takeuchi's understanding of this conception of the transience of all things which are, which he indicates is originally Buddhist, the following sentences are instructive both for its significance for the religious consciousness and its awakening: "All mortal beings are condemned to be finite. But the awareness of the finitude of his being, as well as of everything else in the world, is solely limited to the human being. As it happens, this awareness is his first step toward religious awakening. All this is due to the fundamental and ontological structure of his being."[9] Therefore, although man shares his finitude with all "created things" (to give the expression Takeuchi uses to render the first two Noble Truths of the Buddha which he cites!), he can nevertheless become conscious of this finitude, and as such it represents a finitude different from that of beings and things which cannot become conscious of their finitude. Takeuchi also speaks of it as "three successive stages of religious awakening." The "ontological structure" of "impermanence" in religious consciousness corresponds to "anxiety"; that of "suffering" as attribute, to "suffering" as its experience; and that of nonself, to "absolute negativity."

This interpretation of the three basic sayings of the Buddha, which he cites as statements about general "ontological structures," but in the sense of "stages of religious consciousness or awakening," is what allows him to distinguish his intention from that "of a Buddhist theologian, who presupposes certain dogmatic creeds as absolute," and to acknowledge that Paul Tillich belongs among those theologians from whom a Buddhist can learn something. Thus he sees himself—with his interpretation between "Buddhist doctrine on the one hand and that of Western existentialists on the other"—as a philosopher of religion who "is anxious to be fair to all forms of religious truth." But it is precisely in such a confrontation that he hopes to find a way out of "the labyrinth of nonbeing." To this end he concerns himself especially with a "description of the states of religious consciousness" by means of "the phenomenological method," only thereafter so to "elucidate" in the concluding part of this essay the theory of *pratitya-samutpada* (chain of causation) and the doctrine of *karma-samsara* ("eternal return") that the "Buddhist answer" to the question raised will issue from them.

For the presentation of the "stages of religious consciousness"[10] which constitutes the content of the second section he focuses on the triad "anxiety," "suffering," and "absolute negativity," which he derived in the introduction from the three basic statements of the Buddha. The existentializing of "impermanence" into "anxiety" he explains by the "encounter of being and nonbeing."[11] In order to show what "suffering" means existentially, he latches onto the concept of

---

[9]Ibid., 293.
[10]Ibid., 294ff.
[11]Ibid.

"sin" and "Kant's doctrine of radical evil."[12] Finally, he arrives at "absolute negativity" as "the existential of nonself" by appealing to the "neither/nor" of his teacher Tanabe as a matter which lies "beyond the antinomies of reason."[13]

Takeuchi not only distinguished such a sequence of stages in the whole of religious consciousness, but also established within the individual stages formulations which succeed one another in stepwise fashion. If, according to him, "religious awakening in general occurs when something extraordinary happens in the midst of our daily, ordinary life," this extraordinary can nevertheless appear in different forms and accordingly evoke very different reactions. As such, in the first step of "The Encounter of Being and Nonbeing" Takeuchi follows Kierkegaard in distinguishing "fear" toward definite disruptions of the ordinary orders which are held to be certain from "anxiety" which knows no definite object, but for which being as a whole sees itself threatened by nonbeing and in connection with the question of meaning lapses into the doubt of complete meaninglessness. While he does not attribute religious significance to fear, insofar as the extraordinary supremely manifests the "boredom" of the everyday,[14] he evaluates anxiety as an expressly religious phenomenon because it "transcends" the object-world and is "transformed into transparency."[15] In the "despair of despair," on the contrary," "it drives us to *transdescend* from this transcendence and fall into the abyss of nonbeing,"[16] because here even the resolve of the "atheistic existentialists"[17] becomes meaningless.

The "awareness of the interdependence between the two types of anxiety, that is, between death and meaningless" leads in Takeuchi's view nevertheless immediately to the second, higher step of religious consciousness, "the consciousness of suffering and sin." Suffering is the despair of despair as a condition of one's own inwardness. "As a consequence of myself" this threatening nonbeing is sin. Here we are dealing not merely with the shock of nonbeing but with "the awareness of the shock of the non-self," whose cause I myself am, wherefore accordingly sin is bound up with the "consciousness of guilt and condemnation." This intensive conception of suffering provides Takeuchi an occasion for a longer discussion of the relation of "freedom and destiny," in which he recalls both the Christian conception of death as "the wages of sin" and the Buddhist

---

[12]Ibid., 297ff.
[13]Ibid., 301ff.
[14]Ibid., 295.
[15]Ibid., 296.
[16]Ibid., 297.
[17]Ibid., 296.

connection of samsara and karma, but is also concerned with Kant's idea of radical evil and Pascal's "misery and greatness of human nature."[18]

Although he acknowledges that these thinkers know of a solution to the "antinomies of reason" through a "conversion as repentance," he believes that a real overcoming of the ethical problematic can only be found in Tanabe's "Philosophy as Metanoetics," that is, as repentance (*metanoia*).[19] As an alternative to both Hegel's speculative "as well as" and Kierkegaard's ethical "either/or," he presents the "neither/nor." Neither speculative reason nor ethical effort can solve the problem of man who stands essentially in contradiction to his nature; rather this is possible according to Tanabe and Takeuchi only by assuming that the Absolute—whether God or the Buddha—"negates Himself for the sake of Love and Mercy," with the result that "our repentance of sin means the forgiveness and negation of it by the grace of the Absolute," because its "absolute self-surrender" effects its "power" in us, for in this consists "the innermost cores of Christianity and Buddhism."[20] This "true dialectic," however, is not expressible in "the subject-object relation" of our "logical thinking;" rather, this latter, in his view, is the cause and effect, appearing as the "propensity to evil" in our clinging to the "images of being," including the ones we fashion of ourselves and of the Absolute. This entanglement will be overcome only when the self is conceived as nonself and the Absolute as "absolute void," as this alone corresponds to the nature of sin and divine mercy.

It cannot be said that—in the dialectic which he develops in relation to Nietzsche, Tillich, Bergson, Heidegger and Hegel—Takeuchi succeeds in bringing the nature of "our religious experience" in "commerce with the living God" to the clarity he strives for, and thus it is understandable that in the third section of his essay he attempts to give "the Buddhist answer" to the problematic which in the second part is more truly presented than really solved.[21] He does this in the form of a de-objectified and demythologized existential interpretation of the Buddhist doctrine of the so-called "chain of causes" and of the relation of karma and samsara, being fully aware that he departs from the "authorized opinion of contemporary Japanese scholars" which he regards as a "misunderstanding" of the original doctrine of the Buddha.[22] On the contrary he believes that he can bring the latter into a certain connection with that of Jesus.

Thus we have in this third section three subsections in which Takeuchi develops the existential form of the theory of *pratitya-samutpada* under the per-

---

[18]Ibid., 298ff.
[19]Ibid., 301ff.
[20]Ibid., 301.
[21]Ibid., 304ff.
[22]Ibid., 305n.25.

spective of "Suffering and Repentance in Buddhism," and then in a similar way presents "the true significance of *karman-samsara*," in order in the conclusion to compare "the law of love in Christ and the Buddha" in its convergence and difference.

In respect to *pratitya-samutpada* he emphasizes that in its spiraling sequence of causes and effects it does not deal with a "physical or psychological" explanation of the cause of human misery and the possibility of its overcoming as an objective matter. It is rather the expression for the experience of an "existential boundary situation" which stands under the sign of death and rebirth. If from the experience of the same basic human situation its components are understood as "existential categories," then "the principle of their relation" becomes the "dialectic movement of going-to-the-ground," so that "the recognition of the cause is, at the same instant, its annihilation." In this sense *pratitya-samutpada* in Takeuchi's eyes represents nothing but a "theory of conversion"—for the "religious heart," as he expressly notes; for the transformation of the "negativity, which is now in his innermost self, into affirmation, he ascribes to the "grace and compassion of Buddha."[23]

The resultant question of the "relation between our suffering and Buddha's compassion" gives him an opportunity to expound "the true significance of *karman-samsara*" which he sees "hidden under the mythological garb" of this doctrine.[24] Takeuchi believes he can see this true significance in a twofold manner: one, that by making us "responsible for our acts" it points the way to "liberty and salvation;" and the other, that it becomes the "source of compassion in respect to the karman of all mortal beings." It has both of these effects only if it is understood not only "objectively" but "existentially," as was the sense of its use by the Buddha. Under this aspect he points both to a parallel fateful destiny of the karman doctrine represented by the Buddha and preaching of Jesus, as well to an affinity which stands in opposition to this development in the respective attitude of the Buddha and Jesus. Just as the objectifying misunderstanding of the doctrine of karma led to a "fatalistic and deterministic view of life,"[25] so from the calculation of the eschatology of Jesus into "apocalyptic speculation" there arose a "pessimistic resignation."[26] On the contrary, the Buddha and Jesus filled the "mythological wadi" of the ideas transmitted by them with the "streams of religion" and out of compassion for those who err or

---

[23]Ibid., 306.
[24]Ibid. 307-308.
[25]Ibid., 312-13.
[26]Ibid., 310.

go astray, sent out disciples, to which Takeuchi believes he can find a parallel in the ethical consequences of Plato's cave analogy.[27]

In the concluding section Takeuchi expands this comparison between Buddhism and Christianity in their origins and history in view of what he calls "the law of love in Christ and Buddha."[28] These final deliberations are extraordinarily informative for Takeuchi's existentialistic understanding of Buddhism, while the references to Christianity unfortunately abruptly come to an end. On the other hand, with respect to his position the deliberations and references are very differentiated and afford an exact track of the course of their development, by which we may recognize their religioethical significance as well as their weaknesses.

What Takeuchi is concerned with in the following is already apparent from the first sentence, when—referring to the sending out of the disciples mentioned by him as testimony of the compassion of the Buddha and of Jesus—he explains: "Therefore, the awareness of *karman* and *samsara* brings into existence an openness of the world, where the religious existential communication through this mutual appealing to the Self becomes possible." His goal consists accordingly in the demonstration of an attribute of being, which allows an attitude of the kind of compassion just described to appear possible and meaningful, because it is being-ful. To this end he proceeds in his demonstration from a view of reality which opposes its idea of goal—at least as far as the nature of humanity is concerned—by emphasizing that "in [all] natural tie[s] of love . . . a sting of selfhood" is contained, just as "in our sincere sacrifice for others" there is "something of the arrogance of egoism."[29] According to Takeuchi, it is karma that opens the eyes of the "blind I," reveals to him this "fundamental ground of all life" and gives him the "courage to expose himself" and to abandon his "self-reliance." But this negative effect is connected with a positive one, whose nature Takeuchi designates in Heideggerian terminology as the conversion of his *"Dasein* into *Existenz"* and in which he sees "true blessedness," because from it "a stream of compassion gushes forth which will not stop until all beings are awakened." It corresponds fully to the existential interpretation of his Buddhist tradition when Takeuchi identifies this transformation in the self-understanding of the one who is "awakened" and the way it affects his environment with the "so-called vow to save all beings even if they are of an 'infinite number.' This realization of the vow of Amida in conversion is effected, according to him, when man "confesses the 'solidarity' of his guilt, namely, the unity or connection with the guilt of the infinite number of others . . . and by being taken up in the charitable sphere of grace, he now takes a charitable attitude toward the remorse

---

[27]Ibid., 311.
[28]Ibid., 311-12.
[29]Ibid., 311.

of others as well as himself." Takeuchi sees in this the revelation of the "magnificent compassion and charity (*mahakarunamaitri*) [which ushers] himself and others into the realm of emancipation."

If in this passage he continues in the I-style and explains: "It is from this standpoint of compassion that I can completely deny my arrogance and self-love and so cause others to do the same"; he understands that this provides for us an occasion to ask, who is really the one who saves, who is the subject and who the object of redemption, as man, Amida, and the world take part in these roles? Takeuchi gives us a twofold message in this regard: in the one, he knows that such a question is falsely posed by the fact that he explains that the "standpoint" from which the question can be answered is "strictly speaking" the "standpoint of compassion" [which must be] "in its very nature devoid of any standpoint. For truly compassionate is our heart only when it is entirely absorbed into the suffering of others." In the other he affirms: "Compassion perceives a voice of cosmological signification in all being. All existence and all living are bound to the same life."[30]

The difficulties with this he explains first in the personal realm of the loving encounter of I and Thou, by widening the "contact" "of the instant with eternity," as he finds it expressed in the "eternal return of the same," which is expanded in a discussion of the "relation between the relative and the absolute" into the cosmic.[31] For this purpose he uses the image of a small bird which alights on a solitary pond and thereby generates concentric circles of waves on the surface of the water which, from the place at which the bird touches the water, spread out to the bank and from there again return. The rings, as he interprets the poetic image, represent samsara in which we find ourselves; their flowing out representing its nature as "fate and destiny;" their reversal, "freedom and emancipation." The "happy flow between wave and wave" is said to correspond to the communication which occurs "between the Thou and I" by the "fact that in the center there arose once for all a revelation from the absolute to the relative."[32]

Of this "once for all" Takeuchi had already remarked previously that it is "repeated" in the I-Thou encounter and can occur in the past as well as the future as "a wonder and a mystery," as this gets expressed in a paradoxical way in the idea of the "eternal return of the same."[33] This holds true also of the image of the small bird as "a messenger from the unlimited void." To be sure the "divine-human encounter" intended in this image—an encounter in which "eternity [touches] an instant of time"—occurs in the "*hic et nunc* of religious awakening."

---

[30]Ibid., 312.
[31]Ibid., 313-14.
[32]Ibid., 314.
[33]Ibid., 313.

But "it does not matter where it is located in the commonly accepted time reckoning:" whether "in the past or the present or the future" as "a historical revelation," as may be the case in Christianity, or as the "eternal now" of Christian mysticism and Zen Buddhism, or in the "eschatological expectations" in Christianity and Amida Buddhism. In any case it has to do with a "contingent event," which—in the image of the pond employed—spreads like the waves moving out to all sides.[34]

What matters unconditionally for Takeuchi is the fact that the place of encounter of the absolute and the relative belongs to the "void"; that this encounter, that is, the revelation of Transcendence—despite its "absolute otherness"—is not located in an "intermedium" between the two spheres, but within the "deep void," which as transcendence or the divine contains the world or the "lower dimension" in itself. Therefore he strictly refuses to speak of the absolute or of transcendence merely as an "All-Encompassing (*Umgreifendes*)," and wishes instead use only the term "container." "The divine," he explains, "is a container that contains the lower dimensions within it." Only this view of the relation of the absolute and the relative corresponds to the experience of the "encounter of two persons," in which there is no room for a spectator which as a "third party" would stand between them. The fact that the latter is "a favorite of philosophers" represents "a product of 'discriminatory intelligence,'" of a "thinking that in its effort to have a system draws unconsciously a blasphemous picture of the meeting of the absolute and the relative."[35]

That Takeuchi, in his special kind of evaluation of the standpoint rejected by him, raises the surprising charge of blasphemy and only qualifies it somewhat by the concession that it is possibly unconscious, stems from the fact that he does not see that "the secret affair between the two parties" is preserved by "discriminatory thinking," and the revelation is no longer exclusively a matter of the absolute, but rather is rendered problematic by a "spectator." Therefore he remarks already in the introduction of his image of the little bird that flies down from the sky to a pond, that it deals with a solitary, hidden pond, and that no one may be present because otherwise the "sensitive creature" would not appear.[36]

It is remarkable that Takeuchi reckons neither with the fact that there would be no image of which he makes use if he had not discovered it and presented it to us nor with the fact that he distinguishes between the image as such and the cosmic event intended in it by speaking here of an image and suggests a comparison to his readers. Here we find ourselves with him in the role of the spectator and we participate in his discriminatory thinking, especially when we

---

[34]Ibid., 315.
[35]Ibid., 314.
[36]Ibid., 313.

attempt to imitate the conceptual differentiations of which he makes use in describing the contents of this image. As graphic as the image of the bird that flies hither is, it is just as difficult to imagine this flight as a special event within the "container," if according to his explanation this is simultaneously the "void" and as such an imparticiple whole. For him this difficulty does not exist in so far as he conceives this whole as the "void" in which there are finally no differences, and out of which he permits his little bird to emerge as "messenger."[37]

But it is fortunate that, in contrast to his rejection of discriminating thinking, he nevertheless explains: "The very absolute, while stressing its own otherness against the relative, reveals itself within this partial and relative world, and that at just one point of this partial world, and not in a generality conceived in the mind of the philosopher. Thus the unlimited void reveals itself as the small bird alighting on the point of the water surface, the eternity touching just one moment of time. As the place of divine-human encounter such a part, though only a part of parts, is in truth the whole of wholes."[38] Here a whole series of distinctions is specified by Takeuchi—not only between the absolute and the relative; rather within the latter he still distinguishes "at one point" as "part of the part" the "divine-human encounter," to be sure only finally to declare this equally as "the whole of the whole."

Although here the revelation is completely a matter of the absolute, and the spectator-role of the "philosophic spirit" seems to have been excluded, it can still be asked whether in this system of an existential ontology Takeuchi is not guilty of the same "blasphemy" with which he charged that spirit with respect to the discriminating conceptuality used therein. Nevertheless, more frightening than the critique and anti-critique seems to us the fact that in the quest for being and its meaning we just as unavoidably lapse into paradoxes when we make use of discriminatory thinking as when we employ images—which Takeuchi acknowledges when he speaks of the "paradoxical structure of the encounter or revelation."[39]

"Exactly [at] this point," that is, in the shattering of conceptual-discriminating thinking on the question of being and meaning, as used by philosophical thinking in which Takeuchi also participates in his way, we see with him the standpoint which "for understanding encounter and revelation"—except that we, contrary to him, identify the "part of the part" not with the "whole of the whole," but, in respect to the "ontological difference" between being and Being, cling to the distinctionn between part and whole. Whereas for Takeuchi this deals with a speculative paradox, in which that difference dissolves into nothingness, we are

---

[37]Ibid., 314.
[38]Ibid., 314-15.
[39]Ibid., 315.

dealing with a paradox of experience which consists in the fact that the absolute, although it is the absolute, reveals itself not in the whole, but only in a part of the same: in the man who asks the question of the meaning of being and the meaning of his existence, as this is expressed in the mythology of Christ and Amida as images for the special revelation of the mystery of being in a special human possibility of meaning which is not derivable from the meaning of being.

Takeuchi is basically in agreement with this when, at the end of his essay, he illustrates this special human possibility of meaning by the example of a myokonin who, by willingly bearing it, makes the evil which is done to him an occasion for perceiving his own guilt and thus for experiencing forgiveness in his forgiving.[40] If he here, not incorrectly, points to the "basic difference between the compassion of Buddhism and the love of Christianity" or even to corresponding distinctions within Buddhism, he finds nevertheless that "common to all is the great law of love as it is voiced by Jesus in his commandment, "Love your neighbor and even your enemies," and the "religious heart" itself "contains with itself" and "transforms into the indicative the moral imperative."[41] Although he describes this sequence in the attitude of his myokonin in psychological categories, he thinks nevertheless that it is "conceivable only as a reflection of Buddha's great light." But in contrast to the preceding metaphysical speculation he speaks here now of "Buddha's compassion" as the ground of all being (sin and death) in the "sense of the solidarity of sin" and death "of all human beings."[42] In place of the speculation about the void within which, as we have shown, a "messenger" appearing from it remains problematic, there enters here a religioethical self-understanding of a "follower of the Shin sect," in and through which the realization of the "great compassion" is enacted in the consciousness of the "solidarity of sin."[43]

From the perspective of the enjoining of a speculation concerning emptiness or nothingness in Shinran's Buddhism of grace which is characteristic of this contribution to the Tillich *Festschrift* the way becomes clear in which Takeuchi—in his article on "Modern Japanese Philosophy" which appeared seven years later in the *Encyclopedia Britannica*—sets forth the differences and similarities between Nishida, the founder of the Kyoto School, and his own teacher Tanabe as the latter's great opponent.[44]

Of the "differences" between the two heads of the school indicated by Takeuchi we emphasize the third, which he formulates as follows: "For Tanabe,

---

[40]Ibid., 315ff.
[41]Ibid., 316.
[42]Ibid., 317.
[43]Ibid., 318.
[44]EncB 12 (1966) 962.

the ethical viewpoint is predominant, and from his ethico-social viewpoint he devoted himself to the study of many religions, seeking to unify the truth of the Buddhist Pure Land and Zen sects as well as the truth of Christianity. The fundamental experience of all Nishida's thought, from the beginning to the end, is the immediate realization of Absolute Nothingness."

"But in spite of their differences, their common standpoints of philosophy are more conspicuous," which he sets forth in the following three points:

1. The philosophy of Absolute Nothingness is their common concern; that is, the absolute must be considered first as Absolute Nothingness.
2. The essence of philosophy consists in our religious action; its philosophies differ only in how to interpret this action in the realm of philosophical reflection.
3. The idea of the Eternal Now, and Nothingness in its function of disjunction-conjunction, are the peaks at which the two philosophers can meet and join hands.

As the opposition mentioned is indicative of Takeuchi's philosophy of religion, there is also reflected in the three commonalities which he stresses in the thinking of both philosophers the way in which he attempted to overcome the discrepancy of his own thinking which stands under the influence of both thinkers, and when he says that future Japanese philosophy, whose point of departure is formed from the work of these two thinkers, will direct its interest to a "synthesis of Western and Eastern thinking," he indicates at the same time the nature and intention of his existentialist interpretation of the Buddhist tradition.

3. Existential Interpretation of Early Buddhism

The four essays that appeared in German translation in 1972 under the title *Probleme der Versenkung im Ur-Buddhismus* (*Problems of Contemplation in Early Buddhism*) represent an example of the expansion of the work of Nishida and Tanabe, foreseen by Takeuchi, in terms of the program set forth under the perspective of the encounter of "Buddhism and Existentialism." As the title indicates, he concerns himself here above all with the early history of Buddhism. He does this by no means merely in historical terms, however, but, as he explains with the proximate designation "Problems of Contemplation," in terms of a religiophilosophical, systematic aspect, which corresponds to his religious interests. His intention is to point out that the existential interpretation of the Buddhist tradition which he represents, is not a modern reinterpretation, but corresponds to its traditional form in which it issued from the doctrine of the Buddha. That is exactly what interests us especially in these essays, while we have to reserve judgment on the correctness of his historical statements, and must be content to establish this one thing: Takeuchi understands these phenomena in the conviction that, over against other conceptions, he can—in agreement with his teacher Tanabe—appeal to the Buddha for his religious existentialism and thus portray himself as a true Buddhist.

Typical for this intention which Takeuchi pursues in these essays are the following programmatic sentences at the beginning of the first essay: "In Buddhism philosophy is not originally speculation or metaphysical contemplation. In Buddhism philosophy is metanoesis of thinking, a reversal, or conversion of reflexive thinking in itself into its authentic self, that is, into Enlightenment. Therefore Buddhist philosophy is philosophy in the sense of meta-noetic. It is not metaphysics, but philosophy as overcoming of metaphysics. I should like to call it 'Buddhist existentialism' and enlightenment—the appropriation of the Buddhist spirit in the course of thinking."[45]

To justify this thesis, which he juxtaposes with other conceptions of Buddhism which have spread abroad in the past and the present, Takeuchi not only appeals to the "Buddha's silence" with respect to the famous metaphysical questions,[46] a title which he uses for his essay, but also with respect to the legends of the Buddha's engagement with the question of meaning in meeting an aged man, a sick person, a corpse and an ascetic,[47] he extensively discusses the doctrine of "dependent origination" as a philosophical unfolding of that existential experience in which he sees an "archetype for the religious person." While he holds that "such an existential thinking is no longer to be found among the followers of the Buddha" and charges them with a "degenerate, that is, an objectifying conception of the doctrine that lacks existence," especially in view of the "abhidarmic interpretations,"[48] he thinks that "only Zen Buddhism and the belief in the "Pure Land" can illumine the problem of the depth of existence,"[49] by which he understands under these "problems" the intention "to bring these religious questions into connection with a philosophical answer," and sees in this "the problem of Buddhist philosophy."[50]

To the commendation of Zen and Pure Land Buddhism that stands at the conclusion of the essay devoted to the "Buddha's silence" there is appropriately affixed a longer treatise on "Die Stufen der Versenkung im Ur-Buddhismus" ("Stages of Contemplation in Early Buddhism"),[51] for whose delineation Takeuchi relies on the early Buddhist "General Rules for Spiritual Practice." In contrast to Hinayana's "misunderstanding" of immersion in an "objectifying

---

[45]*Probleme der Versenkung im Ur-Buddhismus*, 1-2.
[46]Ibid., 2-3.
[47]Ibid., 11.
[48]Ibid., 12.
[49]Ibid., 18.
[50]Ibid., 12.
[51]Ibid., 20-62.

thinking," which speaks of "transiency," "without incorporating itself,"[52] Takeuchi wishes to validate "the original 'existential-religious' definition of experience" in the form of an "Illumination of Existence" (*Existenz-Erhellung* [a term of Jaspers']). "A great help is gained from the side of existentialist philosophers and theologians for articulating anew the genuine meaning of early Buddhism in the world of European thinking."[53] In reference to the fact "that for Martin Heidegger human existence is exhaustively interpreted from the preliminary resolve (decisiveness) toward death, and further, that the problem of the self-transcending freedom of man is seen 'homo-excentrically,' that is, from the perspective of neither the theocentric nor the homocentric viewpoint and is directed neither to the theistic nor to the atheistic horizon," he sees the possibility that "the traditional Oriental interpretation of the Absolute as 'Nothingness' can enter into dialogue with the Western notion of the Absolute as 'Being'."[54]

According to Takeuchi philosophical resolve does not satisfy "Being towards death," because therein the question of meaning is not sufficiently taken into account, as is the case with the Buddha. In this sense he juxtaposes Heidegger's question, "Why is there something rather than nothing?" with the Buddha's word: "The world has lapsed into misery. One is born, ages, and dies and separates from existence and is again reborn. But one does not find an escape from this suffering. When will one find a way out of this suffering?" "Only by renouncing life and the world in religious decision"—as Takeuchi explains the meaning of this opposition—"will the anxiety concerning nothingness, or better the doubt in the whirlwind of nothingness, become a question that engages us." What he misses in Heidegger's "slipping away" (*Entgleitung*) "which lets beings sink into the entirety of nothingness," is "the will to escape," the "religious resolve," in which the "anxiety toward death" must be heightened, and by which alone the "detachment" can arise, as is the case in the Buddhist consideration of the "five Skhandas."[55]

For Takeuchi there is a corresponding relationship to the Western philosophy of existence with respect to its intention to overcome the subject-object split of the objectifying thinking of consciousness. On the one hand he shares this intention by reference to the Buddha's sermon which represents the world of objectivity as "standing in flames."[56] On the other, without mentioning it, he apparently judges Heidegger's treatment of this problem to be inadequate, in that—in place of a critical exchange—by means of rich early Buddhist material

---

[52]Ibid,, 27.
[53]Ibid., 28.
[54]Ibid., 28-29.
[55]Ibid., 31.
[56]Ibid., 42-43.

he offers an extensive presentation of the "stages of immersion" by which alone, in his view, this goal is attainable.[57]

But not only can "discursive thinking" be overcome in this way, and "detachment" and "equanimity" be attained;[58] rather the "mystery of the spirit in equanimity" consists in the fact that this "last level of immersion" "encompasses the inward in the outward of everyday activity, and thus can become compassion. "Whereas, according to the Buddhist conception "love" can still be compared with "thirst" and is regarded as "permeated by suffering," the nature of "compassion" directly consists in "universal sympathy" as a cosmic unitary experience of immersion, in which "the microcosm directly agrees with the macrocosm."[59]

This "compassion" strikes me as a little thin. Takeuchi speaks of a "place of the soul" indeed as a space "devoid of air," a "vacuum" and as a "condition where spirit and spirit thus affect one another, like the peaks of a mountain greet each other." Of the "rays which burst forth here," he himself writes that they "contain no warmth, like earthly love," if they wish to spread to all corners and ends of the world."[60] Apparently he realizes its problematic when he concedes that "a certain opposition [obtains] between love and immersion," "which then evokes the development to the Mahayana movement."[61] The objection of Albert Schweitzer, that "love [consists] in social, concrete mutual assistance (love of neighbor)," and is "not consonant with 'world and life renunciation'," he is unable to counter with anything substantial.[62] From our perspective we should like to add to these grounds of ethical dissatisfaction with this conception of compassion as its further cause the dismantling of the subject-object schema of thinking consciousness for which it strives, through which the compassion of both the subject which it confirms as well as the object which it is said to approach, is forfeited.

It is with these problems that Takeuchi is occupied in the two following smaller essays. The subject-object problem which he discusses in the preceding essay he places at the conclusion of the essay on "Die Idee der Freiheit von und durch Kausalität im Ur-Buddhismus" ("The Idea of Freedom from and through Causality in Early Buddhism"),[63] while the fourth which is devoted to the prob-

---

[57]Ibid., 32-56.
[58]Ibid., 54-55.
[59]Ibid., 57.
[60]Ibid., 57.
[61]Ibid., 62.
[62]Ibid., 61.
[63]Ibid., 63-77.

lem of eschatology in the Buddhism of grace, provides him an opportunity once again to raise the question of ethics.[64]

In the first of these two essays Takeuchi presents the true significance of the doctrine of "dependent origination" in a more extensive way than was the case in the contribution to the Tillich *Festschrift*.[65] If this doctrine is understood merely as a theory for explaining all events in terms of a "causal chain" of conceptual-objective knowledge and is so employed, this would be a misunderstanding of its original significance which has as a consequence the embeddedness of persons in the course of things which causes suffering. If, on the contrary, it is understood as an expression of the existential experiencing of "boundary situations," into which we fall in our quest for the meaning of our existence in view of its contradictions, then it presents itself as a "way of salvation" upon which we attain to the freedom from our anxiety about life and our appetites through decisive acceptance of the "boundedness and thrownness" of our existence in a "new self-understanding."[66]

For this existential interpretation of *pratitya-samutpada* Takeuchi appeals to the "Four Noble Truths" of the Buddha[67] as well as to the way in which the young Buddha existentially understood his encounter with "age, sickness and death."[68] As with Jacob Boehme, the "anguish" (*Qual*) has here become a "source" (*Quelle*) of "a new dimension."[69] In a formal, and partly material, respect, as a model for the dialectic of the "Creed of Buddhism"—"All things arise out of the cause (*Ur-sache*), whose cause the Buddha explains in a way that simultaneously illumines nonbeing"—he employs the three factors in Hegel's and Heidegger's concept of ground as "Ground of origin, the going-to-the-Ground of all beings and thereby the annihilation of the Ground itself."[70]

The fact that the epistemological "subject-object relation" forms the crux of Takeuchi's existential-dialectical doctrine of redemption arises from three images which he uses to clarify it. In the first he compares men who "are related to objects and remain fettered in these relations" with a "draught-horse to which blinders are attached," and says of the horse: "It runs straight down the narrow track of the understanding and cannot see the burden it drags behind it." The liberation from the appetites through "the insight into the transiency of all things" he characterizes in a further expansion of this comparison: "We are free from the rela-

---

[64]Ibid., 78-91.
[65]Ibid., 68ff.
[66]Ibid., 73ff.
[67]Ibid., 66-67.
[68]Ibid., 70-71.
[69]Ibid., 66.
[70]Ibid., 65 and 67.

tion to beings which gallop straight ahead, conditioned by the blind will, and can observe being from the perspective of nonbeing, and nonbeing, from being."[71]

Just as in the first image the epistemological viewpoint is bound up with the ethical—and basically with the religious as well—so in the second,[72] in which, by the "light of nothingness" and by its "seizing" (Ergreifen) and "grasping" (Begreifen), he explains that it would assign everything to this side of the subject-object opposition" and is therefore—religiously regarded—"tainted" and carries "the disposition toward evil." Here he compares this situation with an "automobile, whose front windshield is totally covered with a mirror," in which the driver does not see what lies before him, but only the rear view "perspectively" "projected forward to the driver's seat." In the natural sciences and mathematics this is sufficient. "But," continues Takeuchi, "in history, and especially in religion, we have to break through the mirror in order to see what really lies before us. Our mirror of consciousness must therefore be shattered by the genuine encounter with what presses in upon us from the future."[73]

"Shattered"—or as Takeuchi said at first—only "broken through"? According to the following closer description of the function which he ascribes in knowing to the subject-object relation, he apparently means only breaking through the mirror, not a shattering which would render impossible its further use, in that "seizing is the basis on which alone our grasping as a system of knowledge appointed with concepts is possible. This is the reason the blind will, which grasps the object, always stands behind knowledge in the sense of objective knowing. Our 'subject-object' relation is from the beginning dominated by a grasping, an attachment that precedes all our practical as well theoretical attitudes."

At this point Takeuchi has recourse to a third image, in which he compares "the seizing" with the "root of the tala tree" and "the appetites" with its "branches." If the tree is cut down to a "small root," it will again grow out. At the same time it sustains "power and life" from the branches and leaves "of the tree." In this "mutual dependency" Takeuchi sees an image for the "interconnection of the dependent origination of the causal chain and its dependent annihilation," just as this corresponds to the "mutual negation" of the individual elements of the causal chain, that is, their annihilation in their use. Applied to the subject-object schema this means that it is "broken through" in its use, but that this "being broken through" presupposes its use.

Such a restoration through annulling as in the theory of knowledge is represented—according to Takeuchi—by the Buddhist principle of ethics, as he

---

[71]Ibid., 72-73.
[72]Ibid., 75-76.
[73]Ibid., 76.

developed it in the last essay of this collection by means of the "Eschatologie der Jodo-Schule" ("Eschatology of the Jodo School"). In an aesthetic way—as he says—that is comparable to "the triplicate of the absolute, objective and subjective spirit in Hegel," he undertakes here to unfold "the triplicate of the threefold vow (of Amida Buddha), of the threefold period of eschatology and of the threefold transformation of the religious person."[74] In this way there is ascribed to the "foundering" of the longing for meaning and the behavior corresponding to it a decisive significance for attaining the fulfillment of meaning. To the end of the course of history in the kalpa fire[75] which begins with the "time of the right dharma" and leads over "the time of the falsified dharma" to "the time of the last things" there corresponds—in Takeuchi's view—the course of the history of Buddhism which finds its completion according to Hinayana's "self-sanctification" and "immersion in Zen" and in trust in the vow of the grace of Amida, in that in the "foundering" on "one's own groundlessness"[76] eschatology is "existentially" actualized.[77] He emphasizes the indispensability of "encounter" with the name of the Buddha, and therefore, for him and Shinran, with Amida-Buddha's vow[78] and its "invocation" in the "repetition of religious decision";[79] yet he believes that in this way—"from the side of the Jodo School,[80] and yet in agreement with Keiji Nishitani—he can attain an overcoming of the "stages of the 'aesthetic'" in Japanese Buddhism and the mere concern for the interest in the usefulness of the Buddha "on the part of the great mass of folk," who is said to grant them prosperity and help them." The result would be a "cultural synthesis"[81] in which "religious truth is realized in the concreteness of everyday life and our life on earth is made holy and religious "by the annulment of this contradiction in life"—meaning through the "cleft between the 'everyday' and the religious which is produced by eschatology.[82]

Doubtless Takeuchi—as also Nishitani in his own way— succeeds in reaching this goal on the basis of Buddhist "eschatology" and with the help of its interpretation. It is merely questionable whether, for him, this interpretation from the perspective of Shinran and Tanabe is too much accompanied by a need for blessedness growing out the experience of having lost the way, to which it

---

[74]Ibid., 80.
[75]Ibid., 78.
[76]Ibid., 87.
[77]Ibid., 80.
[78]Ibid., 83-84.
[79]Ibid., 85.
[80]Ibid., 91.
[81]Ibid., 89.
[82]Ibid., 91.

corresponds through an equally problematic theory of knowledge, and whether the resulting "cultural synthesis" consists in an enabling which is confident it can "endure and pass through the many miseries of the heart," but not simply in the will to endure at least the external situation and the things which attend it that causes these miseries, but to change them whenever possible as this arises as an essential feature of Western culture out of the problematic of Christian eschatology which yet in a way different from Buddhism has revealed that "cleft" between what is and what should be.

The question as to how this cleft between faith and reality can be overcome—a cleft before which both Buddhism and Christianity find themselves poised in the age of secularization from the perspective of their eschatology—Takeuchi takes up in his latest essay translated into English on "Shinran and Contemporary Thought,"[83] in that he juxtaposes with his Amida faith what in his eyes is a "secularized theology." That and how he can therein appeal to "Early Buddhism" he has attempted to show anew in a still unpublished essay on "The Significance of 'Other-Power' in the Buddhist Path to Salvation." In both presentations there is manifested to us once again in a typical way Takeuchi's proximity to Christianity as well as the Western difference from him—and this in view of a shared problematic—so that an engagement with it is appropriate for bringing to a close our discussion of his Buddhist existentialism.

4. Takeuchi's View of the Significance of Amida Faith in Light of a Secularized Theology

According to a notation of the author,[84] the essay with which we are now concerned represents the second chapter of his book of 1974, *Shinran Today*, in which he unfolded on the basis of Shinran's works a "Logic of Faith-Joy" in view of the depersonalizing effect of the secularization also occurring today in Japan and by taking note of the philosophies and theologies of existence concerned with this problem. In the chapter which lies before us in English translation he manages to speak only briefly about Shinran by citing only his explanation of the seventeen vows concerning the "Great Life" in the *Kyogyoshinsho* in order to use it freely in a decisive way.[85] By means of Arnold Toynbee and Harvey Cox's *Secular City* he describes the sociological causes of modern secularization, and by making use of the example of John Robinson's *Honest to God* and the praise which Bultmann gave to him, of Tillich and Bonhoeffer, and of the debates which followed the Best Sellers of Cox and Robinson, up to the "Death of God theology" he describes the effects for the-

---

[83]EB 13/2 (1980): 26-45.
[84]Ibid., 26.
[85]Ibid., 44.

ology of the "tide of secularization."[86] When he quite generally and thoroughly notes the fact that the traditional notion of a transcendent God has been placed in question as a consequence of secularization, he nevertheless does not overlook the differences in the attempts at a reconstruction of the picture of God arising from it, whether in terms of a pure "inner-worldly" God, in Tillich's distinction between a ground of Being and a ground of meaning in God,[87] or in Bultmann's reduction of the relation of transcendence to existence to the ground of the kerygma, albeit leaving "nature" out of account.[88]

It is precisely this last mentioned point that Takeuchi raised in a visit with Bultmann in 1961, as he reports.[89] In the course of their exchange Bultmann took the little book *The Oxherding Pictures* from the shelf and called it "an admirable book." Its claim that man must forget himself in order to attain to his true self agrees practically with Christian truth. What it lacks is only "the idea, so strong in Christianity, that truth is realized in history." Takeuchi countered that the same is true for "nature" in Christianity, especially Protestant theology; and in reply to Bultmann's question as to what he understood precisely by nature, he [said] he meant "existential Nature, the Nature that must be present when existence becomes true existence and not nature that comes under the spatialized categories of abstract time and space—what existential philosophers would call 'the vulgar world concept'." After some reflection Bultmann agreed with this, but then wished to know what Takeuchi meant by "existential nature." Thereupon the latter reminded him of the "distinction between *soma* and *sarx*" and asked him whether or not "the corporeality of the risen Christ, the *soma* as the place of the resurrection, [is not] a good example of that existential nature." When Bultmann had reflected on it, he said that he could mean something like Heidegger meant with his "quadrate" (*Geviert*), that is, a whole consisting of heaven and earth, gods and man, within which these four elements mutually mirror each other, and he (Takeuchi) affirmed this with certain reservations; but Bultmann decisively rejected it: "Although this *Geviert* is a world wherein truth is disclosed," he rejects this symbol because "there is no place in it for a true encounter with a Thou."

In reporting this conversation Takeuchi touches on his own interpretation of Bultmann's view,[90] by bringing it into connection in a bold move with Heidegger's *Geviert* rejected by Bultmann, and compares it—so understood—not only with Bultmann's concept of the kerygma, but also with Amida Faith under-

---

[86]Ibid., 28ff.
[87]Ibid., 31.
[88]Ibid., 39ff.
[89]Ibid., 40ff.
[90]Ibid., 42.

stood in Shinran's terms.[91] For this he thinks he can appeal not only to Nishida's "Action Intuition" and Tanabe's corresponding viewpoint of a "Practice Faith," but also to Jaspers' "absolute action, wherein all opposition of subject and object melts away and concrete reality appears in its purity on the standpoint of action."[92] Bultmann's contemporizing of the Christ event through the kerygma as something coming from the future, rather than from the past, corresponds to the "worlding" of the world as a "turning" with Heidegger, and similarly his *Geviert* corresponds to the praise of all Buddhas which ensues simultaneously with the pronouncing of the Namu-Amida-Butsu in the Pure Land and in the world. It is in this, according to Shinran, that "Great Life" consists, of which Takeuchi speaks in the manner described as a "religious or symbolic act," whose nature consists in the fact that in it its appellation in the prayer of the believer and the answer of Buddhas who praise Amida in the Beyond resound in unison[93] He does not refrain from mentioning in this connection Shinran's understanding of grace-ful "merit transference" which occurs "in pronouncing the name of Amida" as an "I-Thou encounter."[94]

Although in this essay he expressly acknowledges that he is a "Pure Land believer with extremely conservative markings,"[95] he nevertheless repeatedly stresses the "symbolic" character of his understanding of faith and does not hesitate to concede that to some extent he "demythologizes [its] meanings."[96] If one considers that he acknowledges both Tillich's distinction between the ground of being and existence as well as Bultmann's emphasis upon history in distinction from nature and appeals to Jaspers' connection of "Transcendence and Existence,"[97] we should have accordingly to do in Takeuchi with a self-understanding which knows itself in its enactment as prayer as related to a special revelation of Transcendence and therein experiences the redemption intended in the religious tradition. As he explains in reference to Bultmann, the "Christ event" attested in the kerygma and "the eternal coming of Amida's name from the Pure Land" in the pronouncing of the Namu-Amida-Butsu stand parallel to each other as symbols of the experience of salvation. Both occur in history—but with the difference that Bultmann insists on the skandalon of an origin of salvation in "historical" once-for-all-ness, while Takeuchi speaks of the "eternity" of the salvation event. Accordingly we could, with Takeuchi, find Amida in Christ,

---

[91]Ibid., 43ff.
[92]Ibid., 45.
[93]Ibid., 43.
[94]Ibid., 44.
[95]Ibid., 32.
[96]Ibid., 35.
[97]Ibid., 33.

or Christ in the Amida symbol, which for Christians like Bultmann—not to speak of the exclusive "church-centeredness" of Karl Barth[98]—is not possible. For this reason we cannot exactly agree with Takeuchi if he thinks he can find a "synthesis of standpoints" of Heidegger's *Geviert* as a realization of the world of all Buddhas, who praise the name of Amida and in which all see themselves mutually reflected, with "Bultmann's historical world, [in which] the encounter with the Thou, the meeting with the Name, obtains."[99] "The Name" is just as unexchangeable for Butlmann as it is for Barth. Their narrowness notwithstanding, we should like nevertheless to give preference to the real standpoint of Takeuchi for the sake of the broad consequences which issue from it, even if it must be said that he himself has not made this connection.

That Takeuchi—with all his nearness to an existentially understood Christian theology—is disposed to trace his "religious," that is, Buddhist, existentialism back to the Buddha of "Early Buddhism" and thus to legitimate it Bhuddologically, he has shown once more in his lecture on "Die Bedeutung der 'anderen Kraft' im buddhistischen Heilspfad" ("The Significance of 'Other Power' on the Buddhist Path of Salvation"), which he delivered in the context of a student conference on the theme, "Redemption in the Understanding of Christianity and Buddhism," initiated by the Philosophical-Theological Hochschule of St. Gabriel in Mödling near Vienna in June of 1981.

He refers to Christianity only in so far as he—recalling Rudolf Otto's concept of the numinous and in connection with it, the Indian image of the way of the cat and of the ape—characterizes the difference between Christianity and Buddhism in such a way that in Christianity "the knowledge of the majesty of God" represents the *fascinans*, while in Buddhism the dimension of the *tremendum* "is deepened" into the "abysmal self-consciousness of one's own death and sin" and is "infinitely deepened and expanded" by "samsara and karman." He believes that he can see what is specific about Buddhism—when appeal is made to the introduction of the Mahayana tractate on "The Awakening of Faith"—in the fact that "the dark sea of samsara and karman" has "passed" because it is "null from the beginning," "in the moment when the light shines."

After he had already explained here that Shinran, who represents "the absolute devotee of Other Power," and Dogen, "the truth of redemption through one's own self,"—although "thoroughly opposed—were nevertheless in inward matters more closely related in their personality, mental attitude and thoughts," he explains by means of passages from the Pali canon that in the "young" Buddha the "first conversion" was a "way inward," in that his "revulsion" upon seeing ageing, sickness and death was turned against himself, so that "all his youthful

---

[98]Ibid., 38.
[99]Ibid., 43.

arrogance" "vanished" because of it. In this connection Takeuchi agrees with Mrs. Rhys David's estimate that in his youth the Buddha was not so much surrounded by comfort and contentment—as later representations indicate—but "led the life of knighthood filled with self-mastery, bravery and industry," in order to understand his "religious awakening" in terms of Heidegger's "preliminary resolve" as an attitude in which in a "boundary situation" this fate of transiency is overcome in one's own "responsibility" and thus simultaneously "transcended."

For this existential awareness of the "fundamental fact of human finitude" Takeuchi believes two things are essential. First, that it is not a matter of a reflection on an objective state of affairs in the context of the subject-object split of consciousness, that is, it "does not occur as an experience of thinking," but consists in an "attunement"; and, second, that there is expressed in it not merely a subjective "feeling," but "the transiency of the whole cosmos and of Being." For both factors Takeuchi points to the episodes in which the Buddha explains with reference to a burning city, "Everything burns," and wishes thereby to indicate to his disciples that "the city burns" represents a misunderstanding that issues from the fact that their eyes "burn," that is—like all objectifying thinking—it is evidence of the wish to "grasp," of "thirst," from which all "misery," all suffering originates. On the other hand, in the notion "everything burns," the coinherence of "transiency" and "thirst" is expressed—and at the same time, "the task " of their "overcoming" on the "way of purification."

If the beginning of this path of salvation consists in replacing a mere spectator-like objectifying talk of transiency by its existential appropriation, so it ensues only by entering into a living realization of abandoning of the world of things of "everyday man" in "world-denial," as the Buddha completed this in an exemplary way, but—as Takeuchi acknowledges—also a Francis of Assisi and an Ignatius of Loyola, and as it is described in the legends of Barlaam and Josaphat. The circumstance that with the Buddha's enlightenment "the doctrine of dependent origination" came about and belongs to his Four Noble Truths and also to the "Eightfold Path" allows Takeuchi to see in this doctrine evidence of the "holy longing" that leads to Nirvana, in which the "break through" through "our basic ignorance" can occur. In this way he believes he can interpret—at least partially—the thinkers of German idealism. It is possible to conclude from the suggestion that Takeuchi makes at the conclusion of this lecture that he apparently sees Kant—because of his concept of radical evil and his stress on our "disposition to evil"—as proximate to what he understands by "transcendental existentialism" and therefore to Tariki-piety, while in Schelling's and Hegel's "transcendental idealism" he misses the "break through" which can only be attained through a leap and therefore he categorizes them—like Zen Buddhism—under the Jiriki-religiosity of "self-redemption."

It is in character with the apparent problematic of the development of Takeuchi's thought that he concludes with the question, "How are Jiriki and

Tariki related" in the Eightfold Path as the "peak of the religious consciousness" of Early Buddhism? and answers this question with the sentence: "Early Buddhism holds the key to these questions"—but he neglects to show how this key functions. The basic rejection of the objectifying, discriminating conceptual knowledge, of which he necessarily makes use himself, permits its actual dialectic, which consists in the fact it is both necessary and unsuitable for the nature of the self and of being and for both riddles of meaning, to become a mere seeming dialectic, in which the self-understanding does not succeed to the intended transcending break-through, but remains stuck in the short circuit of an ontologizing of the mood of transiency. The image Takeuchi uses of the "boy, who reaches for the sweets in a jar and remains stuck in the jar and can no longer withdraw his hand," is valid not only of conceptual thinking but also of his Heideggerian existential-ontology.

On the contrary, the critical thinking of reason, which is conscious of the symbolic character of its conceptuality in reference to the self and Being, no longer allows itself to be caught in "the snare" which "is hidden behind the bait," but knows—with the Apostle Paul—that we have "such treasure in earthen vessels" (2 Cor 4:7), and also that therein a transformation is underway (Romans 6–8)—not merely through the fact that "our grasping for things produces a counter-force from the side of things," and not merely through such a general event of Being, but through a special event of Being within and, correspondingly, in our world—an event which the Apostle expresses, for us, mythologically, in the efficacy of the resurrection of Christ and of his Spirit. Takeuchi betrays knowledge of such a special event of Being that is not simply produced by the thing-world but historically, when he explains: "At the end of the transcendental-transdescendental way, the real way to communication is opened between the Buddha and his disciples through a leap."

In view of the parallels which here open up between the Buddha Shakyamuni and the Christ Jesus of early Christianity we can agree with Takeuchi when he is convinced that "here a dialogue and a synthesis of the two spiritual attitudes is both possible and desirable." In this sense it would be necessary to modify the image Takeuchi uses of the key since it is not sufficient to say that the Shin Buddhist sees the key in Early Buddhism and the Christian believes he has found it in primitive Christianity, because both of these historical keys fit only the respective locks of the doors they wish to open, the result being that either both make use of their keys or they must be recast into a Passe-partout which fits both kinds of locks which from antiquity were established on the doors before which they stand. That would surely be the "task of the dialogue, or synthesis of both spiritual attitudes," which Takeuchi contemplates and to which we know ourselves to be obligated. That there are suggestions for both possibilities in his thinking should have been made clear in this chapter devoted to him.

Shizuteru Ueda (b. 1926)

Chapter 8

Shizuteru Ueda (b. 1926)
Breaking through
the Objective Thinking of Substance
in the Trinity of the Selfless Self

1. Doctor of Marburg and Successor of Nishitani

Shizuteru Ueda, born in 1926 in Tokyo, already belongs to the third generation of the Kyoto School. He is Nishitani's pupil and his successor to the Chair of Buddhist Philosophy at Kyoto University. In addition to Nishitani, he also mentions in his essays Suzuki and Hisamatsu. But he also devoted an essay of his own to Nishida and also in another place gets to speak of him. From these the direction Ueda represents in the Kyoto School already becomes apparent. That he is at home in Zen becomes evident from a detailed description and estimation of zazen which occurs in one of his essays, but quite generally from the use he makes of the Zen tradition in his publications as well, and from the significance he assigns to it. In no less than eight of the twelve essays he wrote in German[1]

---

[1]German Essays and Lectures: "Der Zen-Buddhismus als 'Nicht-Mystik' unter besonderer Berücksichtigung des Vergleichs zur Mystik Meister Eckharts," in *Transparente Welt, Festschrift zum sechzigsten Geburtstag von Jean Gebser*, ed. G. Schulz (Bern and Stuttgart, 1965) 291-313.

"Über den Sprachgebrauch Meister Eckharts: 'Gott muss . . . ' Ein Beispiel für die Gedankengänge der spekulativen Mystik," in *Glaube, Geist, Geschichte, Festschrift zum 60. Geburtstag von Ernst Benz*, ed. Gerhard Müller and Wienfried Zeller (Leiden: Brill, 1967) 266-77.

"Der Buddhismus und das Problem der Säkularisierung. Zur gegenwärtigen geistigen Situation Japans," in *Hat die Religion Zukunft?* ed. Oskar Schatz (Graz, Styria, Vienna, Cologne, 1971) 255-75.

"Das Nichts und das Selbst im buddhistischen Denken. Zum westöstlichen Vergleich des Selbsverständnisses des Menschen." *Studia Philosophica: Jahrbuch der Schweizerischen Philosophischen Gesellschaft* 34 (Basel: Verlag für Recht und Gesellschaft, 1974): 144-61.

"Das menschliche Selbst und das Nichts—philosophische Aspekte," *Universitas. Wissenschaftliche Verlagsgesellschaft Stuttgart* (October 1975): 1047-52.

"Der Tod im Zen-Buddhismus," in *Der Mensch und sein Tod*, ed. Johannes Schwärtlander (Göttingen: Vandenhoeck & Ruprecht, 1975) 162-72.

"Das wahre Selbst, Zum west-östlichen Vergleich des Personbegriffs," in *Fernöstliche Kultur. Festschrift für Wolf Haenisch* (Marburg a. L., 1975) 1-10.

he appeals to the famous Zen story of "The Ox and Its Oxherd," in order to explain by its last three pictures the core of his philosophy, namely, "the trinity of the selfless self," as the breakthrough of objectifying thinking, with which he sees Meister Eckhart as already concerned. In his Marburg dissertation[2] Ueda concerned himself exhaustively with this "breakthrough" in Meister Eckhart so as to compare it with that of Zen.

Even with his preoccupation with Eckhart's "mysticism" Ueda was moving in the line of his predecessors, in the same twofold respect and in a more outspoken manner than they. All his teachers were concerned with Meister Eckhart. But while they did it in a more occasional way, Ueda devoted an entire book to him—besides one written in Japanese.[3] Moreover, he wrote this dissertation in German under Ernst Benz in Marburg, which probably none of his teachers would have been able to do. In contrast to his teachers, he needed no translator for his German publications. With the exception of the German essays already mentioned, he has also published more than twenty in Japanese journals, most of which are concerned with Meister Eckhart.

"Das denkende Nicht-Denken. 'Zen und Philosophie' bei Nishida unter besonderer Berücktsichtigung seiner Frühphilsophie der reinen Erfahrung," in *Denkender Glaube. Festschrift für Carl Heinz Ratschow*, ed. Otto Kaiser (Berlin/New York: Walter de Gruyter, 1976) 331-41.

"Das "Nichts" bei Meister Eckhart und im Zen-Buddhismus unter besonderer Berücksichtigung des Grenzbereiches von Theologie und Philosophie," in *Transzendenz und Immanenz. Philosophie und Theologie in der veränderten Welt*. Tagungsbeiträge eines Symposions der Alexander Humboldt-Stiftung, ed. Dietrich Papenfus and Jürgen Söring (Stuttgart/Berlin/Cologne/Mainz: Kohlhammer Verlag, 1977).

"Leere und Fülle: Un-grund und Interpersonalität. Zum Problem des Persongedankens im Zen-Buddhismus," in *Religionen Geschichte Ökumene "In Memoriam Ernst Benz*," ed. Rainer Flasche und Erich Geldbach (Leiden: E. J. Brill, 1981) 205-15.

"Shunyata im Mahayana Buddhismus," *Eranos 1976* (Leiden: E. J. Brill, 1980) 135-63.

Unpublished: "Erfahrung und Sprache." Contribution to the Zürcher Gespräche, 1976.

Contribution on the theme: "Die Macht des Bildes und die Kraft der Ritualisierung" of the fourth conference of the Zürcher Gespräche under the direction of Enrico Castelli and Ernesto Grassi, July 1978.

[2]*Die Gottesgeburt in der Seele und der Durchbruch zur Gottheit. Die mystische Anthropologie Meister Eckharts und ihre Konfrontation mit der Mystik des Zen-Buddhismus* (Gütersloher Verlaghaus Gerd Mohn, 1965).

[3]*Zen Bukkyo: Kongenteki Ningen (Zen Buddhism: Human Nature)* (Chikumashobo, 1973).

Following the example of his teachers, Ueda compared his Zen thinking with Western philosophy and Christian notions both in his dissertation and in the essays which are available to us. After he had done this in the dissertation by means of a comprehensive knowledge—surprising for a Japanese—of Eckhart's Latin and German writings he envisaged in the essays individual themes whose treatment appears like answers to problems which today arise for Buddhism out of the secularization which emerges for it through the engagement with the West. From this state of affairs which arises on the basis of Ueda's German corpus the following take precedence for presenting his thinking which is documented therein. First, we take up his dissertation in which the nature of Zen is worked out in reference to a specific historical formulation of the world of Western culture. Then we deal with the problems with which Buddhism sees itself confronted today by the secularization coming from the West, as Ueda presents this in a lecture devoted to this theme which he delivered in 1970. The essays that arose in the course of the following years we will examine mainly with respect to whether and to what extent a solution can be found to these problems from the nature of Zen unfolded in them in its various aspects, since Ueda himself regards this as the contemporary task of Buddhism. This disposition has the advantage that it not only corresponds to Ueda's intention and validates its actuality, but permits us to consider the essays in the sequence of their appearance.

2. The Book on Eckhart

In these terms we begin our presentation of Ueda's position with a report of his work on Eckhart which represents the fruit of his three year study visit in Marburg and is dedicated to Friedrich Heiler and Ernst Benz. The latter wrote a lengthy "Introduction" to it,[4] in which he fully acknowledged not only Ueda's familiarity—unusual for a Japanese—with the spiritual world of Eckhart, but especially accentuates the fact that—unlike, for example, Daisetz Suzuki—Ueda did not fall into the trap of a "premature identification" of Eckhart's mysticism with that of Zen, but worked out the differences in terms of what was common to these two types of mysticism on the basis of better source materials and a deeper immersion in them.[5]

But in this connection it is necessary to point to yet another difference with respect to the speaking of "myth" and "mysticism." Probably the delineations of Benz concerning "mysticism" in Eckhart and in Zen correspond to the use of this term in the subtitle of Ueda's dissertation: *Die mystische Anthropologie Meister Eckharts und ihre Konfrontation mit der Mystik im Zen-Buddhismus (The Mystical Anthropology of Meister Eckhart and Its Confrontation with Mysticism in Zen*

---

[4]Cf. 11-20 of the dissertation mentioned in n. 2 with the complete title.
[5]Ibid., 19-20.

Buddhism). In his analysis of "the birth of God in the soul" and of "the break-through to Godhead" Ueda determines that the two notions are of a mystical kind, in that the former stands in connection with the tradition of "Christian mysticism," while the latter stems from the "Neoplatonic mysticism of unity."[6]

In this way Ueda gets to show that in his thinking Meister Eckhart reached a position which transcends every kind of mysticism.[7] Similarly he emphasizes that in Zen we are not dealing with a mysticism as a uniting with something, because in Zen there is no such "something" with which a unification could take place. That is exactly the point of the title of an essay which appeared the same year as the dissertation, but which contrasts with its subtitle: "Zen Buddhism as 'Nonmysticism'." It is not in mysticism, but in "nonmysticism" or, as far as Meister Eckhart is concerned, on the way beyond mysticism, that Meister Eckhart—in Ueda's view—is in touch with his Zen masters. Like Nishitani, so Ueda also sees in Christianity, even in its mystical formulations, mere suggestions which could lead to completion on the basis of Buddhism.

It is not our task to subscribe to Ueda's interpretation of Eckhart, much less to verify its soundness. Eckhart's "orthodoxy" is not presently a contested matter, but as Ueda demonstrates by means of numerous references and citations, there is reason enough today in his theological writings as well as in his sermons for quite different evaluations of it.[8] What is of interest to us here is the way in which Ueda compares the position of Meister Eckhart, which in our opinion is worked out with great exactness, with his own Zen philosophy. The comparison is a typical example of the relation between Buddhism and Christianity, as it issues from Zen Buddhism. Ueda supplies this comparison in the last forty pages of his dissertation, and it is highly instructive for our interest.

In a concluding "Gesamtwürdigung der Mystik Meister Eckharts" ("Comprehensive Evaluation of the Mysticism of Meister Eckhart")[9] Ueda once again summarizes the results of both parts of his work, the first of which is devoted to the "Doctrine of the Birth of God in the Soul" and the second to the "Doctrine of the Breakthrough," by characterizing Eckhart's theology as a "mysticism of infinity undergirded by theism."[10] As he has shown when dealing with individual parts, the doctrine of the Trinity forms for Eckhart this "theistic undergirding"—to be sure, in a form which differs in two ways from the conception represented by the Church. First, Eckhart explains that God does not allow his Son to be born only in himself, but at the same time in the soul; and second, that God in his Unity

---

[6]Ibid., 38n12, 32n.15, 111n.30, 145, etc.
[7]Ibid., 140.
[8]Ibid., 38n.12, 89n.19, 93nn.20, 21, 111n.30, 127n.35, 134n.42, esp. 141ff.
[9]Ibid., 140ff.
[10]Ibid., 143.

is "free of the three persons." While the first deviation from dogma leads to a Christ mysticism, the second represents a breakthrough to a suprapersonal "Godhead," which, in lacking attributes, is a "nothingness."[11] As Eckhart shows in his exposition of the story of Mary and Martha (Luke 10:38ff.),[12] this break-through to the "Godhead," which means a "Gott-Lassen," is at the same time a becoming free for the *vita activa* of activity in the world. Eckhart in fact seems to detect in Martha's request that Jesus should send Mary, who is sitting at his feet, away from him so that she might help her, Martha's own concern that her sister might simply "abide with God in a state of bliss" instead of "penetrating further into the Godhead." "Mary should 'arise' from her satisfaction with being united with God and 'abandon' God." He similarly understands Jesus' reply, "One thing is needful," as a reference to the necessity of being-one with God as the One of the Godhead, therefore, as a transcending of being-one, or being-one-with God, who is present in Christ, to a being-one with the trans-personal One. On this basis the care of Martha acquires for Eckhart a positive significance, namely, as a proof that she has become free from concern for God and her soul's salvation so as to be active in the world, as is demonstrated by her kitchen service.

It is evident that in this interpretation of the pericope Eckhart reverses its meaning into its opposite, as Ueda has remarked. But he has no basis for re-proving him for it, for with this apparent reversal of meaning Eckhart—in Ueda's eyes—"reaches very near to the Zen Buddhist thought-world." What he finds objectionable in Eckhart from his Zen standpoint is that he did not carry through to its "ultimate consequences" the tendency latent in his statements about the motifs of birth and breaking through toward an "ascent" "from Christ mysticism to God mysticism and from this to an overcoming of mysticism."[13] Two things hindered him from reaching his goal: on the one hand, his attachment to the con-ceptuality of the personalistic theism of the doctrine of the trinity, by means of which he developed the "doctrine of the birth of God in the soul," and on the other, the neo-Platonic mysticism of infinity of the "doctrine of breaking through to Godhead"—because therein it always deals with a unification of something with something, and not with Absolute Nothingness, in which only "the true man" remains, as is the case in Zen. Because Zen Buddhism is not acquainted with the "personalistic substructure" to which Eckhart holds firm in his doctrine of the soul, and despite its "mysticism of infinity," "both the negative-theological conception of transcendence as well as the return to the reality of the world as

---

[11]Ibid., 144-45.
[12]Ibid., 137ff.
[13]Ibid., 140.

a real breakthrough to true transcendence are carried through much more radically and thoroughly in Zen Buddhism than in Eckhart."[14]

In this connection Ueda correctly refers to parallel differences: the fact that Meister Eckhart—despite his Neoplatonic mysticism of infinity which earned him the reputation of a heretic—made use not only of Christian language, but also piously "received God" in the eucharist,[15] whereas in Zen Buddhism, precisely in respect to the Buddha statue cultically revered in the temple, it is valid to kill the Buddha or quickly pass by him, and to regard the holy writings as "nothing more than dirty scraps of paper."[16]

In an especially impressive way Ueda illustrates the immense difference which obtains between Eckhart and Zen Buddhism—despite their similarities and common features—by a comparison of two pictures: a picture of the visit of Jesus with Mary and Martha painted by a congenial Dutchman, with a picture of a Zen painter in which a man—who is said to be the sixth patriarch of Chinese Zen Buddhism—is cutting bamboo.[17] Copies of both pictures are reprinted in the text. In the first picture Martha busies herself in the kitchen, surrounded by a host of all kinds of fruits and poultry, her depiction according to the manner of a Dutch still life filling half of the picture. In the background one notices between the columns and in perspectival reduction, a group in which Mary sits at the feet of Jesus. The principal figures are clearly Martha and her two helpers who are drawn large in the foreground. In the middle of the diagonal between the two groups there sit two men who apparently find themselves in a reflective conversation about what is transpiring before them. The commentary Ueda gives to this picture could form the content of their thoughts.[18]

He suggests that the "smallness of the form of Jesus" is a "negative expression for the presence of the formless Godhead," while it finds "the positive expression of its presence" "in the form of Martha." "Martha has left God: away from God to the Nothingness of the Godhead and in oneness with it to world-reality. Martha works in the kitchen, that is, she is one with the formless nothingness of the Godhead. . . . However, she is not God, as Jesus is. It is precisely Not-God who is present in Martha. In the same measure that Jesus, the God who became man, is represented as small, is expressed the fact that Nothingness, the ground of God, becomes human in Martha." "The form of Jesus could," according to Ueda, "be completely removed from the painting. That would be the ultimate consequence of the thought." But Eckhart has precisely not drawn this

---

[14]Ibid., 145ff.
[15]Ibid., 150.
[16]Ibid., 146.
[17]Ibid.,
[18]Ibid., 147.

consequence. "Christ, and indeed the heavenly Christ, the Second Person of the Trinity," as Ueda surely knows, "is the central concept of Eckhart's mysticism." For Ueda as a Zen man, to the contrary, the picture contains too much, namely, the form of Jesus—as does the theology of Eckhart corresponding to it.

He juxtaposes this picture, which we can correctly assume to have been painted in terms of Eckhart and the "devotio moderna" influenced by him,[19] with the well-known Zen picture of the man cutting bamboo as a representation of Buddhist sunyata.[20] In contrast to the fullness of objectivities which is characteristic of the first picture, a great emptiness rules here, which is highlighted by means of a few brush strokes of which the painter has made use, and which complete the man who is represented. It is to be judged from the picture previously considered, that here "God has completely disappeared, and with no trace of the divine and no trace of his disappearance remaining." Using the "terminology of Eckhart," Ueda himself comments: "God is here completely 'un-become' . . . there remains only pure emptiness"; and further: "Precisely in the emptiness and as this emptiness is the nothingness of the Godhead, to which God has returned, perfectly present." Just like Martha, "this man as he thus works," is also "the nothingness of the Godhead." But, Ueda emphasizes, "whereas in her work Martha serves Jesus and that means God, the man of the Zen picture works "absolutely," that is completely, without why and "at the same time" for an ordinary task, perhaps for repairing the fence," therefore completely profanely, as belongs to the nature of Zen, "in plain accentuation of the ordinary as such."

This "without why" gives Ueda reason not only to refer for examples to Eckhart's inconsistency in answering the question *Cur deus homo*, but also to counter his unorthodox answer: "because he bore you as his only begotten Son,"[21] with the answer of Dschau-dschou: "An oak tree in the garden," which he is said to have supplied to the question: "What is the meaning of the fact that the patriarch came forth from the West?"[22] Whereas Eckhart's answer, because it excludes a "mediator" of salvation, is—as Ueda thinks—"spiritually related to Mahayana Buddhism," it nevertheless still occurs in Christianity's own logic of the word. The "answer" of the Buddhist, to the contrary, which is no answer in a logical sense, but rather stumps the questioner—and therefore possibly permits him to be brought to "awakening"—corresponds solely to the Buddhist mediation of salvation "outside the doctrine," "directly from heart to heart," and to the same "becoming Buddha," as this occurs with Shakyamuni.

---

[19]Ibid., 146.
[20]Ibid., 148ff.
[21]Ibid., 154.
[22]Ibid., 153ff.

The verse of Angelus Silesius, "The rose is without why; it blooms because it blooms,"[23] could count as a formula of this Buddhist hermeneutic if—contrary to its own principle—it would nevertheless give an answer to the question of why. As Ueda in lengthy discussions presents it,[24] in order to satisfy this hermeneutic actually only "the rose there" must remain. The "cutting off" of everything else amounts to "the deep silence in the great dying," and the "rose" would then become "the incarnation of nothingness in which God un-becomes." Thus this work of Ueda ends up in linguistic-philosophical discussions about "basic questions" of a "structural difference of the language event" in Christian preaching and the "mondo" in Zen Buddhism which consists of "question and rejoinder"—not answers.[25] At the least, Ueda concerns himself with a part of the later investigation which gives attention to it in a work still unpublished, of which we have yet to speak.

First, the consideration that the two pictures interpreted by Ueda in a religious sense, that is, as forms of expression of a relatedness to transcendence—which is always intended—could also be understood also otherwise, namely, as phenomena of the secularization of Christian and Buddhist traditions, provide for us the occasion to concern ourselves with the problem of "secularization" with respect to Buddhism and therewith in connection also with Christianity, as Ueda himself has done in a essay that appeared five years after his dissertation.[26] The fact that the Dutch painter allows Jesus and Mary completely to disappear in the background and places in the foreground the large figure of Martha working in the kitchen, that in the Zen drawing nothing remains of entire Buddhism except the cutting of bamboo, and that according to Ueda Angelus Silesius should only have actually said "the rose there," as then according to him even Jesus in the Dutch painting is "still too much"—all these can be directly understood also as secularization, that is, as the replacement of the sacred with the profane, or in the transformation of the one into the other, in such a way that the latter could not only have a negative force for religion, but could also be of positive significance for a "worldly religion."

3. The Problem of Secularization

The colloquium on the question, "Does Religion have a Future?" which was held in Salzburg in 1970, not only provided Ueda a merely external reason for concerning himself with the problem of secularization; rather in view of the con-

---

[23]Ibid., 157.
[24]Ibid., 158ff.
[25]Ibid., 169.
[26]"Der Buddhism und das Problem der Säkularisierung," 255-75 in *Hat die Religion Zukunft?*

temporary world situation he was under the compulsion of the result of his comparison of Eckhart with Zen Buddhism. Therefore it is not surprising that his essay for this event is dedicated to the theme: "Buddhism and the Problem of Secularization," and that he has in view especially "the contemporary situation of Japan."

In view of this situation Ueda advocates the thesis that Buddhism—in contrast to Christianity—cannot fundamentally be rendered problematic by secularization because it finds no fault with it in its true form, and that therefore from the original, authentic Buddhism alone, which for him consists of Zen Buddhism, can an overcoming of the dangers of secularization of the dehumanizing of man and of the destruction of nature through technology be expected. But he is not blind to the fact that there is a form of Buddhism which is not compatible with the secularization which is inevitable under the influence of Western technology. That is Hinayana Buddhism which in its arhat ideal directed toward a Nirvana beyond represents an continuation of Indian monasticism and whose overcoming is not completed in the Buddha's "middle way" between "world negation" and "world relatedness," but holds firmly to the opposition of samsara and Nirvana as profane and holy, respectively, and precisely in its own choice of the latter for the sake of its salvation falls victim to the egoistic I, from whose blindness the Buddha wishes to become free in immersion and from which he would like to free men as the source of suffering.[27]

In this passage Ueda says nothing of the fact that also in the Buddha's doctrine of the overcoming of suffering something is present of the egoistic self-interest for which he reproaches Hinayana, namely, its primary intention. He is concerned to present a Buddhism which for the sake of nonsuffering does not withdraw from the world of samsara in hope of a Nirvana beyond, but subjects itself to the samsaric world and knows itself in it already to be in Nirvana. According to him it is decisively Mahayana which allows Nirvana to be merged into nothingness and even empties this emptiness, and in consequence of which this "transcendence" which is enacted in thinking is actualized in the Bodhisattva who, foregoing enlightenment, as it were, refuses entry into Nirvana.[28] To illustrate the way in which this "overcoming" of the "difference between Nirvana and samsara in early Buddhism in the most immediate non-differentiation"[29] appears at different times and in different places as a characteristic of Mahayana, Ueda mentions the understanding of Namu-Amida-Butsu on the part of a myokonin who expressed "welcome" in the face of every event, just as the doctrine of Shingon Buddhism, from which he stems, "The concrete is the true," as well as

---

[27]Ibid., 255-56.
[28]Ibid., 257-58.
[29]Ibid., 256.

a modern Zen anecdote according to which Nishitani abruptly asked a theologian who explained to him the Pauline formula, "It is not I, but Christ who lives in me," and then began to smoke, "Who there is smoking, you or Christ?"[30]

After Ueda had delimited Mahayana, and especially Zen Buddhism, from Hinayana in such a way, however, he is still aware of the dangers and weaknesses which could be connected with its worldliness which is withdrawn from the world. "Instead of the withdrawal from the world actually being enacted as a transcending of transcending, that is, as negation of negation of the world, sometimes there occurs only a short-cut to the world—simply being and remaining directly worldly—and even, what is worse, often under the pretext of withdrawal from the world." For this he points to the "worldly function" of Buddhism as "administrative branch office," and to "temple inheritance" in the twentieth century, saying of it that it makes "a temple into a private possession of a family, often into a private museum with beautiful gardens."[31]

To be sure Ueda emphasizes as a positive feature of such phenomena as they are in principle characteristic of cultural life in the sphere of Buddhism that they can form a kind of "nondualist bridge"[32] between Buddhism and the world, and that they can become in a preliminary way a "supplement" which corresponds to its nature.[33] But this possibility presupposes that culture in its totality is understood in this Buddhist sense. That is no longer the case in the modern period of technology in which science and technology attain a kind of sovereignty, and over against religion, raise the claim to absolute truth. In Japan this turn succeeded in "two steps": in 1868, the Meiji period, one heard the solution "Japanese heart, Western science, and technology." Since 1945 there has been the "conscious abandonment of tradition."[34] In view of this situation Ueda asks: "Is Mahayana Buddhism, with its old thoughts of withdrawal from the world, still capable of consorting with the modern industrial society of Japan? Or does this withdrawal itself derive fundamentally from the concept of world in Buddhist thinking?"[35] And he has to concede that "Buddhism is in a very embarrassing situation." For "Buddhism is located in a world that basically ignores Buddhism," and which thinks it can solve "all problems in its own way, even such problems to which"—according to his view—"only religion can give an answer," by offering "tranquilizers" instead of Buddhist renunciation, and the apparatus of

---

[30]Ibid., 259.
[31]Ibid., 261.
[32]Ibid., 264.
[33]Ibid., 263.
[34]Ibid., 267.
[35]Ibid, 267-68.

corporate insurance "instead of the compassionate activity of the Bodhisattva,"[36] to which it should be noted that the latter is still poorly represented in Japan. But as he says on the basis of his presentation of the true Buddhism that it "seems" to "transcend the question of secularization, in that this question seems to it to be "without an object,"[37] so he makes the following comment on the fact that with the "total" secularization of Japan[38] the presupposition of the Buddhist world-view as "contrast and accord" of two "open" possibilities would be lost: "at least it seems to be the case in the modern situation."[39] But as he there juxtaposes reality to the ideal in order to establish that it often does not correspond to it, so here the ideal is juxtaposed to reality in the hope that its losses can be redeemed.

According to Ueda these losses originate on the one hand from an inner deterioration of Buddhism which he diagnoses now no longer merely as a possibility, but is something present, and that consists in the fact that "Buddhist nondifferentiation"—through the omission of the "overcoming of egocentrism and the illusory I" which constitutes its essence—gets easily transformed "into a vague feeling of indifference, haziness, indecisiveness, ambiguity, and so forth, that is, into the so-called Japanese folk character." "Thus the original in-difference"—as Ueda designates this fatal change—which consists in the fact that "the self is not able to differentiate itself selflessly from the other, is transposed into an in-difference" which means "not to distinguish the other egoically from the self"; this leads "to the full expansion of the ego, both in respect to interhuman and social relations as well as in relation to nature." Although Ueda in such a way connects the fateful development with a specific Japanese shaping of Buddhism, he nevertheless stresses emphatically on the other hand that it has intensified and—to use an expression Ueda employs in a good sense—has reached a break-through by a democracy which was dictated to Japan and is misunderstood by it and by thinking in terms of objects and possessions which is connected with the adoption of modern technology—a thinking that has as its consequence the "dehumanizing" of mankind and the destruction of nature.[40]

Over against this fateful development Ueda recalls the attitude toward nature and life of the "old Japanese" who was content with what nature brought him and did not interfere in it destructively. For it nature is not an object, but in the sense of Mahayana "to be simply as it is in itself." This Mahayana conception of nature stands in the most extreme contrast to that of secularistic technology, in that it presupposes a logic quite different from that. In it man and nature are

---

[36]Ibid., 268.
[37]Ibid., 260.
[38]Ibid. 269, cf. 267.
[39]Ibid., 268.
[40]Ibid., 270ff.

"not two," not a subject and an object; rather in consequence of it "being thus as it is in itself"[41] "rules" "in the ground of all beings," and that means, in nature as in man. This "nonduality" can only be expressed logically by saying that with the identity of the two "things" their nonidentity is simultaneously established, and, this means, in the logic of conceptual-objective thinking only in the form of a contradiction. But Ueda has to accept this problematic in Mahayana, because this corresponds in its own way with experiencing a rose is its "such-ness," and because he experiences therein a "hiddenness of being" in which he can in inner freedom become—as it happens—one with the Buddha, with Tathagata, that is, with the one "who comes as he comes and who goes as he goes," in the "thus-ness" (Tathata) which for him is the "truth of being" for the "enlightened one," and not a matter of conceptual knowledge.

From our perspective we remark only that—first—just because a state of affairs cannot be sufficiently grasped conceptually does not mean that, because it is no true knowledge of truth in this sense, it is valid as the "truth of being," and that—secondly—the "security of being (Seinsgeborgenheit)" which according to Ueda is bound up with it can be extremely problematic, not finally because no possibilities issue from it for altering its opposing relationships, but because it remains for man only to acquiesce to these in inner freedom.

If Ueda says that the Buddhist "non-objective experience of nature" lacks the presuppositions for the rise of modern technology" and also the possibility of "Altering nature on the basis of knowledge of its laws,"[42] we can only concur. The Tokaido Express, by which Ueda perceptively illustrates the achievements of technology and the fateful self-deception bound up with it,[43] is just as little a product of the Buddhist spirit as it is of democracy. Even more problematic appears what Ueda has to say on the question, how did it happen that Japan could appropriate "modern technology" despite the lack of necessary assumptions and in opposition to the thought of Buddhism, and what he has to say on over-coming the difficulties which arise from it. In respect to the adoption of the rational thinking of Western science and technology Ueda first notes that Bud-dhism afforded "no direct hindrances,"[44] for according to what he developed earlier, this adoption of rational thinking required no direct sign of its weaknesses nor a manifestation of decay, but can be a proof of its "nondifferentiating differ-entiation" of "worldly" and "Buddhist truth,"[45] by which Buddhism advanta-geously distinguishes itself in this relation from a "religion with another

---

[41]Ibid., 271.
[42]Ibid., 272.
[43]Ibid., 274.
[44]Ibid., 272.
[45]Ibid., 263.

character."[46] What remains is what he thinks about pitiful phenomena from the history of Christianity. In an earlier passage he frankly admits that modern Christian talk about the "coming of age of the world" is not satisfactory to him.[47]

But Ueda is convinced that Mahayana Buddhism can offer a positive as well as a "negative" contribution to the solution of this problem or at least "approaches" to such, and for this purpose points—somewhat surprisingly—to the Sokagakkai and—as to be expected—to Zen Buddhism; he speaks of the first "as a striking example for the restoration of direct human contact in the midst of the cold environment of divided individuals in the large cities," and of the latter "as a conspicuous example for the intangible renunciation which is simultaneously ready for tireless activity in the midst of the noise, haste and agitation of world civilization."[48]

Yet we wonder whether Sokagakkai, especially in its political expression as Komeito, is suited to protect the individual against becoming a mere cipher, and whether the idea that "mankind itself can somehow be set free from entanglement in the acceleration of technology" is being served if, sitting in the Tokaido Express in serene detachment, the Zen Buddhist thinks, "one must grateful to technology." "Technology must be developed further."[49] Also Ueda evidently knows about the questionableness of these "helps," when, subsequent to his presentation of the "non-duality" of Mahanyana logic, he concedes, "The confrontation of Mahayana Buddhism with the mentality of modern natural science, considered from this special angle, remains as a major task that Buddhism has yet to undertake," and when he subsequently reaches the conclusion, "This confrontation ought to be conducted as matter of principle."[50] However, we are dealing here not merely with a "special angle," but with the very problem as such of the Buddhist philosophy he represents, which he defines as a "connection of rationality and mysticism." Although he calls this formulation a "not entirely consistent label of experience,"[51] it nonetheless recalls the title of his dissertation, in which he dealt with the same problematic as here.

4. The Ox and Its Oxherd

In all the following essays Ueda is occupied with the question about the nature of Buddhist thinking in relation to Western, which moves him from the perspective of his heritage from the Kyoto School, except that he no longer entertains

---

[46]Ibid., 272.
[47]Ibid., 266.
[48]Ibid., 275.
[49]Ibid., 275.
[50]Ibid., 273.
[51]Ibid., 273.

problems of the kind represented by secularization, but concentrates on what is central to Zen Buddhist thinking by means of the picture series on "the ox and its oxherd" frequently explained by him—partly in literal repetition—a thinking that occurs in the self and for which the "surroundings" represent only the place of this becoming-a-self. The world also attains here another aspect for the one who has won his true self, but it is not changed thereby, as is expected in biblical eschatology, in an absolute way by an intervention of God, or as this occurs, at least in a relative sense, by man's technical mastery of nature. The "awakened one" does not interfere in the world as is the case with that God of faith or the man of technology. The change is enacted *in* him; but to its nature belongs the fact that he forgets that he has enacted it and that it has happened at all. According to an old Buddhist picture it is more like the case of a ladder to whom one no longer pays attention after he made the ascent. The means of ascent, the ascent and the one who is conscious of the ascent are objectivities which dissolve into nothingness when this goal is reached. Just as little as one, if he is wise, continues to drag around the ladder which has served him or the boat with which he reaches the other shore, so just as little does the one who is immersed in the sphere of nonobjectivity still cling to the objectivities of the means and the way by which he has reached this goal, but lets them—and with them the entire surroundings and himself—be what they are "in themselves"; namely, not objects for him, not his world of objects and not his objective "I," but [views] all of them in his "calmness" in which he finds himself in the nothingness of objectivity in the fullness of the essence, as they truly are in their originality.

For this reason only the last three pictures of the entire series are of significance for Ueda and he only provides detailed commentary for these.[52] These are: the eighth which depicts a completely empty circle; the ninth, in which this circle

---

[52]For the series of pictures often reprinted and commented upon in different forms one is referred to their reproduction in *Der Ochs und sein Hirte*, 3rd ed. (Neske, 1976); in *Eranos Jahrbuch* 23 (1954): 297ff., and 45 (1976) (Leiden: Brill, 1980); in D. T Suzuki, *Manual of Zen Buddhism*, 5th ed. (New York: Grove Press, 1960) 1217ff (in two versions, the second without the Bodhisattva); in Philip Kapleau, *The Three Pillars of Zen* [New York: Doubleday, 1980] 313-25 (in modern representation).

Ueda uses and comments on this series of pictures, or its last three pictures, partly in verbally similar formulations in seven of his essays. First, in "Das Nichts und das Selbst im buddhistischen Denken," 1974, and then—according to their appearance or conception—in "Das menschliche Selbst und das Nichts (partially with repetitions of the preceding essay), "Der Tod im Zen-Buddhismus," "Das wahre Selbst" (all three from 1975), "Leere und Fülle: Shunyata im Mahayana Buddhismus" (1976), "Das 'Nichts' bei Meister Eckhart und im Zen-Buddhismus" (1977), "Die Macht des Bildes und die Kraft der Ritualisierung" (1978) (further references in n. 1).

is filled with stones beside a river and a twig which blooms from it, but without a man standing over against this fullness; and the tenth, in which from the slight oxherd who has anxiously sought and tamed his ox and is finally immersed with it has fortunately become a hefty, beaming "fellow," who is ready to fulfill his Bodhisattva vow which is here signified primarily by the meeting with a youth. The pains of seeking and disciplining the self symbolized in the ox are now forgotten, but to the observer of the series the way described in it for attaining to the true self in nothingness and its fullness of things as they are turns out to be a corresponding relation to itself and the world.

That the way of salvation explained by Ueda by means of these pictures and their accompanying commentary deals practically and concretely with the zazen practice characteristic of Zen Buddhism is evident from the detailed conceptual and praxis-oriented treatment which he devotes to it in one of his lectures on the theme, "Die Macht des Bildes und die Kraft der Ritualisierung (The Power of the Picture and the Power of Ritualization)."[53] Here he connects the last three pictures of the story of the oxherd and his ox with another, that of a "clear, transparent pearl which rolls on by itself," which is said to represent "the universe in its totality in its boundless openness" and at the same time the "total body of the true self of man," as a "fundamental picture" for the "self-assurance" of man "in his awakening to truth." Before he can speak of the "power of ritualization" in zazen he has first to speak of the "power of the picture," as it is understood in Zen. This consists in the fact that, as symbol, it "can make the invisible visible, in such a way that this consists in its "totality" and in the "subject of existence," and as its "self-image" in which both "concern us unconditionally and existentially." For the "rolling by itself," which is said to represent an event of the truth of being and of man" Ueda appeals to the three mentioned pictures which form "a unity" "which represents the perfection on the way of the self-becoming of man" as "the triune truth" of the Buddhist "selfless self." In the three aspects of the traceless unbecoming in nothingness, of selfless flourishing and of the selfless meeting of the other we are dealing with objectifications of what is nonobjectifiable, as is expressed by saying that "the movement from one station to another as such to which it essentially arrives" "is never objective and pictorially fixed," and that therein there even occurs "a dissolution of the pictoriality into transpictorial imagelessness," as is characteristic of the Zen picture. There also occurs therein a "movement from the invisible to the visible and from the visible to the invisible." Precisely because of this "power of the picture" to "make the invisible visible" Ueda warns us not to "confuse the symbolized with the symbol."

---

[53]This lecture was presented in July 1978 to a private circle in Zurich and is still unpublished.

According to Ueda Zen Buddhism corresponds to this nature of the symbol in the "ritualization" peculiar to it, that is, in the "realization and appropriation of that which is shown in it and through the picture, that is, through the corporeal repeatable action to whose style the structure of the relevant picture corresponds," and this happens even in zazen. To the first of the three pictures to which he refers, the picture of absolutely nothing, corresponds "zazen in the narrow sense," that is, as "immersion in a definite sitting position as primary ritualization"; to the second, "the work in nature" bound up with zazen; and to the third, in which it comes to "communication," the dialogue between master and disciple "about a koan." Because zazen in the narrow sense, as ritual sitting, "forms the basis for the whole of Zen praxis," he describes this in all its individual features and externalities, as well as in all the depths of the experiences in which the one practicing participates, from the bowing and counting of breaths to the "attuning to spirit" and the "contemporaneity with the Buddha," by which there is neither only something external nor only internal, but everything forms a whole which dissolves in nothingness.

In tracking the abstract philosophical course of Ueda's thought one must always be conscious of the fundamental significance of the practice of zazen as "personal realization and formation of community" which is represented in the picture series of the ox and the oxherd—even when he does not mention it but is content to comment on the pictures, and also when he philosophizes prior to taking a position on it or draws its consequences. This formal structure of a framing of the said series of pictures by generally leading up to them in the form of a discussion of fundamental problems and by [drawing] effective theoretical and practical consequences which result for him from taking the pictures into account and from the Zen praxis which tacitly they presuppose but not without leaving a trace—this formal structure, I say, is characteristic of all Ueda's essays. They differ in detail only by the extent to which the essential element not so much precedes or follows the course of the argument, but is developed in the explanation of the three pictures. In respect to the content of his Zen philosophy which is represented sometimes in one form and at other times in another, no distinctions can be established. We rather often hear the same thing over and over in a somewhat tiring monotony of stereotypical formulas. Differences in content and special emphases only appear in detail when he takes account of Nishida and basic characteristics of his philosophy, or when a special problem, like that of death, is thematically considered. Even the philosophical-linguistic discussions to which he turns in his last works are already evident in statements in his earlier publications.

5. Nothingness and the Self

Typical for the usual structure of Ueda's essays is his lecture at Basel on "Das Nichts und das Selbst in buddhistischen Denken (Nothingness and the Self in

Buddhist Thinking),"[54] in which he discusses "first the self of nothingness on the side of nothingness and then the self,"[55] in order by way of conclusion to draw consequences for ethical behavior from the "problem of the self,"[56] that is, from the nature of the "true self," developed on the basis of the three familiar pictures—consequences in which the "poisoning of the I" caused by substantializing thinking is said to be overcome.[57]

In the first part Ueda juxtaposes Western substance thinking which arises, according to him, from the "self-substantializing of man" and "attachment to the I which is fundamental to it," with the Buddhist doctrine of "sunyata, according to which everything is essentially empty," and of "pratitya-samutpada, of the co-emergence of everything in fully mutual dependence." For Ueda, the opposition which these two Buddhist doctrines stand in respect both to Western thinking in established concepts and to one another, in that one speaks of "nothingness" and the other of a "universal dynamic of relation, occasions his reference to Buddhist "prajna knowledge," which is "beyond every dualism," in that it both affirms and denies it. Buddhist thinking, like Western, makes use of conceptual designations, too. But it uses them, not as fixed forms which can and must be adhered to, but as "perspectives," which arise immediately out of situations, and are thus variable, but do not even correspond to these, but rather are able "creatively" to give them a new meaning.[58]

As an example of the meaning-giving "thinking-action" which does not issue from the reflection of discursive thinking that clings to the I, but springs directly from the "nothingness of the heart," Ueda mentions the behavior of a guest who while eating on a hot summer day was rescued from a painful situation which had arisen when the host's daughter spilled a glass of water, by placing his hand on the spilled water and saying, smilingly: "Pretty cool!"—not with the intention of excusing his daughter, but wholly without intention as—as Buddhism calls it—"the wonderful act of the nothingness of the heart, which—as Ueda remarks—"is identical with the Buddhist concept of compassion."[59] In order to proceed more abstractly and without following the lines of practical conduct, Ueda explains the nature of non-substantializing Buddhist thinking and through it to what lies beyond dualism by means of the concept of "being-one" and the "subject-object problem."[60] Regarding the "One" to which, according to the doc-

---

[54]*Studia Philosophica* (Basel, 1974): 144-61.
[55]Ibid., 144.
[56]Ibid., 153ff.
[57]Ibid., 158ff.
[58]Ibid., 145ff.
[59]Ibid., 146.
[60]Ibid., 147ff.

trine of Zen Buddhism, all things "return," he explains that the "One" is not the One so long as it stands over against another and splits in two, as is the case in the conceptual fixation both in the antitheses of idealism and materialism as well as those of theism or atheism, or nihilism. This opposition which can not be combined with the One must be "broken through," in that the One becomes nothingness "and at the same time" a plurality, which occurs when one abandons the One "and goes off in two dynamic directions which belong to one another: on the one hand toward nothingness or toward the zero point, and on the other, toward plurality (or: back to plurality)."[61] If the One becomes nothingness for man, he will at once become open to the plurality, to the unity of what is differentiated, as can be experienced in springtime, according to a Zen saying, as a "colorful symphony of Being in openness."[62] Following a famous example, Ueda also discusses the subject-object problem by referring to the example of seeing a flower and explaining how its "immediate presence" can only be seen "in I-less immersion into the flower without objectifying it," that is, "before there arises the distinction of the knowing subject and the known object."[63] This "prior-to-splitting" is "for objectification" "an empty nothingness," which "encompasses" the subject-object field" in its "nonobjectivity," and turns it into a "play area" for the freedom of the "self-less self," within which this can choose and change the "perspectives of the self," free of every absolutization, into a "dynamic mutuality of infinite negation and direct affirmation,"[64] therefore, for example, into infinite nothingness" as is present here-now "at tea," as this is attested by a Zen master, when he answered the question "about ultimate reality," by saying: "Shall we drink a cup of tea?"[65]

After Ueda explains the "self of nothingness" from the side of nothingness in this way, whereby this is not possible, as he said previously, without taking a position on the self, he turns in the second half of this essay to the "problem of the self," in order to show—in a way already familiar to us—by means of the series of pictures of the ox and its oxherd, how man can attain "self-becoming" through nothingness.[66] Although here, in respect to "the resurrection of the self from nothingness to a self-less self," he explains that "this self-lessness of man" is meant, "not in an ethical sense, but in the universal sense of relation as the basic condition of the true self," he connects this "self-less self" quite closely with the "present human self-less self," in that he says in respect to the tenth

---

[61]Ibid., 148.
[62]Ibid.
[63]Ibid., 149.
[64]Ibid., 150ff.
[65]Ibid., 152-53.
[66]Ibid., 154.

station that this "now makes the 'Between' of man and man in its own inner space."[67] Similarly, in the passing from the ninth to the tenth station he speaks of an "interconnected double perspective" of the "Great Knowledge," which entails "seeing through the formal as nothingness," and of the "Great Sympathy," which entails "seeing nothingness directly concretized as the formal."[68]

In the third concluding section, however, Ueda concerns himself with the question, how "hatred between individual men and groups of men" allows "the basic blindness about itself" to be overcome, for which he cites "self-love" and narcissism, and especially "avarice," as examples—thus with questions of ethics. Even the differentiations of this "threefold poisoning of the I" are of an ethical nature, as when he speaks of "forms of compromise of social life," among which "mutual hate" "customarily hides," and of "conative clinging to the I," and when he tracks the concept of "one's own" into the spiritual, and egoism,, into the religious sphere. What he postulates as necessary for overcoming this "basic inversion of the I" is of an ethical sort:" a "transformation of the ground of existence," a "total reversal."[69]

Ueda, however, sees the root of this "basic inversion," that is, "the cause for man's unredemption," not so much in this sphere of the ethical, in which man has to enact a "total reversal," but in "man's substantializing self-grasp"—therefore, despite a certain ethical undertone, in the sphere of thinking, more precisely in the sphere of a definite epistemology of objective thinking which—according to Ueda—is aware of a "consciousness of the I" only in the sense of "I am, for I am," whereas in opposition to it "the true self" in Buddhism says of itself: "I am I, and at the same time: I am not I," or "I am I, because I am not I."[70]

Here one can not only ask, like the Buddhist does in respect to the Pauline formula, "Christ in me," who speaks or acts here? but whether any one at all can speak or act if the I, which speaks and acts, is simultaneously not this I, so that neither the partner in dialogue nor the one speaking, or acting, can know what it is dealing with. How could it be otherwise, if the "consciousness of I" is aware not only of the limits of the objective substantializing of its I and the situation in which it finds itself, as this is to be expected, but rather is absolutely valid as the "basic inversion" and therefore together with the situation in it finds itself, has to die the "Great Death" in nothingness? Indeed, Ueda speaks here simultaneously of the "resurrection" of the "true I" and of a "thinking-acting" which corresponds to the situation and exhibits itself therein as "compassion." But he

---

[67]Ibid., 158.
[68]Ibid., 156.
[69]Ibid., 158ff.
[70]Ibid., 159.

resorts to conceptual-discriminating thinking, when he speaks of "hatred," "basic blindness" and "avarice," and of their concrete-objective effects which are not completely "free of form"; the question arises, on the other hand, who then enacts the "transformation of the ground of existence," the "total reversal," if not that I that sees itself in its thinking and acting as its subject in a situation concerning which it can obtain clarity only with the help of discursive knowledge. Otherwise than in such objective knowledge of the self and the situation—however relative and finally absolutely limited it may be—it arrives at neither the "resurrection of the true self" nor to an attitude that can be distinguished from the outer and inner relativity and arbitrariness of the situation. In any case, Ueda cannot show us how from a self-less self in the theoretical sense there can appear a man who conducts himself self-lessly in the ethical sense. Self-lessness in ethical conduct over against its surroundings presupposes just such a self which in its conduct is conscious that it is the subject which is responsible for its acts. To be sure, this "true self" cannot conceive of itself epistemologically in an objective way, but apart from reflection upon itself and its situation it can attain to neither knowledge of its egoistic attachment to the I nor to its overcoming in the direction of a self-less act.

Ueda actually makes use of conceptual-objective thinking, for otherwise he could not present this doctrine of salvation to us at all, just as we can only enact it by means of this thinking. But instead of appropriately certifying its absolute limits with respect to the nonobjectivity of the self and of being which is evident to him in his enactment of the same in the context of the subject-object schema of thinking consciousness in such a way that the I becomes aware in a way that is no longer objective, of its being determined to selfhood and of its realization as a special revelation of the mystery of Being, he speaks in a problematic conceptual way of the "true self" as a "self-less self" and of the "Being of beings" as "nothingness," whereby both the self-being of the true self as well as its relation to the world in the sense of world formation is rendered problematic, with only a direct, unreflected response corresponding to the situation as "a doing of not doing" in "great sympathy" remaining—a sympathy whose tired resignation can only be somewhat mitigated by the illusory assumption of a harmony which lies at the base of all Being and occurrence.

Less affected by the ethical problematic connected with the ambiguity of his concept of selflessness and of his "Great Yes" to Being as nothingness are, by contrast, Ueda's deliberations on the theme of "Man and his Death,"[71] because here he deals only with the individual human and his destiny, the finitude of which remains, indeed, unchangeable. The situation of unavoidably having to die can be changed only by its anticipation in the "Great Death," that is, through the

---

[71]"Der Tod im Zen-Buddhismus," in *Der Mensch und sein Tod*, 162-72.

liberation from the "false I" which is to be enacted and verified in life—a liberation in which man lives no longer towards death, but "from death."[72] For the unity of death and life which is to be lived by the "I-less" man beyond the opposition of death and life as a "living/dying,"[73] the concepts "immortality" and "eternal life" are not satisfactory, because, as a Buddhist, he always hears them as "attempts at a continuing extension of one's own life."[74] Instead of this, he wants to speak of a "mutual interpenetration of Being and nothingness,"[75] which occurs in the "awakened one" already here and now in a way that reminds us of the way the Apostle Paul speaks of a "resurrection body"—to be sure in another way and with another grounding than happens with him. By taking account of the last two pictures of the ox and oxherd story he even speaks of two different kinds of resurrection bodies. In the ninth picture "nature as it is from itself" is "the first resurrection body of the I-less self." In the tenth picture, however, there appears in the "communion of the common life" between the two figures of the oxherd who has become a Bodhisattva and the youth, a "second resurrection body."[76] That in these two instances we are dealing in this corporealization of the I-less I with a realization of "absolute nothingness" as "Neither Being nor Nothingness," i.e with a "event" which is not to be grasped conceptually, Ueda expresses by saying that at the conclusion he permits the question about dying to fade away "quite simply into astonishment" which expects no answer, as in the sentence "Dying, Oh, whither?"[77]

This talk of death, which ends in a mere "Oh, whither?" which is dissolved therein and at the same time expresses its quintessence brings to mind "The rose, here,"[78] which is alone left as what is essential in Ueda's interpretation of Angelus Silesius' verse which he puts at the end of his dissertation in continuation of Eckhart's "Without why."[79] In such a "primal sentence" he also finds the origin of Nishida's philosophy, and the significance the "Oh" he pursues in Rilke's epitaph.

---

[72]Ibid., 165.
[73]Ibid., 163.
[74]Ibid., 166.
[75]Ibid., 165.
[76]Ibid. 168. Ueda also speaks of these two "resurrection bodies" in the essay on "Das 'Nichts' bei Meister Eckhart und im Zen-Buddhism," 261ff.
[77]Ibid., 170.
[78]*Die Gottesgeburt in der Seele und der Durchbruch zur Gottheit*, 157ff.
[79]Ibid., 155.

6. From Nothingness to Philosophy of Language

Ueda concerns himself with Nishida's philosophy in two works which stem from the year 1976, but in both indeed only with Nishida's *early philosophy*. In the Ludwigsburg essay[80] this early philosophy of "pure experience" is first mentioned in the third section as a "model case" for that with which Eckhart and the three famous pictures deal. The contribution to the Ratschow *Festschrift*,[81] on the contrary, is wholly devoted to the thinking which Nishida represented in his first text and contains at the conclusion even an exposition of the way in which authentic Nishida philosophy developed from this beginning.

In presenting Nishida's early philosophy as a "model case" of a thinking at the base of Zen experience Ueda proceeds in both works from a sentence from the foreword in *A Study of Good* in which Nishida explains: "I should like to explain everything by saying that pure experience is the sole real reality."[82] Ueda sees "contained" in this sentence something "threefold, which represents a movement which proceeds, by stages, in a double direction."[83] The first step is "pure experience."[84] For the second, the statement contained in the sentence is decisive: "Pure experience is the sole real reality."[85] The third step is represented by the whole sentence just as he cites it.[86] Ueda correctly connects "pure experience" as the perception of reality prior to the split of consciousness into subject and object, therefore of a reality which for objective thinking is nothingness, with the enlightenment of Zen experience.[87] This ineffable Zen event of the first step,

---

[80]"Das 'Nichts' bei Meister Eckhart und im Zen-Buddhism unter besonderer Berücksichtigung des Grenzbereiches von Theologie und Philosophie," in *Tranzendenz und Immanenz, Philosophie und Theologie in der veränderten Welt*, 257-66.

[81]"Das denkende Nicht-Denken," in *Denkender Glaube*, 331-41.

[82]"Das 'Nichts' bei Meister Eckhart etc.," 263 and "Das denkende Nicht-Denken," 332 (on these publications see n. 1). In addition to these two essays, Ueda concerns himself with Nishida's early philosophy also in the essay on "Sprache und Erfahrung," always in view of the step-wise unfolding of the event of pure experience.

[83]"Das denkende Nicht-Denken," 334.

[84]Ibid., 334ff.

[85]Ibid., 334ff.

[86]Ibid., 335.

[87]In the essay on "Das 'Nichts' bei Meister Eckhart, etc.," Ueda connects the three steps with the last three pictures of the ox and its oxherd, 260ff., and places before them for comparison a summary of his conception of "Lassen" in Meister Eckhart (257-59). In the essay on "Das denkende Nicht-Denken" he deals with

which is reality only for the one who experiences it, forms the abiding origin of Nishida's entire philosophy, to which he is continually related. As the basic principle of his philosophizing as it is expressed in the formulation of the second step, it represents a statement about something which is essentially ineffable. Ueda calls this formulation of the principle a "primitive sentence," which in its application and unfolding in philosophizing becomes a "basic philosophical principle," as it lies before us in the sentence cited. Moving from the "event" over the "primitive sentence" to the "basic sentence," Nishida's philosophy as a whole, and thus in its first form in which he "attempts" to think back to "the unthinkable through nonthinking," represents in Ueda's eyes a "thinking nonthinking."[88]

That Ueda speaks not merely of a thinking of not-thinking, but of a "Not-thinking," even if he qualifies it in the function of thinking-back as a "thinking," is closely connected with the fact that he wishes thereby to emphasize the "gap" which obtains between the first step and the primitive sentence of the second step as well as between this and the third, and which must eventually be "leapt over"—as this happens—if not already in the movement away from the origin—then at least in the "step back," in philosophy's conscious return to its origin in an "event" in the "person" of the one philosophizing, in this case in the person of Nishida.[89] Although the expression "step back" calls to mind Heidegger's idiom, and with this "leaping over" the dimensional gaps in Nishida, or Ueda, one could think of Heidegger's conception of the "sentence" as a "leaping," Ueda explains that such occurred "in the history of philosophy for the first time in Nishida and as Nishida's philosophy."[90]

He does not hesitate to acknowledge "the tension" which arises in this philosophy from the fact that Nishida "as philosopher is at the same time a practicer of Zen, and as a practicer of Zen is at the same time a philosopher,"[91] and that to him "Zen and philosophy are concerns of life with similar urgency." This is the reason Nishida found himself "in a crucible of the most extreme inner tension" which threatens to split a person in two. But this tension of a "reciprocal questioning of Zen and philosophy"[92] was made "creatively" evident for him in a painstaking appropriation of Western philosophy and of a "lasting confrontation

---

the three steps in a more differentiated way, which is why we here cite from this essay.

[88]"Das denkende Nicht-Denken," 336-40.

[89]Ibid., 337ff.

[90]Ibid., 338.

[91]Ibid., 338 (cited according to the correction of the manuscript in the printed text by Ueda).

[92]Ibid., 338.

with it[93] in a ceaseless struggle to say what is ineffable in experience—which constantly demanded new essays—which stands before us in the nineteen volumes of the principal edition of his works.

Instead of continuing to pursue this development of Nishida's philosophy—which is actually reserved for later—[94] but not without once again referring extensively to its original form, he meanwhile addresses anew the problematic which is here before us in a still unpublished essay on "Erfahrung und Sprache" (Experience and Language) by means of the concept of the "Ur-word" in the context of a linguistic-philosophical discussion. After he has presented the nature of conversation by appealing to Western philosophy of language from Humboldt through Cassirer to Bollnow as a circular movement in the form of an emergence from one's "own language world" to a "thing" which involves conversation, and returns from this to a language in which "the spirit" of the "thing" is itself validated, he asks whether—for the sake of reaching this goal—it can provide the possibility of an extreme movement," "namely, completely outside the world of language and from there back again to the world of language."

In considering the possibility of reaching this goal Ueda calls to mind not only Heidegger's conception of language as the "house of Being," from which man would have to depart lest it become for him a "prison house," but also Merleau-Ponty's "transformation of the spoken word to the speaking word, and beyond to the original silence" (*parole parlé, parole parlante, silence primordial sous le bruit des paroles*). If for Merleau-Ponty this transformation is bound up with a "*modulation de ma propre existence, une transformation de mon être*" which occurs in it, then this corresponds to the existential character of Nishida's "pure experience" which is related to his person, as was advanced by Ueda in the previously mentioned work. Similarly he here finds his favorite notion of "breakthrough"—even a "double breakthrough"—confirmed: "Language is broken through to silence, and this silence is again broken through to speech."

Actually, Ueda can and must speak of a threefold breakthrough, for this "most extreme circular movement" which includes the moment of silence "occurs in us, breaking through us," and signifies "an existential transformation of the speaking subject." But rather than doing that, he is content to let the "twofold breakthrough from the word away to silence and from there again to speech" be a pure "word event," for which the "speaking subject" is only a matter of "place"—to use a term for it coined by the later Nishida, which Ueda is, however, not employing here. Ueda rather sticks with "pure experience," out of whose problematic Nishida attained to his Topos logic. But Ueda is obviously aware of this problematic when he speaks of that "twofold breakthrough" as an

[93]Ibid., 340.
[94]Ibid., 341.

"event" in terms of "pure experience," in which there is by definition no distinction between subject and object, yet he is here the subject of talk about this breakthrough, and "this movement" is enacted by the speaking subject as its object. These difficulties are not obviated by ignoring the subject-being of this "talk" and the postulating of a "simultaneousness" of the "movement, which first makes the word true," with "the existential transformation of the speaking subject." To the degree that the speaking subject is eliminated, the "breakthrough" also loses the "place" at which it is said to occur, and becomes a utopia (*ou-topos*) whose reality only an ecstatic person glosses over.

Besides, it is to be noted that Nishida and his disciple Ueda are dealing with the same problematic, in other forms of notions and thought, with which the Apostle Paul dealt with in glossolalia and which vexed Christian theology in speaking of the word of God and of the Holy Spirit—and now vexes Western philosophy when it thinks it can think and speak "nonobjectively." Only a thinking can bring clarity which is aware that it can appropriately speak of the nonobjectifiable that actually exists only in objectifying conceptuality, and draw consequences from it.

Regarding this matter, of which Ueda is not unaware, it is no mere rhetorical question when he asks with respect to the "event" with which it deals, "Does it really occur?" and says of its connection with "pure experience," that it must be "explained further." He attempts this further explanation in the third chapter of the essay before us, in which he offers his own contribution to the linguistic-philosophical perspectives previously discussed by him—which can be helpful for understanding Buddhist philosophy—on the theme "Das Urwort und dessen Artikulation" ("The Primitive Word and Its Articulation"), and by means of Rilke's epitaph:

> Rose, Oh perfect contradiction. Desire
> To be no one's sleep under so many
> Eyelids.

For Ueda the most decisive thing in this poem is the "Oh." The verses themselves are only the "articulation" of the "Ur-word" or "Ur-sound," whose nature Ueda describes in a very talented way as the "breakthrough of the world of language," in the double sense of that "extreme circular movement" as one from moves away from language beyond absolute silence to language. In the "Oh!" for the sake of whose meaning he now writes with a capital "O" and an exclamation point, language is accompanied back "to something inarticulate, in order to un-become in absolute stillness." It is "the last gasp of breath with which the speech-endowed man dies," in which both the rose and the man "un-become." "At the same time" it is also "the first beginning of the following words of the verse, in which as an "un-verbal fore-word to language" "the way to language is again disclosed"; therefore it is "the resurrection of man who has been robbed of speech." In the "Oh!" is said "everything in one," though it is still not articulated, and in this saying is originally grasped. but still not reflected. It is "the absolute presence," without a something which would be an object for a subject; therefore the "event" of Nishida's "pure experience." As "neither linguistically conceived experience nor speech-less experience," but rather as "the experience of the removal of the word" and in unity with the experience of the birth of the word," the "Ur-word" would correspond accordingly to the "Ur-sentence," in which—in both of the essays referred to above—the "dimensional gap" between this and the "event" is "leapt over."

When Ueda answers the question, "Who actually speaks the 'Oh!' as Ur-word?" he says: "Certainly not the man, or the human I"; rather "the 'Oh!' expresses itself in the "Oh!" The subject of the Ur-word 'Oh!' is the 'Oh!' itself," so the criticism which we offered previously of Ueda's subject-less "speech-event" has become "object-less." It is, however, "simultaneously" confirmed by Ueda himself when he adds in the passage cited: "yet not independent of man, but as the Non-I of the man." Otherwise for Ueda the "non-I" is just the opposite of the "true self," whereas here it has become the "subject of the Ur-word." Univocal conceptual designation is what is needed here. But instead of this, Ueda speaks of an "*ek-static* unity of person, language and reality (or thing)." Not only are "silence and speaking a unity here"; but, according to Ueda, in this "Oh!" "reality and language" can still not be distinguished." But exactly how, also in "other spheres"—"so in the case of the agreement of knowledge with its object"—this "ultimate foundation for a relation to reality and language," is supposed to "grant" that fact," is, however, not shown; except that possibly—as Ueda would like to assume—"the real can be transformed into the unreal and the unreal into the real," whereby "thus-ness" becomes a strange "idea of truth."

But this darkness of the Ur-word does not prevent Ueda from "articulating" it in speech, as happens in Rilke's epitaph, in which the "*un-verbal fore-word*" becomes speech." He explains mysteriously: "With its articulation the 'Oh!' becomes all-saying nothingness, which is now articulated." But what is nothingness to say if it is really nothingness? Thus Ueda now makes use of things and the soul both of which "flash" in a "flashing word of light." Despite the conceptual differentiation of the articulation by this "language prism" into "four modes" and "two dimensions," its nature does not become clearer in Ueda's elucidation, and he concludes it with the concession that different necessary questions emerge "for the articulation of this theme," such as what kind of "event" is "principally" dealt with here, and in which relations its different modes stand to logic—questions for which we had expected answers from Ueda in this essay on "Erfahrung und Sprache," but which he reserved for a "further study" which has not yet been transmitted to us—probably for understandable reasons. In its place he refers us in the notes to different earlier essays of his, whose unsolved questions have obviously been those which provided him the occasion for these linguistic-philosophical deliberations. Thus, despite their spiritual qualities and deep meaning, it cannot be said that Ueda's thinking has become clearer and more repeatable through them, and that his specific contribution to the Kyoto School which is oriented to Western philosophy signifies a real claim to such. Ueda has allied himself with a kind of thinking about language whose talk of "word event" has turned out for coolheaded spirits to be a deceptive "word magic."

In this regard two remarks are in place here: a biographical-spiritual and a fundamental-methodological. First, in view of Ueda's approach to the significance which is ascribed to language by Heidegger, Gadamer, Bollnow, Merleau-Ponty, and others, in respect to the experience of reality, reference should be made to his descent from Shingon Buddhism, because his father was professor at the Koyasan, the holy mountain of Shingon, where Ueda himself taught for a while. There, according to the faith of its adherents, Kukai—the founder of Japanese Shingon Buddhism—perpetually sits immersed in meditation, while the faithful—in a hall before a sea of burning candles—pay their respects to the Sun-Buddha Mahavairocana, whose light penetrates the world and illumines all things. Kukai, however, was not only a magician, but as is evident from his numerous works, also a great thinker about language, who sought to ground its secret, esoteric sense in meditative ways by incisive classifications and differentiations of words and sentences, letters and sounds of the Dharani (Mantric Magical Sayings) and individual sutras. When, for example, he distinguishes the meanings of tone, word and reality," and comprehends them "simultaneously" as "tone-word-reality" in the unity of the Dharma,[95] this reminds us of Ueda's trinity of "event," "Ur-sentence" and "basic sentence" and their "articulation," and the word "Hum" contains a fullness for Kukai, similar to the way Ueda finds it in Rilke's "Oh!,"[96] Thus it can be said that for Ueda Zen Buddhism has preserved a kind of Shingon coinage, whereas it is otherwise for his teachers who connect it with faith in Amida. It is to be said basically and methodologically about the "extreme circularity" of the way from language, through silence and back to language, which is also found in Kukai, that Ueda—with regard to the objectivity of language—stands in opposition to Karl Jaspers' understanding of ciphers, although he shares with him the concept of the "Encompassing."[97] In a notation in his essay last discussed by us Ueda correctly draws attention to "hovering" in Jasper's evaluation of objectivity in the "basic philosophical operation." He

---

[95] *Kukai, Major Works translated by Yoshito S. Hakeda* (New York: Columbia University Press, 1972) 234ff.

[96] Ibid., 246ff.

[97] "Das Nichts und das Selbst im buddhistischen Denkens," 150.

remarks with agreement that Jaspers not only speaks of the "inaccessibility of objectivity," but also of the "simultaneous necessity of 'retracting'," or "turning back from objectivities." But, as it seems to him, this happens in Jaspers without it being apparent to him how this recantation, or turning back is accomplished," and this is the case because, with Jaspers, he emphasizes the existential character of this reversal in "human self-understanding."

In regard to this "hovering," to which Jaspers intentionally clings in this reference in his thinking, one cannot fault Ueda's criticism in respect to the way in which Jaspers speaks of an "objective nonobjectivity" of "objectivities." But in all three of the works in which Ueda speaks of this movement of a back and forth in saying the ineffable, it is equally less apparent to us, and to the degree that he allows the objectivity to dissolve into nothingness, it is even less apparent than with Jaspers who after all, as Ueda notes, holds to objectivity for the sake of bringing this reversal to consciousness—to be sure only "provisionally," as is the case with Ueda. Even in this only preliminary holding fast to the objective thinking of consciousness which is common to both of them there lies the cause of the unclarity of both in this point that is decisive for their entire thinking. For Jaspers this "as a last resort" seems like a vestige of the use of reason as a mere ante-structure for the theology of revelation—a use which he rejects—and, for the same reasons, Ueda does not do justice to the trans-objectivity of the "total nothingness" he postulates. There follows from this immanent critique of Jaspers and Ueda—and for us for other reasons—the necessity, not only of the "last resort" and the "preliminary"; rather we universally and thoroughly hold firm to the indispensable objective thinking of consciousness and speak of what shows itself as nonobjectifiable as its objectifications in symbols—to be sure in a somewhat different way than is the case in Ueda's occasional use of the term symbol.

7. The Ethical Consequences

The problematic character of Ueda's philosophy of language becomes evident not only in its epistemology and metaphysics, but still more in the consequences that issue from it for ethics. This ethical problematic is more difficult to evaluate when Ueda himself at the end of his Basel lecture—as we have seen—ascribes on different occasions essential significance to questions of ethics, as, for example, in the treatment of the story of Mary and Martha in his Eckhart book, in the discussion of the problem of secularization, and in the deliberations on the "threefold poisoning of the I" which requires a "total inversion." If his ethics raises critical questions for us in this connection, it can nevertheless be determined that its problematic character increases in proportion to the extent to which Ueda—in the way presented previously—gives way to a philosophy of language, in consequence of which "language speaks and man can only be present as ecstatic subject." This language-philosophical exclusion of the I is completely in line with the extinction of the I which is attached to things, or hypothesized, that is demanded of the Buddha and represented in all of Buddhism and has as a consequence the same ethical problematic—only in the special form that corresponds to its founding. This distinctiveness of the problematic which has arisen for ethics from a linguistic-philosophical grounding consists in the fact that ethics becomes a kind of cosmic aesthetics for describing good human conduct, in which the beauty of the cosmos is embodied, as this corresponds in a special way to the Japanese as a final refinement of its Confucianist heritage.

A typical example of this authentic Japanese worldly-religious aestheticizing ethics, into which Ueda's Buddhist philosophy of language flows, is the essay "Leere und Fülle: Shunyata im Mahayana-Buddhismus" ("Emptiness and Fullness: Sunyata in Mahayana Buddhism"), which he delivered in 1976 at the Eranos gathering in Ascona.[98] Without a doubt the nature of this place and the universal aesthetics of this institution formed a suitable setting. We take up this essay as the conclusion of our presentation of Ueda's thinking not only because it is his last publication in German, since it only appeared in the *Eranos Jahrbuch* in 1980, but also because all the motifs which have concerned us up to now are once again expressed in it. Once again he adverts to Nishida's "pure experience,"[99] in which—without the interference of an objectifying I—the trees blossom "as they blossom on their own"[100] in true "such-ness,"[101] and once again resounds the "Oh!" from Rilke's epitaph[102] as the "non-verbal fore-word to language";[103] there is talk of *pratitya-samutpada*[104] and of the "breakthrough," as well as of "first"[105] and "second resurrection body,"[106] and naturally again and again of nothingness, and of the "nothingness of nothingness,"[107] of the "self-less self"[108] and of its "tri-uni-ty."[109] Because of the abstractness of these concepts and the derivation of what is meant in them from the "Self-understanding of the East Asian man," whose rendering is not easy in a Western language, Ueda makes use once again—for the seventh time!—of the story of the "Ox and its

---

[98]*Eranos* (1976); *Einheit und Verschiedenheit* (Leiden: Brill, 1980) 135-63.
[99]Ibid., 151.
[100]Ibid., 141.
[101]Ibid., 150.
[102]Ibid., 154.
[103]Ibid., 155.
[104]Ibid., 148.
[105]Ibid., 151.
[106]Ibid., 140.
[107]Ibid., 143.
[108]Ibid., 145.
[109]Ibid., 144.

Oxherd," and just as this series of pictures has already been used as an illustration in a contribution of Suzuki's,[110] it is reproduced here once again. This commentary, which is significantly different from the psychological one Suzuki presents, occupies the entire first half of the lecture, but in comparison to the earlier
one this offers nothing new—with the exception of two formulations which
remind us of Heidegger's idiom: "nature natures,"[111] and "the circle circles,"[112]
but principally of the expanded interpretation of the tenth picture by making
reference to the "ordinary form of greeting among the Japanese."[113]

The illustration by recourse to the Japanese ceremonial, of the "interhuman
relation on the basis of nothingness in which man un-becomes and from which
he rises again"[114]—an illustration that recalls the scene Ueda described earlier of
the glass of water spilled at a table gathering—now especially interests us, because it is characteristic of the ethic that issues from Ueda's philosophy of language. The sequence upon which he here reflects involves the meeting of two
Japanese men on the street who bow deeply before one another and only then,
standing erect after this bowing and turning toward one another, say: "Fine
weather, isn't it?" "Yes, fine!" Ueda sees in the "usual form of meeting and
greeting" in Japan not merely something external and formal which—as he
knows—can also "become decadent," but according to its "original meaning" [he
sees in it] "an elementary expression and a way of enacting human self-understanding in inter-human meeting in which human nature is expressed."[115] If the
meeting described is no mere "courtesy," but is "being-ful," as this gets expressed in the fact that the "bowing before one another" is "sometimes so deep,"
"as in the direction toward the groundlessness of nothingness where there is
neither "I" nor "Thou," then what is expressed actually occurs, and the bowing
is the demonstration of the actuality of what occurs seriously in and through it.
The bowing facilitates a special kind of "I-Thou-Relation," in which two "egos"
no longer stand over against one another in absolute independence, as was otherwise the case.[116] In the bowing as a "kind of immersion into the groundlessness
of nothingness" in which there is "neither 'I' nor 'Thou'," "Absolute independence" becomes penetrated by nothingness and thus becomes an "unending openness" of "nondifferentiation." "Absolute dependence"—to the contrary—is said

---

[110]"The Awakening of a New Consciousness in Zen," *Eranos-Jahrbuch 1954*,
23; *Mensch und Wandlung* (Zurich: Rhein-Verlag, 1955) 302ff.

[111]*Eranos* (1976) 142.

[112]Ibid., 146.

[113]Ibid., 159ff.

[114]Ibid., 159.

[115]Ibid., 159.

[116]Ibid., 160.

to consist in that fact that "each of the two partners" can totally cede to the Thou-side what he experiences in this way on his side, and thus simultaneously "on the basis of that non-differentiation—in a "mutual exchange of role of master."[117]

In view of the being-with-and-in-another of an "absolute independence" in which there is no "I," which he analyzes in paradoxical conceptuality, and of an "absolute dependence" in which the authentic experience is a thing of the other, Ueda himself confesses that the event of greeting can "appear complex in its individual phases and moments," but thinks that "in reality it is actually quite simple." To illumine the conceptual complexity of this intended state of affairs and to show the possibility of its realization in an act that corresponds to it, Ueda refers to the last three pictures of the story of the ox, declaring that: "Taken as a whole this entire greeting is nothing other than the circular movement from the eighth, ninth, and tenth stations of the ox pictures." "Bowing into the depths of nothingness where there is neither I nor Thou" corresponds to the empty circle of the eighth picture; standing erect and turning toward one another, to the tenth in which the Bodhisattva ventures into the market accompanied by a youth. The picture lying between of the circle filled with emerging and blooming nature, Ueda connects with the ordinary words about "fine weather" exchanged in such greeting.

To this illustration of his fair-weather ethics Ueda attaches three essential elucidations. First, "the nondifferentiation of the religious and the ordinary" gets expressed as it is "in Zen Buddhism," because in this way the "ordinary is filled with significance down to the last detail."[118]

Second, he attains now a clear conceptual formulation of the normative self-understanding intended in his Zen philosophy, namely,

> In the dynamic of relation on the basis of nothingness man does not understand himself as a subject substantially identical with itself which only afterwards somehow enters into relation with the other; rather he already understands himself from the relation in which he finds himself. He understands himself already as "partner of the partner," in "ek-sistence," in which "the other is by contrast no other," but in his otherness is the embodiment of the "ek"-ness of the ek-sistence, of the outside-of-itself-ness of the self-less self.[119]

By appealing to the groundlessness of nothingness, Ueda says of this ontologized self-understanding: (1) that "the self and the other . . . are joined in being, so that

---

[117]Ibid.
[118]Ibid., 161.
[119]Ibid., 161-62.

they so joined are "neither two nor one"; and (2) that "this state of affairs" is "no static condition, but always an event" which "in each case has to be concretely enacted and preserved in encounter and communication."

Third, Ueda emphasizes once again that "the self-negation" in which the role of master is given over to the other, represents "no one-sided self-sacrifice," and that it does not deal with a "consciously intentional exchange" in the sense of a "Please, after you," because otherwise it would only be "an act between the I-men," and thus no liberation of the "other from the I-prison" through the self-less self.[120]

From our side, by way of conclusion, we have one affirmative and two critical remarks to make to these deliberations of Ueda. As far as his Zen Buddhist emphasis upon the "nondifferentiation of the religious and the ordinary" is concerned, as it is exemplified in his interpretation of the Japanese ceremonial of greeting by appealing to the ox-pictures, we regard it as a legitimate seculari-zation of Buddhist cult forms through which "the ordinary can actually be filled with significance" down to the last detail—as is no longer to be expected from the repetition of religious praxis that has become archival in a society character-ized by the secularization of its religious tradition. The street must become the place today where the Divine Service occurs as human service.

There is the other question whether, with all that he expresses once again in the essay about the forms and formlessness of his thinking and its contents, he communicates to us the instructions by means of which it is possible—to make use of his world of pictures—to find and tame the ox and to participate in the life of the market in an responsible way. It is to be feared in the contemporary traffic and the hustle and bustle of the world market that the "Oh!" of Ueda's Ur-word could make a sound quite different from the one Ueda hears and acquire a different significance than that ascribed to it by him, if Ueda would expose it to these phenomena. Without speaking in pictures, we think that Ueda in his philosophy of language speaks of things like "absolute independence" and "abso-lute dependence" which do not exist in reality, and of a "Self-less self" which, if were truly self-less, would no longer be a self, just as "nothingness" is no real nothingness so long as we speak of it. No real problems can be solved with the paradoxes of his conceptuality, but at best only those apparent problems of an aesthetic world of language in whose eddy no distinction can any longer be made between deep meaning and nonsense.[121]

---

[120]Ibid., 162.

[121]Such a whirlpool of apparent problems in which one can no longer distin-guish between deep meaning and nonsense is also produced by Ueda in his latest contribution in German which appeared in the Festschrift for Ernst Benz, which carries the title "Un-grund und Interpersonalität," and in which he discusses the

Yet this Zen Buddhist philosophy of language is questionable not only in its epistemological aspect, but—as it is not otherwise possible on this basis—also in its metaphysics and the ethic connected with it. In order to avoid the emergence of a mere "self-sacrifice" from the renunciation of the wish to become master of the other, Ueda must assume that what happens on the side of the I occurs simultaneously on the side of the "Thou," and to be sure "not as a conscious intentional exchange" of the master-slave role, because it would otherwise be only "an act between I-men." Not only I, but the other as well must be freed from the "I-prison," so that the "ek-sisting movement can take place mutually."

"problem of the thought of the person in Zen Buddhism." For a further time he makes use of the last three pictures of the story of the "ox and the oxherd," because he once again finds presented in it "the trinity of the self-less self" (206ff.) and—as before—brings its three aspects into connection with zazen (immersion into and as sitting still), common work and travel in nature and sanzen (conversation with the master in respect to a koan) (208-209). This "three part praxis" gives him reason to emphasize a second time that "Zen dialogue" deals with "no sermon, no talk, no instruction" (208), no "doctrine" (212), but with the awakening of the "existential quest" for the "true self" in "self awakening, that means, to let the other awaken" (208). In his presentation of this "interpersonality" he makes use especially of the third picture which he also illustrates with the typical Japanese manner of greeting (209-10).

What is uniquely new in this essay is a so-called mondo in which it is described how two Japanese drink tea together. One says to the other: "The All is restlessly present here in a cup of tea." Whereupon the other turns over the cup so that the tea spills out and asks: "Where is the All now?" At the answer of the first, "O pity for a cup of such fine tea," the "two laugh at one another" (212).

In the two- or threefold "total transformation of the unusual into the ordinary," which occurs in this "play of truth," (212) Ueda believes he can see an example of the "breakthrough of the plain teaching to living interpersonal realization" (212). In its use as a koan everything depends "on sinking directly into the Between" (214).

If this is taken seriously or put into practice, as he intends, as an "indispensable preparation for dialogue between Christianity and Zen Buddhism," this could actually lead—in a completely different sense than the one described and expected by him, to be sure—to a "spontaneous chorus of laughter at its conclusion" (213). In view of the promised essay which Ueda contributed to this dialogue in earlier years, this is a deplorable ending, so that it is to be hoped that for him it deals with only one "station," which can be "forgotten again" after "the laughter" (213), and that "the old matter of Zen Buddhism in dialogue with Christianity could be expressed differently that is here the case."

This means nothing other than that the goal that is to be attained by way of the ethical conduct is at all times already presupposed as something present. Accordingly, what *is* already corresponds to that which ought to *be*. Preliminary to every event and preservation, the self—through the ontologizing of existence into ek-sistence—is already "the relation of partner to partner" in "non-dual-ity." The standing erect and turning toward one another belong to the greeting, as does the deep bowing, and occurs "so to speak" automatically from it—just as in the series of ox-pictures the one filled with "fine weather" follows the empty circle, as also Ueda allows the two countrymen to greet one another characteristically with "Fine weather!" "Yes, fine weather!" That is the basic tone of Ueda's Zen philosophy, in which there are only clouds of concepts which rapidly dissolve into a nothingness in which life can be well-lived in Rilke's aesthetizing and Heidegger's "overcoming" of the abyssal features of Dasein. *Vale amice!*

Chapter 9

Masao Abe (b. 1915)
Zen Buddhism and Christianity

1. Abe's Literary Legacy:
A Summa of the Zen Philosophy of the Kyoto School

If Nishitani, Hisamatsu, and Takeuchi did not attain the level of creative spiritual power which Nishida and Tanabe manifested in their works, but—as far as originality and literary production are concerned—lagged behind these founders of the Kyoto School, this is even more so in the case of Masao Abe as a representative of the third generation of this school. Whereas Nishitani achieved an impressive systematic presentation of the religious philosophy of Buddhism in his book *Religion and Nothingness*, Hisamatsu worked out the nature of Buddhism as a religious atheism in his voluminous lifework, and Takeuchi as the preserver of the heritage of his teacher Tanabe aimed to connect his philosophy of existence with Ur-Buddhism, in the case of Abe one cannot speak of such an original achievement, as it lies before us in different forms in these representatives of the second Kyoto generation. He is an outspoken disciple of Nishitani and Hisamatsu and, like Takeuchi—if even in a different way—represents a religious existentialism. During and after the Second World War he studied at Kyoto University, was lecturer in the Science of Religion and Ethics for a long time at Otani University, and from 1962 to 1979 was professor on the philosophical faculty of the Pedagogical University in Nara. In these years he worked simultaneously as guest professor at numerous American universities (for example, Columbia/New York, Chicago, Princeton, and Claremont) and participated, so to speak, in all the important congresses of the history and philosophy of religion. Additionally, he is still a leading member on many international committees dealing with the history and philosophy of religion and shares in the editing of many of their respective journals. Moreover, he has frequently been invited to deliver lectures in Japan and America.

In this lecturing on a worldwide scale and in the great number of resulting publications Masao Abe far surpasses his teachers and colleagues[1]—with the

---

[1] Index of the English essays of Masao Abe: "Buddhism and Christianity as a Problem Today," JR 3/2 (1963): 11-22. "Buddhism and Christianity as a Problem Today, Part II," JR 3/3 (1963): 8-31. Review Article: "Paul's Tillich's Christianity and the Encounter of the World Religions," EB 1/1 (1965): 109-22. "Professor Abe's Reply to the Debate," JR 4/2 (1964): 26-57. "Zen and Buddhism,"

exception of Daisetz Suzuki, whose international role he has quite literally assumed. If there can be no second Suzuki, Abe today, through his lectures and journal articles in both America and Europe—at least in academic circles—is nevertheless the best-known representative of Zen philosophy, all the more so since, after two long guest professorships in Princeton and his becoming emeritus in Nara, he serves as professor at the Graduate School in Claremont (California). That he is appreciated in other respects is due not only to the charm of his personality, but above all to his gifts as a teacher and his openness to other conceptions with which he represents his conviction about the truth of Zen Buddhism. If in his interpretation of Buddhist tradition he does not attain to the creative genius of a Suzuki and has worked out and brought together in no great work the aspects and stimuli which were communicated to him by his teacher, but has been content to produce contributions in journals and anthologies, yet these essays represent a self-contained whole in each of which—among one or

---

Japanese Studies 11 (1966): 1-11. "The Ideas of Purity in Mahayana Buddhism," *Numen* 13/3 (1966): 183-89. "Zen and Compassion," EB 2/1 (1967): 54-68. "Christianity and Buddhism—Centering around Science and Nihilism," JR 5/3 (1968): 36-62. "'Life and Death,' and 'Good and Evil' in Zen Buddhism," *Criterion* 9/1 (1969): 7-11. "God, Emptiness, and the True Self," EB 2/2 (1969): 15-30. "A Buddhism of Self-Awakening Not a Buddhism of Faith," in *Anjali: A Felicitation Volume presented to Oliver Hector de Alwis Wijesekera on His Sixtieth Birthday*, ed. J. Tilakasiri (Peradeniya, Ceylon: University of Ceylon, 1970) 33-39. "Zen and Western Thought," *International Philosophical Quarterly* 10/4 (1970): 501-41. "Man and Nature in Christianity and Buddhism," JR 7/1 (1971): 1-10. "Dogen on Buddha Nature," EB 4/1 (1971): 28-71. "Zen and Nietzsche," EB 6/2 (1973): 14-32. "Buddhist Nirvana: Its Significance in Contemporary Thought and Life," *The Ecumenical Review, World Council of Churches* 25/2 (1974): 158-68. "Religion Challenged by Modern Thought," JR 8/2 (1974): 2-14. "Zen as Self-awakening," JR 8/2 (1975): 2-14. "Non-Being and Mu—The Metaphysical Nature of Negativity in the East and the West," *Religious Studies* 11/2 (1975): 181-92. "Mahayana Buddhism and Whitehead,—A View by a Lay Student of Whitehead's Philosophy," *Philosophy East and West* 25/4 (1975): 415-28. "The Crucial Points: An Introduction to The Symposium on Christianity and Buddhism," JR 8/4 (1975): 2-9. "Zen and Buddhism," *Japan Studies* 11/1 (1966): 1-11. "Education in Zen," EB 9/2 (1976): 64-70. "Zen is not a Philosophy, but . . . ," ThZB 33/5 (1977): 261-68. "Emptiness is Suchness," EB 11/2 (1978): 132-36. "The End of World Religions," EB 13/1 (1980): 31-45. "Substance, Process, and Emptiness," JR 11/2-3 (1980): 31-45. "The Problem of Evil in Christianity and Buddhism" (still unpublished). Also 23 articles in Japanese on other themes.

more central themes of Buddhism and in confrontation with the corresponding positions of Western thinking—his view of life and the world has appeared in its basic structure.

Precisely in comparison with the works of other representatives of the Kyoto School two features of the rich material of these essays stand out: first, the simplicity and clarity both in the presentation of Buddhist doctrine and in the stand he takes on the positions of Western thinking, and then the interest manifest in every essay in the encounter with Christianity. What Abe develops in terms of Buddhist notions, terms, and lines of thought is probably nothing new when compared with that of his predecessors and contemporaries. The same is true in the main also of the substance of Western thought which he considers, and of his estimate of it. But Abe is able to illumine much that is dark in it and difficult to follow—without falling into questionable simplifications—and to make it understandable despite its strangeness. Although he completely shares the conception of Christianity that is current in the Kyoto School as well as the objections raised about it, he distinguishes himself from its other representatives by a greater openness for certain characteristics of Christianity in comparison with openly conceded deficiencies of Buddhism. In this he possesses a greater similarity to Tanabe—but with differing emphases of course. If one would like to learn in his essays how the mutual enrichment and deepening of Christianity and Buddhism, which he holds to be both necessary and possible, gets worked out, Abe is the one in the circle of the Kyoto philosophers who represents it most impressively today. Indicative of this is not only his frequent participation in inter-religious conversations and his present activity at a Christian theological school, but also the circumstance that his first essay in English carries the title "Buddhism and Christianity as a Problem of Today," and that with it he opened a "Symposium on Christianity and Buddhism" which extended over a decade in the journal, *Japanese Religions*[2] and is still not concluded, but will probably appear soon in book form.

Because Abe offers a compendium of the Buddhist philosophy of religion of the Kyoto School in his writings, in our treatment of its representatives we have placed him at the end, although he is not the youngest of them; and because the question of the relationship of Zen Buddhism and Christianity which drives us is also his central intention, we have adopted this perspective already in the title of this chapter devoted to him. More than all the others, it is Abe's thought that best lends itself to a presentation of his thinking under this theme.

We proceed in such a way that we first take up the discussion of this symposium by Abe and the positions he refers to in the foregoing section, in order to draw from his remaining essays what can count as its preliminary continuation

---

[2]JR 3/2-3 (1963); 4/2 (1966); 5/3 (1968); 7/1 (1971); 8/4 (1975); 9/1 (1976).

Masao Abe (b. 1915)

and can serve as its extension. In this connection we shall have to ask how Abe understands the Zen Buddhism from which he takes a position with respect to Christianity. For this purpose he not only supplies intellectual references, but also develops in individual essays the relationship of Zen Buddhism to Western thinking and to Christianity in a comprehensive systematic way. Finally we have to consider what is to be expected for him from the Zen perspective for the formation of life and especially for ethics. In all these groupings in which the most important of his essays published in English can be arranged according to the perspectives named, he deals primarily with the question of the relation of Buddhism and Christianity with which he opened the round of talks in *Japanese Religions*, and which pervades his entire literary production as the basic intention of his intellectual concerns. For this reason it seems appropriate for us to present the course of this symposium and then to see how the note struck in it and the themes taken up are preserved and further expanded in the essays which appeared partly concurrently and partly later.

2. The Symposium on Buddhism and Christianity Inaugurated by Abe

The article that opens that symposium consists of two parts which appeared in 1963 in two consecutive issues of *Japanese Religions* under the title "Buddhism and Christianity as a Problem for today."[3] Both the "Methodological Consideration" developed in the first part and the comparative discussion of central Buddhist and Christian notions that forms the second part render conceivable that no fewer than 14 philosophers and theologians—mostly American— reacted to it, partly positively and partly critically. The contributions to this discussion were published, together with Abe's detailed answer, in three issues of *Japanese Religions* in 1964, 1966, and 1968, to be sure under the title "Symposium."[4]

In a foreword to the first of these issues the then editor Tetsuro Ariga remarked, *inter alia*, that Abe had been "an ardent believer of Shin Buddhism, but chiefly under the influence of Dr. Hisamatsu, was being drawn to the side of Zen" and attempts today to reach the "basic truth of religion in which both Zen and the Amida faith in their traditional forms are rooted." He says further that Abe also has a great interest in Christian thinking and has read much theological literature.[5] At a weekend retreat at Kailua Beach which occurred in the context

---

[3]JR 3/2 (1963): 10-22, and 3/3: 8-31.

[4]"A Symposium on Christianity and Buddhism continued: Replies to Professor Abe," JR 4/1 (1964): 5-56; 4/2 (1966): 3-25, and "Professor Abe's Reply to the Debate, Part I," JR 4/2 (1966): 26-57; 2nd part under the title "Christianity and Buddhism centering around Science and Nihilism," JR 5/3 (1968): 36-62.

[5]JR 4/1 (1964): 3-4.

of a meeting of representatives of Buddhism and Christianity in the summer of 1980,[6] Abe confirmed these biographical assertions and added to them the statement that he had originally become an "unbeliever" under the influence of Nietzsche and Marx, and that he was not able to stay with Shin Buddhism because he found it too narrow, and that he had only found in Zen Buddhism the religious openness he sought.

Among the first participants of the Symposium, those of special interest to us are Charles Hartshorne, Winston King, Nels Ferré, I. I. Ramsey and Hans Waldenfels in whose contributions to the discussion Abe also frequently appears.[7] He seizes the opportunity to expand upon the fundamental and material statements of his introduction, and to augment them with new aspects. In an article that appeared in 1971 he gets to speak in particular on the problem of "Man and Nature in Christianity and Buddhism."[8] In an issue that appeared in 1975 he once more summarizes in a concise form "the decisive points" of a decade-long conversation for the purpose of its further expansion. In the same issue there are contributions by Ernst Benz along with Paul Wienphal and Winston King,[9] and in the following year the series of contributions to the discussion is continued by Thomas J. J. Altizer, Fritz Buri, Horst Bürkle, and Hans Waldenfels.[10]

Abe's answer to these essential contributions is still outstanding. But as is apparent from the inauguration of the "East-West-Religions in Encounter" in Hawaii and also from the International Congress of the History of Religion held in Winnipeg the same year, at which the individual participants of the "Symposium" personally met with Masao Abe, the conversation continues, and it is to be hoped that *Japanese Religions* again opens its columns to him, for without a doubt Abe has brought about a very meaningful meeting of Buddhism and Christianity, both through the way he fundamentally conceived and carried out this conversation, as well as through the substance which he has given it by his expositions so far. Both factors—the theoretical and material—make their appearance in an impressive way in the opening essay of the Symposium, in a way to be sure that a certain discrepancy becomes apparent between them—a discrepancy connected with the fact that Abe not only sees problems in Buddhism and Christianity, but that such are also to be found in the manner of argumentation with which he points them out and believes he can eliminate them.

---

[6]Conference on Buddhist-Christian Renewal and the Future of Humanity, University of Hawaii, 15-27 July 1980.

[7]JR 4/1 (1964): 5-56; 4/2 (1966): 3-57; 5/3 (1968): 36-62.

[8]JR 7/1 (1971): 1-10.

[9]JR 8/4-5 (1975): 1-53.

[10]JR 9/1 (1975): 1-56.

In the *first, methodological part* of the article here under discussion Abe explains that it is no longer in order to debate Christianity and Buddhism on the basis of the different doctrines of faith which these religions represent,[11] certainly not in the way it still happens among religious scholars who see in religion something "self-evident."[12] Such a juxtapositioning of Buddhism and Christianity today is "only a part" of the much more comprehensive problem of the challenge to religion whereby "all religions, Buddhism and Christianity included, [are] being exposed to the devastating attack of several anti-religious forces," above all, scientism, Marxism, and nihilism.[13]

But now Abe connects this problem of "antireligionism," over against which Buddhism and Christian are to be seen today in a common defensive front, with a different contemporary problem, namely, with the "problem of the man's self-estrangement" which consists in the fact that "man can no more trust himself and hence finds himself in the vacuum of meaninglessness."[14] Although he does not say so expressly, it must be assumed that he sees the cause of this "general problem" not only in the "anti-religious forces" which he names, but also in the present condition of Buddhism and Christianity when he postulates that they "are today obliged not to remain within the limits of their traditional patterns," but must "break through these limits so as to reveal their purest and most essential qualities," which is only possible if they subject themselves "to the severest kind of self-criticism." This means that with regard to their being under attack as religion they may consider "the truth of religion" as this has occurred in recent years "by especially adopting positions toward Buddhism and Christianity" as we find in the Japanese philosophers of religion, Nishida, Tanabe, Hisamatsu, and Nishitani.[15]

When Abe explains that the question, "Buddhism and Christianity," can only be discussed today under this "double aspect" of their being under a common attack and of the problematic of meaning of modern man, and this in such a way that thereby religion would be able "to overpower all negation," it can nevertheless be asked whether he is dealing ultimately with a repetition of the apologetic which is rejected by him as untimely; and whether this not only continues it in a new form, in that he would like to assume that "the truth of religion" appears only when the "ossified patterns of tradition" are broken through.[16] Abe asks neither whether there are not in the anti-religious phenomena mentioned longings

---

[11]JR 3/2 (1963): 20.
[12]Ibid., 21.
[13]Ibid., 14-15, 22.
[14]Ibid., 14.
[15]Ibid., 15, 21.
[16]Ibid., 22.

for meaning and actualization of meaning, nor whether he can show concretely how the problematic of meaning can be overcome, but they are in his view a "devastating attack"[17] in that they reject religion and even therein acquire for him a positive significance, because in this way Buddhism and Christianity have reason under this aspect of religious hostility which concerns them equally to understand themselves better than before. In a later essay, dated 1974, in which he presents scientism, psychoanalysis, Marxism, and nihilism as "challenges to religion," he can even praise these as "a great grace for religion," in that through this conflict they are led to become "creative [and] productive in the future."[18]

In view of this apologetically colored program of a new view of the relationship of both religions under the sign of their mutual threat, its own problematic becomes evident in his deliberation, and this in a threefold way: First, contrary to his demand that one should not rely on the "historical" externals of doctrine, but interpret them "in a religious-philosophical manner," and that means for Abe existentially,[19] of all things he contrasts such bits of Christian and Buddhist traditional doctrine with one another. Second, he applies the "existential" interpretation only to Buddhist terms, or believes that they can be understood as having had this sense all along, whereas he presents the Christian in its orthodox ossification and, where he considers it in an "existential form," this is anything but existential. The consequence of this is that, third, in a comparison of the two with respect to the present situation the main thing that stands out is only the superiority of the Buddhist position over the Christian one, and that it does not become manifest what Buddhism has to learn from such a Christianity about the deficiencies that attach to it, as previously acknowledged.

This threefold problematic is also exhibited in all its urgency in the *second, substantial part* of Abe's essay.[20] It begins with the Christian doctrine of "creatio ex nihilo" in order to work out a comparison of the "Christian God and the Buddha" and "Nothingness in Christianity and Buddhism," as well as the differences that issue from it on the points that are essential to both.

By appealing to Barth[21] and Bultmann[22] he determines that the doctrine of *creatio ex nihilo* is not to be understood cosmologically in terms of a worldview, or anthropologically, but "existentially," that is, as statements of faith in God as Creator or Redeemer who created the world "out of free will," but in such a way that it is "constantly threatened by nothingness," and that God redeemed man,

---

[17]Ibid., 14.
[18]"Religion Challenged by Modern Thought," JR 8/2 (1974): 14.
[19]JR 3/2 (1963): 17ff.
[20]JR 3/3 (1963): 8-31.
[21]Ibid., 9-10.
[22]Ibid., 12-13.

who does not recognize his "nothingness" of which "original sin" consists, "through his Son who in his death "has assumed man's sinful nihility as his own responsibility."

There arises from this for Abe a double distinction between the "Christian God and Buddha." First, whereas for Christian faith God is "absolutely transcendent Being" and as "eternal life" overcomes "nonbeing and death," the Buddha is in "nondiscriminating wisdom," "beyond being and nonbeing," and is in "realization" of his true "such-ness" which is simultaneously Nirvana. Second, whereas "the transcendent God of creation and revelation" is *"absolutely other* to man and the world," the Buddha "is none other than the Awakened One," who "awakens to his original Self," that is, "the True Self as the absolute *Self*."[23]

At the bottom of this is the difference of the conception of "nothingness in Buddhism and Christianity." Whereas in the latter the "nihility which stamps all creatures with creatureliness, finitude, mortality, and so forth—in contrast to the absolute God who is eternal life—represents a "privative principle" which to the extent that it is to be overcome is merely "relative," in Buddhism it is a matter of "doing away with the dichotomy" in a "nondiscriminating Wisdom," which in its "nondiscrimination" is not to be distinguished from "discriminating mind,"[24] but is "the standpoint of the Absolute Nothingness" which is "beyond relative nonbeing" and "therefore is able to let relative being and relative nonbeing stand and work in their relativity"—as an "absolutely affirmative principle."[25]

It cannot be said that in the compact presentation which he here devotes to the concept of Absolute Nothingness Abe has succeeded in sufficiently clarifying its nature. What is expressed does satisfy him, but sets him in opposition to the "Christian God and his self-negation,"[26] in that by adopting a position on the generation of the Son before creation it emphasizes that in the self-negation of God that occurs in it, it only represents a "higher self-affirmation" that includes it,[27] and that therein—in contrast to the "Great Death"[28] that belongs essentially to the idea of the Buddha—"the dualism is not completely overcome," so that the personalism that belongs essentially to Christianity" is grounded in it.[29]

With the concept of "Christian personalism" Abe comes to speak of "the most crucial points" of his comparison. The first he sees in the fact that Chris-

---

[23]Ibid., 15.
[24]Ibid., 20.
[25]Ibid., 21.
[26]Ibid., 21ff.
[27]Ibid., 23.
[28]Ibid., 24.
[29]Ibid., 25.

tianity, because of the "special position" which it assigns to man "as a being
responsible to God," on the one hand experiences difficulties with modern
science which understands everything "mechanistically," and thus sees itself rendered problematic in its "ideas of a personal God and of divine Providence," and
on the other, it confronts today an "active nihilism" of a Nietzschean stamp
which is determined "to bear with the nihility . . . without God."[30]

In contrast to the state of affairs that is negative for Christianity, the
Buddhist principle of Absolute Nothingness or the nondiscriminating Wisdom is
in his view not unknown to the impersonal rationality of modern science and the
radical negativity of nihilism," and they cannot "destroy" it, "because in
Buddhism man and nature are not distinguished from each other in sharp opposition"; "Buddhism rather opens up a horizon within which both man (self) and
nature may attain emancipation." The Buddhist "naturalness" "provides the *topos*
of the Absolute Nothingness where all relative things may perform their relative
roles, each retaining its own particularity. This is precisely the sphere of nondiscriminating Wisdom which is at the same time Great Mercy "where everything
is 'of itself' and 'as it is'."[31]

In spite of this superiority of Buddhism—emphasized by Abe—in the way
it is possible quite differently from Christianity to establish a relationship to modern science and nihilism "without losing its own religiousness," Abe does not
hesitate to concede that "a difficult problem" arises for Buddhism precisely in
this connection, namely, how it can find the "basis of ethical responsibility and
man's social and historic action," and he admits that Buddhism—"with the exception of Pure Land Buddhism, especially Shin Buddhism"—"does not always
struggle with [these questions] seriously enough." In this connection its personalism and clear distinction between God and man give Christianity an advantage.
It is therefore timely to ask, Abe thinks, "whether and how the problems of
ethics and history can be solved from the standpoint of a completely "nondicho-
tomic" naturalness,[32] but he remarks here that this is possible from the perspective of an appropriately developed doctrine of karma and of the Bodhisattva, if
"in a somewhat different way from Christianity."[33]

Although Abe maintains that a fruitful conversation between Christianity and
Buddhism is possible on the basis of such a two-pronged concession of its problematic with reference to the contemporary spiritual situation, the *numerous
answers* which appear in two successive issues of *Japanese Religions*,[34] are not

---

[30]Ibid., 26-27.
[31]Ibid., 28-29.
[32]Ibid., 29ff.
[33]Ibid., 30n.21.
[34]JR 4/1 (1964) and 4/2 (1966).

very productive. From many sides, which appeal to mystical experience,[35] to Thomas Aquinas,[36] and Teilhard de Chardin,[37] opposition comes to Abe's use of the doctrine of *creation ex nihilo* in terms of Barth's Christological understanding of it as a basic Christian doctrine.[38] It is here objected that in view of nothing-ness and the exclusion of nondiscriminative thinking nothing at all remains that can be affirmed or denied,[39] and over against this negativism reference is made to the positive significance, especially for ethical responsibility, of these phenomena which are considered by Abe to be hostile to religion.[40] We shall not here go into the brief remarks of Hartshorne, for whom Abe is too little rela-tivistic, and the longer response of Waldenfels, because we shall speak later of Process Philosophy in connection with Abe's confrontation with it, and because we have already taken a stand on Waldenfel's position in terms of his book on "Absolute Nothingness" at the conclusion of our chapter on Nishitani.

Even Abe's "Answer to Comment and Criticism"[41] does not lead much further, but mainly consists of repetitions of his earlier statements. It is true that, over against the representatives of Western mystical experience, he correctly em-phasizes that Buddhism "should not be taken as a natural mysticism;"[42] but his equation of a "Christological" with an "existential" understanding of the doctrine of creatio ex nihilo remains a misunderstanding of the intention of both of these ways of understanding.[43] Similarly he reiterates—but this time not correctly—that the dualism in Christianity grounded in the transcendence of God cannot be over-come by the doctrine of incarnation.[44] But from his introduction of the term "soku"[45] in the negation of negation—a term which is characteristic of Buddhist logic—which "as absolute negation is simultaneously absolute affirmation," it becomes apparent how Buddhism attains what Abe misses in Christianity: "the identity" of the "realization of absolute nothingness" with the "realization of the true self"—except he thereby meant the nonobjectifiability of Being and the self, which is not possible, however, without "discriminative thinking," or, more pre-cisely, only by means of recognizing the latter's limitations, which again is that

---

[35]JR 4/1 (1964): 15, 41ff.
[36]Ibid., 38.
[37]Ibid., 24ff.
[38]Ibid., 48ff.
[39]JR 4/1 (1964): 45; 4/2 (1966): 6.
[40]JR 4/2 (1966): 8ff.
[41]JR 4/2 (1964): 30ff.
[42]JR 4/2 (1966): 39.
[43]JR 3/3 (1963): 13ff.
[44]JR 4/2 (1966): 39.
[45]Ibid., 43ff.

very faculty's most characteristic trait and not the business of a "nondiscriminating wisdom," which sacrifices such discriminating thought, and would in this
respect be indistinguishable from a mysticism doing the same, which Abe rejects.
This then is the only justification for Abe's explaining that his answer is "open
to further criticism."[46]

In a "second part of his answer," published two years later,[47] Abe concerns
himself especially with the questions about "Science and Nihilism," stating that
"the Buddhist realization of sunyata or of nondiscriminative thinking" is "not
something in opposition to discriminative thinking," but rather stands "beyond
all discursive or discriminative thinking constructions of the understanding" and
thus "is freed from the opposition between discriminating and nondiscriminating
thinking," but can "in principle" include "in its true nature of emptiness" "all discriminating knowledge." Because in its long history it has never been confronted
"with the autonomous pure reason" by means of which modern Western science
has been in a position to ground itself as "science," it is "a future task of
Buddhism to actualize the possibility of embracing real, scientific rationality in
terms of Non-discriminative Wisdom."[48]

Despite this meaningful reduced estimate of Buddhism with respect to the
relationship of its truth to the scientific thinking of the West, Abe subjects
Teilhard de Chardin,[49] Nietzsche[50] and the Death of God theology[51] to a sharp
critique from the standpoint of Buddhism, showing by these examples that
Western thinking is not in a position to unite science and the Christian religion,
because it cannot overcome the problem of monism-dualism in the "nonduality"
of "emptiness," which is at the same time the "true self."[52]

During a longer interruption of the Symposium there appeared in *Japanese
Religions* an essay from Abe on "Man and Nature in Christianity and Buddhism,"[53] in which he finally comes to speak not only to the questions of dualism
dealt with in the course of the Symposium, by which Christianity distinguishes
itself from Buddhism, and to the problem of personalism connected with it, but
also refers to his previous deliberations with respect to them.[54] In his view the
"homocentric nature of Christian redemption," in consequence of which "man

---

[46]Ibid., 56.
[47]JR 5/3 (1968): 36-62.
[48]Ibid., 40.
[49]Ibid., 40ff.
[50]Ibid., 49ff.
[51]Ibid., 53ff.
[52]Ibid., 48ff.
[53]JR 7/1 (1971): 1-10.
[54]Ibid., 7ff.

alone is created in the image of God" and "can respond to the Word of God," stands in "striking contrast" to the way in which in Buddhism man belongs "in one class" with living and even nonliving beings.[55] In Buddhism the "problem of birth and death" which engages him is seen not only in the "dimension of arising and passing away," but in the still further "cosmological-ontological dimension" of "being and nonbeing," in which man becomes aware "in the depths of his own existence" of his "solidarity" in the "transitoriness common to all beings," both living and nonliving, in such a way, to be sure, that in this "boundary-less dimension of naturalness" "man and nature are equally illumined," because "the impermanence which is as such completely realized is itself transcended."[56] This happens "only to a human being who is fully conscious of himself." "Man alone can be aware of universal transitoriness as such." "In this sense" "Buddhism is concerned in the deepest sense with the individual self, with the person, that is, man as man."[57] But this "homocentrism" is "transcended" in the fact man " 'dies' in the death of his own ego. For only through the death of his own ego is the cosmological dimension, the dimension of [naturalness], opened up to him."

Is man "by realizing impermanence as the essence of everything whatsoever" "freed from its bondage, not only psychologically but also ontologically?" Abe asks himself this question at this place and characterizes the answer to this question as "the crux of the problem." This question is not to be answered in a conceptual thinking in which one thinks "birth and death" can be distinguished from one another "as two different realities" and can view them "from outside" "by taking one of the two as his standpoint," or even from a "third position."[58] In order to attain to "reality," not only "the duality of life and death," but the other "dualities" previously mentioned must be "transcended." Ultimate realty is only reached when one subjects "his own existence" to the all-encompassing "duality of being and non-being," in which one actualizes the "universal transitoriness" and is included in this realization in which "the oneness of realizer and the realized is attained," which is "an ontological, not a psychological awareness par excellence," "absolutely inseparable from its existential and personalistic aspect," as then "the cosmological dimension is opened up, not objectively, but subjectively through one's existential realization of the absolutely universal transitoriness." The "mediating point, or place of confrontation, of the cosmological and the personal aspects," however, "is the death of one's own ego."[59]

---

[55]Ibid., 2ff.
[56]Ibid., 4, 9.
[57]Ibid., 4.
[58]Ibid., 5.
[59]Ibid., 6.

Abe can thus summarize the nature of "Buddhist redemption" by saying that it "is nothing other than awakening to Reality through the death of the ego, i.e. the existential realization of the transiency common to all things in the universe, seeing the universe really *as it is*." In this way "one is liberated from undue attachment to things and ego-self, humanity and the world, and is then able to live and work creatively in the world." It is only this that constitutes the so-called "Buddha nature," which is "in everyone and everything" as the "realization of universal transitoriness or [naturalness] in which every*one* and every*thing* discloses itself as it is truly in itself," and is simultaneously the origin of the "Buddhist life of wisdom and compassion."[60]

Additionally, Abe discusses the relationship in which "Man's finitude and Faith in God" stand to one another in Christianity and in Buddhism. In Christianity, as he determines on the basis of passages from Romans, the finality of man is understood in relation to "divine justice and divine love," before which "death is the wages of sin" and through which this is overcome in "faith in Christ" as the "mediator" and the incarnation of the transcendent God.[61] In Buddhism, on the contrary, death is "only one instance of that transiency which is common to all things whatsoever in the universe"—a transiency that is "so deep that it can not be overcome even by the supernatural," but as such represents the "naturalness" in whose realization one becomes—without a supernatural, transcendent God or a "mediator"—"a real person, that is, an awakened one who has compassion and wisdom for all things in the universe."[62] Besides the existential and personalistic aspect claimed for both,[63] according to Abe both have in common that they "transcend man and nature," but with the difference that in Christianity this proceeds in the direction of the "supernatural God," whereas in Buddhism it proceeds in the direction of "naturalness," which is "identical with the Buddha nature or with 'Suchness'."[64]

3. The Continuation of the Symposium

Nine, or seven, years after his answer to the echo of his article on "Christianity and Buddhism as a Problem for Today," Abe gives an excellent, concise summary of the contents of the course of the Symposium up to that time, as we have taken notice of it above. On the basis of his reformulation of the status of the problem—the placing in question of Christian personalism by science and nihilism, and the ethical problematic of Buddhist nondiscriminating wisdom or

---

[60]Ibid., 7.
[61]Ibid., 8.
[62]Ibid., 9ff.
[63]Ibid.
[64]Ibid., 10.

naturalness—Abe provides the bold watchword for the further course of the Symposium: "We shall have to face our problems as problems, forgetting the conventional ways of distinguishing Buddhism and Christianity."[65]

In the same and the following issue of *Japanese Religions*[66] seven contributions appear which exceed the earlier ones in scope and content, but scarcely correspond in every respect to the intention of the initiators of the Symposium. The authors and the titles of these contributions are, in the order of their appearance:

Ernst Benz (University of Marburg), "Buddhism and Christianity"

Paul Wienphal (University of California), "Religion and Modes of Being"

Winston L. King (Colorado State University), "The Impersonal Personalism and Subjectivism of Buddhist 'Nihilism'"

Thomas J. J. Altizer (State University of New York), "Buddhism and Christianity: A radical Christian Viewpoint"

Fritz Buri (Basel University), "Encounter on the Basis of the Question of Meaning"

Horst Bürkle (University of Munich), "The Actualization of Buddhist Thought and its Relevance for Christian Theology"

Hans Waldenfels (Düsseldorf), "Searching for Common Ways"

To illustrate the course of this conversation with Abe we shall focus only on the contributions of King and Altizer, and of mine as well.

Whereas Wienphal, through an unclear general concept of Being,[67] and Bürkle in an equally unfounded way, attempt to introduce the specifically Christian concept of the "new being in Christ" as the "mystery of faith"[68]—which in any case should be noted as the characterization of their contributions—Winston L. King, in a sharp analysis of Abe's argumentation, refers to its fundamental problematic, which consists in the ontologizing of what Abe understands by existentializing. Thereby he fails to consider that the way in which Abe equates "Christological" and "existential" in respect to Christianity amounts to an obvious misunderstanding of Barth's Christological exposition of the biblical story of creation and redemption which Abe uses as an example of the existential understanding of creatio ex nihilo. King does not criticize this in Abe on this basis, because he himself in his "religious experience" represents a similar, only somewhat less orthodox understanding of Christ.[69] Much more, he engages Abe, reproaching him for the fact that the ontologizing and universalizing of individual

---

[65]JR 8/4 (1975): 6.

[66]JR 9/1 (1976): 1-60.

[67]JR 9/1 (1976): 27ff.

[68]JR 9/1 (1976): 26ff.

[69]JR 8/4 (1975): 37ff.

enlightenment represented by him by appealing to Dogen either does not reach beyond the experienceable sphere of things and the self which is said to be transcended precisely in the Great Death, but at best into its "depths,[70]" or into an "absolute subjectivism" of an "idealistic metaphysics;"[71] all of this shows the unclarity of his concept of transcendence since neither of them corresponds to Abe's intention.[72] To excuse—but not to justify—Abe, reference is made to the Yogacara philosophy also mentioned by King and the notion of a "store-consciousness"[73] in whose tradition Zen philosophy, and especially Abe's teacher Nishitani, stands. The descendants of the Buddha will have to face the fact that they have failed to pay attention to his admonition about metaphysical speculation—a matter to which Bürkle refers by appealing to Hajime Nakamura's misunderstanding of Buddhism.[74] In so far as Waldenfels—as already in his first contribution to the conversation[75]—supposedly attempts once again to solve the problem of immanence-transcendence by a connection of natural theology, or anthropology, and the theology of revelation, in that he does not basically get beyond the concession that it is a problem for Christianity,[76] he can know that with the Buddhists he is "searching for common ways," whereby for him dogma, like metaphysics, is not only the cause for the seeking for a way, but is as well a hindrance to finding it.

From my side, I am not inclined to fault Mahayana Buddhism in general or Abe as a Zen philosopher for their metaphysics, for to speak of a self that deals with the realization of the meaning of its existence is not possible without metaphysics, that is, without taking account of the ground of all Being and of its meaning. In my contribution[77] I rather raise three principal objections against Abe's metaphysics in which he identifies nothingness with "Being-as-it-is," with the "true self" and the Buddha in a supposedly "nonobjectifying knowing:" First, that there is no knowing without objectivity; rather we always confront it already in the subject-object schema of our consciousness. Second, that we can become aware of nothingness only within this structure of our conscious thinking, to be sure as its absolute boundary at the mystery of Being and of its meaning. And, third, that becoming aware of the nonexchangeability of our self in the search for being and meaning represents a special revelation of the mystery of being, whose

---

[70]Ibid., 49-50.
[71]Ibid., 51-52.
[72]Ibid., 52.
[73]Ibid., 44, 52ff.
[74]JR 9/1 (1976): 27ff.
[75]JR 4/2 (1966): 13-25.
[76]JR 9/1 (1976): 50.
[77]JR 9/1 (1976): 12ff.

realization in our being responsible in personal community can be neither institutionalized nor universalized. As symbols, that is, as forms of objective discourse about the nonobjectifiability of being and the self, or as possibilities for an existential understanding of the traditional material that occasions it, I recommend "creation out of nothing" in two different functional ways.

On the one hand, *creatio ex nihilo* can serve as a symbol for the mystery of being as the absolute boundary of objectifying thinking; on the other, of being destined for responsible personhood and the community that is to be formed in correspondence with it—a being destined which is not to be explained, but only clarified in this knowing. For this significance of personal realization of meaning named in the second place both the mythology of the Christ and the Bodhisattva figures can be used, in such a way to be sure that the former must be extracted from an illusory eschatology and the latter, from, circular speculation, but then united into a general human redemptive symbol of the Buddha-Christ.

While I agree with King's warning about an exchanging of existentializing with ontologizing and believe that I comply with it by virtue of these symbols of human self-understanding; the equally pedantic and abstruse discussions of Altizer's[78] are not, in my opinion, doing justice to this concern raised against Abe, given that they fail to clarify how the dichotomy in God, which, in his opinion, represents a Buddhist misconception of Christianity, can meaningfully be replaced by a dualism that could be overcome only from an eschatological perspective. Altizer's metaphysical speculation on the love of God is a *Heilsgeschichte* gone astray in speculation; its untenable nature Abe already uncovered in his answer to the earlier contributions to the Symposium.[79]

Unfortunately, Abe has not declared himself so far on the further contributions to the discussion which were reviewed above. But it is only regrettable in view of the specific status of the discussion which developed with these last contributions to this Symposium. For before and since the temporary conclusion of the Symposium Abe expressed himself on the themes dealt with and the question that arose, in numerous other statements, and this more thoroughly and in greater detail than was possible for him in this series of articles, so that in respect to his conception of Buddhism and his position toward Christianity which issues from it sufficient material is available to us. In this sense we may refer to an essay from his pen which has since appeared in *Japanese Religion*—an essay that derives from the Symposium except that this one—as distinguished from those followed previously—is carried out, not in written, but in oral form and also with other participants.

---

[78]Ibid., 1ff.
[79]JR 5/3 (1968): 53ff.

The article to be mentioned which here carries the title "Zen as Self-Awakening,"[80] consists of Abe's introduction and his report on the discussion that followed it, which already started during the lecture, so that we have to do with the transcription of a conversation as it actually occurred. The immediate onset of questions which were apparently generated by the extremely compact form of Abe's elucidations accounts completely for their explanatory character which a conversation must unavoidably assume on such central questions as are here discussed.

Abe begins his deliberations by explaining to his Protestant and Catholic partners in conversation that it is more conducive for a "real and creative mutual understanding" to consider the differences that obtain between Christianity and Zen than the "affinity" which both have to one another "as religions."[81] Such essential differences between the two he sees in the contrasts of "God-Nothingness, faith-enlightenment, salvation-self-awakening."[82] Although he stresses that he is not concerned to show the "superiority of Zen to Christianity,"[83] he sets out to uncover the problematic character of the Christian position—as he understands it[84] and its overcoming in Zen under all three aspects. Over against the Christian assertion of the uniqueness of God as the Creator, which is embarrassed by the question of the "whence" of this One, he sets Buddhist nothingness which is "beyond the subject-object dualism" in which that question is inevitably posed,[85] as well as even the doctrine of "interdependent origination" (*pratitya-samutpada*) on the basis of which it cannot arrive at the origin of this question and therewith to the embarrassment connected with it.[86] From the perspective of this fundamental Buddhist doctrine he faults not only the Christian doctrine of God but also its Christology for the fact that its God-world, or God-man relation "is not completely reciprocal," and that as far as redemption is concerned, in Zen, man is redeemed not so much from his sin as from his "finitude," which "is so deep and so radical it cannot even be overcome by faith, not even through the work of the divine other power."[87] It is only through the insight which is grounded in enlightenment "that good and evil are like any other thing, interdependently originated," so that no one can be without the other, and between them there obtains "no priority."

---

[80]JR 8/2 (1975): 25-45.

[81]Ibid., 25.

[82]Ibid., 26.

[83]Ibid., 25.

[84]Ibid., 27, 29, 33.

[85]Ibid., 26-27.

[86]Ibid., 28ff.

[87]Ibid., 30-31.

To the intervening question, whether to being "born in enlightenment" there pertains "a priority of good over evil," he answers with the "Pauline thought that the more we try to do good, the more we become aware of the evil in ourselves."[88] A faith that hopes God will solve this problem in the future is only a vain postponement of it that does not do justice to the fact "that I do not *have* an aporia [between good and evil], but that *I am* an aporia in this sense." In the escalation of this dilemma of existential being into nothingness itself he sees at the same time its overcoming, which he describes, in a way typical for his Zen understanding, as follows:

> In the final and deepest realization of the dilemma between good and evil, the structure of my ego collapses and I come to the realization that I am not simply good, nor simply bad. I am neither good nor bad. I am nothing whatsoever. However, this realization is not negative, but positive, because in the full realization of Nothingness we are liberated from the dichotomy of good and evil, life and death. At that point we awaken to our true nature. That is the reason why Zen often asks us to see our "original face" as it is previous to any distinction between good and evil. Enlightenment is precisely to see "one's original face."[89]

In view of this conception of redemption in Zen Abe points out two differences from that of Christianity, one of which is univocal, while the other in his view is not. Univocity obtains insofar as for Zen "the essential point is not faith in God, but realization of Nothingness and awakening to one's true nature." On the contrary: as "the logical conclusion of the Buddhist idea of dependent origination," in consequence of which "not only good and evil, but life and death, God and man, are interdependent," "Buddha—understood as something beyond man—must be killed."

It is a different matter with respect to the understanding of Being and Nothingness in Zen and in Christianity. According to his view it would be "an oversimplification to say that Zen is based on Nothingness, while Christianity is based on God as being, in contrast to nonbeing." If that were so, "Zen and Christianity would be entirely without any correspondence."[90] In order to take account of this "possibility of correspondence" between the two, Abe believes he is able to correct that false distinction by saying that in his view Christianity in its conception of the world and redemption is "not so much ontological as it is axiological"; that is, "the most significant point is not the issue of being and

---

[88]Ibid., 31.
[89]Ibid., 32.
[90]Ibid., 33.

nonbeing, but the question of what I ought to do,"[91] and therefore the question of "righteousness," to be sure in connection with that of "love," and to be sure, according to both factors on the side of God as well as man. In Buddhism to the contrary, above all in Zen, he concedes that "the idea of justice represented by the 'ought to' is rather lacking, or at least very weak." And he concedes further that "Zen's criticism of the Christian view of the one God, based upon the Buddhist idea of dependent origination, does not necessarily hit the core of, or do justice to the essence of Christianity," because it is to be understood not merely ontologically, but axiologically.

Although in this connection he does not expressly apply the term axiological to the Zen Buddhist conception of redemption, it could be concluded from the fact that he explains, "In Zen and Christianity ontological and axiological aspects are inseparably connected," that he understands the Zen Buddhist conception of redemption not only ontologically—as it might seem on the basis of the appeal to dependent origination—but axiologically. The difference between Christianity and Buddhism consists according to Abe in this respect only in a different accenting of both aspects, but in such a way that the "ontological understanding of Nothingness" in Zen and the "axiological emphasis on God's 'ought to' " in Christian faith literally form the "crossing point" of these two [religions].[92] From this situation, which he in conclusion makes more precise by saying that "the strength in Zen is the weakness in Christianity" and that the same holds "vice versa," there results for Abe the necessity as well as the possibility of "[entering] into dialogue."[93]

In the discussion in which this occurs, the major issue is the concept of "person,"[94] and the related consciousness of guilt and the need for redemption[95] or the rendering problematic of ethical action by the becoming nothing of the ego which is demanded by Zen,[96] and positively, the question about attaining to the "true self in zazen practice," which seems to be superfluous when Buddhism emphasizes that one is "already inseparable from self-awakening" and is "already experiencing this as a part of our original being," but even as "the experience of nothingness."[97]

In reference to the "feeling of guilt" as something "unborn," Abe refers on the one hand to the fact that in place of it Buddhism speaks of "suffering" as an

---

[91]Ibid.
[92]Ibid., 34.
[93]Ibid., 35.
[94]Ibid., 37.
[95]Ibid., 35.
[96]Ibid., 36.
[97]Ibid., 41.

"ontological issue," and on the other hand concedes that, in so far as it deals with an "ethical relation between men," it is for Buddhism "not so crucial, even if it is not excluded,"[98] but without more clearly explaining this.

The question, which remains to be dealt with by us, "whether we are absolutely nothingness," and how this is related to our personal being, Abe answers with the counterquestion, what then is meant by this self, and states in longer explanations[99] that it always deals with an "objectification of the non-objectifiable," which for this reason is nothingness—but "not a nothingness that is still something that is only called nothingness," but "true nothingness which cannot be distinguished as a merely negative nothingness from being something," but "neither something nor nothingness," rather "including both," both "root and source" and thus also "the root of your subjectivity, of your life, of your activity in society and history . . . the point of departure for your activity," as Abe concluded his statement about "the true self" in a personal address.[100] But quite apart from the fact that he explains in relation to the formulation frequently used, "I am nothingness, and nothingness is me" that it means "self-awakening," which could be called "the realization of the Buddha," is "dynamic" and consists of "complete openness" and "freedom," he is able to say nothing positive about it; and about all that is meant by it, how it is realized and gets worked out, he is silent.[101]

Abe's answer to the question about the meaning of *zazen* turns out to be just as little positive, in that he on the one hand speaks of an "unbridgeable gap" between a "so-called illusion and a so-called enlightenment," yet on the other, of a "dynamic unity of being on the way and having reached the goal," which could occur at any time "in the process of practice" if we "realize concerning the awareness of the limitations of this approach that we are not simply on the way to enlightenment but have already been in enlightenment." It is significant, although it does not awaken confidence, that Abe at the suggestion of one of the (female) partners in conversation, accepted the interaction of future and present eschatology in the New Testament as a "Christian parallel" to this understanding of zazen.[102]

The problematic character of this alleged correspondence between the not-yet and the already-now of redemption with Zen practice and the early Christian conception of *Heilsgeschichte*, or in that which becomes of it in Christianity, becomes clear when Abe concludes the discussion by posing to the Christian

---

[98]Ibid., 35.
[99]Ibid., 36ff.
[100]Ibid., 37.
[101]Ibid., 43.
[102]Ibid., 42.

faith in God "directed to action" the "ontologically oriented Zen question," what is the ground [of faith in] the one God? and simultaneously explains: "Zen must learn more about this ground of the Christian faith in God," whereby this "learning" is to be understood in the sense of to experience more accurately.[103]

Especially in respect to the difference between Zen and Christianity regarding their ontological, or ethical nature—a difference here noted once again by Abe—not only Buddhist, but also Christians could still learn a thing or two. For in its origin, Christian faith was not by any means "concerned with action," as Abe thinks, and this precisely because of its "ontological orientation," which is quite different from that of Zen, however, namely, of an eschatological kind, one directed toward the activity of God and his Messiah, by which the activity of man is very much restricted, given that, owing to the imminent end of the world, that activity is by no means intent upon changing the world through human action, but is exclusively directed toward surviving the Last Judgment in order to participate in the Kingdom of God, which itself will bring about the great change of the world. While, in consequence of the non-arrival of the Kingdom of God, the supernatural transformation of the world, originally expected for the present world, turned into a hope to be fulfilled in the beyond, there once again emerged, to take its place, but only after its secularization, the idea of a reshaping of the world, but one that now was to be undertaken by humans. Although there are substantial differences in all three attitudes of Christianity toward the world, and in their ontological presuppositions, nonetheless the three alike are different from the Zen Buddhist view in that they do not seek the dissolution of the "I" and the attainment of the "true I," which realizes itself merely in "openness for the world" such as it is, and at the same time in an inner "freedom" from that world, but rather in a state of "personhood" that knows itself to be responsible for its actions, albeit in different ways, each according to the presupposed ontology. Whatever forms these Christian views of Being and the ethical norms resulting therefrom, might present, they clearly differ fundamentally in their structure—even in their forms of mysticism—from Buddhist nothingness and from its corresponding "true self.

Today Buddhism must come to terms with these different forms of Christianity and of their problematic history, even if Abe's Christian conversation partners do not know of this state of affairs, as is evident in the article here reviewed. If in his final word Abe defines Christianity as "justified in its idea of the one God in the sense that He is the living personal God with ethical character, who justifies man in spite of his sinfulness through unconditional love,"[104] and—in view of the expressed opinion—he can count on the agreement of his

---

[103]Ibid., 45.
[104]Ibid., 45.

conversation partners, it nevertheless deals only with a certain conception of Christianity, but in any event with one from which it is to be expected that Zen cannot learn too much in terms of its own deepening.

4. Taking a Position on Whitehead and Tillich

Two articles, one of which one belongs to his first English publications, while the other has just recently appeared, can serve as further examples for the way in which Masao Abe deals with Christianity. These comprise a communication on "Paul Tillich's Christianity and the Encounter of World Religions," in *The Eastern Buddhist* from the year 1975 and Abe's contribution "Substance, Process, and Emptiness" to the conference held in Claremont in October 1979 on "Heidegger, Mahayana Buddhism, and Whitehead," which together with the four other lectures delivered on this occasion have been published in the September 1980 issue of *Japanese Religions*. In contradistinction to the article on "Zen as self-awakening" treated earlier, we have to do in these two works now to be reviewed—unlike in that one—not with a record of a conversational situation, but with Abe's stance on individual positions of Christian theology, or Western philosophy and philosophy of religion from his Buddhist standpoint. We concern ourselves first with the second of the two essays mentioned, his Claremont lecture, because the title of Paul Tillich's book which he reviews gives us reason to introduce a further work of Abe's dedicated to the same theme.

It is especially to be noted of his lecture delivered at Claremont, which consists principally of a confrontation of Whitehead's process philosophy with the Buddhist doctrine of *pratitya-samutpada* in the form in which this doctrine is found in Nagarjuna, that Abe had already dealt with this subject in an earlier publication, which carries the title "Mahayana Buddhism and Whitehead—A View by a Lay Student of Whitehead's Philosophy."[105] As far as the presentation of the points of comparison between the principal matters under debate is concerned, no principal difference obtains between the two articles. Although in the title of this earlier study Abe still described his preoccupation with Whitehead's philosophy as "lay-like," at that time he had already grasped its essentials as he once again presented it fifteen years later—even if somewhat differently. It could be said at best that that self-disclosure—despite its emphasis on the superiority of Buddhism—has since developed to the point that, with respect to the frequent misunderstandings on the Buddhist side, he faces the possibility that "Mahayana Buddhist thinkers can learn a great deal from Whitehead's philosophy," as has been the case prominently in Nishida's philosophy.[106] Of such an application of

---

[105]*Philosophy East and West* (Honolulu: University of Hawaii Press, 1975) 415-28.
[106]Ibid., 427-28.

Whiteheadian philosophy as a "preventative clue against recurrent misunderstandings in interpretation of basic Buddhist ideas[107]—an application which is to
be understood anew in the Mahayana content—there is no longer any trace to be
detected; instead, Whitehead's philosophy here falls completely by the wayside
in face of the now perfectly developed Prajna-paramita logic of Nagarjuna's.

From this concise comparison of the two lectures devoted to the same theme
it is already evident that for the presentation of Abe's view the later is to be preferred to the earlier because of its developed form, but also that we shall have
occasion to remind ourselves of the already mentioned conclusion of the earlier
one, when "the creative and productive dialogue between these" postulated there
by Abe as the goal of a "knowledge of the Western differences" from "Mahayana Buddhism and Whitehead" is promoted, and instead of this the problematic
of the Western standpoint is not only validated in a one-sided way in favor of
Mahayana Buddhism. For with the second opportunity on which Abe concerns
himself with Whitehead, the consciousness of Buddhist superiority appears more
sharply than in the earlier, in that he juxtaposes to process philosophy as its
critique and fulfillment a specific interpretation of the doctrine of "dependent
origination."

In this essay delivered in Claremont[108] Abe pursues a double intention. First,
he is willing to recognize in Whitehead's replacement of the Aristotelian concept
of substance with the notion of a processual becoming "considerable affinity with
Buddhism," insofar as therein the metaphysical basis is stripped from the traditional Christian concept of Creator which is based on Aristotle.[109] Second, however, he sets out to show that Whitehead's idea of process does not attain to the
doctrine of "codependent origination" understood in Nagarjuna's sense, which in
Abe's view alone corresponds to the longing for "redemption" which is common
both to Buddhism and Christianity.[110] But, in a skillful dialectic, Abe also goes
so far as to champion process philosophy over against the Aristotelian metaphysics of Being, only then to unfold over against both the superiority of "dependent
origination" understood in terms of Nagarjuna's "emptiness."

As for the first point—Whitehead's critique of the Aristotelian thinking of
Being—he advances two factors respecting it: the epistemological foundation and
its metaphysical consequences. According to Whitehead, Aristotle's concept of
substance is based on a thinking in the context of a dualistic schema of "subject-
predicate," or "subject-object."[111] For this thinking the subject somehow stands

[107]Ibid., 427.
[108]"Substance, Process, and Emptiness," JR 11/2-3 (1980): 1-34.
[109]Ibid., 9, 11.
[110]Ibid., 15, 23.
[111]Ibid., 6.

"outside of the actual world"[112] and cannot fathom it, but in "its categories" has to do only with "abstractions," which correspond neither to the "flow of events," in which there are no abiding substances, nor to "immediate experience" and its perception and forms of experience. Although Abe from his perspective criticizes Whitehead's replacement of Aristotle's being-like concept of substance by the notion of unceasing becoming and passing away, saying that it basically only deals with a new interpretation of the same, but not with its complete overcoming, he is nevertheless prepared to recognize in it a certain "affinity" to the Buddhist doctrine of "dependent origination." He represents the same Yes and No also in respect to Whitehead's metaphysics. It may well be that as a Buddhist he imposes on him the view that for Whitehead God does not stand over against the world as a transcendent reality, as is the case in Christianity;[113] rather "the world is as immanent in God as God is in the world," so that the relation of both consists in a "becoming-with-one-another" (concrescence), and "ultimate reality" is "not God but creativity."[114] But then Abe reproaches Whitehead for not carrying through his "relational" metaphysics in a thoroughgoing "reciprocal" way, as is the case in Buddhist "dependent origination," in that he still assigns priority to the "One" over against the "many," insofar as he makes a difference between the becoming of the many out of the One and the uniting of the many with the One and permits the former to precede the later in processual happening.[115] This may well correspond to the Christian idea of creation,[116] but it nevertheless represents a inconsistent delimiting of the reciprocity of both factors intended by Whitehead.

In order to clarify the "fundamental difference" which obtains between the two in view of all the "affinity" of Whitehead's process philosophy and Buddhist "dependent origination," Abe points to the fact that the latter—despite the fact that it is formulated in different ways into a "causal chain"—is not to be understood in terms of a causal explanation of events, but as the "nontemporal, logical-ontological" presupposition of all explanations of an event in the context of a cause-effect relation. As Heidegger's "ontological difference between Being and beings" opens the "horizon for the true Metaphysics" in the differentiation of Being and beings," so—thinks Abe—the "codependent-originatological difference is necessary to elucidate the logical ground for the notion of codependent origination thematically in clear distinction from something which happens in terms of codependent origination" (as what is clearly meant by it).

---

[112]Ibid., 8.
[113]Ibid., 15.
[114]Ibid., 10-11.
[115]Ibid., 13, 15.
[116]Ibid., 23.

In—as he says—"somewhat loose parallel to Heidegger's ontological difference" Abe wishes, in relation to the Buddhist doctrine of "codependent origination" to distinguish a twofold applicability: on the one hand, as a so to speak ontical explanation of the causal sequence both as "successive" as well as "simultaneous" and "reciprocal," and on the other, as a "logical-ontological" grounding of the "apparently" logical contradiction in the double conception of causality, for which he coins the concept of "codependent originatology" in contrast to "codependent origination."[117]

According to Abe's own judgment, this distinction only formally represents a parallel to Heidegger's distinction between ontic and ontological, while it is materially of a different kind and this in a twofold respect. With the ontological difference Heidegger wishes in a conceptually univocal distinction between Being and beings to secure the nature of Being as the nonobjectifiable ground of beings and so prevent God from being made into a thing as happens in the so-called causal proof for God. Abe, however, represents a "codependent originatological difference" which makes logically possible the simultaneity of temporally successive, nontemporally simultaneous, reciprocal causality functioning in only one direction, which represents a contradiction for conceptual thinking, by allowing it to function as a cause, which is only possible "in the locus of emptiness."[118] For the difference between Heidegger's Difference and that of Abe, it is significant that in the ontological difference of the later Heidegger the concept of nothingness used by him earlier no longer plays a role, but is rather replaced by that of Being, whereas in its place Abe brings into play the concept of "emptiness" which corresponds to the concept of nothingness, for which he appeals to Nagarjuna's sunyata philosophy.

To the unfolding of the logic of thinking, which is understood to be contradictory to the philosophy of Being of the later Heidegger and to Christian theology as well as to Hinayana,[119] in the "place of emptiness" as the true understanding of the doctrine of "codependent origination" and as the fulfillment of Whitehead's intention to conceive "Being" as "Becoming,"[120] is devoted the great concluding part of his lecture on "Substance, Process and Emptiness."[121] In the detailed pursuit of the individual thinkers of this sunyata logic, whose nature consists in the fact that not only all positions, but even their own negations themselves are negated, Abe shows how the elements of the contraries like "God and man," "good and evil," "life and death," "being and nonbeing," "sacred and

---

[117]Ibid., 18-19.
[118]Ibid., 20.
[119]Ibid., 24.
[120]Ibid., 9, 34.
[121]Ibid., 24-34.

profane," "transcendence-immanence," "absolute and relative" are "completely interdependent and reversible."[122] But for the realization of this transobjectivity of emptiness he not only makes a claim for "wisdom," but sees in it also the facilitation of "compassion."[123] Thus we are dealing here not only with a logical grounding of emptiness, but with an existential realization of the emptying of the self in the form of the Bodhisattva and the extension of his "vow" in praxis that is turned toward the world.[124]

As for the special relationship of this interpretation of the doctrine of "dependent origination" as being "synonymous" with "emptiness,"[125] he is of the view that only in that doctrine could likewise the "mutual relationship between God and man" which is also accepted in the "Judeo-Christian tradition," in the doctrine of creation, be given proper recognition of its real "reciprocity." In contrast to Judaism "the core of the Christian faith" lies as is well known not "in God the creator but in God the redeemer, that is, faith in salvation through Jesus Christ as the son of God."[126] For Abe "this eternal birth of the son within God which is understood as a matter prior to creation represents a much deeper standpoint," in so far as therein "creative being is not understood as the "nature" of God but as his manner of appearance." In this connection he also accords to process philosophy a certain recognition, because it overcomes "the concept of God as creator" and instead of this uses for the foundation of Whitehead's metaphysics "the idea of "creativity" as the basic category."[127]

Abe's elevation of the doctrine of redemption as what is essential in Christianity while pushing into the background its doctrine of creation stands parallel to his claim that the Buddha in his conception of "co-dependent origination" which was won in his enlightenment was primarily concerned "not with the metaphysical structure of the universe but with human suffering and release from suffering."[128] In view of this emphasis on the thought of redemption in Christianity as well as Buddhism one could suppose—irrespective of the differing conceptions of its possibility of realization in both religions—that as the driving motif both in the theological and Christological speculation as well as in the no less complicated interpretation of the doctrine of "dependent origination" in terms of Nagarjuna's sunyata logic, the tendency has been toward a solution of the question of meaning at the expense of the question of being. The common basic

---

[122]Ibid., 23.
[123]Ibid., 28.
[124]Ibid., 33.
[125]Ibid., 21.
[126]Ibid., 23.
[127]Ibid., 24.
[128]Ibid., 15.

intention—even though pursued in different ways—is what connects Abe's treatment of process philosophy with the position he takes on Paul Tillich's writing on *Christianity in the Encounter with World Religions.*

In an even more outspoken way than is the case with his exchange with Whitehead's philosophy of religion, the review which Abe devotes to this writing of Tillich's[129] represents an extension of the "Symposium on Buddhism and Christianity" inaugurated by him, because here is dealing not merely, as in process philosophy, with a secularization of Christianity, but with an emphatic Christian philosophy of religion which sees itself confronted with the same phenomena as Abe conceived them already in the introduction of this symposium and then in the further course as the opposite to the religiosity which according to him connects Buddhism and Christianity. The difference between his estimate of this secularization to that which Tillich represents over against them, consists only in the fact that Abe speaks of them as "anti-religious," whereas Tillich sees in them "quasi-religions," which Abe connects with the fact that Tillich stands over against them only "as an observing participant," while he—Abe—feels "attacked" by them in his religious existence.[130] This difference does not prevent him from emphasizing that he stands over against Tillich's undertaking not only critically but also sympathetically,[131] and that evidence of the "raison d'être of religion" over against the "antireligious powers" is to be expected from a better mutual understanding of Christianity and Buddhism.[132] This expectation which he expressed in the Symposium became more problematic than confirmed by the criticism which he addressed to his conversation partners.

Abe doubtlessly acknowledged of Tillich that he did not regard Christianity as the "absolute religion,"[133] and concedes that Eastern religions, especially Buddhism, offered less "resistance," for example, to Communism than the Western, and that this lack in power of resistance "is partly the fault of their distorted form."[134] But seen as a whole he judges the way in which Tillich juxtaposed the Kingdom of God to Nirvana to be a misunderstanding of the "ontological principles" of both, and in respect to the "ethical consequences" issuing from it and the attitude toward history he regards Buddhism as superior to Christianity.[135] Abe concerns himself most exhaustively with the "ontological principles" of "personal participation" and "suprapersonal identity" by means of which Tillich

---

[129]EB 1/1 (1965): 109ff.
[130]Ibid., 110ff.
[131]Ibid., 110.
[132]Ibid., 112.
[133]Ibid., 112.
[134]Ibid., 121.
[135]Ibid., 113.

thinks he can clarify the difference between the two religions. Precisely on this point, according to Abe, Tillich's position is in need of a basic correction, both as regards his conception of Buddhism as well as the decisive significance of religious self-understanding in respect to ontology. Nirvana—so Abe emphasizes over against Tillich—in no way consists in an "undifferentiated similarity" of man with things, that is, in a loss of personal being, but rather in the "realization of the true self of man as the ultimate ground of his ordinary self and of the world which stands over against it"[136]—this, to be sure, "not in objective determination" of an "objective substantiality," but in "nonsubstantial unification."[137] This "identity" of which only man can be aware in his "self-consciousness" as "transiency which is common to all beings,"[138] is "sunyata, identity with the absolute Mu," in whose "emptiness" the self and all things "are as they really are."[139]

The ethical consequence of this "dialectic nature" of Nirvana[140] as the "true self" and of its "creative profoundness[141] works itself out—according to Abe—in the form of the Bodhisattva who returns out of Nirvana into samsara[142] and its "Great Compassion,"[143] in which this one accepts the other not—as is the case on the Christian love of the neighbor—"in spite of its nature," but "just because of its selfishness."[144] Against the objection that Buddhism in this way does not change the world, Abe asks whether Christianity "does not increase rather than diminish the tensions between peoples," and in this connection points to the "militant elements" of the "militant and triumphing Church" and—as opposite to it—*inter alia* to Taoism as one of the "Eastern 'mystical' religions."[145] On the basis of his interpretation of the significance of the famous stone garden in Kyoto, which is typically different from that of Tillich's, one could say epigrammatically that the experience of this place is more sacred for Abe than the holy preaching of the "prophetic religions" of the West which are praised by Tillich.[146]

Abe's essay on "The End of World Religion," which represents a kind of counterpart to Tillich's treatment of "Christianity and the world religions," is not

---

[136]Ibid., 114.
[137]Ibid., 115.
[138]Ibid., 114.
[139]Ibid., 118.
[140]Ibid., 113.
[141]Ibid., 119.
[142]Ibid., 115.
[143]Ibid., 120.
[144]Ibid., 121.
[145]Ibid., 121.
[146]Ibid., 118-19.

so much an extension of the "Symposium on Buddhism and Christianity"[147] as it is a positive continuation of his exchange with Tillich, but from the Buddhist rather than the Christian standpoint.[148] Corresponding to the double significance of the Greek term *telos* Abe uses here the English expression "end" both in the sense of temporal end as well as of the goal that is determined or to be pursued in respect to the fate of religion, or of individual instances of the same as world religions in history and in the modern situation.[149] Next he comments on these possibilities in the distinction between "nature religions," in which "man, nature, and the gods" are still "undifferentiated"; "ethnic religions," which on the one hand distinguish between these three and on the other attempt to overcome this distinction at the same time through the assumption of something "transcendent or supernatural" distinct from nature; and "world religions," whose founders sought to free religion not only from the "natural," but also from the particular histories of the original forms and thus to bestow on them a "universal" significance, as for example is the case in Christianity through the notion of the "Kingdom of God" and in Buddhism through that of the "Pure Land."[150]

But now Abe emphasizes that if it is common to Western as well as Eastern world religions that "the transcendent truth and supraworldliness"[151] represented in them "can be truly realized" by their believers "only in an individualized consciousness," then this is always possible only on the basis of their cultural heritage, that is, with either a "Western" or "Eastern" stamp.[152] From this state of affairs Abe draws the conclusion that a religion attains the rank of a "world religion" to the degree that it succeeds in expressing its particular truth of salvation in its historical garb in such a way that it is not confined by it, but rather points beyond this, as happened in Christianity in its relation to Judaism and in Buddhism in its relation to Hinduism.[153] The same is held out to Christianity and Buddhism in the modern world situation where religion is threatened by

---

[147]As an extension of the symposium, reference is made to Abe's article "Religion Challenged by Modern Thought," JR 8/2 (1974): 2-14, which offers nothing essentially new with respect to the other articles considered here, which is true also of the recent interview that ensued with Masao Abe and John Cobb, appearing under the title "Buddhist-Christian Dialogue: Past, Present, and Future," in *Buddhist-Christian Studies*, ed. Winston King, East-West Religions Project (Honolulu: University of Hawaii Press, 1981) 12-29.

[148]EB 13/1 (1980): 31-45.

[149]Ibid., 31.

[150]Ibid., 31ff.

[151]Ibid., 33.

[152]Ibid., 35-36.

[153]Ibid., 41ff.

secularization, both for their own self-understanding as well as for their mutual relation. If the powers of secularization are not to mean the "end" of both, they must face up to the "goal" of their destiny, which is "to break through the limits of their respective Occidental or Oriental characters"[154] and must validate anew "their concept of universal redemption," in its deepest sense, so that Christianity "can take root in an Eastern form where it will really be 'at home' in the East, and Buddhism in a Western form in the West." Abe does not fail to emphasize that this is possible neither through a mere change of the outer "garment" nor through an "extension" of the present state, but rather only through an overcoming of the cultural-historical confinement of the universal nature of both of the religions here in question,[155] and he is confident that they are not too old for such a transformation.[156] "Who can say with justification," he asks "that the Logos actualized in Jesus and the Dharma realized by Gautama, have already been exhaustively developed?" Whether or not one believes in the "possibility of Christianity and Buddhism as future universal forms of world religions" is completely dependent on whether one has "direct contact with the Logos and the Dharma."[157]

Quite apart from the individual aspects which Abe unfolds in this essay, its significance consists in the fact that here in religiohistorical and existential argumentation he lays out for Buddhism and Christianity a diagnosis and prognosis in respect to their survival in their present crisis situation. What issues from this as a task for Buddhism forms the content of the remaining essay and lecture materials which we have not previously considered, but to which we now have to turn. Although according to Abe the same goal issues for Christianity as for Buddhism out of the situation described, he however concerns himself so to speak only with the latter, in that he systematically presents and discusses the basic concepts of Buddhist philosophy of religion necessary for its attainment. Nevertheless, he deals with their correspondences in Western thinking and in Christian faith only insofar as they are appropriate for demonstrating by them the superiority—as well as occasionally certain deficiencies—of Buddhism.

5. Abe's Conception of Buddhism as Zen Buddhism

It is connected with the goal set by Abe for Christianity and Buddhism of validating—ultimately independently of their historical heritage—the nature of a universal religion of redemption intrinsic to them, that he takes care to point out within Buddhism Zen Buddhism as the possibility of a meaningful human self-

---

[154]Ibid., 38.
[155]Ibid., 39.
[156]Ibid., 40, 45.
[157]Ibid., 45.

understanding that most particularly corresponds to this destiny. His thorough engagement with the two great Zen Buddhists, Dogen and Rinzai, serves this purpose. When he speaks of Buddhism in the normative sense, he always means—like his revered teacher Hisamatsu—Zen Buddhism. Although we will not enter more closely into these investigations into the history of ideas, they should be mentioned because they form the basis of his systematic presentation of truth of Buddhism represented by him.

In two essays, one of which served as the introduction to a series of lectures on "Zen and Modern Man" held at the Graduate School in Claremont, Abe was concerned to show that Zen is the authentic form of Buddhism which alone really corresponds to its historical origin in the enlightenment of the Buddha.[158] He does this in two essays by appealing to his teacher Shin'ichi Hisamatsu,[159] though he could have appealed also to Daisetz Suzuki who represents the same conception,[160] as this is generally assumed among the adherents of this kind of Buddhism. The difference between Hisamatsu and Suzuki consists only in this, that Hisamatsu sees Zen as "the Buddhism of self-awakening" in sharp contrast to Pure Land Buddhism as a "Buddhism of faith." while Suzuki assumes no principal difference between them except one pertaining to the method of attaining and mediating salvation.[161] Abe, to the contrary, places himself expressly on the side of Hisamatsu and is, with him, of the conviction that Zen alone is useful for "the realization of human existence common to the East and the West."[162]

To the frequently heard question, whether "Zen is a form of Buddhism," Abe would like to "answer both yes and no." "Historically speaking," he concedes that "Zen is a form of Buddhism which was founded by Bodhidharma in China in the sixth century," in so far as the Zen direction "in China and Japan. with its own particular temples, rituals, priesthoods and religious orders" developed from it "side by side with other forms of Buddhism, to which *inter alia* also Pure Land Buddhism belongs—all with "teaching, thought and practice." But at the same time he emphasizes that "Zen is not merely one form of Buddhism," but "rather, in its fundamental nature, is the basic source of all forms of Buddhism." For this second view, more important to him, he appeals to the fundamental sayings with which Zen characterizes its special type: "Not relying on words and letters; an independent transmission outside the teaching of the scriptures; direct

---

[158]"Zen and Buddhism," *Japan Studies* 11/1 (1966): 1-11 [rev. art. in the *Journal of Chinese Philosophy* 3 (1976): 235-52; courtesy of Abe. —Trans.].

[159]Ibid., 8ff.; *Anjali* (1970): 33ff.

[160]Daisetz Suzuki, *Zen and Japanese Buddhism*, 6th ed. (Tokyo: Japan Travel Bureau, 1968).

[161]Ibid., 94ff.

[162]*Anjali*, 33.

pointing to man's Mind; awakening one's (Original) Nature, thereby actualizing Buddhahood."[163]

For the elucidation and at the same time, justification of this self-characterization of Zen as an event of immediate enlightenment Abe presents a comparison between the Buddha Shakyamuni and Jesus as the Christ. Whereas in Christianity the title Christ is only assigned to Jesus, and the believers derive their salvation exclusively from his appearance in history, in Buddhism the Buddha's enlightenment possesses no such once-for-allness that is decisive for the salvation of his devotees; rather, what occurred in him is only of exemplary significance for enlightenment through the Dharma which is granted to each and can make one into a Buddha if he follows Siddhartha on this path.[164] For this he cites from the Samyutta Nikaya the instruction: "O Ananda, be ye lamps unto yourselves. Rely on yourselves, and do not rely on external help. Hold fast to the Dharma as a lamp. Seek salvation alone in the Dharma. Look not for assistance to anyone besides yourselves." "The Dharma is beyond everyone—beyond even Shakyamuni Buddha." "Regardless of [his] appearance or nonappearance . . . in this world, the Dharma is always present[165] and occurs in self-awakening, just as it did with Shakyamuni, in everyone who, like him, completely negates his ego-self."[166]

Additionally, in both treatises Abe gives a summary of the history of Buddhism and of the different interpretations of the tradition which arose in it, as well as a survey of the Trikaya doctrine which arose in this connection—the doctrine of the so-called three bodies of the Buddha, and their diverse accents.[167] With Hisamatsu, whom he extensively cites, he is concerned above all with two things: first, with the difference between Zen Buddhism and Pure Land Buddhism with respect to the use of the Trikaya doctrine and the different conceptions of redemption connected with it; and second, with the nature of Zen as demythologization and existential interpretation of the Mahayana sutra tradition.

As far as the first point is concerned, Abe points out that Zen Buddhism, corresponding to its estimation of the Dharma as the decisive factor among the three phenomenal forms of the Buddha, ascribes special significance to the Dharmakaya, whereas for Pure Land Buddhism Sambhogakaya is central because it sees in it the embodiment of Amida as the Lord of the Pure Land. These different functional roles of the Buddha-body in both forms of Buddhism is connected with the differences of their conceptions of redemption, in that Zen allows redemption to occur already within samsara, while in Jodo Buddhism it

---

[163]*Japan Studies* 11/1 (1966): 1.
[164]Ibid., 2-3.
[165]Ibid., 3.
[166]Ibid., 4.
[167]Ibid., 5ff.; *Anjali*, 35ff.

is fulfilled in the Beyond of its Pure Land. In this way the differences in the Trikaya doctrine and in the doctrine of redemption correspond to each other. They get worked out in the usual distinction of Zen as the "way of holiness" of "self-redemption" (Jiriki) and of Pure Land Buddhism as the "way of faith" of "redemption ab extra" (Tariki), whereby the latter is connected with the acceptance of the situation at the end time (Mappo) and has regard for the weakness of the members of the final generation.[168]

With this difference in the metaphysical and soteriological notions Abe also connects a second characteristic by which Zen distinguishes itself not only from Pure Land Buddhism, but also from other forms of Buddhism and accounts for its special position among them. Whereas these other forms of Buddhism—especially Pure Land Buddhism in the Sambhogakaya—"objectify" the Buddha, that is, make him an object of a faith in a salvation event which completes itself independently of the believers and which it holds to be true, for Zen this event occurs in self-understanding for which it assigns to that only the role of a symbolic expression of an event which is essentially non-objectifiable. Without mentioning Bultmann, Abe sees in this interpretation of the Buddhist sutra tradition in Zen a parallel to the efforts at a dekerygmatizing and existential interpretation of the biblical tradition which is known from the realm of Christianity. By appealing to the same view of Hisamatsu he sees therein not only a correspondence to the original Buddhist self-understanding, but also a possibility for its mediation to modern men. For Hisamatsu, as for Abe, Zen is therefore the sole authentic and appropriate Buddhism.[169]

Although it is regrettable that neither Hisamatsu nor Abe accepts the parallels they determine between their Zen understanding as an overcoming of "Buddhist sutra-dogmatism and Buddhist sutra magic" and the discussion of the hermeneutical problem in theology, because here lies the basis for a real encounter of Buddhism and Christianity, it is nevertheless understandable that they are concerned to clarify and justify the state of affairs indicated by it in modern Buddhism with their own historic heritage. When Abe in this connection already cites Hisamatsu's reference to the famous answer of Bodhidharma to the question of the Chinese emperor Wu about the truth of Buddhism,[170] it is further understandable that for grounding his view, he concerns himself thoroughly with the great thinkers Dogen and Rinzai who established Zen understanding in China in former times and brought it over to Japan, thereby becoming the founders of the Japanese Soto Zen and Rinzai Zen schools, respectively.

---

[168]*Anjali*, 38; *Japan Studies*, 7.
[169]Ibid., 8ff.
[170]Ibid., 10.

A not inconsiderable part of Abe's publications actually consists of translations of, and commentaries on the writings of Dogen, and his essay on "Dogen on Human Nature" arose from his preoccupation with this Zen thinker who was probably the most significant. While we can here disregard the contents of his *Translations of Dogen's Shobogenzo and Bendowa* which were coedited by the deserving curator of *The Eastern Buddhist*, Norman Waddell—translations that appeared with informative introductions and notations in *The Eastern Buddhist*[171]—it is in order to look more closely at the Dogen essay, since it is interesting, not merely historically, but also systematically. It deals essentially with the question whether and in what way man still needs enlightenment for attaining Buddhahood, if, according to Buddhist tradition, "all living beings have the Buddha nature" and the Buddha as the "thus-come-one" (Tathagata) "abides forever without change."[172] This is a question which is somewhat parallel to the problem of natural theology in Christianity, that is, the question of the relation in which the image of God given to man by God stands to the New Creation in Christ, in connection with which it is not to be overlooked that in Christianity the relation between God and man, on the one hand, is destroyed by sin and, on the other, is redeemed through the faith of revelation of a "personal nature," whereas in Buddhism both samsara and enlightenment are of an "impersonal, boundless cosmological dimension."[173] In both, the question is posed as to what significance is ascribed to man or his self-understanding in the context of the event of redemption, which is dealt with in both—even if with different presuppositions and in different forms. This is also the problem Dogen very thoroughly considered in his main work, "A Treasury of the Right Dharma Eye," and in the treatment of which he played a role in the history of Buddhism similar to that of his contemporary Thomas Aquinas—who was a quarter of a century younger—in that of Christianity.[174]

As Abe shows in thorough analysis of text and thoughts, Dogen solved the basic problem of the realization of redemption which he inherited from the form of the teaching taken over by him, by abbreviating the sentence just cited on the general possession of the Buddha nature and on the immutability of the Buddha from the Nirvana sutra in such a way that he understood having-Buddha-nature as "being-Buddha-nature" of all beings—not only the living—and the perma-

[171]EB 4/1 (1971): 124-57; 4/2 (1971): 108-18; 5/1 (1972): 70-80; 5/2 (1972): 129-40; 6/2 (1973): 115-28; 7/1 (1974): 116-23; 8/2 (1975): 94-112; 9/1 (1976): 87-105; 9/2 (1976): 71-87.
[172]"Dogen on Buddha Nature," EB 4/1 (1971): 28-71.
[173]Ibid., 33ff.
[174]Ibid., 29.

nence of the Buddha as "permanent, nonbeing, being, and change."[175] Abe explains in detail that Dogen saw himself obliged to execute this "grammatical" maneuver because he was only able in this way to take account of the nature of the Buddhist conception of redemption that ascribes a special significance to the "cosmological," that is, to what includes all beings, and simultaneously to the "homocentric," that is, to human "self-consciousness," and could appeal to the tradition for its connection of the "homocentric" and "dehomocentric" structures.[176] The connection of these two structures is not possible, however, in an objective thinking of consciousness and of substance, as Abe regards it to be typical for Western thinkers from Descartes and Spinoza on,[177] but only in a nonobjectifiable existential enlightenment,[178] for which there exists between the Buddha nature and all beings neither unity nor duality, but "nonduality," in that it is simply the "All-embracing,"[179] in which all things appear in their true "thusness."[180] For the sake of the nonobjectifiability of the Buddha nature of all beings Dogen can even contest the claim that just any being possesses Buddha-nature,[181] because for objective thinking it is "empty," "nothingness" (*Mu*), and yet is realized in the enlightenment in all things. This world-enlightenment in self-enlightenment occurs, according to Dogen's instruction, in *shikantaza*, that is, in the practice of "only sitting" in immersion which has been practiced in Soto Zen since Dogen's time.[182]

Abe correctly explains that Dogen's notion that "all beings are Buddha nature," "cannot be completely understood without his idea of the 'unity of practice and enlightenment'," and he is equally correct in deducing from this that it arose for Dogen out of the problem experienced by him as young monk on Hiei, namely, "why should one engage in religious practice to overcome illusion," that is, to attain to redemption, "if he is already endowed with the Buddha nature and is originally enlightened?"[183] This "dilemma [in] Mahayana Buddhism, particularly in the T'ien T'ai [Tendai] school with which he started his Buddhist studies," Dogen solves by rejecting the orthodox distinction between "original" and "acquired" awakening as "naturalistic" or even "teleological-idealistic," in each case as an objective thinking of consciousness," and in its stead

---

[175]Ibid., 30-31, 36-37.
[176]Ibid., 34.
[177]Ibid., 39, 40.
[178]Ibid., 45.
[179]Ibid., 38, 43.
[180]Ibid., 51, 62.
[181]Ibid., 46-47.
[182]Ibid., 59.
[183]Ibid., 59.

proclaimed "the unity of practice and enlightenment." Enlightenment is not attained by sitting in immersion (*zazen*), in which "body and spirit fall away;" rather the "unintentionally" enacted sitting (*shikantaza*) is as such already enlightenment, and enlightenment is nothing other than this practice. Both are "beginningless and endless," self-enlightenment and world-enlightenment in one, for which there is neither subject nor object, neither space nor time, and "Every day is a good day."[184]

In view of the significance which Dogen attaches to zazen practice in its identity with enlightenment it is understandable that he was not satisfied with the tenor of the writings in which he presented his Zen philosophy—above all, in the Shobogenzo, and that he provides in individual tractates instructions about the correct way of carrying out the sitting, both with respect to the attitude of mind to be exemplified thereby as well as to the concrete form of the sitting, as they are contained in the Fukanzazengi, the "universal demands of the principles of zazen," translated by Abe and Waddell.[185] In reading this handbook of zazen as it is practiced in Soto Zen as shikantaza, we become rightly aware that zazen practice is the foundation of Zen thinking, and that its enactment seems too difficult to us in many points because we lack its presupposition. Just as certain statements of Christian faith are incapable of being understood by the unbelievers, so for the unenlightened, insights attained on the basis of enlightenment are also incapable of being understood in many respects.

The same difficulty of an understanding enactment obtains for those who in zazen practice have not participated in satori, as well as in respect to the course of thought in Zen thinking of the other stamp, that is, in so-called Rinzai Zen which, as distinguished from Dogen's Soto Zen, makes use of the koan method for immersion (Samadhi). Abe concerns himself with this kind of Zen Buddhism in his essay, "Zen and Compassion," in which he refers to a book of D. T. Suzuki's, which has only appeared in Japanese, on the Lin-chi Lu, "Rinzai's Sayings," and several of the parts translated into English by Suzuki.[186] He amply cites here Suzuki's characterization of Rinzai's "leap" from the "borders of the field of human consciousness" into the "bottomless emptiness" of the "nonobjectifiable absolute subjectivity" of the "true man without rank" as the opposite of Western and Christian thinking," for example, in the following way:

If the Greeks—says Dr. Suzuki—taught us how to reason and Christianity what to believe, it is Zen that teaches us to go beyond logic and not to tarry even when we come up against "the things which are not seen." For the Zen point of view is to find an absolute point where no dualism in whatever

---

[184]Ibid., 60ff., 67.
[185]EB 6/2 (1973): 115-28.
[186]"Zen and Compassion," EB 2/1 (1967): 54-68.

form resides. Logic starts from the division of subject and object, and belief distinguishes between what is seen and what is not seen. The Western mode of thinking can never do away with this eternal dilemma, this or that, reason or faith, man and God, etc. With Zen all these are swept aside as something veiling our insight into the nature of life and reality. Zen leads us into a realm of Emptiness or Void where no conceptualism prevails.[187]

It is characteristic of the significance Abe ascribes to the conception of Rinzai Zen which is represented by him in agreement with Suzuki, that he entitles the essay in which he reviews it, "Zen and Compassion." As in the essay on "the Buddha nature in Dogen" reviewed by us earlier, so here his deliberations also eventuate into a discussion of the practice of compassion (Karuna) which follows from Zen enlightenment.[188] Thus Zen is for him not merely a theoretical business, but also a practical one, in the double sense as practice of zazen and as practice of religio-ethical action.

That this nature of Zen is anything but theoretical explains why Abe could give to his contribution to the Festschrift dedicated to the author by the theological faculty of Basel, the title which on first sight seems somewhat enigmatical: "Zen is not a Philosophy, but. . . . "[189] As he says at the beginning, he wished to explain that Zen may well "embrace a profound philosophy," but that practice is absolutely necessary to its realization, and that, because it "is beyond words and intellect," intellectual understanding cannot be a substitute for Zen's awakening.[190]

As a "key" to understanding this nature of Zen he makes use of the well-known saying of a Chinese Zen master:

> Before I studied Zen, to me mountains were mountains and waters were waters. After I got an insight into the truth of Zen through the instruction of a good master, mountains are to me not mountains and waters are not waters. But after this, when I really attained the abode of rest, mountains are really mountains, waters are really waters.

In order to answer the "crucial question" with which the Zen master concluded this description of his way to truth, "Do you think that these three understandings are the same or different?" he explains these seriatim as follows. In the "first stage" the I stands over against the mountains and waters as different objects. But in this discriminative knowledge they are neither grasped in their nature in themselves but only "from outside," nor are we dealing in this objecti-

---

[187]Ibid., 59-60.
[188]EB 4/1 (1971): 64; 2/1 (1967): 65.
[189]ThZB 33/5 (1977): 261-68.
[190]Ibid., 261.

fying I with the "True Self," but only with an I which objectifies itself in "endless regression." For the true I to appear, the I of the "subject-object-duality" of this first stage must disappear. But with it, its "object disappears as well."[191] That happens in the "second stage" in which there is neither distinction nor objectification, but "all is empty." "This negative realization," says Abe, "is important and necessary in order to disclose ultimate Reality." But, he continues, this overcoming of the distinction of the first stage must still be overcome in the second, because here still a "higher distinction" "between differentiation and non-differentiation" is made. "The negative view must be overcome. Emptiness must empty itself." This happens in the "third and final stage" in which, in a "new form of differentiation," there is still a "higher." "Mountains are really mountains, no more, no less," and through the overcoming not only of the I by the not-I, but also of the latter, "the True Self awakens to itself." "Logically speaking, we have the negation of negation," and that means "affirmation in its absolute sense."[192]

The question posed initially, whether the three stages are identical or different from one another, Abe answers on the basis of this presentation with a both-and. Considered individually, there is "complete discontinuity between them," in that "a great leap is necessary to reach the higher stages." Together they become a "dynamic whole," in consequence of which it is "more than the third and final stage." This "paradoxical" being-with-and-in-one-another of the three stages as such a dynamic whole Abe illustrates with reference to the fact that it is as true that "The willows are green, the flowers are red," as that "Lee drinks wine, Chang gets drunk," or, "I am not I, therefore I am you, and yet I am really I. You are not you, therefore you are me; and yet you are really you." This is, as Abe expressly and repeatedly emphasizes, a matter of Zen enlightenment, to whose nature belongs—in distinction from Hegel's conceptual absolutizing and substantializing of the mind (spirit)—the "bottomless emptiness and the "moment" as past, present and future.[193] Zen is neither "absolute knowledge nor salvation by God, but self-awakening," and "includes a most profound philosophy, although Zen is itself not a philosophy."[194]

If Abe in this way answered the question posed for discussion of the relation of Zen to philosophy, it cannot be said, nevertheless, that he has answered all questions which issue for us from this answer. We learn all the more to appreciate that he has extensively introduced such questions which issue from Western thinking with respect to Zen thinking and concerns himself in

---

[191]Ibid., 262-63.
[192]Ibid., 264.
[193]Ibid., 266-67.
[194]Ibid., 268.

connection with it also with the consequences which issue from it for ethical practice.

6. Zen and Western Thinking

To the most important treatises for the systematic presentation of Abe's Zen philosophy belong doubtlessly the two on "Zen and Western Thought"[195] and "Non Being and Mu. The Metaphysical Nature of Negativity in the East and the West."[196] As the titles of both essays indicate, he discusses in them the basic concepts of Zen in confrontation with Western philosophy and, as on other occasions, he clarifies complicated connections with the help of diagrams.

In the first named and also temporally earlier essay on "Zen and Western Thought," Abe proposes a comprehensive typology of Western thinking in its development from the philosophy of Plato and Aristotle, to Christianity from its biblical origins and in its unfolding in Augustine, Thomas Aquinas and Luther on the one hand and Kant on the other, up to Nietzsche and Heidegger, only to confront it magisterially with the course of Far Eastern thinking, with the Abhidharma of Hinayana and the Prajnaparamita sutras of Mahayana up to the formation of the latter in Nagarjuna and in the Madhyamika school as the foundation of Zen. For this he makes use of the conceptual pairs—not otherwise used by him—of *ji* as a designation for the "actual, phenomenal, particular, temporal, and differentiated," and *ri* with the meaning of the "ideal, noumenal, universal, eternal and undifferentiated,"[197] in order to indicate how in Nagarjuna's transformation of the Buddha's *pratitya-samutpada* into the doctrine of absolute nothingness (*sunyata*) the opposition and the tension between empiricism and idealism, which Western thinking cannot avoid because of its metaphysics of Being, are solved and overcome.

The cause of this problematic of Western thinking Abe sees in the substantializing and objectification of what he designates in his Buddhist terminology as *ri* and for whose application in the context of the Western objectifying thinking of the metaphysics of Being he provides the colophon with a majuscule, written as *Ri*, as he also uses the Japanese term *U*, written as a capital letter in Japanese. On this metaphysical plane he locates not only the Greek concept of Being, but also Kant's term, "Ought,"[198] and the concept of God which is connected with both in Christian theology. The same holds true according to him

---

[195]*International Philosophical Quarterly* 10/4 (1970): 501-41.

[196]*Religious Studies* 11/2 (1975): 181-92. Cf. the summary by Hans Waldenfels, *Absolutes Nichts*, 92-98 [ET: *Absolute Nothingness: Foundations for a Buddhist-Christian Dialogue*, 70-74].

[197]"Zen and Western Thought," 502n.1.

[198]Ibid., 508ff.

of the *heilsgeschichtlich* meaning which Christianity ascribes to the incarnation of the Logos and the cross of Christ,[199] and in Nietzsche's critique of Christianity and its Platonism and in Heidegger's rebuke of the "forgetfulness of being" of Western thinking he sees that its "blind-spot" is still not completely overcome.[200] What occasions his speaking of the "blind spot" of all these ways of thinking is identical with what he develops in other connections we have already reviewed, in respect to the nonobjectifiablity of Being and the self, except that he here all the more applies his principal epistemological-critical point of view[201] to the different formulations of Western philosophy and theology in order to point out from that perspective their insufficiency compared to "Nagarjuna's view of emptiness," which ultimately represents, in his opinion, the only adequate formulation of the Buddha's doctrine of the "non-I and of dependent origination,"[202] and forms as such the basis of Zen and of its claim to be an "independent [spiritual] transmission apart from doctrine or scripture."[203] In this comprehensive confrontation of Western and Eastern thinking four motifs are apparent, which for all their particularity are interconnected in that they issue from each other seriatim. First, as far as the methodology is concerned, Abe presents both in the form of a problem-historical presentation which permeates the entire treatment, by means of several of their main types. The point of departure and driving force of both developments is the perception of an insufficiency of the world in which one lives and the "metaphysical" striving to transcend it.[204] The attempt is made in different ways—second—to respond to this need: in the West by the erection of a Being that sublates what is lacking in beings, in which use is made of conceptual thinking in one way or another—whether by appealing to natural reason or to a supernatural revelation; in the East, on the contrary, precisely by an extinction of this thinking that is directed toward a Being that is somehow represented objectively.

Abe—third—evaluates not only the Eastern but also Western ways of redemption, which are here dealt with, according to the measure of the way in which they are justified in their principles, and thus both work in reference to a certain inner consistency in which later forms correct the deficiencies of the earlier. But while in this context he characterizes the significance of Nagarjuna's "doctrine of the self-emptying emptiness" in such a way that in it—in a way which is valid for all those appealing to it—Buddha's "Middle Way" has found

---

[199]Ibid., 515, 519.
[200]Ibid., 537-38.
[201]Ibid., 536.
[202]Ibid., 504, 511, 512, 519ff., 526.
[203]Ibid., 523.
[204]Ibid., 501ff.

its full philosophical formulation, he not only overlooks the fact that there have always been such appeals in Western cultural history to the truth of its origin, but without hesitation subjects all its phenomena to the judgment of the second and third of the "Noble Truths of the Buddha," in consequence of which all suffering, that is, all deficiencies of existence, derive from the present world of attachment to things and can only be overcome through a liberation from this attachment to any things whatsoever, as this has been perfectly expressed philosophically and practically by Nagarjuna.

From this early Buddhist view it is understandable that Abe can finally only evaluate negatively all conceptual thinking of Being—which is represented by different forms of Western philosophy, theology, and ethics because of its fateful attachment to things—and the attempts that follow from it of a world-transforming action or of its hope for a transformation of the world that is expected from God—as measured by Buddhist non-thinking[205] and its *Wu-Wei* (Non-action).[206] It is all the more surprising—fourth—that at the conclusion of his essay, above all in the discussion with Kant,[207] Abe feels compelled to warn Zen from letting its "Not-thinking," in which it rejects objective thinking for the sake of the non-objectifiablity of the self and of Being, lapse into a "nonthinking as such"[208] and from letting its freedom from "every kind of moral law and principle" become a merely "non- or antiethic."[209] In regard to the first danger he feels required to make the concession that, "Because Zen (at least Zen up until today) has thus not fully realized the positive and creative aspects of human thinking, its position of Nonthinking always harbors the danger of degenerating into mere nonthinking." It follows from this that "Zen today lacks the clue to cope with the problems of modern science, as well as individual, social, and international ethical questions."[210] Finally, he remarks:

> The Zen position of "Nonaction" and "no-business" transcends the standpoint of the "Ought." But it did not necessarily experience a self-conscious confrontation with the moral and ethical "Ought" so keenly realized in the ethical tradition of the West. The fact that, as a result, Zen often harbored the danger of losing its own authentic freedom, of falling into a uncritical dilettantism, and of sinking into a mere nonethic or antiethic, is one that must not be minimized.[211]

---

[205]Ibid., 536.
[206]Ibid,, 534n.18.
[207]Ibid., 535ff.
[208]Ibid., 538.
[209]Ibid., 535.
[210]Ibid., 538.
[211]Ibid., 535.

How these dangers which are connected with the Zen standpoint he represents could be overcome Abe does not show us in the treatise principally devoted to its justification; and when he explains in the concluding sentences that the "historical task" of Zen in the present world situation consists in placing "substantive thinking and subjective thinking, which has been refined and firmly established in the Western world, within the world of its own No-thinking, and [making] them function from "the Origin of Nonattachment" to establish various things," what he elaborates on this problem makes us think of a squaring of the circle. But if he offers no solution to this problem, he nevertheless believes that he can show the way to such by concluding his deliberations with the double demand, that Zen must "embrace the standpoints of Western 'Being' and 'Ought'," just as the West has "been forced to a reexamination" of these concepts. As the special task in the program so formulated of a possible fruitful encounter of Eastern and Western thinking, Zen "must grasp again and renew its own standpoint of 'Nothingness' so as to be able truly to concretize and actualize its No-thinking."[212]

This postulate of a concretizing and actualizing of the standpoint of nothingness within Zen Abe seeks to justify in a treatise which carries the title "Nonbeing and Mu. The Metaphysical Nature of Negativity in the East and West."[213] As far as the social-historical material is concerned to which Abe refers and by means of which he juxtaposes the Zen concept of nothingness (Mu) with the concept of nothingness or Being of Western thinking, his detailed deliberations for the most part coincide with those in the treatise on "Zen and Western Thinking." Thus he appeals here chiefly to Nagarjuna's sunyata philosophy and its conception of "emptiness" as "wondrous being" that "embraces emptiness and fullness."[214] To demonstrate its superiority over all other philosophically or religiously grounded views of world and life he enters upon new ways. The first consists in an exchange with Paul Tillich's famous thesis of the "ontological priority of Being over Non-Being;"[215] the second, in an expansion of this negative-critical argumentation in a positive sense by a "holistic-existential" interpretation of the "Buddhist idea of emptiness."[216]

Abe correctly sees in Tillich's thesis exponents of the Greek metaphysics of being and of Christian theology. With all their distinctiveness, in both ways of thinking which are typical for Western thinking Being, or God, is ranked above beings, not only ontologically, but also valuationally and in an ethical sense. Just

---

[212]Ibid., 539.
[213]*Religious Studies* 11/2 (1975): 181ff.
[214]Ibid., 185-86.
[215]Ibid., 182-83.
[216]Ibid., 188ff.

as for Plato the highest Being is simultaneously the perfect Good, and evil is nonbeing (*me on*), so in Christianity sin is disobedience against God's will which created the world out of nothing.[217] But in its ontological as well as ethical respects this Western thinking of Being represents, in Abe's eyes, a mere "wish projection"[218] which does not correspond to actual reality, but is rather contradicted by it, because life and death "are bound together inseparably," and every overcoming of evil by the Good always appears as "illusory." Therefore he regards the Buddhist notion of samsara and the doctrine of *pratitya-samutpada* in distinction to the dualistic and idealistic forms of Western thinking as "realistic."[219] In Nagarjuna's logic of "emptiness" the contrast between Being and nonbeing, good and evil, is recognized, but is simultaneously overcome in this recognition.[220]

Abe says of this "Buddhist idea of emptiness" which consists of a self-annulling conceptuality, that it could be realized in an authentic sense, not conceptually, but only holistically, subjectively or existentially through the realization of our own existence as a unity of being and nonbeing which is in itself contradictory. This "existential realisation" that consists in the fact that "true Emptiness empties itself," indicates that it is "not a static state that is objectively observable, but a dynamic activity of *emptying* in which you and I are also involved."[221] In Zen this is called the "Great Death," which consists in the "total negation of life-and-death," that is, "beyond the realisation of death as distinguished from life."[222]

This "Great Death" upon which Abe here reflects, represents—as we have already had opportunity to establish on other occasions—a great epistemological problem that is still "holistic" in a different sense from the "holistic nature" which Abe would like to ascribe to it in his Zen thinking, in that it proves to be highly problematic in both an ontological and ethical respect. Neither in his claim to be "not conceptual, but holistic," nor in its development does Abe's thinking correspond to this postulate, for not only is "holistic" a concept, but the "denial of denial" as well, through which he wants to attain to this "emptiness' in logical conceptuality. The denial of its validity presupposes precisely what is said to be made inoperative in it. In the supposed sublation of the contradictoriness of Being with which conceptual knowledge has to do, he still makes use of its aid, just as the "Great Death" and "emptiness," Nirvana and "awakening" are con-

---

217Ibid., 182.
218Ibid., 183.
219Ibid., 190.
220Ibid., 185.
221Ibid., 188.
222Ibid., 190.

ceptual designations, even if they point beyond every objectification. Contrary to the function he assigns to it, "holistic" thinking therefore leads precisely to a contradictoriness of its nature and contents as a whole.

While Abe passes over this epistemological problematic of his holism, in that he thinks he can rescue it in the concept of the "existential"—still a concept!—he now draws out of this existentializing the ontological consequence which he formulates in the sentence: "Indeed there exists nothing whatsoever outside of this dynamic whole of *emptying*."[223] With this, he lapses, not into an ethical idealism—for which he reproaches Western thinking[224]—but into an ontological one by equating the thinking of existence with Being. In certain forms of Western idealism there is actually a trespassing of such ontological boundaries of being-postulating thinking as are connected with ethical postulates and—as we know—Zen philosophy has not remained uninfluenced by such. With all its criticism of post- and neo-Kantian idealism and its transformations up to Heidegger it has yielded too much to this thinking of Being not to borrow from it and become ontologically infected by it. That the "emptying of emptiness" represented by Abe does not deal with an existential self-understanding, but with an ontological misunderstanding of the same is shown precisely in the way in which he juxtaposes Nagarjuna's "emptiness" with the Western concept of Being and, for all his dialectic of "transcending beyond," puts him on a level with it. This ontologizing of the thinking of existence is promoted further by the terminological difficulty that in the English language, of which Abe makes use in the publications available to us, "existentiell" and "existential" are not distinguished, and "realize" can mean both "knowing" in the noetic sense as well as "actualize" in the ontological sphere, which works out fatefully for both in the ethical sphere.

7. The Problem of Ethics

In connection with the mentioned terminological inadequacy the ontologizing or meontologizing of the "emptiness" of the existential (=existentiell) self-understanding in the ethical sphere which is represented in Abe's appeal to Nagarjuna, leads to the establishing of an emancipation "from the existential antinomy of good and evil" and an awakening "to Emptiness prior to the opposition between good and evil," in which the enlightened one can be master of, and not slave to, good and evil."[225] "In this sense," Abe thinks, "the realization of true emptiness is the basis for human freedom, creative activity, and ethical life."[226] Thus his

---

[223]Ibid., 188.

[224]Ibid., 199.

[225]Ibid., 191. On the appeal to Nietzsche, cf. also: "Zen and Nietzsche," EB 6/2 (1973): 14-32.

[226]Ibid.

discussion of the connection which obtains between the metaphysical context and self-understanding that is possible within it develops into an inspection of the ethics that issues from it, as is the case in the materially parallel essay on "Buddhist Nirvana: Its Significance in Contemporary Thought and Life."[227] But while he lets the matter end with suggestions in both places, as also on other opportunities, in the three essays extensively concerned with the problem of ethics in Buddhism at the Eleventh International Congress of the Historians of Religion, held in Claremont in 1965, he deals with the theme "The Idea of Purity in Mahayana Buddhism."[228] Then he devotes a lecture to it in the series of Gooding Lectures delivered by him in Chicago in 1969, on the theme " 'Life and Death' and 'Good and Evil' in Zen."[229] A third time he speaks on "The Problem of Evil in Christianity and Buddhism" in a lecture of this title in Princeton, which he repeated in a somewhat expanded form in July of 1980 at the East-West Encounter in Honolulu.

In the first three of these treatments of the ethical problem in which he—following the theme of the congress to which he lectured—took up the problem under the viewpoint of "purity," or "purification," he proceeds from the fact that in Mahayana Buddhism two conceptions of purity which on first sight are irreconcilable with one another lie before us, in that both an "Original Purity" in consequence of which "everything is pure in itself" is spoken of, as well as an "purity of leaving our defilement," in the sense of a "becoming pure through *dis*defilement."[230] Why is this purification necessary if everything is already pure? Over against such a questioning of the necessity for purification Abe refers to our knowledge of our impurity emotionally, morally and spiritually speaking, and to attempts to relativize them, in which he sees the origin and function of all "rites of purification." But—and this is now his decisive perspective—in this knowing of ourselves as impure and in the attempts to attain a "condition" of purity, we are hopelessly embedded in impurity, from which we should like to become free. In that in objectifying conceptuality we distinguish between "pure" and "impure," we become prisoners of the conceptual world. To be sure—he concedes—it is possible and necessary to "clarify our situation somewhat" with the help of conceptual distinctions. But finally we have to do with the illusory world of an I that falsely puts itself at the center and so falls victim to the error of self-attachment.[231] Likewise, the enlightenment in which one—in accord with the Buddhist conception—in "emptiness" becomes free from all conceptual distinctions, would

---

[227]*The Ecumenical Review* 25/2 (1974): 158-68.
[228]*Numen* 13/3 (1966): 183, 189.
[229]*Criterion* 9/1 (1969): 7-11.
[230]*Numen* 13/3 (1969): 183.
[231]Ibid., 184-85.

still be a deception if one wishes to see in it a means for attaining purity as a goal.[232] As the cause of impurity is the distinction between pure and impure, so purity is realized in the original, that is, authentic sense, when we allow "everything and everyone," including ourselves, "to be respectively just as they are." If the rites of purification are understood in the light of such prajna wisdom which is essentially connected with Karuna, Abe would be prepared to accord them "truly religious significance."[233] The "purification" would then not be enacted through rites which rest on the distinction of pure and impure, but we would effect it in such a way that we purify ourselves from that distinction between pure and impure and thus correspond to "the original purity which is always suitable" to us and all being and things.

But at this point the questionableness of Abe's thinking and the conceptuality of which he makes use become apparent. One can only agree with his de-absolutizing of the conceptuality of objectifying thinking, the relativizing of the success of our moral strivings and the de-mystifying of so-called rites of purification. But the "*existential realization*" of "the Original Purity," of which he rightly says that it is "not an objectively observable state,"[234] is not possible without conceptional distinctions. If in view of its relativity, no distinction is made between the concepts of pure and impure, then speaking about "Original Purity" is meaningless, because then it could not be distinguished from anything, but would be identical "with everything just as it is"—as Abe also says. But can the "existential realization" postulated by Abe still be somewhat united with this identification of "Original Purity" with "everything as it is"—quite apart from the fact that concepts are also used here—since this not only becomes useless, but is impossible in principle if everything "is as it is." "Existential realization" presupposes that something is not yet existentially realized—even if it should only consist in recognizing that everything is as it is. If "existential realization" consists in such recognition, then—if it is not merely an "illusion"—it is different from that which "is as it is," that is, it consists in a purification of our conceptuality from its absolutizations, but also in a use of our conceptuality in its relativity as the means to its enactment in the understanding of ourselves and of environment and to an attitude of self and world forms which correspond to it. For such a "purification" of oneself and its environment, "Original Purity" would be the symbolic expression of its abiding relativity and purposiveness. Instead of an ontology of "emptiness" into which Abe's dialectic of purity and purification issues, definite forms of the biblical-Christian mythology of Christ and speculation would have to appear for this purpose—forms which in existential interpreta-

---

[232]Ibid., 185-86.
[233]Ibid., 188.
[234]Ibid.

tion could serve as language for this understanding of salvation which is to be fundamentally distinguished from Buddhism. Abe does not take this into account in this treatise, although the concept of "Original Purity" with its "perversion" is obviously parallel to the ideas of the original paradisaic condition and its loss through the Fall which in Christian theology form the presuppositions of its doctrine of salvation.

Abe comes to this counterpole in the lecture mentioned in the second place, in which he presents the nature and relation of " 'Life and Death' and 'Good and Evil' in Zen," and juxtaposes it to the way these concepts are conceived in Christianity. While in the context of the dualistically structured Christian *Heilsgeschichte* death is viewed as the enemy of life and since the Fall, as the punishment of God, in Buddhism life and death are two sides of a whole which as such knows no beginning and no end. It may be that in Zen—in a certain correspondence to the "eternal life" of Christian faith—one knows of a fulfillment of existence. But this takes place not in a future Beyond, but in a Here and Now, when the enlightened one dies the "Great Death, in which all "dualistic, objective thinking is dismissed" and henceforth "dies living and lives dying." In that moment of our "living-dying existence, Abe repeatedly explains, "we attain the paradoxical oneness of living and dying which is true of all life," and at the same time become free of it. For Abe this is "the discovery of the 'Great Life', the 'new Life,' in which one can live the living-dying life without becoming shackled by it."

If for this he cites the poem of a Zen master of the early Tokugawa period, that reads

> While living, (to) become a dead man
> Thoroughly dead
> Then do as you will,
> All will be all right,

the other significance of this understanding of the "Great Death" becomes simultaneously apparent in it. Not only is the opposition of life and death dismantled, but the distinction between "good and evil" as well. The ethical, or transethical, consequences of the "Great Death" are indeed suggested, but not developed by Abe at this place. But in comparison with the Pauline conception of "death and resurrection with Christ" which he presents in considerable detail, the parallelism as well as the differences of the doctrine of redemption in Christianity and Zen already become sufficiently evident. Not only—in contrast with Amida Buddhism—is there in Zen no redeemer who brings "new life," but also no judgment for sin. Many difficulties are connected with this doctrinal point also in Christianity, and Abe amply concerned himself with these in the third lecture we mentioned on "The Problem of Evil in Christianity and Buddhism," which discusses Buddhist ethics.

This still unpublished treatise presents principally an expanded repetition of what Abe had represented—in addition to the connections already considered earlier in others—in the two earlier essays which deal with the ethical question. Above all, the presentation of the problem of evil in Christianity here underwent expansion in that he shows by the example of Augustine and Irenaeas, the Manichaeans and Schleiermacher, how Christian theology attempted to solve the riddle of evil and sin in the creation of the good and almighty God in the different forms of so-called theodicies which contradict one another. The insufficiency and inner contradictoriness of these attempts to justify God Abe juxtaposes with the nonattachment to the conceptuality of objectifying thinking in sunyata—which is grounded in "codependent origination"—in which those difficulties of the Christian doctrines of God and creation could not arise. As far as his critique of the attempts at theodicy is concerned, it is not only acknowledged as legitimate, but also in the evident familiarity with Christian theology, it is even remarkable. In reference to his positive deliberations on the opposite Zen Buddhist position, one should recall our critique of this position in reference to the essay reviewed initially. We neither have anything to add to this critique nor is it refuted through the argumentation carried through here in a comprehensive way. Granted, it is difficult to argue with anyone who thinks he can think nonobjectively and on this basis can confuse such questionable judgments of thought with judgments about being and believes he can pass them off as such. But that is a familiar story to which one gradually becomes accustomed in dealing with Buddhists, even if one cannot just accept it, but rather feels obliged to protest time and again, although this seems to fall upon deaf ears.

On the contrary, what is new—not in Buddhist presentations generally, but surely in that of Abe's—is the contrasting of the Buddha's death scene and the cross of Christ and the consequences more or less correctly to be drawn in respect to the conception of redemption which gets expressed therein. But what is certainly new in Abe here—but also more instructive—is his comparison of the so-called Mosaic Decalog with the series of ethical commandments in Buddhism. That divine origin is not to be assigned the latter, and that they do not begin with duties and proscriptions regarding God, but that the commandment not to kill stands in the first place, is already very significant for ethics.

What is most essential and important Abe presents at the conclusion of this lecture, where he asks: "How can we pass judgment and make decisions in respect to our ordinary acts, after we have passed beyond the duality of good and evil; to what principles can one still appeal in such a way that they can be followed in the spirit of this liberating experience?" To this question of the possibility of the grounding of an ethic on the realization of sunyata he replies in three points.

First, he holds firmly to the position that sunyata is "not merely a goal to strive for, but rather forms the foundation of our entire life"—especially the "root and source" from which the duality of good and evil is to be relativized.

Second, the "setting aside of any absoluteness of good and evil" means not only a relativizing, but an "inversion of both valuations." This has as a consequence a "loss of the strengths and intensity of connection with the ethical principles with which one confers meaning and integrity upon life." Even in Christianity there is such a relativizing and inversion of the concepts of good and evil by appealing to the "Will of God." For this Abe refers to the "teleological suspension of the ethical" in Kierkegaard's interpretation of the Abraham-Isaac story and to sayings of Jesus to the effect that he "did not come to call the righteous to repentance, but sinners," and that it is not he but the "Father alone who is just," and that it is valid "to be obedient not to the letter of the Law, but in spirit, that is, in light of the redemption through Jesus Christ." But because faith in "God as ruler over the world and history" and as "the highest Good," and as "just and loving" is presupposed, there is in Christianity still no complete relativizing and inversion of the concepts of good and evil." This "transformation of values" is rather—without "fear of destroying the foundation of ethical life"—reached only in Buddhism "through the realization of the boundless openness of sunyata in which there is no God."

Third, in order to show the illegitimacy of the fear that, through the relativizing and inversion of the concepts of good and evil in the boundless openness of Sunyata, the ethical life could be deprived of its foundation, Abe appeals to the "awakening to boundless openness" as an "extreme experience" through which "the distinction between good and evil is made clearer than before without any limitation," and we become "at the same time" led to the "realization of the sameness of good and evil." Both "aspects" are said to result simultaneously from the awakening to boundless openness—the first, "the more lucid differentiation of good and evil" showing itself in the "Buddhist wisdom" of prajna, while the second, in the form of Karuna, contains "Buddhist compassion." In the "two-fold realization" of both components there results on the one side a recapturing of the "duality of good and evil in the new light of sunyata" as prajna, but on the other, it is not limited to that, because it "is realized in the light of Karuna as un-differentiated unity," and on this is based "the Buddhist ethical life." This "dynamic cooperation" of "distinction and unity, wisdom and compassion" rests on the assumption of the "boundless openness of sunyata as the foundation of our life."

Abe lays great weight on this conception of sunyata as the foundation of the ethical life and our life in general. For if it is not conceived as the "ground and point of departure," but as the "goal and object of our life," Buddhist life would degenerate into the "indifference between good and evil" and its consequence would be an "apathetic attitude toward social evil." This "danger and tendency of degenerating into ethical indifference" is "always latent in Buddhist life," for which there are numerous examples in the history of Buddhism. Therefore he thinks it is "important and meaningful for Buddhism to engage in a sincere ethical and religious dialogue with Christianity."

This is one insight by which Abe—like few others—is led not only in this lecture, but also in the whole of his work and in all the publications that have issued from it. The *summa* of the Zen philosophy of the Kyoto School which he here offers us represents also a challenge to Christian theology which causes it to take up from its side the dialogue with this Buddhist thinking. For this purpose the critical remarks which we have had occasion and opportunity to make in different places in our presentation of the individual representatives of the Kyoto School, are certainly insufficient. The confrontation of Far Eastern Buddhist thinking with Western Christian thinking which we have dealt with here demands rather a comprehensive systematic positional statement to which we hope to make a contribution in our concluding chapter.

Chapter 10

Concluding Position
A Juxtaposition and Connection
of Buddhist and Christian Symbols

1. The Nature of the Problem and the Program Resulting from It

Now that in the main body of this study we have completed our presentation of the eight most characteristic representatives of the Kyoto School especially in respect to their attitude toward Christianity and in this connection have now and then engaged in an immanent critique of their positions, it remains to take account of this philosophy of religion which belongs to the most significant manifestations of contemporary Buddhist thinking in the context of Buddhism as a whole, because it is this—the others less so—that demands the attention of Christian theology and its Western thinking. Taking a fundamental position toward Buddhism as it confronts us here does not reduce the criticism previously expressed to something merely negative, in that, as might be expected, it would consist only of a juxtaposition of presumably insufficient Buddhist solutions of the problems of life and supposedly better Christian solutions. In view of the historical problematic of Christianity's development and the burden of its history such theological arrogance is unwarranted. This is the source of their weak positions which their Buddhist critics like to emphasize—even if the true cause of such remains hidden from them. As we recall from the introductory chapter, there is even in Buddhism such a problem of origins (even if it is quite different from that of Christianity) through which it has become—in all its varied manifestations—something quite different from what it intended to be in its original form.

In both of their problematic origins—in the rise of Christianity and its history as a consequence of the delay of the imminent end of the world and in the different necessary formulations of the Buddha's path to salvation in Hinayana and Mahayana—we are dealing with the question of the meaning of existence and its realization. In Christianity and Buddhism this question has been discussed—albeit differently and antithetically—epistemologically, metaphysically, ethically and from the standpoint of the history of philosophy, as has happened and still happens for example in the philosophy of religion of the Kyoto School. Whether from the perspective of revelation and faith, God and his Messiah, nature and grace, Church and Kingdom of God, or of absorption and enlightenment, Buddha and the Bodhisattvas, Jiriki and Tariki, Pure Land and Nirvana, in every case we are dealing with objectifications of what is nonobjectifiable and this raises the question as to how we may speak appropriately of these matters.

With this problem of the unavoidably objective speaking of things which are essentially not things the material problem of dualism or monism of the divine redemptive activity, or universalism and particularism, arises both in Christianity and Buddhism in connection with the possibility of the realization of meaning. To the extent that we designate objectifications of the nonobjectifiable by the term symbol, in the above spheres of discourse of both Buddhism and Christianity we are dealing both formally and materially with symbols.

In this way we have named three factors which are important for the proposed concluding systematic stance toward the philosophy of religion of the Kyoto School and its attitude toward Christianity.

First, the problematic relationship in which this philosophy of religion as a formulation of Buddhist tradition stands to its historic origin and which binds it *mutatis mutandis* to the problematic of Christian origins. Establishing this fact is more important for its evaluation of Christianity than for Buddhist philosophy's own self-conception. In Buddhism the problematic of historic origins plays a role only in Amida Buddhism because it appeals to a once-for-all vow of the Bodhisattva Dharmakara. Despite the fact that Amida Buddhism understands this tradition as mythology, this problem is solved for it, or has the possibility of being solved, since it can see this vow as a mythological expression for a special kind of self-understanding which saves through a specific relationship to Transcendence, as Zen Buddhism does in relation to the entire Buddhist tradition, as far as it makes use of it. The matter is quite different with the Christianity with which these Buddhists—both Zen and Shin Buddhists—are concerned, insofar as they are dealing with a Christianity—in Catholic or Protestant, ancient or modern forms—which does not reckon with its historic problematic or solves it in a questionable manner, as it meets them in the prevailing theology and above all in the mission. Over against this Christianity misunderstood on the basis of its own self-misunderstanding we shall have to take into account a Christianity which reckons with its historical problematic whereby a completely different situation arises for discussion.

Consideration of this conception of Christianity which differs considerably from the traditional one will become operative in respect to the *second* factor connecting the two partners in discussion, which consists in the fact that they ground their positions epistemologically—if indeed in a mutual systematic with material differences—and construct a metaphysic in order to draw consequences from them for their ethic and to derive a philosophy of history and culture. Under these four enumerated aspects which are equally essential for the unfolding of the content of truth by Buddhist philosophy of religion as for a self-understanding of Christian theology suitable for today, we have to extend the foregoing discussion and to provide a satisfactory conclusion to both parts which took account of their good intentions.

Third, that can only occur if account is taken of the symbols which are present on both sides in all four spheres; even so this task is beset with difficulties as it represents an aid to understanding. The difficulty of an agreement on the use of symbols rests on the fact that they, as objectifications of what is non-objectifiable in the tradition, play a further role only in the objectivity which belongs to their nature and in this way cannot be misunderstood, but rather serve to emphasize the opposition and exclusive validity of their content. On the contrary they can be helpful if despite their differences they can validate their mutual function as statements of a self-understanding related to Transcendence.

This significance of statements of self-understanding in relation to Transcendence—a significance belonging essentially to all symbols—is best exhibited in the two recognized symbols of Enlightenment and Holy Spirit. Explained epistemologically, these two symbols serve as formal criteria for the truth content of the material, metaphysical, soteriological, and historical-philosophical symbols of Buddhism and Christianity.[1]

This understanding of symbol we have to explain initially by means of the two aforementioned epistemological symbols of Buddhism and Christianity in order to apply it to those of Buddhist and Christian metaphysics, soteriology and philosophical history of Buddhism and Christianity, respectively; in doing so we must constantly take account of the historical problematic of both phenomena.

The execution of the program therewith introduced demands for its justification a look at several different kinds of positions.

2. Other Positions on the Relation between Christianity and Buddhism

In respect to this final systematic chapter as well as the methodological introductory chapter it is quite understandable that only one voice speaks in the colossal chorus of voices which in the course of time and especially in the present time

---

[1]Although the concepts of being and meaning are fundamental for the structure and content of our thinking as well as for that of Paul Tillich, ours is likewise principally different from his because we distinguish between the formal and material, while Tillich does not make this distinction either in his concept of symbol or in his typology resting upon it; rather he fills his formal aspects with the contents of faith which cannot be justified through correlation and made usable as the basis of a dialogue. Cf. Paul Tillich, *Das Christentum und die Weltreligionen*, separately printed from *Ges. Werke*, vol. 5 (Stuttgart: Evangel. Verlagswerk, 1964) and Fritz Buri, "Die Bedeutung des Sein-Sinn-Problems für interkulturelles religiöses Verstehen," ThZB 34/5 (1978): 277-91; on the concept of symbol, cf esp. *Dogmatik als Selbstverständnis des christlichen Glaubens*, 1:265-312.

have sounded on the question of the relation between Christianity and Buddhism in historical investigations and fundamental positions, and that it is received by their representatives—because of the basic perspective employed and the consequences issuing from it—as only an amplified dissonance within the existing cacophony of voices which one ignores as far as possible or attempts to set aside by pointing out its alleged weaknesses and to drown out by different kinds of sounds. We should like nothing better than a discussion with those—and they are numerous—who hold antithetic positions which digress from, ignore, or reject ours.

If we here decline to engage other conceptions of the nature of Buddhism and Christianity and the relation in which they stand to one another, this is due to the fact that that would demand an even greater investigation than that which we have devoted to the philosophy of religion of the Kyoto School, and that as far as my position on different types of Christian theology is concerned, one should consult my *Dogmatik als Selbstverständnis des christlichen Glaubens* and other works. That in my conception of Christianity and in dialogue with the representatives of the Kyoto School I rely on this work, and that on other matters I find myself constantly in calm or often inwardly intense conversations with my theological critics, is well known among scholars.

But putting aside an explicit engagement with positions rejected by us does not absolve us of the necessity of referring to the status of the present discussion and illustrating it by some of the most important names and publications, limiting ourselves to such as concern themselves not only proximally but thematically with Zen Buddhism as it is represented in the Kyoto School. We neglect its treatment by authors such as Eugen Herrigel, Philip Kapleau, Karlfried Graf Dürckheim, and others because they lack a specifically Christian standpoint. For similar reasons we do not initiate a presentation of the philosophy of Zen Buddhism which Toshihiko Izutsu published in Tehran in 1977 under the title "Toward a Philosophy of Zen Buddhism."[2] Since we have already concerned ourselves with Hans Waldenfels in our presentation of Nishitani's philosophy of religion, we limit ourselves to the mention of the most important positions of four Jesuits at Sophia University in Tokyo and a half dozen quite dissimilar attitudes of Protestant theologians.

---

[2](Tehran: Imperial Iranian Academy of Philosophy, 1977); review by Robert E. Carter, EB 13/2 (1980): 127-30. Now also in German translation: *Philosophie des Zen-Buddhism* (RoRoRo: Taschenbuch, 1979).

The three Eranos Lectures of Toshihiko Izutsu expand on this: "The Field Structure of Zen Buddhism," *Eranos* 47 (1978); "Between Image and No-Image: Far Eastern Ways of Thinking," *Eranos* 48 (1979); "The Nexus of Ontological Events," *Eranos* 49 (1980).

On the Christian side Heinrich Dumoulin has most exhaustively dealt with Zen Buddhism in historical perspective and in a systematic manner in numerous greater and lesser publications, such as, for example, *Zen, Geschichte und Gestalt (Zen, History and Form)*[3]; *Östliche Meditation und christliche Mystik (Eastern Meditation and Christian Mysticism)*[4]; *Christlicher Dialogue mit Asien (Christian Dialogue with Asia)*[5]; *Christianity meets Buddhism*[6]; *Mumonkan, Die Schranke ohne Tor (Mumonkan: The Cabinet without a Door)*[7]; *Der Erleuchtungsweg des Zen im Buddhismus (The Way of Enlightenment in Zen Buddhism)*[8]; *Begegnung mit dem Buddhismus. Eine Einführung (Encounter with Buddhism: An Introduction)*[9]; and in countless contributions in journals, Festschriften, and collected works. Dumoulin would like to find in Zen Buddhism as well as in Christianity a "natural theology" which can reach its fulfillment only in a "supernatural Christian mysticism of grace." Like other Catholic authors he appeals to the Missionary Decree of Vatican II for his positive attitude toward Buddhism.[10]

While Dumoulin is hesitant regarding a connection between Christian and Buddhist elements, however, his colleagues at Sophia University go farther in their "ecumenical" endeavors—not as far as doctrine is concerned which must naturally remain Catholic, but in the *praxis pietatis*—like the Irish Jesuit William Johnston who sees the "Christian contemplative" and the "Zen monk" sitting only on different "Zabuton" (cushions), that is, different traditions, but thereby directed to the same "still point" in the "ground of the soul",[11] with the result that for the Buddhists Jesus becomes a "Zen Master"[12] and "the Christian Mystic" becomes "another Christ" on the basis of the incarnation of the cosmic Christ.[13]

The other German Jesuit, who has earned the attestation of Satori (Enlightenment) from his Zen Master and changed his name to Hugo Makibi Enomiya-Lasalle, goes still further—not dogmatically for that is not possible, but

---

[3](Bern: Francke, 1959).

[4](Freiburg/Munich: Karl Alber, 1966).

[5](Munich: Max Huber, 1970).

[6](LaSalle IL, 1974).

[7](Mainz: Grünewald, 1975).

[8](Fischer Taschenbuch, 1976).

[9]Herderbücherei, vol. 642 (1978); with Bibliography.

[10]*Östliche Meditation und christliche Mystik*, 37.

[11]*Der ruhende Punkt* (Freiburg: Herder, 1974) 146; German trans. of *The Still Point: Reflections of Zen and Christian Mysticism* (New York: Fordham University, 1970).

[12]Ibid., 208.

[13]Ibid., 171.

practically in the use of Zen practice in Christian meditation. With his innovations which appear to traditional Christians as daring experiments and which he carries out in his own Zen Center and propagates in numerous courses and writings which have appeared in several languages and in some instances in many editions (e.g., *Zen-Weg zur Erleuchtung [The Zen Way to Enlightenment]*[14]; *Zen-Buddhism*[15]; *Zen-Meditation für Christen [Zen Meditation for Christians]*),[16] *Zazen und die Exerzitien des Heiligen Ignatius [Zazen and the Exercises of St. Ignatius]*),[17] he has won the recognition of the general of his order in his contribution to the comprehensive *Festschrift* dedicated to Father Lassalle on his eightieth birthday, namely, *numen musō. Ungegenständliche Meditation (numen musō: Non-Objective Meditation)*,[18] in which are found articles of his fellow Jesuits Karl Rahner and Johannes Baptist Lotz as well other such international authorities in the field of religious studies as Hajime Nakamura, Zwi Werblowsky, Raimundo Panikkar, and Carl Friedrich von Weizäcker, all of whom attest to the worldwide recognition Enomiya Lassalle has found with his endeavors.

A fourth Jesuit of Sophia University I would finally mention is the Japanese Kakichi Kadowaki who in his book *Zen and the Bible. A Priest's Experience*[19] interprets biblical texts in the sense of Zen koans and for this goal commends a "reading with the body" or "body reading" and not only finds this "body reading" as "a new hermeneutics" already in Nichiren,[20] but also uses the Ignatian *Exercitia spiritualia* as the structure of a Zen-Sesshin.[21] In contrast to the somewhat tumultuous style and content of his book, Kadowaki demonstrates in the essay "Ways of Knowing. A Buddhist-Thomist Dialogue,"[22] that he knows his way around in Scholastic conceptuality.

Six representatives of Protestant theology considered here display a connection between Buddhism and Christianity which in principle is philosophically, biblically, and dogmatically quite different from that of the Jesuits just mentioned: Käsemann's student Seiichi Yagi, the disciple of Nishida and Karl Barth,

---

[14](Vienna, 1960; 5th ed., 1977).

[15](Cologne: Bachem, 1966; 3rd ed., 1974).

[16](Weinheim: O. W. Barth Verlag, 1968; 3rd ed., 1973).

[17](Cologne, 1975).

[18](Mainz: Grünewald, 1978).

[19](London: Routledge and Kegan Paul, 1980); first appeared in 1977 in Japanese, now also in German: *Zen und die Bibel* (Salzburg: Otto Müller, 1980). The *Buddhist Sermons on Christian Texts* by R. H. Blith (South San Francisco: Heian International Pub. Co., 1976) represents a "Buddhistic" companion to this.

[20]Ibid., 115ff.

[21]Ibid., 127-80.

[22]NAJTh 20/21 (1978): 53-93.

Katsumi Takizawa, the American Whiteheadian John Cobb, the follower of Tillich Masatoshi Doi, the Baptist missionary Tucker Callaway, and the religion scholar of "Free Christianity" Gustav Mensching.

While Kadowaki,[23] as well as Takizawa and Doi, were originally Buddhists and became Christians, Seiichi Yagi—according to his own report—having become disillusioned with his orthodox, pietistic Christianity while a student in Marburg, experienced "Enlightenment"[24] in the vicinity of Kassel on the way back from a visit with a friend of his father's, Wilhelm Gundert, who had given him a copy of his translation of *Bi-Yän-Lu*. In Japan Yagi became acquainted with Takizawa[25] through his exchange of writings and through his dismissal as teacher in a theological school because of his "Buddhism" and his "liberalism." Since then Yagi has become a successful theological journalist and teaches at the International Christian University at Mitaka/Tokyo, as well as other places. In Europe he has become known as the coeditor of the collective work *Gott in Japan*,[26] to which he contributed not only translations and commentaries, but also an article "Buddhist Atheism and the Christian God."[27] Besides several German and English essays on New Testament and religiophilosophical themes, especially instructive is his contribution on "Buddhism and Christianity" in an issue of the *Northeast Asian Journal of Theology* devoted to this theme and the conversation with John Cobb which is attached to the same article in this issue.[28]

In the essay which forms the object of this conversation Yagi formulates the following "thesis" which states the central intention of his philosophy of religion as well as the possibility of making it correspond to his view: "Egoism and the discriminating intellect are united in their roots. Christianity testifies to the life in which egoism is overcome, whereas Buddhism knows the thinking which has overcome the discriminating intellect. In this sense Christianity and Buddhism

---

[23]*Zen and the Bible*, 3ff.

[24]Details about this "Kassel Experience" in August of 1958 are to be found in the critical description of Yagi's Christology in the Basel dissertation of the Korean Sun Hwan Pyun: "The Problem of the Finality of Christ in the Perspective of Christian-Zen Encounter: Carl Michalson and Seiichi Yagi" (1975) 181-82, which—corresponding to its title—presents in more than 400 pages an extremely informative treatment of our theme based on Japanese sources, and with a rich bibliography.

[25]Cf. the reports about this by Sun Hwan Pyun in his diss. 212-39, and Kenzo Tagawa, "The Yagi-Takizawa Debate," NAJth (March 1969): 41-59.

[26](Munich: Christian Kaiser, 1973).

[27]Ibid., 160-91.

[28]NAJTh 20-21 (1978): 1-30 and 31-52.

complement each other in the breaking down of the union between egoism and the discriminating intellect."[29]

The central concept in Yagi's Christianized Buddhism or Buddhologized Christianity is the concept of "integration" as the symbol of a "field" of immanent transcendence in which the conceptual thinking attached to things should be superseded by a "[loving] knowing."[30] But for this construction he not only makes use of the discriminating intellect which he identified with "egoism" but in his "field theory" which operates with poetic images and with *pratitya-samutpada* one no longer knows who the subject and object of this love may be and whether both can actually exist in this "harmony" of a "being," which is at the same time "nothing"—a harmony which is indistinguishable from a "chaos."

No less confused seems the "Immanuel" speculation which Katsumi Takizawa develops in his *Reflexionen über die universale Grundlage von Buddhismus and Christentum (Reflections on the Universal Foundation of Buddhism and Christianity)*[31] and elsewhere in the essay " 'Rechtfertigung' im Buddhismus und Christentum" ("Justification in Buddhism and Christianity"),[32] in which he attempts to bring into relationship Nishida's philosophy and the theology of Karl Barth as mutual corrections and expansions of each other. In view of his interpretation of religion, Christianity, and Buddhism it is equally understandable that he believes he is able to find in the form of the "sensei" in Soseki's "Kokoro" traces of the portrait of Jesus in the Gospels,[33] and that as professor at the Royal Kyushu University he long delayed receiving baptism.[34]

The questions "Can a Christian be a Buddhist, too?" and "Can a Buddhist be a Christian, too?" also interested John Cobb, as is evident from his two essays

---

[29]Ibid., 1.

[30]Ibid., 6ff.; *Gott in Japan*, 167ff. Cf. Yagi's contribution in *numen musō* (see above n. 18): "Selbsterwachen und Liebe, Zur Überwindung des objektivierenden Denkens," 268-85.

[31]*Studien zur interkulturellen Geschichte des Christentums*, vol. 24 (Frankfurt/Bern: Verlag Peter Lang, 1980) with Takizawa's biography and bibliography, pp. 180ff.

[32]*Evangelische Theologie* 39 (1979): 182-95, On Takizawa's theology cf. also his "Nachwort" in Walter Böttcher's, *Rückansicht, Perspektiven japanischen Christentums* (Stuttgart: Kreuz Verlag, 1973): 154-73, and his contribution to *Gott in Japan*, "Zen-Buddhismus und Christentum im gegenwärtigen Japan," 139-59.

[33]" 'Kokoro' of Soseki and the Gospels," unpub. ms. (1977).

[34]"Was hindert mich noch, mich taufen zu lassen?" in *Antwort—Karl Barth zum siebzigsten Geburtstag* (Zollikon-Zurich: Evangel. Verlag, 1956) 911-25.

which carried these titles.[35] He thinks "that we can help the Buddhists to realize the truth of Buddhism in a fuller measure," but to do so we have to advocate a Christianity understood in Whitehead's sense, as he does. He "believes that Christianity in its present form can make no claim for universal validity" and therefore he regards the "most important step to be undertaken at once by the Christian mission" to be a "self-alteration of Christianity" in the manner undertaken by him on the basis of Process Philosophy.[36]

But like John Cobb who since the publication of his Christology *Christ in a Pluralistic Age*[37] has neglected the further execution of this program, so Masatoshi Doi, sometime professor at Doshisha University and director of the NCC in Kyoto, in his book *Search for Meaning through Interfaith Dialogue*[38] and former essays, allowed this program to become central in methodological reflections and reports on conversations between Christians and Buddhists, which no longer continue.

Less irenic is the Southern Baptist missionary Tucker Callaway in his book *Zen Way—Jesus Way*,[39] dedicated to his "teacher and friend" Daisetz T. Suzuki. Despite his great understanding of "the logic of Zen" and moving accounts of his experiences in Zen temples and conversations with Zen folk he can only view the "Zen Way" and the "Jesus Way" as opposites. Thus he concludes his expositions with the position "For the Zen-man the Zen Way and the Jesus Way are Not-Two. For the Jesus-man the Zen Way and the Jesus Way are absolutely and irreconcilably Two," and for this he cites the deep sentence of the Diamond Sutra, to the effect that, if the one who vows to redeem all beings "[attains] the highest Enlightenment," "all beings are already delivered," although one "knows not a single being has ever been delivered' because one cannot be called an

---

[35]John B. Cobb, "Can a Christian Be a Buddhist, Too?" JR 10/3 (1978): 1-20; "Can a Buddhist Be a Christian, Too?" unpub. ms. Cf: "Buddhism and Christianity as Contemporary," NAJTh 20-21 (1978): 19-30, and EB 13/2 (1980): 16-25.

[36]"Buddhism and Christianity, Dialogue between Drs. John Cobb and Seiichi Yagi," NAJTh 20/21 (1978): 51. On Cobb's process theology, cf. John B. Cobb, Jr. and David Ray Griffin, *Process Theology: An Introductory Exposition* (Philadelphia: Westminster Press, 1976); also my critical presentation of his "Christian natural theology" in *Gott in Amerika* (Bern: Verlag Paul Haupt and Tübingen: Katzmann Verlag, 1970) 123-35.

[37](Philadelphia: Westminster Press, 1975).

[38](Tokyo: Kyo Bun Kwan, 1976); cf. also "Interfaith Dialogue Methodological Reflections" in JR 7/2 (1971): 1-17.

[39](Rutland VT and Tokyo: Charles E. Tuttle Co. and Zurich: Boxerbooks, Inc., 1976).

"Enlightened One" if he should "believe in the existence of himself, other selves, or any beings," and the words of Jesus from the Gospel of John: "I am the way, the truth and the life; no one comes to the Father, but by me."[40]

Meanwhile, in the work of the post-Bultmannian New Testament scholar Yagi, a sentence arose like an erratic boulder among the rubble of his form-critical exegesis and existential interpretation: "The promised Kingdom has not come, indeed appears not to be coming"—a sentence he only uses to illustrate the "temptation" which comes to the one believing in "being destined for integration,"[41] on the contrary the references to the delay of the Kingdom of God are used throughout the entire book of the recently deceased religious scholar Gustav Mensching, entitled *Buddha und Christus—ein Vergleich* (*Buddha and Christ—A Comparison*),[42] as the justification for the necessity of his new interpretation of the culturally conditioned world of ideas of biblical eschatology in the sense of Rudolf Otto's concept of religion. Although Mensching—in contrast to the previously named Protestant and Catholic theologians—did not concern himself with the Kyoto School, we mention him in this connection because he is the only one among them who attempts in his own way to take account of the perspective of "thoroughgoing eschatology" which we have employed in our critical comparison of Buddhism and Christianity. The understanding of early Christian eschatology represented by us excludes its use as a *heilsgeschichtlich* justification of a hope for a future overcoming of the remaining difficulties in the dialogue between Christianity and Buddhism as conducted, for example, by Dumoulin.[43]

An orientation to the present state of the discussions between Buddhism and Christianity in general with which we are dealing and in whose context the preoccupation with Zen Buddhism, in particular with the Kyoto School, forms an essential component is likewise briefly provided by Dumoulin[44] and extensively from comprehensive knowledge by Joseph Spae in his latest work *Buddhist-Christian Empathy*,[45] as well as by an issue of Concilium dedicated to the theme of "Buddhism and Christianity" which appeared in June/July of 1978. Copious bibliographies on this theme are contained in the special issue of the *Northeast Asia Journal of Theology*,[46] entitled "Theology in Dialogue with Buddhism,"

---

[40]Ibid., 241. Cf., by the same author, "Selflessness in Buddhism and Christianity," *Studies in the Christian Religion* 33/4 (Kyoto: Doshisha University, 1965): 17-31.

[41]*Gott in Japan*, 181-82.

[42](Stuttgart: Deutsche Verlags-Anstalt, 1978).

[43]E.g., in *Östliche Meditation und christliche Mystik*, 287-88.

[44]*Christlicher Dialog mit Asien*, 9ff.; *Begegnung mit dem Buddhismus*, 17-18.

[45]The Chicago Institute of Theology and Culture, 1980.

[46]NAJTh 20/21 (1978): 111-16.

previously cited, as well as in the book by Joseph Spae with extensive bibliographical notes.[47] An account of a visit of Zen monks to German monasteries in 1979 and lectures which were delivered at the Vatican on this occasion have been published by Hans Waldenfels under the title "Begegnung mit dem Zen Buddhismus."[48] Notto R. Thelle reports on Protestant as well as interconfessional contacts with Buddhism and their history in various issues of *Japanese Religions*[49]—a journal which is principally informative for the conversation between the two religions.[50]

Apart from their respective orientations, this list of authors and the references to the literature on the theme of "Christianity and Zen Buddhism" should suffice to justify our decision in this study devoted to the presentation of the Kyoto School, not to engage in an analysis of the global echo which it has already found and the spiritual realms within which it has been expressed, but—in accordance with our intention as stated in the program developed in the introduction to this chapter—to limit ourselves to taking a preliminary definitive position on this phenomenon and the interconnections in which it stands for us.

3. Enlightenment and Holy Spirit

In both Buddhism and Christianity these two concepts have played both a negative and a positive role. The negative consists in the fact that by means of these it has been possible to demarcate the sphere of discriminating, objective knowl-

---

[47]*Buddhist-Christian Empathy*, 245-52, as well as the index to literature in Hans Waldenfels, *Absolutes Nichts*," 208-21 [ET: *Absolute Nothingness: Foundations for a Buddhist-Christian Dialogue*, 190-203].

[48](Düsseldorf: Patmos Verlag, 1980). Instructive reports of their visits to Zen monasteries and experiences in them are given by Else Madelon Hooykaas, in *Zazen* (Weilheim: Otto Wilhelm Barth, 1972), and Janwillem van de Wetering, in *The Empty Mirror, Experiences in a Japanese Zen Monastery*," (Boston: Houghton Mifflin, 1974). More recently—and in contrast to these, negatively critical—cf. Harvey Cox, *Licht aus Asien, Verheissung und Versuchung östlicher Religiosität* (Stuttgart: Kreuz Verlag, 1978) [orig. English]. An excellent presentation of Zen Buddhism in 101 outstanding photographs and an equally impressive commentary is the work *The Zen Life. Text by Koji Sato, photographs by Sosei Kuzunishi* (Japanese ed., Kyoto: Tankosha, 1966; English ed., New York and Tokyo: John Wetherhill, 1972, 1977).

[49]JR 8/3 (1975): 68-84; 10/1 (1977): 63-70; 10/3 (1978): 53-74; 10/4 (1978): 46-65; 85-86.

[50]Along with *Japanese Religions* the other journals to be mentioned in this connection are *Monumenta Nipponica, Philosophy East and West*, and *The Eastern Buddhist*.

edge. On the positive side they have served to characterize Prajna or Faith-Knowledge once they have been separated from the sphere of discursive reasoning.

On both sides these two concepts are equally problematic in both applications—even if partly in different ways. Distinguished negatively, the problematic consists in the fact that it is precisely that discriminating objective knowledge which one wants to keep separate from the sphere of Enlightenment, or the Holy Spirit. Isn't it still a matter of discriminating thinking to be delimited and explained as no longer belonging to a definite point? It is for precisely this reason that it must be estimated that negatively as well as positively, Prajna, or Faith-Knowledge, somehow belongs to it. Should this happen, the autonomy of Prajna-Knowledge and the Theonomy of Faith-Knowledge would be abandoned. There would be no Enlightenment or Faith-Knowledge apart from rational understanding.

To avoid admitting this, Zen Buddhists say that one cannot know whether one has achieved Enlightenment, and that the one who claims to be enlightened is surely not enlightened. This does not, however, prevent their patriarchs from transmitting the "Seal of Enlightenment" and attesting to their own Enlightenment from a Zen master. In Christianity the attempt is made—unless a *sacrificium intellectus* is openly or secretly demanded—somehow to bring the human and the divine spirit into relation with one another, the best arrangement being the subordination of the former under the latter. There are here, as in Buddhism—though in a more pronounced way—established successions of spiritual authority and corresponding institutions.

This liquidation or differentiation of the negative function of the concept of Enlightenment or Holy Spirit nevertheless has consequences for its positive function. Apparently the Nothing of Buddhism is not as empty as it would like to assume, especially if it asserts without possessing a criterion for doing so, that in it things show how they are real. If one disavows a criterion for this "manifestation of themselves in reality," there is no guarantee that this is the case. The situation is no better for the Christian faith-knowledge if in distinction from Buddhist Enlightenment it appeals to testimony and to the activities of the Holy Spirit. Either Spirit is allowed to be self-authenticating, in which case every criterion is abandoned and one submits to blind trust, or in view of the manifoldness and objectivity—even irrationalities—of appeals to the Holy Spirit the claim is made for material representations of the sphere of the Holy Spirit over against discriminating conceptual thinking and rational criteria.

This epistemological problem once again illustrated by the concepts of Enlightenment and Holy Spirit—a problem met with in Buddhism and Christianity only in different ways, but in the same degree—is solved for us only by being recognized as insoluble. There are boundaries of objectifying conceptual knowledge—boundaries which such knowledge certainly recognizes. In this way the spheres of the objectifiable and the nonobjectifiable which cannot be separated from each other are dealt with by means of special principles of knowledge. To be sure, spheres of our inner and outer experience can be distinguished in which—in varying degrees—the understanding and the heart are addressed and have to speak, and we employ different methods in the sciences according to their respective areas of objects. But as we have to make use thereby of the whole spectrum of discriminating objectifying thinking—a spectrum ranging from daily experiences and the problems of technology and society to the most subtle philosophical speculations and the deepest religious thoughts—and move completely within the subject-object schema of our consciousness, even so the boundaries of our thinking consciousness can appear at any place on the spectrum if we ask about the Being of the Being with which we have to do and consider that it is we who raise the question for the sake of its meaning.

For the awareness of the not only relative but absolute boundaries of objectifying thinking and the related insight into the unconditionality of the representation of that which essentially cannot be objectified we can legitimately make use of the symbols of Enlightenment and the Holy Spirit without remaining trapped in the epistemological problematic previously described. Enlightenment and the Holy Spirit are the formal symbols for the capacity of every concept of discriminating thinking which represents an objectification of what is nonobjectifiable to become a symbol. As the formal symbols of all material symbols they have continually to take account of their presupposition and their use. Material symbols can only correctly be used under the sign of the formal symbols of Enlightenment and the Holy Spirit. Without this sign they are merely objects of rational thinking which are not transparent to the Nonobjectifiable intended in them. In Enlightenment and through the Holy Spirit they nevertheless become transparent to the Nonobjectifiable. Thus Enlightenment and Holy Spirit are the symbols of true symbolism.

Because of this common function we can combine the symbols of Enlightenment and Holy Spirit into one symbol—despite their different heritage—and speak of Enlightenment in Holy Spirit or of an enlightened spirit, of spirit-enlightenment.[51] For they are even used in this sense in Buddhism and Christianity.

---

[51]For the connection of the two symbols in enlightenment of man in his inner composition through the Gospel as the testimony of the acts of God's Spirit in Christ attention should be given to 1 Cor 2:10-14 and 2 Cor 4:3-6, and to Acts 9:17-18; 10:10-34, 44-47 as a suitable illustration of this. From these biblical origins the two symbols are combined into a functional unity in the course of the history of Christianity not only by the spiritualists who have time and again appeared in various forms; but even the orthodox of all times teach the enlightenment of the human spirit through the Holy Spirit. Both this as well as

Quite apart from the monistic structure of the spirit-world in which it is found, the Buddhist use of the symbol of Spirit can be distinguished from the Christian only by the fact that it abandons the expression "holy" which appears conceptually and legitimately in its objective fulfillment in traditional Christian usage. Characteristic of this attitude of Buddhism is the answer which Bodhidharma gave to Emperor Wu's question "What is the highest meaning of holy truth?": "Open expanse—nothing holy."[52] This answer would be applicable to Christian discourse about the Holy Spirit, if it really deals with the Holy Spirit.

If in our formulation "Enlightenment in the Holy Spirit" nevertheless we do not abandon the designation "holy," it is for two reasons. First, because the relation of the spirit-world to Transcendence is thereby expressed; and second, because thereby reference is made to the sanctifying, soteriological-ethical significance of the special characteristic of Transcendence to become open and active. We can speak of this by means of the respective material symbols of the Buddhist and Christian doctrine of redemption—especially in respect to those of Transcendence.

4. The Nothing as the Mystery of Being and the Buddha-Christ as Lord of the True Self

In Buddhism the three concepts Nothing, Buddha, and True Self are used synonymously, that is, as designations for one and the same thing. The True Self is Buddha, and both are at the same time Nothing. To attain the True Self is the goal of the Buddhist way of salvation by which through Enlightenment one

---

the inner light (*lumen internum*) to which the mystics gave special weight, became in the time of the Enlightenment and of Idealism the light of reason, or of Absolute Spirit. In the monism which replaced the early Christian and traditional Christian dualism between the spirit of the world and the Spirit of God, in consequence of which what is real is the rational (Hegel), this modern Western conception of Spirit and of enlightenment proved to be related to those of the Far East, both of Brahmanism, Confucianism, and Taoism on the one hand and of speculative Buddhism on the other. An excellent documentation of the latter can be found in n. 26 of chap. 1 on *The Awakening of Faith* in the form of a kind of catechism of questions and answers of the "Mind-Only-Buddhism" of the "new Wisdom school" of the Prajna-Paramita-Sutras (Edward Conze, *D. T. Suzuki on Indian Mahayana Buddhism*, ed. with an intro. by Edward Conze, Harper Torchbooks [New York: Harper & Bros., 1968] 62, 112ff.) whose effect in contemporary Japanese Zen Philosophy is still to be determined.

[52]This story which is often and favorably cited in Buddhist literature is to be found, among other things, in the first example of Bi-Yän-Lu translated into German by Wilhelm Gundert.

enters into Nirvana. The one enlightened becomes a Buddha and enters into Nirvana. Whether this goal is understood existentially as a possibility in time or is represented mythologically as postmortal, in either case we have to do with an overcoming of the absurdities of existence (*Dasein*) and its fulfillment of meaning. In its unenlightened condition existence is embedded in the absurdity of unending becoming and perishing. For the one who is enlightened, however, this sorrowful world of samsara is extinguished, even if he finds himself still in its midst.

In Christianity something comparable to this series of Buddhist concepts encounters us in the concepts of the original creation out of nothing, of Christ as the Lord of the New Creation and of the redeemed one who as a New Creature attains to his true self. Yet we must not overlook the fact that in Christian dogmatics these three concepts stand in a relation to one another different than the Buddhist and that they principally do not form a unity and are not understood as synonyms; rather, either because or in spite of their interrelation they are respectively understood as special figures. The Creator of the original Creation and of its unfolding is quite different from the Lord of the New Creation, and neither represents Nothing; rather the primal state and final kingdom are forms of Being to be distinguished from the powerlessness of Chaos. That holds true for the final Kingdom no less than for the original Creation, in that in the original Creation the power of Chaos, as is evident from its effects, is only conquered in a preliminary way and will be overcome only at the end of history. But as in the beginning Being appears in the place of Non-Being, so at the end this dissolves not into a Nothing but in place of the form corrupted through the Fall its perfected form appears which—after the exclusion of every possibility of a new Fall—is yet more perfect than the original.

Even in Christianity conceptions appeared which approach an identification of the three things in question. There is already in the New Testament the idea that Christ is not merely the Lord of the New Creation,[53] but already in the first Creation plays the role of the mediator of Creation; and even in the later conception of salvation history the continued creation is regarded as standing not only under the providence of God, but even as the realm of Sovereignty of the exalted Lord.[54] The exaltation of the Redeemer to deity posed great difficulties for the

---

[53]Col 1:16-17.

[54]Old Protestant Dogmatics speaks not only of the three offices of Christ (*tres munera*), the prophetic, the highpriestly and the royal, but in the last named also distinguishes further between the *regnum potentiae*, by virtue of which Christ participates in God's rule over the world; the *regnum gratiae*, which he exercises in and by means of the Church; and the *regnum gloriae*, which he will establish upon his Return, until he gives it over finally to God. For the

Christian faith, to be sure, because it stood in tension with the biblical conception of Creation and in contradiction to the philosophical concept of God. The discussions about the Trinity and incarnation of Christ and the fate of the respective doctrines bear eloquent witness to this fact.[55]

The same problem with respect to the relation of God to the person of the redeemer arose even in regard to the relation of both divine persons to humanity. While an identification of the Creator with humanity as his creatures seemed impossible without abandoning the nature of both, it was believed possible—even already in the New Testament—to speak of an ontological connection of humanity at least with Christ, of a being in Christ.[56]

From the exchange of the subject of Christ and the "I" in Paul's Christ mysticism, in which a distinction is still made between the two subjects, there later arose out of the distinction—on the basis of the substance metaphysics and an extension of the incarnation to all flesh, which gave rise to the cosmic aspect of early Christian cosmology—a union of humanity with Christ, and only then on the basis of the union of the Son with the Father[57] even the possibility of a union of human beings with God.[58]

Despite the obvious relationship between this God- or Christ-mysticism and the Buddhist equation of the Buddha and the True Self, we should not overlook the distinction which exists between the two. This distinction to which today's Buddhists refer more emphatically than is the case with representatives of Christian mysticism, consists in the fact that it always deals with a union with something, with God or Christ—in secular Western mysticism with a union with the self or Being, while for the Buddhists the True Self, which awakens to its original Buddha-being, dissolves into the Nothing which is the Buddha. These mystics agree with the Buddhists only insofar as they follow the way of knowledge similar in many respects to that of the Buddhists as a way of attaining their goal: a way of becoming free from the representations of objective consciousness into

---

connection between this doctrine of the threefold Sovereignty of Christ, which begins with his exaltation, and the three aspects of God's continuing creation (*creatio continua*) in his conserving (*conservatio*), accompanying (*concursus divinus*), and ruling (*gubernatio*) activity, cf. Fritz Buri, *Der Pantokrator* (Hamburg: Herbert Reich-Verlag, 1969) 46ff., and the elaboration of this program in *Dogmatik als Selbstverständnis des christlichen Glaubens*, 3:120ff.

[55]Cf. ibid., 3:579ff., and 2:116ff.

[56]Cf. Albert Schweitzer, *Die Mystik des Apostels Paulus* (Tübingen, 1930) 122ff. [ET: *The Mysticism of Paul the Apostle* (New York, 1931) 121ff.].

[57]John 17:21-22.

[58]Cf. Martin Werner, *Die Entstehung des christlichen Dogmas* (1941) 389-90 [ET: *The Formation of Christian Dogma* (1957) 165ff.].

a—as they say—nonobjective thinking, which, they—like those—assert, leads to the true view of things and their final interconnection, even if in a finally ineffable, and therefore generally unprovable, way.[59]

Just as little as a thinking that does not think remains thinking, does a thought Nothing remain a Nothing. Nonobjectifying thinking, like an objectified Nothing, is a contradiction in itself, and if the expression "not" or "nothing" is anywhere in place, it is because here not and nothing are thought. This is the basis of the mutual questionableness of Christian mysticism and Buddhist Sunyata philosophy. In their way they both document their questionableness by speaking separately of God, Christ, and the Self, or of Nothing, Buddha, and the True Self, despite their asserted identity, and thereby objectify the Nonobjectifiable which they intend.

This criticism is anything but negative. For with the recognition of the unavoidableness of this objectification of the Nonobjectifiable found on both sides, the possibility arises of the overcoming of the problematic bound up with both series of triads, namely, of a positive understanding. Nothing and Creation, redemption and selfhood, and their representations are objectifications of Non-objectifiable realities which can be laid hold of only in objectifications of consciousness, imaging, and thinking. The terms of both sets of three correspond exactly with what we have defined as the nature and function of symbol. Understood and used in this way they arrive at their correct significance in which they represent at the same time a not unessential correction of their traditional employment in Buddhism and in Christianity.[60]

The concept of the True Self characteristic of both Buddhism and Christianity is the legitimate symbol of the destiny of the human self to be able to understand itself. To this end the self must objectify itself, stand over against itself. It is not in a position to understand itself without such objectification. In its enactment this self-objectification is nevertheless not objectifiable, because therein the self is simultaneously subject and object. Therein it observes itself and yet at the same time not only observes itself. For this enactment of self-understanding which in its Nonobjectifiablity makes use of objectifying conceptuality, the concept of the True Self can serve as a symbol. The True Self is the self fulfilling its destiny to understand itself. Without this enactment of its self-understanding it is not the True Self. Only as this being which seeks to understand itself is it a True Self. Of this specific human possibility intended in this symbol for the

---

[59]Particularly instructive is Shizuteru Ueda, in his Eckhart book, 140ff., where he shows that even Meister Eckhart, because of the "theistic substructure" of his "mysticism of infinity," does not attain to the "Nothing" of Zen.

[60]The exposition of this matter in connection with Christianity forms the 3rd vol. of *Dogmatik als Selbstverständnis des christlichen Glaubens.*

True Self—a possibility it can even miss—there is still more that can be said. Here we are concerned primarily with the relation between the two other symbols of the Nothing and of the Buddha, or of Creation and the Christ, and with the significance which these two symbols rightly acquire.

In contrast to the symbols of the True Self, Nothing, and Creation or creature, Buddha and the Christ are symbols not of human immanence but of Transcendence, to which we experience ourselves related in our self-understanding. In a certain sense, to be sure, even the symbol of the True Self is a symbol of Transcendence insofar as we experience our destiny in it. But while this destiny embodied in the True Self has to be actualized in the human self, in those two other pairs of symbols the origin of this destiny is meant. In this respect however an apparent difference obtains between the Buddhist and Christian use of these terms. Whereas in the Buddhist understanding of the symbol of the True Self—for the sake of the identity of the three things—the Nothing and the Buddha essentially belong to it as its transcendental dimension, Christian theology here makes a dimensional difference: *Deus Deus, creatura creatura est.*[61] Between the two there exists even in the Catholic speculation about *analogia entis* "a greater dissimilarity in all similarity."[62] In Christian theology, although with different nuances, a distinction has been made from time immemorial between two revelations of God, namely, a so-called general, natural, revelation which takes place in the sphere of human reason which however does not lead to salvation, that is, to a solution to the question of meaning; and a so-called special, supernatural saving revelation in Christ. For traditional Christian faith the question of meaning is finally insoluble apart from the latter. Nature and history indeed point to manifold structures of meaning, but precisely in their manifoldness they oppose one another and represent more of an enigma than a univocal meaning of our existence in the world. Only the question, Why is there this existence?, that is, the question of being, is thought to be answerable with full certainty. Everything that is owes its existence to God the Creator, whose creation it is, and everything that happens, happens according to His will, is his work. Salvation, the fulfillment of meaning in particular and in general represents on the contrary something special; it is a matter of the revelation of God in Christ and of his saving work in history. Theology is not content with the present creation, but rather proclaims a future New Creation in which the partially or fully hidden God, the *Deus absconditus*, will only then be revealed in his glory.

---

[61]Oecolampadius to Hedio, which can be read on the front wall of the interior of the Cathedral Hall of the Bishop's Court in Basel.

[62]Denziger, *Enchiridion* 806; cf. Fritz Buri, *Dogmatik als Selbstverständnis des christlichen Glaubens*, 3:635ff.

This "Christian" solution to the problem of meaning is however bound up with difficulties, in that a series of new problems issue from it. The primary among these, with respect to the Creator God and His creation, is the fact that the world-transcendence of a demonstrable God becomes problematic, in that he becomes a piece of the world and appears to be burdened with its problematic of meaning. This applies no less to the appeal to the revelation of the Redeemer God in Christ, in that this can only make the vain attempt to defend itself from the charge of being a mere postulate of a very natural satisfaction of a need only through the replacement of objective rational knowledge by a similarly objective faith-knowledge. The price it pays for this is that, like revealed theology, natural theology expresses its content as objectivities of understanding, or faith, instead of becoming aware therein of the limits of conceptual knowledge or seeing in it symbols of self-understanding.

If Buddhism suffers the same fate in its Trikaya Buddhology, in this connection it is nevertheless better than when it allows the personifications of the Buddha and of his Buddhas to dissolve into nothing and thus avoid objectification. But it thereby also loses the possibility of employing them as symbols of self-understanding, and this all the more when it identifies the true self with the Nothing. For with its characterization of the Nothing as "neither Nothing nor Being" it would have an appropriate expression for the fact that every pronouncement about Being contains a self-contradiction, because it makes it into a being; therefore it can represent a symbol of the awareness of the absolute limits of objective conceptual thinking both in respect to Being and also to the self. Similarly, in setting out from the self which suffers under Dasein's fracture of meaning and which is in quest of the meaning of existence it would possess the possibility not merely of sinking into the silence of Nothing, but of making the true Self into the very place at which in the midst of the Nothing a person will become aware that he is determined to be a special being which can become aware both of the mystery of Being which for his knowledge is a Nothing as well as of an illumination of this mystery which occurs in himself. This illumination consists in becoming aware of this mystery and is therein something quite different from this mystery which requires silence on his part: the mystery of his obligation and ability to ask about its meaning and about the possibilities open to him for the realization of the meaning of his existence in the world. It is not the meaning of total existence that is illumined, but the meaning of being-a-self amidst the mystery of Being and its riddle of meaning in which the one who so understands himself experiences himself to be so thoroughly entangled.

For this special revelation of the meaning of the mystery of Being the Buddha, or—in view of the manifold modes of the revelation of the mystery of Being—the Buddhas, could be a symbol. Despite their different heritage and names their proper function then would be same as that of the correctly understood symbol of the Christ in the Christian tradition. Such a collective view of the Buddha and Christ symbol could preserve Christianity from the exclusive claim that—contrary to its historical problematic—its central figure is a symbol of a falsely understood universal salvation. But it could also prevent Buddhism from identifying the Buddha absolutely with the Nothing and of dissolving the Self into the Nothing. The Buddha-Christ would then as a special entity be distinguished both from the Nothing, or the mystery of Being, and from the True Self, to some extent standing between them as the mediator of a special revelation of the mystery of existence as well as of the human possibility of becoming a self.

Neither the Nothing nor the mystery of Being would accordingly be the meaning of human existence. In Nothing no meaning is to be found, unless perhaps it is the placing in question of every expressible meaning, and the mystery of Being contains the enigma of all existence. The True Self is rather the "place" of the revelation of the meaning of existence, because in it the question of meaning bursts forth and because in it it is always to be answered. It must decide how it will understand itself. It can neither avoid this decisive move by silence, nor will it be relieved of this by a god. To be sure, in its quest for the meaning of Being it experiences itself as surrounded by the Nothing in which all objectifications of its thinking finally fail, and in its replies to the question of meaning in the context of a mythology can appeal to divine revelation. But as in its questioning it has to do not simply with the Nothing, but with this questioning, it distinguishes itself from the silence of the Nothing, so it is itself in each case that appeals to divine revelation.

In one case as in the other—whether in becoming speechless before the mystery of Being which for objectifying thinking is a Nothing or in the enactment of its likewise nonobjectifiable self-understanding in which it is determined in relation to the meaning of its existence—the self experiences itself as related to realms with which it cannot simply be identified, because it thereby would not only fail to recognize their nature, but would forfeit itself. This epistemological Nothing-character has much in common with the mystery of Being. But in an ontological sense they are both not Nothing; rather the mystery of Being is mystery because it is experienced as such, and the true Self occurs in that in its awareness of being destined for self-being it distinguishes itself from that Nothing of the mystery of Being as well as experiences itself as related to it, and this in a twofold manner: first, negatively, in that it cannot understand itself to be the origin of the mystery of Being, not even in the sense that this is to be sought in the fact that its epistemological capacity is limited to what is objectifiable; and then positively, in that in this limitedness it experiences its thinking as encompassed by the mysterious Nothing of Being, and this in such a way that even its own nonobjectifiability is enclosed in this mystery.

The matter, in respect to which Christian theology correctly speaks of the twofold revelation of Transcendence, may accordingly be explained, and it may even have clarified the way in which the distinction between the two modes of God's revelation is to be understood. It is one and the same mystery of Being, both when we are left speechless in respect to the quest for the Being of beings and its meaning as a whole, and when it is revealed to us in such a special way that we get to engage these questions, and indeed in such a way that we have to perceive the present possibilities of meaning theoretically and practically.

The Christian doctrine of the Trinity may serve as a symbol of the dual-istically structured metaphysic issuing from this twofold revelation of transcendence insofar as, as a whole, it represents a mystery inaccessible to reason, while in the individual parts of the *opera Trinitatis ad intra et ad extra* lying at the heart of the riddles of meaning it points nevertheless to the possibilities of the realizations of human existence grounded in Transcendence—something which is not the case in the Nothing-Monism of the Buddhist Trikaya doctrine. To be sure even the doctrine of the Trinity conceives of the *opera Trinitatis ad extra* as indivisible and points to the fact that every individual possibility of meaning in the world is encompassed by the mystery of Being and has to take it into account in its actualization. But within Transcendence itself its individual persons are distinguished from each other as special types of functions. Over against this substantializing, Buddhist emptiness would be preferred, but not in such a way that the self which avails itself of this speculation for the enactment of its self-understanding would dissolve into the Nothing. In the enactment of its self-understanding the self would not perceive itself as a Nothing, but as the "place" of a special disclosure of the mystery of Transcendence in becoming aware of its being destined for personhood in community, as this is symbolized in the mutual interpenetration of the individual persons of the Trinity (*perichoresis*).

A correspondence to this understanding of the doctrine of the Trinity as a symbol of the twofold revelation—of the mystery of Being and its enigma, and of the special possibility of the meaning of human existence—can be found in what Shin'ichi Hisamatsu described as the "heart" or "heart of Nothing," "the heart of the Buddha."[63] The Nothing would correspond to the mystery of Being which represents a Nothing for our grasp; the "heart of the Nothing" or the "Buddha-heart," to the special revelation of the possibility of the meaning of our existence in the world in Christ, of Being-in-Christ, in which Christ—or the Buddha—would be "the heart of the True Self."

It is true that both symbols can be distinguished in the fact that Christ as the Second Person of the Trinity is neither identical with God nor indeed with the Nothing, as is the case with the "Buddha-heart," but is a symbol of a self-under-standing which is not fused with Transcendence but experiences itself as related to Transcendence. In this experience of itself as related to Transcendence the self

---

[63]Shin'ichi Hisamatsu, *Die Fülle des Nichts*, 39ff.

remains differentiated from Transcendence and becomes one neither with God nor Christ, while in Buddhism the Buddha and the self are held to be identical and dissolve together into the Nothing.

In both cases a decisive meaning is apparently ascribed to the self, its nature and its conduct corresponding to their different understanding of Transcendence: in the one case, as a relatedness to Transcendence or as a self-understanding of such a relatedness to Transcendence; in the other, as an identity of the self with the Buddha in the Nothing. From this it follows that self-understanding, as much as it is determined by a conception of Transcendence presupposed in its enactment, is at the same time of special significance for the conception of the *Gestalt* of Transcendence. That justifies our focusing on those symbols which in Buddhism and Christianity speak of the nature and function of the self.

5. The Buddha-Nature and Human Image of God, of Bodhisattva-Being and Being in Christ

The two pairs of concepts—Buddha-nature and the human-Divine Image, and Bodhisattva-Being or Being in Christ—are to be distinguished on the one hand by the fact that the former deals with basic determinations of human nature, while the concepts of the second pair are of a soteriological and ethical kind. On the other hand in the two pairs of concepts we have to do at the same time with the equally basic distinctions which obtain between Buddhism and Christianity in their respective anthropologies. These material distinctions are not to be overlooked in the three realms that were mentioned.[64]

Regarded anthropologically, the distinction consists in the fact that according to the Buddhist conception the Buddha-nature is ascribed to all beings, not only to human beings, but also to animals, plants, and stones. Christianity, on the contrary, speaks only of the Image of God in human beings, that is, it represents it as a trait which distinguishes them from all other beings. If on the contrary Buddhism assigns the Buddha-nature to every being living and dead, this is an essentially anthropological assertion which claims that no fundamental distinction obtains between human beings and all other beings.

To be sure Buddhism understands by the Buddha-nature something quite different from what Christianity understands by the Image of God, and this material difference between the view that the characteristic of being is ascribed to every being and that which reserves it for human beings constitutes the actual difference between Buddhist and Christian anthropology. In the eyes of the Buddhists the essence of the Buddha-nature consists in the Nothing, and in the Nothing every thing is identical to the Buddha. Only in their *thingness* are these

---

[64]Cf. Fritz Buri, *Dogmatik als Selbstverständnis des christlichen Glaubens*, 3:41ff.

entities to be distinguished from one another. But this is a consequence of the discriminating thinking from which—according to the Buddhists—all ill (*Unheil*) originates and which can be overcome only through the *Aufhebung* of this thinking in Enlightenment.

In Christianity, on the other hand, the capacity for discriminating reasoning—above all other endowments—belongs precisely to the original Image of God which human beings, to be sure, partially or even fully forfeited in the Fall. But although with this Fall a discriminating knowledge or a craving for such is involved, this nevertheless does not—as in Buddhism—form the cause of ill. It is rather—and remains so despite its weakened condition due to the Fall—a neutral matter with respect to salvation. The real threat to human beings arises—as at the beginning of their history—only through the supervention of the sinful will which craves objective knowledge of its consequences, that is, for the sake of the knowledge of good and evil, and makes further use of it even in its condition weakened by sin.[65]

On this basis discriminating knowledge stands in a kind of twilight in Christian faith. On the one hand it belongs to the creaturely human faculty without which human beings could not even know the command of God, and on the

---

[65]An interesting parallel to the assumption of a residual Image of God in human beings even after the Fall is afforded by the "Store-Consciousness" (*Speicher-Bewusstsein* = *Alajavijnana*) of the Yogacarin. Although these two notions stand in a relationship of some difference, they nevertheless correspond to each other in their nature and function, as well as even in the problematic bound up with them which here and there has occasioned much discussion. Cf. Conze, *D. T. Suzuki on Indian Mahayana Buddhism*, 160ff. [ET: 168ff.]. A discussion of this important concept of Buddhist psychology can be found in Keiji Nishitani, "The Standpoint of Zen," English translation by John C. Maraldo, still unpublished. See above.

As it was deemed necessary in Buddhism to assume a "Store-Consciousness" to establish a kind of core of the person despite the dissolution of consciousness into the five skhandas, as rebirth demanded it in accord with karma, so in Christianity the doctrine of redemption demanded a personhood not completely destroyed by the Fall to whom sin could be reckoned and the salvation deed of Christ could become efficacious. Both instances could result either in ill or salvation—in ill, through attachment to things or through a part of self-redemption which restricts grace; in salvation, as the foundation of Buddhist self-redemption or as a point of contact for the divine event of redemption.

It is remarkable that this correspondence between a residual *Imago Dei* and *Alajavijnana* continues to go unnoticed in the subsequent confrontation of Christianity and Buddhism.

other, this endowment can become the occasion and means of disobedience against God, so that it forms for them simultaneously blessing and curse. In Christian faith the role of reason is burdened with two other difficult problems which are strongly interrelated: the problem of free will and the question about the source of evil in God's good creation. In the course of the history of doctrine free will has taken many different forms according to the measure which assigned to the damage caused by the Fall and the kind of resolution which each believed found by taking account of freedom and bondage (*Unfreiheit*) in human behavior. Still unanswered, the question of the origin of sin and its connection with evil, that is, the question of theodicy, nevertheless persists.

If Christianity is thereby plagued with the opposition between a monism of a good Creator God and a dualism of God and the Devil, on the Buddhist side the difficulty is no less great, in that the question is posed as to how non-Enlightenment is possible if the Buddha-nature as being-enlightened constitutes the nature of all things. Briefly concluded: Not-being-enlightened is Enlightenment, Enlightenment is Not-being-enlightened; this contradiction cannot be expelled from the world, and yet at the same time, with it, even the Buddhist path of salvation which consists in the attainment of Enlightenment becomes illusory. To the Buddhist way of argumentation which leads ad absurdum there corresponds on the Christian side the postulating of faith-knowledge which finally leaps over the rules of logic and deteriorates into arbitrariness and one-sidedness.

In the dilemma in which theology—from the vantage point of its metaphysical presuppositions—sees itself threatened in relation to these questions, recourse has been had to that which approaches the Buddhist doctrine of the Nothing—even if differently conceived—as when evil was spoken of in the sense of the platonic *Meon*, or when the Nothing was thought of as What-God-did-not-will.[66] Another similarity presents itself in the assumption of a paradisiacal innocence in the condition before the Fall and the "innocent play" of the Enlightened beyond good and evil.[67] The difference consists in the fact that that which there is considered to have been lost is here considered yet to be attained, and further, that whereas in Christianity, in place of the innocence lost through sin, there appears the justification which shows up at the Last Judgment on the basis of the reconciliation effected by Christ, in Buddhism it is a matter of attaining, not

---

[66]Cf. Karl Barth, *Church Dogmatics*, III/3 para. 50; "Gott und das Nichtige," 327ff. [ET: "God and Nothingness," 289ff.].

[67]So especially Keiji Nishitani, in chaps. 3-6 of *Religion and Nothingness*: "Nihility and Sunyata," "The Standpoint of Sunyata," "Sunyata and Time," and "Sunyata and History."

something lost, but the insight of Enlightenment, that the Buddha-nature was never lost.

The doctrine that the Buddha-nature cannot be lost, or the erroneous claim that it can be lost, and even the Enlightenment—which discloses this error—and its consequences for the behavior of the Enlightened are represented most beautifully in the series of pictures entitled "The Ox and its Oxherd" which is a virtual counterpart to the Catholic Stations of the Cross and similarly aids meditation.[68]

With this the soteriological and ethical aspects have appeared which are bound up with the anthropological pair of concepts and which we have already discussed relative to conceptual pair, Bodhisattva-Being and Being-in-Christ. Both pairs highlight commonalities as well as differences, and problems peculiar to each as well.

Now it remains to indicate two formal commonalities. One consists in the fact that Bodhisattva-Being and Being-in-Christ are conditions of being found on the path to salvation or in a process of salvation which is not lasting but moves toward a goal. This goal—and that is the second common feature—transcends everything earthly and human, in that for the Bodhisattva it culminates in becoming a Buddha and for the one who is in Christ, in participation in a new completed form of the world which is quite differently conceived—but in any case not in becoming a Christ in a way parallel to becoming a Buddha. For unlike the Buddhist who becomes a Buddha, the Christian never becomes a Christ—either on the way or at the goal. It is all the same whether the Christ is in me or I am in the Christ—the Christian and the believer do not become one, but remain distinct from each other. That "God will be all in all," as it says in 1 Cor. 15:28, is nevertheless still something quite different from Nirvana or merely the end of an age of the world; it is rather a final creation with no rival. Having said as much, we have finally arrived at the differences of the two ways of thinking.

To be sure there remain certain commonalities in relation to the course and realization of the process of salvation. Like the arhat who abjures the world and thereby becomes a supernatural being, the one who is in Christ does, or experiences, this, and there is formed in him a nature which is no longer attached to the world. Both ways of salvation are also similar in the fact that they designate precise preliminary steps for fulfillment, e.g. the Pure Land before extinction in Nirvana, or conditions on earth or beyond before the Last Judgment and Glorification. But even in the latter the Blessed remain distinct from God. With but one exception, the Christ, they do not return from the Beyond, as the Bodhisattvas do, in that they renounce remaining in or even entering into Blessedness in order

---

[68]Cf. the treatment of this series of pictures by Shizuteru Ueda, above.

mercifully to embrace weak, erring human beings and so become cultically honored by them as Bodhisattvas or as Buddhas, as the Catholic Church honors the saints.

In this connection it could be asked whether and how far, formally regarded, the Christian Redeemer is comparable with the Buddha, or one of the Buddhas, with Amida, say, or not rather with a Bodhisattva. Jesus as a man and as the returning Exalted One would be much like a Bodhisattva; as the Exalted One and as the Second Person of the Trinity, on the contrary, he would stand at the threshold of the Buddha—if indeed the latter were not at the same time—despite his three bodies—the Absolute Nothing. It is apparent here that Buddhology and Christology are constructed precisely from quite different perspectives and in a quite different manner, and in their conceptuality cannot be made directly to coincide. The principal difference in this regard consists in the fact that in Christology the terms are sharply defined and therefore the dogmatic problems appear to be sharper—precisely in the solutions which are attempted in the respective doctrinal formulations, while Buddhism—for the sake of the rejection of discriminating thinking and even on the basis of the developmental history of Buddhism—in this regard carelessly displays a great confusion.

With all the ambiguity of its conceptuality, in consequence of which everything can also mean something else, that is, its partial or complete opposite, there is one problem which Buddhism has not been able to avoid: the problem of redemption by one's own powers or redemption through the power of another. It is the same problem which appears in Christianity as the question of the justification or making-righteous of the sinner by God's grace alone or with human cooperation through good works. As in Buddhism, Zen- and Amida-Buddhism stand opposite each other as representatives of self- and other-Redemption, so in Christianity certain forms of a Reformation doctrine of grace stand opposite the Catholic synergism of nature and grace which by the former is branded as "works-righteousness." But on both sides there are mediating positions between the two extremes: in Buddhism there is Zen with its recognition of the Nembutsu as a koan and, alternatively, the Buddhism of grace with its understanding of Sunyata as the renunciation of one's own work.[69] In Christianity the Reformed estimation of good works as a test of thankfulness for experienced grace[70] or as a sign of election[71] and the Catholic emphasis upon prevenient grace in the

---

[69]Cf. D. T. Suzuki, "The Koan Exercise and the Nembutsu," 146ff., in *Essays in Zen Buddhism: Second Series*, 4th ed. (London: Rider and Company, 1974).

[70]So, e.g., in the 3rd section of the Heidelberg Catechism, "Of human thankfulness."

[71]The so-called *Syllogismus practicus* which is found not only, but above all, in later Calvinism. Cf. Karl Barth, CD II/2, 367ff. [ET 335ff.].

process of salvation[72] correspond to these neutralizing attempts. In the latter this cooperation of nature and grace is so differently developed that it is evident that we have to do all along the line more with compromises than with real solutions to the problem.

Shakyamuni, who commanded his disciples to tread "the middle path," is quite different from the Buddha of Nirvana or Amida of the Pure Land, just as the Jesus of the Sermon on the Mount is quite different from the Jesus who sits at the right hand of God, who uses all his influence with God the Father so that his own might enjoy the benefits which he had achieved for them. Just as the "middle path" is not intended as a mean between self- and other-redemption, but a sanctification to be effected without assistance; so likewise Jesus did not consider his ethical instructions to be a substitute for defective ethical performances, but rather intensified the demands of the Jewish law and judged their fulfillment as indispensable for surviving the Last Judgment.[73]

The differences in ethics which arise with Shakyamuni and Jesus derive from the worldview which each presupposes and the possibilities of redemption foreseen in each. With Shakyamuni the cosmic presupposition consists in the doctrine of *pratitya-samutpada*, which allows a redemption only through the extinction of the desire of life and simultaneously demands a universal compassion apart from attachment to the things with which one is connected. With Jesus, to the contrary, it is the end-time situation which demands a radical love of neighbor as well as makes it possible. In Buddhism this becomes different to the degree that the Hinayana arhat ideal, which already represents a misunderstanding of the "middle path," gives way to the metaphysicalizing of the Buddha and the transformation of the holy ones concerned with their own perfection into helping figures of the Bodhisattva. Because of the delay of the Parousia and its own continued existence, Christianity was driven to a similar modification of its ethical demands and a dogmatic transfiguration of Christ's redemptive work. While Jesus wishes to bring about the new Aeon through his suffering and death, his redemptive work was interpreted in later times in the sense of an institution of sacraments whose consumption was said to ensure access to Blessedness in the beyond.[74]

---

[72]This grace of God which precedes every human striving for holiness (*gratia praeveniens*) was made into dogma in the degree on Justification and the relevant canon 3 (Denz. 1525, 1553) of the Council of Trent in 1547.

[73]Matt 5:17ff.

[74]Thus already in John 3:5; 5:24ff.; 6:40 et al. Cf. Albert Schweitzer, *Die Mystik des Apostels Paulus*, 340ff. [ET: *The Mysticism of Paul the Apostle*, 349ff.] and Martin Werner, *Die Entstehung des christlichen Dogmas*, 396ff. [ET: *The Formation of Christian Dogma*, 167ff.] and elsewhere.

In this connection, out of the ethic of the Kingdom of God an otherworldly ethic arose, whose flight from the world was nevertheless again overcome by an untenable secularization in whose this-worldliness man and his cultural activity increasingly displaced God and his saving activity. Although the modern Western ideal of humanity with its ideas of innate human worth already represents a product of the secularization of biblical-Christian salvation-history, it seems to be more closely related to the Bodhisattva ideal and the concept that the Buddha-nature belongs to all beings than to its own historical heritage, which—it must be said—is also connected with its link to non-Christian antiquity. What nevertheless distinguishes Western culture from the Buddhist world now as before is the Hinayana denial of the world and the Mahayana metaphysics. Meanwhile the Far East is today witnessing a massive secularization under the influence of Western science and technology in respect to which Buddhism must examine the meaning of its metaphysics and the meaning of a critical attitude toward the world and a different attitude toward the world resulting from it, as is especially the case in the Kyoto School.

This preview of possible future developments causes us to make a necessary as well as an essential limitation in respect to the Buddha-nature and Imago Dei, as well as to Bodhisattva-Being and Being-in-Christ. We have hitherto spoken of these as concepts and treated them as objects of conceptual thinking. But now we shall treat these expressions—Buddhist as well as Christian—as statements which give information as to how and in what way they wish to be understood as the meaning of human existence with regard to the enigmatical meaning of the mystery of Being. Their ideas and concepts deal with self-understanding, and they even effect self-understanding with the help of these ideas and concepts. When they lapse into difficulties and contradictions, as shown above, or fall into errors and nonsense and contend with each other about the tenability of their positions, this rests on the fact that neither the human self which they contest nor that to which they experience themselves related can be conceived in the concepts of discriminating knowledge, but transcend it. This is true whether the self and its relationships are conceived in the sphere of immanence or of an objectified Transcendence, as the Nothing or as a supernatural world, as identical with or different from one another, monistically or dualistically. In each case we are dealing with concepts which are as unavoidable and indispensable for the enactment of self-understanding as they are inaccessible and problematic for its expression. The nature of symbol consists precisely in this fact, as we have developed it in the epistemological section and as it has already proven itself for us in respect to the metaphysical statements.

Buddha-nature and Imago Dei, as well as Bodhisattva-Being and Being-in-Christ, are symbols of the True Self, of its nature and its being determined for a life appropriate to its relatedness to Transcendence. The statements about its nature and the behavior resulting therefrom appear differently in accord with the

Transcendence to which the self is related in each. But as the criterion for the truth of the Buddha-nature and the Imago Dei consists in their relatedness to Transcendence which exceeds all their objectifications, so the attitude appropriate to it consists in the never-ending quest for what Bodhisattva-Being and Being-in-Christ must mean in every individual situation. As the Buddha-nature and Imago Dei are perverted in each of their objectifications, this happens likewise in Bodhisattva-Being and Being-in Christ if the attempt is made to establish generally valid rules and criteria for them and then to use them as a generally definable norm for ethical conduct.

Buddha-nature, no less than Imago Dei, is constantly in danger of falling victim to the original sin of being desired as a possession, and of being seen as something one may have at one's disposal. But even at the very point of recognizing their perversion and their impending loss, both reveal themselves anew in their true form as being finally impossible to lose. The problematic of all their conceptual objectifications, pointed out above, will have sufficiently shown this fact. For this reason, however, this problematic must not be judged only negatively, but rather positively; because it is precisely in the failure of the conceptual apprehension of these qualities that the symbolic nature of the objectivity thus put to use is rendered visible; and in that light also the real essence of those qualities becomes apparent. Under this formal aspect, which embraces all differences as to content, Buddha-nature and Imago Dei can thus not be played off against each other, as is often done, but must be viewed synoptically, as symbols of self-understanding in whose enactment we experience ourselves, governed by the transcendent nature of that understanding.

The same applies also of the other pair of concepts or symbols, except that—due to their more soteriological and ethical orientation— they—unlike the first, expressly anthropological pair—deal not so much with our original destiny, but rather with the course we still have to pursue toward its fulfillment. Yet Bodhisattva-Being and Being-in-Christ are to be described not as symbols of what has been attained, or even of enactments of self-understanding which are constantly to be newly undertaken in the specific present, but rather of their future realization in our conduct determined by them. Because of this orientation toward the future one could speak of an eschatological character of Bodhisattva-Being and Being-in-Christ, as this is expressed in their orientation toward the Pure Land or Nirvana, or to the reign of Christ or the Kingdom of God. These eschatological symbols of Buddhist soteriology and ethics, no less than the anthropological ones, are concerned with the present, in that they deal not with a purely future event, but with an eschatological event already breaking into the present. that is, with an eschatology presently being actualized, as is certainly the meaning of Bodhisattva-Being and Being-in-Christ.

In this regard the two symbols no longer stand opposed to each other; rather in their synoptic view the problematic of their conceptuality for both even proves fruitful: with its all-merciful Bodhisattvas Mahayana Buddhism corrects the deficient Hinayana Arhat ideal as an attitude that is unrealizable in the world and that stands in contradiction to the "middle path." The Catholic Church accepts the consequences of the delay of the Parousia, institutionalizes itself in the world and introduces the cult of the saints. But both the "Great Vehicle" and the "Great Church" can justify the transformations of their traditions only by appealing to reinterpretations of their origins. Hence arises for both the problem of self- and other-redemption. The extreme attempts at redemption offered in Shinran's Buddhism of grace and Luther's *sola gratia* prove to be ethically problematic and susceptible to secularization, in which the factor of grace no longer prevails, but is expected in the progress which is said to depend on human effort alone. With this we arrive once more at the point of departure of the two series of developments—except that now it is no longer the ideal of holiness, but the secular ideal of progress that is unfeasible, and that it is no longer the delay of the Parousia but the dangerous course of technology that forms the basis for disappointment.

The cause of this problematic which pervades the history of Buddhism and Christianity in different forms, yet in the same way, is to be sought nowhere else than in the previously mentioned objectification of symbols of self-understanding of the person who seeks the meaning of his existence in the world—a self-understanding which in its enactment is dependent upon conceptuality, yet is not objectifiable as such—and in the misconception of a natural or supernatural manipulability of the fulfillment of his destiny—a misconception that arises from a misunderstanding of his true situation. But neither in Bodhisattva-being, nor Being-in-Christ, can it truly be a question of objectifications of self-redemption, or of redemption from without, or their connections in any given conceptual constructions, but rather will it be a question of symbols of a self-understanding which, in its inner enactment as well as in its external conduct, which it can control, comprehends itself as being dependent on a merciful fate, which it cannot control, and on a special revelation of the mystery of being; and on the latter's granting the success of our own ineluctable commitment. Understood in this symbolism the Bodhisattva in no way belongs merely to Buddhism, just as little as Being-in-Christ can arise only on the turf of Christianity. If the Christian rightly understands his Being-in-Christ, even the Bodhisattva-Buddhist has a place in it, and in this "Great Vehicle" of the true Being-in-Christ even that will no longer appear strange but as familiar. If anywhere, here is the "place" where "East and West" do not remain merely "East and West," but share a common future.[75]

---

[75]"East is East and West is West, and never the twain shall meet" (Rudyard Kipling). Used as a motto by Rudolf Otto in *Westöstliche Mystik* (1926); now in Gütersloher Tagenbücher, Siebenstern 318.

Now we arrive at the fourth aspect of our comparison of Buddhism and Christianity in their historical development, namely, the philosophical, to whose treatment we have assigned the symbols of the silence of the Buddha and the Cross of Christ.[76]

6. The Silence of Buddha Shakyamuni
and the Cross of Christ

This pair of concepts or symbols has both formal and material significance for our theme. Formally it reaches beyond the plateau of our comparison of Buddhism and Christianity insofar as the epistemological view, which we have already developed relative to the symbols of Enlightenment and Holy Spirit and then utilized in our treatment of the metaphysical and anthropological-soterio-logical-ethical aspect, attains its most powerful symbolic expression. Now we must distinguish from this formal function the significance of its material content for the conception of its history, and with it, of its culture and community. We wish first to consider the specific historical-philosophical importance of the silence of Buddha and of the Cross of Christ in order definitively to present several fundamental remarks on the relationship of Buddhism and Christianity in their contemporary encounter in reference to their general significance.

At the conclusion of the preceding section we spoke of the philosophical aspect of the comparison of these two religions by pointing out the eschatological character of Bodhisattva-Being and Being-in-Christ and discussing its fate in the history of Buddhism and Christianity. We have to expand what was set forth in this connection concerning a possible conferral of meaning in the self-understanding of the individual and its realization, by establishing the consequences

---

[76]On the relation of epistemological, metaphysical, and ethical aspects to the philosophy of culture and history to be unfolded in what follows, cf. Fritz Buri, "Encounter on the Basis of the Question of Meaning," *JR* 9/1 (1976): 12-25; "Die Bedeutung des Sein-Sinn-Problems für inter-kulturelles religiöses Verstehen," *ThZB* 34/5 (1978): 277-91. On the background of Albert Schweitzer's view of the relationship of ethics and culture in the history of the West and in that of the East, especially in view of the role which is assigned in the former to biblical-Christian eschatology and its problematic, cf. Albert Schweitzer, *Kultur und Ethik* (1923), *Das Christentum und die Weltreligionen* (1924), *Die Weltanschauung der indischen Denker* (1935) (today in *Gesammelte Werke* in 5 vols., Zurich: Buchclub Ex Libris, vol. 2) and Martin Werner who in his dogmatic works expands both the historical view of Schweitzer and its significance for the philosophy of culture, and in whose second part has unfolded the program of a Christian faith-culture which stands at the end of part 1 of his *Der protestantische Weg des Glaubens*.

which issue from this individual realization of meaning from the standpoint of community and by discussing the question of the significance which belongs to the course of history and its goal with respect to the meaning of existence and its actualization.

In this regard only the problematic of their respective cosmologies is common to Buddhism and Christianity. Individually and as a whole, their eschatology is very different, even if certain correspondences are to be established both in individual ideas and concepts, and in their problematic as a whole.

Such a correspondence between Buddhist and Christian eschatology presents itself in the central ideas of Nirvana and the Kingdom of God. As Buddhism speaks of being freed from the world of samsara in terms of Nirvana, so Christianity sees in the Kingdom of God the goal which God traces out in the history led by him both for the elect as well as for the whole of creation. With this general characterization of the two eschatologies we have already signalled their fundamental difference from which their individual differences arise.

Buddhism not only knows no Lord of history, but no history at all which could be directed by such a one toward a goal or proceed on its own to a final goal. Rather it views all happening in a universal connection incorporating the whole realm of Being. But this happening has neither a beginning nor an end, but constantly repeats itself in successive dissolutions of one world into another in eternal recurrence. In their rebirths even the living beings participate in this cosmic circular course until desire of life by which they are entangled in samsara is extinguished and they are themselves extinguished in Nirvana which can happen within one, or in the course of many, kalpas.

In contrast, the Kingdom God brings a once-for-all end to a world created once by God, whether through a total transformation of what now exists or through a New Creation which replaces it. In the framework of this final cosmic event the destiny of the individual attains its goal, in that he participates in it through transformation or resurrection and in the judgment either enters into eternal blessedness or is condemned to hell. In contrast to extinction in Nirvana what is essential here is the restoration and preservation of personal being.

Besides all these differences in details there are also parallels between both eschatologies, as in the distinction of stages in the final condition, in consequence of which believers in Amida first enter the Pure Land and afterward into Nirvana, just as the believers belonging to Christ first participate in his reign and afterward enter into the Kingdom of God, when the Son surrenders his sovereignty to the Father.[77] More important still than these mythological ideas of the Beyond are those actualizations in the here and now of earthly existence for Buddhist and Christian self-understanding. As the Buddhist prepares his future

---

[77]1 Thess 4:13ff.; 1 Cor 15:20.

karmic condition in his present existence and can already experience Nirvana in Enlightenment while still in the body, so may those who decide for Christ while still alive suffer with him and die to their old nature and so be certain of their surviving the Last Judgment. Even as Amida allows his merits to go to his followers, so, too, the Christians appeal to the fact that the active and passive obedience to God representatively achieved for them by Christ will be credited as their righteousness. In place of a redemption through the power of another, Zen Buddhists speak of the "Great Death" which each must die and of the Enlightenment that comes to them as "resurrection." But there are parallels to this dying and rising in the present life even in the New Testament and Christian notions about faith—except that here the "Great Death" consists not, as in Zen Buddhism, in the "Great Doubt" but, to the contrary, in a faith that cannot be shaken by the evidences of reason—a faith in whose light the wisdom of the world appears as foolishness.[78] Despite the fact that in these diverse forms of an actualization of eschatological notions their mythical language is retained, we know from both Buddhism and Christianity also of heavenly realms in which dwell God and the gods, future and past Buddhas and Bodhisattvas, or Christ in his preexistence and after his ascension, as well as of corresponding underworlds with their demons and the damned.

These mythologies of the Beyond, especially those of Indian and Tibetan Vajrayana Buddhism[79] and of Japanese Shingon Buddhism which is related to it[80] represent a rich field of research for psychology and depth psychology, whose

---

[78]1 Cor 1:20ff.

[79]Conze, *D. T. Suzuki on Indian Mahayana Buddhism*, 166ff. [ET: 174ff.]; *Das Totenbuch der Tibeter*, Diederichs gelbe Reihe (1975); *Das Erbe Tibets* (Bern: Kümmerly und Frey (1972) 149ff.

[80]The best orientation to the nature of Japanese Shingon Buddhism is to be found in the work of its founder Kukai, called Kobodaishi: *Kukai: Major Works Translated, with an Account of His Life and a Study of His Thought*, by Yoshito S. Hakeda (New York: Columbia University Press, 1972), and in the picture album, published in the Shogakkukan, about the Koyasan, the Holy Mountain of Shingon-Buddhism, Kukai's place of activity.

The other form of esoteric Buddhism in Japan, Tendai Buddhism, was founded by Kukai's contemporary, Dengyo Daishi, on the Heisan. Cf. Bruno Petzold, Dengyo Daishi and German Theology," EB 2 (1922/1923): 348-57 (a review of his writings on Tendai Buddhism newly edited in 1979 is to be found in EB 13/2 (1980): 135ff.) and Ui Hakuju, "A Study of Japanese Tendai-Buddhism," in *Philosophical Studies of Japan* (Tokyo: Japan Society for the Promotion of Science, 1954) 1:33-74.

findings can be used even in psychotherapy.[81] In contrast to these perspectives which operate according to the principle of "nothing else but"—and even to the so-called demythologizing—the method of existential interpretation applied by us in the above discussion sees in this material mythology and "at the same time" symbols of self-understanding which in its enactment can be no further psychologized. It deals with "demythologizing" only insofar as for us the myths play not merely the role of objectifications of consciousness and of conceptual thinking, but of symbols of an self-understanding which is nonobjectifiable in its enactment and which in its objectivity points to its nonobjectifiable content and its relation to Transcendence.

In contrast to the orthodox forms of Buddhism and Christianity, which regard the contents of their mythologies as supernatural objectivities, and to their secularizations for which these mythologies are "passé," Zen Buddhism corresponds to our principle of the nondemythologizing existential interpretation of mythology as the appropriate language of self-understanding. A comparison of different types of commerce with mythology—whether psychologizing, orthodox, secularistic, or even existential—makes it apparent that we are not only dealing here with a hermeneutic which utilizes the formal principle, but that the mythologies in question, or their disenfranchisement, are also of significance for the self-understanding that results therefrom, and not only, as we have seen in the previous section, in respect to the specific situation of the individual and its relation to its environment, but—and this is what interests us—in respect to the understanding of history and the judgment about its goal, its meaningfulness or final lack of meaning. This judgment on the nature of history is not without significance for the conception of personal and social actualization of meaning. In view of the problematic which manifests itself therein the fundamental question arises as to what significance can be assigned to history in respect to the question of meaning—whether the meaning of our existence depends on the meaning of history, or whether and how it can in any sense be independent of it, and what that would mean for the conception of both.

For both points of view—the phenomenological, under which the determinable connection between the picture of history and the picture of existence has to be conceived, and the normative which in view of the situation proves itself to be necessary—the conceptions of history represented in Buddhism and Christianity comprise an exemplary sphere of application.

---

[81]Cf. E. Fromm, D. T. Suzuki, R. de Martino, *Zen-Buddhism und Psychoanalyse*, Suhrkamp Taschenbuch 37 (1972), with bibliographies in the notes; C. G. Jung's introduction to D. T. Suzuki's *Die grosse Befreiung*, 4th ed. (Zurich: Rascher, 1958).

The cyclical conception of history arising out of the doctrine of reincarnation, which yields a redemption only as release from this samsara in Nirvana, proves to be pessimistic in respect to the attitude toward history and negative with respect to the estimation of the human possibilities for actions which change the course of history. At best, history can be the realm in which human beings free themselves and their environment from this entrapment and thereby secure a better karma for their next reincarnation. But before their entry into Nirvana they and their surroundings remain under the grip of the law of karma, and their extinction in Nirvana can only consist for them in an escape from this fate in which, after their rescue, the rest of the world remains embedded. In their Nirvana state they could be thought of as redeemed only insofar as they no longer knew about it in this state. For if they still knew about it, they would no longer be in Nirvana.

Out of the insufficiency of the arhat ideal which is concerned only with its own salvation and the knowledge of interrelatedness of all beings there arose in Mahayana Buddhism the notion of the Bodhisattva, and in the Buddhism of the Pure Land the figure of the all-compassionate Amida. But neither the Bodhisattvas nor Amida invalidate the fateful character of history through their compassion, but presuppose it in their redeeming activity and only thereby confirm it, in that the Bodhisattvas expressly act only within samsara, and Amida only invalidates it within the Pure Land, while outside it goes on as usual. While the Bodhisattvas after all intervene actively in the sphere of the unredeemed only to a certain degree and through their actions realize a meaning within it, for Amida—except in his own redemptive activity—such a separation from activity which corresponds to a norm and activity which does not correspond to that it would represent a misunderstanding of human pride which he extinguishes by his grace which justifies sinners. Both conceptions of redemption moreover appeal to the logic of the identity of absolute contradictories, in consequence of which samsara is Nirvana, by which the condition of the world is recognized as hopeless—as it is—and every change appears as illusory.

In its traditional form the Christian conception of history exhibits a great similarity with that of Buddhism and its problematic on one side, and a great dissimilarity on the other. Agreement and difference arise from the completely different foundations of their conceptions of history. While behind the Buddhist conception lie the doctrines of the reincarnation and of the universal relation of all things in "their dependent origination," for its view of history Christianity appeals to a redemptive history directed by God which encompasses both the Fall and its negative consequences as well as the dualism of the original and fallen creation and its dissolution through the saving work of Christ—partly already in time and in a completed form at the end of time. Because history stands under the curse of the defection and salvation can be effected only through God, history as a whole and the possibility that human beings can change it for the better, are here just as pessimistically and negatively evaluated as in Buddhism. In respect both to his own individual salvation in the future and that of his fellows one can exercise a good or evil influence through his actions. As the Bodhisattvas refuse Nirvana for the time being out of compassion for those who suffer, so Christ abandons his divinity in order to accomplish his redemptive work on earth in the form of a servant, and after his exaltation will return once again for the final struggle with the powers of evil, and his holy ones will join the one who appealed to them for their support. But it deals with this, not merely like that of the Bodhisattvas as it were, with the appearance and disappearance of individual islands in the sea of despair (*Unheil*) in whose infiniteness their vow to save all fades away, and not even like that of Amida with a sanctioning of what survives by the grace of being accepted into his Pure Land. Although there is something similar in certain forms of a Christian faith in the savior and the Beyond, Christianity regards everything that happens on earth relative to salvation or its lack in connection with a history which proceeds towards the realization of its redemptive goal under God's direction, quite irrespective of whether this consists in an eternal blessedness of the elect or of the eternal condemnation of the non-elect, or reconciliation of all.

History, and whatever pertains to the reaching of its goal, is evaluated more optimistically in the secularization which this faith in redemptive history has experienced in modern Western scholarship, because here the pessimism about the present world due to sin is replaced with a faith in progress, in consequence of which human beings achieve what must otherwise be expected in vain as a miracle of God. But actually what we have here is only one illusion replaced by another whereby the profaneness of the present time in comparison with the time of traditional Christian redemptive history is still more strange to reality, because it nullifies the problematic of the meaning of human existence which that redemptive history with its dualism always takes into account. Thus it is not surprising that the knowledge of the illusory character of modern cultural optimism either leads to nihilism or to attempts to restore the Christian tradition in some kind of modernized forms. But just as nihilism contains a contradiction in itself and cannot exist alone in its self-absolutizing, so those attempts at restoration cannot be convincing, because that which they wish to validate once again is already the product of the expectation about history held by Jesus and primitive Christianity which is shown by the actual course of history to be illusory, that is, because of their unwillingness to acknowledge the fiasco to which Christianity paradoxically owes its history. While the delay of the Parousia represents an exponent of the actual problem of the meaning of history, Christianity in a measure loses the truth of its origin when it succeeds in dissolving this problematic in a supernatural or even a natural history of redemption.[82]

A comparison of the Western conception of history with the Buddhist indicates that the basically different metaphysics of history underlying each has an effect on the ideas of the nature of history, so far as they are of significance for the individual's realization of meaning, but also on the transindividual spheres of the formation of social relationships, namely, politics, science, art, religion, and culture. As transitory and insignificant as what humans create in these spheres may seem—measured by the Eternal and in view of the salvation of the individual contained in them—these are only human creations, outlasting the generations, which lend their stamp to history in its individual epochs and comprise its essence. Even taking into account their respective negative attitudes toward the world, Buddhism and Christianity display an impressive array of human cultural creations.[83] Quite apart from the fact that even a negative attitude toward the world can have a creative cultural and world-forming effect, as can be observed in Buddhism and Christianity in rich measure, so both nevertheless possess moments which occasion a positive posture toward the world. In Buddhism this world-affirmation has different sources, such as the bonding of all beings in dependent origination, the effort to permit things to show themselves as they are, and naturally the compassion for all being. In Christianity a positive estimation of the world issues from the fact that it places God's creation in the custody of human beings, who are guided to its end by the commandment of love.

But these possibilities of a positive attitude toward the world assume in Buddhism and Christianity not merely a different form corresponding to their different grounding, but on both sides they are bound up with characteristic problems. From his presuppositions the Buddhist sees no need to have a world-transforming attitude as this is commanded of the Christian as the ally of God in the struggle against the powers of evil. But just as the former must constantly be on guard lest he become attached to the objects of his compassion, so the latter faces the danger of letting his actions encroach on God's activity, of

---

[82]Cf. Fritz Buri, "Heil in permanenter Säkularisierung. Ein Beitrag zur Hermeneutik der Säkularisierung," *Kerygma und Mythos*, 6/9 (Hamburg: Herbert Reich, 1977): 255-65.

[83]For the significance which is ascribed especially to Zen Buddhism, one may consult in particular D. T. Suzuki, *Zen and Japanese Culture* (London: Routledge and Kegan Paul, 1959), and in general Edwin O. Reischauer and John Fairbank, *East Asia: The Great Tradition*, 6th ed. (Boston and Tokyo, 1969), and Hajime Nakamura, *Ways of Thinking of Eastern Peoples*, 3rd ed. (Honolulu: East-West Center, 1968).

mistaking his will for God's, and of making the Kingdom of God into a cultural ideal. In both cases it is not easy to establish the boundaries between what is permitted and what is not, between what is commanded and what is forbidden. If one can accuse Buddhism of a lack of external measures for establishing social justice, one can also accuse Christianity of an excess of external reforms at the expense of inwardness.

On the contrary the relation of Buddhism and Christianity to science in the modern sense is plainly different—at least in respect to its origin and development in the previous century. Today, however, the Far East is no less concerned with its problematic consequences than the West. Equally problematic are the connections with politics which presently engage Buddhism and Christianity—contrary to their doctrines and their observance. Even religious art can serve not only to honor God and his Son or Buddha and Bodhisattvas. In both cases religion can degenerate into magic, and appears to be most helpful in this regard.

With all the diversity of their metaphysical grounding and their problems the Buddhist and Christian conceptions of history nevertheless have this in common, that they aim to bring the meaning of human existence into connection with history as a whole and to establish it in this context and thus to justify their respective conceptions. Through the picture which is composed from history—quite irrespective of whether it proves to be positive or negative to the meaning of the whole, or consists in a combination of both assessments—it is hoped to obtain a guarantee for the possibility of a fulfillment of the meaning of existence. If the judgment on the meaning of history turns out to be positive, as in the case of the speculations concerning the cosmic Buddha or that of the Buddhist Consciousness-Only-Doctrine and of the Absoluteness of Spirit in German Idealism, as well as in the Christian doctrine of Providence, there is the expectation of obtaining an innerworldly guarantee of the fulfillment of human longing for meaning. If, to the contrary, the fragility of this immanent historical construction of meaning is recognized, there ensues a flight to what lies beyond history, which is conceived in the mythological forms of the Pure Land and of Nirvana or of the "other shore" or of the Christian heaven and their opposing pictures of hells and purgatories. As images of the goal of life these notions also belong to the realm of history. The combinations of the doomed present and the redemptive future in the eschatological overcoming of reincarnation in Nirvana, or of the fallen creation through a new creation, correspond to its nature as a temporal passage of events. The *futurum* of these notions can even be transformed into a *nunc aeternum*, as is the case in the equation of samsara and Nirvana and in Christian mysticism or in defiant self-assertion in an self-absolutizing nihilism.

All these pictures of history and even of its dissolution into nonhistory represent attempts at a metaphysical or redemptive guaranteeing of the meaning of human existence. They are housings in which human beings believe they are able to escape "homelessness" in the world; even the homelessness can be made into a home as is the case when from the message of the end of the world is constructed a system of belief as the foundation of the Church.

"Homelessness" and "End of the World" are slogans which permit us to turn to Shakyamuni and his silence and to Jesus and his cross in place of our demonstrations of Buddhist and Christian conceptions of history. The silence of Shakyamuni and the cross of Jesus are actually symbols by means of which the problematic of the meaning of history presented above can emerge, and this in such a way that this problematic is not obviated but becomes understandable as the meaning of the riddle of history.

Like Shakyamuni who was not content to leave his palace but maintained his homelessness in his silence about the questions of metaphysics, so Jesus was not content to preach the nearness of the end of the world, but got himself crucified to turn the tide of the Aeons. That silence and this cross are the keys for understanding the meaning of history. In the building of its metaphysic of history Buddhism lost this key, as did Christianity in that of its redemptive history. These palaces must be demolished if one is to find enlightenment in silence, and this can be effected in the cross through the Holy Spirit. In this sense the silence of the Buddha and the cross of Christ not only represent symbols of the meaning of history, but as such they encompass those which became apparent to us in epistemology as well as those which we deemed essential for metaphysics and for anthropology, soteriology and ethics, in that they confer a final enlargement and deepening upon their formal and/or material structures.

Silence is the most appropriate symbol for the experience of the boundaries of conceptual knowledge regarding the mystery of Being and its riddle in human history and in each individual historical situation. We can just as little discover in nature a final ground and meaning as in history. Although individual structures of meaning are not lacking in both realms, it is not possible to establish in them a universal meaning. What we are and can be cannot be derived from them, because we experience ourselves as gripped in this mystery of meaning and entangled in its riddle of meaning. Silence is therefore the symbol of its essence because it is silent before our questions. Thus it is clear why this which stands over against us in silence and demands our silence is also designated as the Nothing.

Yet this Being or Nothing is not only silent, but also speaks, addressing us in its mystery and in its enigmatic nature, both around and even within us. We would not speak of it if it did not around and in us address us through its mysterious and enigmatic nature and thereby induce us to speech and speechlessness. In its depth dimension the history of humanity is such a speaking of transcendence and a speaking with it, even if it is not understood as such and often cannot be understood as such. As should be evident in the above, a human being is a being who understands and can be understood, but can also misunderstand himself and others. Failure to understand oneself and one another belongs to the riddles of history, just as the understanding of one's own and the alien self belongs to the special revelation of the meaning of the mystery and enigmatic nature of history. Human beings are those who can understand and misunderstand; and history is to be distinguished from nature—whose appearances can only be explained and understood but which cannot explain and understand themselves—by the fact that it is the sphere of humans beings who seek and understand meaning. As such it represents the sphere of the special revelation of the mystery of its being a being—always against the background of the residual enigmatic nature of its total meaning.

If the concept of revelation which we have already used to designate the sphere of the quest for meaning and its distinction from that in which nothing happens, that is, the distinction between nature and history, so we will only become aware of the relatedness of our existence in nature and history to transcendence if we become conscious of the indisponibility of this distinction in its emergence and extinction and take notice of the fact that it concerns the meaning of our existence, its gain or loss. It is even apparent here that therein it deals not merely with a theoretical, but also with an extremely practical matter, namely, with a relation to transcendence which is not merely to be enacted emotionally or intellectually, but wishes to be realized by us in our behavior. In this connection we always stand in danger of destroying nature or becoming its victim. What arises out of it as history is repeatedly swallowed up by it, and in its silence is lost—happily or unhappily—the echo of the voices of past races and the call of the living to a better future.

In the sections on the metaphysics and soteriology of Buddhism and Christianity we have seen how both have their symbols for these different kinds of relatedness to transcendence: Buddhism, in the Nothing, in the Buddha and in the true self of the Bodhisattva; Christianity, in God the Creator, in Christ and in Being-in-Christ. We have also seen how they systematize their notions of transcendence in the doctrines of Trikaya and the Trinity, and what problems for ethics arise for them out of their notions of transcendence. While this need not be repeated here, we should call it to mind because—as shown above—these positions come to a head in the philosophy of history and here finally a position is taken with respect to them.

For this reason we have to connect the Buddhist and Christian positions—from their epistemological presuppositions to the ethical consequences of their metaphysics, anthropology and soteriology—with their central symbols of the silence of the Buddha and the cross of Christ, respectively, and in such a way that these are no longer restricted to the historical-philosophical aspect.

Our intention of extending the significance of these two symbols individually to the whole of Buddhism and Christianity seems counterindicated by the fact that the cross of Christ is as strange to Buddhism as the silence of the Buddha is to Christianity. Buddhists customarily deny the cross of Christ as a theory of sin and blood-sacrifice incompatible with their whole conception of redemption, just as Christians confront the silence of the Buddha with the revelation of God in his word.

Just as what is rejected there may prove to be a distortion of the symbol of the cross which Buddhism rightly repudiates, so Christianity might come to a unanimous understanding of the silence of the Buddha, because it knows not only of God's speaking, but also of his silence, and in its speaking of God there are even phenomena on both sides for whose deepening interpretation the symbols of the opposite side could be useful, and there are estimates of such a modus operandi which are just as capable as they are inadequate for a stronger valida-tion. In this, both the symbols of the silence of the Buddha and the cross of Christ would become effective, each in a twofold way—a negative and a posi-tive—and at the same time become expanded and only then unfolded in their significance.

Epistemologically considered, the silence of the Buddha is primarily a symbol of the Being of beings and of his Nothing-Essence for our conceptual knowledge. This cross of the limits of our knowledge we have to accept and endure in order to become aware of the reality of the true self which is as some-thing that is as little generally provable in general as that which Christ intended with his death on the cross, but which as such ought to be in this form an illu-sion. No self-deception—to the contrary—is the experience of being freed for true selfhood for the one who shares this experience through the crucifixion of the objective "I." Therein the Zen Buddhist and the Christian symbols of the "Great Death" and the "resurrection" to the true self correspond to each other, in a way in which the *Noli me tangere* of the Johannine Christ is valid of the latter as well as the former.[84]

But as in Buddhism this true self does not remain limited to the individual who experiences it, but there proceeds from it an enlightenment of the world, in which this true self first manifests itself in its true being, so for the Christians

---

[84]John 20:17; but even the disappearance of Christ in Emmaus (Luke 24:31) and the rebuke, in the story of the ascension, of the disciples who gazed at the Lord being taken up by a cloud, are in any case connected with the promise of his bodily return (Acts 1:11). In the story of unbelieving Thomas two moments are connected—the touching of the scars of the resurrected one and believing without seeing (John 20:27ff.). In Buddhism, to the nonobjectifiablity of the presence of the Buddha there corresponds the famous warning: "Do not tarry where the Buddha dwells. . . . Make haste to where the Buddha does not dwell" (Hisamatsu, *Die Fülle des Nichts*, 49).

personal Being-in-Christ extends to the body of Christ which is to be realized through its behavior in the world as a new creation. In this event redemption through one's own power and through the power of another are not to be distinguished; rather it represents for self-understanding a grace which encompasses both modes of operation, for which—if not falsely objectified—the grace of Amida and the grace of Christ can be a symbol.[85] In this view the Bodhisattva

---

[85]To the Pauline paradox "Work out your own salvation with fear and trembling; for God is at work in you, both to will and to work for his good pleasure" (Phil. 2:12, 13) there corresponds exactly the nature of faith (*shin-jin*) in Jodoshin Buddhism which is very well conceived by Ryogi Okochi and Klaus Otte in their translation and discussion of the *Tan-ni-sho* (Bern: Origo Verlag, 1978), when they wrote of it: "It is on one side through and through the willful and existential decision of each individual. On the other, it is taught that faith is not 'my faith,' but a gift of Amida-Tathagata and that saying the nembutsu is again also caused by Amida-Tathagata. . . . Actually the event of faith 'in me' can be expressed neither actively nor passively; it eventuates 'from nature,' from the 'self' or from itself. At the same time it is concretely experienced by the individual. So thinks Shinran when he speaks of 'the natural spontaneity' of faith and of saying the nembutsu. Here even the opposites of 'Ji-riki—Ta-riki' (self power—other power) is overcome" (164). Cf. the explanation of Shinran's concept of faith by D. T. Suzuki in his edition of Kyogyoshinsho, as Amida's gift and as being-faithful (215) and Morris J. Augustine, "Faith and Religion in Japan," JR 10/3 (1978): 21-52. If Paul, in the passage cited, continues with "Do all good things without grumbling or questioning, that you may be blameless and innocent, children of God without blemish in the midst of a crooked and perverse generation, among whom you shine as lights in the world," and in view of the possible martyrdom which he and his followers faced concludes this disheartening warning with the words "I am glad and rejoice with you all. Likewise you should be glad and rejoice with me" (Phil 2:14ff.), even so this activity of his faith directed toward the "Day of Christ," as a light in the existing world and as the basis of the joy of the hearts of the faithful, corresponds to what Shinran said of "naturalness," "natural spontaneity" (*jinen*) and "joy in faith" (*shingyo*) effected through Nembutsu (Suzuki, ibid., 216). On this point, also, Okochi and Otte correctly note: "Shinran equates 'Tariki' (other power) with 'Jinen.' With this his religious thought takes a step further, i.e., than the rest of Pure Land Buddhism, in order to avoid the danger of notional objectification of Amida's Tariki" (150). For Christianity as well as Buddhism, the problem of nature and grace arises only out of false objectifications of symbols of faith, which in the enactment of its self-understanding is certainly dependent on concepts, but cannot therein be objectified. In this sense this problematic belongs essentially to faith

can similarly be understood as one being-in-Christ and the one being-in-Christ as a Bodhisattva. Both have crucified the self that is only concerned with itself and thereby become a true self in compassionate love.

From this intentional application of our two symbols to the anthropological, soteriological, and ethical sphere we can derive the understanding of its correct significance for metaphysics. It is not for nothing that in Buddhism one speaks of the Nothing, of the Buddha, and of the Buddha-nature, although the three are identical. Similarly, in the mystery of the Trinity three persons are distinguished

---

in Amida and in Christ. As for what they have in common in respect to their works in the existing world in view of the future, Okochi and Otte again note correctly: "The Pure Land is established by the vow of the Buddha (in Jodo-Buddhism: Amida Buddha) to rescue and awaken there all suffering beings. This Land is by no means conceived substantially and constructively, as though it lies outside or above this world. Thus it is generally taught in Buddhism: if the human heart is purified, such a one lives, while in the midst of this E-do" (i.e., in the impure land; Early Christian = in the present evil age), "nevertheless already in the Pure Land" (Pauline = in Christ, that is, in the turning point of the Aeons set in motion since the resurrection of Christ) (151).

Because Buddhism lacks this dynamic conception of history which rests on the assumption of a cosmic redemptive event in progress, it emphasizes all the more an inwardness detached from things, while Christianity has paid the price of secularization for directing itself toward world change—because of the illusory nature of its notion. In any case the authors have not recognized this connection. Otte, to the contrary, thinks he can overcome the historical problematic of Christianity and solve the problematic of the meaning of human existence, in that he argues in a "reason illumined by faith" that "the absurd cross of Christ has been transformed once for all by God in the resurrection." His partner in dialogue seems to be nearer to reality when he recalls in this connection the "enslavement of the heart" and the "Nothing" in Buddhism (135ff., esp. 156).

As a positive expansion to this criticism directed at Otte's "enslavement" in the "once for all" and at the way in which his partner envelops himself in a Buddhist "Nothing," attention should be given to the beautiful book of Silvia Ostertag, *Einswerden mit sich selbst, Ein Weg der Erfahrung durch meditative Übung* (Munich: Kösel-Verlag, 1981), at the conclusion of which this student of Dürckheim's, in a chapter entitled "Ein initiatischer Weg und christlicher Glaube," describes in persuasive, repeatable *openness*, how Zazen showed her the way to understand the mass, and how participation in the Eucharist can mean the same as participation in the Zazen practice—not as something "at one's disposal" but as mediation of life in community, in which Christ joins "even as an other and unnamed reality."

despite their essential oneness. In their conceptual inconceivability the identity of the different manifestations of transcendence corresponds to the silence of the Buddha and to the inconceivable self-abandonment of God in the crucifixion of his only-begotten Son. Buddhism knows not only about the Nothing, as Christianity knows not only a *Deus absconditus*; for both know as well of a special revelation of this metaphysical mystery in the realm of incarnation, redemption, and the conduct of the redeemed person in the world, in which the symbols of the silence of the Buddha and the cross of Christ attain their positive significance. The Buddha's silence points to the indisposibility of this special revelation and activity of Being, or mystery of the Nothing and its enigma, and Christ's cross points to recognition of the indisposibility demanded of us. In relation to transcendence this recognition of its final inconceivability is nevertheless positive, because only therein does it appear as truly transcendent, so that it does not forfeit its transcendence in becoming immanent in the Buddha nature, or the Imago Dei, but rather is only then properly revealed.

The same twofold function—negative and positive—also belongs to the symbols of the silence of the Buddha and of the cross of Christ in respect to the Buddhist and Christian historical-philosophical notions about the cessation of samsaric rebirth in Nirvana or the end of the present sovereignty of demons in the Kingdom of God.

Shakyamuni was silent before questions about an individual and universal metaphysic of history, and Jesus died on the cross conscious of having been abandoned by God.[86] Just as the former was resigned to silence and thereby disappointed those interested in posing metaphysical questions, so Jesus goes to the cross without his disciples understanding the significance of this undertaking. In both instances the inquiring disciples received only answers which related to their conduct: from Shakyamuni the direction that they must bring the desire of life to extinction on the "Eightfold Path" in order to attain to Enlightenment; from Jesus, the command to follow him in forsaking life in order to attain to eternal life.[87]

On the basis of the experiences undergone by both communities of discipline in obedience to these mostly negative messages, their determinate representatives

---

[86]If one of the words of Jesus on the cross could be regarded as original, it would be the cry of despair strikingly transmitted in his saying: "My God, my God, why hast thou forsaken me?" (Mark 15:34 and Matt 27.46), while the ones preserved in Luke and John are to be regarded as attempts at an edifying mitigation of the end of the life of Jesus. The fiasco of this end cannot be toned down by appealing to the fact that that word stems from Psalm 22 which not only expresses despair, but also its overcoming through trust in God's help.

[87]Matt 16:21ff., and par.

elevated their earthly masters to heavenly beings, as in the appearances of the eternal Buddha, or the incarnation of the pre-existent Son of God; the former, to the Lord of the Pure Land or identity with Nirvana, and the latter, to Lord of his Kingdom which he finally gives over to God that God may be all in all. The positive effect of the Buddha's silence and of Christ's cross consists in their facilitation of the realization of these goals.

But like the negative aspects of these modes of conduct of Buddha and Jesus, so also their positive side stands in closest relation with the self-understanding of both masters and their disciples. In neither case are we dealing with a self-contained metaphysic of history independent of any self-directed understanding on the part of its representatives, but with symbols of self-understanding which arise out of its enactment and become efficacious in its repetition. We think it is not possible to understand the symbols of Buddha's silence and Christ's cross in any other way than as normative statements about the meaning and goal of history. In such an understanding and use of these symbols we do not run the danger of wishing to derive from them theories about the future of history which turn out afterwards to be illusory wish projections, as has happened in the course of their history on both the Buddhist and Christian sides and still happens when Nirvana and the Kingdom of God are juxtaposed to each other as incompatible opposites. Doubtless the position on history will vary according to whether it sees in the signs of one or the other objectifications of these matters. But precisely in contrast to these uses which rest on a misunderstanding of these notions, the symbols of the Buddha's silence and the cross of Christ prevail as criteria of their correct understanding. They fail this test so long as a philosophy of history understood under the sign of these symbols is not affected by Shakyamuni's aversion to metaphysical questions and Jesus' reluctance with respect to apocalyptic notions, but is rather justified through the attitudes of both.

In any event we have to make concessions regarding both the philosophical-historical significance of both symbols and our understanding of the symbols which were regarded as determinative for the spheres we have just dealt with.

First, this understanding of Buddhist and Christian symbols is enlightening and achievable only for those who feel at home in the traditional realms of both symbolic worlds, but not for those who have "deceased" in the narrow confines of their own world of symbols or terms, of which one could say "Let the dead bury their own dead."[88]

Second, we concede that the existential content of the self-understanding and its consequences for the meaningful possibilities of our existence which were unfolded above in quite different ways by means of Buddhist and Christian symbols are by no means limited to the symbolic realms here articulated. These matters

---

[88]Matt 8:22.

can also appear outside of the spheres of their origin, above all, even where the mentioned symbols have lost their religious character and fallen victim to secularization. From their beginnings Buddhism and Christianity have been secularizing phenomena, albeit in different ways: Buddhism as the secularization of Brahmanism and Hinduism, Christianity by its entry into a history it did not foresee. As such, they have spawned a wealth of religious symbols. Irrespective of these considerations, normative symbols of the self-understanding in vogue at the time have arisen as a result of their later processes of secularization. To the degree that these are poorer in substance in comparison with those of earlier times, they are no longer burdened with its problems—also others have possibly taken their place. Just as misunderstandings and perverse uses of such symbols customarily occasion their secularization, so out of a new self-understanding new symbols can enter in to replace those which have become questionable.

Now we have to reckon with both concessions, or with the consequences issuing from both: namely, the modern impossibility of a religious provincialism and also the increasing presence of a secular world in which the mutually opposed claims of Buddhism and Christianity to an exclusive and at the same time universal significance for salvation have become an anachronism.

Although we are convinced that the understanding of Buddhist and Christian symbols developed here can be achieved as a possible understanding of normative self-understanding not only by Buddhists and Christians, but by modern persons as such, regardless of provenience, so we nevertheless find ourselves between all three fronts, and our understanding of symbol is rejected by confirmed Buddhists, Christians and secularists alike. But even if we have to have the woeful experience in these latter instances, which Karl Jaspers once expressed in the sentence: "There is no talking with religious warriors,"[89] so we take confidence in view of the previously assumed possibility in Jaspers' favorite saying from the Seventh Letter of Plato to the effect that the truth can occur "among good friends in good hours." In our case this would be the hour in which—"in loving struggle"—also a Jaspersian expression!—the Buddha-Christ proves to be the Lord of the True Self. But because these "good hours" are of the nature of eternity, none of these in time can be the last. This means, that with the conclusion of this treatment the examination of this confessional formula undertaken by us is not finished, but has only been opened.

---

[89]Karl Jaspers, *Der philosophische Glaube angesichts der Offenbarung* (Munich: Piper Verlag, 1962) 88. [ET: *Philosophical Faith and Revelation*, trans. E. B. Ashton (New York: Harper & Row, 1967) 45.]

Appendix 1

Nothingness and the True Self in Light of the Problem of Meaning and Being

A lecture delivered at the Fourteenth International Congress of Historians of Religion, Winnipeg (17-22 August 1980)

At a recent meeting of Buddhists and Christians in Hawaii a Japanese, before beginning his lecture, asked the audience, because the lectern was a little too high considering his stature, "Can you see me?" Then he ducked behind the lectern for a moment, so that he completely disappeared behind the lectern, only to emerge again an instant later. And, in fact, one could see better than before. That was not, however, merely a jest, which made the audience laugh, nor simply a visual aid. Rather, in that little scene this Buddhist—consciously or unconsciously—had shown us a basic structure of his thinking. And—I believe—not only of his Buddhist thinking, but of thinking as such, including the so-called Western type: the subject is obstructed by an object. It disappears into the nonobjective state, yet reemerges from the Nothing; and only now do we recognize what things are all about in truth.

Regardless of our tradition, in thinking we are always dealing with objects which are intended by a subject, to which the subject is related and which seem to be related to the subject. Thinking always occurs within a subject-object relation. That is not just the starting point; rather, we are constantly in a diffuse state of unity with our surroundings, as perhaps in awakening from sleep. We don't know where we are, and what is actually wrong with us. But as we become clearly conscious and begin to orient ourselves by thinking about our situation, our world becomes split into a subjective and an objective sphere, and as long as we think, we are not able to escape this subject-object split. Without it we would again sink into a kind of sleeping or dreaming, or even lapse into hallucinations. There may even be beautiful dreams and great intimations which mediate to us such a state. But it is only in the clear consciousness of thinking in the subject-object split that we are able to judge the significance of such experiences, and to distinguish between deception and truth, illusion and reality.

As we saw in the scene depicted at the outset, a ducking into the nonobjectifiability of the object world can be a visual aid for knowing the objectifiablity in its true suchness. At this point Far Eastern Buddhist and Western Christian thinking begin to part company. In this way we should be dealing in each case with a thinking of both traditions which misunderstands itself. On the contrary a thinking that corresponds to its definition remains within the immutably fixed boundaries of the objectifiability of the subject-object split of consciousness, knows about nothingness in the nonobjectifiability of Being and the true self, and speaks of it in symbols as the equally unavoidable and appropriate objectifications of the nonobjectifiable.

It is this that we want to explain in the following discussion of the problem of Being and meaning. We proceed, not from specific mythological or speculative dogmatic positions, by making use of a thinking in objective conceptuality, which is also used for the intellectual enactment of their positions by their representatives, even if they reject it, and for whose critique we also offer our philosophical categories. It is in this sense that we conceive the concept of Being in what follows.

Being can have a twofold significance. It can be understood as the sum of all beings or as what makes each being into a being, namely, the Being of beings. In both instances the grasp of Being appears inconclusive; in the first instance only relatively, in that the horizon of the knowable being gets extended, and thus knowledge reaches no conclusion, regardless of the fact that—despite its attempt at objectivity—it remains limited in perspective. In the second instance, however, which deals not with the whatness of Being but with the question, Why is there something rather than nothing at all? an unfathomable depth as the mystery of Being is disclosed for conceptual knowledge to every individual being.

Under both aspects, in our objectifying thinking we are dealing with a Nothing: under the first, with the Nothing as the ever Unknown and Unthought behind the horizon that encompasses our knowing; under the second, with the absolute Nothing of the depth of the Being of being—a depth that is constantly impenetrable and eludes every grasp. To the former there corresponds in Christian theology the concept of creation as the designation of all beings as creatures in a *creatio continua*; to Buddhism, by contrast, the concept of *pratitya-samutpada* as "dependent origination" without beginning or end. In contrast to the latter, moreover, theology speaks of an original creation *ex nihilo* which is problematic as a rational assertion, while for Buddhism, *pratitya-samutpada*, which dissolves all substantiality is identical with Emptiness (Sunyata).

Objectifying thinking, however, founders not only on the question of Being, but also on the question of its meaning. True, individual instances of meaningful, regular and appropriate attributes of beings and their courses can be established. But for persons who are totally in quest for the meaning of Being for the sake of the meaning of their existence, to them all total constructions of meaning prove to be wishful illusions. This is due to the conflicts of meaning which are experienced in their own bodies and spirits. Just as we cannot speak of the absurdity of Being in view of what is objectively established as meaningful, just so we cannot speak of a preestablished harmony of the cosmos in view of the objectively experienced contradictions of suffering, sin, and death. Thus, for sensible thinking, there is joined to the mystery of Being the equally insoluble riddle of meaning.

No less than Being, the self which is in quest for Being and its meaning proves to be a Nothing for conceptual-objective thinking, and this—like Being—takes two directions, and is enigmatical in both as in its meaning. True, the self can be analyzed inwardly and outwardly in objectifying conceptuality, that is, psychologically and sociologically, and in this way objectively demonstrable facts can be established in respect to human nature and the circumstances of its surroundings. On the basis of such information and of the capabilities which are at his disposal, a person is in a position to make his personal and social life more meaningful, to create culture out of nature and to permit fate to become history. And he can probably experience himself in his finiteness to be related to Transcendence and to understand himself and his existence not only scientifically, but also philosophically and religiously.

But in our objectifications of our own self and that of others we never behold the subject of these objectifications, but only its representations in the subject-object scheme of our thinking consciousness. More than is the case with natural events, all human cultural creations are unavoidably bound up with contradictions, religion can become a *fabrica idolorum*, and philosophy an idle pseudoenlightenment.

This problem of the human self and its realization is reflected in both Buddhist and Christian anthropology, and this is as true for both in respect to epistemology and the resultant instructions for practical, life-constituting behavior, as well as to their metaphysical foundations. Under all three aspects Buddhism and Christianity seem to possess answers to these human questions about the meaning of life in the world; yet in their instructive traditional forms they are so constituted that they are more likely to put in question the nature of the person seeking answers to these questions than really to answer them.

In the first place, Christianity tells us that our reason is darkened through the Fall, or is at least so completely incapacitated that we are not in a position to answer the question of the meaning of our existence, but for that answer must rely on God's revelation which is known in faith. But as it can happen to this knowledge of faith which rests upon revelation, the opinions of theologians greatly diverge. They consist of compromises between the extremes of a rational faith that absolutizes itself over against revelation and a revelatory faith whose subject is the Holy Spirit. What then is left of a criterion of truth that takes account of human fallibility?

Buddhism puts us in a similar predicament with its doctrine of Sunyata if we measure it by the criteria of objective thinking. How are emptiness and selfhood related? Where does emptiness begin and the self cease? Is there still a self in emptiness, and is the emptiness empty if there is still a self? Isn't Sunyata as a doctrine of emptiness a contradiction in itself? What is the criterion of enlightenment if the claim to be enlightened is a sign of nonenlightenment? How then is attestation of enlightenment possible; and, lacking a positive criterion, are we not left with arbitrariness?

Second, from this epistemological problematic, parallel difficulties result in traditional Christianity and Buddhism for the evaluation of practical behavior and its possibilities. In Christianity we have to do with debates about good works and grace, about the actual or declared justification of the sinner, and with the problems of the justice, omnipotence and omnibenevolence of God and or predestination; in Buddhism, with the distinction between jiriki and tariki, self-redemption or other-redemption of the vow of Amida Buddha, which have here and there generated special forms of churches and sects.

Behind this ethical problematic both sides exhibit different conceptions of the world and of history. Christianity represents a salvation history standing under the guidance of God—a salvation history in which, according to the Last Judgment, there are the elect and the nonelect. Buddhism holds to the endless series of ever new kalpas standing under the same conditions—a series structured by karma and "dependent origination." Both conceptions produce equally discordant versions in respect to the ethics derived from them, in that, on the one hand, they demand a human mode of acting corresponding to them and, aa the same time, make that conduct seem no longer valid.

In the third place, however, both moments of these anthropologies—moments which are epistemologically and ethically-historically conceived—peak in a metaphysics in the form of a doctrine of the Trinity, or a doctrine of Trikaya, in which an attempt is made to take account both of the historical appearance of Jesus of Nazareth and the Buddha as Shakyamuni, and of the different ways God and the Buddha act. In Christianity, both in respect to the Trinity and to humans the concept of the person plays a decisive role. Accordingly, the relation of the three divine persons to one another, and that of divine and human nature in the personality of the redeemer, as well as that of body, soul and spirit in terrestrial humans and their relation to God, the Father, the Christ, and the Holy Spirit—these three become problematic and give rise to objective speculations. In Buddhism, on the other hand, Buddha and the true self are identified with nothingness in a no less questionable manner.

Whereas the application of the concept of person in Christian theology evokes the critical question whether man is not so much created in the image of God as rather that God is formed in the image of man, it is questionable on the Buddhist side how one comes to speak of Buddha and his three bodies, of the many Buddhas and Bodhisattvas and of the true, enlightened and the unenlightened self, if for the enlightened the nature of all these three entities is nothingness. Apparently, the discriminating thinking of the unenlightened is here at work! And—to return once again to the ethical question—how can a metaphysical selfless self be dealt with ethically and selflessly? What is the subject of the selfless action, or does selflessness consists of nonselfless action, and is the same problematic role ascribed to enlightenment as to the "declared righteousness of the godless" in Paul (Romans 4:5) and in Shinran and in the Tannisho?

But enough of the problematic! It seems to me that what I have just presented, like the lectern of my friend Masao Abe mentioned at the beginning, has escalated into a lectern of objectivity on which there lies a manuscript of objectivity and, standing behind it and lecturing, I now likewise have reason to ask: "Can you see me?" Are we, because of all such objectivities, still in a position to know what we are dealing with in these objectifications of what is ultimately nonobjectifiable? In order to make this possible there must now recur what consciously or unconsciously was intended by Abe Sensei's momentary disappearance into nonobjectifiablity and his reemergence into objectivity as a visual aid. To state this without the image: the problematic of Christian and Buddhist doctrine which developed objectively must now in its unavoidable objectivity momentarily disappear into nothingness in order to reappear as speech about the nonobjectifiable intended therein and thus to be understood as its symbolism, that is, as the objectification of what is nonobjectifiable.

As such an existential visual aid I cite the answers which Bodhidharma gave to King Wu-ti's question about "the holy truth of Buddhism": "Open expanse, nothing holy, " and to the question who he was: "I don't know." To that I would add what the Apostle Paul said of himself: "I live, but not I, Christ lives in me" (Gal 2:20) and "In Christ the world is crucified to me and I to the world" (Gal 6:14).

With the visual and interpretive aid I think it would be possible to see the Buddha-Christ as the special revelation of the mystery of Being—which for our grasp is nothingness—as "the Lord of the true self," and that Bodhisattvahood and being-in-Christ could be understood as individual, particular possibilities of meaning within the abiding enigma of Being.

But unlike what is reported in that scene of the Bodhidharma I do not disappear into incomprehensiblity; rather I am ready, like Paul on the Areopagus (Acts 17), to address myself to your questions about Nothingness and the true self in light of the problem of Being and meaning.

Appendix 2

Dialogue as Theological Principle

A lecture delivered at the opening of the Religiotheological Student Meeting, 10-13 June 1981, on "Redemption in the Understanding of Christianity and Buddihism," at St. Gabriel, Mödling near Vienna.

To introduce our dialogue on the Christian and Buddhist understanding of redemption I should like to say a word about "dialogue as a theological principle." I must confess that initially I have several objections to this formulation of the theme, for it contains a twofold ambiguity. For one thing, is it supposed to mean that in the theology of *dialogue* as principle it holds that theology is principally dialogue, or should "dialogue as *theological principle*" signify that dialogue in theology is acceptable only insofar as it is theologically qualified, that is, that dialogue does not have to define what theology is, but theology decides whether and to what extent dialogue can prove acceptable. Both can be meant in the formulation of our theme. On the other hand—which is connected with it—it leaves open the question which dialgoue is appropriate: whether the *intra- and interhuman dialogue* of a meeting like ours, or the *dialogue of God with humans and of humans with God*, to which the concept "theological" apparently refers, and how the relation of this Vertical to that Horizontal is to be conceived.

In reflecting on this issue it occurred to me how relevantly and appropriately this theme is formulated. For the first of the two questions resulting from it is characteristic of a central problem of the contemporary *theology of mission*, and the second, of the situation in which Christian theology has always found itself. In all the contemporary readiness for dialogue there is the fear that dialogue could imperil the message the Church is commisioned to deliver, and wishes to permit it only insofar as it can serve its proclamation. But how one is to speak of the Word of God represents a *basic problem of theology* that is timeless. Yet both questions not only play an important role in Christianity, but also concern non-Christians since the position taken on the first question determines how they are confronted in missions, and because, even if they deny the second problem in the position taken on the first question, it deals in some kind of way with the problem of Transcendence. For this reason the theme seems to me to be fully appropriate to the situation, and I have accepted it in the form in which it was proposed to me, even if I am aware that the treatment I would devote to it perhaps does not correspond in all respects to what those who entrusted it to me had in mind.

I will proceed in such a way as to develop the nature and structure of the intra- and interhuman dialogue and the questions that issue from it so as to consider the answers theology is prepared to give to these questions on the basis of its vertical dialogue. After setting forth the problematic of taking sides with the theology of revelation on the plane of intra- and interhuman dialogue, we will take a look at the corresponding counterpositions of Buddhism and their problematic in order finally to find the principle of any dialogue as a consequence of this state of affairs in the problematic of the nature of dialogue.

I. The Essential Structures of Intra and Inter Human Dialogue and the Problems Associated with It

The four question and problems to be dealt with are as follows:

1. The question of Being which opens out to the mystery of Being;
2. The question of meaning which leads to the riddle of meaning;
3. The question of the self in which the self proves to be inconceivable; and
4. The question of a meaningful copresence which can rest content with no form of the same.

These questions deal with the deepest problems of epistemological theory and metaphysics, anthropology, social ethics, and philosophy of history—and of course, theology. I should like to engage, though not extensively, the philosophical disciplines mentioned here—disciplines which deal with these problems and are concerned with their solution. That means that I locate myself in quiet engagement with them, in that—in place of their solutions—I derive the insolubility of these problems from the essential structures of the intra and interhuman dialogue. And I do this in an elementary way.

I begin with the *question of Being*, although, except in philosophy and theology, it mostly does not stand at the beginning. But in dialogue—whatever the signs that attend it—it immediately breaks open and permeates it in every aspect.

Put into a simple scheme, dialogue consists of two subjects and an object. The subjects may even consist of several subjects, each of which as a consequence of dialogues have become subjects of groups and, like individual subjects, stand opposed to one another and in relation to an object which can consist of different objects to which dialogue can belong in all cases.

Primarily the two subjects are each in dialogue with each other—not with themselves as object (of that we shall speak later)—but in a dialogue about their relation to an object which stands over against them externally, and which represents for them an object of their representational or thinking consciousness. In this intrahuman dialogue a subject would not be a subject unless in its consciousness it possesses an idea of such an object located outside itself and have thoughts about it. It is subject in relation to an object different from it, just as the object is object only in relatedness to a subject. Neither one can exist without the other. Both only become what they are in relatedness. Whether and what they are apart from this relatedness to one another we cannot know. Only in the consciousness of the difference of subject and object and their mutual connection can we know about subject- and object-being. The question, What is the status of the subject in itself in the situation in which we find ourselves with the awakening of our consciousness? we may leave aside for the moment. But we can ask ourselves regarding the objects of our consciousness, in what relationship they stand to the objects of the outerworld intended in our representing and thinking. The question can be answered only insofar as we take into account the fact that we know about them only in the framework of the subject-object schema of our consciousness and that we can state something about their being and being-with this presupposition. Within the boundaries of our consciousness we are in a position to arrange such objectifications into representational forms and systems of concepts, and to define them more precisely. But in view of the different kinds of objects we are not only confronted with the problem of methods, that is, with the questions, whether they deal with an objective explanation of something quantitative and measurable—an explanation that aims at universal demonstrability, or with a subjective interpretation of something qualitative and experienceable—an interpretation calling for a certain congeniality. Rather, within these disparate ways of knowing we can only make relatively valid statements, with the result that for our objective notions and conceptual thinking about what is therein intended, there always remains something ultimately indefinable in itself, a mystery, which, the more we try to know it, becomes only more mysterious.

Insofar as we have not already found ourselves more or less consciously in it, there intrudes here the *interhuman*, in that from the contents of our consciousness and for the sake of its meaning, we communicate with another self and accept reciprocal communications from it in order in this way to expand the horizon of our consciousness and, on the basis of comparison, to obtain pertinent facts. Thereby we have not only the experience that in this way our knowledge is enriched, purified, and deepened, but is also put into question and made uncertain, but rather that even the mystery of Being—instead of vanishing—becomes ever more impenetrable and overwhelming. Because of this, only in individual moments do we become aware of the consiousness that now becomes the basic structure of our consciousness as such: that in every being—and thus also in our being—we are dealing with the mystery of Being.

With this widening of the question of Being into the question of meaning, emerge the other questions which belong to the essential structure of intra and inter human dialogues, namely, the question of the self and the question about the mandatory formulation of togetherness.

This is especially the case with the *question of meaning* which is closely connected with the question of Being, because the question of meaning is already presupposed in the question of Being, and this in a twofold way: first, in such a way that we permit an individual being to attain its significance by arranging it into an interconnection of significance in which it exercises a sense-giving

another? What is the meaning of the moment? What will happen eventually? In some manner we must give form to this togetherness in which we find ourselves—and we give it form even if we neglect conscious forms.

In just this way we are dealing with the fourth essential structure of intra- and interhuman dialogue: the *problematic of the realization of meaning in social existence.* We are dependent upon the possibilities of existence that lie at hand, and we stand before definite forms of these pssibilities—forms which we have not created. There are traditions and institutions which assist us in assigning meaning to existence, but can even contradict what we intend by meaning. In the social forms, whether adopted or fashioned by us, we perceive their insufficiency in the tension between the selfhood they should serve and the being-for-another which they demand. How is community as the actualization of the meaning of dialogue possible?

Here we have presented in the most concise form the basic structures of the intra- and interhuman dialogue and its problems in their essential interconnection.

2. The Answers to the Questions of Inner- and Interhuman Dialogue Which Emerge from the Vertical Dialogue of Theology

It is certainly the case that theology, past and present, occurs on the plane of intra- and interhuman dialogue—and this in "menschlich-allzumenschlich" ways. Since its inception and in its essence it appeals to another dialogue, the dialogue between God and humans, humans and God, which forms a vertical to what we have just considered. The right angle in which this specifically theological dialogue stands to what is universally human can also be diminished so that the vertical approaches the horizontal. Such approximations are manifest in the history of theology and its current forms. But if God is to remain God, and humans humans, then the vertical must not become the horizontal. For the sake of God and humans the relationship in which they stand to one another must always be brought back into plumb.

That means, not that both intersect only at a point, as the image has been used. Such a conception has always led to an impoverishment of theology. Theology has something to say not only at one point "straight down from above" (perpendicularly). It is not so linear, but represents a plane which intersects the plane of human dialogue at a series of points, in a series of intersections which as such form a line. This is evident from the fact that according to the series, answers are forthcoming for theology to all four problems which have emerged from the analysis of inner- and interhuman dialogue, from which at its intersections and for the entire length of it a dialogue arises between those in dialogue. For the theological partner has not only something to say by way to the problems which we have found in the inner- and interhuman dialogue, but the theologian must be responsible to his vertical relation, which he actualizes in prayer, liturgy, and cultus, as well as in respect to the secular instances of the horizontal to which he also belongs, and there not only new solutions emerge, but *new problems*. Schematically, the dialogue looks like this:

1. Theology sees the mystery of Being of the question of Being in the light of the thought of creation and thereby comes to deal with the problem of revelation and reason.
2. For solving the riddle of meaning it takes account of salvation history, whereupon the problem of revelation becomes the problem of faith and history.
3. The question of the self is answered with the doctrine of the *imago Dei* and the doctrine of grace, both of which also have their problems.
4. In light of the problems of the shape of society and world it refers to the Church as the body of Christ and its fulfillment in the Kingdom of God which again raises the problems of biblical eschatology.

We shall now attempt to give brief explanations of this dialogical situation between the vertical and horizontal dimension in which dogmatics in its entirety fundamentally comes up for discussion.

On the first point: *The mystery of Being as creation and the question of divine revelation.* In the different forms in which creation is spoken of in the Bible—from the use of mythological material which Israel borrowed from its environment to express its self-understanding as the elect people of God, and beyond that, from its transformation in the wisdom literature and in the later Jewish apocalyptic and the idea stemming from it of a new creation in the New Testament—we are dealing not so much with the question of Being and its mystery as with the question of meaning and its enigma, and with the question of Being only insofar as meaning is necessary for the realization of beings, and in connection with it, the question is raised about their origin and the maintenance of their existence. But all these notions of creation are primarily forms of expression of the meaning of beings and attempts to answer them. From the tehom, the Babylonian Tiamat, and the serpent in paradise—notions which we find at the beginning of the Bible—to "the old dragon, the ancient serpent, which is the devil and Satan" in the Book of Revelation and in all the forms which come between—all these deal with the power of chaos which is hostile to God and with whom God is in conflict and which he himself or through his Messiah will overcome.

Insofar as in these conceptions of creation conceived in the form of a conflict with the dragon a condition of being is already presupposed, God plays therein the role of a demiurge who constructs the world from preexisting material. In order to distinguish its concept of God and doctrine of the origin of the world from other such mythologies and speculations and to exhibit it as superior to these, there emerged in Christian theology the doctrine of creation out of nothing which derived from Gnostic ideas and to which one can appeal only in questionable ways to passages on the margin of biblical tradition, because the latter is not interested in the philosophical question of Being. But the doctrine of *creatio ex nihilo* does provide an answer to the question of Being, "Why is there something and not nothing?" It deals, not with the question of meaning, but of Being. *Creatio ex nihilo* can actually be understood as a speculative expression for the mystery of Being.

But with this conception of the question of Being *new problems* arise for theology. We mention only a few of these: What is this *nihil*? If appeal is made to biblical revelation, doesn't this *nihil* still deal with a kind of unformed matter, that is, with a kind of Platonic *me on* rather than with an *ouk on*, and doesn't the latter represent an unbiblical philosophical speculation? If only *creatio ex nihilo* is valid as creation in an authentic sense—doesn't *creatio continuo*—a divine preservation of creation, for which appeal is made both to the Bible and reason— still deal with creation in an authentic sense, because therein something pre-existent which is to be preserved is always presupposed, with the result that we find ourselves back at the level of mere theories of a constructor of the world? But not only in the hairsplitting over concepts in which one is here entangled does the problem of meaning appear in the form of the question of the significance; but that problem also asserts itself in the form of the question of value, namely, that which is also to be preferred, on account of its Being, to something that does not exist.

According to the biblical portrayal and the judgment of reason the condition of creation is not as it should be; rather what is meaningful is confronted by what is meaningless. The teleology of the divine plan of creation and of the striving of reason is threatened by what is opposed to God and unreasonable. Thus in both a formal and material respect theology sees itself confronted with the problem of *reason and revelation*, and is not able to solve the mystery of Being into which the question of Being flows in intra- and interhuman dialogue, but rather leads through its amalgamation of the same with the question of meaning only more deeply into it—an amalgamation that derives from the biblical idea of the conflict with dragons.

But theology, from the vertical direction of the dialogue in which it is grasped as theology and from which it takes a stand on the questions of the dialogue of the horizontal, intra- and interhuman plane, is not only oriented to the question of meaning, but also to faith which can see in the salvation history of the biblical revelaton the *solution of the riddle of meaning*.

As in the biblical story of creation and in the doctrine of creation which appeals to it, theology comports with the problem of Being, so both, from the beginning and in the entire length and breadth of the development of this basic view, are interested in the question of meaning and in overcoming the riddle of meaning in which human existence in the world is embedded. The Bible refers to the riddle of meaning in the narrative of the Fall under whose curse theology sees the entire history of humankind, and from which imperfections and suffering is derived, whereas in the Old Testament this myth plays no such role; rather the disobedience of the people of God and their punishment is rectified over and again by the concluding of new covenants of God with his people. The series of the covenants which receive special weight in Reformed theology, peak—according to the New testamnent—in the new covenant which God concluded with his elect in the atoning death of his Son, and which is said to bring salvation and deliverance to all who believe on it.

But if for theology the question of the role of the Fall in God's plan of redemption represents a problem, namely, whether and to what extent it is foreseen and caused by him, this is all the more the case with the question of the significance which is to be ascribed to this completion of the decisive saving act of the Son of God as the Messiah. For this is described in the New Testament as an end-time event of cosmic proportions whose status is proclaimed being-in-process is already rendered questionable by the fact that theology already finds itself in the New Testament in a history which, according to the presuppositons of its faith, ought no longer to exist. Actually Christian theology owes its existence to the delay of the inbreak of the Kingdom of God which in the New Testament is expected imminently. In order to be able to preserve the salvation event believed by it as the solution of the question of meaning, it must transform it into an event of faith, to assert its vertical dimension, embodied in the dogma of the God-manhood of the redeeemer, in the horizontal dimension of world and human history, which it has hardly succeeded in making believable despite all the different attempts undertaken in the course of its history for this purpose. In the discussion of the problem of *faith and history*, before which it always sees itself poised, it is apparent that in its discourse about creation and new creation theology is always dealing with objectifications which are essentially unobjectifiable, because not only Being which is here being discussed but also the human who asks the question of the meaning of his Being and would like to realize it, cannot be objectified; neither the one nor the other is possible without objectification. Here we find the problematic of every anthropology which makes its appearance in the *anthropolgy of theology*.

In contradistinction to scientific and philosophical anthropologies which do not use these concepts or somehow intellectualize them, theology speaks from its biblical heritage of the image of God which was to some extent lost through sin and is to be renewed through a divine act of grace, and—to some degree—of a cooperation from the human side demanded for this renewal of his original nature. That these are two aspects of the same problem is apparent in the fact that the power of *sin* and the power of *grace* stand in reciprocal relation with each other. The greater the damage to the image of God through sin, the less possible it is for humans actively to cooperate in attaining salvation. Conversely, the greater the significance humans assign to faith, the greater the estimation of the damage the image of God has suffered through sin.

In this ambivalence of nature and grace—so long as the nature of the two powers is not defined too proximally and the relation in which they stand to each other is allowed to remain open and not allowed to escalate to the assertion of an absolute self-redemption nor oppositely to an absolute redemption from the outside, but does not think it can establish what humans can do to attain salvation out of their own powers and how much they are in need of grace—the problem posed above could correspond to what we have established as the result of dialogue concerning the self on the intra- and interhuman plane. The ambivalence, if not more closely defined, would then be an expression of the final nonobjectifiability of the self.

But theological anthropology is not content with such a completely open ambivalence of its elements because it believes that, on the basis of its vertical dialogue, it can know something more precisely of their respective nature and power and thus can also can precisely circumscribe the relationship in which they stand with respect to each other. In theology self-redemption is out of the question because on the basis of its revelatory foundation it can view it only as an expression of human hubris as a consequence of the Fall. As much as sola fide and sola gratia may underlie the biblical seriousness of sin and praise of grace, even so this formula is highly erroneous and misleading. In any case we cannot appeal to the gospel for it, and the Apostle Paul, who is thought to be its source, expressly warned about it (Rom 6:1; 7:7). Thus we are left only with the assumption of a residual image of God after the Fall, on the basis of which man is in a position to cooperate with grace to some extent, and through grace to fulfill good works which would then be rewarded in the Last Judgment. The lack of unity among the Christian confessions in respect to the anthropological and soteriological doctrines and their inner contradictions are too well known to think that we can find in them something other than self-refutations of objectifications of the nonobjectifiable mission of humans.

What is true with respect to the individual and his mission is also true of the social doctrines and forms of the Christian faith. On the one hand, decisive influences from the ideas of covenant and of the expectation of the Kingdom of God, from the Decalogue and the Sermon on the Mount, have shaped the ethics and philosophy of history of the West and have operated in them both positively and negatively in respect to the humanization of society. From them have arisen sacrificial love and fanatical utopianism alike, as well as hostile powers of sacred and secular institutions, culture and questions about it. Present earthly realities have issued from images of hell in ideas of the Beyond, and the search for "lost Paradise" is in vain.

What we have described essentially and comprehensively as the problematic confronting theology in the position it takes regarding the mystery of Being and

its riddle of meaning, the question of the self and a social ideal corresponding
to its nature is a concern not only of Chrstianity and the Western world,
but—despite different presuppositions and different attempts at a solution—no
less so of Buddhism and the significance which has been ascribed to it, past and
present, in the Far East. This social destiny rests not only on the fact that it is
affected by this problematic under the influence of Western thought stamped by
Christianity, and that many Westeners are currently seeking answers to their
questions in the wisdom of the Far East, but that also as a consequence of
modern world intercommunication it has brought it about that Buddhism must
deal with the same ultimate questions as Christianity.

This situation gives us the occasion to point out

3. The Parallelism between the Way
the Questions are Dealt with in Buddhism
and Its Answers to the Respective Problematic of Christianity

In view of the major relevant materials and the great difference of the questions
and answers contained in it and also of the problems connected with it, we can
deal, in what we can develop in the context of this opening paper—but more so
in our theological discussions—only with suggestions of the matter in question
in a few catchwords. The relation of Christianity and Buddhism which forms the
object of our meeting seems to be characterized by a threefold parallelism:

1. in relation to the four basic questions with which Buddhism as well as
   Christianity ultimately have to do;
2. with respect to the answers which Buddhism gives to them and through
   which it places Christianity in question no less than it already proves itself
   as problematic; and
3. in the fact that it—like Chrsitianity—turns out to be problematic in its own
   way.

First, concerning the commonality of concern with the four basic questions.
The *question of Being*—which Christianity answers with the doctrine of creation
in which it speaks of the mystery of Being in the creation out of nothing, in the
continued creation and as its goal in the new creation—Buddhism answers with
the doctrine of *pratitya-samutpada*, of the *dependent origination*, without beginning and without end, in which, for the enlightened, the causal nexus dissolves
into emptiness (*sunyata*). To the way in which Christianity sees the cause of the
problem of meaning in the Fall and proclaims the overcoming of its unredeemed
consequences in a salvation history culminating in the Christ event, there corresponds in Buddhism the *Four Noble Truths* of Shakyamuni on the cause of the
suffering of all existence in ignorance of desire and of the Eightfold Noble Path
upon which, in nirvana, the liberation from embeddedness in the karma of
samsara is said to be possible. Both doctrines of salvation deal with both the

question of the nature of true self and the question of the significance which obtains for its procedure for attaining an ideal social form of existence. Whereas Christianity sees *the true self* in the image of God and its enactment in Being-in-Chirst, in this connection Buddhism employs the ideas of the Buddha *nature* and *becoming-Buddha*. In respect to *true mutual existence* Christianity speaks of love (*Agape*), the Body of Christ, and the Kingdom of God, and to the contrary, Buddhism speaks of the *compassion* (*karuna*) of the *Bodhisattva*, as well as of *nirvana* and the *Pure Land*.

Second, the correspondences deal not only with points of contact between Christianity and Buddhism, but with materially opposing doctrines and in such a way that Buddhism in its critique of Christianity considers itself superior, believing it can see in its own position an *overcoming of the problematic of Christian dogma*. In the way in which it regards *pratitya-samutpada* as enlightenment, in whose emptiness things can appear in their true form supposedly without deformation by human consciousness, the problem of immanence and transcendence associated with Christianity and also its difficulties with the connection between reason and revelation does not exist. The vertical of the Holy Spirit whose agreement with the "inner light" represents the problem of Christian mysticism is replaced in Buddhism with a *universal enlightenment*. Thus, here the problem of faith and history, with which the biblical-Christian conceptions of salvation history are burdened, plays no role. The true self is no possession which one can partially or wholly lose and correspondingly has to be restored by a divine act of grace.Only in such discriminating thinking can persons deceive themselves about their own nature.In the transobjective knowledge of enlightenment corresponding to the nonobjectifiability of the self the Buddhist says neither that he is enlightened nor that he is not enlightenened; rather he conceals it in silence or attempts to embarrass Christians who appeal to the word of Paul, "It is not I, but Christ who lives in me" (Gal 2:20), with the ironic question, Who then is the subject in this case? From their side the Buddhists are not embarrassed by the delay of a completion of history because history for them does not represent something determinable, being without beginning and end.

Third, it should be pointed out that not only has Western thinking, generally and from a Christian perspective, turned in particular to such details, just as they are in use in the Far East and have been constructed in specific ways by Buddhists, but that the latter lapse into *similar difficulties* from which they hold themselves to be free and for which they reproach the former. In the Far East and the West a so-called *nonobjective thinking* has actually proven in the discussion to be *objectless*. One still speaks, but knows thereby neither what is spoken nor who is actually speaking here. Whereas objectifying thinking somehow knows of its relative and absolute limits and within them takes account of possible illusions, in enlightenment-world of contemplation just as with the appeal to the Word of God all such criteria are dispensed with and the danger arises of speaking of what is objectified as something nonobjectifiable and of the latter as something objectifiable. This fate is evident in Buddhism in the opposition of Jiriki and Tariki as norm or as theme, no less so than in the debate about good works in the Christian doctrine of grace, and on both sides results in the question of structure of the world and of life. In the Christian doctrine of creation and its eschatology both world affirmation and world denial, profane and spiritual fanaticism, produce institutions which to some degree fancy that they possess salvation—institutions which are rendered problematic by the fact that they appeal to the same source. Similarly the Zen Buddhst, in his *equation of samsara and nirvana*, regards himself as freed from the world and at the same time surrenders to it, being in the present state concerned with himself and the world, whereas the believer in Amida hopes some day to enter into the Pure Land by trusting in the *vow of Amida* or knows himself to be in it altready. But both forms lead to the same ambiguity in reference to attitudes toward the world and self, as is the case also in Zen Buddhism. The Buddhist might charge that Christians, in their love of self and neighbor, nevethless remain in the grip of self-love and of attachment to things as the cause of all suffering, and they might not only view them as a sign of being unredeemed, but put opposite this Christian concept of love the selfless compassion of karuna, in that the Buddhist derives the selflessness of this concept in an ethical sense from an ontological understanding of this concept and grounds both modes of understanding in *pratitya-samutpada*. But the question arises whether, if all are already enlightened in emptiness, becoming a Buddha embodying the selfless compassion is still necessary, and how such selfless compassion is possible at all, if there is neither a subject of his practice nor an object of his perception. Obviously the difference between the empirical and the true self is no less problematic than the relation of Christ and the I in the Apostle Paul's understanding.

I am aware that Buddhism is ready with answers to all these critical questions, just as Christianity has regarded the objections which have been raised against it as misunderstandings long overcome by its theology. Christian theology and Buddhist philosophy—if they do not simply talk insistently to one another and therein talk at cross-purposes with one another, but are willing to listen to one another—consist in large measure of apologetics against objections rightly or wrongly raised against them; in both instances this makes the dialogue between them neither especially refreshing nor fruitful.

What from this state of affairs, which has been discussed in relation to Christianity and Buddhism, is forthcoming as a principle of a genuine dialogue between these two entities? I think that can consist in nothing other than the acknowledgement of the problems of dialogue as they encounter us as specific formulations of its four basic elements in theology and Buddhology which both excludes and requires one another. What this points to therefore is neither a theological nor a Buddhist principle of dialogue, but

4. The Problematic of Dialogue as Principle of Dialogue

in philosophical theology and Buddhist philosophy, as it can be presented as a summary of the previous discussion in the following schema:

If we say philosophical theology, we find ourselves already engaged with this *first, epistemological and metaphysical viewpoint of the question of Being*. For with this proximate designation we intend a theology which explains its mythological tradition as the objective expression of the self-understanding which is not objectifiable in its enactment, as this occurs today also in the so-called Kyoto School with the Buddhist tradition. In this theology or philosophy one is in the presence of a tradition which—for all the interpretation one may give it—one has not personally created and which from its perspective speaks of the origin and nature of all beings: the Christian, in the form of the doctrine of creation; the Buddhist, in terms of *pratitya-samutpada*. The former objectifies transcendence on the basis of revelation and reason; the latter dissolves all objectification in the emptiness of the wisdom of enlightenment. If the doctrine of creation also speaks of a beginning and end, it nevertheless does not mean by this, philosophically understood, something fixed in space and time, but—just like the doctrine of the beginningless and endless origin in dependent origination which transcends the causal nexus—the conceptual incomprehensibillity of the moment which simultaneously is and is not. Whereas creation puts more emphasis on the being of beings, but also knows of their transiency, *pratitya-samutpada* deals with the emptiness in which nevertheless the fullness of beings is in their being-thus—just as they issued from the hand of the creator. In the dialogue with their own tradition and in the reciprocal dialogue in which their representatives become aware of the problematic of their modes of expression and once more—dubiously—speak of revelation and enlightenment, the two conceptions correspond to each other as both legitimate and inadequate symbolism of the *mystery of Being* which is simultaneously fullness and emptiness.

This intentional commonality in dialogue about the question of Being is the model which operates in the definition of the positions taken on the other three aspects of the Christian and Buddhist dialogue situations—primarily in the *Christological* or *Buddhalogical* which deal with the question of meaning and the riddle of meaning. The opening up of the question of meaning already ensues in view of a special formation of creation or the fullness of Being which consists in the fallen state of creation, or in suffering which all existence fulfills. The dissolution of the riddle of meaning all the more demands a special event; the salvation history centered in Christ, or becoming-a-Buddha. Whereas the Christological salvation history takes place as a breaking in from transcendence into immanence and—despite its universal character—seems to be limited to the elect, in comparison with this, becoming-a-Buddha represents a breakthrough into immanence and—despite the emphasis upon man as its place—encompasses all being, because all beings possess a Buddha nature. The problems of predestination or naturalism which for both conceptions result from the objectification of their specific characteristics, could be overcome by understanding Christ and the Buddha as symbols, that is, as essentially inadequate but necessary objectifications of nonobjectifiable Being and the self; thus they could be combined into the *Buddha-Christ* by assimilations which correspond to their intention and which can be established in their own objectifications. Accepting the problematic of dialogue bound up with it would become a principle which facilitates dialogue.

The same is true of the *anthropological-soteriological question* of the nature of the true self in general and of the possibility of its realization in particular. The differences in the doctrines of grace among the Christian confessions and between redemption by one's own power (Jiriki) and by other-power (Tariki) in Buddhism could become symbolizations of the experiences of individual actualizations of meaning in Being-in-Christ or Bodhisattva-Being which can be analyzed into individual components of these ideas and examined for their validity, but cannot be shown in their entirety, but enacted in a specific self-understanding and can be constituted as its effects in the structure of existence.

In respect to the social- and world-shaping effects of the conceptions of redemption we encounter in Christianity and in Buddhism the two phenomena which stand opposed to one another and are also self-contradictory—phenomena which for this reason need one another for the fulfillment of their essential determination: the Church as the institution of the community of love established by God and oriented to the coming of his Kingdom, and the compassionate shared suffering of all living beings that are subject to the karma of samsara, a suffering to be annulled in nirvana. Buddhism is not wholly wrong in seeing in the way the Christian is to love his neighbor and in its foundation in the ecclesiastical institution of salvation a bit of self-assertion and attachment to things, from which, according to it, all suffering comes. But it must also be asked what in its view remains of a self that could through its conduct prepare a karma or improve upon one; whether and to what extent the compassion of the Boddhisattva is different from the mutual suffering of all beings and is distinguished from it only by explaining to the other sufferers the cause of their suffering rather than preparing an end to the suffering whether it be by the self extinguishing of its karma in continuing samasara or in the Pure Land—which is precisely the problematic of Buddhist eschatology. Whereas the Christian view transcends history with its expectation of the fulfillment of love only to be shattered by it, the Buddhist view in its compassion remains stuck in an eternal return of the same. This problematic can only be overcome by virtue of a love without saving guarantees and a compassion which risks the problematic character of love. As a symbol of such a self-conception in community one could consider a Kingdom of God as nirvana and a nirvana as the Kingdom of God.

Now I am aware of the problematic of such notions not only in view of this fourth, but also of the three preceding combinations of symbols. Although these combinations have emerged for me from the dialogue with the dialogue situations in which the representatives of the individual components of this pair of symbols find themselves, they could prove to be not only beneficial, but also perplexing, for the further development of the dialogue in both spheres. The symbols of which we make use in dialogue as the language of our self-understanding, are not our creation; rather we take them from the tradition in the character of a definite content, a form which in the course of history can also become empty or encrusted as a whole. In any case they can appear to those who do not live in a tradition of symbols—as such traditions are always constituted—as such an encrusted or even empty form. Today, as Christian and Buddhists we have to reckon with such persons. If we have troubles with our own traditional symbols, it is not surprising that non-Christians and non-Buddhists have difficulty understanding our language. In the age of secularism the religious symbols stemming from the sphere of the numinous appear strange.

For this reason I would like to conclude my remarks on the problematic of dialogue and on their application as its principle, by calling attention to the possibility of a *translation* of the respective symbols out of their sacrality into images taken from the secular—images which could at the same time serve as criteria for the objective content of the symbols to be translated.

> For the immanence-transcendence problem in the epistemolgical-metaphysical subject-object scheme the following could serve as a symbol: *the transparence of glass which arises when arenaceous quartz is fired.*
>
> For the problem of meaning in Christology and Buddhology: *spontaneous flames at night*, and being consumed like the flame in the illumined without asking about the end of the night.
>
> For the anthropological-soteriological problem of the actualization of the self as self- or outside-redemption: *experiencing oneself as destined and granted to be a flame.*
>
> For the normative structure of togetherness in the world: *the knowledge of being unconditionally responisble for one another*, and the experience of eternity in the present moment of self-decision.

At these four points we do not simply remain in the horizontal of intra- and interhuman dialogue; rather here occurs its vertical as well, and at the intersection of both there results dialogue as salvation event in the true and full sense—formulated as a "theological principle": God assuming human form in man's becoming human, or according to Plato's expositions in the Seventh Epistle, "Truth occurs among friends in good hours."

Supplement

The Newest Publications on Our Theme

After the manuscript of this work was finished, two treatises appeared which—in addition to others only briefly mentioned by me (pp. 385ff.)—are so close to it, both as to their content and the goal of its treatment that it seemed unavoidable that I should introduce them in this supplement, although I seem to be in express opposition to them and must decisively speak against them while at the same time appreciating their significance for our common concern. The two treatises are the Bonn dissertation "Das 'Selbst' im Mahayana-Buddhismus in Japanischer Sicht und die 'Person' im Christentum im Lichte des Neuen Testaments" ("A Japanese view of 'Self' in Mahayana Buddhism and the 'Person' in Christianity in Light of the New Testament"),[1] written by the Japanese Masumi Shimizu under the direction, first of Gustav Mensching and then, after his death, of Hans-Joachim Klimkeit; and, the essay by Wolfhart Pannenberg scheduled for, but not delivered at, the Student Meeting on "Redemption in Christianity and Buddhism," organized by the Philosophical-Theological College of St. Gabriel in Mödling, and published together with the other contributions to the Conference: "Auf der Suche nach dem wahren Selbst, Anthropologie als Ort der Begegnung zwischen christlichem und buddhistischem Denken" ("The Search for the True Self: Anthropology as the Place of the Encounter between Christian and Buddhist Thought)."[2]

As the titles of the two studies indicate, they closely approximate my intention, and this commonality is further strengthened by the fact that for their comparison of Buddhism with Christianity, both, as I do, appeal to the representatives of the Kyoto School—Shimizu to all, with the exception, oddly, of Tanabe—Pannenberg at least to Hisamatsu and Masao Abe. Beyond the comparative intention and the appeal to the religious philosophy of the Kyoto School serving this purpose—as well as their orientation to Zen and Shin—my work has nothing in common with that of the two authors, but stands basically opposed to them, both with respect to their evaluation of the Buddhism considered and to the conception of Christianity confronting it. On the one hand, I stand much more critically opposed to Buddhism considered epistemologically, meta-physically, ethically, and historically than do Shimizu and Pannenberg, considering it more comprehensively than they through the use of these perspectives. On the other, I am content not merely like Shimizu with gaining several "points of convergence"[3] and unlike Pannenberg, with the working out of a possible

---

[1](Leiden: E. J. Brill, 1981).
[2](Mödling: Verlag St. Gabriel, 1982).
[3]Shimizu, 140ff.

"relation to the Buddhist Mahayana tradition" from the perspective of a not essentially corrected Lutheran faith in justification,[4] but rather hold to the position that on the basis of my understanding of Buddhism and Christianity, "the Buddha-Christ as the Lord of the True Self" can be plainly validated.

Although on the basis of their appeal to the representatives of the Kyoto School, Shimizu and Pannenberg agree to some extent in their conception of the nature of the Buddhist religious philosophy, the presentation of the former being more extensive and thorough than that of the latter who is content to use features which are, to be sure, essential, but generally held, they both fundamentally differ with respect to their conception of Christianity. For the "Christianity" which she compares with Buddhism, Shimizu appeals almost exclusively to a selection of passages from the "Johannine and Pauline writings,"[5] and for their interpretation she relies—with few exceptions—just as exclusively on Catholic exegetes and dogmaticians in the background of whom, for most of these as for her, stands Heidegger. She believes she can disregard the historical-critical investigation of the New Testament[6] as well as of eschatology—the former on general grounds, the latter on practical.[7] In view of this restriction of sources the assertion— for all its appeal to revelation—that "Christianity *is* God's self-utterance (*sic!*)" looks odd.[8] But apparently it is not so much a theological reason which causes her to derive what she understands by 'Christianity' above all from Johannine and Pauline passages, but the expectation of finding in them a structural parallel to the logic of *soku hi* which she worked out in the first part of her work as the characteristic peculiarity of Buddhist thinking and in which she believes she can see the possibility of a liberation from the Cartesian thinking of self-consciousness with its constricted I.

Although for her Christian understanding of the person Shimizu occasionally appeals to *Pannenberg's* ideas of the person and its Christology,[9] in the present essay Pannenberg's understanding does not prove to be as "self-less" as the Buddhist self and he is not ready to permit the nature of persons seeking their identity to become immersed in nirvana and therein to find its true self. In contrast to such an extinction of objectifying self-consciousness, persons—according to him—"experience" or "perceive" their redemption rather in faith in something outside the self,[10] thus in something over against them, namely, a fact of salva-

---

[4]Pannenberg, 145, 134.
[5]Shimizu, 95ff.
[6]Ibid., 96, 177n.79.
[7]Ibid., 205.
[8]Ibid., 144.
[9]Ibid., 172n.19, 177nn.75, 77.
[10]Pannenberg, 135, 139.

tion— the death and resurrection of Jesus—which occurs in history as a "once for all" event. Admittedly, he sees here "convergences" between the "inward self"[11] hidden in the "natural" person and only knowable in faith and the "Buddha-nature" which is present in all beings and actualized in enlightenment, and also between the death and resurrection with Christ in the community of his body[12] and the "Great Death" and the awakening to Buddha-being. He also attempts to understand transcendence in the incarnation as its appearance in immanence.[13] And like the Buddhist who, when he makes statements about the ineffable, lapses into contradictions for whose justification he must make use of a self-contradictory logic because in its alleged overcoming of contradiction it disclaims it, so Pannenberg, with his Lutheran doctrine of justification lapses into difficulties which are evident, for example, in the fact that he believes that he must—on psychological grounds—diminish the notion of sin, without which that doctrine becomes invalid,[14] and that he who otherwise emphasizes time in the salvation event,[15] makes of the "eschatological hope"[16] "God's eternal affirmation of his creation," that is, the "experience of an eternal affirmation through divine love."[17]

This is not the place to engage in debate with Pannenberg's theology of history. It deals with a mythological speculation whose experiential grounding in the "human experience of nonidentity and inauthenticity"[18] consists in the "transiency of creation" and as sin, as well as in the "Christian longing for the transfiguration of this world through the glory of God."[19] "Redemption" then consists in the fact that in his experience of his problematic of meaning man believes that this problematic is to be overcome through "the transformative affirmation of man through God's love.," for whose "transformative and historical dynamic" Pannenberg appeals to the fact that "the identity of the human person, its authentic self, is actualized outside our self in Christ."[20]

Regardless of the fact that the global character, which Pannenberg claims for the love of God, is proclaimed in the New Testament in anything but a univocal way, there being in its eschatology not only the elect but also the rejected, and

---

[11]Ibid., 134, 136.
[12]Ibid., 133.
[13]Ibid., 139.
[14]Ibid., 129-30, 146.
[15]Ibid., 134.
[16]Ibid., 144.
[17]Ibid., 143.
[18]Ibid., 145.
[19]Ibid., 144.
[20]Ibid., 145.

that Jesus dies only for the former—I say, despite this fact, that the experience of inauthenticity and the "divine affirmation of the individual" belong to quite different realms, and that their combination in the Lutheran doctrine of justification, as Pannenberg knows, represents more of a problem than its solution; at best, as he also says, it is a "search for the true self," but without the guarantee that, as he thinks, "on the path of such seeking it is nevertheless somehow already present."

Quite the opposite of Pannenberg's expectation that with his "Lutheran tradition" he finds himself "in the convergence with the Buddhist critique of the self-assertion of the empirical I,"[21] the Buddhist critique—and not incorrectly—comes into play just at this point, and here speaks of the "self-assertion of the empirical I" and sees its cause in the "dualistic objectification" of this Christology and soteriology mentioned by Pannenberg, but which, despite his concerns, is not overcome.[22]

Finally, the endeavor of *Masumi Shimizu* to achieve a series of points of convergence between Buddhism and Christianity hastens to establish the conclusion that "the danger for Western reflection on the person" consists in the fact that it understands "spiritual individuality" too thing-like and substance-like. At the same time she warns Buddhism of the opposite "danger that the reference to the self is not sufficiently emphasized and reflected upon, with the result that thereby 'being-with' is easily changed into 'being closed in upon oneself'."[23] In these warnings—addressed to Christianity and to Buddhism, respectively—in regard to possible perversions of their nature there is simultaneously expressed the intention by which she is guided in her discussions of the Mahayana notion of the true self and the idea of the person in Christian faith. That the New Testament basis which she uses is too small to warrant the claim of representative validity for Christianity for the understanding of the person derived from it, we have already noted. Basically the same is to be said against this view of a definite Catholic theology, as against Pannenberg's Lutheranism. Both fail to take account of eschatology in the New Testament and the significance which is ascribed to its problematic of the history of Christianity. Shimizu fails completely, and Pannenberg takes account of it only in the way of the attempts to overcome this problematic of origin typical for the history of Christianity. The effect of this is that both its normative significance for the human understanding of the self and its reference to transcendence and ethical and historical-philosophical consequences are not noticed. For this one should turn to the introductory and

---

[21]Ibid.

[22]Shimizu, 139.

[23]Ibid, 144; cf. 83.

concluding chapters of our investigation where this matter has become adequately articulated by us.

What interests us in the work of Masumi Shimizu and needs discussion is the Buddhist "logic of soku hi" as the "identity of the contradictory" which she presents and explains in a major way by means of the similar texts and above all by making reference to the same representatives of the Kyoto School which we have consulted in our comparison of Buddhism and Christianity. We can only agree with her presentation of this logic, even if we regret that she uses these citations from our mutual sources only as an illustration of *soku hi*, instead of making use of them, as we have done, to point out the problematic of this logic. For Shimizu these thinkers are, so to speak, sacrosanct and play for her only the role of overcoming the egocentrism (derived from Cartesianism) of Western thinking and the damning results of its subject-object split. This frontal attack against a kind of thinking shared by her with these Buddhist philosophers would necessitate taking a critical position toward one's own position and could only prove helpful for the discussion. She would then remark that in her endeavor she—like her authorities—makes use of this thinking to overcome objectifying thinking, but in a manner in which she forfeits the possibility of attaining to the real overcoming of what is half wrongly or rightly repudiated by them. This is a kind of argumentation which I, in my presentation of individual representatives of the Kyoto School, have brought out on different occasions and in different directions, with the result that in the following I have nothing new to say, but can only refer to what is presented in chapters 2 through 9.

If I restate here again, summarized in the main points and with reference to the work under discussion, I should like to begin, so to speak, with a personal appeal to its author. She is certainly aware that in this work she is dealing with objects which she distinguishes from one another, designates them with concepts, and introduces an interconnection which corresponds to the laws of customary logic. She finds herself confronted by the subject-object split of consciousness and makes use of this discriminating conceptual knowing of its objects when she speaks of an ego-less thinking and of its nonobjectifiable entities which deal with self, Being, God, Buddha, and their nature and power. Otherwise than in this way these entities would not be available to her, and she could not speak of them at all, but would have to be silent about them. But neither is she silent, nor do the philosophers and sources to which she appeals remain silent, but with all these she speaks of the ineffable and—once again like these—does so in the con-ceptuality of objectifying thinking of the subject-object split of consciousness and in its logic which clings to the identity of the designations employed and in the logic based on the injunction against contradiction in the combination of these designations.

But here in Shimizu and in the school to which she appeals and the tradition from which she comes together with them, there occurs a short conclusion which proves to be ruinous for thinking, in that for thinking she extinguishes its subject-object split, and, as well, in the enactment of thinking replaces the lack of contradiction demanded by it with an explanation of the validity of contradiction. That both are possible in the "contemplation" of meditation practice, and that a state of "ecstasy" can be possible, is not to be contested when one considers the witnesses present in the tradition. In parallel to the demand of Christian theology, that faith is necessary for the understanding of revelation Shimizu explains that statements which appeal to the experience of enlightenment can only be understood on the basis of an "experience of enlightenment."[24] With this the discussion naturally comes to an end, for it is equally unlikely for one to discuss with "believers" as with the "enlightened."[25] But these would also have to countenance the second objection, that their experiences of faith and enlightenment could be psychologically explainable illusions, testimonies of a wish-conditioned assertion, and that in these respective statements they make use of the very logic which they repudiate, in that they could be distinguished from it without using conceptual differentiation as a means. In order not to have to permit this objection to be valid for herself and vis-à-vis others, and to prevent its self-certainty from being made questionable, they, like the Cartesian rationalist who declares of himself: "I am I because I am I,"[26] will say: "I am enlightened because I am enlightened," and thus commit the same error for which they reproach him.

The effective difference between the collapse in the thinking of the Cartesian who succeeds by identifying thinking and Being and that of the "enlightened one" who succeeds by extinguishing the I in nothingness, consists in the fact that the former, who thanks to the conceptuality of his discriminating thinking can be aware of its boundaries and can come to speak of Being as an inconceivable mystery and of the self as the "place" at which the mystery of Being is revealed in a special way—as the becoming revealed of the mystery of Being in man's being destined to responsible personhood, which is possible only in symbols as objectifications of what is nonobjectifiable. The enlightened one, on the contrary, sinks into transcenceless nothingness which, when he "awakens" therein, is to be understood in an identity with the Buddha as his own Lord.[27] For him, nothingness could become a symbol of the mystery of Being which represents for our grasp a nothingness, and the Buddha-nature a symbol of its special revelation in human self-understanding. But because he renounces discriminating thinking and the possibility of using its conceptuality to become aware of its boundaries and to enact his self-understanding as its symbolic language, he is robbed

---

[24]Ibid., 49.
[25]Karl Jaspers, *Der philosophische Glaube angesichts der Offenbarung*, 88.
[26]Shimizu, 92, 130.
[27]Ibid., 40.

of the possibility which consists of human salvation. If in view of the figures of Christian theology, past and present, it cannot unfortunately be said that they made use of the possibility, yet—in contrast to the Buddhist doctrine of anatta and sunyata—there was available to them in their doctrine of the Trinity and Christology the possibility of so speaking of God that therein the mystery of Being and its riddle of meaning, and in Christ the latter's special revelation and "the Buddha-Christ as the Lord of the true self" could be expressed as a symbol for human understanding, as I have developed this in my treatment of the religious philosophy of the Kyoto School, with which I know myself as much connected as in opposition—compared to the development it found in Masumi Shimizu, and at greater distance from Wolfhart Pannenberg. For this reason I welcome both authors as a background upon which the intention of my view of the relation of Buddhism and Christianity in the context of the discussion of this problem can stand out in sharper relief, which is what occasioned this supplement.

I shall refrain from a more extensive development of this point of departure of my basic critique, for which Shimizu's citations of characteristic passages from the presentation of Kyoto philosophy and its appeal to men like Rinzai, Dogen, and Shinran, would afford ample material, and limit myself to adducing some of the obvious weaknesses of this philosophy which necessarily issue from its epistemological principles. They are

- the erroneous idea that things would "show themselves as they are" if only we become free of the subject-object split of consciousness;
- the false ontologizing of self-understanding in a nirvana-speculation;
- the putting in question of the postulated ethics of compassion, or love, through the sleight-of-hand removal of the empirical I which is necessary for its practice;
- the complete lack of an understanding of history, which takes account of the problematic of the meaning of human existence in the world, in an illusory acceptance of a universal harmony in the here and now.

These are a few of the elements to which I have devoted sufficient attention in the treatment of their appearance in the Kyoto philosophers, so that I need here only refer to the respective expositions.

Shimizu's understanding of Christianity seems to me to be no less burdened with this problematic than her presentation of Buddhist thinking—the former being presented only in other terminology—so that the points of convergence she highlights between the two phenomena form "convergence points" of their common problematic which, however, if they are recognized as such, could serve "to enrich the dialogue which we should all take to heart,"[28] as Shimizu says so beautifully in the last sentence of this book.

To the two undertakings here critically evaluated—and of equal significance—which are parallel to my present book there has appeared a third treatise from the same era which—although conceived from a completely different viewpoint, no less than the two treated here, represents a challenge—as do they—to my conception of Buddhism, and therefore should not be omitted. This is the investigation which *Alfonso Verdu* devoted to the historically problematic development of Buddhism from its origin to the formation of Kegon (Hua-Yen) and Zen (Ch'an) philosophy in China. It carried the promising title *The Philosophy of Buddhism, a "Totalistic" Synthesis.*[29] He had previously published an investigation of "Early Buddhist Philosophy in the Light of the Four Noble Truths,"[30] and for his specific view of Buddhism he relied on the work of *Garma C. C. Chang*, "The Buddhist Teaching of Totality." The Philosophy of Hua Yen Buddhism,[31] distancing himself essentially from its concept of totality by developing this into his concept of "Totalism" by means of a dialectic of "perspectives" into a "doctrine of universal complementarity." When he appeals for this to Plotinus,[32] Leibniz,[33] and Whitehead,[34] as well as to the theory of relativity[35] and quantum physics,[36] this reminds us of John Cobb's Process Theology[37] and Masao Abe's attention to Whitehead,[38] except that he (Alfonso Verdu) in contrast to the latter (Masao Abe), does not essentially go beyond Whitehead, but identifies Buddhist philosophy with Abe's principle of relationality. In this relationalism he agrees with Harold H. Oliver's "A Relational Metaphysic,"[39] from which issues a relational view of Buddhism.[40]

---

[28]Ibid., 145.

[29]Studies in Philosophy and Religion 3 (The Hague: Martinus Nijhoff Publishers, 1981).

[30](Washington DC: University Press of America 1979).

[31](Pennsylvania State University Press) 36-37.

[32]*The Philosophy of Buddhism*, 36-37.

[33]Ibid., 152-53.

[34]Ibid., 127, 152-53.

[35]Ibid., 38.

[36]Ibid., 153, 157, 167.

[37]Cf. chap. 10, 389-90.

[38]Cf. chap. 9, 346ff.

[39]Studies in Philosophy and Religion 4 (The Hague: Martinus Nijhoff Publishers, 1981).

[40]"Theses on the Relational Self and the Genesis of the Western Ego," ThZB 33/5 (1977): 326ff., 332ff. [Reprinted in Harold H. Oliver, *Relatedness: Essays*

Under this fundamental aspect of a reciprocal complementarity of opposed expressions, Buddhism for Verdu represents, both in his history and in the doctrine unfolded in it, a totality which includes all differences and thus overcomes all partial absolutizations, a universal totality. In presenting the historical development he proceeds from the opposition of the dharma theory of the Hinayana[41] in its legacy from Shakyamuni[42] and the subjective idealism of the early Mahayana,[43] in order to attain, chiefly in Ashvagosha's "Awakening of Faith" in Mahayana and in the Lankavatara Sutra, a total system of Tathata, the thusness in its various manifestations.[44] Verdu sees its normative systematic doctrine represented in the three forms of Buddha-being, the *nirmanakaya*,[45] the *sambhogakaya*,[46] and the *dharmakaya*.[47] In the nirmanakaya as the continuation of the historical Buddha he believes he can find the entire multiplicity of the various schools of Buddhism in the form of the problem-historical development of its essential contents as mutual partial aspects of a Buddhist truth[48] and sets this forth in all its details in several tables,[49] for which his familiarity with Sanskrit, Chinese, and Japanese stand him in good stead. The triadic sequences in which he arranges the various schools in their relatedness to each other and their succeeding one another, reminds us of the threefold rhythm of Hegel's self-unfolding of the absolute spirit, which causes Verdu to reject the claim of "Hegelianizing Buddhism or Buddhizing Hegel." Although he deems a comparison of the great minds of the East and of the West to be legitimate, he regards the system of Hua-Yen to be superior to that of Hegel. Whereas Hegel proceeds from "pure thinking," "The Awakening of Faith in Mahayana," to which Verdu especially appeals, takes its departure from something that is "ontologically 'real'," namely, from the "absolute being of thusness as the eternal essence and substance."[50] This forms the point of departure, whereas the subject-object split of knowing, which for Verdu corresponds to Hegel's self-alienation of the spirit, but as "unknowing," represents the cause of suffering, and must be

---

in Metaphysics and Theology (Macon GA: Mercer University Press, 1984) 33-46.
—Trans.]

[41]*The Philosophy of Buddhism*, 5ff.
[42]Ibid., 87ff.
[43]Ibid., 18ff.
[44]Ibid., 29ff.
[45]Ibid., 87ff.
[46]Ibid., 139ff.
[47]Ibid., 147ff.
[48]Ibid., 87ff.
[49]Ibid., 39ff.
[50]Ibid., 36-37.

overcome through the "restoration of the original infinity" in enlightenment, which thanks to the "mutual interpenetration" of all things, is of cosmic proportions.[51] In Verdu's view, to this stage of enlightenment[52] there corresponds the dharmakaya in the Trikaya doctrine of the completed Buddha-being which corresponds to this stage of enlightenment, whereas the bodhisattva, by virtue of its sambhogakaya nature,[53] is only on the way to it.

While this overcoming of the subject-object split of conceptual thinking through its extension into a cosmic monistic speculation may appropriately designate the state of affairs which has occasioned our critique throughout all our discussions of Buddhist positions. Verdu does not concern himself with the religious philosophy of the Kyoto School; rather, from this circle refers only to D. T. Suzuki as the translator of and commentator to, the Lankavatara sutra.[54] But insofar as the representatives of this school appeal to the tradition treated by Verdu, our critique is valid for that which Verdu works out as "the philosophy of Buddhism" and in which he simultaneously sees *the* philosophy and also his philosophy by understanding it in the sense of current process philosophy and in relational physics and metaphysics.

Despite our basic rejection of this construction—both in respect to the classical forms of Buddhism and the forms of Western philosophy[55] cited by Verdu as the correspondences which confirm it—we do not hesitate to take note of a certain methodic relationship between his procedure and ours. With all his familiarity with Buddhist thinking and a remarkable execution of its structures and intention, Verdu stands outside the object of his analysis when he also emphasizes, that for a complete understanding the presuppositions are his "own personal point of view,"[56] a thinking in Heidegger's sense,[57] and further, "meditation"[58] and a "Hear this silence of emptiness, as it resounds through the entirety of modulations of the universe."[59] The Trikaya doctrine in whose framework Verdu permits his "Philosophy of Buddhism" to be completed, is not so highly rated by all Buddhists as by him, and measured by this standard many of the forms of Buddhism he discusses would not represent genuine Buddhism, but in

---

[51]Ibid., 50-51.
[52]Ibid., 147ff.
[53]Ibid., 139ff.
[54]Ibid., 76, 177n.16, 179n.8, 191n.76.
[55]Ibid., 152ff., 158, 167-68.
[56]Ibid., 45.
[57]Ibid., 3, 156, 158, 183.
[58]Ibid., 162.
[59]Ibid., 170.

their historical appearance, manifestations of the absolutization of partial truths rejected by it.

But with all our efforts to enter into them, we also stand outside the Buddhist intellectual world if we wish to bring them into connection with Christianity, and we see ourselves over and again repulsed at decisive points by its representatives, not to speak of the Christians who view this as a risky undertaking. The Buddha-Christ, to which I have attained in my encounter with the religious philosophy of the Kyoto School and which I maintain over against its representatives as well the theologians concerned with them as the symbol of its possible future, will appear problematic to many in the Far East as well as the West, and Verdu also will not know what to make of it. With his complementary universal relationality he finds himself in a much more advantageous situation with respect to Buddhism and to a process philosophy embellished by salvation history. Additionally, with representatives of a theology of revelation, as they have been set forth in this supplement, he will, in view of his metaphysical monism of salvation—if differently established and differently developed—have to consider his own understanding. Over against all these monisms of salvation—whether supposedly scientific or whether arrived at by means of rational speculations or on the basis of revelations of faith—the Christ—stemming from the dualistic biblical eschatology as a symbol for the solution of the problematic of Being and meaning in the enactment of a nonillusory self-understanding, represents *the* alternative: in his connection with the Buddha-symbol, an invitation to its adherents to become aware of their truth, and for Christians, instructions for proper speaking with Buddhists. Both can occur, but much previous idle talk must give way to a silence before the mystery of transcendence out of which the Lord of the true self can be revealed, who then can carry many—possibly new—names. That the Apostle Paul proclaimed to the Athenians an "unknown God"—hitherto unknown to them—and is reported to have said in the words of the poet, "We are his offspring,"[60] could then be understood in Christian or Buddhist ideas, for example, creation and final judgment as being destined for responsibility and "awakening from the dead" as "awakening out of ignorance," that is, in both instances in an existential interpretation of mythology, which pervades our entire book as a cantus firmus.

The situation worked out in this supplement is thus characterized by the fact that in it three or four positions stand opposed: two rejected on the basis of Christian presuppositions, of which the one would like to deepen Buddhism in a Christian sense on the basis of mysticism (Shimizu), while the other, on the basis of a Lutheran doctrine of justification, determined that it is insufficient for salvation. Next a purely humanistic position, disregarded by Christianity, which

---

[60]Acts 17:22ff.

by means of a universal theory of relationality is identified with the "philosophy of Buddhism" (Verdu), and—last but not least—the reference to self-understanding represented by me—which is related to the transcendence of the mystery of Being and its riddle of meaning and to its special revelation as the possibility of the meaning of human existence, for whose enactment I—in critical examination and connection of what corresponds to them—find the illumining symbols both in Christianity and Buddhism. In view of the current conversation between the two worlds and their future the confrontation of these positions seems to me to merit a supplement.

The Buddha-Christ as the Lord of the True Self.
The Religious Philosophy of the Kyoto School and Christianity.
by Fritz Buri
translated by Harold H. Oliver

Mercer University Press, 6316 Peake Road, Macon, Georgia 31210-3960.
Isbn 0-86554-536-7. Catalog and warehouse pick number: MUP/H410.
Text and interior design, composition, and layout by Edmon L. Rowell, Jr.
Cover and dust jacket design and layout
    by Edmon L. Rowell, Jr. and Marc A. Jolley.
Camera-ready pages composed on a Gateway 2000
    via dos WordPerfect 5.1 and WordPerfect for Windows 5.1/5.2
        and printed on a LaserMaster 1000.
Text fonts: TimesNewRomanPS 10/12; display font: TimesNewRomanPS bf;
    dust jacket display font: OzHandicraft BT.
Printed and bound by Braun-Brumfield Inc., Ann Arbor, Michigan 48106,
    via offset lithography on 50# Natural Hi-Bulk ppi 400.
Smyth sewn and cased into Roxite B 53575 (black linen) cloth,
    one-hit foil stamping on spine and c. 4 with gold foil ES19.
Dust jacket on 100# enamel printed two colors (PMS 172 red/yellow;
    PMS 2607 violet/red/black) and film laminated.

[June 1997]

060297elr